Time Out

Venice

Verona, Treviso & the Veneto

timeout.com/venice

D0026970

Penguin Books

PENGUIN BOOKS

Published by the Penguin Group
Penguin Books Ltd, 80 Strand, London WC2R ORL, England
Penguin Books USA Inc., 375 Hudson Street, New York, New York 10014, USA
Penguin Books Australia Ltd, 250 Camberwell Road, Camberwell, Victoria 3124, Australia
Penguin Books Canada Ltd, 10 Alcorn Avenue, Toronto, Ontario, Canada M4V 3B2
Penguin Books (NZ) Ltd, cnr Rosedale and Airborne Roads, Albany, Auckland, New Zealand

Penguin Books Ltd, Registered Offices: Harmondsworth, Middlesex, England

First published 1999
Second edition 2001
Third edition 2003
10 9 8 7 6 5 4 3 2 1

Colour reprographics by Icon, Crowne House, 56-58 Southwark Street, London SE1 1UN
Printed and bound by Cayfosa-Quebecor, Ctra. de Caldes, Km 3 08 130 Sta, Perpètua de Mogoda, Barcelona, Spain

Edited and designed by
Time Out Guides Limited
Universal House
251 Tottenham Court Road
London W1T 7AB
Tel + 44 (0)20 7813 3000
Fax + 44 (0)20 7813 6001
Email guides@timeout.com
www.timeout.com

Editorial
Editor Anne Hanley
Deputy Editor Rosamund Sales
Listings Editor Patrizia Lerco
Proofreader Tamsin Shelton
Indexer Jackie Brind

Editorial Director Peter Fiennes
Series Editor Ruth Jarvis
Deputy Series Editor Jonathan Cox
Guides Co-ordinator Anna Norman

Design
Group Art Director John Oakey
Art Director Mandy Martin
Art Editor Scott Moore
Senior Designer Lucy Grant
Designer Sarah Edwards
Scanning/Imaging Dan Conway
Ad Make-up Glen Impey
Picture Editor Kerri Littlefield
Deputy Picture Editor Kit Burnet
Picture Desk Trainee Bella Wood

Advertising
Group Commercial Director Lesley Gill
Sales Director Mark Phillips
International Sales Manager Ross Canadé
Advertisement Sales (Venice) Fabio Giannini
Advertising Assistant Sabrina Ancilleri

Administration
Chairman Tony Elliott
Chief Operating Officer Kevin Ellis
Managing Director Mike Hardwick
Group Marketing Director Christine Cort
Marketing Manager Mandy Martinez
US Publicity & Marketing Associate Rosella Albanese
Group General Manager Nichola Coulthard
Chief Financial Officer Rick Waterlow
Guides Production Director Mark Lamond
Production Controller Samantha Furniss
Accountant Sarah Bostock

Features in this guide were written and researched by:
Introduction Anne Hanley. **History** Anne Hanley (*Secret agents*, *Trading with the enemy* Gregory Dowling). **Venice Today** Cat Bauer. **That Sinking Feeling** Fabio Giannini. **Architecture** Diana Niklaus, Lee Marshall. **Venetian Painting** Frederick Ilchman. **Literary Venice** Gregory Dowling. **Accommodation** Chiara Barbieri (*Best hotels*, *Island luxury* Lee Marshall). **Sightseeing** Gregory Dowling (*Long weekend*, *Checks & balances*, *The garden of Eden* Anne Hanley; *Peggy G* Lee Marshall). **Eating Out** Michela Scibilia & Lee Marshall (*Best restaurants*, *Bacari*, *The purple artichokes of Sant'Erasmo*, *Wines of the north-east* Lee Marshall). **Cafés, Bars & Gelaterie** Jill Weinreich (*Bar talk* Anne Hanley). **Shops & Services** Pamela Santini. **Glass** Louis Berndt. **Festivals & Events** Gaby Lewin, Anne Hanley. **Children** Gregory Dowling & Patrizia Lerco. **Film** JoAnn Titmarsh, Lee Marshall. **Galleries** Chiara Barbieri. **Gay & Lesbian** Salvatore Mele, Thom Price. **Music & Nightlife** Kate Davies. **Performing Arts** Emma Molony, Chiara Barbieri. **Sport & Fitness** JoAnn Titmarsh. **The Veneto - Getting Started** Anne Hanley. **Palladian Villas** Frederick Ilchmann, Patrizia Lerco. **Padua** JoAnn Titmarsh, Gus Barker. **Verona** Michael Thompson, Rita Baldassare. **Vicenza** Michael Thompson, Lee Marshall. **Treviso & Northern Veneto** Michael Thompson, JoAnn Titmarsh. **Directory** Gaby Lewin, Pamela Santini, Chiara Barbieri.

Maps LS International Cartography, via Sanremo 17, 20133 Milan, Italy.

Photography by Adam Eastland except: page 7, 13, 14, 16, 34, 37, 38, 39, 40 AKG London; page 65 Corbis; page 66, 68 A. Bevilacqua; page 67 Turismo Venezia; page 69 David Heald.

The Editor would like to thank the Locanda San Trovaso, the Dowling family and special thanks to Lee and Clara Marshall.

Contents

Contents

Introduction

To get some idea of the uniqueness of Venice, try this mental exercise. Think of a small town near you, a town in which 60,000 or so unexceptional people go about their unremarkable business and live their ordinary lives. Now imagine that the main thoroughfares have been replaced by canals, the traffic by a flotilla of bobbing boats; that the minor roads have become narrow alleys, echoing with the voices and ringing with the footsteps of those unexceptional people. In your mind's eye, transform all the cinemas into museums and galleries holding a disproportionately high percentage of the world's art treasures; put churches – again, many containing artistic gems and almost all of them architectural treasures in their own right – in the place of supermarkets and shops.

Not easy, is it? And fertile as your imagination may be, you're going to be very hard pushed indeed to envisage Brentwood, Essex, or Trenton, New Jersey, as the hub of a once-glorious maritime empire, lording it over the known world's shipping routes. Just as you may struggle to believe that Venice is the kind of place where hassled workers rush to get to the supermarket before it shuts and where 'motorists' curse traffic wardens who slap fines on their carelessly parked 'vehicles'... though these vehicles are waterborne. But they do.

Unique and breathtakingly splendid Venice may be – and whether you're a first-time visitor or a frequent caller, this will burst upon you each time you cross the lagoon to the city – but it is also workaday and real. And herein lies its charm. The visit that merely whisks you round its best-known sights is a reductive visit. Not time wasted, of course, but an opportunity missed: an opportunity to savour the weirdness of doing ordinary things in a truly extraordinary place. Get over your awe and into your stride, and head for those bits of Venice that other visitors never reach. For this is the real Venice, where you eat well and drink cheaply and find gems that become personal lodestones. Anyone can make it to St Mark's or the Accademia, but only the adventurous few enjoy that particularly Venetian mix of rustic and cultural pleasure to be had while listening to lapping canal water as they picnic on the grass after a visit to the great former cathedral of San Pietro in Castello.

There's a literary flavour to this third edition of the *Time Out Venice Guide*. Though Venice has produced very few writers of its own, it has long been – and still is – much written about. By heading for the sights (both major and minor) and live-in backstreets mentioned in our series of **Literary locations** feature boxes, you'll not only leave the beaten tourist track behind but experience the city through the lives and characters of novelists and playwrights who have worked here, and still do. The latest writers to turn their attention to the lagoon city – Donna Leon, for example, and Sally Vickers – have thrown off the Venice-as-dream aura that pervaded much of Venice-centred literature of the past. Their Venice has a lived-in feel to it.

Perhaps this is it's a sign of changing attitudes. If it is, the city authorities will be happy. Faced with the prospect of Venice becoming little more than a historical and artistic theme park, trampled beneath the feet of landmark-seeking hordes making their way through an otherwise deserted lagoonscape, they have long been striving to encourage the remaining pockets of real life to stay on. And so should we. A Venice 'Experience' would be a sorry thing.

ABOUT TIME OUT GUIDES

This is the third edition of the *Time Out Venice Guide*, one of the expanding series of Time Out guides produced by the people behind London and New York's successful listings magazines. Our guides are written and regularly updated by resident experts who have striven to provide you with all the most up-to-date information you'll need to explore the city or read up on its historic and artistic background, whether you're a local or a first-time visitor.

THE LIE OF THE LAND

We've divided Venice by *sestieri*, the city's six 'quarters'. Note that house numbers in Venice don't begin and end in each street. They start in one arbitrary spot in any given *sestiere* and continue, apparently at random, to the last house in that district. Venetian addresses are, therefore, almost useless for the purposes of locating your goal. To make your task easier, our listings include first the official address (*sestiere* and number), followed by the name of the street. Each listing also has

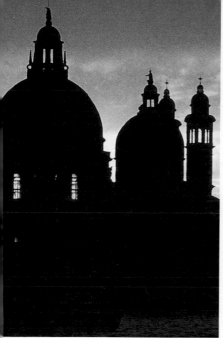

a map reference, indicating the page and square on which it will be found in our maps at the back of the book.

ESSENTIAL INFORMATION

For all the practical information you might need for visiting the area – including visa and customs information, details of local transport, a list of emergency numbers and a directory of useful websites – turn to the Directory chapter at the back of this guide. It starts on page 274.

THE LOWDOWN ON THE LISTINGS

We have tried to make this book as easy to use as possible. Addresses, phone numbers, transport information, opening times and admission prices are all included. However, there's nothing simple about finding your way around the Venetian labyrinth. Moreover, small shops and bars often do not keep precise opening hours, and arts programmes can change at the last moment. Before you go out of your way, we'd strongly advise you to phone ahead to check opening times and other particulars. Bear in mind, too, that Venetians have a very flexible attitude to spelling and will swing back and forth between Italian and dialect names for streets and *campi*; sometimes

There is an online version of this guide, as well as weekly events listings for 35 international cities, at **www.timeout.com**

locals have no idea of the 'official' name of their street, preferring to use the traditional one. We have given the most commonly used names; be prepared, however, to have to do some guess-work. While every effort has been made to ensure the accuracy of the information contained in this guide, the publishers cannot accept responsibility for any errors it may contain.

PRICES AND PAYMENT

In the listings, we have noted which of the following credit cards are accepted: American Express (AmEx), Diners Club (DC), MasterCard (MC) and Visa (V). Some venues will also accept other cards, such as Delta, Switch or JCB.

The prices we've listed in this guide should be treated as guidelines, not gospel. If prices vary wildly from those we've quoted, ask whether there's a good reason. If not, go elsewhere. Then please let us know. We aim to give the best and most up-to-date advice, so we want to know if you've been badly treated or overcharged.

TELEPHONE NUMBERS

The area code for Venice is 041. You must use this prefix whether you are dialling from inside or outside the city. If you are calling from abroad, the international code for Italy is 39, followed by the whole prefix, including the 0. For more information on phones, *see p288*.

MAPS

Street maps of Venice and the islands of Murano, Burano and the Lido are included in the map section at the back of this book. There's a comprehensive street index for Venice too. A map of the Veneto region is provided on page 228, and plans of Padua, Verona and Vicenza are given in those chapters.

LET US KNOW WHAT YOU THINK

We hope you enjoy the *Time Out Venice Guide*, and we'd like to know what you think of it. We welcome your tips for places to include in future editions and take note of your criticism of our choices. There's a reader's reply card at the back of this book for your feedback, or you can email us at guides@timeout.com.

Advertisers

We would like to stress that no establishment has been included in this guide because it has advertised in any of our publications and no payment of any kind has influenced any review. The opinions given in this book are those of *Time Out* writers and entirely independent.

In Context

Features

OPEN YOUR EYES.

Have a better look at Venice, saving time and money with Venice Card.

Buy your prepaid card before leaving.

For further information please visit our website www.venicecard.it
or call +39 041.27.14.747

VENICE card THE ONLY KEY TO VENICE'S HEART.
www.venicecard.it

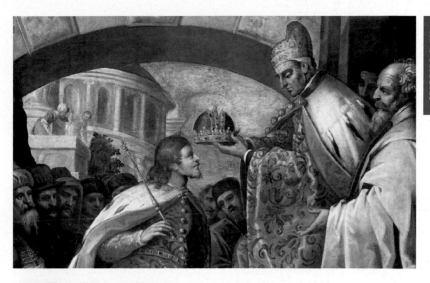

History

A city state built on water that became a world trading hub, built an empire in the process, then lost it.

For a city state that would last for more than 1,000 years – half of those in more or less total control over the shipping routes of the eastern Mediterranean – Venice's origins were decidedly unheroic. The city was born out of terror: terror of the barbarians who invaded the collapsing Roman Empire in the fifth century, and terror of the unpredictable, ugly moods of the Adriatic.

The brutality of Visigoths, Huns, Ostrogoths and Lombards drove thousands of town-dwellers out on to the muddy, flood-prone islets and sandbanks of the lagoon that would later become known as the Laguna Veneta. Enormous public works were necessary almost from the beginning to shore up the islands and make them habitable. Huge amounts of timber had to be cut down and transported from coastal pine forests; the trunks were sunk deep into the mud as foundations for buildings in villages scattered on islands all over the lagoon. But above all, the rivers, including the fast-flowing Brenta and Piave, which drain the eastern Dolomites and which threatened to silt up the lagoon, had to be tamed and diverted.

LIFE ON THE LAGOON

This battle against nature helped to unite the lagoon-dwellers into a close-knit community and into a republic that was to become one of the strongest and most stable nation states in European history. The fight never ended. Even in the 18th century, when the French were advancing on the lagoon and the Venetian Republic was near the end of its own decline and fall, the government invested its last resources in the construction of the *murazzi*, the massive sea walls that run between the Lido, Pellestrina and Chioggia.

Although the islands of the lagoon hosted only transient fishing hamlets until the collapse of the Roman Empire, the surrounding area had been one of the richest in the Empire. Padua, Verona, Aquileia and Altino were among the most prosperous cities in Roman Italy; many smaller towns – Vicenza, Concordia and Belluno – were of almost equal importance. With the final disintegration of any semblance of public order and security in the later sixth century, their inhabitants finally fled for their lives. Those from Aquileia and Concordia

Mark 1, Theodore 0

Theodore of Amasea (or of Euchaita, or Theodore Tyro or Prince Theodore el Shatebi) was born some time in the third century somewhere in Asia Minor, to a father who was a soldier in the Roman army and who may have been married to the princess of a local tribe.

According to the traditions of the Coptic church – for whom Theodore is still an important saint – his Christian father fled his nagging pagan wife while Theodore was young. But the flame of Christianity burned strong within the child and he soon rejected the family idols. He went on to become a brave soldier in the Roman army, but Theodore annoyed his chiefs by converting his comrades-in-arms with his miraculous feats, which included slaying a demon-possessed dragon – generally portrayed as a crocodile – with a nasty habit of devouring the younger inhabitants of the Persian mountain town where he was stationed. Finally his devotion became too much for his superiors to bear, and he was beheaded and made a martyr in 306 (or maybe 313). He was buried near his father's grave in Egypt,

only for his remains to be purloined later and shipped to Brindisi in southern Italy.

Why Theodore was Venice's first patron saint is unclear. But for a city with expectations as great as Venice's, he soon came to be viewed as unfittingly small fry in the sanctity stakes. Rome had the top apostle; Venice would settle for nothing less than an evangelist.

Theodore was quickly replaced when some wily merchants nabbed St Mark's body in Alexandria, Egypt, wrapped it up in pork to stop Muslims and Jews from probing too closely into the contents of their swag bag, and brought it triumphantly back to Venice in 829. To justify the theft, probably apocryphal accounts of a visit to Venice by saints Mark and Paul were embroidered for all they were worth (despite the fact that in the first century the travelling saints would have found little but deserted islands in a swampy lagoon). It was here, Venetian legend recounts, that Jesus appeared to Mark and announced 'pax tibi Marce Evangelista meus' (peace to you Mark, my evangelist) – the words inscribed on the book held by the Lion of St Mark.

gravitated towards the islands of the Grado lagoon, between Venice and Trieste. The inhabitants of Altino and Treviso made for the islands of Murano, Burano, Mazzorbo and Torcello in the northern section of the lagoon. Paduans pitched up on the central island of Rivo Alto ('high banks'), soon abbreviated to Rialto – the first nucleus of historical Venice. Chioggia drew fugitives from Este and Monselice.

These influxes were meant to be temporary. But as economic life on the mainland collapsed, the lagoon islands came to be thought of as permanent homes. They offered enormous potential in the form of fish and salt, commodities that even in times of chaos were basic necessities. Once settled in the lagoon, the fugitives could also enjoy the relative peace and tranquillity that would be denied to the peoples of mainland Europe for centuries to come.

BYZANTINE CONNECTIONS

In 552 Justinian I, the emperor of Byzantium, was determined to reconquer Italy from the barbarians. His first object was the city of Ravenna. But his troops were confronted with an almost insuperable problem: they had made their way overland, via the Dalmatian coast on

the eastern side of the Adriatic, but were blocked by the barbarian Goths who controlled the mainland to the north of Venice. The only way they could attack and take Ravenna was to bypass the Goths, travelling across the lagoon from the town of Grado. The Byzantine commander Narsete requested help to ship his men across.

Already by this time, the lagoon communities had adopted a practice that was to mark Venetian diplomacy through its 1,250-year history: staying as far as possible from – and, where possible, profiting by – other people's quarrels. Justinian's request presented a dilemma: helping him would be seen as a declaration of war against the Ostrogoths in Ravenna, with whom the lagoon communities had reached a comfortable *modus vivendi* assuring safety on the mainland for their traders. Yet the Eastern emperor was offering vast monetary and political rewards for transporting his troops.

The communities eventually threw in their lot with Byzantium. Justinian conquered Ravenna, and marched on to Rome. From this time on the communities of the lagoon became vassals of the Eastern Empire, with its capital in Constantinople. Venice would remain

technically subject to the Byzantine emperors until well after the Sack of Constantinople – an attack led by Venetians – during the Fourth Crusade in 1204.

DOGE CITY

It was not until AD 697, under the growing threat of the barbarian Lombards who controlled the mainland, that the communities scattered around the lagoon – now officially recognised by Byzantium as a duchy – decided to convert their fragile confederation into a stronger, much more centralised state. In this year (or maybe not: some historians have dismissed the story as a Venetian myth) they elected one Paoluccio Anafesto to be their first doge, as the dukes of Venice became known. Yet right from the beginning *il doge* was very different from the other feudal strongmen of Europe.

In the first application of a system that would be honed into shape over the centuries (*see p76* **Checks & balances**), the doge was elected for life by a council chosen by an assembly that represented all the various social groups and trades of the island communities. Technically, therefore, the leadership was elected democratically, although the strongest groups soon formed themselves into a dominant oligarchy. Yet democracy of a kind survived in the system of checks and balances employed to ensure that no one section of the ruling elite got its hands on absolute power. Venetians, fearing the creation of an immovable hereditary monarchy, hedged the office of doge about with all kinds of limitations.

The first ducal power struggle took place in 729. The doge in question, Ipato Orso, achieved the duchy's first outstanding victory as a military power when he dislodged the Lombards from Ravenna. Success, though, went to Orso's head, and he attempted to transform the doge's office into a family heirloom. Civil war wracked the lagoon for two years, ending only when a furious mob forced its way into Orso's house and cut his throat. Troubles continued with the two succeeding doges: both were accused of tyranny, and were not only deposed and exiled but also ceremonially blinded.

A MERCANTILE EMPIRE

Despite moments of near-anarchy, the lagoon dwellers were already becoming a major economic power in the upper Adriatic, the eastern Mediterranean, the Black Sea and North Africa. Craftsmen were sent abroad to Dalmatia and Istria to study the art of shipbuilding; they learnt so swiftly that by the seventh century the construction and fitting-out of seagoing vessels had become a thriving industry. Mercantile expansion and technical advances went hand in hand, as tradesmen brought back materials and techniques from far-flung places – especially from the Middle and Far East, where technical and scientific knowledge and culture was far in advance of the West.

In 781 Pepin, son of the Frankish king Charlemagne, invaded Italy and attacked the Lombards. Wariness of involving the lagoon in mainland struggles still dominated the duchy's policy and it played for time, unsure whether to sacrifice the alliance with Byzantium to this new and powerful player on the European scene. In the end, however, Pepin's designs on Istria and Dalmatia – now part of the Venetian sphere of influence – caused relations to turn frosty. Exasperated by the duchy's fence-sitting, Pepin attacked its ally, Grado, on the mainland, executing its cardinal by hurling him from the town's highest tower. He then proceeded to take all the mainland positions around Venice, and besieged the lagoon communities from the sea.

In the mid eighth century the confederation had moved its capital from Heraclea in the northern lagoon to Malamocco on the Adriatic coast, where it was now at the mercy of Frankish naval forces. At this crucial juncture, in 810, a strong, effective leader suddenly emerged in the form of an admiral, Angelo Partecipazio. He immediately abandoned the besieged capital of Malamocco; almost overnight, the capital was moved to the island archipelago of Rialto in the centre of the lagoon.

Partecipazio's next move was a stroke of military genius. He ordered his fleet to head out of the lagoon through the strait of Malamocco to attack Pepin's ships, then to feign terror and head back into the lagoon. In hot pursuit, the deep-keeled Frankish ships ran aground on the sandbanks of the lagoon, allowing the locals, with their intimate knowledge of deep-water channels, to pick off the crews with ease until thousands had been massacred.

After his great victory against the Franks, Partecipazio was elected doge. During his reign, work began on a ducal palace on the site of the current one, and the confederation of islands that made up the lagoon duchy was given the name 'Venetia'. Around the same time, the flourishing city of Torcello began to decline, as the surrounding lagoon waters silted up and malarial mosquitoes took over.

These were also the years when Venice set about embroidering a mythology worthy of its ambitions. After two local merchants stole the body of St Mark from Alexandria and brought it to Venice – traditionally in the year 829 – the city's previous Byzantine patron, St Theodore, was unceremoniously deposed and the Evangelist – symbolised by a winged lion – set up in his place (see p8 **Mark 1, Theodore 0**). A shrine to the saint was erected in the place where St Mark's basilica would later rise.

Angelo Partecipazio's overwhelming success in both military and civic government led to another tussle for power. Before he died in 827, he made certain that his son Giustiniano would succeed him. When Giustiniano died two years later, his younger brother Giovanni was elected doge, despite mounting dissent and jealousy from rival families. It was a measure of Partecipazio's importance that his surname was to feature repeatedly in the ducal roll of honour over the next century, but the family was never allowed to achieve the hegemony that the Medici dynasty enjoyed in Renaissance Florence. In Venice, any sign of arrogance or dynastic ambition was greeted either with banishment or worse; one doge with aspirations beyond the role assigned to him, Pietro Candiano, was thrown to the dogs at the end of the tenth century.

The development of the vast Venetian empire grew out of the mercantile pragmatism that dominated Venetian political thinking. Expansion was embarked upon for two main reasons: to secure safe shipping routes, and to create permanent trading bases. Harassed by Slav pirates in the upper Adriatic, the Venetians set up bases around the area from which to attack the pirate ships: gradually, they took over the ports of Grado and Trieste, then expanded along the coastlines of Istria and Dalmatia. In some cases, Venetian protection against pirates was requested; in others, 'help' arrived unbidden.

With the coast well defended, the Venetian Republic tended not to bother to expand its territories into the hinterland. There was, for many centuries, a certain mistrust of terra firma; Venetian citizens were not even allowed to own land outside of the lagoon until 1345.

Secret agents

Venice, Henry James wrote, is a city of secrets. At the same time it is a city whose inhabitants have always made the ferreting out of other people's secrets their business. Few illicit affairs or shady deals go unremarked in Venice; and if solid facts are lacking as a basis for gossip, vague rumours will do instead.

Some attribute this tendency to the clammy intimacy of the city's geography, but Venetians were probably already swapping gossip as the first poles were driven into the mud. Over the centuries the city's rulers took care to exploit this tendency in – as they saw it – the interests of state security.

A Tribunal of Inquisitors was set up after the war against the Venetian Republic instigated by the allies of the League of Cambrai (1508; see also p16); at the time the city was in a condition of excusable paranoia, with enemies apparently lurking on all sides. There were three Inquisitors, two from the Council of Ten and one from among the Counsellors of the Doge; their appointment lasted a year. As Venice's system of government (see p76 **Checks & balances**) became more markedly oligarchic, the Inquisitors became increasingly powerful, relying upon armies of agents in Venice and wherever the Republic had interests. Allegations of foul play could be dropped into special lion-mouthed postboxes, but anonymous denunciations were heeded only if they concerned major matters of public order. In general, the Inquisitors preferred to rely on reports from hand-picked agents. They were chosen either for their ability to blend

CRUSADE FOR TRADE

The Crusades presented Venice with its greatest opportunity yet for expanding trade routes while reaping a profit. Transporting crusaders to the Holy Land became big business for the city. More importantly, the naïve crusaders were easy prey for the professional generals – the *condottieri* – who commanded Venice's army of highly trained mercenaries: the eager defenders of the faith were, as often as not, used to extend and consolidate the Venetian empire.

Never was this truer than in the case of the Fourth Crusade, which set off proudly from Venice in 1202 to reconquer Jerusalem. The Venetian war fleet was under the command of Doge Enrico Dandolo, who although 80 years old and completely blind, retained his capacities as a supremely cunning leader, outstanding tactician and accomplished diplomat. He persuaded other European crusader leaders to take time out to conquer the strategic Adriatic port of Zara, thus assuring Venice's control of much of the Dalmatian coastline. Even more surprisingly, they allowed themselves to be talked into attacking Constantinople.

Venice's special relationship with the Eastern Empire had always had its ups and downs. In 1081 and 1082 Venice had done the Byzantine emperor a favour when it trounced the

DE NON TE SECRETE CONTRO CHI OCCVLTERA GRATIE ET OFFICII O COLLVDERA PER NASCONDER LA VERA RENDITA D ESSI

in among the classes they were watching over, like the decayed nobleman Pietro Corner who kept an eye on the upper classes, or simply for their powers of observation; one of the most industrious of the 18th-century agents was a certain GB Manuzzi, who had been a jeweller, and whose sharp, evaluating eyes were always on the lookout for suspicious behaviour; for over 20 years he provided the Inquisitors with daily denunciations of chicanery and shiftiness on the part of his fellow-citizens, all in the most exquisite handwriting.

These agents were, of course, paid for their efforts. But study the reams of secret reports in the State Archives (*see p110*), and it soon becomes clear that many of the spies were not motivated by greed alone. The dogged persistence with which the agents followed up domestic scandals – hovering in doorways, questioning servants, noting secret arrivals and departures – suggests more than mere professional assiduity. The important thing clearly is to know – and, of course, it is all the more satisfactory if one's knowledge concerns those in a higher walk of life than one's own.

It was the duty of these agents (who included, for a while at least, Giacomo Casanova) to keep the state informed of all dangers of sedition, from whatever quarter. This did not only mean looking out for foreign intrigue or lower-class discontent; it was equally important that an eye should be kept on the Venetian nobility. Any nobleman who behaved with less than the dignity to be expected of his rank brought the whole class (and thus the whole system) into disrepute. Thus it was that strict dress rules were imposed: nobles must neither indulge in excessive displays of wealth, which might provoke envy and rivalry, nor must they dress in such a way that they could be confused with the lower ranks. And so these agents' reports are full of sightings of noblemen wearing excessively foppish wigs or, conversely, wearing middle-class *tabarri* rather than officially approved *toghe*. There seems little doubt that for many of these spies it was the chance to catch the upper classes out that constituted the main attraction of the job.

Of course, as the amount of such trivial information swelled, its usefulness decreased proportionately. In the end, it was not difficult for the Venetian government to accede to Napoleon's demand to abolish the Inquisitors; they had, after all, proved totally ineffectual in preventing the downfall of the Venetian Republic. East Germany's Stasi could have learned from this lesson.

menacing Normans in the southern Adriatic. In return, it was granted duty-free trading rights throughout the Empire. But in 1149 those trading privileges were withdrawn in disgust at Venetian arrogance during a siege of Corfu.

As the Fourth Crusade set out, Dandolo saw that this was an ideal opportunity to remove the Byzantine challenge to Venetian trade hegemony once and for all. He pulled the wool over his fellow crusaders' eyes, with the noble argument that the Eastern emperor must be ousted and replaced by someone willing to reunite the eastern Orthodox and western Roman churches.

They acquiesced, but there was nothing noble about the brutal, bloody, Venetian-led sacking of the Constantinople on 13 April 1204, nor about the horrendous pillaging that ensued. Far outstripping all their colleagues in greed and callousness, the Venetians looted all the city's greatest treasures, including the celebrated quartet of antique Greek horses that was transported back to Venice and placed above the main entrance of St Mark's basilica (*see p71*). Innumerable other artefacts – jewellery, enamels, golden chalices, statuary, columns and precious marbles – were plundered: they are now an inseparable part of the fabric of the *palazzi* and churches of Venice.

But the booty was only a minor consideration for the Venetians and their pragmatic doge: the real prize was the one handed out when the routed Byzantine empire was carved up. The Venetians were not interested in grabbing huge swathes of territory that they knew they couldn't hold. This was left to the French and German knights, who, indeed, lost it within a few decades. Putting their intimate knowledge of eastern trade routes to excellent use, the Venetians hand-picked those islands and ports that could guarantee their merchant ships a safe passage from Venice to the Black Sea and back. These included almost all the main ports on the Dalmatian coast, certain strategic Greek islands, the sea of Marmora and a number of strategic Black Sea ports.

For many years after the conquest of Constantinople, Venetian ships could sail from Venice to Byzantium without ever leaving waters controlled by the city. The Serene Republic, La Serenissima, had finally become a major imperial power. The city marked the turn of events by conferring a new title upon its doge: *Quartae Partis et Dimidiae Totius Imperii Romaniae Dominator* – Lord of a Quarter and Half a Quarter of the Roman Empire.

SOME MORE EQUAL THAN OTHERS
In 1297, in what came to be known as the *Serrata del maggior consiglio*, the leaders of the Venetian merchant aristocracy decided to limit entry to the Grand Council to those families already in the club. Membership of the Maggior Consiglio was restricted to those who had held a seat there in the previous four years, or to descendants of those who had belonged at any point since 1172. Under these rules, only around 150 extended families were eligible for a place, but the number of council members leapt to some 1,200.

Up-and-coming clans were understandably indignant at the thought of being forever excluded from power and from a coveted place in the *Libro d'Oro* – the Golden Book – of the Venetian aristocracy. In 1310 a prosperous merchant named Baiamonte Tiepolo harnessed the discontent in a rebellion against the aristocratic oligarchy. Had Tiepolo's standard-bearer not been felled by a loose brick knocked carelessly out of its place by an old lady who was watching the shenanigans from her window in the Merceria, the uprising may have succeeded. But his troops fled in panic, the uprising was savagely crushed, and the much-feared Council of Ten was granted draconian police and judicial powers. An extensive network of spies and informers was set up to suppress any future plots.

> ## 'Vast fortunes were built up and lavished on building, furnishing and decorating great *palazzi* and churches.'

In 1354 Doge Marino Faliero made a bid to undermine the powers of the Venetian oligarchy while increasing and consolidating his own powers as a permanent hereditary leader. This plot, too, was mercilessly suppressed and Faliero was beheaded.

The Council of Ten – along with the Venetian Inquisition that had been set up after the Tiepolo plot – wielded its special powers most effectively after the Faliero incident, ensuring that this was the last serious attempt to attack the principle of rule by elite. It was at this time that lion's-head postboxes first appeared at strategic points around the city: Venetians were encouraged to drop written reports of any questionable activity through their marble mouths.

LIVES OF THE RICH AND FAMOUS
While Venice's mercantile power was at its zenith from the 13th to the 15th centuries, vast fortunes were built up and lavished on building, furnishing and decorating great *palazzi* and churches. It was at this time that the city took on the architectural form still visible today. For sheer luxury, Venice's lifestyle was unequalled anywhere else in Europe.

Bellini's view of Venetian festivities.

In the 14th and 15th centuries, Venice was one of the largest cities in Europe, with an estimated population of between 150,000 and 200,000, many connected with the city's booming mercantile activities. International visitors were astounded by its opulence and economic dynamism.

Salt had long ceased to be Venice's main trading commodity. When ships set sail from Venice for the Middle East, their holds were crammed with Istrian pine wood, iron ore, cereals, wool and salted and preserved meats. These were traded for finely woven textiles, exotic carpets, perfumes, gold and silverware, spices, precious stones, ivory, wax and slaves: with a virtual monopoly on all these sought-after commodities, Venice was able to sell them on to the rest of Europe at enormous profit.

The Venetian aristocracy liked to live in some comfort. 'The luxury of any ordinary Venetian house,' wrote one traveller in 1492, 'is so extraordinary that in any other city or country it would be sufficient to decorate a royal palace.' Domestic luxury was not confined to the city. The Venetians were also investing huge amounts of money in their summer villas on the mainland, which often surpassed their city establishments in magnificence, designed and decorated as they were by the leading Veneto architects and painters.

Venetians lavished the same kind of attention on their appearance. Venetian women were famous for the unbridled luxury of their clothing. Fortunes were spent on furs, the richest and most gorgeous textiles woven with gold and silver thread, and jewellery. Their perfumes and cosmetics were the envy of all Europe, as were the beauty and fascination of the estimated 12,000 courtesans who dominated much of the social and cultural life of the city in the 15th century.

So dedicated were Venetians to the cult of love and earthly pleasures, that the patriarch, Venice's cardinal, was driven to issue orders forbidding the city's nuns from going out on the town at night in ordinary clothes.

Sumptuous festivals of music, theatre and dance were almost daily occurrences. The visit of a foreign ruler, a wedding or funeral of a member of the nobility, a religious festival, a naval or military victory, or delivery from an epidemic were all excuses for public celebrations involving days of festivities and huge sums of money. The city's foreign communities – Jews, Armenians, Turks, Germans, French and Mongols, many of them permanent residents – would celebrate their national or religious feast days with enormous pomp.

Despite the wealth of the city, and the full employment created by its trades and industries (at full stretch, the shipyard was capable of launching one fully equipped ship every day), life was not easy for the city's poor, who often lived in damp, filthy conditions. Epidemics were frequent: more than half the city's population is estimated to have died in the Black Death of 1348-9. Social tension and discontent were rife.

GENOAN RIVALRY

The enormous wealth of the Venetian Republic and of its rapidly expanding empire inevitably provoked jealousy among the other trading nations of the Mediterranean – above all with the powerful maritime city state of Genoa, Venice's main rival in its trade with the East.

The Genoese had already clashed with the Venetians in 1261 when the former obliged the Byzantine emperor by helping to evict Venice's high-handed merchants from Constantinople. Skirmishes between the two Italian powers continued throughout most of the 14th century, regularly flaring up into major battles or periods of open warfare, and often resulting in disastrous defeats for Venice.

By 1379 the situation had become desperate for La Serenissima. The Genoese fleet and army had moved into the Gulf of Venice in the upper Adriatic and, after a long siege, had taken Chioggia, at the southern end of the lagoon.

From here the Genoese attacked and occupied much of the lagoon, including Malamocco and the passage to the open sea. Venice was under siege and began to starve.

Then, in 1380, the city worked another of its miracles of level-headed cunning. Almost the whole of the Genoese fleet was anchored inside the fortified harbour of Chioggia. Vittor Pisani, the admiral of the Venetian fleet, ordered hundreds of small boats to be filled with rocks. Panicked by a surprise Venetian attack on the mouth of the port, the Genoese failed to notice that the small boats were being sunk in the shallow port entrance, preventing any escape. The tables had been turned and Venice besieged the trapped Genoese fleet until it surrendered unconditionally. Genoa's days as a great naval power were over.

THE BEGINNING OF THE END

Ironically, however, this victory was to spell the beginning of the end for La Serenissima. For though the Republic had reached the height of its prosperity and had re-acquired its supremacy in the East, concentrating its energies on fighting Genoa was to prove a fatal foreign policy mistake. Venice's leaders badly underestimated the threat posed by the emergence of the Turks as a military power in Asia Minor and the Black Sea area. Convinced – wrongly and ultimately fatally – that diplomacy was the way to deal with the threat from the East, Venice turned its attention to conquering other powers on the Italian mainland.

For centuries Venice had followed a conscious policy of neutrality towards the various powers that had carved up the Italian mainland. The European political upheavals from the end of the 12th century to the end of the 14th century put paid to that neutrality. The bitter rivalry between Venice and the other Italian maritime states, especially Pisa and Genoa, inevitably brought it into conflict with their powerful mainland allies: the pope, the Scaliger dukes of Verona and a succession of Holy Roman emperors.

> ### 'The city state sank gradually into dissipation and decline.'

The defeat of the vast Scaliger empire (which included much of the Venetian hinterland) by Count Gian Galeazzo Visconti of Milan in 1387 brought Milanese power much too close to the lagoon for comfort: it was not only Venetian security that was under threat, but access to all-important trade routes through north-eastern Italy and across the Alps into northern Europe

The Provinces Pay Homage to Venetia.

beyond as well. Venice began a series of wars that led to the conquest in 1405 of Verona and its enormous territories, of Padua, Vicenza and a number of other significant towns.

By 1420 Venice had annexed Friuli and Udine; by 1441 La Serenissima controlled Brescia, Bergamo, Cremona and Ravenna as well. The land campaign continued until 1454, when Venice signed a peace treaty with Milanese ruler Francesco Sforza. Though Ravenna was soon to slip from Venice's grasp, the remainder of the Republic's immense mainland territories were to remain more or less intact for almost 300 years.

Even as the Venetian Republic expanded on the mainland, events were conspiring to bring La Serenissima's reign as a political power and trading giant to a close. In 1453 the Ottoman Turks swept into Constantinople, and Venice's crucial trading privileges in what had been the Byzantine empire were almost totally lost. In 1487 Vasco da Gama rounded the Cape of Good Hope; in 1489 he became the first European to reach Calcutta by sea, shattering Venice's monopoly on the riches of the East. The arrival of Portuguese ships laden with spices and textiles in Portuguese ports caused a sensation in Europe and despair in Venice. The Venetians hastily drew up plans to open a canal at Suez to beat the Portuguese at their own game, but the project came to nothing.

Instead, cushioned by the spoils of centuries and exhausted and drained by 100 years of almost constant military campaigns, the city state sank gradually over the following two centuries into dissipation and decline.

But, as was only to be expected from a city as lavish as Venice, the decline was glorious. For most of the 16th century few Venetians behaved as if the writing was on the wall. Such was the extent of the enormous wealth that the city had built up that the economic fallout from the Turks' inexorable progress through the Middle East went almost unnoticed at first. Profits were not as massive as before, but the rich remained

very rich and the setbacks in the East were partly counter-balanced by exploitation of the newly acquired territories.

As revenue gradually declined through the 16th century, spending on life's little pleasures increased, producing an explosion of art, architecture and music. Titian, Tintoretto, Veronese and Giorgione were among the artists working hard in the city (*see chapter* **Venetian Painting**). Meanwhile, Palladio, Sanmicheli and Scamozzi were changing the face of architecture (*see chapters* **Architecture** *and* **Palladian Villas**). The city rang out to the music of the Gabriellis.

Trading with the enemy

In the Doge's Palace, a grandiose painting by Andrea Vicentino celebrates the naval Battle of Lepanto. In it, Venice is portrayed as Defender of the Faith, a solitary bulwark protecting Christian civilisation from the ravages of bloodthirsty Turkish hordes. From 1453 – when Christian Constantinople fell to the Muslim Ottoman Turks – onwards, Venice was, according to this official version of history, engaged in a life-and-death struggle with the Ottoman Empire, which treacherously tried to rob the Republic of its legitimate possessions in the eastern Mediterranean.

The wars, with their sporadic acts of barbarism (on both sides), were real enough, but they were not the whole story. Commercial relations between the two empires continued for centuries, disrupted but never completely severed by outbreaks of hostilities. Periods of peace lasted much longer than the conflicts (the longest such lull being between 1573 and 1645), but even in the midst of war, trade often found a way of proceeding.

In the Middle Ages, Venice had been the city with the closest ties to Christian Constantinople; the tradition continued when the Turks turned the city into Istanbul. Venice always maintained a *bailo* (representative) in Istanbul and the Turks had their own *fondaco* (emporium; *see p64*) on the Grand Canal. No other European city trafficked and traded so intensely with Istanbul; in the 16th century well over half of Venice's grain came from lands under Ottoman rule, and it also imported wool, hides and textiles. Just as Venice had been the first city in Europe to adopt the Byzantine table-fork, it was now the first to start drinking Turkish 'black water', or coffee. Sultan Mahomet II invited the artist

Gentile Bellini to Istanbul, where he spent two years that furnished him with exotic backgrounds for his paintings.

The two countries would never have admitted it, but they even cooperated militarily at times, when it was to the advantage of both, as in taking joint action against pirates. In 1480 Venice did not lift a finger when the Turks occupied Otranto in south-eastern Italy; indeed, it was even hinted (probably unfairly) that it was Venice that had suggested the move to Istanbul, as an act of revenge against the region's Aragonese rulers. When Persia – supposedly a European ally – attacked Turkey in the early 16th century, Venice refused to ally herself with the attacker; in 1535 she even went so far as to congratulate Suleiman the Magnificent on a victory over the Persians.

Officially, of course, the Republic abhorred Islam, and considered its devotees as damned souls. However, this did not stop the historian Niccolò Contarini, who became doge in 1630, from studying the cohesion of the Ottoman Empire and concluding, with Machiavellian approbation, that 'Mahomet had succeeded better than anyone else in organising religion to bring the multitude to himself and to extend the state'. A *bailo*, Giambattista Donà, published a book on the literature of the Turks – in 1688, the year that Francesco Morosini, the last Venetian victor over the Turks, was elected doge.

All in all it was hardly surprising that Pope Clement VIII, when trying to whip up support for a final Crusade in 1601, should have declared to the Venetian envoy: 'We would be happy if you behaved with as much respect to the Apostolic See and the person of the Pope as you do to the Turks.'

Tintoretto gives Venetian officials ringside seats at the Resurrection. *See p15.*

Meanwhile, on the mainland, Venice's arrogant annexation of territory had not been forgotten by the powers that had suffered at its hands. When Venice took advantage of the French invasion of Italy in the final years of the 15th century to extend its territories still further, the Habsburgs, France, Spain and the papacy were so incensed that they clubbed together to form the League of Cambrai, with the sole aim of annihilating Venice.

They came very close to doing so. One Venetian rout followed another, some Venetian-controlled cities defected to the enemy and others that did not were laid waste. Only squabbling within the League of Cambrai stopped Venice itself from being besieged. By 1516 the alliance had fallen to pieces and Venice had regained almost all its territories.

Its coffers almost empty, its mainland dominions in tatters, Venice was now forced to take stock of the damage that was being done by the Turks (*see p15* **Trading with the enemy**). A short-sighted policy of trying to keep the Ottoman Empire at bay by diplomacy had already had devastating effects on Venice's position in the eastern Mediterranean.

In 1497, as the Ottomans stormed through the Balkans, coming almost within sight of the belltowers of Venice, La Serenissima had been obliged to give up several Aegean islands and the port of Negroponte; two years later it lost its forts in the Peloponnese, giving the Turks virtual control of the southern end of the Adriatic. And if Venice felt jubilant about securing Cyprus in 1489 by pressuring the king's Venetian widow Caterina Cornaro into bequeathing control of the island, the legacy in fact involved the Republic in almost

constant warfare to keep the Turks off this strategically vital strip of land.

In 1517 Syria and Egypt fell to the Turks; Rhodes followed in 1522; and by 1529 the Ottoman Empire reached across the southern Mediterranean as far as Morocco. The frightened European powers turned to Venice to help repulse the common foe. But mistrust of the lagoon city state was deep and, in their determination to keep Venice from deriving too much profit from the war against the Turks, the campaign itself was botched.

In 1538 a Christian fleet was trounced at Preveza in western Greece; in 1571 Venice led a huge European fleet to victory against hundreds of Turkish warships in the Battle of Lepanto, in what is now the Gulf of Corinth. But despite the massive propaganda campaign of self-congratulation and self-glorification that followed, it became apparent that the victory was hollow and that the Turks were as strong as ever. In a treaty signed after the battle in 1573, Venice was forced ignominiously to hand over Cyprus, its second-last major possession in the eastern Mediterranean (Crete, the final one, fell in 1669).

By the 17th century the Venetian government was no longer under any illusion about the gravity of its economic and commercial crisis. In a report issued by the Savi alla Mercanzia, the state trading commission, dated 5 July 1610, it was noted that 'our commerce and shipping in the West are completely destroyed. In the East only a few businesses are still functioning and they are riddled with debt, without ships and getting weaker by the day. Moreover, and this must be emphasised, only a small quantity of goods is arriving in our city, and it is becoming increasingly difficult to find buyers for them. The nations that used to buy from us now have established their businesses elsewhere. We are facing the almost total annihilation of our commerce.'

Venice was down but not quite out, however, and some heroic attempts were made to regain the empire that had been so disastrously mauled in the 16th century by the Turks. In 1617 a successful campaign was fought against the Uskoks, pirates financed by the Austrian Habsburgs, who had territorial ambitions in Istria and along the Dalmatian coast; in the process, some resounding blows were struck against the Turks of the region too. Between 1681 and 1687 Francesco Morosini, the brilliant commander of the Venetian fleet, succeeded in reconquering much of the territory that had been taken by the Turks in the preceding century, including Crete and the Peloponnese. But these moments of glory, celebrated with colossal pomp and ceremony in Venice itself, were invariably short-lived.

> ### 'Masked nuns from fashionable convents were a common sight at the city's gambling houses.'

Exhausted by debts and the sheer effort of its naval campaigns, the Venetian Republic lacked the resources needed to consolidate its victories in the newly reconquered territories.

In 1699, the Treaty of Carlowitz had restored much of Venice's territory in the East, along with many of its trading privileges. But by 1718 the Venetian Republic was once again struggling to keep its head above water as the Austrians and Turks forced it to cede most of these same territories in the humiliating Treaty of Passarowitz.

DECAY AND DECADENCE
By the time the Venezia Trionfante Café (now Caffè Florian, see p164) opened for business in piazza San Marco in 1720, the Republic was virtually bankrupt and its governing nobility had grown decadent and politically inert. But decadence was good for the city's growing status as the party capital of Europe.

Aristocratic women of all ages and marital states were accompanied in their gadding by handsome young cisibei (male escorts), whose professions of chastity fooled nobody. Masked nuns from fashionable convents were a common sight at the city's gambling houses and theatres; party pooping church officials who tried to confine nuns to barracks at the convent

by the church of San Zaccaria were met with a barrage of bricks on at least one occasion.

Priests, too, were not slow to join in the fun: composer-prelate Antonio Vivaldi's supposed affairs with members of his famous female choir were well publicised. Father Lorenzo Da Ponte, Mozart's great Venetian librettist, was better known for his amorous conquests than for his piety. And though Giacomo Casanova, the legendary embodiment of sexual excess, never actually donned a cassock, he had been a promising student of theology before he realised where his true vocation lay.

Bankrupt, politically and ideologically stagnant and no longer a threat to any of its former enemies, Venice directed its final heroic effort to survive not against those erstwhile foes but against the forces of nature. Even as Napoleon prepared to invade Venice in 1797, the city was spending the meagre funds left in its coffers on building the vast murazzi, the long stone and marble dyke designed to protect the city from the worst ravages of unpredictable Adriatic tides (see chapters **That Sinking Feeling** and **The Lido to Chioggia**).

FRANCE AND AUSTRIA TAKE OVER
On 12 May 1797 the last doge, Lodovico Manin, was deposed by the French. Even before the Republic had bowed to the inevitable and voted itself out of existence, the French had handed control of the lagoon city over to Austria under the terms of the Treaty of Loeben. (Manin consigned his doge's cap to the victors, saying, 'Take this, I don't think I'll be needing it any more.')

In 1805 Napoleon changed this state of affairs, absorbing Venice back into his Kingdom of Italy. Until 1815, when the French emperor's star waned and Venice once again found itself back under Austrian control, Napoleon's Venetian plenipotentiaries were given free rein to dismantle churches, dissolve monasteries and to redesign bits of the city, including the wide thoroughfare that is now known as via Garibaldi, together with its adjoining public gardens.

The last, ill-fated spark of Venice's ancient independent spirit flared up in 1848, when lawyer Daniele Manin (no relation of the last doge) led a popular revolt against the Austrians. An independent republican government was set up, holding out against siege and bombardment for five heroic months. It was doomed to failure from the outset, however, and the Austrians were soon firmly back in the saddle, keeping their grip on this insignificant backwater until 1866, when a weakened Austria, badly beaten on other fronts by the Prussians, handed the city over to the newly united Italian state.

Key events

c450 First settlers arrive in lagoon, fleeing invading forces of barbarian hordes.
520 Lagoon communities recognised by Ostrogoth Emperor Theodoric as having best merchant fleet in the Adriatic.
552 Lagoon communities allow troops of Eastern Emperor Justinian I to pass through the lagoon to attack Ravenna, placing lagoon within the Byzantine sphere of influence.
697 First doge (duke) elected as Lombard barbarians rampage through mainland and threaten communities' capital at Heraclea.
729 Doge Ipato Orso seeks to make dukedom hereditary, sparking two-year civil strife.
c742 Capital moved to Malamocco; lagoon communities have virtual monopoly on eastern Adriatic trade.
810 Frankish forces besiege lagoon from the sea after a long land campaign against mainland allies; Admiral Angelo Partecipazio moves capital to Rialto, lures deep-keeled Frankish boats into shallow lagoon and massacres Franks; lagoon duchy named Venetia; economic and building boom begins.
829 Two Venetian merchants bring stolen body of St Mark from Alexandria; St Mark becomes Venice's patron saint, deposing the Byzantine St Theodore in an act of defiance towards the Eastern Empire.
1000 Venetian fleet destroys Dalmatian pirates, securing trading bases and taking absolute control of Adriatic sea routes.
1063 Work begins on St Mark's basilica.
1081-2 Venice beats Normans in southern Adriatic, earning gratitude of Byzantine Empire, which grants Venice the right to unrestricted trade throughout the Empire and waives customs tariffs.
1147-9 Venice helps Byzantium drive Normans from Corfu but is so aggressive that a period of enmity follows, with Venetian traders being ejected from Constantinople.
1202-4 Doge Enrico Dandolo heads Fourth Crusade, which sacks Constantinople; Venice acquires many Aegean islands; substantial Venetian colony remains in Constantinople.
1261 Byzantine emperor, aided by Genoese, evicts Venetians from Constantinople; grants Genoa trading privileges formerly held by Venice; Venice and Genoa periodically at war for 20 years.
1297 Electoral laws tightened to keep power in patrician hands and limit effective power of doges, in *Serrata del maggior consiglio*.

1310 Disgruntled merchant Baiamonte Tiepolo leads unsuccessful uprising to overthrow doge; Venetian Inquisition founded.
1348 Black Death leaves two thirds of Venice's population dead.
1381 Venice ends long-running skirmishes with Genoa in decisive battle at Chioggia; Peace of Turin ends Genoese influence in eastern Mediterranean.
14th-15th centuries Venice expands inland, annexing modern Veneto and Venezia-Friuli-Giulia regions, fighting series of wars that reshapes the political power balance on mainland and stokes antagonism of other Italian powers against Venice.
1453 Turks take Constantinople, ending Venice's trading privileges.
1479 Venice loses Negroponte and some Aegean islands to Turks.
1499 Turks seize Venetian forts in Peloponnese, control entrance to Adriatic.
1508 League of Cambrai defeats Venice at Agnadello.
1527 City hit by plague; building work begins on Santa Maria della Salute.
1571 Venice and forces of Habsburg ally Charles V beat Turks at Lepanto.
1606 Centuries-old antagonism between Venice and Vatican culminates when whole city is excommunicated in argument over temporal powers of the pope; interdict lifted one year later.
1669 Crete, Venice's last possession in eastern Mediterranean, falls to Turks.
1699 Venice takes control of Morea (Peloponnese) after campaign to expel Turks.
1718 Venice returns costly, unprofitable Morea to the Turks.
1797 Last doge, Lodovico Manin, deposed by Napoleonic French troops; Venice handed over to Austria.
1805 Napoleon annexes Venice to his Kingdom of Italy.
1815 Venice returns to Austrian control.
1846 Railway bridge built linking Venice to mainland.
1848-9 Venetian patriot Daniele Manin sets up provisional republican government.
1866 Austrians, after defeat by Prussia, hand Venice over to newly united Italy.
1932 First road bridge built.
1966 Venice badly damaged by flooding.
1992 Venice granted metropolitan status.
1996 La Fenice opera house gutted by fire.

Venice Today

Venice may be a preserved chunk of history, but behind those façades is a living city.

To the dilettante, Venice is an ailing enchantress, hitching up her skirts to avoid *acqua alta* (high water; *see chapter* **That Sinking Feeling**) as hordes of visitors flock to pay their last respects. Reports of suffocating mass tourism and inexorably rising water levels constantly reinforce this image.

But, like many true beauties, Venice has depth below its surface. It is two parallel worlds: that of the tourist and that of the Venetians. Behind the heavy wooden doors of its *palazzi*, or tucked into the labyrinths of its *calli*, everyday Venetian life goes on. Those residents who have refused to join the mass exodus to the mainland – what Venetians haughtily call *la campagna* (the country) – are hopelessly smitten by their timeless seductress, for better or for worse. These devotees (with help from the rest of the world) are working diligently to ensure that their 1,500-year-old temptress – the most magical city on the planet – remains vibrant and alive, albeit with a few nips and tucks.

Beyond island Venice is another world again, that of the Veneto. While La Serenissima continues to hold the world in her thrall, the terra firma side of the lagoon has come – quietly but steadily – into its own: besides being one of Italy's biggest economic success stories, it now has a burgeoning tourist industry, with annual arrivals expected to rise from the current 58 million visitors to 70 million in the next three or four years, making it the most visited region in all of Italy.

Things were not always so rosy. Venice had slipped far into decline before the city capitulated to Napoleon's troops in 1797. Under Austrian rule (1815-66), it was relegated to the status of a picturesque, inconsequential backwater. But if the city suffered, the fate of its former mainland territories was even worse: with no industry to speak of, agriculturally behind the times, the Veneto ran the semi-feudal south a close race for the title of Italy's own Third World. Between 1876 and 1901, almost 35 per cent of the 5.2 million desperate Italians who sought a better life abroad were fleeing from the crushing poverty of the Veneto and the neighbouring Friuli region.

Massive industrialisation in Venice's mainland Porto Marghera area after World War I and – more extensively – World War II served to shift the more impoverished sectors of the population from agricultural to urban areas. But the poverty remained. As recently as 1961, 48 per cent of homes in the north-east had no running water, 72 per cent had no bathroom and 86 per cent had no heating.

What the people of the Veneto did have, however, was a deep-rooted attachment to their traditional crafts, and a cussedness of character unmatched anywhere else in Italy. In the past, both proved detrimental: in the age of heavy industry, small-scale manufacturing was a sure-fire loser; and when captains of heavy industry sought meek vassals to man the furnaces, many of the natives of the Veneto who protested were forcibly deported to populate Fascist new towns in the malarial swamps south of Rome.

ECONOMIC MIRACLE

It was not, in fact, until the 1970s that north-eastern determination came into its own. With a growing trend towards industrial downscaling, those family-run workshops that had tightened their belts and ridden out the bad times gradually became viable business concerns. So Giuliana Benetton's humble knitting machine gave birth to a global clothing empire based in Treviso, and the metal-working lessons imparted to Leonardo del Vecchio in his orphanage spawned Luxottica, the world's biggest producer of spectacle frames, in Belluno, and Ivano Beggio progressed from tinkering with bikes in his father's cycle shop in Noale to running Aprilia, where 60 per cent of Europe's 250cc motorbikes are churned out.

Theories explaining the north-eastern miracle are as numerous as they are unconvincing. Most sociologists and economists agree, however, that the region's historical links across the Alps to Austria, Germany and eastern Europe and its family ties to successful emigrants further afield gave it a vocation for export unmatched anywhere else in Italy. Through the mid to late 1990s, one-third of the country's huge balance of trade surplus was generated in the north-east.

Back in Venice, the city that once lorded it over the whole of the eastern Mediterranean, the situation was bleaker. The odd boat was still being constructed in small shipyards, a few glass-blowing workshops were still active on the island of Murano and a small fishing fleet was still operative. As terra firma became

increasingly industrialised, blue-collar workers looked across the water for employment. Then, realising that housing there was cheaper, dryer and easier to park in front of, they moved out in an exodus that has brought the population of island Venice plunging from around 170,000 in 1946 to about 65,000 today.

Still, for an area about the size of New York's Central Park, that's a respectable figure. Add to that a sizeable student population, a dedicated group of ex-pats and part-time residents, plus the thousands of workers who commute to Venice from the mainland each day, and the result is a solid base of locals that gives Venice its distinct flavour.

'For all its quaintness, Venice strives to make its voice heard in the modern world.'

THE LIVING CITY

The stalwarts who remain cite many reasons for their endurance: the beauty, the culture, the quality of life, the lack of cars. Granted, many cheese shops have succumbed to mask-makers and many butchers have fallen victim to Murano glass; but compared to the corporate cookie-cutter megastores that exist in other major cities, even these tourist-oriented outlets – when coupled with the remaining family-owned wine shops, pastry shops and vegetable stands – make Venice seem downright cosy. Provincial it may be, but provincialism has its perks. The city is remarkably safe, give or take a pickpocket or two: children walk to school unattended; and an unescorted woman can wander home in the wee hours of the morning, without encountering anything more threatening than a flirtatious local blade.

Moreover, the ramifications of living in a car-less society cannot be underestimated. And forced to walk or hop the vaporetto, the small-town nature of Venice helps to cultivate relationships. It is almost impossible to saunter down the street and not bump into acquaintances, duck into a bar, toss back a coffee or a spritz (see p167 **Rosy to hazy**) and catch up on the current gossip... a favourite Venetian pastime.

For all its quaintness, Venice strives to make its voice heard in the modern world. A left-leaning oasis in an increasingly conservative north-east, the city adorns its vaporetti with ads demanding a halt to the death penalty, rather than promoting the usual multinational giants. A letter drafted by Mayor Paolo Costa urging President George Bush to change his

position on the Kyoto treaty was signed by mayors all over the world. The Centro Pace (Peace Centre), an agency instituted by the city council in 1983, now has more than 35 member-organisations under its umbrella. The myriad international associations dedicated to restoring and safeguarding the city's historical fabric believe that conflicts are laid aside by those involved in their cultural initiatives. In the 2001 fiscal year, very diverse private institutions throughout the world stumped up over €1.2 million for projects to restore and promote Venice's treasures.

Likewise in the arts, 21st-century Venice is loath to content itself with passively showcasing the vast hoard of wonders contained in its galleries and churches: the city council, businesses and cultural associations are striving to ensure that Venice shrugs off her reputation as historic theme park and features on the list of the world's most vibrant cultural centres.

'Day trippers contribute little to the city, economically speaking, yet their presence is overwhelming.'

In 1999 the Biennale (*see p206*) enlarged its umbrella to cover not only film, the visual arts and architecture, but also the performing arts, attracting international performers in music, dance and theatre. The cavernous Arsenale (*see p90*), where Venice once built its great warships, has been undergoing a gradual restoration programme, with some areas now used as a venue for cultural events and exhibitions; there are further plans to transform its 46 hectares into a centre for qualified research and production relating to maritime technology. Every year, the Fondazione Giorgio Cini (*see p128*) plays host to major intellectuals, artists, scholars, politicians and economists who visit the island of San Giorgio Maggiore for conferences, study encounters or concerts. A joint project involving the Fondazione Cini and the Biennale breathed new life into that same island's Teatro Verde, a 1,200-seat open-air theatre nestled among cypress trees with a splendid view of the lagoon.

COPING WITH THE TOURISTS

However, there's no getting away from the fact that part of Venice's magical and other-worldly quality derives from its demography: with a population that appears to be composed entirely of visitors, at least in the main tourist centres, real life is largely hidden from view.

Venice attracts 12 million visitors annually, of which 80 per cent are day-trippers in groups:

during peak holidays, this can translate into as many as 150,000 people. It is this stressful dawn-to-dusk mass that saps the city's resources. They contribute little to the city, economically speaking, yet their presence is overwhelming: Venetian residents can get understandably peeved when, rushing for an appointment, they find the calle ahead blocked by a mob of spellbound foreigners, their leader shepherding the group with a flower-on-a-stick.

Though Venice also attracts a more sophisticated traveller, who spends an average 3.8 days in the city – more than in either Florence (2.5 days) or Rome (2.6 days) – it is to the masses that city hall has begun to turn its attention after years of indecision. Tour buses and boats are now charged an admission fee in an attempt to help meet the cost of maintaining Venice's delicate infrastructure. A new, ultra-modern airport (*see p274*) can serve 6.5 million passengers a year, making it the third largest airport in Italy.

Still on the drawing board – though slated for construction in the not-too-distant future – are Frank Gehry's design for the Venice Gateway project, a new 30,000-square-metre (100,000 square-foot) complex that will enlarge the dockyard at the airport and include a hotel, conference hall and meeting rooms; and Santiago Calatrava's bridge across the Grand Canal, a glass and Istrian stone construction linking the train station to piazzale Roma and, hopefully, providing further relief at clogged arrival areas (*see p31* **The shock of the new**).

The current administration is committed to reopening the fairways leading to Venice's port – one of the world's biggest cruise-ship docks with 18,000 workers, 10,000 ships in annual transit, and a yearly turnover of €1.3 million – and has ambitions to build a 2,000-car garage, joining the port to the other parking areas of Tronchetto and piazzale Roma by monorail. More surreal is Mayor Costa's pet project, on which much scorn has been poured by environmentalists, for an underground railway, passing beneath the lagoon direct from the airport to Murano (*see p135*) and the Arsenale, thus allowing visitors and the thousands of mainland residents who commute to island Venice daily to bypass the current access points.

That the lagoon city exists at all is evidence of the determined nature of the Venetian folk. Throughout the centuries, Venetians have consistently refashioned themselves to fit their circumstances. These most recent innovations are resulting in an influx of business travellers and cultural enthusiasts who are discovering Venice's latest transformation: into an eternal city that embraces its past, while gazing steadily toward the future.

Th at Sinking Feeling

Venice is in peril. But can the city be saved?

Is Venice sinking? To be frank, yes. Though the term is far from adequate to describe the effects of the huge range of phenomena – natural and man-made, local and global – that are making the waters of La Serenissima's lagoon lap over her pavements.

You'll need some idea of Venetian construction techniques and the city's unique relationship with its lagoon to understand how things came to reach the pass they are at today. All of the buildings of Venice rest on a stratum of compacted clay known as *caranto* – the remains of the ancient Venetian plane, which subsided aeons ago. On top of the *caranto* are silt and sand deposits of variable depths. On the mainland side of the lagoon, the sand is just a few metres deep; further out towards the Adriatic there are tens of metres of the stuff.

When the lagoon's earliest inhabitants got down to building their first permanent dwellings, they drove their sharp-ended stakes of larch and oak through the more recent, less compact deposits and into the solid clay base. It was these stakes that were to bear the weight of all that would be built on the 118 islands that make up Venice. Lack of oxygen in the clay saved the wood from the ravages of decomposition, and turned the stakes hard as rock. As you walk through Venice's *calli*, you are, in effect, striding across the top of a petrified forest.

Throughout Venice's history, water has been its life-blood and its means of defence. According to the 16th-century Edict of Ignatius – engraved on a black marble plaque that hung above the door of the Magistero alle Acque (*see p103*) and now visible in the Museo Correr, *see p75*) – Venice was 'founded on water, surrounded by water, and protected by water in lieu of walls'. Penalties for citizens profaning these watery 'walls' were draconian.

Today, the ever-changing lagoon environment faces three possible destinies. If erosion and sedimentation counter-balance each other effectively, the lagoon will survive. If, on the other hand, too many solids are deposited by the river- and seawater that flow into the lagoon, the lagoon bed will rise: in the (very) long term, Venice would become a land-locked jewel in a grassy plain. But if the sea is allowed to get the upper hand, it will reclaim the city for itself, absorbing the lagoon into the Adriatic.

Since time immemorial, safeguarding and conserving the delicate balance upon which the lagoon – and Venice itself – depend has proved a tricky problem. In the 14th century, major works were undertaken to reroute some of the rivers – the Brenta and numerous smaller waterways – that flowed directly into the lagoon, thus avoiding deposits of solids that would have filled it in. This strategy had the added benefit of raising salinity levels and thus driving away (some of the) mosquitoes.

In the first years of the 16th century, the city created the Magistrato alle Acque, an office with the sole task of safeguarding the lagoon environment. The Magistrato initiated more major engineering works through the years, culminating in the second half of the 18th century with the construction of the *murazzi* – sea walls in Istrian stone still visible along the coast (*see p132*) – and the closure of two of the five outlets to the sea. Under French and Austrian rule during the early 19th century, projecting jetties, complete with lighthouses, were positioned in such a

way as to use sea currents to erode 'natural' channels through which deep-keeled ships could sail into the shallow lagoon.

The 20th century was not kind to the Venetian lagoon. From the end of World War II until 1980, this fragile environment was left to its own devices. No, worse: it was actively destroyed. In the frenetic, profit-driven years of the Italian industrial miracle (*see p20*) from the 1950s to 1970s, a fatal mix of neglect and speculation wreaked untold damage. *Acqua alta* – those high tides that drive the lagoon level higher than Venice's pavements – became a rule rather than an exception as the industrial district across on the mainland expanded, tapping immense quantities of water from aquifers (water-bearing layers of soil or rock) that extended right below Venice itself; in very few years, the city sank ten centimetres (four inches). Floods occurred in piazza San Marco, one of the city's lowest points, 40 times a year instead of the usual six or seven. To compound the problem, global warming and melting ice caps helped drive the world's sea levels up by 11 centimetres (4.3 inches) during this period – a phenomenon known as eustatic change.

Channels 18 metres (59 feet) deep were hacked into the lagoon bed to permit petrol tankers (1,200 transit each year) and cruise ships to pass through, with risks to the environment. Landfill was used to create and/or enlarge islands such as Sant'Elena, Sacca Fisola and Tronchetto. Pollution levels sky-rocketed too: 3.5 million tonnes of industrial waste water containing chloride, mercury, dioxin and other toxins were being dumped into the lagoon daily, and this on top of the household grey- and blackwater that naturally finds its way into the canals and the lagoon of this city with no waste treatment plant to mention, giving it its oh-so-characteristic odour, especially in the dog days of summer.

Lagoon statistics

Size of Venetian lagoon: 549sq km.
Sea water entering the lagoon from the Adriatic daily: 400 million cubic metres.
Fresh water entering the lagoon from rivers yearly: 900 million cubic metres.
Height of 'normal' high tide: 60cm above zero level.
Height of *acqua alta*: more than 80cm above zero level.
Height of *acqua alta eccezionale*: (exceptionally high tide): more than 110cm above zero level.
City pavements under water during *acqua alta*: three per cent.
City pavements under water if high tide reaches 140cm: 90 per cent.

Out in the lagoon, formations that had been there for millennia began to change. Slowly but steadily, *velme* (outcrops exposed only at low tide), *barene* (low-lying outcrops submerged only by particularly high tides) and *ghebi* (the arabesque canals that wend their tortuous way across the body of water) began to disappear.

In a very short period, the lagoon became saltier, deeper, flatter and dirtier than it had ever been before. And every year, the *acqua alta* situation became more dramatic.

Venice's tides are measured against the *zero mareografico* (zero sea level), a height established by convention at the Punta della Dogana (*see see chaper* **Dorsoduro**). When the lagoon waters rise 80 centimetres (32 inches) above this zero level, it's *acqua alta*. A rise of 110 centimetres (43 inches) and it's an *acqua alta eccezionale*. In November 1966 it reached 194 centimetres (76 inches), with the worst flooding the city had – and has – ever seen, causing inestimable damage to Venice's urban fabric

and artistic treasures. For the last ten years of the 20th century, tides in November, December, February and April rose above the one metre level an average 130 times. Which means almost every day, and sometimes twice a day.

This excessive rise and fall in water levels, coupled with vibrations from boat engines, is responsible for the *moto ondoso*, the worst enemy of Venetian foundations. As the water rises above normal levels, larger and larger sections of house walls become water-logged. As the water recedes again, the walls, still full of water, weigh increasingly heavily on foundations. Which, sooner or later, must give.

Current research shows that Venice is subsiding at a steady – but reassuringly slow – rate of one millimetre a year. There's nothing, however, nearly so comforting about the rates at which the sea is rising. Worst-case prophets foresee a leap of 49-57 centimetres (19-22 inches) in sea levels globally by 2100. For Venice, that would mean *acqua alta* twice a day, every day.

Stemming the flow

Proposals for keeping Venice afloat are almost as numerous as the visionaries, experts and politicians who have applied their minds to the problem over the years. The job of safeguarding the lagoon environment – not to mention sifting through and implementing chosen schemes – has fallen to the Consorzio Venezia Nuova. Under this body's guidance, initiatives have been launched to raise the height of canal-side *fondamenta* pavements, dredge silt from ever-more-shallow canal bottoms, reinforce 46 kilometres (29 miles) of sea walls, patch up the jetties by the *bocche di porto* (sea entrances) and severely limit transit by petrol tankers through the lagoon.

But the biggest, most expensive and unquestionably most controversial project adopted by the Consorzio Venezia Nuovo is known as **MoSE** (Modulo Sperimentale Elettromeccanico). First mooted in the early '80s, over the ensuing years this project has been alternately approved as the only means of saving Venice from the waves and rejected as a costly ecological nonsense. But as this guide went to press, the centre-right national government finally looked set to stump up the cash for the project. And a whole lot of cash it is too.

MoSE will consist of a series of 79 hollow steel barrages – each five metres (16 feet) deep, 20 metres (70 feet) wide and 30

metres (100 feet) high – to be installed between the Adriatic and the lagoon (21 at Lido-Treporti, 20 at Lido-San Nicolò, 20 at Malamocco, 18 at Chioggia). When tides are within acceptable levels, the barrages will lurk on the sea bottom filled with seawater. But if the wind gets up and waters show signs of rising too high, air will be pumped into the barrages and they will shoot up to stem the flow into the lagoon. The MoSE scheme will take about eight years to put into place, Consorzio says. And it will cost some 3.7 billion.

Environmental groups are vociferously against the scheme: it's unwarrantedly expensive, they say, and its environmental impact will be immense.

The alternatives? Well, Venice could go on raising its pavements as it has done throughout history... though how long it can go on 'burying' its buildings is a moot point. There are, however, more 'natural' solutions, environmentalists argue, that when used together could reduce tides by an estimated 40 centimetres (16 inches). These include raising ground levels at the *bocche di porto* – thus reducing the volume of seawater able to flow into the lagoon – and hacking away levées built over the ages to stop high tides sweeping into far-flung areas of the lagoon set aside for fishing... perfect overflow areas for tidal excesses.

IUAV università degli studi

A university with a tradition of excellence in architecture
In the most unique city in the world

faculty of architecture

The goal of the faculty of architecture is to prepare professionals to design, control and manage the processes of physical transformation of space and environments where man lives, through the study of the architectural project in its figurative-formal and technical-construction aspects.

- undergraduate degree in architectural science (three years)
- undergraduate degree in construction (three years)
- graduate programme in architecture (two years)

tel + 39 (0) 41 257 1735
fax + 39 (0) 41 257 1795
www.iuav.it/architettura
architettura@iuav.it

faculty of arts and design

It is difficult to "train artists", but it is possible to teach art "practices" and propose an education which combines experience in workshops and theoretical courses.
The programmes offer third-level education for careers as artists, curators, directors, set-designers and theatre producers.
Design graduates may seek employment as industrial designers, editorial graphic designers, or work in multimedia communications.

- undergraduate degree in industrial design (three years)
- undergraduate degree in visual arts and theatre (three years)
- graduate programme in product design (two years)
- graduate programme in visual and multimedia design (two years)
- graduate programme in visual arts (two years)
- graduate programme in theatre (two years)

tel + 39 (0) 41 257 1321
fax + 39 (0) 41 257 1326
www.iuav.it/design-arti
design.arti@iuav.it

faculty of urban and regional planning

The faculty of urban and regional planning offers programmes in areas of planning, design and urban, regional and environmental regeneration.
The undergraduate programmes prepare students for careers as analysts and junior planners, qualified to work in planning and government.
The graduate programme prepares experts who may work as independent professionals with extensive expertise.

- undergraduate degree in urban and regional planning science (three years)
- undergraduate degree in territorial information systems (distance learning) (three years)
- graduate programme in urban and regional planning (two years)

tel + 39 (0) 41 524 2312
fax + 39 (0) 41 524 2535
www.iuav.it/pianificazione
pianificazione@iuav.it

www.iuav.it

Architecture

Venetians borrowed and stole to make something unique.

In his overlong but immensely enjoyable work *The Stones of Venice* (1853), John Ruskin set out to discredit 'the pestilent art of the Renaissance' in favour of 'healthy and beautiful' Gothic. The swathe of radical new designs taking shape in the lagoon city (*see p31* **The shock of the new**) must have the opinionated critic turning in his grave. For Ruskin and his stiff-collared Victorian cronies did as much as anyone to turn the city into an architectural sacred cow, untouchable by the unclean hand of innovation. Yet if there's one city in the world where the concept of architectural purity simply doesn't apply, it's Venice.

Venice's architecture, like much else in the maritime republic, is based on borrowings, assimilations and daylight robberies. Not content with drawing architectural inspiration from Constantinople and Rome, and decorating its *palazzi* with looted treasures, it also looked beyond the lagoon for its architects. Of the four architects who can claim to have altered the fabric of the city, two are out-of-towners: Tuscan-born Jacopo Sansovino, and Andrea Palladio, from Padua. The native talents – early Renaissance master Mauro Codussi and baroque wonderboy Baldassare Longhena – usually get second billing. In fact Codussi

was completely unknown until his name was unearthed from archives towards the end of the 19th century.

MEDIEVAL AND BYZANTINE

It all started in Torcello, where the cathedral of **Santa Maria Assunta** (*see p140*), founded in 639, is the oldest surviving building on the lagoon. It has been remodelled since then – notably in the ninth and 11th centuries – but still retains the simple form of an early Christian basilica. Next door, the 11th-century church of **Santa Fosca** (*see p139*) has a Greek-cross plan – also found in **San Giacomo al Rialto** (*see p103*), which is traditionally thought to be the earliest church in Venice (though the present structure dates mainly from 1071). The portico of Santa Fosca exhibits a feature that recurs in the first-floor windows of 12th-century townhouses such as **Ca' Loredan** or **Ca' Dona della Madonetta**, both on the Grand Canal – stilted arches, where horseshoe-shaped arches are supported on slender columns.

The history of Venetian domestic architecture in this early period can be charted by following the development of the arch, which is the most typically Venetian of all structural devices. This is understandable in a city built

Santi Giovanni e Paolo.
See p29.

on mud, where load-bearing capabilities were a prime consideration. In the latter part of the 13th century the pure, curved Byzantine arch began to sport a point at the top, under the influence of Islamic models – early examples of this can be seen in the heavily restored **Albergo del Selvadego** in calle dell'Ascensione, **San Marco**, and **Palazzo Vitturi** in campo Santa Maria Formosa. Soon this point developed into a fully fledged ogee arch – two concave-convex curves meeting at the top – a northern Gothic trait, but one that has also been found in southern Indian cave art from as early as the third century BC.

SAN MARCO

Meanwhile, the **Basilica di San Marco** (*see pp71-4*) was into its sixth century of growth. Founded in 829-32 by the Partecipazio family, the original church was modelled on the Church of the Apostles in Constantinople. This first church burnt down, but had been rebuilt by 1075. The main body of the church – and its Greek-cross plan surmounted by five domes – dates from the 11th century; but it was embellished extensively over the next four centuries, sometimes with curious results (note the curved Byzantine arches on the façade surmounted by hopeful Gothic ogees). Two humbler 12th-century churches, **San Giacomo dell'Orio** (*see p110*) and **San Nicolò dei Mendicoli** (*see p116*), both feature squat belltowers apart from the church – a key feature of the Veneto-Byzantine style.

GOTHIC AND LATE GOTHIC

In the 14th and 15th centuries Venetian architecture developed an individual character unmatched before or since. It was at this time – when Venice had beaten Genoa for control of eastern Mediterranean sea routes, and when the republic was engaged in large-scale terra firma expansion – that the city's own Arab-tinged version of Gothic came into its own.

By the mid 14th century the ogee arch had sprouted a point on the inside of its concave edge – producing the cusped arch, which distributes the forces pressing down on it so efficiently that Ruskin decreed that 'all are imperfect except these'. By the beginning of the 15th century, this basic shape had been hedged around with elaborate tracery and trefoils (clover-shaped openings) and topped with Moorish-looking pinnacles in a peculiarly Venetian take on the flamboyant Gothic style, which reached its apotheosis in the façades of the **Palazzo Ducale** (*see pp77-9*) and the **Ca' d'Oro** (*see p95*) – both completed by 1440. The Palazzo Ducale was a prime example of the Venetian faith in tradition for architecture:

a design first initiated in the 1340s – possibly by stonemason Filippo Calendario – was duplicated faithfully over the following century – The florid **Porta della Carta** (1438; *see p77*) is a prime example.

CHURCHES AND SCUOLE

Outside of St Mark's, church architecture mainly reflected the traditional building styles of the orders who commissioned the work: the cavernous brick monuments of **Santi Giovanni e Paolo** (completed in 1430; *see p87*) and the **Frari** (1433; *see pp113-4*) are classic examples of, respectively, the Dominican and Franciscan approaches. Both have a Latin cross plan, a façade pierced by a large rose window and a generous sprinkling of pinnacles. More individual are some smaller churches such as **Santo Stefano** (*see p82*) – with its wooden ship's keel roof – and the earliest *scuole* (*see p61*), such as the **Scuola Vecchia della Misericordia** (*see p97*), with its ogee windows and oddly Flemish-style roof gable. Both involved the collaboration of Giovanni and Bartolomeo Bon, who also worked on the Ca' d'Oro. These talented mid-15th century sculptors and masons are among the first named 'architects' recorded during this period.

THE VENETIAN PALAZZO

Majestic Grand Canal palaces such as **Ca' Foscari** (begun in 1452) and **Palazzo Pisani Moretta** continued to indulge the need for elaborate tracery windows, but behind the façade the structure went back centuries.

The Venetian palazzo was not only a place of residence; in this mercantile city, it was also the family business headquarters, and the internal division of space reflects this.

The standard layout consisted of a ground floor with storerooms surrounding a long, open *androne* – used as an entrance to the rooms above, and for loading, unloading and storing commodities; a first-floor *piano nobile* – with high ceilings – where the family had its living quarters, bisected by a huge *salone* running the whole length of the building. Above this was a floor of servants' quarters, offices and more storerooms. In the grandest *palazzi*, the *piano nobile* was sometimes spread over two floors, with the lower one reserved for receiving guests.

On the roof, between those funnel-shaped chimneys, there may have been a raised wooden balcony or *altana*, where clothes were dried and Titianesque beauties came to bleach their hair in the sun. In a city where space was at a premium, courtyards were almost unheard of; at most, the *androne* itself might become a sort of roofed-in courtyard, as at the Ca' D'Oro or **Ca' Rezzonico** (*see p120*).

EARLY RENAISSANCE

Venetians were so fond of their own gracefully oriental version of Gothic that they held on to it long after the New Classicist orthodoxy had taken over central Italy. For the second half of the 15th century, emergent Renaissance forms existed alongside the Gothic swansong. Sometimes they merged or clashed in the same building, as in the church of **San Zaccaria** (*see p88*), which was begun by Antonio Gambello in 1458 in the purest of northern Gothic styles but completed by Mauro Codussi in the local Renaissance idiom he was then elaborating; the transition is embodied in the façade, which is Gothic below, Renaissance above.

Next to nothing is known about Codussi's background, save that he may have trained under Giovanni Bon. What is certain is that in 1469 he was appointed *protomagister* (works manager) for the church of **San Michele in Isola** (*see p134*), the Franciscan monastery on what is now the city's cemetery island. Within ten years he had completed the first truly Renaissance building in the city. The austere Istrian marble façade with its classical elements has something pre-Palladian about it, though the curves of the pediment and buttresses are pure Codussi, adapted from a late Gothic model. Flexibility was the keyword for Codussi; **Santa Maria Formosa** (*see p87*) is the most Tuscan of his churches, but in **San Giovanni Crisostomo** (built by 1504; *see p95*) he adopted a Greek-cross plan common to the earliest Venetian churches. His *palazzi*, such as **Palazzo Corner Spinelli** or **Palazzo Vendramin Calergi** on the Grand Canal, were equally influential, but equally adapted to local traditions.

LOMBARDESQUE STYLE

Codussi took over a number of projects begun by Pietro Lombardo, who represents the other strand of early Renaissance architecture in northern Italy. This was based on the extensive use of inlaid polychrome marble, Corinthian columns and decorated friezes, in a style that owes much to Lombardo's training as a sculptor of funerary monuments. Lombardo's masterpiece is the jewel-like church of **Santa Maria dei Miracoli** (*see p102*), but he also designed – with the help of his sons Tullio and Antonio – the lower part of the façade of the **Scuola Grande di San Marco** (*see p89*), with its delightful *trompe l'oeil* relief work. The Lombardesque style, as it was known, was all the rage for a while, producing such photogenic charmers as tiny, lopsided **Ca' Dario** on the Grand Canal (1487-92; *see p68*).

HIGH RENAISSANCE

Codussi's influence lingered well into the 16th century in the work of architects such as Guglielmo dei Grigi and Scarpagnino, both of whom have been credited with the design of the **Palazzo dei Camerlenghi** (1525-8) next to the Rialto bridge. It was around this time that piazza San Marco took on the shape we see today, with the construction of the **Procuratie Vecchie** (*see p70*) and also the **Torre dell'Orologio** (*see p79*), both to designs by Codussi and both demonstrating that in the centre of civic power, loyalty to the myth of Venice tended to override architectural fashions and impose a faintly antiquarian style that looked back to the city's Veneto-Byzantine origins.

SANSOVINO AND SAN MARCO

It was not until the late 1520s that something really new turned up, in the form of Jacopo Sansovino, a Tuscan sculptor and would-be architect. Perhaps it was the influence of his new-found friends Pietro Aretino and Titian that secured him the prestigious position of *proto* of St Mark's only two years after his arrival, despite his lack of experience; certainly the gamble paid off, as Sansovino went on to create a series of buildings that changed the face of the city. He began to refine his rational, harmonious Renaissance style in designs for the church of **San Francesco della Vigna** (begun in 1532; *see p86*) and **Palazzo Corner della Ca' Grande** on the Grand Canal, Venice's first Roman-style palazzo, which owes a heavy debt to Bramante. But it was in piazza San Marco that Sansovino surpassed himself, in three buildings all planned in the course of two years, 1536 and 1537. **La Zecca** (*see p80*) – the state mint – with its heavy rustication and four-square solidity, is a perfect financial fortress. The **Biblioteca Marciana** (*see p74*) next door (completed in 1554, also known as the Libreria Sansoviniana), which faces the Doge's Palace, is his masterpiece, disguising its classical regularity beneath a typically Venetian wealth of surface detail. Finally, the little **Loggetta** at the base of the Campanile showed that Sansovino was also capable of a lightness of touch that derived from his sculptural training.

PALLADIAN PRE-EMINENCE

Michele Sanmicheli, primarily a military architect, built the imposing sea defences on the island of Le Vignole, and two hefty Venetian *palazzi*, the **Palazzo Corner Mocenigo** (1559-64) in campo San Polo and the **Palazzo Grimani** (1556-75) on the Grand Canal. But it was another out-of-towner, Andrea Palladio, who would set the agenda for what was left of

The shock of the new

Decades of architectural foot-dragging have given way to frenzied activity on the lagoon where some of the world's top names are turning blueprints to bricks and mortar.

Inaugurated in summer 2002, the new **airport** terminal is billed as a high-tech interpretation of Venice's Arsenale (*see p90*) by local architect Giampaolo Mar. The usual airport lighting and surplus of retailers make it feel like a shopping mall, but this airport certainly demonstrates Venice's commitment to new construction.

Spanish superstar Santiago Calatrava's sleek design for a fourth **bridge over the Grand Canal** will create a much-needed pedestrian link between the bus and rail stations. The bridge is scheduled for completion by early 2004.

London-based architect David Chipperfield won the 1998 competition for the **expansion of San Michele** (*see p134*), the cemetery island. His clean, boxy complex of tomb buildings and gardens will remain architecturally distinct from the island's existing fabric without disturbing the prevailing serenity.

Frank Gehry – responsible for Bilbao's Guggenheim Museum – could be leaving his mark in another Guggenheim city, although this time not at the Peggy Guggenheim Collection (*see p123* **Peggy G**). He won the 'Venice Gateway' competition in 1998 with plans for a twisty complex of buildings providing the new airport with a boat terminal, hotel and convention centre. Hopes are high that his project will make it to construction.

The **IUAV** (the University Institute of Architecture, www.iuav.it), currently located

near piazzale Roma, offers architectural aficionados a host of lectures, conferences and exhibits. Don't miss the entry atrium by Carlo Scarpa. The new seat of the university, designed by the Spanish-Italian team of Enric Miralles and Benedetta Tagliabue, will bring a dynamic profile to the previously inaccessible zone of San Basilio (near Santa Marta).

Venice's best showcase for cutting-edge design is the **Biennale di Architettura** (*see p206* **The Biennale**), where some of the world's hottest architects and installation artists present their visions for the future. This exhibition runs from the second week of September to the first week of November in even-numbered years.

---

the 16th century (*see chapter* **Palladian Villas**). A star in his adopted town of Vicenza, the man who invented the post-Renaissance found it difficult to get a foothold in a city that valued flexibility above critical rigour. But he did design two influential churches: **San Giorgio Maggiore** (begun in 1562; *see p129*); and the **Redentore** (1577-92; *see p128*). Anyone who considers Palladio's designs to be over-simplistic should observe the subtle play of levels and orders on the exterior. The church of the **Zitelle** (*see p127*), also on the Giudecca, was built to Palladio's plans after the architect's death.

Palladio's pupil and follower Vincenzo Scamozzi designed the **Procuratie Nuove** (*see p70*) to complete the north side of piazza

San Marco, which he helped to finish. At the same time, Antonio Da Ponte was commissioned to design a stone bridge at the **Rialto** (*see p103*) in 1588 after designs by Michelangelo and Palladio had been turned down.

BAROQUE

The examples of Sansovino and Palladio continued to be felt well into the 17th century, though buildings such as **Palazzo Balbi** (1582-90) on the Grand Canal, by Alessandro Vittoria, showed the first signs of a transition to baroque opulence. But it wasn't until the arrival on the scene of Baldassare Longhena in the 1620s that Venice got twirly bits in any abundance. Longhena was a local boy who first made his mark with the **Duomo** (*see p133*) in Chioggia. But it was with the church of **Santa Maria della Salute** (*see p125*) that he pulled out all the stops, creating perhaps the greatest baroque edifice outside of Rome. Commissioned in 1632, and 50 years in the making, this huge church dominates the southern reaches of the Grand Canal. Longhena's circular structure updates the Palaeochristian church plan so as to give it a theatrical vocation.

While La Salute was going up, Longhena was also busy designing a series of impressive *palazzi* for rich clients, including the **Palazzo Belloni Battagia** at San Stae and the huge Grand Canal hulk of **Ca' Pesaro** (begun in 1652; *see p106*). He also designed the façade of the **Ospedaletto** (1667-74; *see p85*), with its grotesque telamons.

This was a taste of things to come: the overwrought façade developed in the 1670s through the exuberance of the **Gli Scalzi** (*see p97*) and **Santa Maria Del Giglio** (*see p83*) churches – both the work of Longhena's follower Giuseppe Scalzi – to the bombastic drama of **San Moisè** (*see p83*), a kitsch collaboration between Alessandro Tremignon and sculptor Heinrich Meyring.

NEOCLASSICISM

During the 18th-century decline, tired variations on Palladio and Longhena dominated the scene. Domenico Rossi adorned Palladian orders with swags and statuary in the façades he designed for the churches of **San Stae** (1709-10; *see p111*) and the **Gesuiti** (1715-28; *see p101*). Sumptuous palaces continued to go up along the Grand Canal; one of the last was the solid **Palazzo Grassi** (*see p82*), built between 1748 and 1772. It was designed by Giorgio Massari, the most successful of the city's 18th-century architects. Massari also designed the church of **La Pietà** (*see p91*) – the Vivaldi church – the oval floorplan of which strikes a rare note of originality (though it may have been copied from a church by Sansovino that was swept away by Napoleon). The **Palazzo Venier dei Leoni** – now home to the Peggy Guggenheim Collection (*see p123* **Peggy G**) – also dates from the mid 18th century. If it had ever been finished, this huge palazzo would have been as boring as Palazzo Grassi, but funds ran out after the first storey, giving Venice one of its most bizarrely endearing landmarks.

Giannantonio Selva's **La Fenice** opera house (1790-2; *see p83*) – still being rebuilt after the devastating fire of 29 January 1996 – was one of the Serene Republic's last building projects. Napoleon's arrival in 1797 marked the destruction of many churches and convents, but

also began a series of clearances that allowed for the creation of the city's first public gardens, the **Giardini Pubblici**, and the nearby via Garibaldi. Piazza San Marco took on its present-day appearance at this time, too, when the Procuratie Vecchie and Nuove were united by the neoclassical **Ala Napoleonica** (*see p70*). Restoration rather than building dominated the Austrian occupation of Venice (1815-66). One important project, though, put an end to the city's long history of isolation: the construction of the railway bridge linking Venice to Mestre (1841-2).

SINCE THE RISORGIMENTO

Curiously, the years when Venice became a part of modern Italy were also the years when it began to rediscover its Gothic and Byzantine past. An example is the **Palazzo Franchetti** next to the Ponte dell'Accademia, a 15th-century edifice redesigned in neo-medieval style (1878-82) by opera composer and librettist Camillo Boito. One of the city's most elegant neo-Gothic constructions is the **cemetery** of San Michele (1872-81; *see p134*), the pinnacle-and-arch brick facing of which dominates the northern lagoon view. Another landmark from the same period is the **Molino Stucky** (1897-1920; *see p127*), a huge pasta mill and grain silo at the western end of the Giudecca designed in turreted Hanseatic Gothic style by Ernest Wullekopf. The turn of the century was also a boom time for hotels, with the **Excelsior** on the Lido (1898-1908) setting the eclectic, Moorish-Byzantine agenda.

MODERN ARCHITECTURE

Venice's modern architecture is limited. Only locally born modernist Carlo Scarpa (1906-78) – a master of multifaceted interiors – has had a chance to build up a body of work, with the entrance and garden-patio of the **Biennale** gardens (1952; *see p206* **The Biennale**), the Olivetti showroom (1957-8) in piazza San Marco, and the ground-floor reorganisation of the **Museo Querini Stampalia** (1961-3; *see p85*). There are also one or two adventurous public housing projects around outlying areas of the city or lagoon, such as Giancarlo De Carlo's low-income housing on the island of Mazzorbo (1979-86), an asymmetrical arrangement inspired by the colourful domestic architecture of Burano.

But with a slew of exciting new projects well into pre-production (*see p31* **The shock of the new**), the usual excuse given for architectural stasis, shortage of space, becomes ever less convincing. The resistance to change engendered by Ruskin – a resistance that is now breaking down – may have been the real stumbling block to Venice's vocation to innovation.

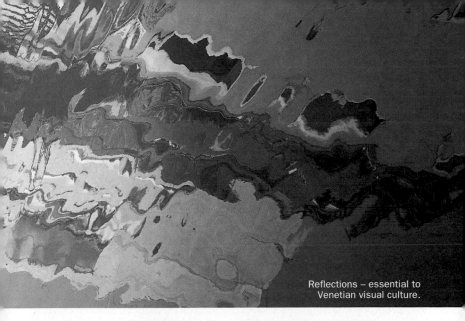

Venetian Painting

Venice is the city where you'll finally understand painting.

From the mid 15th century until the fall of the Republic in 1797, Venice was a centre of the art world, a magnet for talented artists and sophisticated collectors. Even today, artists are lured to Venice by its unique lagoon setting and the superabundance of magnificent paintings designed especially for this singular context… the self-same draws that artists have acknowledged for centuries.

Painters as different as El Greco, Rubens and John Singer Sargent have been transformed by their experience of viewing, for the first time, the great panels and canvases that abound in Venice. Velázquez made a bee-line for the lagoon city during his first visit to Italy in 1629 (he didn't even bother to visit Florence). As he stood open-mouthed before the enormous pictures by Titian, Veronese and Tintoretto, the Spaniard suddenly awoke to the full extent of the possibilities of painting.

The attentive traveller can recreate such artistic epiphanies by observing carefully both technique and setting, since the two are intertwined more in Venice than anywhere else on the globe. Leave the madding crowd at San Marco behind, and you'll soon begin to come across superb pictures in obscure churches:

glowing altarpieces and pulsating canvas *laterali* (paintings for side walls of chapels). Seeing these pictures in their original sites reveals how aware painters were of the relation of their works to the surrounding architecture, light and existing artwork. Yet, exceptionally, the paintings also relate to the physical context of Venice itself. What makes Venetian painting distinctive – the decorated surfaces, asymmetry, shimmering light effects and, above all, warm tonalities – can also be found in the lagoon environment. Venetian visual culture in the Renaissance encompassed the richness of Byzantine mosaics and Islamic art, the haphazard arrangement of streets and canals with their strong shadows, and light experienced through haze or reflected off moving water.

Venetian painting has its roots in mosaics. The glittering 12th- and 13th-century mosaics of the Basilico di San Marco or the cathedral in Torcello provided a visual model of shimmering splendour and a repertory of stories that later painters drew upon for narrative paintings. Although the making of mosaics was entrusted to specialists, important painters contributed designs.

Purveyor of pomp: **Gentile Bellini**'s *Procession in Piazza San Marco*.

THE END OF MEDIEVAL ANONYMITY

Venetian church interiors were once covered with frescos; the damp Venetian climate has meant that very few survive. The official history of Venetian painting begins in the 1320s with the first painter to emerge from medieval anonymity, **Paolo Veneziano** (c1290-1362), who worked in egg tempera and gold leaf on wood panel. He championed the composite altarpiece, which would become one of the key formats of Venetian painting. His polyptychs, such as *The Coronation of the Virgin* in the Accademia (*see p122*), were ornately framed, compartmentalised works featuring sumptuous fabrics, a preference for surface decoration and pattern over depth, and a seriousness – or stiffness – derived from Byzantine icons. A love of drapery and textile patterns proved to be a Venetian constant, still visible in Veronese's paintings in the 16th century and in Tiepolo's in the 18th century.

Although many painters worked in Venice in the century after Paolo, the next major legacy was that of a team, **Giovanni d'Alemagna** (John of Germany) and his brother-in-law **Antonio Vivarini**, who were active in the mid 15th century. Their three altarpieces in San Zaccaria (*see p88*), dated 1443, one in San Pantalon (*see p114*), and a large canvas in the Accademia demonstrate the transition from Gothic to Renaissance. All have benefited from recent restorations that recapture the original courtly elegance and three-dimensional details in *pastiglia* (raised ornament). Although Italian art historians give precedence to Antonio, the sudden decline in the quality of his works after Giovanni's death in 1450 indicates that his partner was the brains behind the operation. Antonio's younger brother **Bartolomeo Vivarini**, who ran the family workshop from the 1470s until about 1491, learned Renaissance style from both painting and sculpture, as seen

in the lapidary figures in the altarpiece (1474) in the Cappella Corner of the Frari (*see p113*).

By the next generation, the main players had become more clearly defined. From around 1480 **Giovanni Bellini** directed the dominant workshop in Venice. Most of Bellini's sizeable output, stretching from the late 1450s until his death in 1516, was painted on wood panel rather than the newer canvas. He cornered the market in small devotional panels commissioned by cultivated private clients. The important group of early Bellini pictures in the Museo Correr (*see p75*) and the many variations on the Madonna and Child theme in the Accademia show how varied and moving these subjects could be. Equally impressive is Bellini's stunning series of altarpieces. In these he perfected the subject of the *Sacra Conversazione* (Sacred Conversation), where standing saints flank a seated figure, usually the Virgin Mary, within a setting that evokes the gold mosaics and costly marbles of the Basilica di San Marco. The inner glow afforded by the new medium of oil paint allowed Bellini to model his figures with an astonishing delicacy of light and shadow. One can follow his progress through a series of altarpieces that remain in situ: in Santi Giovanni e Paolo (*see p87*), the Frari, San Zaccaria and San Giovanni Crisostomo (*see p95*). A letter home by German painter Albrecht Dürer in 1506 shows that Bellini's fame was great in his own lifetime: 'Giovanni Bellini is very old but he is still the best painter of all.' (Dürer would agree that Bellini deserves a cocktail named after him.)

Giovanni's elder brother, **Gentile Bellini**, enjoyed even greater official success: from 1474 until his death in 1507 he directed the decoration of the Palazzo Ducale, replacing crumbling frescos with huge canvases. He also performed a diplomatic role for the Venetian government by travelling to Constantinople in

1479 to paint for the Ottoman sultan. Although his Palazzo Ducale canvases were destroyed by fire in 1577, his *Procession in Piazza San Marco* (1496; pictured p34), now in the Accademia, shows his ability to depict sumptuous public spectacle with choreographed verve.

Three painters born in the second half of the 15th century and active in the 16th are worth seeking out. **Cima da Conegliano** (c1459-1517) offers a stiffer style than Bellini, with figures standing in dignified repose against crisp landscapes. Cima's best altarpieces, in the Accademia, and at San Giovanni in Bragora (*see p91*), the Madonna dell'Orto (recently restored, *see p99*) and the Carmini (*see p121*), all demonstrate a mastery of light.

Vittore Carpaccio (c1465-1525) specialised in narrative works for the *scuole* (*see p61*). These canvases tell a story from left to right, and offer enough miscellaneous detail to immerse the viewer in the daily life of Renaissance Venice. Two intact cycles from around 1500 are among the treasures of Venetian painting: the St Ursula cycle in the Accademia, and that of St George and St Jerome in the Scuola di San Giorgio degli Schiavoni (*see p93*). A striking *Supper at Emmaus* (1513) in the church of San Salvador, recently restored and now attributed to Carpaccio, continues the anecdotal detail in a surprisingly monumental vein.

'It can be argued that the modern concept of the painting was born in Venice around 1500.'

Lorenzo Lotto (c1480-1556), active throughout the first half of the 16th century, spent much of his career outside Venice: he was an entrepreneur who knew how to create markets in provincial centres. His best altarpieces in Venice, in the Carmini and Santi Giovanni e Paolo, combine an uncanny accuracy in rendering landscape or cloth with a deeply felt spirituality. His impressive portraits, such as the *Portrait of a Youth* in the Accademia, employ an unusual horizontal format and convey a seemingly modern melancholy.

INTRODUCING ATMOSPHERE
At the beginning of the 16th century, Venetian painting took a dramatic turn. Three of Bellini's pupils – Giorgione, Sebastiano del Piombo and Titian – experimented with new secular subject matter and new ways of handling paint. **Giorgione** (c1477-1510) remains one of the great enigmas of art. No other reputation rests on so few surviving pictures. The hard contours and emphasis on surface pattern seen in earlier

Venetian painting have softened in his work, and for the first time the atmosphere becomes palpable, like damp lagoon air. Two haunting pictures in the Accademia, *The Tempest* and *La Vecchia*, may be deliberately enigmatic, more concerned with mood than story. It can be argued that the modern concept of the painting was born in Venice around 1500. For the first time, three conditions that we now take for granted were met: these works were all oil on canvas, painted at the artist's initiative, and not for a specific location.

Sebastiano del Piombo (c1485-1547) left his mark with a similar emphasis on softened contour and tangible atmosphere. His major altarpiece, painted some time around 1507 and still in San Giovanni Crisostomo, shows a *Sacra Conversazione* in which some of the figures are seen in profile, rather than head on, and hidden in shadow. Even more exciting is a set of standing saints painted as organ shutters, now in the Accademia, which show an unprecedented application of thick paint (*impasto*).

Events conspired to boost the early career of **Titian** (Tiziano Vecellio, c1488-1576) when, in the space of only six years (1510-16), Giorgione fell victim to the plague, Sebastiano del Piombo moved to Rome and Giovanni Bellini died too. Titian soon staked his claim with a dynamic *Assumption of the Virgin* for the high altar of the Frari (1518). There he dominated the enormous space by creating the largest panel painting in the world. Although Titian gained fame throughout Europe for his portraits and mythological paintings, no examples of these survive in Venice. The lagoon city is, however, the place to appreciate *in situ* the 70-year span of his religious work. These include a second altarpiece in the Frari (the *Madonna di Ca' Pesaro*, which is a *Sacra Conversazione* rotated on its axis), the virile St Christopher fresco in the Palazzo Ducale (*see p77*) and the ceiling paintings in the sacristy of the Salute (*see p125*).

For a decade (c1527-39) Titian had a true rival in **Pordenone** (1483?-1539), a painter of muscular figures engaged in violent action. Now, for the first time in decades, Pordenone's work can be appreciated in Venice. The recently restored *Saints Christopher and Martin* in the church of San Rocco (*see p114*) and the confrontation in the reopened church of San Giovanni Elemosinario (*see p105*), where Pordenone's bulging figures on the right altar square off against the soft edges of Titian's high altar show an urgent style that had great appeal. Yet once again Titian reaped good fortune when his adversary suddenly died.

By the 1560s, in works such as the extraordinary *Annunciation* in San Salvador (*see p81*), Titian's handling of paint had become so loose that forms were not so much defined by contours as caressed into being. Line was replaced by quivering patches of warm colouring. Canvas, which had originally been seen as a cheap and durable substitute for fresco or wood, was now a textured surface to exploit. Contemporaries swore that the old artist painted as often with his fingers as with the brush. Nowhere is this tactile quality more apparent than in Titian's final painting, a *Pietà*, originally intended for his tomb, and now in the Accademia. Left unfinished at his death during the plague of 1576, this picture summarises the Venetian artistic tradition, with its glittering mosaic dome and forms so dissolved as to challenge the very conventions of painting.

Instead of mourning Titian's death, Jacopo Robusti (c1518-94) – better known as **Tintoretto** – probably breathed a sigh of relief. Though he rose to fame in the late 1540s, he had to wait until he was 58 years old before he could claim the title of Venice's greatest living painter. Yet Tintoretto was canny enough to learn from his rival. He supposedly inscribed the motto 'The drawing of Michelangelo and the colouring of Titian' on the wall of his studio. Tintoretto's breakthrough work, *The Miracle of the Slave* (1548), now in the Accademia, offered a brash attempt at this synthesis, combining Michelangelo's confident muscular anatomies with Titian's shimmering paint surface. Borrowing the figure types and violent compositions of Pordenone, Tintoretto's aggressive and tumultuous canvases marked the end of the decorative narrative painting tradition perfected by Carpaccio.

Unlike Titian, Tintoretto is an artist who can only be appreciated in Venice. Among the dozens of works in his home town, the soaring choir paintings in the Madonna dell'Orto (c1560) or the many canvases at the Scuola Grande di San Rocco (*see p115*), dated 1564-87, amaze in their scale and complexity. Tintoretto offered his clients free pictures or steep discounts, revealing a knack for marketing. His many workshop assistants, including two sons and a daughter, allowed him to increase production to unprecedented quantities. Like his contemporaries Bassano and Veronese, Tintoretto went even further than Titian in the liberation of the brush stroke. Rough brushwork and impasto served as a sort of signature for these artists. The tradition of bravura handling that goes from Rubens to Delacroix to De Kooning begins with the action painters of 16th-century Venice.

Paolo Veronese (1528-88) made his impact in Venice with a love of rich fabrics and elegant poses that contrasts with Tintoretto's agitated figures. Veronese's savoir faire is best seen in the overpopulated feasts he painted for monastery refectories. The example now in the Accademia got its painter into hot water. When confronted by the Inquisition in 1573 over a *Last Supper* in which figures of 'buffoons, drunkards, Germans, dwarves' apparently insulted church decorum, Veronese pleaded artistic licence. He cleverly got around the Inquisition's command to alter the picture by changing the title to *Feast in the House of Levi* (pictured p38). Veronese's wit can also be seen in one of the few great 16th-century

Made to order

A striking percentage of Venice's greatest paintings remain in their original settings. Many, moreover, were ingeniously designed to blend in with, stand out from or take advantage of their particular setting; painters would cleverly adapt their pictures to conform to lighting conditions, surrounding architecture and other, 'competing' artworks.

The simplest adaptations continued the design of an altarpiece's stone frame within the architecture of the painted scene; Bellini's altarpieces for the churches of San Zaccaria and San Giobbe (the latter painting now in the Accademia) created powerful illusions of depth.

Other paintings respond to natural light. **Cima da Conegliano**'s altarpiece in the Madonna dell'Orto, for example, shows John the Baptist – 'sent to bear witness to that light that was the true light' – gazing upward toward the actual light coming through a window.

Sensitivity to a painting's setting reached a new sophistication with **Titian**'s altarpieces in the Frari, both of which presuppose that they will be approached from the main entrance. Titian designed his huge *Assumption* (1516-18) over the high altar to be seen first from the nave, through the arch of the Gothic choir screen. From closer in, the compositional sections of the painting parallel the architectural divisions of the window tracery behind. More complicated is the *Madonna di Ca' Pesaro* in the left aisle. This altarpiece features a grouping of saints rotated off-centre so that the painting can be understood both from head-on and as one approaches from the left. Note how the red and white paving and the huge grey columns in the picture resemble those in the church itself.

mythological paintings remaining in Venice: *The Rape of Europa* in the Palazzo Ducale, with its leering, slightly comical bull. His supreme ensemble piece is in San Sebastiano (*see p118*), a church that features altars, ceilings, frescos and organ shutters all painted by Veronese, as well as the artist's tomb.

Venetian painting was also practised outside Venice: **Jacopo Bassano** (c1510-92) was an artist based in a provincial centre who kept pace with the latest innovations. Although his work is best seen in his hometown of Bassano del Grappa (*see p267*), canvases in the Accademia and an altarpiece in San Giorgio Maggiore (*see p129*) display characteristic Venetian flickering brushwork and dramatic chiaroscuro.

With the following generation, the golden age of Venetian painting drew to a close. The super-prolific **Palma il Giovane** (c1548-1628), who completed Titian's *Pietà*, now in the Accademia, created works loosely in the style of Tintoretto. His finest pictures, such as the *Crucifixion* in

Tintoretto built upon the innovations of Titian with his extraordinary paintings (1564-87) in the Scuola Grande di San Rocco. On the upper floor, through the doorway into the Sala del Albergo, one gets a remarkable first glimpse of the central group in the panoramic *Crucifixion* (pictured). At the altar end in the Sala Superiore all the surrounding canvases on wall and ceiling – from the *Last Supper* to the *Miracle of the Loaves and Fishes* – are about bread and spiritual food. On the lower floor, notice how Tintoretto brilliantly repeated in the bending branches of the landscape in the *Flight into Egypt* the form of the windows in the room. Perhaps Tintoretto's cleverest adaptation was achieved in the *Last Supper* in San Giorgio Maggiore. When viewed from the intended viewing position – just before entering the railed presbytery – the table in the painting is perpendicular to the viewer, an extension of the real high altar. Moreover, as one moves toward the choir (and changes point of view from average worshipper to privileged monk), the painted table and the disciples seem to pivot within the painting.

As this guide went to press, restorers were working on one of the greatest Venetian painterly stand-offs, in the church of San Giovanni Crisostomo. Around 1507 **Sebastiano del Piombo** painted a pioneering *Sacra Conversazione* for the high altar, in which the central figure of St John Chrysostom was seen in a shadowy profile, lost in his reading. Six years later, Sebastiano's teacher, the aged **Giovanni Bellini**, finished an altarpiece for the right altar responding to the young upstart. Bellini matched Sebastiano's red and white paving, and then made sure to have his central bearded figure of St Jerome – equipped with a nifty reading stand – face his counterpart at the high altar. Although Bellini may have been born more than 50 years before his student, with this juxtaposition he proved that an old dog could come up with new tricks.

Paolo Veronese's *Feast in the House of Levi. See p36.*

the Madonna dell'Orto or those in San Giacomo dell'Orio (*see p110*) or the Oratorio dei Crociferi (*see p102*), all date from the 1580s. After the deaths of Veronese and Tintoretto it seems that the pressure was gone and the quality of Palma's work took a nose dive.

BAROQUE AND ROCOCO

In the years that followed, the baroque in Venice was represented largely by out-of-towners (**Luca Giordano**, whose recently restored altarpieces adorn the Salute) or by bizarre posturing (**Gian Antonio Fumiani**'s stupefying canvas ceiling in San Pantalon). Exaggerated light effects ruled the day. It was only at the beginning of the 18th century, as Venetian political and economic power slipped away, that Venetian painting experienced a resurgence. In the first half of the century, **Giambattista Piazzetta** (1683-1754) produced a ceiling painting in Santi Giovanni e Paolo and a sequence of altarpieces (particularly those in Santa Maria della Fava, *see p81*, the Gesuati, *see p101*, and San Salvador), all demonstrating restrained elegance and a muted palette of gold, black and brown. He enlivened otherwise static compositions by placing the figures in a zigzag arrangement.

   Giambattista Tiepolo (1696-1770), the greatest painter of the Venetian rococo, adapted Piazzetta's zigzag scheme for use with warm pastel colours. In his monumental ceilings in the Gesuati, the Pietà (*see p91*) and Ca' Rezzonico (*see p120*), Tiepolo reintroduced fresco on a large scale after more than two centuries of canvas ceilings. Perhaps the most satisfying place to view his work is the upper room of the Scuola Grande dei Carmini (*see p121*), where the disproportionately low ceiling provides a close-up view of his technique.

The essence of the Venetian rococo is to be found in the sites where architecture, sculpture and painting were employed to form a unified whole: the Gesuati, Santa Maria della Fava, San Stae (*see p111*) and Ca' Rezzonico.

'By the time of Napoleon's conquest, Venetian painting, like Venetian military power, was a spent force.'

In the 18th century, both local and foreign collectors provided a constant demand for portraits and city views. A woman artist, **Rosalba Carriera** (1675-1757), developed a refined style of portrait using pastels. **Canaletto** (1697-1768) and **Guardi** (1712-93) offered views of Venice, respectively in sharp focus and softly blurred. The popularity of these landscape paintings as Grand Tour souvenirs means that although examples exist in the Accademia and Ca' Rezzonico, both artists are seen at their best in Britain. A different aspect of 18th-century painting, and perhaps Guardi's masterpiece, can be seen in the astonishingly delicate *Stories of Tobias* (1750-3) decorating the organ loft in the church of Angelo Raffaele (*see p117*). **Pietro Longhi** (1702-85) was a sort of Venetian Hogarth, painting amusing, naïve genre scenes in which the social life of his day was gently satirised.

   By the time of Napoleon's conquest in 1797, Venetian painting, like Venetian military power, was a spent force. The capital of the art world in the 19th century was Paris. Over the following 200 years, Venice's unique setting and collections have remained a magnet for foreign artists; Venice now exhibits painters, rather than producing them.

Literary Venice

The city as a setting; and the city as metaphor.

Creative as they were in other fields, the Venetians singularly failed to excel in literature. Venetian writing tended to come in the form either of self-vaunting reminiscences (**Giacomo Casanova**'s memoirs for example), or lively renderings of Venetian gossip (the plays of **Carlo Goldoni**). More meditative forms – poetry and the novel – are noticeable by their absence. Nevertheless, the city-state was always pleased to have other writers visit or live here – particularly if their presence enhanced its image.

In the 14th century the poet **Petrarch** left his library to Venice in gratitude for its hospitality; Venice promptly mislaid it, which speaks volumes about the city's literary sensibility. It was not, in fact, till the advent of printing (**Aldo Manuzio** set up his pioneering Aldine Press here in 1495) and its lucre-generating potential, that Venice really awoke to the virtues of books. By the 16th century, partly thanks to the relative laxity of its censorship, Venice was one of the most important centres of the European printing trade, with over 100 active presses producing books in dozens of different languages. Apart from anything else, printed books were then objects of great beauty – and catching the eye was (and still is) Venice's speciality.

But if Venice hasn't bred many writers, it has succeeded in attracting them. And often enough disgusting them. This is particularly true of English writers, who have been swaying between love and loathing, romantic admiration and puritan disapproval, for centuries.

SHAKESPEARE'S VENICE
Venice really enters English literature with **Shakespeare**. The Bard never actually set foot here, but nonetheless the city of *The Merchant of Venice* and *Othello* is a more fully realised place than, say, the Sicily of *Much Ado About Nothing*. Clearly, Venice was already as powerful an image abroad as New York is today; the Rialto bridge and gondolas could be mentioned as casually as Brooklyn Bridge and yellow cabs. Shakespeare's Venice is very much a mercantile city. There are no sunsets over the lagoon, no gondola serenades. Venice is the city of deals, exchanges and bonds – and of law, which must never be impeached because the Republic's survival depends on it, 'Since that the trade and profit of the city/Consisteth of all nations'. But it is also a place of licentiousness and scheming, where people are not necessarily what they seem. To use Iago's definition of Desdemona, the typical citizen of the Republic is a 'super-subtle Venetian'.

TRAVELLERS' TALES

The first detailed description by an English visitor was that of insatiable literary traveller **Thomas Coryat**, who set out on foot from Odcombe in Devon in 1608. Coryat furnishes one of the first of many gobsmacked-tourist descriptions of Venice: 'Such is the rarenesse of the situation of Venice, that it doth even amaze and drive into admiration all strangers that upon their first arrival behold the same.' He records the precious stones and marbles, assesses the belltower, counts the churches. Everything is tested and measured (he flings his arms round pillars), including the famous courtesans: 'As for herself, she comes to thee decked like the queen and goddess of love… Also the ornaments of her body are so rich, that except thou dost even geld thy affections… she will very near benumb and captivate thy senses. For thou shalt see her decked with many chains of gold and oriental pearl like a second Cleopatra.'

It's difficult not to see an association with the city here – enchantingly bedecked in riches. But Coryat gives fair warning: 'If thou shouldest wantonly converse with her, and not give her that *salarium iniquitatis*, which thou hast promised her… she will either cause thy throat to be cut, or procure thee to be arrested…' Just in case we were getting the wrong idea, he adds hastily: 'I believe thou wilt cast an aspersion of wantonness upon me and say that I could not know all these matters without mine own experience. I answer thee that although I might have known them without my experience, yet for my better satisfaction, I went to one of their noble houses (I will confess) to see the manner of their life, and observe their behaviour.' The eternal tourist, watching the glass-blowing but never buying.

In the more cynical 18th century, wariness predominated over bedazzlement. Venice was viewed less as a real place and more as a

Literary locations Byron

Byron created two Venices. One is the melodramatic setting of his 'serious' poetry, a city haunted by the memories of former glories and sinister intrigues. The other – celebrated in his vastly more entertaining 'light' poetry – is the lively city of gossiping salons and theatres he himself frequented.

Lovers of the gloomy *Childe Harold*, *Marino Faliero* and *The Two Foscari* can get their thrills in the **Doge's Palace** (*see p77*) – or, more particularly, on the **Bridge of Sighs**, which, as Ruskin rather dismissively said, was 'the centre of the Byronic ideal of Venice'. Byron was blithely unpedantic in his attitude to history; the last line of *Marino Faliero* tells us that 'the gory head rolls down the Giants' Steps' – the **Scala dei Giganti**, *see p78*, which were not built until a century and a half after the execution of the doge in question. Elsewhere, *Marino Faliero* addresses the **monument to Bartolomeo Colleoni** (*see p85*) outside Santi Giovanni e Paolo – an anachronism Byron airily acknowledges in his preface.

Anyone more interested in the poet's rhyming romp *Beppo* can best savour its atmosphere by visiting Venice at Carnevale, when they can enjoy the 'fiddling, feasting, dancing, drinking, masquing/And other things which may be had for asking'. They can also visit the historic **Ridotto**, Venice's 18th-century casino, now part of the Hotel Monaco & Grand Canal.

metaphor – usually a negative one. English travellers set their burgeoning sense of national self-importance against Venice's decline. This admonitory use of the city was to culminate in the works of **John Ruskin**, whose theory of architecture – elaborated at enormous length in *The Stones of Venice* – sprang out of his need to demonstrate that the Venetian Gothic architecture of the 13th and 14th centuries was a sign of moral and intellectual health, while the classicism of the Renaissance and its elaboration in the baroque was the objective correlative of the city's slide into decadence.

During the period of the Grand Tour the English came to Italy as to a great museum, picking up fragments of culture, works of art and Italian vices. Venice gets one contemptuous mention in **Alexander Pope**'s *Dunciad*, as a place of dissoluteness, while **Edward Gibbon** was even more dismissive: 'The spectacle of Venice afforded some hours of astonishment and some days of disgust… stinking ditches dignified with the pompous denomination of Canals; a fine bridge spoilt by two rows of houses upon it, and a large square decorated with the worst Architecture I ever yet saw.'

And even those who came specifically in search of its dissolute pleasures were soon fed up. **James Boswell** wrote: 'For the first week I was charmed by the novelty and beauty of so singular a city, but I soon wearied of travelling continually by water, shut up in those lugubrious gondolas.'

CITY OF DREAMS AND DECADENCE

Enthusiasm returned with the Romantics. Suddenly, decadence was the whole point. Where Gibbon had snorted, writers such as **William Beckford**, **Lord Byron** and **Percy Shelley** thrilled. They went in search of shudders by visiting the prisons of the Palazzo Ducale; they saw romance in the double aspect of decay and splendour.

Byron's twofold reaction to Venice (*see* **Literary locations: Byron**) makes him the most interesting expatriate writer of the period.

In his immensely fashionable poem *Childe Harold's Pilgrimage* – a sort of cross between *A Year in Provence* and *Fear and Loathing in Las Vegas* – he draws Venice as a dream; the city is depopulated, seen at 'airy distance'. Its past is melodramatic: dungeons, the Council of Ten, vendettas, anonymous denunciations. It is a purely literary creation, based more on a self-propagating writerly tradition than on observation. He continued to mine this Venetian seam in his lugubrious historical verse dramas *The Two Foscari* and *Marino Faliero* (both 1821).

But in *Beppo* Byron draws a very different picture, describing Venice at Carnevale time: a menacing Turk turns out to be a lost husband; and when this husband finds his wife has taken a lover, no knives are pulled; instead they discuss the situation over coffee and all three settle down to live together happily ever after.

Throughout the 19th century travellers drifted through Venice in their closed gondolas, apparently having no contact with the inhabitants. In their accounts of their visits, they fall into swoons or trances; the city casts its spell, enchants them or mesmerises them. 'Je végète, je me repose, j'oublie,' murmurs George Sand tipsily. It is Turner's Venice they describe: a dreamscape where the buildings seem less substantial than the dazzling light and shimmering water, where the *palazzi* and churches merge mirage-like into their reflections.

In **Charles Dickens**' *Pictures From Italy* the chapter devoted to Venice is entitled 'An Italian dream'. Dickens recounts the experience of floating through the city, even through St

Byron lived in Venice from 1817 to 1819. His first residence was an apartment in **Piscina di Frezzeria**, located behind the Napoleonic Wing of St Mark's Square; the building (No.1673; map p307 A4) is fairly undistinguished and has no commemorative plaque. Here he met his first Venetian love, Marianna Segati… his landlord's wife. He moved subsequently to **Palazzo Mocenigo** on the Grand Canal (*see p68*), where he lived in grand style with a menagerie of dogs, monkeys and foxes, not to mention his awe-inspiring mistress, Margarita Cogni, 'tall and energetic as a pythoness, fit to breed gladiators from'.

A more unexpected side to Byron can be found on the island of **San Lazzaro degli Armeni** (*see p141*), whose monks proudly show visitors the study where Byron took lessons in their language. As he noted in a letter to a friend: 'Venice & I agree very well – in the mornings I study Armenian – & in the evenings I go out sometimes – & indulge in coition always.'

Greater imagination is needed to enjoy the other location with strong Byronic associations: the **Lido** (*see p130*), where the poet kept horses, since he loved cantering along what was then a deserted beach. Shelley's poem *Julian and Maddalo*, describes one such ride that the two poets shared in this 'waste/And solitary place'.

Mark's, which loses its solidity and is described in terms of colour and perfumes. In the end, he gives up trying to describe and merely babbles: 'unreal, fantastic, solemn, inconceivable throughout…' Or, as he put it elsewhere: 'Opium couldn't build such a place…'

The strongest reaction to all this came from Ruskin. He can be prejudiced, inconsistent and sometimes plain barmy, but his great virtue is his determination to tell the truth – to be honest about his own feelings. Perhaps the greatest contribution he made to Venetian studies was his continual emphasis on the physical reality of the place. In an age when most visitors were continuing to see it through a golden haze of romantic enchantment, Ruskin focused his attention on the stones of Venice – the crumbling, corroded bricks and marble.

THE AMBIVALENT CITY

Every major writer on Venice thereafter – **Marcel Proust, WD Howells, Henry James** – had to struggle to break free from Ruskin. It took some courage to like the baroque with Ruskin's fulminations ringing in one's ears. But gradually a new taste arose, one in which the famous ambivalence of Venice played a key role, attracting writers such as **John Addington Symonds** and **Frederick Rolfe** – the self-styled 'Baron Corvo' – who, in between liaisons with gondoliers, described an androgynous city. At the same time the mysterious secrecy of the city was perfect for a novelist such as James, who wrote: 'Venice is the refuge of endless strange secrets, broken fortunes and wounded hearts.' He was perhaps also attracted by a city whose topography was almost as labyrinthine as his own syntax.

After World War I it was time for a fresh onset of disgust, with **DH Lawrence** and **TS Eliot** seeing the city as irredeemably commercial and sordid. Lawrence pictures it as the 'Abhorrent green, slippery city/Whose Doges were old and had ancient eyes'. Eliot describes a city where 'the rats are underneath the piles'. Both Eliot and **Ezra Pound** reworked, in a different light, Ruskin's moral disapprobation. But after he was released from a US hospital for the criminally insane, where he had been confined for his active wartime support for Mussolini's Fascist regime, Pound chose to divide most of his last years (1958-72) between Venice and Rapallo. As he once put it: 'Venice is an excellent place to come to from Crawfordsville, Indiana.' He lies buried in the cemetery island of San Michele (*see p134*).

Recent literature and cinema have mostly remained faithful to the *Childe Harold* version of Venice: sex, lies and dirty canals. The city is murky, treacherous and damp in novels by

Murky, treacherous and damp.

Ian McEwan, Barry Unsworth and Lisa St Aubin de Téran, and in Nicholas Roeg's manneristically melodramatic film *Don't Look Now* (based on a short story by **Daphne du Maurier**; *see p202* **Celluloid Venice**). The detective novels of American writer **Donna Leon** are equally melodramatic in plot (and have operatic epigraphs to prove it), but are firmly set in workaday Venice: the aquatic dream-city seems almost down-to-earth.

Perhaps the finest summation of the two contrasting visions of the city can be found in the narrative poem *The Venetian Vespers* (1979), by the American poet **Anthony Hecht**, whose psychologically disturbed protagonist seems to have chosen the city as his place of residence precisely because its internal contrasts so perfectly match his own inner lacerations.

Romance returns in two recent novels with Venetian settings. In *An Equal Music* **Vikram Seth** revives the dream-vision of the 19th-century writers, tempering it with Carpaccio-esque humour and presenting appreciative views of such off-the-beaten-track suburbs as Sant'Elena. The recent bestseller by **Sally Vickers**, *Miss Garnett's Angel*, gives us a refreshingly ungloomy Venice; awe prevails for the protagonist of this novel, who finds her rigid atheism shaken by the almost paradisiacal qualities of what appears to be a city of angels.

It's too early to say whether this heralds a new wave of wonder; what is certain is that real writers are never going to be put off by the thought that there's nothing new to say about Venice. After all, you could say the same thing about falling in love.

Accommodation

Accommodation

There are plenty of new places to lay your head, but prices remain high.

So many hotels, hostels and B&Bs blossomed in Venice to accommodate the tourist boom of the 2000 holy year that the city found itself with arguably more rooms for tourists than residents. A rash of refurbishments meant that quality, too, increased somewhat. But for all its huge selection, Venice remains a seller's market: the city's enduring popularity ensures that establishments fill up regardless of what's on offer. Good accommodation deals are thin on the ground, and value for money in this unique city is a relative concept.

Selecting your district carefully will enhance your enjoyment (for information on Venice's *sestieri*, see the sightseeing chapters of this guide). San Marco will satisfy you with the plush or horrify you with the brash. The more tranquil areas of Castello will prove a relief on hot crowded summer days. Residential Dorsoduro has such luxuries as neighbourhood bread and grocery shops.

Genre, too, has a bearing: the modern annexe or extreme refurbishment will provide more mod cons than the old palazzo with bouncy floors and cranky plumbing, but it may be a little short on Venetian magic.

Venice's urban features will do the rest. When booking, it pays to bear in mind that narrow alleys can throw your room into permanent penumbra; and echos bouncing off walls can be very noisy if the alley happens to be an important thoroughfare. Inner courtyards provide some relief from the city's hot streets, especially if shaded by trees. Any view will push up the price of your room. But before you shell out for that 'canal view', ascertain how much of a view it is: you may end up paying a huge supplement for a small sliver of Grand Canal only visible out of the bathroom window.

By and large, most hotels will exchange currency and, for an extra charge, organise babysitting, laundry and dry-cleaning. Baby cots or supplementary beds can often be squeezed into bedrooms, although expect to pay an extra 20-40 per cent on top of the room price. Where breakfast is **not** included in the price of the room, this is specified in the listings below.

> ▶ Each listed hotel is marked on the maps at the back of the guide: look for the blue numbers after each entry.

LAST-MINUTE OPTIONS

The best way to ruin your stay in Venice is to show up with no hotel room booked, even in what elsewhere would count as the low season.

If you have nowhere to lay your head, make for an **AVA** (Venetian Hoteliers Association) bureau at the Santa Lucia railway station, piazzale Roma or the airport: staff will help you track down a room, charging a small commission that you can claim back on the price of your first night.

If you're not fussy about the state of your room or don't mind a hike down the corridor to the bathroom, try the cheaper hotels in the area around the station (which despite the plethora of tacky souvenir shops is cleaner and safer than in most cities). If you're really desperate, there's always Mestre on the mainland – by no means a bad bet if you're travelling by car; hotels there are usually cheaper and it's only a ten-minute hop across to Venice by train or bus. But don't let anyone try to convince you that it's the same as staying in Venice: it very definitely isn't.

For last-minute bookings from home, AVA has a detailed online information and booking service as well: www.veniceinfo.it. On the www.venicehotel.com site is a large, though not exhaustive, directory of hotels, B&Bs and campsites that can be booked online.

LOCATING YOUR HOTEL

Getting lost in Venice is all too easy, especially if you're a newcomer to the city. Make sure you obtain detailed directions before you arrive: ask your hotel for the nearest vaporetto stop, easily identifiable campo (square) and/or landmark (such as a church). Alternatively, you'll need a map and a fiendishly good sense of direction.

MONEY-SAVING

Many hotels post off-season or midweek offers on their websites: it pays to check these out.

Some hotels (*see p48* **Locanda delle Acque**; *p56* **La Calcina**; *p56* **Messner**) offer apartments for longer stays; these are true money-saving options, especially for groups or families. Cleaning and breakfast are not always included in the price: enquire beforehand.

Alternatively, www.viewsonvenice.com and www.veniceapartment.com are good online resources if you fancy a more residential approach to the city.

The **Danieli**. *See p49.*

San Marco

Deluxe

Gritti Palace ●

*San Marco 2467, campo Santa Maria del Giglio
(041 794 611/fax 041 520 0942/www.
luxurycollection.com/grittipalace). Vaporetto
Santa Maria del Giglio.* **Rates** €391-€503 single;
€589-€755 double; €2140-€3692 suite. Breakfast
€50. **Credit** AmEx, DC, MC, V. **Map** p307 B3.
Queen Elizabeth (the current one) opted to stay here,
which says it all really. Expect no postmodern frills,
just a studied air of old-world charm and nobility.
Refined and opulent, adorned with antiques and
fresh flowers, each room is uniquely decorated. The
reception desk is one of the finest. A courtesy boat
ferries guests to the Starwood group's sports facilities on the Lido. An aperitif on the vast canal terrace
is an experience in itself.
Hotel services *Air-conditioning. Babysitting.
Bar. Conference facilities. Currency exchange. Dry-
cleaning. Fax. Garden. Laundry. Lift. Multilingual
staff. No-smoking rooms. Restaurant. Safe. Theatre
reservations. Tours arranged.* **Room services**
*Air-conditioning. Fax point (in suites). Hairdryer.
Minibar. Radio. Room service (24hr). Safe.
TV (satellite).*

Luna Hotel Baglioni ●

*San Marco 1243, calle Larga dell'Ascensione
(041 528 9840/fax 041 528 7160/www.
baglionihotels.com). Vaporetto Vallaresso.* **Rates**
€215.60-€391.60 single; €332.20-€651.20 double;
€464.20-€1575.20 suite. **Credit** AmEx, DC, MC, V.
Map p307 B4.

Accommodation

Conveniently situated for aperitivi in Harry's Bar
(*see p165*), this is the oldest hotel in Venice, dating
back to the late 15th century. But after a modern
makeover with rather too much shiny marble, this
fact is not immediately obvious, except in the conference room, which still has its original fresco and
stuccoed decoration. A quarter of the rooms have
views of the Giardinetti Reali, the lagoon and across
to Palladio's church of San Giorgio Maggiore.
Hotel services *Air-conditioning. Bar. Conference
facilities (for up to 100). Currency exchange.
Dry-cleaning. Fax. Internet point. Laundry. Lift.
Multilingual staff. No-smoking rooms. Restaurant.
Safe. Theatre reservations. Tours arranged.* **Room**
services *Air-conditioning. Fax point (in suites).
Hairdryer. Jacuzzi (in suites). Minibar. Radio. Room
service. Safe. TV (satellite).*

Expensive

Saturnia & International ●

*San Marco 2398, via XXII Marzo (041 520 8377/
fax 041 520 7131/www.hotelsaturnia.it). Vaporetto
Vallaresso.* **Rates** €152-€280 single; €216-€396
double. **Credit** AmEx, DC, MC, V. **Map** p307 B3.
A friendly atmosphere pervades this hotel in a 14th-
century building. The interior has been done up in
a faux-Renaissance style (beamed ceilings, damask-
covered walls) with touches of Charles Rennie
Mackintosh. There is a nice roof terrace with a view
on to the basilica of Santa Maria della Salute.
Hotel services *Air-conditioning. Babysitting. Bar.
Conference facilities (for up to 60). Currency
exchange. Dry-cleaning. Fax. Garden. Laundry. Lift.
Multilingual staff. No-smoking rooms. Restaurant.
Safe. Solarium. Theatre reservations. Tours
arranged.* **Room services** *Air-conditioning.
Hairdryer. Minibar. Room service. Safe. TV (satellite).*

Moderate

Ala ●

*San Marco 2494, campo Santa Maria del Giglio
(041 520 8333/fax 041 520 6390/www.hotelala.it).
Vaporetto Santa Maria del Giglio.* Closed 3wks Jan.
Rates €90-€170 single; €155-€280 double; €170-€320
deluxe. **Credit** AmEx, DC, MC, V. **Map** p307 B3.
The bedrooms – where decor ranges from classical to
modern – have a variety of views, some on to campo
Santa Maria del Giglio, others on to a little side canal
with the Grand Canal itself further in the distance.
Hotel services *Air-conditioning. Babysitting. Bar.
Currency exchange. Dry-cleaning. Fax. Internet point.
Laundry. Lift. Multilingual staff. No-smoking rooms.
Safe. Theatre reservations. Tours arranged.* **Room**
services *Air-conditioning. Hairdryer. Minibar. Safe.
TV (satellite).*

Bel Sito & Berlino ●

*San Marco 2517, campo Santa Maria del Giglio
(041 522 3365/fax 041 520 4083/belsito@iol.it).
Vaporetto Santa Maria del Giglio.* **Rates** €85-€125
single; €115-€192 double. **Credit** MC, V. **Map** p307 B3.

Venice-proof.

How to find the hotel of your dreams in one click

1. Connect to Venicehotel.com
2. Select by area, category or type
3. Choose from monthly special offers
4. Enter the hotel website via direct link and book

Fast. Simple. Worth it.

Venicehotel.com
The best Venice hotels used to the Internet

Equidistant from the Accademia and piazza San Marco, with what remains of La Fenice nearby, the Bel Sito's rooms are decorated in faux 18th and 19th-century style, half of them looking out on to the church of Santa Maria del Giglio.
Hotel services *Air-conditioning. Bar. Currency exchange. Fax. Laundry. Multilingual staff. Safe. Theatre reservations. Tours arranged.* **Room services** *Air-conditioning. Hairdryer. Minibar (in 50% of rooms). Room service. TV (satellite).*

De l'Alboro

San Marco 3894B, corte dell'Alboro (041 522 9454/fax 041 522 8404). Vaporetto Sant'Angelo. Closed 3wks Jan. **Rates** €80-€160 single; €140-€210 double. **Credit** AmEx, DC, MC, V. **Map** p307 B3.
In a peaceful spot sandwiched between Palazzo Grassi and Palazzo Fortuny, the De l'Alboro is off the main tourist route but within easy reach of the Rialto bridge and campo Santo Stefano. The bedrooms are clean though rather plain.
Hotel services *Air-conditioning. Babysitting. Bar. Currency exchange. Dry-cleaning. Fax. Laundry. Lift. Multilingual staff. Safe. Theatre reservations. Tours arranged.* **Room services** *Air-conditioning. Hairdryer. Minibar. Safe. TV.*

Do Pozzi ❼

San Marco 2373, via XXII Marzo (041 520 7855/ fax 041 522 9413/www.hoteldopozzi.it). Vaporetto Santa Maria del Giglio. **Rates** €75-€130 single; €130-€210 double. **Credit** AmEx, DC, MC, V. **Map** p307 B3.
This hotel has a homely, friendly feeling. Some of the rooms are a bit cramped, but there is an enchanting attention to detail. It's situated very near to piazza San Marco, but off the main tourist track, down a little alley to a lovely outdoor courtyard with an ancient well in the middle where guests can have their meals.
Hotel services *Air-conditioning. Babysitting. Bar. Courtyard. Dry-cleaning. Fax. Laundry. Lift. Multilingual staff. Restaurant. Safe. Tours arranged.* **Room services** *Air-conditioning. Hairdryer. Minibar. Room service (24hr). TV (satellite).*

Flora ❽

San Marco 2283A, calle Bergamaschi (041 520 5844/fax 041 522 8217/www.hotelflora.it). Vaporetto Vallaresso. **Rates** €145-€180 single; €185-€230 double. **Credit** AmEx, DC, MC, V. **Map** p307 B3.
In the vicinity of piazza San Marco, the Flora offers a dreamy, tranquil stay in the palazzo adjacent to the so-called Desdemona's house. The decor is classical Venetian. There is a warm cosy bar and a small garden with wrought-iron tables and a fountain in the middle. Staff are helpful.
Hotel services *Air-conditioning. Babysitting. Bar. Currency exchange. Dry-cleaning. Fax. Garden. Laundry. Lift. Multilingual staff. Safe. Theatre reservations. Tours arranged.* **Room services** *Air-conditioning. Hairdryer. Safe. TV (satellite).*

Bel Sito: faux 18th-century style. See p45.

Locanda Art Deco ❾

San Marco 2966, calle delle Botteghe (041 277 0558/ fax 041 270 2891/www.locandaartdeco.com). Vaporetto San Samuele or Sant'Angelo. **Rates** €67-€120 single; €80-€175 double. **Credit** AmEx, DC, MC, V. **Map** p307 A3.
On a street renowned for its antique shops, just off campo Santo Stefano, the small, friendly Art Deco is a good find. The welcoming entrance hall and the classically decorated bedrooms are dotted with original pieces of 1930s and '40s furniture.
Hotel services *Air-conditioning. Fax. Multilingual staff.* **Room services** *Air-conditioning. Hairdryer. Internet connection. TV.*

Locanda Novecento ⓫

San Marco 2683/84, calle del Dose (041 241 3765/ fax 041 521 2145/www.locandanovecento.it). Vaporetto Santa Maria del Giglio. **Rates** €150-€200 single; €165-€230 double. **Credit** AmEx, DC, MC, V. **Map** p307 B3.
Wooden floors, ethnic textiles, Middle Eastern rugs and Far Eastern cupboards make the Novecento a special location from where to begin enjoying the city. There are nine individually decorated rooms with modern comforts, plus spacious, cosy reading and sitting rooms and a tiny leafy courtyard for the summer breakfasts. The staff is friendly and very helpful.
Hotel services *Air-conditioning. Babysitting. Courtyard. Fax. Laundry. Multilingual staff. Theatre reservations. Tours arranged.* **Room services** *Air-conditioning. Datapoint. Minibar. Safe. TV (satellite).*

There's a great view from the **Locanda delle Acque**.

Budget

Domus Ciliota ⑫

San Marco 2976, calle delle Muneghe (041 520 4888/fax 041 521 2730/www.ciliota.it). Vaporetto Sant'Angelo or San Samuele. **Rates** €70-€85 single; €90-€106 double. **Credit** MC, V. **Map** p307 A3.
This former convent has been transformed into a bed and breakfast offering half-board treatment as well. The modern decor is distinctly reminiscent of university lodgings, which may explain why it's so popular with students and backpackers. With so many bedrooms, it's a good stand-by when Venice is packed.
Hotel services *Multilingual staff. Fax. Conference facilities (for up to 100).* **Room services** *Air-conditioning. TV (satellite).*

Gallini ⑬

San Marco 3673, calle della Verona (041 520 4515/ fax 041 520 9103/hgallini@tin.it). Vaporetto Sant'Angelo. Closed lat Nov-mid Feb. **Rates** €37-€104 single; €78-€171 double. **Credit** MC, V. **Map** p307 A3.
The Gallini has a great variety of rooms, ranging from some that are expensive for this category to a few ultra-cheap ones with shared bathrooms. Some bedrooms on the top floor have views over the rooftops; one even has a private (though not particularly glamorous) little roof terrace.
Hotel services *Air-conditioning. Currency exchange. Fax. Multilingual staff. Safe. Theatre reservations. Tours arranged.* **Room services** *Air-conditioning (in 20% of rooms) Hairdryer. Room service. TV (in some rooms).*

Locanda delle Acque ⑭

San Marco 4991, calle delle Acque (041 241 1277/ fax 041 241 4112/www.locandadelleacque.it). Vaporetto Rialto. **Rates** €100-€140 double. **Credit** AmEx, DC, MC, V. **Map** p307 A4.

Hidden in the midst of the shopping area between Rialto and San Marco and handy for all the city's main sights, this friendly establishment offers graceful, comfortable rooms. The top-floor rooms give on to a pleasant roof terrace with a great view over neighbouring rooftops. Breakfast is served at the next-door restaurant. The Locanda also handles apartments for rent.
Hotel services *Multilingual staff. Fax. Safe.* **Room services** *Minibar. TV.*

Locanda Fiorita ⑮

San Marco 3457, campiello Nuovo (041 523 4754/ fax 041 522 0843/www.locandafiorita.com). Vaporetto Sant'Angelo. **Rates** €65-€78 single; €115-€125 double. **Credit** AmEx, MC, V. **Map** p307 A3.
This small family-run hotel between campo Santo Stefano and campo Sant'Angelo has refurbished rooms (though some have bathrooms in the corridor – make it clear when booking which you'd prefer) and beamed ceilings; two rooms have wonderful views through the hotel's vine-covered entrance to the airy campiello.
Hotel services *Currency exchange. Fax. Internet connection. Multilingual staff. Safe. Theatre reservations.* **Room services** *Air-conditioning. Hairdryer. Room service (24hr). TV (satellite).*

San Samuele ⑯

San Marco 3358, salizada San Samuele (tel/fax 041 522 8045). Vaporetto San Samuele or Sant'Angelo. **Rates** €26-€45 single; €46-€100 double. Breakfast €4.50. **No credit cards. Map** p307 A3.
Most of the rooms in this lovely hotel have window boxes full of cascading flowers overlooking the art gallery-lined salizada San Samuele. This clean and friendly establishment is a notch above most of its fellow one-stars, though all the single rooms have bathrooms in the corridor.
Hotel services *Fax. Multilingual staff. Safe. Theatre reservations.*

Castello

Deluxe

Danieli 🕧

Castello 4196, riva degli Schiavoni (041 522 6480/ fax 041 520 0208/www.starwood.com/italy).
Vaporetto San Zaccaria. **Rates** €385-€423 single; €642-€856 double; €856-€2350 suite. Breakfast €30-€50 extra. **Credit** AmEx, DC, MC, V. **Map** p308 B1.
Right next to the Doge's Palace, the Danieli is split between an unprepossessing 1940s building and the 14th-century Palazzo Dandolo: a room in the latter is definitely preferable if it's atmosphere and grandeur you're after. The rooms are sumptuously decorated with Rubelli and Fortuny fabrics, antique furnishings and marble bathrooms. There are spectacular views across the lagoon from the stunning roof terrace. The Starwood group's sports facilities and beach on the Lido can be used. Balzac, Dickens, Proust and Wagner all stayed here.
Hotel services *Air-conditioning. Babysitting. Bar. Conference facilities. Courtesy boat. Currency exchange. Dry-cleaning. Fax. Laundry. Lift. Multilingual staff. No-smoking rooms. PC rental. Restaurant. Safe. Theatre reservations. Tours arranged.* **Room services** *Air-conditioning. Fax point. Hairdryer. Minibar. Radio. Room service (24hr). Safe (in most rooms). TV (satellite).*

Expensive

Ca' dei Conti 🕧

Castello 4429, fondamenta del Remedio (041 277 0500/fax 041 277 0727/www.cadeiconti.com).
Vaporetto San Zaccaria. **Rates** €155-€310 single; €207-€413 double; €310-€620 suite. **Credit** AmEx, DC, MC, V. **Map** p308 A1.
In a historic palazzo situated on a quiet canal between Santa Maria Formosa and San Marco, this hotel is small but has all the comforts you'd expect in a four star. The rooms are tastefully decorated in Venetian style with particular attention paid to fabrics. There's a wonderful little terrace from which to survey the surrounding rooftops too.
Hotel services *Air-conditioning. Babysitting. Fax. Laundry. Multilingual staff. Safe. Theatre reservations. Tours arranged.* **Room services** *Air-conditioning. Hairdryer. Internet connection. Minibar. Radio. Room service. Safe. TV (satellite).*

Colombina 🕧

Castello 4416, calle del Remedio (041 277 0525/fax 041 277 6044/www.hotelcolombina.com). Vaporetto San Zaccaria. **Rates** €130-€350 single; €170-€390 double. **Credit** AmEx, DC, MC, V. **Map** p308 A1.
Close to piazza San Marco but far from the crowds, the Colombina has decor that is a modern take on the usual Venetian: the Murano chandeliers are here, but the overall effect is understated. The bathrooms have lashings of marble, and some rooms have balconies with views over the canal beneath the Bridge of Sighs.

Hotel services *Air-conditioning. Babysitting. Bar. Conference room. Currency exchange. Dry-cleaning. Laundry. Lift. Multilingual staff. Theatre reservations. Tours arranged.* **Room services** *Air-conditioning. Minibar. Hairdryer. Internet connection. Room service (24hr). Safe. TV (cable and satellite).*

Locanda Vivaldi 🕧

Castello 4150/52, riva degli Schiavoni (041 277 0477/ fax 041 277 0489/www.locandavivaldi.it).
Vaporetto San Zaccaria. **Rates** €180-€380 single; €210-€440 double; €360-€650 suite. **Credit** AmEx, DC, MC, V. **Map** p308 B2.
Located partly in the house where composer Antonio Vivaldi lived, and next to the church now solely devoted to his music, the Locanda offers tastefully, classically decorated rooms with lashings of modern comforts (many rooms have jacuzzis) and views of the island of San Giorgio from the magnificent roof terrace.
Hotel services *Air-conditioning. Babysitting. Bar. Conference facilities. Laundry. Multilingual staff. Restaurant. Safe. Theatre reservations.* **Room services** *Air-conditioning. Internet connection. Jacuzzi (some rooms). Minibar. Radio. Room service (24hr). Safe. TV (satellite).*

Londra Palace 🕧

Castello 4171, riva degli Schiavoni (041 520 0533/fax 041 522 5032/www.hotelondra.it).
Vaporetto San Zaccaria. **Rates** €275-€585 double; €485-€790 suite. **Credit** AmEx, DC, MC, V. **Map** p308 B1.

The best Hotels for...

Out-and-out island luxury
Cipriani (*p57*); **San Clemente Palace** (*p57*); **Sofitel Venezia in Isola** (*p57*).

Art deco details
Ca' Pisani (*p55*); **Locanda Art Deco** (*p47*).

A bit of green
Accademia-Villa Maravege (*see p55*); **Flora** (*p47*); **Giorgione** (*see p53*); **Locanda Novecento** (*p47*); **Metropole** (*p50*).

A literary air
La Calcina (*p56*); **Danieli** (*p49*); **Des Bains** (*see p58*).

Lagoon views
Bucintoro (*p51*); **Luna Hotel Baglioni** (*p45*); **Ostello di Venezia** (*p58*).

Grand Canal views
Ala (*p45*); **Locanda ai Santi Apostoli** (*p53*); **Locanda Sturion** (*p54*); **Marconi** (*p54*); **San Cassiano-Ca' Favoretto** (*p54*).

The **Metropole** has a gorgeous garden.

Elegant but restrained, the Londra Palace offers traditional rooms with antiques, paintings and the occasional piece of 19th-century Biedermeier furniture. Tchaikovsky composed his fourth symphony during a stay here in 1877. You can compose your masterpiece while sunbathing on the roof terrace.
Hotel services *Air-conditioning. Babysitting. Bar. Currency exchange. Dry cleaning. Fax. Laundry. Lift. Multilingual staff. Restaurant. Safe. Theatre reservations. Tours arranged.* **Room services** *Air-conditioning. Hairdryer. Internet via TV. Minibar. Radio. Room service (18-hour). Safe. TV (satellite).*

Metropole 22
Castello 4149, riva degli Schiavoni (041 520 5044/fax 041 522 3679/www.hotelmetropole.com). Vaporetto San Zaccaria. **Rates** €145-€300 single; €210-€570 double; €390-€725 suite; €104 extra for lagoon view. **Credit** AmEx, DC, MC, V. **Map** p308 B2.
The hotel's gorgeous garden offers a refuge from the tourist trudge of the riva degli Schiavoni: the only sounds are the occasional bells of neighbouring churches and water trickling in the fountain. The elegant rooms are furnished with antiques from the owner's collection. There are views over the lagoon (at a price), the canal behind, or on to the garden. Large reading and sitting rooms on the ground floor.
Hotel services *Air-conditioning. Babysitting. Bar. Car park. Conference facilities. Currency exchange. Dry cleaning. Fax. Garden. Laundry. Lift. Multilingual staff. No-smoking rooms. Restaurant. Safe. Theatre reservations. Tours arranged.* **Room services** *Air-conditioning. Hairdryer. Internet connection. Minibar. Room service (24hr). Safe. TV (satellite).*

Savoia & Jolanda 23
Castello 4187, riva degli Schiavoni (041 520 6644/522 4130/fax 041 520 7494/www.hotels avoiajolanda.com). Vaporetto San Zaccaria. **Rates** €130-€207 single; €190-€398 double; €320-€590 suite. **Credit** AmEx, DC, MC, V. **Map** p308 B1.

A hotel of two different but equally lovely halves, the Savoia offers rooms with balconies and views across the watery expanse of the Bacino di San Marco to Palladio's church of San Giorgio Maggiore in one direction, or, on the landward side, facing back towards the glorious façade of San Zaccaria. The decor in both bedrooms and reception rooms manages to be pleasantly luxurious without going over the top.
Hotel services *Air-conditioning. Babysitting. Bar. Currency exchange. Dry cleaning. Fax. Laundry. Lift. Multilingual staff. No-smoking rooms. Restaurant. Safe. Theatre reservations. Tours arranged.* **Room services** *Air-conditioning. Hairdryer. Internet connection. Minibar (in 70% of rooms). Room service (24hr). Safe. TV (satellite).*

Moderate

Casa Querini 24
Castello 4388, campo San Giovanni Novo (041 241 1294/fax 041 241 4231/www.locandaquerini.com). Vaporetto San Zaccaria. Closed 3wks Jan. **Rates** €73-€119 single; €124-€166 double. **Credit** AmEx, DC, MC, V. **Map** p308 A1.
Outdoor tables and the tiniest reception area welcome you to this friendly hotel in a small square between bustling campo Santa Maria Formosa and San Marco. The stairs lead up to six comfortable bedrooms, all pleasantly decorated in sober Venetian style. The rooms are spacious, but some look over an uninspiring side alley.
Hotel services *Air-conditioning. Fax. Internet connection. Multilingual staff. Safe. Theatre reservations. Tours arranged.* **Room services** *Air-conditioning. Minibar. Safe. Telephone. Minibar. Radio. Room service (18-hour). Safe. TV (satellite).*

Locanda La Corte ⑩

*Castello 6317, calle Bressana (041 241 1300/
fax 041 241 5982/www.locandalacorte.it). Vaporetto
Fondamenta Nove.* **Rates** €78-€120 single; €114-
€176 double; €155-€210 suite. **Credit** AmEx, DC,
MC, V. **Map** p308 A1.

In a 16th-century small palazzo, La Corte has 14 elegant rooms and two suites with a pleasant little
courtyard where breakfast is served in summer. It's
delightfully far away from noisy tourist trails.
Hotel services *Air-conditioning. Babysitting.
Courtyard/garden. Fax. Multilingual staff. Theatre
reservations. Tours arranged.* **Room services** *Air-
conditioning. Email connection. Minibar. TV (satellite).*

Scandinavia ㉕

*Castello 5240, campo Santa Maria Formosa
(041 522 3507/fax 041 523 5232/www.scandinavia
hotel.com). Vaporetto Rialto or San Zaccaria.* **Rates**
€130-€206 single; €150-€310 double. **Credit** AmEx,
DC, MC, V. **Map** I 4C.

On the lively and quintessentially Venetian square
of Santa Maria Formosa, this hotel is done up in
pseudo 18th-century style with lashings of Murano
glass. The rooms are all doubles and cosy, with overpriced views over the campo and on to Mauro
Codussi's wonderfully curvaceous church (*see p87*).
Hotel services *Air-conditioning. Bar. Currency
exchange. Fax. Multilingual staff. Safe. Theatre
reservations.* **Room services** *Air-conditioning.
Hairdryer. Minibar. Room service (24hr). Safe.
TV (satellite).*

Budget

Bucintoro ㉖

*Castello 2135, riva San Biagio (041 522 3240/
fax 041 523 5224). Vaporetto Arsenale.* Closed
Dec-Jan. **Rates** €62-€93 single; €125-€167 double.
Credit MC, V. **Map** p308 B2.

All the rooms in this friendly family-run hotel have
stunning views across the lagoon to the island of San
Giorgio Maggiore with its Palladian church: for such
a setting, it's amazingly good value. Some bedrooms
have no bathrooms of their own, but facilities on the
same floor: specify what you want when booking.
Always a favourite among artists due to its proximity to the Biennale grounds.
Hotel services *Bar. Fax. Garden. Multilingual
staff. Safe. Theatre reservations.* **Room services**
Hairdryer. Room service.

Casa Fontana ㉗

*Castello 4701, campo San Provolo (041 522 0579/
fax 041 523 1040/www.hotelfontana.it). Vaporetto
San Zaccaria.* **Rates** €60-€110 single; €80-€170
double. **Credit** AmEx, DC, MC, V. **Map** p308 B1.

It's a relief to leave the confusion of campo San
Provolo behind you and enter this family-run hotel.
The decor is rather olde worlde. Some rooms have
balconies and some at the top have a view over the
Romanesque campanile of San Zaccaria.
Hotel services *Bar. Fax. Safe. Theatre
reservations.* **Room services** *Fan. TV (satellite).*

Casa Linger ㉘

*Castello 3541, salizada Sant'Antonin (041 528
5920/fax 041 528 4851/hotelcasalinger@libero.it).
Vaporetto Arsenale.* Closed Dec. **Rates** €40-€80
double without bathroom; €47-€120 double with
bathroom. **Credit** MC, V. **Map** p308 B2.

A long, narrow flight of stairs leads up to this
unassuming little hotel, in which most of the rooms
are airy and spacious. All the bedrooms are double,
and some have bathrooms in the corridor (check
when booking). Breakfast is served in the rooms. It's
on a busy street with a true down-home Venetian
atmosphere, although it is quite a hike from the
nearest vaporetto stop.
*Hotel services Fax. Multi-lingual staff. Safe.
Room services. TV (on request).*

La Residenza ㉙

*Castello 3608, campo Bandiera e Moro (041 528
5315/fax 041 523 8859/www.venicelaresidenza.com).
Vaporetto Arsenale.* **Rates** €60-€95 single; €100-
€155 double. **Credit** MC, V. **Map** p308 B2.

With its genteel old-fashioned air, La Residenza is
undoubtedly great value, and has the advantage of
being away from the noisy crowds, but within easy
walking distance of San Marco. An ample, stucco-
decorated reading room (where breakfast is served)
welcomes you on the first floor. And alhough the
palazzo is one of the few in the city that hasn't
undergone restoration, the bedrooms have all been
recently refurbished.
Hotel services *Fax. Multilingual staff. Theatre
reservations.* **Room services** *Air-conditioning.
Minibar. Safe. TV.*

Locanda Silva ㉚

*Castello 4423, fondamenta del Rimedio (041 522
7643/fax 041 528 6817/www.locandasilva.it).
Vaporetto San Zaccaria.* Closed Jan. **Rates** €40-
€70 single; €65-€105 double. **No credit cards.**
Map p308 A1.

A large hotel with spacious rooms, the Silva is
situated in a convenient, quiet canal-side street just
off the buzzing square of Santa Maria Formosa.
Some rooms have bathrooms in the corridor: check
when booking.
Hotel services *Fax. Multilingual staff. Safe.*

Hostels

Foresteria Valdese ㉛

*Castello 5170, calle lunga Santa Maria Formosa
(041 528 6797/fax 041 241 6924/www.
chiesavaldese.org/venezia). Vaporetto San Zaccaria
or Rialto.* **Rates** €22 dormitory bed; €54-€70 room
with bath. **No credit cards. Map** p308 A1.

Just off the lively campo Santa Maria Formosa, in a
wonderful palazzo with high ceilings and flaking
frescos, this really is a beautiful spot. An impressive
flight of stone stairs leads up to dormitories, double
rooms and self-catering flats. The hostel is run by
Waldensian Evangelicals and generally attracts
slightly older guests.

Cannaregio

Expensive

Bellini 🟥

Cannaregio 116, Lista di Spagna (041 524 2488/ fax 041 715 193/www.boscolohotels.com). Vaporetto Ferrovia. **Rates** €180-€390 single; €220-€445 double. **Credit** AmEx, DC, MC, V. **Map** p304 B1.

Glitzy, glam and very imposing, with its silk damask wallpaper with matching curtains, inlaid marble and Murano chandeliers. It's the only deluxe hotel conveniently close to the station, though this means it's slap-bang in the centre of an area that is noisy, thronged with tourists, and distant from the main cultural sights and better restaurants.
Hotel services *Air-conditioning. Bar. Currency exchange. Dry-cleaning. Fax. Laundry. Lift. Multilingual staff. No-smoking rooms. Safe. Theatre reservations. Tours arranged.* **Room services** *Air-conditioning. Hairdryer. Minibar. Radio. Room service. Safe. TV (satellite).*

Giorgione 🟥

Cannaregio 4587, campo dei Santi Apostoli (041 522 5810/fax 041 523 9092/www.hotelgiorgione.com). Vaporetto Ca' d'Oro. **Rates** €105-€175 single; €150-€400 double; €250-€400 suite. **Credit** AmEx, DC, MC, V. **Map** p305 B4.

Just off the busy campo Santi Apostoli, the Giorgione exudes warmth and comfort rather than luxury and glitz. The older 15th-century palazzo joins the newer part around a flower-filled courtyard with a pretty central lily pond. Some split-level rooms have terraces overlooking the rooftops and the courtyard below.
Hotel services *Air-conditioning. Babysitting. Bar. Currency exchange. Dry-cleaning. Fax. Internet point. Garden. Laundry Lift. Multilingual staff. No-smoking rooms. Safe. Theatre reservations.* **Room services** *Air-conditioning. Hairdryer. Minibar. Radio. Room service. Safe. TV (satellite).*

Moderate

Locanda ai Santi Apostoli 🟥

Cannaregio 4391/A, campo Santi Apostoli (041 521 2612/fax 041 521 2611/aisantia@tin.it). Vaporetto Ca' d'Oro. Closed 2wks Dec. **Rates** €160-€310 double. **Credit** AmEx, DC, MC, V. **Map** p305 C3.

A large door from the busy Strada Nuova leads you into the wonderful courtyard of this palazzo. A lift or a sweeping flight of stone stairs leads to the third floor, where the 12 double rooms, all spacious and individually decorated, are located. Book in advance for the two with a view over the Grand Canal.
Hotel services *Air-conditioning. Babysitting. Bar. Currency exchange. Fax. Laundry. Lift. Multilingual staff. No-smoking rooms. Safe. Theatre reservations. Tours arranged.* **Room services** *Air-conditioning. Hairdryer. Internet connection. Minibar. Radio. Room service. TV.*

Budget

Adriatico 🟥

Cannaregio 224, Lista di Spagna (041 715 176/ fax 041 717 275). Vaporetto Ferrovia. **Rates** €45-€93 single; €65-€130 double. **Credit** DC, MC, V. **Map** p304 B2.

Extremely basic and somewhat noisy it may be, but the Adriatico is clean. There's a tiny breakfast room.
Hotel services *Fax.* **Room services** *Hairdryer. TV (satellite).*

Locanda Ca' San Marcuola 🟥

Cannaregio 1763, campo San Marcuola (041 716 048/fax 041 275 9217/www.casanmarcuola.com). Vaporetto San Marcuola. **Rates** €52-€129 single; €62-€180 double. **Credit** AmEx, DC, MC, V. **Map** p304 B2.

Strategically positioned just a few steps from the vaporetto stop. Rooms are spacious and comfortable, although an overabundance of pastel-coloured Venetian decor pervades the house.
Hotel services *Fax. Internet connection. Multilingual staff. Safe.* **Room services** *Air-conditioning. Minibar. Safe. TV (satellite).*

Florida 🟥

Cannaregio 106, calle Priuli dei Cavaletti (041 715 253/fax 041 718 088/www.hotel-florida.com). Vaporetto Ferrovia. **Rates** €73-€113 single; €90-€160 double. **Credit** AmEx, DC, MC, V. **Map** p305 B4.

The Florida offers quiet, simple, though somewhat small rooms very conveniently located in a calle right outside the train station and opposite the vaporetto stop.
Hotel services *Fax. Multilingual staff.* **Room services** *Air-conditioning. PC connection on request. TV (satellite).*

Guerrini 🟥

Cannaregio 265, calle delle Procuratie (041 715 333/ fax 041 715 114). Vaporetto Ferrovia. **Rates** €65-€100 single; €90-€130 double. **Credit** AmEx, DC, MC, V. **Map** p304 B2.

Set in a quiet alley, this hotel is handy for the station without being too close to the noisy, crowded Lista di Spagna. The decor is simple.
Hotel services *Fax. Multilingual staff. Safe. Theatre reservations.* **Room services** *Room service (24hr).*

Rossi 🟥

Cannaregio 262, calle delle Procuratie (041 715 164/ fax 041 717 784/rossihotel@interfree.it). Vaporetto Ferrovia. Closed 6 Jan-Carnevale. **Rates** €52-€67 single; €75-€90 double. **Credit** MC, V. **Map** p304 B2.

For a one star near the busy, noisy and generally to be avoided area around Santa Lucia railway station, this is quite a find. Large and acceptably clean, it is at the end of an alleyway just off the tourist-trap Lista di Spagna.
Hotel services *Currency exchange. Fax. Multilingual staff. Safe. Theatre reservations.* **Room services** *Air-conditioning. Fan.*

Accommodation

Al Vagon ⓾

Cannaregio 5619, campiello Riccardo Selvatico
(tel/fax 041 528 5626/www.hotelalvagon.com).
Vaporetto Ca' d'Oro. Closed Jan. **Rates** €60-€120
single; €70-€130 double; €80-€150 double 'superior'.
Breakfast €6. **Credit** MC, V. **Map** p305 C4.
Just off campo Santi Apostoli a minute's walk
from Rialto, this hotel is cheap and cheerful with
basic but not overly cramped rooms, all of which
have their own bathrooms.
Hotel services *Fax. Restaurant. Safe. Theatre*
reservations. **Room services** *Air-conditioning*
('superior' rooms). Safe. TV.

Hostels

Ostello Santa Fosca ⓭

Cannaregio 2372, fondamenta Daniele Canal (tel/fax
041 715 775). Vaporetto San Marcuola. **Rates** €18-
€21 per person. **Credit** MC, V. **Map** p305 B3.
This student-run hostel is not best-known for its efficiency, so make sure you have double confirmation
of your booking.

San Polo & Santa Croce

Moderate

Locanda Sturion ⓬

San Polo 679, calle dello Sturion (041 523 6243/
fax 041 522 8378/www.locandasturion.com).
Vaporetto Rialto. **Rates** €70-€150 single;
€120-€250 double. **Credit** AmEx, MC, V.
Map p305 C3.
Established in the late 1200s by the doge as an inn
for visiting merchants, this hotel is still thriving –
and it's not surprising, given the location. The
Sturion has undoubtedly one of the best-value Grand
Canal locations, though only two bedrooms and the
breakfast room have a view. The other spacious
rooms give on to a quiet calle. It's a long haul up
steep stairs, however, and there's no lift.
Hotel services *Air-conditioning. Concert*
reservations. Fax. Internet point. Multilingual
staff. **Room services** *Air-conditioning.*
Hairdryer. Minibar. Radio. Room service (24hr).
Safe. TV (satellite).

Marconi ⓭

San Polo 729, riva del Vin (041 522 2068/fax 041
522 9700/www.hotelmarconi.it). Vaporetto Rialto.
Rates €55-€228 single; €70-€325 double. **Credit**
AmEx, DC, MC, V. **Map** p305 C3.
The Marconi welcomes you with reception rooms
done out in a wonderful olde-worlde bachelor style;
the rooms are simpler. Two of them look out on to
the Grand Canal; the others, on the other hand, have
the advantage of being much quieter. There are
some outdoor tables for morning coffee before a
stroll through the Rialto market.
Hotel services *Air-conditioning. Babysitting.*
Currency exchange. Dry cleaning. Fax. Laundry.
Multilingual staff. Theatre reservations. Tours

Locanda La Corte. *See p51.*

arranged. **Room services** *Air-conditioning.*
Hairdryer. Internet connection. Minibar. Radio.
Room service. Safe. TV (satellite).

San Cassiano – Ca' Favretto ⓮

Santa Croce 2232, calle de la Rosa (041 524 1768/
fax 041 721 033/www.sancassiano.it). Vaporetto
San Stae. **Rates** €60-€217 single; €70-€310 double.
Credit AmEx, MC, V. **Map** p305 C3.
The rooms of this 14th-century Gothic building are
elegant; some of the reception rooms, and a lovely
verandah, look out over the Grand Canal. It's diffi-
cult to find, but very much worth the search.
Hotel services *Air-conditioning. Babysitting. Bar.*
Fax. Courtyard. Laundry. Multilingual staff. No-
smoking rooms. **Room services** *Air-conditioning.*
Hairdryer. Minibar. Radio. Room service (24hr).
Safe. TV (satellite).

Budget

Casa Peron ⓯

Santa Croce 84, salizada San Pantalon (041
710 021/fax 041 711 038/casaperon@libero.it).
Vaporetto San Tomà. Closed 7 Jan-mid Feb. **Rates**
€45-€85 single; €70-€85 double. **Credit** AmEx, DC,
MC, V. **Map** p304 C1.
This simple, clean hotel is very conveniently located
within the university area with the shops, restaurants and bars of campo Santa Margherita close at
hand. All the rooms have showers, though some are
without toilets: check when booking.
Hotel services *Multilingual staff. Safe.*
Room services *Air-conditioning (some rooms).*

Dalla Mora ⓰

Santa Croce 42, salizada San Pantalon (041 710
703/fax 041 723 006/hoteldallamora@libero.it).
Vaporetto San Tomà. **Rates** €57 single; €67-€88
double. **Credit** DC, MC, V. **Map** p304 C1.

At the end of a side-calle giving on to a narrow canal, Dalla Mora is simple, basic, and conveniently located near campo Santa Margherita and its many bars and restaurants. Some of the double bedrooms share bathrooms in the corridor: check when booking.
Hotel services *Fax. Telephone.*

Iris

San Polo 2910, calle del Cristo (tel/fax 041 522 2882/www.irishotel.com). Vaporetto San Tomà.
Closed Jan. **Rates** €70-€93 single; €98-€135 double. **Credit** AmEx, DC, MC, V. **Map** p306 A2.
In a quiet area between the Frari and San Tomà, the Iris has a pleasant courtyard and simple bedrooms. Some rooms share a bathroom on the floor: check when booking. The restaurant next door belongs to the hotel.
Hotel services *Bar. Fax. Theatre reservations.*
Room services *Air-conditioning. Hairdryer. TV (satellite).*

Locanda Marinella

Santa Croce 345, rio terà dei Pensieri (041 275 9457/fax 041 710 386/www.locandamarinella.com). Vaporetto piazzale Roma. **Rates** €55-€110 single; €85-€170 double. **Credit** AmEx, MC, V.
Map p304 C1.
Strikingly new and modern, and located a stone's throw from piazzale Roma and its car parks, the Marinella is a recent and pleasant addition to Venice's hotel scene. Its spacious, comfortable rooms are ideal for late arrivals or early departures.
Hotel services *Fax. Multilingual staff. Safe. Theatre reservations.* **Room services** *Air-conditioning. Hairdryer. Minibar. Safe. TV (satellite).*

Salieri

Santa Croce 160, fondamenta Minotto (041 710 035/fax 041 721 246/www.hotelsalieri.com). Vaporetto Ferrovia or piazzale Roma. **Rates** €43-€65 single; €55-€115 double. **Credit** AmEx, MC, V.
Map p304 C1.
This simple, family-run place situated between the railway station and piazzale Roma is handy if you get into Venice late. Some rooms give on to the canal leading to the architecture university, others on to a garden. A few bedrooms share bathroom facilities in the corridor: check when booking.
Hotel services *Fax. Multilingual staff. Telephone. Theatre reservations.*

Dorsoduro

Expensive

Ca' Pisani

Dorsoduro 979A, rio Terà Foscarini (041 277 1478/ fax 041 277 1061/www.capisanihotel.it). Vaporetto Accademia. **Rates** €204-€285 double; €234-€330 'superior' double; €279-€381 suite. **Credit** AmEx, DC, MC, V. **Map** p306 B2.
The Ca' Pisani's luxurious, designer-chic rooms in 1930s and '40s style – a refreshing change from the usual fare of glitz, gilt and Murano glass – make this

one of the best hotels in Venice. It's conveniently located behind the Accademia, with friendly staff and large rooms. There's a restaurant (La Rivista, *see p161*) with tables outside in the summer, a sauna, a roof terrace and a discount at the gym round the corner.
Hotel services *Air-conditioning. Babysitting. Bar. Currency exchange. Dry-cleaning. Fax. Laundry. Lift. Multilingual staff. Restaurant. Safe. Sauna. Solarium. Spa. Theatre reservations. Tours arranged.* **Room services** *Air-conditioning. Minibar. PC connection. Radio. Room service. Safe. TV (satellite).*

Moderate

Accademia – Villa Maravege

Dorsoduro 1058, fondamenta Bollani (041 521 0188/fax 041 523 9152/www.pensioneaccademia.it). Vaporetto Accademia. **Rates** €80-€122 single; €128-€270 double. **Credit** AmEx, DC, MC, V.
Map p306 B2.
This wonderful, secluded 17th-century villa, which used to be the Russian embassy, has two shady, leafy gardens, one of which surrounds a Palladian-style annexe. Breakfast is served in one of the gardens or in the wood-panelled breakfast area. The rooms are stylishly done out with marble floors.
Hotel services *Air-conditioning. Babysitting. Bar. Currency exchange. Dry-cleaning. Fax. Garden. Internet point. Laundry. Multilingual staff. Safe. Tours arranged.* **Room services** *Air-conditioning. Hairdryer. Room service. Safe. TV (satellite).*

Agli Alboretti

Dorsoduro 884, rio Terà Foscarini (041 523 0058/ fax 041 521 0158/www.aglialboretti.com). Vaporetto Accademia. Closed 3wks Jan. **Rates** €104 single; €180 double. **Credit** AmEx, MC, V. **Map** p306 B2.
This hotel with a vaguely nautical air also has its own restaurant and pretty outdoor eating area, where breakfast is served in summer. The simply decorated rooms are comfortable, if rather small. The staff are very helpful.
Hotel services *Air-conditioning. Bar. Fax. Garden. Laundry. Multilingual staff. Restaurant. Safe.* **Room services** *Air-conditioning. Hairdryer. Internet connection. Room service (24hr). TV (satellite).*

American

Dorsoduro 628, fondamenta Bragadin (041 520 4733/fax 041 520 4048/www.hotelamerican.com). Vaporetto Accademia. **Rates** €75-€180 single; €100-€300 double. **Credit** AmEx, MC, V. **Map** p307 B3.
In the peaceful residential area of Dorsoduro, the American has generally spacious rooms decorated in antique Venetian style and recently refurbished. Some rooms have verandas adorned with fresh flowers facing on to the delightful rio di San Vio.
Hotel services *Air-conditioning. Babysitting. Bar. Concert reservations. Fax. Garden. Internet point. Laundry. Multilingual staff. Safe. Tours arranged.* **Room services** *Air-conditioning. Hairdryer. Minibar. Room service (24hr). Safe. TV (satellite).*

La Calcina 54

Dorsoduro 780, fondamenta delle Zattere (041 520 6466/fax 041 522 7045/www.lacalcina.com). Vaporetto Zattere or Accademia. **Rates** €55-€106 single; €99-€182 double. **Credit** AmEx, DC, MC, V **Map** p306 B2.

The hotel where Ruskin stayed in 1877, while writing *The Stones of Venice*. It's a great location: the Redentore church across the water can be admired while sipping cocktails on the terrace on the canal. Rooms have been recently refurbished but not over-modernised, with wooden floors and classic 19th-century furniture. Apartments are also available.
Hotel services *Air-conditioning. Bar. Fax. Laundry. Multilingual staff. Restaurant.* **Room services** *Air-conditioning. Hairdryer. Room service. Safe.*

Locanda San Barnaba 55

Dorsoduro 2486, calle del Traghetto (041 241 1233/ fax 041 241 3812/www.locanda-sanbarnaba.com). Vaporetto Ca' Rezzonico. **Rates** €70-€110 single; €120-€170 double; €160-€210 suite. **Credit** AmEx, MC, V. **Map** p306B2.

With its welcoming atmosphere and 13 comfortable, individually decorated rooms (a simple mix of antique furniture and textiles), the San Barnaba is arguably the best hotel in this price range in this area. There's a small courtyard and roof terrace, and no bridges to cross to get to the nearest vaporetto stop.
Hotel services *Air-conditioning. Babysitting. Bar. Fax. Garden. Multilingual staff. No-smoking rooms. Theatre reservations.* **Room services** *Air-conditioning. Hairdryer. TV.*

Messner 56

Dorsoduro 216, fondamenta Ca' Balà (041 522 7443/fax 041 522 7266/www.hotelmessner.it). Vaporetto Salute. Closed 3wks Dec. **Rates** €90-€110 single; €115-€160 double. **Credit** AmEx, DC, MC, V. **Map** p307 B3.

A recent refurbishment was rather over-zealous, and the Messner's immaculately clean rooms may be too modern for many tastes. The location, the shady garden and the warm, welcoming and helpful staff make up for the loss of atmosphere. Two next-door buildings have become part of the hotel, which also manages some apartments in the area.
Hotel services *Air-conditioning. Bar. Currency exchange. Fax. Garden. Internet point. Multilingual staff. No-smoking rooms. Restaurant. Safe.* **Room services** *Air-conditioning. Hairdryer. Safe. TV (satellite) in 50% of rooms.*

Seguso 57

Dorsoduro 779, Zattere (041 528 6858/fax 041 522 2340/pensioneseguso@tiscali.it). Vaporetto Zattere or Accademia. Closed Dec-mid Feb. **Rates** €120-€183 single; €190-€230 double. **Credit** AmEx, MC, V. **Map** p306 B2.

A renowned hotel with sunny outdoor seats and dark, cosy reception rooms. Obligatory half board, with few exceptions in the summer, seems to attract rather than put off the many regulars, despite the rather mundane food on the plate.

Hotel services *Babysitting. Bar. Dogs welcome. Fax. Lift. Multilingual staff. Restaurant. Safe.* **Room services** *Room service (24hr).*

Budget

Alla Salute da Cici 58

Dorsoduro 222, fondamenta Ca' Balà (041 523 5404/fax 041 522 2271/www.hotelsalute.com). Vaporetto Salute. Closed 2wks Dec, Jan-Carnevale. **Rates** €50-€115 single; €70-€135 double. **Credit** MC, V. **Map** p307 B3.

This pleasant hotel with simple, modern rooms is a stone's throw from the major sites, but well away from the hubbub; it's perfectly situated for summer strolls along the Zattere. Rooms in the new annexe are unquestionably smarter than those in the older building, where bathrooms need renovation.
Hotel services *Bar. Currency exchange. Fax. Garden. Multilingual staff. No-smoking rooms. Safe.* **Room services** *Air-conditioning (some rooms). Hairdryer (some rooms).*

Antica Locanda Montin 59

Dorsoduro 1147, fondamenta delle Eremite (041 522 7151/fax 041 520 0255/www.locandamontin.com). Vaporetto Accademia or Zattere. **Rates** €50-€70 single; €80-€135 double. **Credit** AmEx, DC, MC, V. **Map** p306 B2.

It's difficult to get a booking in this sweet seven-bedroom locanda overlooking a delightful canal. It owes its popularity to the fact that it is also home to one of Venice's most famous – though very over-rated – restaurants.
Hotel services *Bar. Garden. Restaurant. Safe.*

Ca' della Corte 60

Dorsoduro 3560, corte Surian (041 715 877/fax 041 722 345/www.cadellacorte.com). Vaporetto San Tomà. **Rates** €95-€130 single; €105-€165 double. **Credit** AmEx, DC, MC, V.

Though distant from any vaporetto stop, the Corte's vicinity to piazzale Roma in a quiet residential area, its six modern, comfy rooms up a narrow flight of stairs, and its enthusiastic staff make the hike worthwhile. Breakfast is served in bedrooms. Though credit cards are accepted, the owners prefer cash.
Hotel services *Babysitting. Fax. Internet point. Laundry. Theatre reservations.* **Room services** *Hairdryer. Minibar. TV (satellite).*

Locanda San Trovaso 61

Dorsoduro 1351, fondamenta delle Eremite (041 277 1146/fax 041 277 7190/www. locandasantrovaso.com). Vaporetto Zattere. **Rates** €90 single; €110-€125 double. **Credit** AmEx, MC, V. **Map** p306 B2.

Located on a quiet fondamenta near a gondola-maker's workshop, the San Trovaso has a friendly, family feel and spacious, homey bedrooms (none of which have television). Cash payment is required for the pretty rooms in the new annexe across the alley.
Hotel services *Multilingual staff. Roof terrace. Theatre reservations.* **Room services** *Fan.*

Island luxury

There's so little space available in island Venice and so many bureaucratic hoops for would-be developers to jump through that the opening of a large-scale luxury hotel is an epochal event. The fact that two huge, brand-new, top-notch ones are being inaugurated in 2003 has, therefore, something of a miracle about it.

The locations – and they certainly have something divine about them – came in the shape of deserted lagoon islands, a great untapped real estate resource within a gondola's row of San Marco. Some of these are no more than mud-banks; around 70 are important enough to have names. A few, because of their size, or their proximity to the *centro storico*, have been built up, and lived on, and abandoned – often more than once.

San Clemente in the southern lagoon is typical of the mixed religious and military use of most of these island outposts: over time it has been a hospice for Holy Land pilgrims, a powder store, an ecclesiastical prison for unruly priests and, more recently, a mental hospital. Though it is not keen to publicise the fact, it is the buildings of this last complex that the THI hotel group has reworked to create the **San Clemente Palace** hotel: 205 rooms and suites and four restaurants, a business centre, beauty farm, swimming pool and tennis courts – not to mention a three-hole practice golf course, in the extensive, landscaped grounds.

And the 17th-century church hasn't been forgotten either: its retro-Renaissance façade and fine baroque altars have been painstakingly restored.

Just a short boat-hop away, Sacca Sessola is an artificial island created in 1870 using mud from the dredging of the maritime port. Originally a garden island, Sacca Sessola later became a hospital and TB sanatorium. The crumbling 1920s buildings – some with original art deco details – have been renovated and turned into the **Sofitel Venezia in Isola**, a 324-room mega-hotel with an eye on the business market (the new complex also includes a conference centre for up to 440 delegates). The hotel boasts two swimming pools and a five-room presidential suite with a huge private terrace. Both hotels (will) offer non-stop *navette* (shuttle boats) to and from piazza San Marco – for those who can bear to leave their island retreats.

San Clemente Palace

Isola di San Clemente (041 241 3484, www.thi.it). **Rates** 190 single; 230- 570 double; 410- 930 suite. Opening April 2003.

Sofitel Venezia in Isola

Isola di Sacca Sessola (041 520 4388, www.sofitel.com). Rates €369-€569 single; €419-€619 double; suites €619-€979; presidential suite €3,000. Opening February 2003.

Pantalon

Dorsoduro 3942, crosera San Pantalon (041 710 896/fax 041 718 683/www.hotelpantalon.com). Vaporetto San Tomà. Closed Jan. **Rates** €50-€170 single; €80-€240 double. **Credit** AmEx, DC, MC, V. **Map** p306 A2.

Located within university territory, the Pantalon has recently been over-refurbished in pastel Venetian style. On the plus side, the roof terrace is very pleasant.
Hotel services *Air-conditioning. Currency exchange. Dry-cleaning. Fax. Laundry. Multilingual staff. Solarium. Theatre reservations. Tours arranged.* **Room services** *Air-conditioning. Hairdryer. Minibar. Radio. Room service. Safe. TV (satellite).*

Tivoli

Dorsoduro 3838, crosera San Pantalon (041 524 2460/fax 041 522 2656/www.hoteltivoli.it). Vaporetto San Tomà. Closed mid Dec-mid Jan. **Rates** €31-€122 single; €68-€144 double. **No credit cards. Map** p306 A2.

This relatively large, if somewhat unatmospheric, hotel is a good place to seek out if you're daunted by Venice's topography, as it's conveniently located right by the vaporetto stop. It has a small but pretty courtyard, which some of the rather dark rooms look on to. Some single rooms have shared bathrooms.
Hotel services *Fax. Garden. Safe.* **Room services** *Hairdryer. Internet connection. Room service (24hr). TV (satellite).*

La Giudecca

Deluxe

Cipriani

Giudecca 10, fondamenta San Giovanni (041 520 7744/fax 041 520 3930/www.cipriani.orient-express.com). Hotel boat from Vaporetto Vallaresso stop. Closed early Nov-late Mar. **Rates** €499-€755 single; €813-€1248 double; €1683-€3946 suite; €6,360-€8,043 Palladio Suite. **Credit** AmEx, DC, MC, V. **Map** p307 C4.

A **Youth Hostel** with a view.

Set in three acres of verdant paradise on the eastern tip of the Giudecca island, the Cipriani has tennis courts, an Olympic-sized pool, a private harbour for your yacht and a higher-than-average chance of rubbing shoulders with your favourite film star. The rooms are exquisitely decorated, many with marble bathrooms. If this seems too humdrum, take an apartment in the neighbouring 15th-century Palazzo Vendramin, complete with butler service and a private garden. Despite the possibility of unlimited use of the motorboat to San Marco, many guests choose not to leave the premises, begging the question: do they come here for Venice or for the Cipriani itself? **Hotel services** *Air-conditioning. Babysitting. Bar. Car park. Conference facilities. Courtesy boat. Currency exchange. Dry-cleaning. Fax. Garden. Gym. Internet point. Laundry. Lift. Marina. Multilingual staff. Restaurant. Safe. Sauna. Solarium. Swimming pool. Tennis courts. Theatre reservations. Tours arranged.* **Room services** *Air-conditioning. Fax and PC point. Internet connection. Hairdryer. Jacuzzi. Minibar. Radio. Room service (24hr). Safe. TV (satellite).*

Hostels

Istituto Canossiano ⑥⑤
Giudecca 428, fondamenta del Ponte Piccolo (tel/fax 041 522 2157). Vaporetto Palanca. **Rates** €15 per person. Breakfast not incl. **No credit cards.** **Map** p306 C2.
This is a women-only hostel run by lovely, friendly nuns. It is simple and clean, and one of the cheapest places to sleep in Venice. The price includes sheets and blankets. On the down side, guests must be in by 10.30pm (10pm in the winter), and there's no breakfast served.

Ostello di Venezia (Youth Hostel) ⑥⑥
Giudecca 86, fondamenta delle Zitelle (041 523 8211/fax 041 523 5689/vehostel@tin.it). Vaporetto Zitelle. **Rates** €16.50 per person; €8 dinner. **No credit cards.** **Map** p307 C4.
A vaporetto ride away from the main island, this youth hostel offers stunning and unique views across the lagoon towards the church of Santa Maria della Salute and San Marco. Written reservations are needed, especially during the summer months. Unadventurous but very cheap meals are served.

The Lido

For hotels in Chioggia, *see p133.*

Deluxe

Des Bains ⑥⑦
Lungomare Marconi 17, Lido (041 526 5921/fax 041 526 0113/www.starwood.com/italy). Vaporetto Lido. Closed early Nov-mid Mar. **Rates** €192-€413 single; €440-€660 double; €580-€1490 suite. **Credit** AmEx, DC, MC, V. **Map** p311.
Thomas Mann wrote, and Luchino Visconti filmed, *Death in Venice* in this glorious art deco hotel set in its own park. Des Bains has a private beach just across the street and access to tennis courts, a golf course and riding facilities. A water taxi ferries guests to San Marco every half hour. **Hotel services** *Air-conditioning. Babysitting. Bar. Conference facilities. Car park. Courtesy boat (free to Venice; €24 to airport). Currency exchange. Dry-cleaning. Fax. Garden with pool. Gym. Laundry. Lift. Massage parlour. Multilingual staff. No-smoking rooms. Restaurant. Safe. Tennis courts. Theatre reservations. Tours arranged.* **Room services** *Air-conditioning. Fax & PC point. Hairdryer. Minibar. Radio. Room service). TV (satellite).*

Excelsior ⑥⑧
Lungomare Marconi 41, Lido (041 526 0201/fax 041 526 7276 /www.starwood.com/italy). Vaporetto Lido. Closed early Nov-late Mar. **Rates** €410-€675 single; €484-€846 double; €1295-€2445 suite. **Credit** AmEx, DC, MC, V. **Map** p311.
The early-1900s pseudo-Moorish Excelsior hosts hordes of celebrities when the Venice Film Festival (*see p202*) swings into action each September (the festival headquarters is just over the road). Demand a sea-facing room for a view of beach happenings and the Adriatic beyond. The Excelsior's beach huts are the last word in luxury. There are tennis courts and a water taxi to San Marco. **Hotel services** *Air-conditioning. Babysitting. Bar. Car park. Cellphone rental. Conference facilities. Courtesy boat. Currency exchange. Dry-cleaning. Fax. Garden. Laundry. Lift. Multilingual staff. No-smoking rooms. Restaurant. Safe. Theatre reservations. Tours arranged.* **Room services** *Air-conditioning. Hairdryer. Minibar. Radio. Room service (24hr). Safe. TV (satellite).*

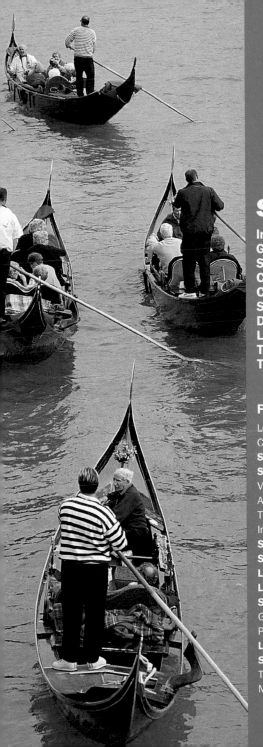

Sightseeing

Features

Introduction

Leave your maps (but not your guide book) at home: Venice is one big sight.

You don't need a map to find the sights in Venice; the whole city is a sight. You won't accidentally end up in its boring suburbs; they're on the other side of the lagoon. Even the 'tacky' bits of Venice have their own surreal charm.

Naturally, the city has its highlights. The **Basilica di San Marco** (*see p71*) is one of Christendom's greatest churches; the **Gallerie dell'Accademia** (*see p122*) contain an unparalleled selection of Renaissance art; and the **Rialto** (*see p65*) is a potent symbol of mercantile energy as well as a fine bridge. But one of the joys of Venice consists in leaving the main routes – and getting lost.

When you do get lost, don't be alarmed: the *calli* will close in around you; you'll come to innumerable dead ends and find yourself returning inexplicably to the same (wrong) spot over and over. But eventually you'll hit a busy thoroughfare. Until that happens, enjoy the feel of village Venice – or, more appropriately, island Venice. The city is made up of over 100 islands, and every one has something – magnificent or quaint, historic or charmingly local – to offer. The real knack to enjoying Venice is to take your time.

Venice is divided into six *sestieri*, which on the map look like fairly random divisions. But they are worth getting to grips with, first because all addresses include the *sestiere* name, and second because each district has a different flavour. Cradled by the great lower bend of the Grand Canal is the *sestiere* of San Marco, the heart of the city; east of here is Castello, one of the most lived-in areas; stretching to the west and north is Cannaregio, whose western stretches are among the most peaceful parts of Venice. South of the Grand Canal is San Polo, bristling with churches; to the west is Santa Croce, short on sights but not atmosphere; while further to the south is Dorsoduro, one of the city's most elegant and artsy districts, with its wide Zattere promenade looking across to the long residential island of the Giudecca – the honorary seventh *sestiere*.

CHURCHES

Venice grew up originally as a host of separate island-communities, each clustered around its own parish church. The bridges were an afterthought. Despite Napoleon's clearance work (*see p93* **Venice and Napoleon**), there are still well over 100 churches in Venice, at least half of them in regular use. They contain an inestimable heritage of artistic treasures. Most of the major churches have reliable opening times; hours in minor churches depend on the good will or whim of the priest or sacristan. It's well worth exploring these, too, since there is not a single one that does not contain some item of interest, whether it be a shrivelled relic or a glowing Madonna with *bambino*. In general, early morning and late afternoon are the best times for church-crawling. But it's best never to pass an opportunity by: if you see one open without a service under way, go in and poke around. No Sunday opening times are given in listings for churches that open only for mass.

MUSEUMS AND GALLERIES

On the whole, Venice's museums and galleries adhere to the basic pre-modern requirement that a museum should be a passive container for beautiful and/or instructive things. But some of those things are very beautiful indeed, especially in treasure troves such as the **Gallerie dell'Accademia**. Instruction can be fun, too. The **Museo Storico Navale** (*see p91*) provides a colourful introduction to Venice's maritime past, while a grasp of the elaborate mechanism of Venetian government (*see p76* **Checks & balances**) will turn the slog around the **Palazzo Ducale** (Doge's Palace; *see p77*) into a voyage of discovery.

Then there are the curiosities – **Ca' d'Oro** (*see p95*), where a patchy gallery with the occasional gem is housed inside one of the city's most extraordinary architectural frames; and the eclectic **Museo della Fondazione Scientifica Querini Stampalia** (*see p85*), a private foundation with a fascinating collection of scenes of 18th-century Venetian life and a glorious Bellini (the painter, not the cocktail).

For something completely different, visit the ultra-new **Telecom Italia Future Centre** at San Salvador (*see p81*), where you can avoid getting lost by touring the city on a touch-screen computer, with Titian and Marco Polo as your guides; this opportunity for virtual touring has had no appreciable effect on the crush in piazza San Marco.

SCUOLE

A unique blend of art treasure house and social institution, Venice's *scuole* (schools) were devotional lay brotherhoods subject to the state rather than the Church. The earliest were founded in the 13th century; by the 15th century there were six *scuole grandi* and as many as 400 minor *scuole*. The *scuole grandi* had annually elected officers drawn from the 'citizen' class (those sandwiched between the governing patriciate and the unenfranchised *popolani*). While members of the *scuole grandi* (such as **Scuola di San Rocco**, *see p115* and **Scuola di San Giovanni Evangelista**, *see p111*) were mainly drawn from the wealthier professional classes, the humbler *scuole piccole* were either exclusively devotional groups, trade guilds or confraternities of foreign communities (such as **Scuola di San Giorgio degli Schiavoni**, *see p93*). When done with providing funds for dowries and scholarships, the wealthier confraternities turned to building and beautifying their own meeting houses (the *scuole* themselves) in a less-than-humble spirit of self-promotion.

The *scuole* were dissolved by Napoleon in 1806, and most of the buildings were put to new uses. Only three survived or were refounded in the mid 19th century, with their artistic treasures intact. *Oratori* were an earlier and more mystic product of the religious enthusiasms that affected Venice between the 11th and the 13th centuries.

Admission & tickets

In summer, expect to queue to enter the Accademia and the Palazzo Ducale (Doge's Palace). Other museums rarely present any overcrowding problems except during special exhibitions. April and May are traditional months for Italian school trips: this can mean sharing your Titians and Tintorettos with gangs of bored teenagers.

Entry to all state-owned museums is, theoretically, free for EU citizens under 18 and over 65. Charges and concessions at city-run and privately owned museums vary; it pays to carry whatever ID cards you can muster (student card, press card and so on).

For one week each spring – designated the *Settimana dei Beni Culturali* (Cultural Heritage week) – all state-owned galleries and museums are free. See www.beniculturali.it for details.

Multi-entrance tickets

For **Rolling Venice** and the **Venice Card**, *see p289*.

Many of Venice's landmarks offer multi-entrance tickets, which cut costs if you are planning to visit all the sights covered by any given ticket. The most comprehensive of all is the **Carta dei Musei di Venezia**, which should be available from spring 2003 (*see p290* **Museum Card**). Other schemes include:

Musei Civici Veneziani

Venice's city-owned museums offer multi-entrance tickets in different forms and prices, all of which can be bought at participating establishments. No credit cards.
● **Musei di Piazza San Marco** (Palazzo Ducale, Biblioteca Marciana, Museo Correr, Museo Archeologico) €9.50; concessions €5.50.
● **Area del Settecento** (museums of the 18th century: Ca' Rezzonico, Palazzo Mocenigo, Casa Goldoni) €8; concessions €4.50.
● **Area del Moderno** (Ca' Pesaro-Galleria Internazionale d'Arte Moderna and Palazzo Fortuny, from spring 2003) €6; concessions €4.
● **Musei delle Isole** (Glass Museum and Lace Museum) €6; concessions €4.
● **Museum Pass** (all the above museums) €18; €12 concessions.

Note that the Musei di Piazza San Marco can only be entered on a cumulative ticket. For the others, individual tickets are available.

Information on sights covered by the scheme can be found on www.museicivicineveziani.it.

State Museums

The Gallerie dell'Accademia (*see p122*), Ca' d'Oro (*see p95*), and Ca' Pesaro-Museo Orientale (*see p108*) can be visited on a multi-entrance ticket costing €9.50 (€4.75 concessions) from participating sights. No credit cards.

Chorus

The following churches belong to the Chorus scheme (041 275 0462/www.chorus-ve.org), which funds upkeep and restoration by charging for entry:
San Marco: Santa Maria del Giglio (*see p83*), Santo Stefano (*see p82*).
Castello: Santa Maria Formosa (*see p87*), San Pietro in Castello (*see p92*).
Cannaregio: Santa Maria dei Miracoli (*see p102*), Sant'Alvise (*see p101*), Madonna dell'Orto (*see p99*).
San Polo & Santa Croce: San Polo (*see p105*), San Stae (*see p111*), I Frari (*see p113*), San Giacomo dell'Orio (*see p110*), San Giovanni Elemosinario (*see p105*).
Dorsoduro: Gesuati (*see p126*), San Sebastiano (*see p118*).
Giudecca: Il Redentore (*see p128*).

There's a fee of €2 for each church; or you can invest in a multi-entrance ticket (€8; €5 students under 30). Single- and multi-entrance tickets can be bought in participating churches and at VeLa shops (*see p188*). Churches are equipped with audioguides in English (included in the multi-entrance ticket price for all Chorus churches except the Frari; 50¢ for visitors buying single-entrance tickets). No credit cards are accepted.

Sightseeing

The woman of today can find items from prestigious Italian and foreign fashion houses and a wide range of coordinates, from our own production, of handmade and Italian design.
We present our view of the world, of fashion and of everyday life at home, without forgetting the things of the past, which have played such a vital role in creating the present.
We are waiting for you.

www.potpourri.it - info@potpourri.it

The Grand Canal

Hop on a vaporetto to appreciate the *palazzi* lining this most stately high street.

No city has a more stately high street than Venice. The Canal Grande, three and a half kilometres (two and a half miles) in length, snakes through the city with wide curling loops that give the *sestieri* (districts) their shape. A trip from the railway station to piazza San Marco (about half an hour) is not only interesting aesthetically, but also gives you an idea of how the city functioned in its historic heyday – and, indeed, how it functions today.

The canal is still the main thoroughfare of Venice; in the great days of the city's trading empire it would have been alive with cargo boats from all over the Mediterranean. A Grand Canal address was not only socially but commercially desirable; and the architecture of the *palazzi* that line it is as practical as it was impressive. Most of the notable buildings were built between the 12th and 18th centuries. When a family decided to rebuild a palazzo, they usually maintained the same basic structure – for the good reason that they could build on the same foundations. This resulted in some interesting style hybrids: the Grand Canal offers many examples of *palazzi* in which Veneto-Byzantine or Gothic features are incorporated into the Renaissance or baroque.

For centuries the *palazzi* generally followed the same plan: a main water-entrance opening on to a large hall with storage space on either side; a *mezzanino* with offices; a *piano nobile* (the main floor – sometimes two in grander buildings) consisting of a spacious reception hall lit by large central windows and flanked on both sides by residential rooms; and a land-entrance at the back. Over the centuries all kinds of architectural frills and trimmings were added, but the underlying form was stable – and, as always in Venice, it is form that follows function.

In the following description of the most notable *palazzi*, many names recur, for the simple reason that families expanded, younger sons inheriting as well as older ones. Compound names indicate that the palazzo passed through various hands. Originally the term 'palazzo' was reserved for the Doge's Palace. Other *palazzi* were known as Casa or Ca' for short: this is still true of some of the older ones, such as Ca' d'Oro.

This chapter deals mainly with canal-side *palazzi*. Churches and museums facing on to the canal are covered elsewhere in the guide: in these cases, cross-references are given. For information on the *vaporetti* that ply the Grand Canal, *see p276*.

Sightseeing

Palazzo Vendramin Calergi, winter home of the Casino. *See p65.*

Left bank

From the railway station to San Marco

❶ Vaporetto stop Ferrovia

At the foot of the Ponte degli Scalzi is the fine baroque façade of the **Scalzi** church (*see p97*), recently restored.

ⓐ Ponte degli Scalzi

Unusually narrow **Palazzo Flangini** is a 17th-century building by Giuseppe Sardi. Despite picturesque stories of quarrelling brothers, it owes its shape to the simple fact that the family's money ran out.

❶ **Riva di Biasic**

Grand Canal

ⓐ
Ponte degli Scalzi
ⓐ
❶ **Ferrovia**

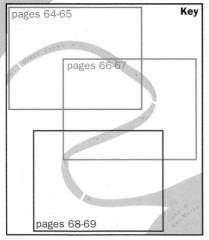

pages 64-65   **Key**

pages 66-67

pages 68-69

Right bank

From the railway station to the Salute

Before the Scalzi bridge is the church of **San Simeone Piccolo**, with its high green dome and Corinthian portico. For those arriving in Venice it's a picturesque introduction to the city.

The **Ponte degli Scalzi**, which leads across to the station, was built in stone by Eugenio Miozzi in 1934.

ⓐ Ponte degli Scalzi

❶ Vaporetto stop Riva di Biasio

Just before the rio del Megio stands the **Fontego dei Turchi**, a 19th-century reconstruction of the original Veneto-Byzantine building, which was leased to Turkish traders in the 17th century as a residence and warehouse. Some of the original material was used but the effect as a whole is one of pastiche. Once lived in by the poet Torquato Tasso, it's now the Natural History Museum (due to reopen in 2004).

The **Depositi del Megio** (state granaries) have a battlemented plain brick façade. The sculpted lion is a modern replacement of the

Just before the wide Cannaregio Canal is the church of **San Geremia**; from the Grand Canal, the apse of the chapel of Santa Lucia is visible.

Standing with its main façade on the Cannaregio Canal is **Palazzo Labia**, the 18th-century home of the seriously rich Labia family. The story goes that parties ended with the host throwing his gold dinner plates into the canal to demonstrate his wealth; the servants would then be ordered to fish them out again. A famous fancy-dress ball thrown here in 1951 by a Mexican millionaire continued this tradition of conspicuous consumption. The building is now the regional headquarters of the RAI (the

➋ San Marcuola

The neo-Gothic **Pescaria** fish market.

original, destroyed at the fall of the Republic. The church of **San Stae** (*see p111*) has a baroque façade by Domenico Rossi, with exuberant sculpture.

➋ Vaporetto stop San Stae

On the rio di Ca' Pesaro, and with a magnificent side wall curving along the canal in gleaming marble, is **Ca' Pesaro** (*see p106*), a splendid example of Venetian baroque by Longhena.

After two smaller *palazzi* stands the **Palazzo Corner della Regina**, with a rusticated ground floor featuring grotesque masks, some just above water level. It was built for a branch of the Corner family, who were descended from Caterina Cornaro, Queen of Cyprus; Caterina was born in an earlier house on the site. The present palazzo dates from the 1720s.

The covered fish market or **Pescaria** has occupied a site here since the 14th century. The current neo-Gothic construction, however, was only built in 1907, replacing an iron one. Beyond this is a building with an endless parade of arches along the canal; this is the longest

Italian state broadcaster). It contains suitably sumptuous frescos by Tiepolo.

➋ Vaporetto stop San Marcuola

The next building of note is **Palazzo Vendramin Calergi**, an impressive Renaissance palazzo designed by Mauro Codussi in the first decade of the 16th century. It uses his characteristic arched windows incorporating twin smaller arches. Porphyry insets decorate the façade. Wagner died here in 1883. It is the winter home of the Casinò (*see p142* **Chancers**).

A fairly uneventful stretch ends at the **Ca' d'Oro** (*see p95*), the most gorgeously ornate Gothic building on the Grand Canal. Restoration work on this palazzo came to an end finally in 1984, after 20 years of labour. However, for all its ornaments, it is sober in comparison with its original appearance, when its ▶

➋ San Stae

facade on the Grand Canal and belongs to Sansovino's **Fabbriche Nuove**, built in 1554-6 for Venice's financial judiciary; it now houses the Court of Assizes.

Just beyond this stands the **Fabbriche Vecchie** by Scarpagnino, built after a fire in the early 16th century.

Before the Rialto bridge, the **Palazzo dei Camerlenghi** (1523-5) is built around the curve of the canal; the walls lean noticeably. It was the headquarters of the Venetian Exchequer, with a debtors' prison on the ground floor.

ⓑ Ponte del Rialto

The **Ponte di Rialto** was built in 1588-92 by the aptly named Antonio Da Ponte. Until the 19th century it was the only bridge over the Grand Canal. It replaced a wooden one, which can be seen in Carpaccio's painting of *The Miracle of the True Cross* in the Accademia (*see p122*). After the decision was taken to build it, 60 years passed, during the course of which designs by Michelangelo, Vignola, Sansovino and Palladio were rejected. Da Ponte's simple but effective project eventually got the green light, ▶

Sightseeing

▶ probably because it maintained the utilitarian features of the previous wooden structure, with its double row of shops. The bridge thus acts as a logical continuation of the market at its foot. Palladio's design was far more beautiful, but made no provision for the sale of counterfeit Nike shoes and plastic gondolas.

❸ Vaporetto stop San Silvestro

Beyond the San Silvestro vaporetto stop are a few houses with Veneto-Byzantine windows and decorations.

Before the rio San Polo is the 16th-century **Palazzo Cappello Layard**, once the home of Sir Henry Austen Layard, archaeologist and British ambassador to Constantinople.

A little way before the San Tomà stop is the **Palazzo Pisani Moretta**, a large Gothic palazzo of the 15th century, often hired out for Hollywood-style parties

❹ Vaporetto stop San Tomà

Palazzo Balbi (1582-90), with obelisks (an indication that an admiral lived here), is the seat of the Veneto Regional Council.

The rio Ca' Foscari turns into the rio Novo, a canal dug in the 1930s to provide a short cut to the car park and station; traffic seriously undermined the foundations of the buildings along the canal, so public transport stopped using the rio Novo in the 1980s. Looking down the rio, you can see the archways of the city's fire station. Between the fire station and Palazzo Balbi is a minor building, on a site once scheduled to hold Frank Lloyd Wright's Centre for Foreign Architectural Students. In the end his designs were judged too radical for so conspicuous a spot.

Immediately beyond the rio Ca' Foscari come three magnificent mid 15th-century Gothic *palazzi*. The first and largest is **Ca' Foscari** (being restored as this guide went to press, and hidden behind a huge photographic reproduction of itself). It was at Ca' Foscari that Henry III of France was lavishly entertained in 1574 – so lavishly that his reason seems to have been knocked permanently askew. Doge Francesco Foscari died here of a broken heart after being ousted from office. The palazzo is now the

headquarters of Venice's Università Ca' Foscari. The next two are the **Palazzi Giustinian**; Wagner stayed in one of them in the winter of 1858-9, composing part of *Tristan und Isolde*. The horn prelude to the third act was inspired by the mournful cries of the gondoliers.

Ca' Rezzonico (*see p120*) is a baroque masterpiece by Longhena, begun in 1667 for the Bon family, then sold to the Rezzonico family. Robert Browning died here, while staying with his profitably married but otherwise talentless son Pen, who bought the palazzo with his wife's money. Later guests included Whistler and Cole Porter. The building now contains the museum of 18th-Century Venice.

❺ Vaporetto stop Ca' Rezzonico

Just after the Ca' Rezzonico stop is the 15th-century **Palazzo Loredan**. The last palazzo before the Accademia Bridge houses the British Vice-Consulate.

Once the church and monastery of Santa Maria della Carità, the **Gallerie dell'Accademia** now boasts an unrivalled collection of Venetian paintings (*see p122*).

❻ Vaporetto stop Accademia
❻ Ponte dell'Accademia

After four fine Renaissance *palazzi* comes campo San Vio, one of the few *campi* on the Grand Canal. In the corner is the Anglican church of **St George**. To one side of the campo is the 16th-century **Palazzo Barbarigo**, disfigured by some tacky 19th-century mosaics. Next is the pretty Gothic **Palazzo da' Mula**.

A little beyond that is the single-storey **Palazzo Venier dei Leoni**. Work ground to a halt in 1749 when the family opposite objected to their light being blocked by such a huge pile. ▶

❹ **San Tomà**   **Sant'Angelo** ❺

The **Ca' d'Oro**: ornamented but comparatively sober. *See p65.*

The **Rialto**: simple, effective and *with* plastic gondolas.

ⓑ
Ponte di
Rialto
ⓑ

Rialto ④

San Silvestro

At the foot of the Rialto bridge is the **Fondaco dei Tedeschi**, a huge residence-cum-warehouse leased to the German community from the 13th century onwards. The present building was built by Spavento and Scarpagnino in 1505-8 after a fire. The façade once had glorious frescos by Titian and Giorgione – now in a sad state of repair in the Ca' d'Oro gallery (*see p95*). The Fondaco is now the main post office.

ⓑ Ponte del Rialto

Just before the Rialto stop is **Palazzo Manin Dolfin**, with a portico straddling the *fondamenta*. The façade is by Sansovino (late 1530s); the rest was rebuilt by Ludovico Manin, the forlorn last Doge of Venice (*see p17*). It now belongs to the Bank of Italy.

④ Vaporetto stop Rialto

Palazzetto Dandolo is a Gothic building that appears to have been squeezed tight by its neighbours. Enrico Dandolo, the blind doge who led the ferocious assault on Constantinople in 1204 (*see p11*), was born in an earlier palazzo that stood on this site.

Palazzo Farsetti and **Palazzo Loredan** are Veneto-Byzantine buildings that now house the city hall and various municipal offices. Though heavily restored, these two adjoining *palazzi* are among the few surviving examples of the 12th-century Venetian house, with its first-floor polyforate window.

Palazzo Grimani is one of the largest *palazzi* on the Grand Canal. Its creator, Michele Sanmicheli from Verona, was famous for his military architecture, and this building is characteristically massive and assertive. The Grimani family were *nouveaux riches*, and the story goes that they wanted each one of their windows to be larger than the front door of the palazzo that used to stand opposite.

Seven *palazzi* further on, before the rio Michiel, stands the pink **Palazzo Benzon**, home of Countess Marina Querini-Benzon, a great society figure at the end of the 18th century. Byron was charmed by her when she was already in her sixties. She inspired a popular song, *La biondina in gondoleta*, which the gondoliers used to sing before international tourism imposed the unfittingly Neapolitan *O' Sole Mio*.

Before the Sant'Angelo vaporetto stop is the small-scale **Palazzo Corner**, built in the last decade of the 15th century by Mauro Codussi. It is one of the most beautiful early Renaissance buildings in Venice, with a rusticated ground floor, elegant balconies and the characteristic double-arched windows seen in **Palazzo Vendramin Calergi** (*see p65*).

▶ decorative features were gilded or painted in ultramarine blue and cinnabar red. It has an open loggia on the *piano nobile*, like the Doge's Palace, but unlike any other palazzo after the Byzantine period.

③ Vaporetto stop Ca' d'Oro

Just before the rio dei Santi Apostoli is **Palazzo Mangilli Valmarana**, built in 1751 for Joseph Smith, the British consul, who amassed the huge collection of Canaletto paintings that now belongs to the Queen. The building is now the Argentinian Consulate.

Beyond the rio dei Santissimi Apostoli stands the **Ca' da Mosto**, once the site of the Leon Bianco (white lion) Hotel; this is one of the earliest Veneto-Byzantine *palazzi* on the Grand Canal. It still has three of the original five arches of its water-entrance and a long array of Byzantine arches on the first floor.

▶

▶ Art collector Peggy Guggenheim lived here from 1949-79; she was the last person in Venice to have her own private gondola. The building now contains the **Peggy Guggenheim Collection** (*see p123* **Peggy G**). Check out the brass horse and rider (1948) by Marino Marini overlooking the canal.

Next but one comes the pure, lopsided charm of the Renaissance **Ca' Dario**, built in the 1470s, perhaps by Pietro Lombardo, with decorative use of coloured marbles and chimney pots. Venetians say the palazzo is cursed; certainly the list of former owners who have met sticky ends is impressive.

Palazzo Salviati is a 19th-century building with gaudy mosaics advertising the products of the Salviati glassworks.

The former abbey of **San Gregorio** is the last building before the Salute stop, with a fine 14th-century relief of St Gregory over a Gothic doorway. (Beyond can be seen the apse of the former church of the same name.)

Sant'Angelo ●

❹ **San Tomà**

▶ ❺ **Vaporetto stop Sant'Angelo**

A little beyond the *traghetto* (*see p276*) station for San Tomà stand the four **Palazzi Mocenigo**, with blue and white poles in the water. The central double palazzo (16th century) was where Byron and his menagerie of foxes, monkeys and dogs lived in 1818-19; he wrote to a friend: 'Venice is not an expensive residence… I have my gondola and about 14 servants… and I reside in one of the Mocenigo palaces on the Grand Canal; the rent… is two hundred a year (and I gave more than I need have done).'

Just before the San Samuele vaporetto stop is heavy, grey-white **Palazzo Grassi** (*see p82*), designed by Giorgio Massari. This was the last of the great patrician *palazzi*, built in grand style in 1748-72 when the city was already in terminal decline. It was bought by Fiat in the 1980s and restored at the speed and enormous expense that only huge PR-conscious corporations can allow themselves.

San Samuele ❻

❺ **Rezzonico**

Accademia ❻   ◉ **Ponte del Accademia** ◉

❼ **Vaporetto stop Salute**

In triumphant position, at the very opening of the Grand Canal, stands the wonderfully curvy church of **Santa Maria della Salute** (*see p125*). Baldassare Longhena's audacious baroque creation (1671) took 50 years to build. Every year on November 21 (*see p196*) a procession from the basilica di San Marco makes its way across a specially-erected bridge of boats to the church. Beyond the church is the Patriarchal Seminary.

Ca' Dario: former owners met sticky ends.

⑥ Vaporetto stop San Samuele

The **Ca' del Duca** incorporates in one corner a part of the rusticated base and columns of a palazzo that Bartolomeo Bon was going to build for the Cornaro family. In 1461 it was bought by Francesco Sforza, Duke of Milan, but fortunately the bombastic plan for the site was abandoned.

In 1932 the iron **Ponte dell'Accademia** built by the Austrians was replaced by a 'temporary' wooden one. When this was discovered to be on the point of collapse in 1984, the Venetians had grown too fond of it to imagine anything else spanning the canal, so it was rebuilt exactly as before.

⑥ Ponte dell'Accademia

At the foot of the bridge is **Palazzo Franchetti**, built in the 15th century but much restored and altered in the 19th; it's now used as a conference centre.

Immediately beyond this are two **Palazzi Barbaro**, which have literary associations. The first one – 15th-century Gothic, with a fine but battered Renaissance water entrance – still partly belongs to the Curtis family, who played host to Henry James at intervals between 1870 and 1875. The building was the model for Milly Theale's palazzo in *The Wings of the Dove.*

Just before one of the few Grand Canal gardens comes the bashful **Casetta delle Rose**, set back behind its own small trellised garden. Canova had a studio here; and Gabriele D'Annunzio, who set one of his most sensuous novels, *Il Fuoco* ('Fire'), in Venice, stayed in the house.

The massive rusticated ground floor of the **Palazzo Corner della Ca' Grande** (now the Prefecture) influenced Longhena's baroque *palazzi*. The highest of High Renaissance, the imposing pile was commissioned in 1537 from Sansovino for Giacomo Cornaro, and built after 1545. Never one to mince words, Ruskin called it 'one of the worst and coldest buildings of the central Renaissance'.

Palazzo Venier dei Leoni. *See p66.*

⑦ Vaporetto stop Santa Maria del Giglio

After Campo Santa Maria del Giglio comes the long 15th-century Gothic facade of **Palazzo Gritti**, now one of Venice's poshest hotels.

Three *palazzi* further on is the narrow Gothic **Palazzo Contarini Fasan**, traditionally, but quite arbitrarily, known as Desdemona's house. It has beautiful balconies with wheel-tracery.

The **Europa & Regina** hotel was once the home of Kay Bronson, an American society hostess whose hospitality was much appreciated by Henry James.

The last notable building is **Ca' Giustinian**, built in the late Gothic style of the 1470s, and once a hotel where Verdi, Gautier, Ruskin and Proust stayed; George Eliot's honeymoon here was ruined when her husband fell off the balcony into the Grand Canal and nearly died.

At the corner of calle Vallaresso is the self-effacing **Harry's Bar** (*see p165*), the near-legendary Venetian watering-hole, founded by Arrigo Cipriani senior in the 1930s.

⑧ Vaporetto stop Vallaresso

Just beyond the vaporetto stop lie the pretty Giardinetti Reali (*see p71*) and piazza San Marco.

⑧ **Vallaresso**

⑦ **Santa Maria del Giglio**

⑦ **Salute**

The left bank ends with the **Dogana di Mare** (Customs House, 1677), with its tower, gilded ball, weather vane figure of Fortune and spectacular view out across the Bacino di San Marco towards the Lido. (Eastward-facing, the view is best savoured at sunrise.) Ships wanting to enter Venice would have their cargoes examined by customs officials, who were based here. The warehouses before the Punta della Dogana are from the 19th century. Plans to convert them into state-of-the-art exhibition space for overflow from the Peggy Guggenheim Collection are at a standstill at the moment, due to opposition from the Seminary next door.

Sightseeing

San Marco

A bustling *sestiere* surrounds the 'drawing room of Europe'.

Piazza San Marco may appear to be the heart of the city, but that title belongs not so much to the square itself – impressive as it is – as to the bustling *sestiere* of the same name. Three main thoroughfares link the key points of San Marco, forming a rough triangle: one from piazza San Marco to the Rialto bridge, one from the Rialto to the Accademia bridge, and one from the Accademia to piazza San Marco. This is classic visitor's Venice, its main streets packed to rib-cracking capacity with short-stay tourists 'doing' the sights. But stray into the centre of the triangle and you'll feel far off the beaten track.

Piazza San Marco

Napoleon famously referred to the square as the 'drawing room of Europe'. His description catches some of the quality of the place: it may not be homey, but it is a supremely civilised meeting place, with architecture that is impressive but not intimidating. Byzantine rubs shoulders with Gothic, late Renaissance and neo-classical. Napoleon intended to embellish this open-air salon with a statue of himself in the centre of the western wing. The work remained in front of the Palazzo Ducale for a few years but never made it into the piazza (*see p93* **Venice & Napoleon**): the Venetians have always kept the square clear of public monuments (sometimes stooping to mendacity to do so – *see p85* **Monument to Bartolomeo Colleoni**). This is typical of Venice, where individual glory was always kept firmly in second place to communal progress.

The north side of the square dates from the early 16th century. Its 'troops of ordered arches' (to quote John Ruskin) take up a motif suggested by an earlier Byzantine building that can be seen in Gentile Bellini's painting *Translation of the Relics of the Cross* in the Accademia gallery (*see p122*). Here resided the procurators of St Mark's, who were in charge maintenaning the basilica – hence the name of this whole wing, the **Procuratie Vecchie**. At its eastern end is the **Torre dell'Orologio**.

Construction of the **Procuratie Nuove** on the other side of the square went on for most of the first half of the 17th century; it was built to designs by Vincenzo Scamozzi on the model of the **Biblioteca Marciana** around the corner. Napoleon, of course, had to join the two wings

at the far end – not for the sake of symmetry but in order to create the ballroom that was lacking in the Procuratie Nuove, which had become the imperial residence. So, in 1807, down came Sansovino's church of San Geminiano and up went the **Ala Napoleonica**, which now houses the **Museo Correr**. The cafés under the arches have their history, too; but before you take your weight off your feet here, bear in mind that a cup of coffee at an outside table will double your day's expenses.

The **Campanile** and **Basilica di San Marco** (St Mark's basilica) close off the square in all its splendour to the east.

PIAZZETTA DEI LEONCINI

On the north side of the basilica is this small square, named after two small marble lions that have been rubbed smooth by generations of children's bottoms. The large palazzo at the far end of the square is the 19th-century residence of the patriarch (cardinal) of Venice.

LA PIAZZETTA

Between the basilica and the lagoon, the Piazzetta, as it is so economically known, is the real entrance to Venice, defined by two free-standing columns of granite (from Syria or Constantinople). Generations of foreign visitors disembarked here, to be immediately struck by all that pomp and magnificence. The area directly in front of the **Palazzo Ducale** (Doge's Palace) corresponded to the modern-day parliamentary lobby. Known as the *broglio*, it was the place where councillors conferred and connived (hence the term 'imbroglio'). Opposite the palace are entrances to the **Biblioteca Marciana/Libreria Sansoviania**, the little-visited **Museo Archeologico** and **La Zecca**, now the main city library.

The man who erected the two columns in the 12th century supposedly asked for the right to set up gambling tables between them. The authorities agreed, but soon put a damper on the jollity by using the pillars to string 'em up (criminals, that is) for public edification – which is why superstitious locals avoid walking between them. The winged lion on top of the easternmost column is in fact a chimera from Persia, Syria or maybe China; the wings and book are Venetian additions. St Theodore, who tops the other one, was Venice's first patron saint (*see p8* **Mark 1, Theodore 0**).

BY THE LAGOON

West of the Piazzetta are the **Giardinetti Reali** (Royal Gardens), created by the French, who had the old granaries pulled down to provide a view for the royal residence that they had set up in the Procuratie Nuove. The dainty neo-classical coffeehouse by Gustavo Selva is now the city's main tourist office (*see chapter* **Directory: Tourist information**), with a small bookshop attached.

By the Vallaresso vaporetto stop is Harry's Bar (*see p165*), the most famous watering hole in the city, founded in the 1920s. Ernest Hemingway, Orson Welles and many other famous drinkers have contributed to the legend of the place and the price of the food.

Going the opposite way from the Piazzetta, you cross the **ponte della Paglia** (Bridge of Straw). If you can elbow your way to the side of the bridge, there is a photo-op view of the **Bridge of Sighs**, famous in legend and poetry as linking the Palazzo Ducale to the prisons and thus, supposedly, offering a last glimpse of the outside to the condemned wretches. From the Bridge of Straw there is also a superb view of the Renaissance façade of the Palazzo Ducale, by Antonio Rizzo, which even Ruskin – a fan of the Byzantine and Gothic – was forced to admire against his will.

TICKETS

The museums around piazza San Marco (but not the paying parts of the basilica) must be visited on a multi-entrance ticket. *See p61* **Musei Civici Veneziani/Musei di piazza San Marco**.

Basilica di San Marco

Piazza San Marco (041 522 5205). Vaporetto San Zaccaria or Vallaresso. **Open** *Apr-Oct* 9.45am-5pm Mon-Sat; 2-5pm Sun. *Nov-Mar* 9.45am-4.30pm Mon-Sat; 2-4.30pm Sun. Before 9.45am private prayer and mass only, from the piazzetta dei Leoncini door. *Loggia & Museo Marciano* Apr-Oct 9.45am-5pm daily. Nov-Mar 9.45am-4.30pm daily. **Admission** free. *Chancel & Pala d'Oro* €1.50; €1 concessions. *Loggia & Museo Marciano* €1.50; €1 concessions. *Treasury* €2; €1 concessions. **No credit cards**. **Map** p307 A4.

Throughout history, the Basilica di San Marco has provoked extreme reactions. Some, like John Ruskin, pitch head first into purple prose: 'The crests of the arches break into a marble foam, and toss themselves far into the blue sky in flashes and wreaths of sculpted spray.' Others, resentful of its opulence, take the dissenting view. Mark Twain described it as a 'vast and warty bug taking a meditative walk'. The church is often seen as the living testimony of Venice's links with Byzantium. But it is also an expression of the city's independence. In the Middle Ages any self-respecting city state had to have a truly important holy relic. So when two Venetian

merchants swiped the body of St Mark from Alexandria in 828, concealed from prying Muslim eyes under a protective layer of pork, they were going for the very best – an Evangelist, and an entire body at that. Fortunately, there was a legend (or one was quickly cooked up) that the saint had once been caught in the lagoon in a storm, and so it was fitting that this should be his final resting place.

It is perhaps equally fitting that this most sacred monument, symbol of the city, is built around a piece of plunder, however divinely sanctioned. The Venetians, who had started out with nothing but salt and fish, had by necessity become traders, but they never looked askance at a bit of straightforward loot-ing as well. The basilica – like the city as a whole – is encrusted with trophies brought back from Venice's greatest spoliatory exploit, the Sack of Constantinople in 1204, during the free-for-all that went under the name of the Fourth Crusade.

The present basilica is the third on the site. It was built mainly between 1063 and 1094, although the work of decoration continued all the way through to the 16th century. The church only became the Cathedral of Venice in 1807, ten years after the fall of the Republic; until then the bishop exerted his authority from San Pietro in Castello (*see p92*).

Next door to the Palazzo Ducale, Venice's most important church was associated with political as much as spiritual power. Venetians who came to worship here were very aware that they were guests of the doge, not the pope, and the basilica was an integral part of the city's self-glorifying mythology.

The great triumphal arches of the façade are an expression of civic pride; and even the Venetians' sincere devotion to their patron saint, which mate-rially supported the costly decoration lovingly bestowed on the building over the centuries, had a strong nationalist element.

Exterior

The first view of the basilica from the western end of the square is an unforgettable experience. It is particularly impressive in the evening, when the mosaics on the façade glow in the light of the setting sun (as they are mostly 17th- and 18th-century replacements, the distance improves them). The façade consists of two orders of five arches, with clusters of columns in the lower order; the upper arches are topped by the fantastic Gothic tracery that inspired Ruskin to reach for those metaphors.

The only original mosaic is the one over the north door, *The Translation of the Body of St Mark to the Basilica*, which contains the earliest known repre-sentation of the church; it dates from around 1260. Of curiosity value is the 17th-century mosaic over the south door, which shows the body of St Mark being filched from Alexandria and the Muslims reel-ing back in disgust from its crafty pork wrapping.

The real treasures, though, are the sculptures, par-ticularly the group of three carved arches around the central portal, a masterpiece of Romanesque work. The inner curve of the outer arch is the liveliest, with

Sightseeing

its detailed portrayals of Venetian trades, crafts and pastimes such as shipbuilding, hunting and fishing. The upper order, with its fine 14th-century Gothic sculpture by the Dalle Masegne brothers and later Tuscan and Lombard sculptors, can be seen from the Loggia (*see p73*).

The south façade, towards the Palazzo Ducale, was the first side seen by visitors from the sea and is thus richly encrusted with trophies proclaiming Venice's might. There was a ceremonial entrance to the basilica here as well, but this was blocked by the construction of the Zen Chapel (*see below*) in the 16th century. At the corner stand the Tetrarchs, a fourth-century porphyry group of four conspiratorial-looking kings. These come from Constantinople, and are usually accepted as representing Diocletian and his Imperial colleagues. However, popular lore has it that they are four Saracens turned to stone after an attempt to burgle the Treasury.

The two free-standing pillars in front of the Baptistry door, with Syrian carvings from the fifth century, come from Acre, as does the stumpy porphyry column on the corner, known as the *Pietra del Bando*, where decrees of the Signoria were read. It bore the brunt of the fall of the Campanile in 1902 (*see p75*); hence its rather battered appearance.

The north façade, facing piazzetta dei Leoncini, is also studded with loot. One example is the carving of 12 sheep on either side of a throne bearing a cross, a Byzantine work of the seventh century. Note the beautiful 13th-century Moorish arches of the Porta dei Fiori, which enclose a Nativity scene.

The narthex (entrance porch) has an opus sectile marble floor; a small lozenge of porphyry by the central door is said to mark the spot where the Emperor Barbarossa paid homage to Pope Alexander III in 1177. The influence of Islamic art comes through in the few remaining grilles that cover the wall niches where early doges were buried. Above, a series of fine 13th-century mosaics by Venetian craftsmen in the Byzantine style shows scenes from the Old Testament.

Interior

Come every day for the rest of your life, with a small portable helicopter, and you just might begin to feel that you have seen everything contained in this cave of wonders. Failing that, make more than one visit, preferably at different times of day, to appreciate the varying effects of light on the mosaics.

The lambent interior exudes splendour and mystery, even when bursting with tourists. It is in many ways an exercise in obsession: for centuries the Venetians continued to add to its treasures, leaving not an inch uncovered.

The form is that of a Greek cross, surmounted by five great 11th-century domes. The surfaces – all the surfaces – are covered by more than four square kilometres (1.5 square miles) of mosaics, the result of 600 years of labour. The finest pieces, dating from the 12th and 13th centuries, are the work of Venetian craftsmen influenced by Byzantine art but develop-

ing their own independent style. The chapels and Baptistry were decorated in the 14th and 15th centuries; a century later, replacements of earlier mosaics were made using cartoons by such artists as Titian and Tintoretto. However, most of these later mosaics are fundamentally flawed by the attempt to achieve the three-dimensional effects of Renaissance painting.

In the apse, *Christ Pantocrator* is a faithful 16th-century reproduction of a Byzantine original. Beneath, in what may be the oldest mosaics in the church, are four saint-protectors of Venice: St Nicholas, St Peter, St Mark and St Hermagoras. The central dome of the Ascension, with its splendidly poised angels and apostles, dates from the early 13th century. It is said to have influenced fresco painting in the area as well as the sculptures on the façade. The Passion scenes on the west vault (12th century) are a striking blend of Romanesque and Byzantine styles. The Pentecost dome (towards the entrance) was probably the first to be decorated; it shows the *Descent of the Holy Spirit*. Four magnificent angels hover in the pendentives.

Worth seeking out is the scene of the *Miraculous Rediscovery of the Body of St Mark* in the right transept. This refers to an episode that occurred after the second basilica was destroyed by fire, when the secret of the whereabouts of the body was lost. The Evangelist obligingly opened up the pillar where his sarcophagus had been hidden (it's just opposite and is marked by an inlaid marble panel). Notice, too, the spectacular 12th-century marble, porphyry and glass mosaics on the floor, which has been much restored.

Baptistry & Zen Chapel

The Baptistry contains the Gothic tomb of Doge Andrea Dandolo and some interesting mosaics such as the famous image of Salome dancing, but has long been closed. Special permission (041 522 5202) is needed to visit it and the adjoining Zen Chapel, with its bronze 16th-century tomb of Cardinal Zen.

Chancel & Pala d'Oro

The Chancel is separated from the body of the church by the iconostasis – a red marble rood screen by the Gothic sculptors Jacobello and Pier Paolo Dalle Masegne, with fine naturalistic statues of the Madonna, the apostles and St George. Access to the Chancel is via the San Clemente chapel to the right, with a mosaic showing merchants Rustico di Torcello and Buono di Malamocco, apparently about to FedEx the body of St Mark to Venice. St Mark's sarcophagus is visible through the grate underneath the altar. It was moved here from the 11th-century crypt in 1835; the crypt remains a popular venue for society weddings, though it's closed to the rest of us.

The indigestibly opulent Pala d'Oro (Gold Altarpiece) is a Byzantine work and, just for a change, was acquired honestly. It was made in Constantinople in 976 on the orders of Doge Pietro Orseolo I and further enriched in later years with amethysts, emeralds, pearls, rubies, sapphires and

Long weekend

Time tight? Stopover short? With the exception of the **Rialto** bridge (*see p65*), Venice's must-sees are also, unfortunately, its must-queues – in high season at least. So check out waiting times at top attractions. Then be prepared to opt for Plan B.

The **Basilica di San Marco** (St Mark's basilica, *see p71*) is a sight to behold but queues form even before the church opens to visitors. Bear in mind that the main body of the church (though not the *loggia* or museum) is open for prayers well before the sightseeing multitude arrives; a quiet, respectful dawn visit amid the praying old ladies is an awe-inspiring experience.

If the line at the **campanile** (*see p75*) in front of the basilica is daunting, take a vaporetto to **San Giorgio Maggiore** (*see p129*) and ascend the belltower there: the view is arguably better, and you get the added bonus of a handful of paintings by Tintoretto in the church.

The **Palazzo Ducale** (Doge's Palace, *see p77*) is an impressive testimony to the workings of the Venetian state. Avoid a long wait by booking a guided tour; you'll pay extra, but gain privileged access. The same trick works at the **Accademia** (*see p122*), repository of countless treasures of Western art. But for a less overwhelming artistic experience – plus a pleasant hike through Venice's streets – a careful selection of churches will suffice.

The **Frari** (*see p113*) is the place for Titian, Donatello and Giovanni Bellini; **Santi Giovanni e Paolo** (*see p87*) for Giovanni Bellini, Lorenzo Lotto and Paolo Veronese; and the above-mentioned San Giorgio Maggiore for Tintoretto.

But Venice is as much about water as it is about art. For full immersion, a round-trip on vaporetto 4 or 5 (they follow the same route in opposite directions) will whisk you up/down the **Grand Canal** (*see p63*), up/down the **Giudecca canal** and on an interesting trawl through the Venetian equivalent of an industrial underbelly. And if there's no time or funds for a gondola ride, compensate by resorting to a *traghetto* (*see chapter* **Directory: Getting Around**).

topaz, topped off with a Gothic frame and resetting in 1345. It's a worldly corner of the church, this. Set in the frame of the curving sacristy door are bronze busts of its maker, Sansovino, and his friends, Titian and Aretino, who helped to get him out of prison in 1545 (*see p74* Biblioteca Marciana). Aretino was a poet and playwright who moved to Venice in 1527 after scandalising Rome with his 'Lewd Sonnets'. A great satirist and hedonist, he is said to have died laughing at a filthy joke about his sister.

The left transept contains the chapel of the Madonna Nicopeia (the Victory-Bringer), named after the tenth-century icon on the altar – another Fourth Crusade acquisition that Byzantine emperors used to carry into battle. She is still much revered: early in the morning, praying Venetians can often be seen here confiding in her.

The St Isidore chapel beyond, with its 14th-century mosaics, is reserved for private prayer and confessions; visitors are asked to show the maximum discretion if they do enter. The same goes for the Mascoli chapel. The altarpiece, featuring Saints Mark and James, with the Virgin between them (in this unusual representation the Virgin appears to sway, with a graceful bend round about her midriff), is a striking piece of Gothic statuary. The chapel's mosaics, thought to be mostly by Michele Giambono and dating from 1430-50, have a definite Renaissance look to them, with classical architecture featuring in their backgrounds.

Loggia & Museo Marciano

Of all the pay-to-enter sections of the basilica, this is definitely the most worthwhile – and it's the only part of the church that can be visited on a Sunday morning. Up a narrow stairway from the narthex are the bronze horses that vie with the book-bearing lion of St Mark as the city's symbol; here, too, is Paolo Veneziano's exquisite Pala Feriale, a painted panel that was used to cover the Pala d'Oro on weekdays. The Loggia also provides a marvellous view over the square. The original bronze horses are now kept indoors. They are the greatest piece of loot – apart from the body of St Mark himself – in the whole city. They were among the many treasures that Venice brought back from the Sack of Constantinople, where they had stood above the Hippodrome, advertising a great day out at the races.

The horses' origins are uncertain. For many years they were attributed to a Greek sculptor of the fourth century BC, but the idea that they may be an original Roman work of the second century AD has recently come into favour: the half-moon shape of their eyes is said to have been a Roman characteristic. They were at first placed in front of the Arsenale (*see p90*), but around 1250 they found their place of honour on the terrace of the basilica, supreme expressions of Venetian pride.

In 1797 it was Napoleon's turn to play looter, and the horses did not return to Venice until after his defeat at Waterloo. Apart from the parentheses of

The Doge's Palace. *See p77.*

the World Wars, during which they were put away in safe storage, they remained on the terrace until 1974, when they were removed for restoration. Since 1982 they have been on display in a room inside the basilica, with perfect but soulless copies replacing them on the terrace.

Treasury

This contains a hoard of exquisite Byzantine gold and silver work – reliquaries, chalices, candelabras – most of it Crusade plunder. If you can stand the glitter, the highlights are a silver perfume censer in the form of a church and two 11th-century icons of the Archangel Michael.

Biblioteca Marciana/ Libreria Sansoviniana

San Marco 13A, piazzetta San Marco (041 520 8788/http://marciana.venezia.sbn.it). Vaporetto San Zaccaria or Vallaresso). **Open** *Apr-Oct* 9am-7pm daily (ticket office closes 5.30pm). *Nov-Mar* 9am-5pm daily (ticket office closes 3.30pm). **Admission** by multi-entrance ticket (*see p61* Musei di Piazza San Marco). **Map** p307 B4.

Opposite the seat of government stands the symbol of learning and culture, the city's library (*marciana* means 'of Mark'). In 1468 the great humanist scholar Cardinal Bessarion of Trebizond left his collection of Greek and Latin manuscripts to the state.

This time the Venetians didn't lose them, as they had done with Petrarch's library (*see p39*), although they didn't get round to constructing a proper home for them until 1537. Jacopo Sansovino, a Florentine architect who had settled in Venice after fleeing from the Sack of Rome in 1527, was appointed to create the library. Palladio described it as the 'richest and most ornate building since antiquity'.

With this building, Sansovino brought the ideas of the Roman Renaissance of Bramante and Michelangelo into Venice, although, with its abundance of statuary, he also appealed to the Venetian love of surface decoration. His original plan included a barrel-vault ceiling. This collapsed shortly after construction, however, and the architect was immediately clapped into prison. His friends Titian and Aretino had to lobby hard to have him released.

The working part of Venice's main library is now housed in La Zecca (*see p80*) and contains 750,000 volumes and around 13,500 manuscripts, mainly Greek. The Libreria Sansoviniana – now a museum – is entered from the Piazzetta. A monumental staircase with stucco decoration leads up to the anteroom, in which a partial reconstruction has been made of Cardinal Grimani's collection of classical statues, as arranged by Scamozzi (1596). On the ceiling is *Wisdom*, a late work by Titian.

In July 1902 the whole thing fell down. Some blamed old age, weak foundations and lightning damage; others, such as crusty old British travel writer Augustus Hare, put it down to 'gross neglect and criminal misusage'. The Campanile was tidy in its collapse, imploding in a neat pyramid of rubble; the only victim was the custodian's cat.

It was rebuilt exactly 'as it was, where it was', to use the formula of the town council (recently exhumed for the rebuilding of the La Fenice opera house, see p83). Holy Roman Emperor Frederick III rode a horse to the top of the old version in 1451; these days, visitors take the lift. The view through the anti-suicide grate is superb, taking in the Lido, the whole lagoon and the Dolomites in the distance.

Sansovino's little Loggetta at the foot of the tower, which echoes the shape of a Roman triumphal arch, was also rebuilt, jigsaw-fashion, using bits found in the rubble. During sessions of the Grand Council, guards recruited from the Arsenale used to keep watch here. In the 18th century the Loggetta took on a more popular function as the place where the state lottery was drawn.

Museo Archeologico

San Marco 17, piazzetta San Marco (041 522 5978). Vaporetto San Zaccaria or Vallaresso. **Open** *Apr-Oct* 9am-7pm daily (ticket office closes 5.30pm). *Nov-Mar* 9am-5pm daily (ticket office closes 3.30pm). **Admission** by multi-entrance ticket (*see p61* Musei di Piazza San Marco). **Map** p307 B4.

This seldom-visited collection of Greek and Roman art and artefacts is interesting not so much for the quality of the individual pieces as for the light they cast on the history of collecting. Assembled mainly by Cardinal Domenico Grimani and his nephew Giovanni, mainly from Roman finds, the collection is a discerning 16th-century humanist's attempt to surround himself with the classical ideal of beauty; as such these statues were much copied by Venetian artists. Among the highlights are the original fifth-century BC Greek statues of goddesses in Room 4, which are among the few such works known to the Italian Renaissance, the Grimani Altar in Room 6, and the intricate cameos and intaglios in Room 7 or Room 12 (depending on temporary exhibitions).

Museo Correr

San Marco 52, piazza San Marco/sottoportego San Geminian (041 522 5625). Vaporetto Vallaresso. **Open** *Apr-Oct* 9am-7pm daily (ticket office closes 5.30pm). *Nov-Mar* 9am-5pm daily (ticket office closes 3.30pm). **Admission** by multi-entrance ticket (*see p61* Musei di Piazza San Marco). **Map** p307 A4.

The Museo Correr is Venice's civic museum, dedicated to the history of the Republic – which means that it acts as a storeroom for all the bits and pieces that didn't fit in elsewhere. Based on the private collection of Venetian nobleman Teodoro Correr (1750-1830), it is elevated beyond mere curiosity value by the second-floor gallery, which is essential viewing for anyone interested in Venetian early Renaissance painting. The museum is housed in the Ala

The main room has a magnificent ceiling, with seven rows of allegorical medallion paintings, produced by a number of Venetian Mannerist artists as part of a competition. Veronese's *Music* (sixth row from entrance), perhaps the least Mannerist in style, was awarded the gold chain by Titian. In a room off the staircase landing is Fra Mauro's Map of the World (1459), a fascinating testimony to the precision of Venice's geographical knowledge, with extraordinarily accurate depictions of China and India.

Campanile

San Marco. Vaporetto San Zaccaria or Vallaresso. **Open** *Apr-Sept* 9.30am-30mins before sunset daily. *Nov-Mar* 9.30am-3.30pm daily. **Admission** €6; €3 concessions. **No credit cards**. **Map** p307 A4.

Venice's most famous landmark – and at almost 99m (325ft) the tallest building in the city – was originally built between 888 and 912. Its present appearance, with the stone spire and the gilded angel on top, dates from 1514. The Campanile served both as a watchtower and a belltower. It provided a site for public humiliations: people of 'scandalous behaviour' were hung in a cage from the top. More wholesome fun was provided by the *volo dell'anzolo*, when an intrepid *arsenalotto* (Arsenale shipwright) would slide down a rope strung between the Campanile and the Palazzo Ducale to mark the end of Carnevale.

Sightseeing

Checks & balances

Determined to prevent one family or faction getting uppity, Venice created a complex administrative system of checks and balances:

Maggior consiglio (Great Council) – the Republic's parliament, with around 500 elected members, which in turn elected (and provided the candidates for) most other state offices, including that of doge.

Minor consiglio (Lesser Council) – elected by and from the Maggior consiglio, this six-man team advised – or kept tabs on – the doge.

Senato (Senate) – known until the late 14th century as the *pregadi*, the *senato* was the upper house of the Venetian parliament; by the 16th century it had some 300 members.

Collegio dei savi (College of Wise Men) – group of experts, elected by the *senato*, who staffed special committees to oversee all aspects of internal, marine and war policy.

Quarantie – the three supreme courts; the 40 members were chosen by the *senato*.

Consiglio dei dieci (Council of Ten) – appointed by the *senato*, the council's extensive network of spies brought any would-be subversives to a closed-door trial in which defence lawyers were forbidden. In time, the increasingly powerful *Consiglio dei dieci* would have the Venetian Inquisition to assist it in its task.

Pien collegio (Full College) – made up of the *minor consiglio* and the *collegio dei savi*, this became Venice's real government, eventually supplanting the *senato*.

Serenissima signoria (Most Serene Lordships) – made up of the Minor consiglio, the heads of the three *quarantie* courts and the doge, this body was vested with ultimate executive power.

Il doge (the Duke) – elected for life in a complicated, cheat-proof system of multiple ballots, the sumptuously robed Duke of Venice was glorious to behold. He could not, however, indulge in business of his own, receive foreign ambassadors alone, leave Venice without permission, or accept personal gifts. If his city state tired of him, he could be thrown out of office.

With his whole extended family banned from high office for the term of his reign, many doges hailed from less politically adept Venetian clans. Most, moreover, were old and tired by the time they donned the *biretta*, the distinctive horned hat (the average age of doges between 1400 and 1570 was 72). However, the doge was the only official privy to all state secrets and eligible to attend meetings of all state organs; he could, if he played his cards right, have a determining effect on Venetian policy.

Napoleonica, the wing that closes off the narrow western end of the piazza, and in the Procuratie Nuove. Napoleon demolished the church of San Geminiano to make way for this exercise in neo-classical regularity, complete with that essential imperial accessory, a ballroom. The spirit of these years is conserved in the first part of the collection, dedicated to the beautifully soulless sculpture of Antonio Canova, who was born in Possagno (*see p267*) and whose first Venetian commission – the statue of Daedalus and Icarus, displayed here – brought him immediate acclaim. Some of the works on display are Canova's plaster models rather than his finished marble statues.

The historical collection beyond here, which occupies most of the first floor of the Procuratie Vecchie (*see p70*), documents Venetian history and social life in the 16th and 17th centuries. Among the globes, lutes, coins and robes, interesting light is thrown on various aspects of life in the Republic. Room 6 features Lazzaro Bastiani's famous portrait of Doge Francesco Foscari (c1460). The next room is dedicated to ducal elections, with a collection of gilded wooden hands that look like props from a De Chirico painting. These were used to count votes. Room 11

has a collection of Venetian coins, plus Tintoretto's fine *St Justine and the Treasurers*. Beyond are rooms dedicated to the Arsenale (*see p90*): a display of weaponry and some occasionally charming miniature bronzes – a favourite and much-collected art form of the Venetian Renaissance.

The bulk of one's critical energy should be saved, however, for the Quadreria picture gallery upstairs – perhaps the best place in the city to get a grip on the development of Venetian painting between the Byzantine stirrings of Paolo Veneziano and the full-blown Renaissance storytelling of Carpaccio. Rooms 24 to 29 are dedicated to Byzantine and Gothic painters – note Paolo Veneziano's fine *St John the Baptist* and the rare allegorical fresco fragments from a 14th-century private house in Room 27. Room 30 fast-forwards abruptly with the macabre, proto-Mannerist *Pietà* of Cosme Turà; beyond here, the Renaissance gets into full swing, with Antonello da Messina's *Pietà with Three Angels*, haunting despite the fact that the faces have nearly been erased by cack-handed restoration. The Bellinis get Room 36 to themselves – note the rubicund portrait of Doge Giovanni Mocenigo, painted by Gentile Bellini just before his departure for Constantinople in 1475. The gallery's most fascinating work, though, must be Vittorio Carpaccio's *Two Venetian Noblewomen* – long known erroneously as *The Courtesans* – in Room 38. These two bored women are actually not angling for trade: they're waiting for their husbands to return from a hunting expedition. This was confirmed when *A Hunt in the Valley* from the Getty Museum in Los Angeles was revealed to be this painting's other half. Back downstairs, past the frankly missable Museo del Risorgimento (of interest only to students of 19th-century freemasonry), the civic collection continues with rooms dedicated to the state barge, the *Bucintoro*, to Venetian festivities and to the city's trade guilds. The last two rooms show how Venetians enjoyed themselves, with paintings of fairground trials of strength and some portable gambling accessories.

Palazzo Ducale (Doge's Palace)

San Marco 1, piazzetta San Marco (041 522 4951/ bookings 041 520 9070). Vaporetto San Zaccaria. **Open** *Apr-Oct* 9am-7pm daily (ticket office closes 5.30pm). *Nov-Mar* 9am-5pm daily (ticket office closes 3.30pm). **Admission** with multi-entrance ticket (*see p61* Musei di Piazza San Marco). **Guided tours** 11.30am Sun; €6. *Itinerari Segreti tour* (book at least 2 days in advance, 041 520 9070) 9.55am, 10.45am, 11.35am daily in English; 9.30am, 11.10am daily in Italian; €12.50, €4-€7 concessions. **No credit cards. Map** p307 A4.

An unobtrusive side door halfway down the right wall of the nave in San Marco leads straight into the courtyard of the Palazzo Ducale (Doge's Palace). Today's visitors take a more roundabout route, but that door is a potent symbol of the entwinement of Church and state in the glory days of La Serenissima. If the basilica was the Venetian Republic's spiritual nerve centre, the Doge's Palace was its political and judicial hub. The present site was the seat of ducal power from the ninth century onwards, though most of what we see today dates from the mid 15th century. Devastating fires in 1574 and 1577 took their toll, but after much debate it was decided to restore rather than replace – an enlightened policy for the time.

The architectural form of the building testifies to Venetian confidence in the impossibility of invasion or attack: whereas Renaissance seats of government in other Italian towns look like castles, this is very definitely a palace. It is the great Gothic building of the city, but is also curiously eastern in style, achieving a marvellous combination of lightness and strength. The ground floor was open to the public; the work of government went on in the more closed part above. This arrangement resulted in a curious reversal of the natural order. The building gets heavier as it rises: the first level has an open arcade of simple Gothic arches, the second a closed loggia of rich, ornate arcading. The top floor is a solid wall broken by a sequence of Gothic windows. And yet somehow it doesn't seem awkward.

The Piazzetta façade was built in the 15th century as a continuation of the 14th-century waterfront

façade. On the corner by the ponte di Paglia (Bridge of Straw) is an exquisite marble relief carving, the *Drunkenness of Noah* from the early 15th century, while on the Piazzetta corner is a statue of Adam and Eve from the late 14th century.

The capitals of the pillars below date from the 14th to the 15th centuries, although more than a dozen of them are 19th-century copies (some of the originals are on display inside). On the waterfront side (ninth pillar from the left) is what appears to be a boy eating an ice-cream cone; don't disappoint your kids by telling them it's really a chicken leg.

The Porta della Carta (or 'Paper Gate' – so called because this was where permits were checked), between the palace and the basilica, is a grand piece of florid Gothic architecture and sculpture (1438-42) by Bartolomeo and Giovanni Bon. The statue of Doge Francesco Foscari and the lion are copies dating from 1885; French troops smashed the originals when they occupied the city in 1797.

Behind the palace's fairy tale exterior the machinery of empire whirred away with the same kind of assembly-line efficiency that went into the building of ships over at the Arsenale (*see p90*). Anyone really interested in the inner workings of the Venetian state should take the 90-minute *Itinerari segreti* tour. This takes you into those parts of the palace that the official route does not touch: cramped wooden administrative offices; the chambers of the

Titian's well-hidden **St Christopher**. *See p78.*

Cancelleria segreta, where all official documents were written up in triplicate by a team of 24 clerks; the chamber of the three heads of the Council of Ten, connected by a secret door in the wooden panelling to the Sala del Consiglio dei Dieci, and the torture chambers beyond.

The tour ends up in the leads – the cells underneath the roof from which Casanova staged his famous escape (probably by bribing the guard, though his own account was far more action hero; *see p108* **Literary locations: Casanova**).

Following reorganisation, the main visit – for which an audioguide (€5.50) is recommended – now begins at the Porta del Frumento on the lagoon side of the palace, rather than at the main Piazzetta entrance via the Porta della Carta. The Museo dell'Opera, just to the left of the ticket barrier, has the best of the 14th-century capitals from the external loggia; the ones you see outside are copies.

In the main courtyard stands the Arco dei Foscari – another fine late Gothic work, commissioned by Doge Francesco Foscari in 1438, when Venice was at the height of its territorial influence. It was built by Antonio Bregno and Antonio Rizzo; Rizzo also sculpted the figures of Adam and Eve (these, too, are copies; the originals are inside the palace), which earned him gushing accolades and led to his appointment as official architect in 1483, after one of those disastrous fires. Rizzo had time to oversee the building of the overblown Scala dei Giganti (where doges were crowned) and some of the interior before he was found to have embezzled 12,000 ducats; he promptly fled, and died soon after.

The official route now leads up the ornate Scala d'Oro staircase by Jacopo Sansovino, with stuccoes by Vittoria outlined in 24-carat gold leaf.

First floor: Doge's apartments

And to think this is supposed to be the domestic side of the operation. In reality, the doge's private life was entirely at the service of La Serenissima, and even his bedroom had to keep up the PR effort. These rooms are sometimes closed or used for temporary exhibitions; when open, the Sala delle Mappe (also known as the Sala dello Scudo) merits scrutiny.

Here, in a series of 16th-century maps, is the known world as it radiated from Venice. Just to the right of the entrance door is a detailed map of the New World with Bofton (Boston) and Isola Longa (Long Island) clearly marked. Further on, it's worth seeking out Titian's well-hidden fresco of St Christopher, which, astonishingly, took the artist a mere three days to complete.

Second floor: State rooms

This grandiose series of halls provided steady work for all the great 16th-century Venetian artists. Titian, Tintoretto, Veronese, Palma il Vecchio and Jacopo Bassano all left their mark, though the sheer acreage that had to be covered, and the subjects of the canvases – either allegories or documentary records of the city's pomp and glory – did not always spur them to artistic heights.

The Sala delle Quattro Porte was where the *Collegio* – the inner cabinet of the Republic – met before the 1574 fire. After substantial renovation it became an ambassadorial waiting room, where humble envoys could gaze enviously at Andrea Vicentino's portrayal of the magnificent reception given to the young King Henry III of France in 1574 (the triumphal arch that you can see in the picture was put up overnight). The Anticollegio, restored in part by Palladio, has a spectacular gilded stucco ceiling, four Tintorettos and Veronese's blowsy *Rape of Europa*. Beyond here is the Sala del Collegio, where the inner cabinet convened.

The propaganda paintings on the ceiling are by Veronese; note the equal scale of the civic and divine players, and the way that both Justice and Peace are mere handmaidens to Venice herself. But for real hubris you have to stroll into the next room, the Sala del Senato, where Tintoretto's ceiling centrepiece shows *The Triumph of Venice*. Here the Senate, which by 1450 had grown from 60 to an unwieldy 300 members, met to debate questions of foreign policy, war and commerce, and to hear the reports of returning Venetian ambassadors.

Beyond are the Sala del Consiglio dei Dieci and the Sala della Bussola, where the arcane body set up specifically to act as a check on the doge considered matters of national security. In the former, note Veronese's ceiling panel *Juno Offering Gifts to Venice*. By the time this was painted in 1553, the classical gods had started to replace St Mark in Venice's self-aggrandising pantheon.

Here the itinerary (which is liable to change with little warning) heads through a bristling armoury, whose ingenious instruments of war impressed early visitors. But, as one 17th-century tourist pointed out, the collection was established so that 'if the People should conspire against the Nobles, and make any Attempt against them while they are sitting, they might be furnished with Arms upon the Spot to defend themselves'.

First floor: State rooms

The Sala dei Censori now leads down to a *liagò* (covered, L-shaped loggia), which gives on to the Sala della Quarantia Civil Vecchia (the civil court) and the Sala del Guariento. The latter's faded 14th-century fresco of *The Coronation of the Virgin* by Guariento (for centuries hidden behind Tintoretto's *Paradiso* in the Sala del Maggior Consiglio) looks strangely innocent amid all this worldly propaganda. The shorter arm of the *liagò* has the originals of Antonio Rizzo's stylised marble sculptures of Adam and Eve from the Arco dei Foscari. Next comes the Sala del Maggior Consiglio – the largest room in the palace. It had to be big, as by 1512, according to historian Marin Sanudo, 2,622 patrician men were entitled to sit on the *maggior consiglio* (Greater Council). This was in effect the Republic's lower house – though with the top-heavy Venetian system of government, this council of noblemen had fairly limited powers. Before the fire of 1577, the hall had been decorated with paintings by Bellini, Titian, Carpaccio and Veronese – a choice collection that was so costly to commission that in 1515 a group of patricians complained about the expense. When these works went up in smoke, they were replaced by less exalted works – with one or two exceptions. Tintoretto's *Paradise* on the far wall, sketched out by the 70-year-old artist but completed after his death in 1594 by his son Domenico, is liable to induce vertigo, as much for its theological complexity as its huge scale. But this massive choral composition – which members would have had plenty of time to contemplate during the Council's protracted voting sessions – drew a deliberate comparison between the celestial hierarchy (as featured in Dante) and Venice's equally complex but equally inviolate power structure (*see p76* **Checks & balances**). In the ceiling panels are works by Veronese and Palma il Giovane; note, too, the frieze of ducal portraits carried out by Domenico Tintoretto and assistants, with the black veil marking the place where Marin Falier's face would have appeared had he not conspired against the state in 1356.

On the left side of the hall, a balcony gives a fine view over the southern side of the lagoon. A door leads from the back of the hall into the Sala della Quarantia Civil Nuova and the large Sala dello

Goldoni looks on amused in **campo San Bartolomeo**. *See p80.*

Scrutinio, where the votes of the *maggior consiglio* were counted; the latter is flanked by vast paintings of victorious naval battles, including a dramatic *Conquest of Zara* by Jacopo Tintoretto and *Battle of Lepanto* by Andrea Vicentino.

Criminal courts & prigioni

Backtracking through the Sala del Maggior Consiglio, a small door on the left leads past the Scala dei Censori to the Sala della Quarantia Criminale – the criminal court. The next room retains some original red and gold leather wall coverings. Beyond is a small room that has been arranged as a gallery, with Flemish paintings from Cardinal Grimani's collection, originally hidden from public view. The hysterical religious mysticism of Bosch's *Inferno* strikes an odd note here: though rational, Venice was not immune to religious fanaticism. The route now leads over the Bridge of Sighs to the Prigioni Nuove, where petty criminals were kept. Lifers were sent down to the waterlogged *pozzi* (wells) in the basement of the palazzo itself. By the 19th century most visitors were falling for the tour guide legend that, once over the Bridge of Sighs, prisoners would 'descend into the dungeon which none entered and hoped to see the sun again', as Mark Twain put it. But when this new prison wing was built in 1589, it was acclaimed as a paragon of comfort; in 1608 English traveller Thomas Coryat remarked, 'I think there is not a fairer prison in all Christendom.'

Some of the cells have their number and capacity painted over the door; one has a *trompe l'œil* window, drawn in charcoal by a bored inmate. On the lowest level is a small exercise yard, where an unofficial tavern used to operate. Up the stairs beyond is a display of Venetian ceramics found during excavations, and more cells, one with a fascinating display of cartoons and caricatures left by 19th-century internees.

Back across the Bridge of Sighs, the tour ends on the lower floor in the Avogaria – the offices of the clerks of court. Next to this a bookshop has been set up (open 9am-4pm), with a good selection of works on Venice. On the ground floor is a welcome (though not particularly cheap) cafeteria; beyond the cafeteria are the old kitchens, where the restored mechanism from the Torre dell'Orologio (Clock Tower, *see below*) can be seen, together with the statues of the Magi and the Angel (usually only seen during Ascension week), all waiting to be replaced in the restored tower; it is likely to be a long wait.

Torre dell'Orologio

San Marco 147, piazza San Marco (041 522 4951/ www.museiciviciveneziani.it). Vaporetto San Zaccaria. **Map** p307 A4.

The clock tower, designed by Maurizio Codussi, was built between 1496 and 1506; the wings were an addition, perhaps by Pietro Lombardo. Above the clock face is the Madonna. During Ascension week and at Epiphany, the Magi come out and bow to her every hour, in an angel-led procession. At other times of year, the burly Moors on the roof, made of gunmetal and cast in 1497, strike the hour. Another

Moore – Roger – sent a villain flying through the clock face in the film *Moonraker*. In 1999 the clock was restored. However, the building as a whole has been hidden since 1998 behind a lifesize photograph of itself and, owing to legal wrangling with the proprietors of the adjoining buildings, restoration work has proceeded in somewhat leisurely fashion.

The official reopening date is now 2004, but don't hold your breath. When it does reopen it will only admit small groups with prior bookings. In the meantime the original mechanism and statues can be seen in the Palazzo Ducale (*see p77*).

La Zecca

San Marco 7, piazzetta San Marco (041 520 8788). Vaporetto Vallaresso. **Open** 8.10am-7pm Mon-Fri; 8.10am-1.30pm Sat. **Admission** free. **Map** p307 B4.
The Mint, designed by Sansovino, was completed by 1547. It coined Venice's famous gold ducats – later referred to as *zecchini*, precursor of the English 'sequins'. It is more impregnable in appearance than the neighbouring Biblioteca Marciana (*see p74*), though the façade had to accommodate large windows on the *piano nobile* (for relief from heat) and open arches on the ground floor, where the procurators of St Mark's owned a number of cheese shops. The architect's son, author of the first famous guidebook to the city, described the building as 'a worthy prison for all that precious gold'. It now houses most of the contents of the civic library.

Piazza San Marco to the Rialto

Piazza San Marco is linked to the Rialto by the busiest, richest and narrowest of shopping streets: the Mercerie. The name is plural, since it is divided into five parts: the Merceria dell'Orologio, di **San Zulian** (on which stands the church of the same name), del Capitello, di **San Salvador** (with its homonymous church, in the beautiful cloisters of which is the spanking new **Telecom Italia Future Centre** visitors' installation) and del 2 Aprile.

Mercerie means 'haberdashers', but we know from John Evelyn's 1645 account of 'one of the most delicious streets in the world' that in among the luxury textile emporia were shops selling perfumes and medicines too.

Most of the big-name fashion designers are to be found here now, and most of Venice's short-stay tourists too. The ponte dei Baretteri (the Hatmakers' Bridge), in the middle of the Mercerie, is, by the way, a minor record holder in Venice: there are six different roads and alleys leading directly off the bridge. (*See also p99* **Take it to the....**)

The Mercerie emerge near campo San Bartolomeo, the square at the foot of the Rialto, with the statue of playwright Carlo Goldoni looking amusedly down at the milling crowds.

Street wise

See also p279 **Street wise**.
Bissa (calle della)
Venetian for grass-snake, on account of the street's tortuousness, though there's no lack of rivals for the distinction.
Bo (calle del)
Venetian for ox, after a *spezier* (spice-shop) with a golden ox on its sign.
Buso (fondamenta)
Venetian for 'hole'; the blander theory attributes the name to the cramped dimensions of the place; an earthier tradition recounts that a ferry from this fondamenta was used to transport prostitutes.
Cuoridoro (sotoportego, corte dei)
Not hearts of gold (*cuori d'oro*) but gilded leather (*cuoi d'oro*), after a local workshop.
Dai (sotoportego, ponte, fondamenta dei, rio,)
From *dadi* (dice), suggesting that they were either played with or sold here.
Guerra (ponte della)
One of a number of bridges where punch-ups between the rival factions of the city were tolerated by the authorities.
Rimedio (fondamenta, calle, ponte del)
Probably the family name of a malmsey-seller, but it was popularly believed that this sweet wine was an all-round remedy.
Salvadego (calle del)
Wild-man (*selvatico* in Italian), after a tavern of the same name.
Strazze (calle delle)
Ragmen; in 1773 this category of workers had 57 shops throughout the city and their own altar in the church of San Zulian (*see p81*).

This square, together with the nearby campo San Luca, is where young Venetians meet up and hang out of an evening. Most Italian towns have their corso where the citizens parade at *passeggiata* time; Venetians, perhaps because they are always walking, are a little more static in their evening encounters.

Calle dei Stagneri leads out of the campo to the 18th-century church of **Santa Maria della Fava** (technically in the sestiere of Castello).

San Salvador

Campo San Salvador (041 270 2464). Vaporetto Rialto. **Open** 9am-noon, 3-6pm Mon-Sat; 4-6pm Sun. **Map** p307 A4.

If you can't make it to Florence on this trip, come to San Salvador instead, which has one of Venice's most Brunelleschi-esque interiors: a pass-the-baton effort begun by Giorgio Spavento in 1506, continued by Tullio Lombardo and completed by Sansovino in 1534. But even though the geometrical sense of space and the use of soft-toned greys and whites exude Tuscan elegance, the key to the church's structure is in fact a combination of three domed Greek crosses, which look back to the Byzantine tradition of St Mark's. The church contains two great Titians, the *Annunciation* at the end of the right-hand aisle (with the signature 'Tizianus fecit, fecit', the repetition was intended either to emphasise the wonder of his unflagging creativity, or is a simple typo – take your pick) and the *Transfiguration*, on the high altar (which conceals a silver reredos, revealed on request).

There's also some splendid Veneto-Tuscan sculpture, including Sansovino's monument to Doge Francesco Venier, situated between the second and third altar on the right. Here, too, at the end of the right transept, is the tomb of Cristina Cornaro, the hapless Queen of Cyprus (died 1510), a pawn in a game of Mediterranean strategy that ended with her being forced into abdicating the island to Venetian rule. By way of compensation she was palmed off with the town of Asolo (*see p267*) and the title 'Daughter of the Republic'.

Santa Maria della Fava

Campo della Fava (041 522 4601). Vaporetto Rialto. **Open** 8-11.30am, 4.30-6.30pm Mon-Sat. **Map** p307 A4.

St Mary of the Bean – the name refers to a popular bean-cake that was turned out by a bakery that used to stand nearby – is on one of the quieter routes between the Rialto and San Marco. This 18th-century church is worth visiting for two paintings by the city's greatest 18th-century artists, which neatly illustrate their contrasting temperaments. Tiepolo's *Education of the Virgin* (first altar on the right) is an early work, painted when he was still under the influence of Giovanni Battista Piazzetta; but the bright colours and touchingly human relationships of the figures are nonetheless in great contrast with the sombre browns and reds of the latter's *Virgin and Child with St Philip Neri* (second altar on the left). In Piazzetta's more earnest painting, which still bears traces of Counter-Reformation gravity, the lily, bishop's mitre and cardinals' hats show the worldly honours rejected by the saint.

San Zulian

Mercerie San Zulian (041 523 5383). Vaporetto Vallaresso or San Zaccaria. **Open** 8.30am-noon, 3-6pm Mon-Sat. **Map** p307 A4.

The classical simplicity of Sansovino's façade (1553-5) is offset by a grand monument to Tommaso Rangone, a wealthy and far-from-self-effacing showman-scholar from Ravenna, whose fortune was made by a treatment for syphilis, and who wrote a book on how to live to 120 (he only made it to 80 himself). He unilaterally declared his library to be one of the seven wonders of the world, and had himself prominently portrayed in all three of Tintoretto's paintings for the Scuola di San Marco (now in the Accademia, *see p122*). The interior has a ceiling painting of *The Apotheosis of St Julian* by Palma il Giovane, here in Tintoretto mode, and a more Titianesque *Assumption* by the same painter on the second altar on the right, which also has good statues of St Catherine of Alexandria and Daniel by Alessandro Vittoria. The first altar on the right has a *Pietà* by Veronese. San Giuliano (Zulian to Venetians), curiously, is one of only two churches in Venice that you can walk all the way around (the other is the Angelo Raffaele in Dorsoduro, *see p117*.)

Telecom Italia Future Centre

San Marco 4826, campo San Salvador (www.futurecentre.telecomitalia.it). Vaporetto Rialto. **Open** 10am-6pm Tue-Sun. **Admission** free. **Map** p307 A4.

The Italian telephone company acquired the 16th-century cloisters of the monastery of San Salvador after World War I. In the 1980s it embarked upon a thorough restoration of the buildings to provide a prestigious showcase for its latest offerings. The Future Centre opened in September 2002 and offers a tour through the latest innovations in information

Florid Gothic at **Santo Stefano**. *See p82*.

Sightseeing

technology. The first cloister contains 100 computers with cutely playful lessons on various aspects of Venetian art and history, in Italian and English. Don't miss the splendid refectory with a 16th-century frescoed ceiling.

The Rialto to the Accademia Bridge

The route from the Rialto to the Accademia passes through a series of ever-larger squares. From cosily cramped campo San Bartolomeo, the well-marked path leads to campo San Luca with its bars and cakeshops. Beyond this is campo Manin with its 19th-century statue of Daniele Manin, leader of the 1848 uprising against the Austrians (*see p17*). An alley to the left of this campo will lead you to the **Scala del Bòvolo**, a striking Renaissance spiral staircase. Back on the main drag, the busy calle della Mandola takes you into broad campo Sant'Angelo with its dramatic view of **Santo Stefano**'s leaning tower; off calle della Mandola to the right is the Gothic **Palazzo Fortuny**, once home to the Spanish fashion designer Mariano Fortuny.

Just before the Accademia bridge, campo Santo Stefano is second only to piazza San Marco in the *sestiere* in size. Until 1802, when part of a stand collapsed, this was where *corse al toro* (bullfights) took place. Nowadays, the tables of three bars scarcely encroach on the space where small children play on their bikes (officially banned in the city, but a blind eye is turned) or kick balls around the statue of Risorgimento ideologue Nicolò Tommaseo, known locally as *Cagalibri* (bookshitter) for reasons that are obvious when the monument is viewed from the rear. At the Accademia end of the square is the freshly restored 18th-century church of **San Vidal**. On the Grand Canal to the north-west of campo Santo Stefano is campo San Samuele, with a deconsecrated 11th-century church and the massive **Palazzo Grassi**, now an exhibition centre.

Palazzo Fortuny

San Marco 3780, campo San Benedetto (041 520 0995). Vaporetto Sant'Angelo. **Open** during exhibitions 10am-6pm Tue-Sun (hours subject to change). **Admission** varies. **No credit cards**. **Map** p307 A3.

With the museum closed for long-term reorganisation (due to reopen in 2004), the only way to see the charming 15th-century palazzo that belonged to Spanish fashion designer Mariano Fortuny (1871-1949) is to catch an exhibition. These are usually photographic, photography being one of Fortuny's interests, alongside theatrical set design, cloth dyes and elegant silk dresses.

Palazzo Grassi

San Marco 3231, campo San Samuele (041 523 1680/www.palazzograssi.it). Vaporetto San Samuele. **Open** during exhibitions 9am-7pm Tue-Sun (hours subject to change). **Admission** varies. **Credit** MC, V. **Map** p306 A2.

This superbly regular 18th-century palazzo on the Grand Canal was bought by Fiat in 1984 and converted by architect Gae Aulenti into a high-profile exhibition space. Since then it has unleashed one blockbuster show after another, doing for civilisations such as the Celts, Mayans and Etruscans what Fiat does for cars. It is a light and well-organised space with a good shop, bookshop and café, and the quality of the exhibits is often so high that one forgets the over-the-top packaging.

Santo Stefano

Campo Santo Stefano (041 522 5061). Vaporetto San Samuele or Accademia. **Open** *Church* 9am-7pm daily. *Sacristy* 10am-5pm Mon-Sat; 1-5pm Sun. **Admission** *Church* free. *Sacristy* €2. *See also p61* Chorus. **Map** p307 A3.

Santo Stefano is an Augustinian church, built in the 14th century and altered in the 15th. The façade has a magnificent portal in the florid Gothic style. The large interior, with its splendid ship's keel roof, is a multicoloured treat, with different marbles used for the columns, capitals, altars and intarsia, and diamond-patterned walls, as on the Palazzo Ducale. On the floor is a huge plaque to Doge Morosini (best known for blowing up the Parthenon) and a more modest one to composer Giovanni Gabrielli. On the interior façade to the left of the door is a Renaissance monument to Giacomo Surian by Pietro Lombardo and his sons, decorated with skulls and festoons. In the sacristy are two tenebrous late works by Tintoretto: *The Washing of the Feet* and *The Agony in the Garden* (The *Last Supper* is by the great man's assistants) and three fanciful works by Gaspare Diziani (*Adoration of the Magi, Flight into Egypt, Massacre of the Innocents*). From the first bridge on the calle that leads from the campo towards piazza San Marco, there's a good view of the apse of Santo Stefano with a canal passing underneath it.

San Vidal (or Vitale)

Campo San Vidal (041 522 2362). Vaporetto Accademia. **Open** for concerts only. **Map** p307 B3.

This early 18th-century church, with a façade derived from Palladio, was for years used as an art gallery. It has now been restored and, like the church of the Pietà (*see p91*), hosts concerts. Over the high altar is a splendid Carpaccio painting (1514) of St Vitalis riding what appears to be one of the bronze horses of San Marco. The third altar on the right has a painting by Piazzetta (*Archangel Raphael and Saints Anthony and Louis*).

Scala Contarini del Bòvolo

San Marco 4299, corte dei Risi (041 270 2464/asa@patriarcato.venezia.it). Vaporetto Rialto. **Open** *Apr-Oct* 10am-6pm daily. *Nov-Mar* 10am-4pm Sat,

Sun. *Christmas & Carnevale* 10am-4pm daily.
Admission €2.50 with guided tour; €2 groups.
No credit cards. Map p307 A3.
Follow the signs for the Scala del Bòvolo from campo Manin and you will emerge in a narrow courtyard entirely dominated by this elegant Renaissance spiral staircase, built c1499 by Giovanni Candi. Spiral staircases are called *scale a chiocciola* (snail staircases) in Italian; *bòvolo* is Venetian dialect for snail. It was restored in 1986 and has recently been opened to the public; the view from the top makes the climb worthwhile.

From the Accademia to piazza San Marco

The route from Santo Stefano back to piazza San Marco zigzags at first, passing through small squares, including campo **Santa Maria del Giglio** (aka Santa Maria Zobenigo) with the most boastful church façade in Venice. It winds past banks and hotels, along with a few top-dollar antique shops, to end in wide via XXII Marzo, with an intimidating view of the freshly restored baroque statuary of **San**

Self-glorification at **Santa Maria del Giglio**.

Moisè. To the left from here are the gutted remains of Venice's once-glorious opera house, **La Fenice**. Press on and you are ready for the greatest view in the world: piazza San Marco from the west side.

Santa Maria del Giglio

Campo Santa Maria Zobenigo (041 275 0462/ www.chorus-ve.org). Vaporetto Santa Maria del Giglio. **Open** 10am-5pm Mon-Sat; 1-5pm Sun. **Admission** €2 (*see also p61* Chorus). **No credit cards. Map** p307 B3.
This church's façade drew the censure of Ruskin for its total lack of any Christian symbols (give or take a token angel or two). Built between 1678 and 1683, it's really a huge exercise in defiant self-glorification by Admiral Antonio Barbaro, who was dismissed by Doge Francesco Morosini for incompetence in the War of Candia (Crete). On the plinths of the columns are relief plans of towns where he served, including Candia; his own statue (in the centre) is flanked by representations of Honour, Virtue, Fame and Wisdom. The interior is more devotional. You may not have heard of the painter Antonio Zanchi (1631-1722), but this is definitely his church. Particularly interesting is *Abraham Teaching the Egyptians Astrology* in the sacristy, while the Cappella Molin has *Ulysses Recognised by His Dog* (an odd subject for a church). The chapel also contains a *Madonna and Child*, which is proudly but probably erroneously attributed to Rubens. Behind the altar there are two paintings of the Evangelists by Tintoretto, formerly organ doors.

San Moisè

Campo San Moisè (041 528 5840). Vaporetto Vallaresso. **Open** 3.30-7pm daily. **Map** p307 B4.
The baroque façade of San Moisè has been lambasted by Ruskin ('one of the basest examples of the basest school of the Renaissance') and just about everybody else as one of Venice's truly ugly pieces of architecture. Inside, an extravagant piece of baroque sculpture occupies the high altar, representing not only Moses receiving the stone tablets but Mount Sinai itself. Near the entrance is the grave of John Law, author of the disastrous Mississippi Bubble scheme that almost sank the French central bank in 1720.

Teatro La Fenice

San Marco 1983, campo San Fantin. Vaporetto Santa Maria del Giglio. **Map** p307 A3.
All that remains of Venice's great opera house, where operas by Rossini, Verdi, Stravinsky and Britten opened, is the façade on to the square, built by Gianantonio Selva. The rest went up in flames on the night of 29 January 1996, and it wasn't an accident. The theatre – named 'The Phoenix' – is at last showing some signs of rising from the ashes. The official reopening date is September 2003, but it would be unwise to do any breath-holding. In the meantime the Teatro Malibran has been restored and reopened (*see p217*).

Sightseeing

Castello

This huge district is half grand *palazzi* and churches, half old industry.

Venice's largest *sestiere*, Castello (castle) is thought to have been named after a fortress on the island of San Pietro, one of the earliest inhabited sites in the lagoon. Stretching almost from the Rialto bridge to Sant'Elena in the far east, Castello encompasses grander areas such as those around Santi Giovanni e Paolo and San Zaccaria, which were closely linked with centres of power, as well as more workaday ones around the Arsenale, once home to Venice's most important industries.

Northern & western Castello

The Bridge of Sighs marks the border between the *sestieri* of San Marco and Castello, so the quaint **Museo Diocesano di Arte Sacra** and the stately **San Zaccaria**, although closely associated with San Marco, actually belong to Castello. But the true heart of northern and western Castello lies inland from here: campo **Santa Maria Formosa** (literally 'Shapely St Mary'), a large, bustling, irregular-shaped square on the road to just about everywhere. It has a fine church, a small market, a couple

of bars and an undertaker's. Nearby is the quintessentially Venetian museum cum library of the **Fondazione Querini Stampalia** (*see also p205* **La Querini**). Constantly buzzing with Venetians and tourists, the square is surrounded by *palazzi* that range in style from the very grand to the very homely. It is, in fact, Castello in miniature.

For grandeur, head north-east from here towards campo **Santi Giovanni e Paolo**. This square is second only to piazza San Marco in monumental magnificence. The Gothic red brick of the Dominican church is beautifully set off by the glistening marble on the *trompe l'œil* façade of the **Scuola di San Marco** and the bronze of the equestrian **monument to Bartolomeo Colleoni** gazing contemptuously down.

It's a short walk through narrow *calli* from Santi Giovanni e Paolo to the fondamenta Nuove, where the northern lagoon comes into view. Murano and further-flung Burano and Torcello (*see p137* and *p139*) are visible on clear days, as are the foothills of the Dolomites. The cemetery island San Michele is always in sight, acting as a grim *memento mori* for patients in the hospital.

The lovely Romanesque cloister of the **Museo Diocesano di Arte Sacra**. *See p85.*

Eastwards from Santi Giovanni e Paolo, a road called Barbaria delle Tole passes the extraordinary baroque church of the **Ospedaletto** by Baldassare Longhena, with its alarmingly teetering façade adorned by leering faces. This long road will take you into one of the least touristy areas of the city. Here, beyond the old gasworks, is the imposing **San Francesco della Vigna**, an austere church the remoteness of which is part of its charm.

Monument to Bartolomeo Colleoni

Campo Santi Giovanni e Paolo. Vaporetto Fondamenta Nove. **Map** p306 A1.

Colleoni was a famous *condottiere* (mercenary soldier), who left a legacy to the Republic on condition that a statue be erected to him in front of St Mark's. Not wishing to clutter up St Mark's Square with the statue, but loath to miss out on the money, Venice's wily rulers found a solution to their conundrum in 1479 when they hit upon the idea of giving him a space in front of the Scuola di San Marco. Geddit? In order, perhaps, to make up for this flagrant deception, the Republic did Colleoni proud, commissioning the Florentine artist Andrea Verrocchio to create an equestrian statue that is widely agreed to be one of the world's finest. On Verrocchio's death it was completed, together with the pedestal, by Alessandro Leopardi (1488-96). It is not a portrait, since Verrocchio never saw Colleoni, but a stylised representation of military pride and might. Colleoni's coat of arms (on the pedestal) includes three fig-like objects, a reference to his name, which in Italian sounds very similar to *coglioni* – testicles.

Museo della Fondazione Querini Stampalia

Castello 5252, campo Santa Maria Formosa (041 271 1411/www.querinistampalia.it). Vaporetto Rialto. **Open** *Museum* 10am-6pm Tue-Thur, Sun; 10am-10pm Fri, Sat. *Library* Reading room & catalogues 4pm-midnight Mon-Fri; 2.30pm-midnight Sat; 3-7pm Sun. **Admission** Museum €6; €4 concessions. *Library* free. **Credit** DC, MC, V. **Map** p308 A1.

This Renaissance palazzo and its art collection were bequeathed to Venice by Giovanni Querini, a 19th-century scientist, man of letters and successful silk producer. He came from one of the city's most ancient families, which was permanently excluded from running for the dogeship after Marco Querini's involvement in the 1310 Bajamonte Tiepolo plot (*see p12*). Giovanni Querini specified in his will that a library and reading room should also be created here that would open 'particularly in the evenings for the convenience of scholars', and that the foundation should promote 'evening assemblies of scholars and scientists'. The Querini Stampalia still exudes something of its founder's cultural generosity and ecumenicism: the first-floor library is a great place to study on misty autumn evenings, and the Foundation organises conferences, debates and

A local Madonna looks over Castello.

concerts (5pm, 8.30pm Fri, Sat; included in admission price). The ground floor and gardens, were which redesigned in the 1960s by Carlo Scarpa, offer one of Venice's few successful examples of modern architecture. On the second floor, the gallery contains some important paintings, including Palma il Vecchio's portraits of Francesco and Paula Querini, for whom the palace was built in the 16th century, and a marvellous *Presentation in the Temple* by Giovanni Bellini. It also has a fascinating series of minor works, such as Gabriele Bella's 67 paintings of Venetian festivals, ceremonies and customs, and a selection of Pietro Longhi's winning scenes of bourgeois life in 18th-century Venice.

Museo Diocesano di Arte Sacra

Castello 4312, ponte della Canonica (041 522 9166). Vaporetto San Zaccaria. **Open** 10.30am-12.30pm Mon-Sat. **Admission** free (donations accepted). **Map** p308 B1.

An odd hotchpotch of a collection, which can seem haphazard until you realise its purpose: to act as a storeroom and restoration clinic for works of art from local churches and monasteries. It's difficult to say what will be on view at any time, but items that have nowhere else to go include the 15th-century Cross of the Patriarch from San Pietro in Castello. There is also a series of stolen and recovered marble sculptures from the former convent of San Clemente, one of the abandoned islands of the lagoon. The thieves shoved rubber tyres over *Faith*

Sightseeing

and *Charity* and used a motorboat to drag them along the bottom of the lagoon; you can still see the tyre marks at the back. There is also a pretty Romanesque cloister.

San Francesco della Vigna

Campo San Francesco della Vigna (041 520 6102). Vaporetto Celestia. **Open** 8am-12.30pm, 3-6.30pm Mon-Sat; 3-6.30pm Sun. **Map** p308 A2.

San Francesco may be off the beaten track, but the long trek over to the down-at-heel area beyond the gasworks, where the church's Palladian façade is half-concealed by the surrounding buildings, is well worth it. In 1534 Jacopo Sansovino was asked by his friend Doge Andrea Gritti to design this church for the Observant Franciscan order. The Tuscan architect opted for a deliberately simple style of building, to match the monastic rule adopted by its inhabitants. The façade (1568-72) was a later addition by Andrea Palladio; it is the first example of his system of superimposed temple fronts.

The dignified, solemn interior consists of a single broad nave with side chapels, which are named after the families who paid for them – and who held no truck with Franciscan notions of modesty and self-effacement. The Cappella Giustiniani on the left of the chancel holds a marvellous cycle of sculptures by Pietro Lombardo and school, moved here from an earlier church on the same site. In the nave, the fourth chapel on the right has a *Resurrection* attributed to Paolo Veronese. In the right transept is a fruity, flowery *Madonna and Child Enthroned*, a

signed work by the Greek artist Antonio da Negroponte (c1450). From the left transept a door leads into the Cappella Santa, which contains a *Madonna and Saints* by Giovanni Bellini (1507, perhaps assisted by Girolamo da Santacroce). From here it is possible to visit the monastery's two peaceful Renaissance cloisters. Back in the church, the fifth chapel on the left is home to Paolo Veronese's first Venetian commission, the stunning *Holy Family with Saints John the Baptist, Anthony the Abbot and Catherine* (c1551). The second chapel has three powerful statues of saints Roch, Anthony the Abbot and Sebastian by Alessandro Vittoria (1565).

Santa Maria dei Derelitti (Ospedaletto)

Barbarie delle Tole 6691 (041 270 2464/asa@ patriarcato.venezia.it). Vaporetto Fondamenta Nove. **Open** 3.30-6.30pm Thur-Sat. **Admission** (incl guided tour) €2. **No credit cards.** p308 A1.

The church was built in 1575 within the complex of the Ospedaletto, a hospice for the poor and the aged. There is still an old people's home on the site. Between 1668 and 1674 Baldassare Longhena gave the church its staggering façade, complete with bulging telamons (architectural supports in the shape of male figures) and leering faces. The interior contains interesting 18th-century paintings, including one of Giambattista Tiepolo's earliest works, The *Sacrifice of Isaac* (fourth on the right). The hospice contains an elegant music room with frescos by Jacopo Guarana (1776); concerts are occasionally given here.

Street wise

See also **Street wise** in *chapter Directory.*

Do Pozzi (campo)
'Two wells'; the campo only has one now, but two can be seen carved on its side.

Gatte (campo, salizada delle)
Female cats; apparently a corruption of *salizada dei Legati*, after the Papal Legates lived here.

Giazzo (calle del)
Ice (*ghiaccio* in Italian) was sold here, at least as far back as 1661.

Gorne (campo, rio delle)
'Gutters', from the huge marble gutters protruding from the Arsenale walls.

Mendicanti (ramo, calle, ponte, fondamenta dei)
'Beggars', from a hospice and church built in the 17th century for the poor.

Morte (calle della)
'Death'; according to legend state executions were carried out in this narrow alley in the early days of the Republic.

Occhio Grosso (calle del)
Large eye; in 1566 a certain Zuan Carlo Occhio Grosso lived here.

Osmarin (fondamenta dell')
'Rosemary'; from a family of this name, rather than the plant itself.

Prete Zoto (corte del)
A lame (*zoppo* in Italian) priest apparently lived here.

Giuffa (ruga)
Named after either a community of Armenian merchants from Julfa, or a band of thugs (*gagiuffos* in a document of 1283) who terrorised the area.

Barbaria de le Tole
Tole are planks (*tavole* in Italian); various explanations are offered for *barbaria*: the wild appearance of the area, the presence of numerous barbers' shops, the barbaric behaviour of the carpenters, the fact that the planks were destined mainly for 'Barbaria' (the Barbary Coast).

Details from the **Ospedaletto** (*see p86*)...   ...and **Santa Maria Formosa**'s campanile.

Santa Maria Formosa

Campo Santa Maria Formosa (041 275 0642/
www.chorus-ve.org). Vaporetto San Zaccaria or
Rialto. **Open** 10am-5pm Mon-Sat; 1-5pm Sun.
Admission €2 (*see also p61* Chorus) **No credit
cards. Map** p307 A3.

In the pre-Freudian seventh century, St Magnus,
Bishop of Oderzo, had a rather pleasant vision in
which the Virgin appeared as a buxom (*formosa*)
matron, and a church was built in this bustling
square to commemorate the fact. The present church
was designed by Mauro Codussi in 1492 and has
something fittingly bulgy about it. It has two
façades, one on the canal (1542), the other on the
campo (1604). The baroque campanile has a
grotesque mask, memorably reviled by Ruskin but
now recognised as a portrait of a victim of von
Recklinghausen's disease – the condition that affected the Elephant Man. Codussi retained the Greek
cross plan of the original church in his own
Renaissance design; the spatial effects reveal how
strong the Byzantine tradition remained in Venice.
The first chapel in the right aisle has a triptych by
Bartolomeo Vivarini, *The Madonna of the
Misericordia* (1473), which includes a realistic
Birth of the Virgin.

The altar in the right transept was the chapel of
the Scuola dei Bombardieri, with an altarpiece of
St Barbara, patron saint of gunners (a heaven-sent
stun gun in the shape of a lightning bolt saved

Barbara's life when it struck her father as he prepared to kill her), by Palma il Vecchio. The model
was apparently the artist's daughter. George Eliot
described it as 'an almost unique presentation of a
hero woman'. Half-hidden by the elaborate high
altar is one of the few works on show in Venice by
a woman artist: an 18th-century *Allegory of the
Foundation of the Church, with Venice, St Magnus
and Santa Maria Formosa* by Giulia Lama. She has
been described as a pupil of Giovani Battista
Piazzetta, but Piazzetta's only known portrait from
life (in the Thyssen-Bornemisza collection in
Madrid) is of Giulia Lama: its tenderness suggests
she was more than a mere pupil.

Santi Giovanni e Paolo
(San Zanipolo)

Campo Santi Giovanni e Paolo (041 523 5913).
Vaporetto Fondamenta Nove. **Open** 8am-
12.30pm, 3.30-7pm Mon-Sat; 3-6pm Sun.
Map p308 A1.

Santi Giovanni e Paolo was founded by the
Dominican order in 1246 but not finished until
1430. Twenty-five doges were buried here between
1248 and 1778; from the 15th century onwards all
ducal funerals were held here. The vast interior –
101m (331ft) long – is a single spatial unit; the
simple columns serve to enhance the unity of the
whole, rather than dividing the body of the church
into separate aisles. The monks' choir was removed
in the 17th century, leaving nothing to impede our

view. Santi Giovanni e Paolo is a historical artefact, packed with monuments not only to doges but also to Venetian heroes. The entrance wall is entirely dedicated to a series of funerary tributes to the Mocenigo family. The grandest – the masterpiece by Pietro, Tullio and Antonio Lombardo – belongs to Pietro Mocenigo, who died in 1476: the doge stands on his own sarcophagus, supported by three warriors representing the three ages of man. The religious reference above – the three Maries at the sepulchre – seems almost an afterthought.

Renaissance elegance continues in the second altar on the right, which features an early polyptych by Giovanni Bellini (1465) in its original frame. Continuing down the right side of the church, the huge baroque mausoleum by Andrea Tirali (1708) has two Valier doges and a *dogaressa* taking a bow before a marble curtain. Tirali also designed the Chapel of St Dominic, notable for its splendid ceiling painting by Giovani Battista Piazzetta of *St Dominic in Glory* (c1727). The right transept has a painting of *St Antonine Distributing Alms* (1542) by the mystically minded Lorenzo Lotto, who asked only for a decent funeral as payment – but then died far away in Loreto. On the right of the chancel, with its baroque high altar, is the Gothic tomb of Michele Morosini, which Ruskin, predictably, loved. Opposite is the tomb of Doge Andrea Vendramin, by the Lombardo family, which the architectural arbiter just as predictably

Gothic-Renaissance **San Zaccaria**.

hated. Just to confirm his prejudice, he climbed a ladder and was shocked to discover that the sculptor had not bothered to carve the unseen side of the face.

The rosary chapel, off the left transept, was gutted by fire in 1867, just after two masterpieces by Titian and Bellini had been placed here for safe keeping. It now contains paintings and furnishings from suppressed churches. The ceiling paintings, *The Annunciation, Assumption* and *Adoration of the Shepherds*, are by Paolo Veronese, as is another *Adoration* to the left of the door.

San Zaccaria

Campo San Zaccaria (041 522 1257). Vaporetto San Zaccaria. **Open** 10am-noon, 4-6pm Mon-Sat; 4-6pm Sun. **Map** p308 B1.

Founded in the ninth century, this church has always had close ties with the Doge's Palace. Eight Venetian rulers were buried in the first church on the site, one was killed outside, and another died while seeking sanctuary inside. This is another holy booty church: the body of St Zacharias, the father of John the Baptist, was brought to Venice in the ninth century, at the same time as that of St Mark; it still lies under the second altar on the right. The current church was begun in 1444 but took decades to complete, making it a curious combination of Gothic and Renaissance. The interior is built on a Gothic plan – the apse, with its ambulatory and radiating cluster of tall-windowed chapels, is unique in Venice – but the architectural decoration is predominantly Renaissance. Similarly, the façade is a happy mixture of the two styles. Inside, every inch is covered with paintings, of varying quality. Giovanni Bellini's magnificently calm *Madonna and Four Saints* (1505), on the second altar on the left, leaps out of the confusion. The Chapel of St Athanasius in the right aisle contains carved 15th-century wooden stalls and *The Birth of St John the Baptist*, an early work by Tintoretto. The adjoining Chapel of St Tarasius (open, together with the sacristy, same hours as the church, admission €1) was the apse of an earlier church on the site; it has three altarpieces by Antonio Vivarini and Giovanni d'Alemagna (1443) – stiff, iconic works in elaborate Gothic frames that are in keeping with the architecture of the chapel. Definitely not in keeping are the frescoed saints in the fan vault by the Florentine artist Andrea del Castagno. Although painted a year before the altarpieces, they have a realistic vitality that is wholly Renaissance in spirit.

Attached to the church was a convent (now a Carabinieri barracks), where aristocrats with more titles than cash dumped female offspring to avoid having to rake together a dowry. The nuns were not best known for their piety. While tales of rampant licentiousness may have been exaggerated, a painting in Ca' Rezzonico (*see p120*) shows that such convents were considered sophisticated salons rather than places of contemplation.

The **Giardini Pubblici...** and turtles guarding the **monument to Garibaldi**. *See p90.*

Scuola Grande di San Marco (Ospedale Civile)

Campo Santi Giovanni e Paolo (041 529 4111). Vaporetto Fondamenta Nove. **Open** 24hrs daily. **Map** p308 A1.

This is one of the six *scuole grandi*, the philanthropic confraternities of Venice (*see p61*). It's now occupied by the city hospital, which extends all the way back to the lagoon. The façade (being restored at time of writing) by Pietro Lombardo and Giovanni Buora (1487-90) was completed by Mauro Codussi (1495). It has magnificent *trompe l'œil* panels by Tullio and Antonio Lombardo (protected from stray footballs by perspex panels), representing two episodes from the life of St Mark and his faithful lion. Over the doorway is a lunette of *St Mark with the Brethren of the School* attributed to Bartolomeo Bon.

Southern & eastern Castello

If Venice's fairytale charm is getting too much, head for eastern Castello. The low-rise, close-clustered buildings of this working-class area housed the employees of the Arsenale – Venice's dockland – most of which now lies poignantly derelict.

Like the London's East End or New York's Brooklyn, eastern Castello had its foreign communities, as local churches testify. There's **San Giorgio dei Greci** (Greeks), with its adjoining **Museo dell'Istituto Ellenico** icon museum, and the **Scuola di San Giorgio degli Schiavoni** (Slavs), with its captivating cycle of paintings by Vittorio Carpaccio. Indeed, the great promenade along the lagoon – the **riva degli Schiavoni** – was named after the same community.

Inland from the Riva is the quaint Gothic church of **San Giovanni in Bragora** and, further back in the warren of streets, the church of **Sant'Antonin**, undoubtedly the only church in Venice in which an elephant has been shot. The unfortunate animal escaped from a circus on the Riva in 1819 and took refuge in the church, only to be finished off by gunners summoned from the Arsenale.

Back on the riva degli Schiavoni is the church of **La Pietà**, where Vivaldi was choir master; it is now frequently used for concerts. Head on eastwards past the Ca' di Dio, once a hostel for pilgrims setting out for the Holy Land and now an old people's home, and the Forni Pubblici (public bakeries), where the biscuit (*bis-cotto*, literally 'twice-cooked') – that favourite, scurvy-encouraging staple of ancient mariners – was reputedly invented.

Crossing the bridge over the rio dell'Arsenale, you can see the grand Renaissance entrance to the huge **Arsenale** shipyard, once a hive of empire-building industry and closely guarded secrets, now an expanse of crumbling warehouses and empty docks, parts of which are occasionally brought to life by temporary exhibitions.

Just beyond the rio dell'Arsenale, the model-packed **Museo Storico Navale** charts Venice's shipbuilding history lovingly. A little further on, the wide via Garibaldi forks off to the left. This road and the nearby **Giardini Pubblici** are a legacy of the years of French occupation in the early 19th century (*see p92* **Venice & Napoleon**).

For proof that Venice is not a dead city, head here in the morning to catch the bustle at the market close to the **monument** to Garibaldi, a dignified statue perched on a rocky island in the middle of a turtle-filled pond. Otherwise, take an evening stroll and join Venetians en masse, from kiddies on tricycles to old men propping up the bars.

Via Garibaldi leads eventually to the island of **San Pietro**, where the former cathedral stands forlornly among modest, washing-garlanded houses. For centuries before relocating to St Mark's, the bishop (later patriarch) of Venice was relegated here, at a safe distance from the decision-making centre. Nowadays the island has a pleasant backwoods feel to it; on the feast of saints Peter and Paul (29 June), locals spill on to the patchy grass in front of the church for the nearest thing Venice offers to a village fête, complete with al fresco dining, dancing, music and gallons of wine. Bring your clogs.

Back on the lagoon, the riva degli Schiavoni changes its name after the rio dell'Arsenale to become the riva dei Sette Martiri, named after seven partisans executed here in 1944. Created in 1936, this long, wide section is often dwarfed by moored cruise ships. By the vaporetto stop of the same name, you'll find the shady **Giardini pubblici**, public gardens that took the place of four suppressed convents. A Renaissance archway from one has been reconstructed in a corner. In another corner lies the entrance to the **Biennale**; the international pavilions, ranging in style from the seedy to the pompous, used to remain locked up except for those few weeks every two years when a major contemporary art bonanza (*see p206*) is set up; however, other recently created events such as the Biennale dell'Architettura mean the pavilions get more frequent airings and the gardens are not left exclusively to local junkies.

The riva ends in the sedately residential district of Sant'Elena. This, in Venetian terms, is a 'modern' district. In 1872, work began to fill in the *barene* (marshes) that lay between the edge of the city and the ancient island of

Sant' Elena, with its charming Gothic church, which now stands just the other side of the football stadium (*see p93*). Sant'Elena has a distinctly suburban feel to it: children play and dogs are walked in grassy expanses dotted with holm oak and pine trees. It's the ideal spot for an evening drink as the sun sets dramatically over the lagoon.

Arsenale

Campo dell'Arsenale. Vaporetto Arsenale.
Map p308/p309 B2-3.

The word *arsenale* derives from the Arabic *dar sina'a*, meaning 'house of industry': the industry, not to mention the efficiency, of Venice's Arsenale was legendary. When the need arose, the *arsenalotti* could assemble a galley in just a few hours. Shipbuilding activities began here in the 12th century, and before long all Venice's galleys were constructed within its confines. At the height of the city's power, 16,000 men were employed. Production continued to expand until the 16th century, when Venice entered its slow but inexorable economic decline.

The imposing land gateway by Antonio Gambello (1460) in campo dell'Arsenale is the first example of Renaissance classical architecture in Venice, although the capitals of the columns are 11th-century Veneto-Byzantine. The gateway was modelled on a Roman arch in the Istrian city of Pola. The winged lion gazing down from above holds a book without the traditional words *Pax tibi Marce* (Peace to you, Mark), perhaps a sign that it was installed when Venice was at war. Outside the gate, four Greek lions keep guard. Those immediately flanking the terrace were looted from Athens by Doge Francesco Morosini in 1687; the larger one stood at the entrance to the port of Piraeus and bears runic inscriptions on its side, hacked there in the 11th century by Norse mercenary soldiers in Byzantine service. The lion, whose head is clearly less ancient than its body, came from Delos and was placed here to commemorate the recapture of Corfu in 1716.

Since shipbuilding ceased in 1917, the Arsenale has remained navy property. Officers in smart uniforms cut fine figures against the brickwork but appear to put the decaying facilities to no practical use. Exhibitions, theatrical performances and concerts are now occasionally put on in the cavernous spaces within its walls, such as the Artiglierie and the grandiose Gaggiandre, dockyards designed by Sansovino.

In campo della Tana, on the other side of the rio dell'Arsenale, is the entrance to the Corderia, or rope factory, an extraordinary building 316m (1,038 ft) long. In recent years this vast space has been used to house the overflow from the Biennale (*see p206*) and for other temporary exhibitions.

Museo dell'Istituto Ellenico

Castello 3412, ponte dei Greci (041 522 6581). Vaporetto San Zaccaria. **Open** 9am-5pm daily. **Admission** €4; €2 concessions. **No credit cards.** **Map** p308 B1.

The Byzantine side of Venice is played up in this temple of icons. The adjacent church of San Giorgio dei Greci was a focal point for the Greek community, which was swollen by refugees after the Turkish capture of Constantinople in 1453. There has been a Greek church, college and school on this site since the end of the 15th century, and the museum is an essential adjunct to the centre for Byzantine studies next door. The oldest piece in the collection is the 14th-century altar cross behind the ticket desk. The icons on display mainly follow the dictates of the Cretan school, with no descent into naturalism, though some of the 17th- and 18th-century pieces make jarring and often kitsch compromises with Western art. The best pieces are those that are resolute in their hieratic (traditional-style Greek) flatness, such as *Christ in Glory Among the Apostles* and the *Great Deesis* from the first half of the 14th century. Also on display are priestly robes and other Greek rite paraphernalia.

Museo Storico Navale

Castello 2148, campo San Biagio (041 520 0276). Vaporetto Arsenale. **Open** 8.45am-1.30pm Mon-Fri; 8.45am-1pm Sat. **Admission** €1.55. **No credit cards. Map** p308 B2.

Housed in an old granary, this museum dedicated to ships and shipbuilding is a treasure trove. It continues an old tradition: under the Republic, the models made for shipbuilders in the final design stages were kept in a special building inside the Arsenale. Some of the models on display here are survivors from that original collection. The ground floor has warships, cannons, explosive speedboats and dodgy looking manned torpedoes, plus a display of ships through the ages. On the first floor are ornamental trimmings and naval instruments, plus a series of impressive models of Venetian ships, including a huge 16th-century galleass. Here, too, is a richly gilded model of the *Bucintoro*, the doges' state barge. The second floor has uniforms, more up-to-date sextants and astrolabes, and models of modern Italian navy vessels. On the third floor there are models of Chinese and Korean junks, cruise ships and liners, and a series of fascinating naïve votive paintings, giving thanks for shipwrecks averted or survived. A room at the back has a display of gondolas, including a 19th-century example with a fixed cabin, and the last privately owned gondola in Venice, which belonged to Peggy Guggenheim (*see p123* **Peggy G**).

La Pietà (Santa Maria della Visitazione)

Riva degli Schiavoni (041 523 1096). Vaporetto San Zaccaria. **Open** for concerts only (information APT offices, *see chapter* Directory). **Map** p308 B1.

Attached to the girls' orphanage of the same name, the church of La Pietà was most famous for its music. Antonio Vivaldi, violin master and choir master here in the first half of the 18th century, wrote some of his finest music for his young charges. The present building by Giorgio Massari was begun in 1745, four years after Vivaldi's death. Music inspired its architecture: the interior, which is reached by crossing a vestibule distinctly resembling a theatre foyer, has the oval shape of a concert hall. It is still used as such. The ceiling has a *Coronation of the Virgin* by Giambattista Tiepolo (1755).

San Giorgio dei Greci

Fondamenta dei Greci (041 523 9569). Vaporetto San Zaccaria. **Open** 9am-1pm, 3-5pm Mon, Wed-Sat; for 10.30am service only Sun. **Map** p308 B1.

By the time the church of San Giorgio was begun in 1539, the Greeks were well established in Venice and held a major stake in the city's numerous scholarly printing presses. Designed by Sante Lombardo, the church's interior is fully Orthodox in layout, with its women's gallery, and high altar behind the iconostasis. A heady smell of incense lends the church an Eastern mystique, enhanced by dark-bearded priests in flowing robes. The distinctive campanile is decidedly lopsided. Next to the church are the Scuola di San Nicolò (now the Museo dell'Istituto Ellenico; *see p90*) and the Collegio Flangini (now seat of the Istituto Ellenico di Studi Bizantini e post-Bizantini), both by Baldassare Longhena.

San Giovanni in Bragora

Campo Bandiera e Moro (041 270 2464/ asa@patriarcato.venezia.it). Vaporetto Arsenale. **Open** 3.30-5.30pm Mon-Sat. **Map** p308 B2.

San Giovanni in Bragora (the meaning of *bragora* is as obscure as the date of the foundation of the first church on this site) is an intimate Gothic

San Giorgio degli Schiavoni. See p93.

structure. The church where composer Antonio Vivaldi was baptised (the entry in the register is on show), San Giovanni also contains some very fine paintings. Above the high altar is the *Baptism of Christ* (1492-5) by Cima da Conegliano (which can 'only properly be seen by standing on the altar', according to Victorian traveller Augustus Hare), with a charming landscape recalling the countryside around the painter's home town of Conegliano (*see p269*). A smaller Cima, on the right of the door to the sacristy, shows *Constantine Holding the Cross and St Helen* (1502). To the left of the door is a splendidly heroic *Resurrection* (1498) by Alvise Vivarini, in which the figure of Christ is based on a statue of Apollo, now in the Museo Archeologico (*see p75*).

San Pietro in Castello

Campo San Pietro (041 275 0642/www.chorus-ve.org). Vaporetto San Pietro. **Open** 10am-5pm Mon-Sat; 1-5pm Sun. **Admission** €2 (*see also p61* Chorus). **No credit cards. Map** p309 B4.

Until 1807, San Pietro in Castello was the cathedral of Venice, and its remote position testifies to the determination of the Venetian government to keep the clerical authorities well away from the centres of temporal power. The island of San Pietro may be connected to the rest of Venice by two long bridges, but even today it has a distinctly insular feel to it. There has probably been a church here since the seventh century, but the present building was constructed in 1557 to a design by Andrea Palladio. San Pietro's lofty interior looks as if it has seen better days, but it contains some minor gems. The body of the first patriarch of Venice, San Lorenzo Giustiniani, is preserved in an urn elaborately supported by angels above the high altar: a magnificent piece of baroque theatricality designed by Baldassare Longhena (1649). In the right-hand aisle is perhaps the church's most interesting artefact, the so-called 'St Peter's Throne', a delicately carved marble work from Antioch containing a Muslim funerary stele and verses from the Koran. The baroque Vendramin Chapel in the left transept was again designed by Longhena, and contains a *Virgin and Child* by the prolific Neapolitan Luca Giordano. Outside the entrance to the chapel is a late work by Paolo Veronese, *Saints John the Evangelist, Peter and Paul*. San Pietro's canalside 'church green' of scrappy grass under towering trees and a punch-drunk campanile in white marble is a charming place to relax and have a picnic.

Venice and Napoleon

Venetians are great ones for harbouring historic grudges. Early in 2002, the Museo Correr (*see pp75-7*) purchased a statue of Napoleon that had stood in front of the Doge's Palace from 1811 to 1814. Had it bought a monument to Osama bin Laden the outcry could hardly have been louder. Angry readers of the local *Gazzettino* daily suggested that the statue be locked up in the ducal prisons.

The Napoleonic occupation of Venice lasted just nine years (the Austrians were here for 56), but the humiliations inflicted on the city by the Corsican bully left the deepest scars. It wasn't just the fact that Napoleon put an end to the 1,000-year-old Venetian Republic in 1797; this they might have been able to forgive. But Napoleon's callous reneging on promises of liberty and equality after toppling Venice's aristocratic regime was beyond the pale.

The regime had collapsed with extraordinary ease. As France and Austria waged war across Venetian terra firma, the Venetian Senate stuck to its traditional neutrality. But uprisings against the French on the mainland were exploited by Napoleon, who accused Venice of stirring up the populace against him. When a ship of the French fleet, the provocatively named *Liberateur d'Italie*, was fired upon while entering the lagoon, Napoleon had the excuse he needed to fly into a strategic rage. He would, he said, 'be an Attila to the Venetian state'.

Napoleon demanded immediate introduction of democracy and (the final humiliation) services of thanksgiving in St Mark's. On 12 May 1797 the *Maggior consiglio* was summoned to vote on the ultimatum. Aware that there was little point in resisting, the last doge, Ludovico Manin, proposed capitulation. As council members cast their votes, a round of shots fired by departing Dalmatian troops was mistaken for a French attack: the motion was accepted swiftly and almost unanimously.

The new French-backed municipal government had little success in whipping up enthusiasm among a populace that resolutely refused to consider itself 'liberated'. Moreover, blockaded by the British in the Adriatic and deprived of revenue from its mainland territories, the municipality was in dire economic straits. Reforms were mainly symbolic: removal of winged lions and aristocratic coats of arms from public places, name changes (campo San Polo became piazza della Rivoluzione; the Caffè Florian

Sant'Elena

Servi di Maria 3, campo Chiesa Sant'Elena (041 520 5144). Vaporetto Sant'Elena. **Open** 5-7pm Mon-Sat. **Map** off p307 C4.

The red-brick Gothic church of Sant'Elena is reached by a long avenue alongside the precarious-looking mesh of scaffolding that constitutes Venice's football ground (*see p223*). Though it contains no great works of art (the church was deconsecrated in 1807, turned into an iron foundry, and not opened again until 1928), its austere Gothic nakedness is a relief after all that Venetian ornament. In a chapel to the right of the entrance lies the body of St Helen, the irascible mother of the Emperor Constantine and finder of the True Cross. (Curiously enough, her body is also to be found in the Aracoeli church in Rome.)

Scuola di San Giorgio degli Schiavoni

Castello 3259A, calle dei Furlani (041 522 8828). Vaporetto San Zaccaria. **Open** Apr-Oct 9.30am-12.30pm, 3.30-6.30pm Tue-Sat; 9.30am-12.30pm Sun. *Nov-Mar* 10am-12.30pm, 3-6pm Tue-Sat; 10am-12.30pm Sun. **Admission** €3; €2 concessions. **No credit cards**. **Map** p308 A2.

The Schiavoni were Venice's Slav inhabitants, who had become so numerous and influential by the end of the 15th century that they could afford to build this *scuola* or meeting house by the side of their church, San Giovanni di Malta. The *scuola* houses one of Vittore Carpaccio's two great Venetian picture cycles. In 1502, eight years after completing his St Ursula cycle (now in the Accademia, *see p122*), Carpaccio was commissioned to paint a series of canvases illustrating the lives of the Dalmatian saints George, Tryphone and Jerome. In the tradition of the early Renaissance *istoria* (narrative painting cycle), there is a wealth of incidental detail, such as the decomposing virgins in *St George and the Dragon*, or the little dog in the painting of *St Augustine in His Study* (receiving the news of the death of St Jerome in a vision) – with its paraphernalia of humanism (astrolabe, shells, sheet music, archaeological fragments). It's worth venturing upstairs to see what the meeting hall of a working *scuola* looks like. San Giorgio degli Schiavoni still provides scholarships, distributes charity and acts as a focal point for the local Slav community. The upper floor is the setting of a particularly embarrassing scene in Vikram Seth's novel *An Equal Music*.

became the less snappy Café of Patriotic Brotherhood) and a new democratic vocabulary ('servants' had to be called 'domestics'). True, the gates of the Ghetto were torn down and the Inquisition abolished. But the new administration tarnished its libertarian credentials when it made the cry of '*Viva San Marco!*' (long live St Mark!) punishable by death.

Venetian diffidence soon proved well founded when it emerged that Napoleon, even before taking the city, had secretly promised Venice and its territories to the autocratic Austrians in return for non-intervention in his war on the British. But before handing the city over, he took a last opportunity to plunder its finest treasures, including the famous bronze horses, which were packed off to the Tuileries.

Seven years later, after a series of victories over the Austrians, the French returned. Venice was absorbed in 1805 into Napoleon's Kingdom of Italy, remaining under French rule until 1814 during which time it was subjected to the Napoleonic code and democratic principles. Religious houses were closed, and workers' corporations and forms of private assistance were dismantled in favour of state-run entities.

The ex-Scuola di San Marco (*see p89*) and the Dominican convent of Santi Giovanni e Paolo were combined to create the new Civic Hospital.

The overhaul didn't stop there. Sansovino's church of San Geminiano in St Mark's Square was torn down to provide the Royal Palace in the Procuratie Nuove with a suitably grand ballroom. In like fashion the State Granaries were demolished and replaced with the Giardinetti Reali (Royal Gardens; *see p71*), so that the palace enjoyed a view of the lagoon. In Castello, several churches and monasteries were razed to create the Giardini Pubblici (*see p90*) and a canal was filled in to provide a sweeping thoroughfare (the present via Garibaldi) giving access to the gardens.

The monasteries of San Zaccaria (*see p88*) and San Salvadore (*see p81*) were turned into barracks and the Scuola della Carità became the Accademia di Belle Arti (*see p122* **Gallerie dell'Accademia**). Perhaps the most positive innovation was the creation of the city's first cemetery on the island of San Cristoforo (now joined to San Michele; *see p134*), though even this was only accomplished by pulling down the 15th-century church of that name.

Cannaregio

The classic first view of Venice: step off the train and there's the Grand Canal.

Cannaregio has always been the point of arrival for visitors from the mainland. Its name derives either from the *canne* (reeds) that grew there abundantly or from Canal Regio, the 'regal canal' by which newcomers used to enter the city.

The *sestiere* is second in size only to Castello, stretching across the north-west of the city from the railway station almost to the Rialto bridge. Cannaregio was settled well before AD 1000, when the first dwellings were built on the islands of San Giovanni Crisostomo and Santi Apostoli, close to the Rialto. The areas adjacent to the Grand Canal were built up next. The city then extended northwards, engulfing the convents and monasteries – the Misericordia, the Madonna dell'Orto, the Servi, Sant'Alvise – on what had been, until then, remote islands.

When the railway bridge was built in the 19th century (followed by the road bridge in the 1930s), the mainly residential and religious nature of the *sestiere* changed. A large slaughterhouse (now converted into university facilities) was built at the northern end of the Cannaregio Canal. Abandoned churches and convents were taken over by industry. In the 1860s it was decided to create a new pedestrian route, the strada Nuova, by cutting a great swathe through the *sestiere*, roughly parallel to the Grand Canal, to funnel travellers swiftly from the station to the Rialto. Despite these changes, most of Cannaregio still maintains its atmosphere of undisturbed calm.

From the station to the Rialto

Few railway stations provide first-time visitors with such an immediate feast for the eyes. You step off the train and practically into the Grand Canal. After this visual treat, however, the first stretch of the pedestrian route from station to centre is rather a let-down: beyond the magnificent baroque façade of the **Scalzi** church lies a quivering hive of tacky souvenir stalls, grotty bars and downmarket hotels on and around the Lista di Spagna.

The squalor is, mercifully, circumscribed. Heading away from the station towards the Rialto, the Lista leads to the large campo San Geremia, overlooked by the church of the same name (containing the shrivelled body of St Lucy) and **Palazzo Labia**, now occupied by

the RAI (Italian state television). The palazzo contains frescoes by Tiepolo, visible by appointment (041 781 277/fax 041 524 0675, 3-4pm Wed-Fri, admission free).

Once over the Cannaregio Canal (*see p96* **Along the canal**) – by way of a grandiose bridge with obelisks – the tack is replaced by Venetians going about their daily business… dodging tourists to do so. Off to the right, in a square giving on to the Grand Canal, is the church of **San Marcuola**, with an unfinished façade. A bit further on, the more picturesque church of **La Maddalena**, inspired by the Pantheon in Rome, stands in a small square with an assortment of fantastic chimney pots.

Beyond this, the wide strada Nuova begins. Off to the left is the church of **San Marziale**, with whimsical ceiling paintings; on the strada Nuova itself stands the church of **Santa Fosca**, another mainly 18th-century creation. Down a calle to the right is the entrance to the **Ca' d'Oro**, Venice's most splendid Gothic palazzo.

The strada Nuova ends by the church of **Santi Apostoli**; the route to the Rialto soon becomes reassuringly narrow and crooked, passing the church of **San Giovanni Crisostomo** and the adjacent courtyard of the **Corte Seconda del Milion**, where Marco Polo was born. Some of the Veneto-Byzantine-style houses in the courtyard would have been there when he came into the world in 1256. The corte also has a splendidly carved horseshoe arch, much admired by Ruskin.

There's a plaque commemorating the great traveller on the rear of the **Teatro Malibran**, formerly the Teatro di San Giovanni Crisostomo, one of Venice's earliest theatres and opera houses. The theatre was reopened in 2001 (*see also p217*), its slow-moving restoration fast-tracked after the city's main opera house, La Fenice (*see p83*), was destroyed by fire.

Ca' d'Oro (Galleria Franchetti)

Cannaregio 3932, calle Ca' d'Oro (041 523 8790/ guided tours in Italian 041 520 3652/www. artive.arti.beniculturali.it). Vaporetto Ca' d'Oro. **Open** 8.15am-2pm Mon; 8.15am-7.15pm Tue-Sun. *Courtyard* Apr-Oct 8.15am-6.45pm Tue-Sun. **Admission** €3.50; €1.50 concessions (*see also p61* State Museums). **No credit cards**. **Map** p305 B3. In its 15th-century heyday, the façade of this pretty townhouse on the Grand Canal must have looked a psychedelic treat: the colour scheme was light

Sightseeing

Horseshoe arch, **Corte Seconda del Milion.**

blue and burgundy, with 24-carat gold highlights. Though the colour has worn off, the Grand Canal frontage of Ca' d'Oro – built for merchant Marin Contarini between 1421 and 1431 – is still the most elaborate example of the florid Venetian Gothic style besides the Doge's Palace. Inside, little of the original structure and decor has survived the depredations of successive owners. The pretty courtyard was reconstructed with its original 15th-century staircase and well-head a century ago by Baron Franchetti, who assembled the collection of paintings, sculptures and coins that is exhibited on the first and second floors. The highlight of the collection is Mantegna's *St Sebastian*, one of the painter's most powerful late works; the Palladian frame contrasts oddly with the saint's existential anguish. The rest is good in parts, though not necessarily the parts you would expect. A small medal of Sultan Mohammed II by Gentile Bellini (a souvenir of his years in Constantinople) is more impressive than the worse-than-faded frescoes by Titian and Giorgione removed from the Fondaco dei Tedeschi (see p67).

San Giovanni Crisostomo

Campo San Giovanni Crisostomo (041 522 7155).
Vaporetto Rialto. **Open** 8.30am-noon, 3.30-7pm Mon-Sat; 3.30-7pm Sun. **Map** p305 C4.
This small church by Mauro Codussi is dedicated to St John Chrysostomos, archbishop of Constantinople, and shows a fittingly marked Byzantine influence in its Greek cross form. It contains two

great paintings. On the right-hand altar is *Saints Jerome, Christopher and Louis of Toulouse*, signed by Giovanni Bellini and dated 1513. This late work is one of his few Madonna-less altarpieces and shows the Old Master ready to experiment with the atmospheric colouring techniques of such younger artists as Giorgione. On the high altar hangs *Saints John the Baptist, Liberale, Mary Magdalene and Catherine* by Sebastiano del Piombo (c1509), who trained under Bellini but was also influenced by Giorgione. Henry James was deeply impressed by the figure of Mary Magdalene: she looked, he said, like a 'dangerous, but most valuable acquaintance'. On the left-hand altar is *Coronation of the Virgin*, a fine relief (1500-02) by Tullio Lombardo.

As this guide goes to press the interior of the church is being restored; the paintings are in the meantime being stored at the Accademia (see p122).

San Marcuola

Campo San Marcuola (041 713 872). Vaporetto San Marcuola. **Open** 10am-noon, 5-6pm Mon-Sat. **Map** p304 B2.
There was no such person as St Marcuola; the name is a local mangling of the over-complicated Santi Ermagora e Fortunato, two early martyrs. The church, designed by 18th-century architect Giorgio Massari, has just been beautifully restored (completed in July 2002) and its gleaming interior comes as a surprise after the unfinished brick façade. It contains some vigorous statues by Gianmaria Morleiter and a *Last Supper* by Tintoretto (1547) in

Along the canal

For Venetians, only the grandest of their waterways are canals; the others are *rii* (rio in the singular). For centuries the main route into Venice from the mainland, the Cannaregio Canal is fitted out in suitably impressive fashion with wide *fondamente* on each side and several imposing *palazzi*. It's spanned by two stately bridges, the **ponte delle Guglie** (Bridge of the Obelisks, 1823), and the **ponte dei Tre Archi** (*pictured*), the only three-arch stone bridge in Venice, built by Andrea Tirali in 1688. Heading

towards the lagoon from the ponte delle Guglie on the right-hand fondamenta, you pass the *sottoportico* leading to the Jewish Ghetto (*see p100* **In the Ghetto**).

Beyond this stands the **Palazzo Nani** (No.1105), a fine Renaissance palazzo dating from the 16th century. Two hundred metres (700 feet) further on is the **Palazzo Surian-Bellotto** (No.968): in the 18th century this was the French embassy, where Jean Jacques Rousseau worked – reluctantly – as a secretary. Beyond,

---

the chancel, his first treatment of what was later to become one of his favourite subjects. Opposite is a 17th-century copy of another Tintoretto (*Christ Washing the Feet of His Disciples*); the original can be found in Newcastle.

San Marziale
Campo San Marziale (041 719 933). Vaporetto San Marcuola or Ca' d'Oro. **Open** 4-6.30pm Mon-Sat; 8.30-10am Sun. **Map** p305 B3.
The real joy of this church is its ceiling, with its four luminous paintings by the vivacious colourist from Belluno, Sebastiano Ricci (1700-05). Two of them depict *God the Father with Angels* and *St Martial in Glory*; the other two recount the miraculous story of the wooden statue of the Madonna and Child that resides on the second altar on the left – apparently, it made its own way here by boat from Rimini. The high altar has an equally fantastic baroque

extravaganza: a massive marble group of Christ, the world and some angels looms over the altar while St Jerome and companions crouch awkwardly beneath.

Santi Apostoli
Campo SS Apostoli (041 523 8297). Vaporetto Ca' d'Oro. **Open** 7.30-11.30am, 5-7pm Mon-Sat. **Map** p305 C4.
According to tradition, the 12 apostles appeared to the seventh-century Bishop of Oderzo, St Magnus, telling him to build a church where he saw 12 cranes together – a not uncommon sight when Venice was little more than a series of uninhabited islands poking out of marshes. The ancient church was rebuilt in the 17th century. Its campanile (1672), crowned by an onion dome added 50 years later, is a Venetian landmark. The Cappella Corner, off the right side of the nave, is a century older than the rest of the structure. It was built by Mauro Codussi for the

Santa Maria delle Penitenti, with its unfinished façade, was formerly a home for the city's fallen women.

On the left bank is the **Palazzo Priuli-Manfrin** (Nos.342-3), another Tirali creation from 1735, in a neo-classical style of such severe plainness that it prefigures 20th-century purist art.

The imposing 17th-century **Palazzo Savorgan** (No.349) – now a school – has huge coats of arms and reliefs of helmets; the owners were descended from Federigo Savorgnan who, in 1385, became the first non-Venetian to be admitted to Venice's patrician ruling clique.

Behind it is the **Parco Savorgnan**, a charming public garden that is one of Venice's better-kept secrets. A little further on, the **ponte della Crea** spans a canal that was covered over for centuries, only to be re-excavated in 1997.

After passing the **ponte dei Tre Archi** (with the Renaissance church of **San Giobbe** off to the left) the fondamenta continues to the ex-slaughterhouse, built in the 19th century by the Austrians. Long used by a rowing club, it has recently been taken over and revamped by Venice University's economics faculty.

San Giobbe

Campo San Giobbe (041 524 1889). Vaporetto Ponte Tre Archi. **Open** 10am-noon, 3-6pm Mon-Sat; 3.30-6pm Sun. **Map** p304 A1.

Job (Giobbe) – like Moses and Jeremiah – has been raised by Venice to the status of saint, despite his Old Testament pedigree. The church named after him was built to celebrate the visit in 1463 of St Bernardino of Siena, a Franciscan friar and high-profile evangelist. The first Venetian creation of Pietro Lombardo, it introduced a new classical style, immediately visible in the doorway (three statues by Pietro Lombardo that once adorned it are now in the sacristy). The interior of what was probably the first single-naved church in Venice is unashamedly Renaissance. Members of the Lombardo family are responsible for the carvings in the domed sanctuary, all around the triumphal arch separating the sanctuary from the nave, and on the tombstone of San Giobbe's founder Cristoforo Moro, in the centre of the sanctuary floor. The name of this doge has given rise to associations with Othello, the Moor of Venice; some imaginative souls have even seen the mulberry symbol in his tombstone (a moro is a mulberry tree as well as a Moor) as the origin of Desdemona's handkerchief, which was 'spotted with strawberries'. The church's artistic treasures – altarpieces by Giovanni Bellini and Vittore Carpaccio – are now in the Accademia (*see p122*). An atmospheric *Nativity* by Gerolamo Savoldo remains, as does an *Annunciation with Saints Michael and Anthony* triptych by Antonio Vivarini. The Martini Chapel, the second on the left, is a little corner of Tuscany in Venice. Built for a family of silk-weavers from Lucca, it is attributed to the Florentine Bernardo Rossellino. The terracotta medallions of Christ and the Four Evangelists are by the Della Robbia studio – the only examples of its work in Venice.

deposed and depossessed Queen Caterina Cornaro of Cyprus (*see p16*); she was buried here in 1510 alongside her father and brother but subsequently removed to San Salvador (*see p81*). On the altar is a splendidly theatrical *Communion of St Lucy* by Giambattista Tiepolo; the young saint, whose gouged-out eyes are in a dish on the floor, is bathed in a heavenly light. The chapel to the right of the high altar has remnants of 14th-century frescoes. As this guide goes to press half of the church was under scaffolding for restoration.

Gli Scalzi

Fondamenta degli Scalzi (041 715 115). Vaporetto Ferrovia. **Open** 9am-noon, 3.30-5.30pm Mon-Sat; 3.30-5.30pm Sun. **Map** p304 B1.

Officially Santa Maria di Nazareth, this church is universally known as Gli Scalzi after the order of Carmelitani Scalzi (Barefoot Carmelites) to whom it belongs. They bought the plot in 1645 and commissioned Baldassare Longhena to design the church. The fine façade (1672-80) is the work of Giuseppe Sardi; it was paid for by a newcomer to Venice's ruling patrician class, Gerolamo Cavazza, determined to make his marble mark on the landscape. The interior is striking for its coloured marble ('a perfect type of the vulgar abuse of marble in every possible way,' wrote Ruskin sniffily) and massively elaborate baldachin over the high altar. There are many fine baroque statues, including the *St John of the Cross* by Giovanni Marchiori in the first chapel on the right and the anonymous marble crucifix and wax effigy of Christ in the chapel opposite. An Austrian shell that plummeted through the roof in 1915 destroyed the church's greatest work of art, Tiepolo's fresco, *The Transport of the House of Loreto*, but spared some of the artist's lesser frescos, *Angels of the*

Passion and *Agony in the Garden,* in the first chapel on the left and *St Theresa in Glory,* which hovers gracefully above a hamfisted imitation of Bernini's sculpture, *Ecstasy of St Theresa,* in the second on the right. In the second chapel on the left lie the mortal remains of the last doge of Venice, Lodovico Manin.

North-western Cannaregio

If you're tired of the crowds, there's no better place to get away from it all than the north-western areas of Cannaregio. Built around three long parallel canals, it has no large animated squares and (with the exception of the **Ghetto**; *see p100* **In the Ghetto**) no sudden surprises – just occasional views over the northern lagoon.

That's not to say it doesn't have its land-marks, including the *vecchia* (old; 14th-century) and *nuova* (new; 16th-century) **Scuole della Misericordia**, the 'new' one being a huge building by Sansovino, its façade never completed. Long used as a gym, it now awaits conversion into an auditorium; plans to create a multimedia music archive and museum seem to have been shelved. Behind the *scuole,* the picturesque campo dell'Abbazia, overlooked by the baroque façade of the **Abbazia della Misericordia** and the Gothic façade of the Scuola Vecchia, is one of the most peaceful retreats in Venice; on the façade of the latter you can still see the outlines of sculptures by Gothic master Bartolomeo Bon, which are now in London's Victoria & Albert Museum.

Statue of St Christopher, **Madonna dell'Orto**.

On the northernmost canal are the churches of the **Madonna dell'Orto** and **Sant'Alvise**, as well as many fine *palazzi.* The palazzo at the beginning of the fondamenta along this canal, Palazzo Contarini dal Zaffo, was built for Gaspare Contarini, a 16th-century scholar, diplomat and cardinal. Behind, a large garden stretches down to the lagoon; in its far corner stands the **Casinò degli Spiriti** (best seen from fondamenta Nuove). Designed as a meeting place for the 'spirits' (wits) of the day, the name and the lonely position of the construction have given rise to numerous ghost stories.

The Madonna dell'Orto area may have been the home of an Islamic merchant community in the 12th and 13th centuries, centring on a since-destroyed Fondaco (meeting-place and storehouse) degli Arabi. Opposite the church of Santa Maria dell'Orto is the 15th-century Palazzo Mastelli, also known as Palazzo del Camello because of its relief of a turbaned figure with a camel. The Arabic theme continues in the campo dei Mori ('of the Moors') across the bridge, named after the three stone figures set into the façade of a building, all wearing turbans. The one with the comically prominent iron nose – dubbed 'Sior Antonio Rioba' – was the Venetian equivalent of Rome's Pasquino: disgruntled citizens or local wits would hang their rhyming complaints on him overnight, or use him as a pseudonym for published satires. The three figures are believed to be the Mastelli brothers, owners of the adjacent palazzo, who came to Venice as merchants from the Greek Peloponnese (then known as Morea – which offers another explanation of the campo's name).

Madonna dell'Orto

Campo Madonna dell'Orto (041 275 0642/www. chorus-ve.org). Vaporetto Madonna dell'Orto. **Open** 10am-5pm Mon-Sat; 1-5pm Sun. **Admission** €2 *(see also p61* Chorus). **No credit cards. Map** p305 A3. The 'Tintoretto church' was originally dedicated to St Christopher (a magnificent statue of whom stands over the main door), the patron saint of the gondo-liers who ran the ferry service to the islands from a nearby jetty. However, a cult developed around a large, unfinished and supposedly miraculous statue of the Madonna and Child that stood in the nearby garden of sculptor Giovanni de Santi; in 1377 the sculpture was solemnly transferred into the church (it's now in the chapel of San Mauro), and the church's name was changed to the Madonna of the Garden. It was rebuilt between 1399 and 1473, and a monastery was constructed alongside. The beau-tiful Gothic façade is similar to those of the Frari *(see pp113-4)* and Santi Giovanni e Paolo *(see p87),* although the false gallery at the top is unique. The sculptures are all fine 15th-century works. But it is the numerous works by Tintoretto that have made

Take it to the bridge

Venice's 400 or so bridges (in this variously spanned city, manifold definitions of the word 'bridge' make computation tricky) include a number of curiosities. Venetian bridge-watching makes for a fascinating study in human ingenuity... and can keep bored offspring happy with a city-wide game of I-spy. (The *sestieri* where bridges are located are given in brackets.)

Bridges without parapets
Ponte Chiodo (Cannaregio); ponte del Diavolo (Torcello).

Bridges without steps
The (nameless) bridge at the Giardini (Castello) – you can cross this without realising it's a bridge; the bridges over the rio di Sant'Elena.

Pugnacious bridges
Ponte dei Pugni at San Barnaba (Dorsoduro), ponte della Guerra at San Zulian (San Marco), ponte Santa Fosca (Cannaregio): these bridges all have white marble footprints, indicating the starting points for the more-or-less organised punch-ups between the city's rival factions.

A bridge with three arches
The ponte dei Tre Archi (Cannaregio) spans the Cannaregio Canal.

A bridge that's also a church
The apse of Santo Stefano (San Marco).

A bridge that's also a campo
Campiello dei Meloni (San Polo).

A bridge that's also a road
Via Garibaldi (Castello) – a canal was covered, rather than filled in, to create this street.

A single bridge spanning two canals
Ponte Pasqualigo e Avogadro from campiello Querini to fondamenta del Remedio (Castello); there are just two flights of steps and one level span, but it crosses the rio di Santa Maria Formosa and the rio del Remedio.

The tightest cluster of bridges
The complex of bridges across the rio Novo beside piazzale Roma (Santa Croce) known as Tre Ponti (three bridges); the interlocking bridges are, in fact, five, and from them there is a view of 12 other bridges.

The bridge offering the widest choice of directions
Ponte dei Barrettieri in the Mercerie (San Marco), with six roads and alleys leading off it.

The longest (pedestrian) bridge
This is not one of the Big Three over the Grand Canal, but ponte di Sacca Fisola, at the western end of the Giudecca (around 65 metres, 217 feet); it is followed by the two bridges to the island of San Pietro (Castello), both around 50 metres (160 feet).

The newest bridge
From the Ca' Rezzonico vaporetto stop to the museum itself (*see p120*), built for the reopening of the museum in 1996. (*See also p31* **The shock of the new**).

The only bridges where it is possible to step from one to the other without touching the pavement in between
Ponte dei Preti and ponte del Paradiso (Castello) near campo Santa Maria Formosa.

The only bridge not facing the lagoon from which there is a view of the campanile of San Marco
Ponte del Lovo (San Marco), between campo San Bortolo and campo San Luca.

The first stone bridges
Ponte di Canonica (between San Marco and Castello) and ponte San Provolo (Castello), built to provide a safer journey from piazza San Marco to San Zaccaria after the assassination of Doge Pietro Tradonico in AD 864.

The first iron bridge
Ponte della Corona (1850, Castello), near campo Santi Filippo e Giacomo.

the Madonna dell'Orto famous. Tradition has it that the artist began decorating the church as penance for insulting a doge: in fact, it took very little to persuade Tintoretto to get his palette out, and the urgent sincerity of his work here speaks for itself.

Two colossal paintings dominate the side walls of the chancel. On the left is *The Israelites at Mount Sinai*; some have seen portraits of Venice's artistic top four (Giorgione, Titian, Veronese and Tintoretto himself) in the bearers of the Golden Calf, although there is no documentary evidence for this, nor for

the identification of the lady dressed in blue as Mrs Tintoretto. Opposite is a gruesome *Last Judgement*. Like Dante and Michelangelo, Tintoretto had no qualms about mixing religion and myth: note the classical figure of Charon ferrying the souls of the dead. Tintoretto's paintings in the apse include *St Peter's Vision of the Cross* and *The Beheading of St Paul* (or Christopher, according to some), both maelstroms of swirling angelic movement. On the wall of the right aisle is the *Presentation of the Virgin in the Temple*, a calmer, more reverential work. It was

In the Ghetto

Map p304 A2

The word ghetto (like arsenal and ciao) is one that Venice has given to the world. It originally meant an iron foundry, a place where iron was *gettato* (cast). Until 1390, when the foundry was transferred to the Arsenale, casting was done on a small island in Cannaregio. In 1516 it was decided to confine the city's Jewish population to this island; there they remained until 1797.

Venetian treatment of the Jews was by no means as harsh as in many European countries, but neither was it a model of open-minded benevolence. The Republic's attitude was governed by practical considerations, and business was done with Jewish merchants at least as early as the tenth century. It was not until 1385, however, that Jewish moneylenders were given permission to reside in the city itself. Twelve years later, permission was revoked amid allegations of irregularities in their banking practices. For a century after that, residence in Venice was limited to two-week stretches.

In 1509, when the Venetian mainland territories were overrun by foreign troops, great numbers of Jews took refuge in the city. The clergy seized the opportunity to stir up anti-Jewish feeling and demanded their expulsion. Venice's rulers, however, had begun to see the economic advantages of letting them stay, and in 1516 a compromise was reached. In a decision that was to mark the course of Jewish history in Europe, the refugees were given residence permits but confined to the Ghetto.

Restrictions were many and tough. Gates across the bridges to the island were closed an hour after sunset in summer (two hours after sunset in winter), reopening at dawn. During the day, Jews had to wear distinctive badges. Most trades other than moneylending were barred to them. One exception was medicine, for which they were famous: Venetian practicality allowed Jewish doctors to leave the Ghetto at night for professional calls. Another was music: Jewish singers and fiddlers were hired for private parties.

The Ghetto became a stop on the tourist trail. In 1608 traveller Thomas Coryat came to gaze at the Jews – never having seen any in England – and marvelled at the 'sweet-featured persons' and the 'apparel, jewels, chains of gold' of the women.

The original inhabitants were mostly Ashkenazim from Germany; they were joined by Sephardim escaping from persecution in Spain and Portugal and then, increasingly, by Levantine Jews from the Ottoman Empire. These latter proved key figures in trade between Venice and the East, particularly after Venice lost so many of her trading posts in the eastern Mediterranean. By the mid 16th century the Levantine Jews, the richest community, were given permission to move from the Ghetto Nuovo to the confusingly named Ghetto Vecchio (the 'old Ghetto', the site of an earlier foundry); in 1633 they expanded into the Ghetto Nuovissimo.

Nonetheless, conditions remained cramped, and the height of the buildings in the campo del Ghetto Nuovo shows how the inhabitants, unable to expand in a horizontal direction, did so vertically, creating the first high-rise blocks in Europe. A recent study has calculated that at certain periods overcrowding was such that the inhabitants must have had to take it in turns to sleep. Room was found for five magnificent synagogues, however, each new influx of immigrants wanting its own place of worship. The German, Levantine and Spanish synagogues can be visited as part of the **Museo Ebraico** tour.

With the arrival of Napoleon in 1797, Jews gained full rights of citizenship; many chose to remain in the Ghetto. In the deportations

---

painted as a deliberate response to Titian's master-piece on the same theme in the Accademia, and is more characteristically mystical in tone.

The Contarini Chapel, off the left aisle, contains the artist's beautiful *St Agnes Reviving the Son of a Roman Prefect*. Once again, it is the swooping angels that steal the show in their dazzling blue vestments. Tintoretto, his son Domenico and his artistically gifted daughter Marietta are buried in a chapel off the right aisle. When the Tintorettos get too much for you, take a look at Cima da Conegliano's freshly restored masterpiece *Saints John the Baptist, Mark, Jerome and Paul* (1494-5) over the first altar on the right. The saints stand under a ruined portico against a sharp wintry light. There used to be a small *Madonna and Child* by Giovanni Bellini in the chapel opposite but it was stolen in 1993.

Sant'Alvise

Campo Sant'Alvise (041 275 0642/www.chorus-ve.org). Vaporetto Sant'Alvise. **Open** 10am-5pm Mon-Sat; 1-5pm Sun. **Admission** €2 (*see also p61* Chorus). **No credit cards. Map** p304 A2.

during the Nazi occupation of Italy in 1943, 202 Venetian Jews were sent to the death camps, including the chief rabbi and 20 inmates of an old people's home. The Jewish population of Venice and Mestre now stands at about 500, though only around a dozen Jewish families still live in the Ghetto. The Ghetto remains, however, the centre of spiritual, cultural and social life for the Jewish community; there's a museum, a library, a kosher restaurant, a bakery and a nursery school. Orthodox religious services are held in the Scuola Spagnola in the summer and in the Scuola Levantina in winter.

Museo Ebraico

Cannaregio 2902B, campo del Ghetto Nuovo (041 715 359). Vaporetto Ponte delle Guglie or San Marcuola. **Open** *June-Sept* 10am-7pm Mon-Fri, Sun; guided tours hourly 10.30am-5.30pm. *Oct-May* 10am-6pm Mon-Thur, Sun; 10am-30mins before sunset Fri; guided tours hourly 10.30am-4.30pm. **Admission** *Museum only* 3; 2 concessions. *Museum & synagogue tour* 8; 6.50 concessions. **Credit** MC, V. **Map** p304 A2.

Venice's Jewish community has been enjoying a renaissance recently, and this well-run museum and cultural centre – founded in 1953 – has been spruced up accordingly, with the addition of a bookshop. In the small museum itself there are ritual objects in silver – Trah finials, Purim and Pesach cases, menorahs sacred vestments and hangings, and a series of marriage contracts. To get the most out of the experience, the museum should be visited as part of the guided tours in English and Italian. These take in three synagogues – the Scuola Canton (Ashkenazi rite), the Scuola Italiana (Italian rite) and the Scuola Levantina (Sephardic rite).

A pleasingly simple Gothic building of the 14th century, Sant'Alvise's interior was remodelled in the 1600s with extravagant, if not wholly convincing, *trompe l'oeil* effects on the ceiling. On the inner façade is a *barco*, a hanging choir of the 15th century with elegant wrought-iron gratings, formerly used by the nuns of the adjacent convent. Tiepolo's huge *Road to Calvary* on the right wall of the chancel is a vivid work, with ill-suited circus-pageantry, complete with trumpets and prancing horses. Eight charmingly naïve biblical paintings in tempera, fancifully

attributed by Ruskin to the ten-year-old Carpaccio, which used to be in the sacristy, are currently being restored; when they return they will probably be hung in the church (on the main-entrance wall). Those looking for a picnic spot will find a garden nearby, complete with picturesque classical 'ruins'.

North-eastern Cannaregio

North-eastern Cannaregio is more intriguingly closed in, with many narrow alleys (including the Venetian record holder, calle Varisco, 52 centimetres (20 inches) wide at its narrowest point), charming courtyards and well-heads, but no major sights, with the exception of the spectacularly ornate church of **I Gesuiti**, the **Oratorio dei Crociferi** and, further east, the miniature marvel of **Santa Maria dei Miracoli**. Titian had a house here, with a garden extending to the lagoon; the courtyard where the house was located is raised to the dignity of a 'campo' and named after the artist.

I Gesuiti

Campo dei Gesuiti (041 528 6579). Vaporetto Fondamente Nove. **Open** 10am noon, 4-6pm daily. **Map** p305 B4.

The Jesuits were never very popular in Venice and it wasn't until 1715 that they felt secure enough to build a church here. Even then they chose a comparatively remote plot on the edge of town. But once they made up their mind to go ahead, they went all out: local architect Domenico Rossi was given explicit instructions to dazzle the Venetians. The result leaves no room for half-measures: you love it or you hate it, and for the past couple of centuries, most people have done the latter, considering the result the ultimate in church kitsch. The exterior, with a façade by Gian Battista Fattoretto, is conventional enough; the interior (freshly restored) is anything but. All that tassled, bunched, overpowering drapery is not the work of a rococo set-designer gone berserk with brocades: it's plain old green and white marble. Bernini's altar in St Peter's in Rome was the model for the baldachin over the altar, by Fra Giuseppe Pozzo. The statues above the baldachin are by Giuseppe Torretti, as are the rococo archangels at the corners of the crossing. Titian's *Martyrdom of St Lawrence* (1558-9), over the first altar on the left side, came from an earlier church on this site, and was one of the first successful night-scenes ever painted. According to writer WD Howells – who labelled the church 'indescribably table-clothy' – the saint is the only person in the building not to suffer from the cold.

Oratorio dei Crociferi

Cannaregio 4905, campo dei Gesuiti (041 270 2464/ asa@patriarcato.venezia.it). Vaporetto Fondamente Nove. **Open** *Apr-Oct* 10am-12.30pm Fri; 3.30-7.30pm Sat. *Nov-Mar* by appointment. **Admission** €2. **No credit cards. Map** p305 B4.

Founded in the 13th century by Doge Renier Zeno, the oratory is a sort of primitive *scuola* (*see p61*), with the familiar square central meeting hall but without the quasi-masonic ceremonial trappings. Palma il Giovane's colourful cycle of paintings shows Pope Anacletus instituting the order of the Crociferi (cross-bearers), and dwells on the pious life of Doge Pasquale Cicogna, who was a fervent supporter of the order.

Santa Maria dei Miracoli

Campo Santa Maria dei Miracoli (041 275 0462/ www.chorus-ve.org). Vaporetto Rialto or Fondamente Nove. **Open** 10am-5pm Mon-Sat; 1-5pm Sun. **Admission** €2 (*see also p61* Chorus). **No credit cards. Map** p305 C4.

Arguably one of the most exquisite churches in the world, Santa Maria dei Miracoli was built in the 1480s to house a miraculous image of the Madonna, reputed to have revived a man who had spent half an hour underwater in the Giudecca Canal, and to have cancelled all traces of a knife attack on a woman. The building is the work of the Lombardo family, early Renaissance masons who fused architecture, surface detail and sculpture into a unique whole. Pietro Lombardo may have been a Lombard by birth but he soon got into the Venetian way of doing things, employing Byzantine spoils left over from work on St Mark's to create a work of art displaying an entirely Venetian sensitivity to texture and colour. There is an almost painterly approach to the use of multicoloured marble in the four sides of the church, each of which is of a slightly different shade. The sides have more pilasters than are strictly necessary, making the church appear longer than

Street wise

See also **Street wise** *in chapter* **Directory**.

Braccio nudo (corte)
'Naked arm', probably from the name of a shop.
Cavallo (corte del)
'Horse'; the bronze equestrian statue of Colleoni (*see p85*) was cast here.
Cenere (calle)
'Ash'; it was collected here, for use in various industrial processes.
Proverbi (calle larga dei)
A house with two proverbs carved on its balconies once stood here.
Scala Matta (corte)
'Crazy staircase'; with no staircase worthy of this title to be found in the vicinity, the origin of this name is lost in the mists of time.

it really is. Inside, 50 painted ceiling panels by Pier Maria Pennacchi (1528) are almost impossible to distinguish without binoculars. Instead, turn your attention to the church's true treasures: the delicate carvings by the Lombardi on the columns, steps and balustrade. Look out for the child's head that so distressed Ruskin, who wondered how any sculptor, after creating something this lifelike, could be so 'wanting in all human feeling as to cut it off, and tie it by the hair to a vine leaf'.

I Gesuiti, whose decor divides opinions. *See p101.*

San Polo & Santa Croce

The densely packed heart of ancient Venice.

These two *sestieri* nestle in the bulge south of the upper loop of the Grand Canal, with San Polo occupying roughly the bottom portion and Santa Croce the top. Probably only postmen know exactly where boundary lies.

But it makes little difference because the real dividing line here is the rio San Polo, which changes its name three times as it slices its watery way through the two *sestieri* in a north south direction. To the east of this boundary line is the dense ancient heart of the city, squeezed tight around the Rialto market; the only large-scale buildings in this area face on to the Grand Canal (*see also chapter* **The Grand Canal**). To the west, on the other hand, lies a once-rural area, radiating out from the magnificently grandiose religious complex of the Frari (*see p113*) and the *scuole* of San Rocco (*see p115*) and San Giovanni Evangelista (*see p111*).

The Rialto markets

It is generally agreed that the name Rialto derives from 'Rivoaltus' (high bank), and it was on this point of higher ground at the very centre of the Grand Canal that one of the earliest settlements was founded in the fifth century. The district has been the commercial heart of the city since the market was moved here from campo San Bartolomeo in 1097. The present layout of the market and adjacent buildings is the result of an overall reconstruction project by Scarpagnino after a fire in 1514, which destroyed the whole area.

As usual in Venice, the project made use of the previous foundations, so the present street-plan probably reflects quite faithfully the earliest urban arrangement, with long, narrow parallel blocks running behind the grand *palazzi* along the riva del Vin, and smaller, squarer blocks further inland for the market workers.

At the foot of the Rialto bridge, where the tourist stalls are thick on the ground, stands – to the south – the **Palazzo dei Dieci Savi**, which housed the city's tax inspectors (it is now used by the ancient but extant lagoon water authority, Il Magistrato alle Acque) and – to the north – the **Palazzo dei Camerlenghi**, which housed the finance department.

Beyond, the small church of **San Giacomo di Rialto** (known affectionately as San Giacometto) is generally agreed to be the first

of the city's churches (tradition has it that it was founded in 421). All around it stretch the markets, around which commercial and administrative buildings and areas of low-cost housing mushroomed after trade was shifted from across the canal. Despite an over-abundance of souvenir stalls, the Rialto market remains the best place to buy your fruit, veg and – for those who can take the sight of fish in their squirming death-throes – seafood.

The larger streets and squares are named after the merchandise that is still sold there (Naranzeria – oranges; Casaria – cheese; Speziali – spices; Erberia – vegetables), while the narrower alleys mostly bear the names of ancient inns and taverns (some still in operation), such as 'The Monkey', 'The Two Swords', 'The Two Moors', 'The Ox', 'The Bell'; then as now, market traders hated to be too far from liquid refreshment.

On the other side of campo San Giacomo, behind the fruit stalls, is a 16th-century statue of a kneeling figure supporting a staircase leading up to a small column of Egyptian granite, from which laws and sentences were pronounced. It was to this figure – the *Gobbo di Rialto* (the Hunchback of the Rialto, although he is, in fact, merely crouching) – that naked malefactors clung in desperate and bloody relief, since the statue marked the end of the gauntlet they were condemned to run from piazza San Marco as an alternative to gaol.

The ruga degli Speziali leads to the **Pescaria** (fishmarket; open Tue-Sat morning). The present neo-Gothic arcade (1907) replaced the iron structure of the previous century. Beyond the market extends a warren-like zone of medieval low-rent housing interspersed with proud *palazzi*; this area is traversed by two main pedestrian routes from the Rialto bridge, one running westward, more or less parallel to the Grand Canal, towards campo San Polo, and the other zigzagging north-westwards via a series of small squares towards campo San Giacomo dell'Orio and the station.

San Giacomo di Rialto

San Polo, Campo San Giacomo (041 522 4745).
Vaporetto Rialto. **Open** 9.30am-noon, 4-6pm Mon-Sat. **Map** p305 C3.
The traditional foundation date for this church is that of the city itself: 25 March 421. It has undergone several radical reconstructions since its foundation,

Sightseeing

the last in 1601. Nonetheless, out of respect for the history of the building, the original Greek- cross plan was always preserved, as were its minuscule dimensions. The interior has columns of ancient marble with 11th-century Corinthian capitals. According to Francesco Sansovino (son of the architect and author of the first guide to the city in 1581), the brick dome may have been a model for the domes of St Mark's. In 1177 Pope Alexander III granted plenary indulgence to all those who visited the church on Maundy Thursday; among the eager visitors every year was the doge. The special role of this church in Venetian history was given official recognition after 1532, when Pope Clement VII bestowed the patronage of the church on the doge, effectively annexing it to the Ducal Chapel of St Mark's.

West from the Rialto

The route to campo San Polo traverses a series of straight, busy shopping streets, passing the recently reopened church of **San Giovanni Elemosinario** and the deconsecrated church of **Sant'Aponal**, which has fine Gothic sculpture on its façade. To the south of this route, towards the Grand Canal, stands the church of **San Silvestro**, with a good Tintoretto, while to the north is a fascinating network of quiet, little-visited alleys and courtyards.

Curiosities worth seeking out (take calle Bianca Cappello from campo Sant'Aponal) include **Palazzo Molin-Cappello**, birthplace of Bianca Cappello, who in 1563 was sentenced to death in absentia for eloping with a bank clerk but who managed to right things between

herself and the Most Serene Republic by subsequently marrying Francesco de' Medici, Grand Duke of Tuscany. North-westwards from here is campiello Albrizzi, overlooked by **Palazzo Albrizzi**, which contains one of the most sumptuous baroque interiors (closed to the public) in Venice.

Nearby is one of Venice's early red-light zones; the district of Ca' Rampana was notorious enough to have passed on its own name (*carampana* means 'slut') to the Italian language. Just round the corner is the ponte delle Tette, or the Tits Bridge (*see p105* **Street wise**).

After the shadowy closeness of these *calli*, the open expanse of campo San Polo comes as a sudden sunlit surprise. This is the largest square on this side of the Grand Canal and in the past was used for popular occasions such as bull-baiting, religious ceremonies, parades and theatrical spectacles as well as weekly markets. Venue of an open-air film season in the summer (*see p201*), its main day-to-day function is that of a vast children's playground.

The curving line of *palazzi* on the east side of the square is explained by the fact that these buildings once gave on to a canal, which was subsequently filled in. They still have a water-entrance, on the other side, which means that when they were first built access was by boat or bridge only. The two **Palazzi Soranzo** (Nos.2169 and 2170-1) are particularly attractive Gothic buildings with marble facing and good capitals. In the 18th century these houses had three bridges leading to them.

A five-light window at **Palazzo Agnusdio**. *See p106.*

Street wise

See also p279 **Street wise**.

Amor degli amici (calle dell')
'Love of (male) friends'; perhaps a reference to a group of local homosexuals; but *see also* Donna Onesta.

Anatomia (corte dell')
An anatomy theatre stood in this area from 1671 to 1800.

Bella Vienna (campo, calle della)
After a 19th-century café of this name.

Carampane (calle, rio terrà delle)
Corruption of Ca' Rampani (house of the Rampani family); the area became a semi-official red-light zone in the 17th century. *Carampana* came to mean 'slut' in Italian.

Chiovere (campiello, corte delle)
Area used for drying dyed cloth, from nails (*chiovi – chiodi* in Italian), used to fix cloths.

Donna onesta (ponte, fondamenta di)
'Honest woman'. Explanations abound: the tiny sculptured face of a woman in a house over the bridge was once pointed out as being Venice's only 'honest woman'; a local prostitute was famous for carrying on her trade with singular honesty; the wife of a sword-maker, raped by a client of her husband's, stabbed herself in desperation with one of her husband's daggers – though

another version of this last says she was saved in extremis by a friend of her husband, who stabbed the assailant before the dirty deed was done (*see also* Amor degli amici).

Furatola (calle, ponte della)
A *furatola* was a tiny shop selling fried fish; from *foro* (small hole), or from the *furari* (thieving) that went on in such places.

Parrucchetta (ponte, fondamenta)
'Little wig'; a local seller of animal-fodder was famous for his absurdly large wig.

Saoneri (calle dei)
'Soap-makers'.

Sbianchesini (sottoportico, calle dei)
'Whitewashers'.

Scimia (calle della)
'Monkey'; after an *osteria* of this name.

Scoazzera (campiello, rio terrà della)
'Rubbish-dump'; *scoazze* is Venetian for rubbish.

Sole (calle del)
'Sun'; from a hostelry of this name.

Squartai (ponte dei)
The quartered remains of criminals were hung here.

Tette (ponte, fondamenta delle)
'Tits'; prostitutes were officially encouraged to display their wares here.

In the north-west corner is a view of **Palazzo Corner** (the main façade is on the rio di San Polo), a 16th-century design by Sanmicheli. Novelist Frederick Rolfe stayed here – until his English hosts read the manuscript of his work, *The Desire and Pursuit of the Whole*, which contained vitriolic portraits of their friends. They turned him out of the house, thus earning a place for themselves in this ultimate grudge novel. One of Casanova's most boasted acts of revenge took place in calle Bernardo, to the north of the campo, when he beat up a bullying bailiff, having made his first prison escape (from the fortress island of Sant'Andrea) to do so.

San Giovanni Elemosinario

San Polo, ruga vecchia San Giovanni (041 275 0462/www.chorus-ve.org). Vaporetto San Silvestro or Rialto. **Open** 10am-5pm Mon-Sat; 1-5pm Sun. **Admission** €2 (*see also p61* Chorus). **No credit cards**. Map p305 C3.
This small Renaissance church – a Greek-cross structure contained within a square – was reopened in 2002 after remaining closed for an unexplained 20 years. It was founded in the ninth or tenth

century but rebuilt after a fire in 1514, probably by Scarpagnino. On the high altar is a painting by Titian of the titular saint, St John the Alms Giver. (The saint's body is preserved in the church of San Giovanni in Bragora, *see p91*.) In the left aisle is a medieval fragment of sculptural relief (12th or 13th century) of the Nativity, which shows an ox reverently licking the face of the Christ child.

San Polo

Campo San Polo (041 275 0462/www.chorus-ve.org). Vaporetto San Silvestro/San Tomà. **Open** 10am-5pm Mon-Sat; 1-5pm Sun. **Admission** €2 (*see also p61* Chorus). **No credit cards**. Map p304 C2.
The church of San Polo faces away from the square, towards the canal, although later buildings have deprived it of its façade and water-entrance. The campanile (1362) has two 12th-century lions at the base, one brooding over a snake and the other toying with a human head, which Venetians like to think of as that of Count Carmagnola, who was beheaded for treachery in 1402. This basically Gothic church was extensively altered in the 19th century, when a neo-classical look was imposed on it. Some of this was removed in 1930, but the interior remains an awkward hybrid. Paintings include a

Last Supper by Tintoretto to the left of the entrance, and a characteristically snappily named Tiepolo: *The Virgin Appearing to St John of Nepomuk.* Giambattista Tiepolo's son, Giandomenico, is the author of a brilliant cycle of *Stations of the Cross* in the Oratory of the Crucifix (entrance under the organ), being restored as this guide went to press, but visible. He painted these – and the ceiling paintings – at the age of 20.

San Silvestro

San Polo, Campo San Silvestro (041 523 8090). Vaporetto San Silvestro. **Open** 7.30-11.30am, 4-6pm Mon-Sat. **Map** p305 C3.

This church was rebuilt in the neo-classical style between 1837 and 1843. It contains a *Baptism of Christ* by Tintoretto over the first altar on the right (c1580), with the River Jordan represented as a mountain brook. Opposite is *St Thomas a Becket Enthroned* by Girolamo da Santacroce (1520), with the saint in startling white robes against a mountain landscape; the other two saints are 19th-century additions. Off the right aisle (ask the sacristan to let you in) is the former School of the Wine Merchants; on the upper floor there's a chapel with 18th-century frescos by Gaspare Diziani. Opposite the church is the house (No.1022) where Giorgione died in 1510.

North-west from the Rialto

The north-western route from the Rialto (follow the yellow signs to Ferrovia) takes you zigzagging past the fishmarket, through campo **San Cassiano**. The uninspiring exterior of the church here is matched by a heavily decorated interior. Then cross the bridge into campo **Santa Maria Mater Domini** with its Renaissance church. Before entering the campo, it's worth admiring the view from the bridge of the curving marble flank of **Ca' Pesaro** – seat of the **Museo Orientale** and **Galleria d'Arte Moderna** – on the Grand Canal. On the far side of this square, which contains a number of fine Byzantine and Gothic buildings, the yellow road sign, in true Venetian fashion, indicates that the way to the station is to the left and to the right.

The quieter route to the right curls parallel to the Grand Canal. The road towards Ca' Pesaro passes **Palazzo Agnusdio**, a small 14th-century house with an ogival five-light window decorated with bas-reliefs of the Annunciation and symbols of the evangelists; the house used to belong to a family of sausage-makers who were given patrician status in the 17th century.

Many of the most important sights face on to the Grand Canal, including the 18th-century church of **San Stae** and the **Fondaco dei Turchi** (the Warehouse of the Turks, which houses the city's long-closed Natural History Museum, due to reopen in 2004). On the wide

road leading towards San Stae is **Palazzo Mocenigo**, containing a collection of textiles and costumes. A short distance away is the quiet square of **San Zan Degolà** (San Giovanni Decollato), with its well-preserved 11th-century church. From here, a series of narrow roads leads past the church of **San Simeone Profeta** to the foot of the Scalzi bridge across the Grand Canal.

Leave campo Santa Maria Mater Domini by the route to the left, on the other hand, and you'll make your way past the near-legendary **Da Fiore** eaterie (*see p157*) to the house (No. 2311) where Aldo Manuzio (Aldus Manutius) set up the Aldine Press in 1490, and where humanist Erasmus came to stay in 1508. To the right by a building with a 14th-century relief of *Faith and Justice* above its doorway, the rio terrà del Parrucchetta (*see p105* **Street wise**) leads to the large leafy campo **San Giacomo dell'Orio**. The church has its back and sides to the square; when the church was built, the main entrance was from the water.

Ca' Pesaro – Galleria Internazionale d'Arte Moderna

Santa Croce 2076, fondamenta Ca' Pesaro (041 524 0695). Vaporetto San Stae. **Open** *Nov-Mar* 10am-5pm Tue-Sun. *Apr-Oct* 10am-6pm Tue-Sun. **Admission** €5.50; €3 concessions; includes Museo Orientale (*see also p61* Musei Civici Veneziani). **No credit cards. Map** p305 B3.

This museum was re-opened in November 2002 after lengthy and careful restoration. The grandiose palazzo was built in the second half of the 17th century for the Pesaro family (celebrated in Titian's great painting *La Madonna di Ca' Pesaro* in the Frari), to a project by Longhena. When Longhena died in 1682 the family entrusted the completion of the project to Gian Antonio Gaspari, who concluded it in 1710, sticking largely to the original blueprint. The interior of the palazzo still contains some of the original fresco and oil decorations, although the family's great collection of Renaissance paintings was auctioned off in London by the last Pesaro before he died in 1830. The palazzo passed through various hands until its last owner, Felicita Bevilacqua La Masa, bequeathed it to the city for use as a modern art museum. Into it went the city's collection of modern art, gleaned over the years from Biennale exhibitions (*see p206* **The Biennale**). Between 1908 and 1924 its mezzanine floor played host to the renowned Bevilacqua La Masa exhibitions, which gave hanging space to a generation of young Italian artists, as well as providing healthy competition for the Biennale.

The museum now covers a century of mainly Italian art, from the mid 19th century to the 1950s. On the stately ground floor are a number of 20th-century Italian sculptures, including a monumental *Eve* by Francesco Messina and a bronze *Cardinal* by Giacomo Manzù.

Plump apses at **San Giacomo dell'Orio**. *See p109*.

Literary locations Casanova

Giacomo Casanova di Seingalt (as the 18th-century Love Machine liked to style himself) wandered wherever the urge took him, and it seemed to take him everywhere. His brazenly candid memoirs, *The Story of My Life*, roam all over Europe; those parts devoted to his home town show an equally lustful restlessness.

There seems hardly a Venetian courtyard or alley where Casanova did not have some kind of intimate encounter. What follows is necessarily an abbreviated list of places with particularly Casanovan associations.

San Marco

The illegitimate son of an actress and a member of the patrician Grimani family, Casanova was born in a house in **calle Malipiero** in San Marco (**map** p306 A2; the exact house is uncertain). The nearby **corte Teatro** marks the former site of the Grimani-owned Teatro di San Samuele where his mother performed.

Towards the Grand Canal is the **corte del Duca Sforza**, where Teresa Imer lived; she was a young actress with whom Casanova was discovered in compromising circumstances by the aged but doting Venetian senator, Malipiero, who set upon

him with a stick. Angela Tosello, the desired but unattained daughter of his priest-tutor, lived in **corte Nani**; the 18-year-old Casanova found release for his frustration in his first full sexual encounter with two obliging sisters, Nanetta and Marta Savorgnan, who lived in **salizzada San Samuele**.

The **Doge's Palace** (*see p77*) was the site of Casanova's much-vaunted second prison break. After a whole string of scandals Casanova was warned to leave Venice. Following his usual self-destructive impulses, he failed to pay heed and was promptly whisked off to the *piombi*, the prisons under the lead roof of the palace. The escape, together with a cowardly monk and a plump count – described in fascinating detail in his memoirs – involved much foreplanning, a rudimentary iron spike, torn-up sheets and a good deal of athletic roof-scrambling. Sceptics have suggested that it was probably achieved by a less sensational but much simpler bribe to the jailer, but it seems a pity to spoil a good story.

San Polo

Campo San Polo, on the other side of the Grand Canal, was the site of two important events. It was in **calle Bernardo**, to the north

---

The first rooms on the *piano nobile* contain atmospheric works by 19th-century painters such as Ippolito Caffi and Guglielmo Ciardi and some striking sculptures by Medardo Rosso. In the central hall are works from the early Biennali up to the 1930s, including pieces by Gustav Klimt and Vassily Kandinsky, alongside more conventional vast-scale 'salon' paintings. Room 4 holds works by Giorgio Morandi, Joan Miró and Giorgio De Chirico. After rooms devoted to international art from the 1940s and '50s, the collection winds up with works by post-war Venetian experimentalists such as Armando Pizzinato, Giuseppe Santomaso and Emilio Vedova.

Ca' Pesaro – Museo Orientale

Santa Croce 2070, fondamenta Ca' Pesaro (041 524 1173). Vaporetto San Stae. **Open** 10am-5pm Tue-Sun. **Admission** €5.50; €3 concessions; includes Galleria d'Arte Moderna (*see also p61* Musei Civici Veneziani). **No credit cards. Map** p305 B3.
If Japanese art and weaponry of the Edo period (1600-1868) are your thing, you'll love this eclectic collection, put together by Count Enrico di Borbone – a nephew of Louis XVIII – in the course of a round-the-world voyage between 1887 and 1890. After the count's death the collection was sold off to an

Austrian antique merchant; it bounced back to Venice after World War I as reparations. The Museo Orientale might seem an odd attraction for such a monocultural city as Venice, but if you come here after the Palazzo Ducale and the Museo Correr, all this ceremonial paraphernalia will seem oddly familiar. The collection features parade armour, dolls, decorative saddles and case upon case of curved samurai swords forged by smiths who had to perform a ritual act of purification before putting their irons in the fire. There is a dwarf-sized lady's gilded litter, and lacquered picnic cases that prove that the Japanese obsession with compactness pre-dates Sony. The final rooms have musical instruments, and eastern miscellanea, including Chinese crockery and Indonesian shadow puppets.

Palazzo Mocenigo

Santa Croce 1992, salizzada San Stae (041 721 798). Vaporetto San Stae. **Open** *Apr-Oct* 10am-5pm Tue-Sun. *Nov-Mar* 10am-4pm Tue-Sun. **Admission** €4; €2.50 concessions (*see also p61* Musei Civici Veneziani). **No credit cards. Map** p304-5 B2-3.
Small but perfectly formed, the Palazzo Mocenigo will not come top of anyone's museum list, but it is a good place to while away half an hour. The

of the campo, that Casanova beat up Razzetta, the bailiff of the Grimani family. The attack was in revenge for Razzetta's persecution of Casanova; the bailiff had of course been acting on the instructions of the Grimanis, but Casanova was not so foolish as to attempt a direct assault upon an important aristocratic family. It was Razzetta himself who had rowed Casanova to his first brief imprisonment on the fortress island of Sant'Andrea, from which he escaped to make the attack. The escape was cleverly planned, and included an apparently unassailable alibi; he feigned a twisted ankle and then bribed a boatman to row him from the island during the night and back again after the assault.

The other San Polo association was more propitious. It was while playing the violin at an aristocratic wedding-feast in **Palazzo Soranzo**, a splendid Gothic palazzo on the campo, that Casanova first met Senator Bragadin; the aged senator offered Casanova a ride in his gondola, and on the way home suffered a stroke; showing great coolness Casanova had the gondoliers stop and called a surgeon, saving the man's life. The senator ended up by adopting Casanova, who lived in his palace near **campo Santa Marina** (across in the sestiere of Castello, it can be seen from

ponte Storto leading out of the corte seconda del Milion) for nine years, during which he succeeded in convincing the alchemy-loving Bragadin and two equally good-hearted and gullible friends of his own occult powers.

The Lagoon

Murano was the scene of one (or rather two) of his most passionate love-affairs. Casanova actually proposed marriage to a young girl named Caterina Capretta, known in his memoirs as CC. Probably acting upon advice from Bragadin, who didn't want to lose Casanova, her father promptly had her sent off to the convent of **Santa Maria degli Angeli** on Murano. Casanova's frequent visits to the church brought him to the attention of another nun, referred to as MM (still unidentified), who suggested an assignation in a *casino* on the island. Casanova, wallowing in his customary titillating mixture of guilt and desire, was not hard to persuade. He soon realised that he was providing a free spectacle for the voyeuristic owner of the *casino*, the French ambassador; Casanova did his best to give satisfaction to all concerned, who soon also included the young but not so innocent CC, who was quite happy to join in sexual threesomes.

museum serves a double purpose. The interior gives a fine illustration of the sort of furniture and fittings an 18th-century Venetian noble family liked to surround itself with. The Mocenigo family (which also owned a complex of *palazzi* on the Grand Canal) provided the Republic with seven doges, and the paintings, friezes and frescos by late 18th-century artists such as Jacopo Guarana and Gian Battista Canal glorify their achievements. In the rooms off the main salone, which in typical Venetian fashion runs the length of the building, the neo-classical influence already makes itself felt. Here, too, are the dusty display cases that serve the museum's other function: to chronicle Venetian 18th-century dress. An *andrienne* dress with bustles so horizontal you could rest a cup and saucer on them, antique lace and silk stockings, a whalebone corset – it's a patchy but charming collection, with a library.

San Cassiano

San Polo, campo San Cassiano (041 721 408). Vaporetto San Stae. **Open** 9am-noon Tue-Sat. **Map** p305 C3.
This church has a singularly dull exterior and a heavily decorated interior, with a striking ceiling (freshly restored) by the Tiepolesque painter Constantino

Cedini. It contains three major Tintorettos in the chancel: *Crucifixion, Resurrection* and *Descent into Limbo*. The *Crucifixion* is particularly interesting for its viewpoint; as Ruskin puts it: 'The horizon is so low, that the spectator must fancy himself lying full length on the grass, or rather among the brambles and luxuriant weeds, of which the foreground is entirely composed.' In the background the soldiers' spears make a menacing forest against a stormy sky. Off the left aisle is a small chapel with coloured marbles and inlays of semi-precious stones. On the wall opposite the altar is a painting by Antonio Balestra, which at first glance looks like a dying saint surrounded by *putti*. On closer inspection it transpires that the chubby children are, in fact, hacking the man to death: the painting represents *The Martyrdom of St Cassian*, a teacher who was murdered by his pupils with their pens. This, of course, makes him the patron saint of schoolteachers.

San Giacomo dell'Orio

Santa Croce, campo San Giacomo dell'Orio (041 275 0462/www.chorus-ve.org). Vaporetto Riva di Biasio. **Open** 10am-5pm Mon-Sat; 1-5pm Sun. **Admission** €2 (*see also p61* Chorus). **No credit cards. Map** p304 C2.

Relief from baroque excesses at **San Zan Degolà**. *See p111.*

Campo San Giacomo dell'Orio (St James of the wolf, the laurel tree, the rio or the Orio family – take your pick) has a pleasantly downbeat feel, with its trees, bars and children. It's dominated by the church with its plump apses and stocky 13th-century campanile. As with most older Venetian churches, the main entrance faces the canal rather than the campo. The interior is a fascinating mix of architectural and decorative styles. Most of the columns have 12th- or 13th-century Veneto-Byzantine capitals ; one has a sixth-century flowered capital and one is a solid piece of smooth *verde antico* marble, perhaps from a Roman temple sacked during the Fourth Crusade. Note, too, the fine 14th-century ship's-keel roof. The Sacrestia Nuova, in the right transept, was built in 1903 on the site of the Scuola del Sacramento. This was the original home of the five gilded compartments on the ceiling with paintings by Veronese: an *Allegory of the Faith* surrounded by four *Doctors of the Church.* Among paintings in the room is *St John the Baptist Preaching* by Francesco Bassano, which includes a portrait of Titian (in the red hat).

Behind the high altar is a *Madonna and Four Saints* by Lorenzo Lotto, one of his last Venetian paintings. There is a good work by Giovanni Bonconsiglio at the end of the left aisle, *St Lawrence, St Sebastian and St Roch*; St Sebastian is conventionally untroubled by his arrow, but St Roch's plague sore has an anatomical precision that is quite unsettling; the saint is without his usual sore-licking dog. The third of these saints, St Lawrence, also has a chapel all to himself in the left transept, with a central altarpiece by Veronese and two fine early

works by Palma il Giovane. As you leave, have a look at the curious painting to the left of the main door, a naïve 18th-century work by Gaetano Zompini, showing a propaganda miracle involving a Jewish scribe who attempted to profane the body of the Virgin on its way to the sepulchre. His hands were promptly lopped off by divine intervention; they can be seen sticking to the coffin.

San Simeone Profeta
Santa Croce, campo San Simeone Profeta (041 718 921). Vaporetto Ferrovia. **Open** 8am-noon, 5-6.30pm Mon-Sat. **Map** p304 B1-2.
More commonly known as San Simeone Grande, this small church of possibly tenth-century foundation underwent numerous alterations in the 18th century. The interior preserves its ancient columns with Byzantine capitals. To the left of the entrance is Tintoretto's *Last Supper*, with the priest who commissioned the painting standing to one side, a spectral figure in glowing white robes. The other major work is the stark, powerful statue of a recumbent St Simeon, with an inscription dated 1317 attributing it to an otherwise unknown Marco Romano. The prophet is 'represented in death; the mouth partly open, the lips thin and sharp, the teeth carefully sculptured beneath; the face full of quietness and majesty, though very ghastly', as Ruskin puts it.

San Stae
Santa Croce, campo San Stae (041 275 0462/www. chorus-ve.org). Vaporetto San Stae. **Open** 10am-5pm Mon-Sat; 1-5pm Sun. **Admission** €2 (*see also p61* Chorus). **No credit cards. Map** p305 B3.

Stae is the Venetian version of Eustachio or Eustace, a martyr saint who was converted to Christianity by the vision of a stag with a crucifix between his antlers (St Hubert had a similar experience). This church on the Grand Canal has a dramatic late baroque façade (1709) by Swiss-born architect Domenico Rossi. The form is essentially Palladian but enlivened by a number of vibrant sculptures, some apparently on the point of leaping straight out of the façade. Venice's last great blaze of artistic glory came in the 18th century, and the interior is a temple to this swansong. On the side walls of the chancel, all the leading painters operating in Venice in 1722 were asked to pick an apostle, any apostle. The finest of these are: Tiepolo's *Martyrdom of St Bartholomew* (left wall, lower row); Sebastiano Ricci's *Liberation of St Peter*, perhaps his best work (right wall, lower row); Pellegrini's *Martyrdom of St Andrew*; and Piazzetta's *Martyrdom of St James*, a disturbingly realistic work showing the saint as a confused old man in the hands of a loutish youth.

Santa Maria Mater Domini

Santa Croce, campo Santa Maria Mater Domini (041 721 408). Vaporetto San Stae. **Open** 10am-noon Tue-Fri. **Map** p304 C2.

This church, recently restored by the Venice in Peril fund, is set just off the campo of the same name, which has a number of fine *palazzi*. It was built in the first half of the 16th century to a project by either Giovanni Buora or Maurizio Codussi. The façade is attributed to Jacopo Sansovino; the harmonious Renaissance interior alternates grey stone with white marble. The *Vision of St Christine* on the second altar on the right is by Vincenzo Catena, a spice merchant who seems to have painted in his spare time. St Christine was rescued by angels after being thrown into Lake Bolsena with a millstone tied round her neck; in the painting she adores the Risen Christ, while angels hold up the millstone for her. In the left transept hangs *The Invention of the Cross*, a youthful work by Tintoretto.

San Zan Degolà (San Giovanni Decollato)

Santa Croce, campo San Giovanni Decollato (041 524 0672). Vaporetto Riva di Biasio. **Open** 10am-noon Mon-Sat. **Map** p304 B2.

The church of Headless Saint John, or San Zan Degolà in Venetian dialect, stands in a quiet campo near the Fondaco dei Turchi; it's a good building to visit if you want a relief from baroque excesses and ecclesiastical clutter. It was restored and reopened in 1994 after being closed for nearly 20 years and preserves much of its original 11th-century appearance. The interior has Greek columns with Byzantine capitals supporting ogival arches, and an attractive ship's-keel roof.

During the restoration a splendidly heroic 14th-century fresco of *St Michael the Archangel* came to light in the right apse. The left apse has some of the earliest frescos in Venice, Veneto-Byzantine works of the early 13th century.

From the Frari to piazzale Roma

At the heart of the western side of the two *sestieri* lies the great Gothic bulk of **Santa Maria Gloriosa dei Frari** (*see* **I Frari**, *p113*), with its 70-metre (230-foot) campanile, matched by the Renaissance magnificence of the **church** and **Scuola di San Rocco**. These buildings contain perhaps the greatest concentration of innovative and influential works of art in the city outside piazza San Marco and the Accademia (*see p122*).

But there's more to it than just art: the monastery buildings of the Frari contain the State Archives, a monument to the Venetian reluctance ever to throw anything away. In 300 rooms, about 15 million volumes and files are conserved, relating to all aspects of Venetian history, starting from the year 883. It is said that only the Spanish archives at Simancas approach them in scope and detail. Faced with this daunting wealth of information, ranging from ambassadors' dispatches on foreign courts to spies' reports on noblemen's non-regulation cloaks, grown historians have been reduced to quivering wrecks.

Beyond the archives is the **Scuola di San Giovanni Evangelista**, one of the six *scuole grandi* (*see p60*) that played such an important part in the complex Venetian system of social checks and balances. The courtyard is protected by a screen with a magnificent eagle pediment and a frieze of leaf-sprays by Pietro Lombardo, while the building itself contains a double staircase by Maurizio Codussi.

North of here runs rio Marin, a canal with *fondamente* on both sides, lined by some fine buildings; these include the late 16th-century **Palazzo Soranzo Capello**, with a small garden (to the rear) that figures in D'Annunzio's torrid novel *Il Fuoco* and Henry James' more restrained *The Aspern Papers*, and the 17th-century **Palazzo Gradenigo**, the garden of which was once large enough to host bullfights.

South-west of the Frari is the quiet square of **San Tomà**, with a church on one side and the **Scuola dei Caleghri** (cobblers) opposite; the *scuola* (now a library) has a protective mantle-spreading Madonna over the door and above it a relief by Pietro Lombardo of *St Mark Healing the Cobbler Annanius*, who became bishop of Alexandria and subsequently the patron saint of shoemakers. Directly south of here is campo **San Pantalon**; its church has an extraordinary Hollywood-rococo interior.

Just off the square of San Tomà is Palazzo Centani, the birth place of Carlo Goldoni, the prolific Venetian playwright (*see p112*

Sightseeing

Literary locations Goldoni

Given the Venetian love of spectacle and gift for conversation, it is no surprise that the city's one undisputed writer of genius should have been a playwright.

Carlo Goldoni (1707-93) began by writing *intermezzi*, sketches which were set to music. Then, for the Teatro San Samuele, he started producing tragicomedies. It soon became clear, however, that comedy was his natural medium.

As Goldoni embarked on his career, the Venetian stage was dominated by the *Commedia dell'arte* tradition, whose stock characters had grown tired and stultified. The playwright knew better than to attempt any brusque changes with a Venetian audience; his move away from clichés was gradual. In the early plays – such as the eternally popular *Servant of Two Masters* – he kept stock figures such as Arlecchino (Harlequin) and Pantaleone (Pantaloon) but transformed them into more rounded characters.

Naturally, actors used to improvising around a skeleton plot were unhappy at having to learn lines. But audiences were enthusiastic about the new offerings, and Goldoni soon signed a contract with the Teatro Sant'Angelo.

In his velvet revolution, Goldoni gradually changed Pantaleone from an old buffoon into a wise merchant, a mouthpiece for Venetian pragmatism, and filled his stages with everyday figures speaking a vigorous dialect.

But there's nothing like success to stir up resentment, and soon Goldoni was under attack from less talented but vociferous rivals. To confound his critics, Goldoni staged an unprecedented publicity stunt: in 1750 he announced his intention to produce 16 new plays in a single season.

He pulled it off, and even managed a couple of masterpieces: *La bottega del caffè* (The Coffee Shop) and *Il bugiardo* (The Liar). There was to be no resting on laurels, however, in the competitive world of Venetian theatre. He continued to furnish plays at breakneck speed, providing the same bewildering mixture of mediocre hackwork alongside works of sheer genius, such as *La locandiera* (The Innkeeper, 1753), which contains one of the greatest female roles in the whole of Italian theatre.

In a new contract in 1753 with the Teatro San Luca, Goldoni undertook to provide a more reasonable eight comedies a year. Further vitriolic broadsides from conservative writer, Carlo Gozzi (author of such fables as *Turandot*), who denounced him for his sordid realism and his disrespect towards the aristocracy, forced Goldoni to follow fashion for a while. But alongside the exotic dramas set in a fabulous East, he wrote some of his best dialect comedies, including *Le baruffe chiozzotte*, about quarrelling fishwives in Chioggia (*see p132*).

The never-ending bitterness of Venetian theatrical rivalry eventually wore him down, and Goldoni accepted an offer of work in Paris, where he had already won the sincere acclaim of no less a writer than Voltaire. In 1762 he bade farewell to Venice, only to find on his arrival at the Comédie Italienne that the Italian actors there were still rigidly set in the ways of the *Commedia dell'arte*. French audiences showed a decided lack of enthusiasm for innovations. Before long, Goldoni was supporting himself by teaching Italian at court.

Disillusioned, the playwright turned to reminiscing instead: between 1784 and 1787 he wrote the three volumes of his *Mémoires*, a fascinating if not entirely reliable account of his life. When his small state pension was suppressed after the Revolution, he fell into severe penury. He died on 6 February 1793, just one day before the National Assembly voted to restore his pension in recognition of 'the reformation of the theatre he had carried out with such success in Italy'.

Literary locations: Goldoni). The house, which has an attractive Gothic courtyard with a fine well-head and staircase, contains a small museum and library (**Casa Goldoni**) devoted to the writer and to Venetian theatre.

Heading west from the Frari, the route leads past the church and *scuola* of San Rocco, treasure-houses for Tintoretto lovers, and ends up in a fairly dull area of 19th-century housing, which replaced medieval gardens and orchards. At the edge of this stands the baroque church of **San Nicolò dei Tolentini**; the adjoining former monastery houses part of the Venice University Architecture Institute (*see p31* **The shock of the new**).

If you're looking for a picnic spot, you could do better than the rather forlorn **Giardino Papadopoli**, a small park with Grand Canal views that stands on the site of the church and convent of Santa Croce. The name survives as that of the sestiere, but the church is one of many suppressed by the French at the beginning of the 19th century.

All that remains of Santa Croce is a crenellated wall next to a hotel on the Grand Canal. The garden was much larger until the rio Novo was cut in 1932 and 1933 to provide faster access from the new car park to the St Mark's area. The decision was much contested at the time; as the canal had to be closed to regular waterborne traffic in the early 1990s owing to subsidence in the adjacent buildings, it would seem that the protesters had a point.

Beyond the garden there is little but the carbon-monoxide kingdom of piazzale Roma and the multi-storey car parks.

One last curiosity is the complex of bridges across the rio Novo known as Tre Ponti (three bridges); there are, in fact, five interlocking bridges (*see p99* **Take it to the bridge**).

Casa di Carlo Goldoni e Biblioteca di Studi Teatrali

San Polo 2794, calle dei Nomboli (041 244 0317).
Vaporetto San Tomà. **Open** *Apr-Oct* 10am-5pm
Mon-Sat. *Nov-Mar* 10am-4pm Mon-Sat. **Admission**
€2.50; €1.50 concessions (*see also p61* Musei Civici
Veneziani). **No credit cards. Map** p304-5 B2-3.
This museum is really only for specialists, although the attractive Gothic courtyard, with its carved well-head and staircase is worth seeing. On the first floor there are reproductions of prints based on Goldoni's works and a few 18th-century paintings; the best item is a splendid 18th-century miniature theatre complete with puppets of *Commedia dell'arte* figures, standing in for the ones that Goldoni remembered so fondly from his childhood. The library on the upper floor has theatrical texts, studies and original manuscripts.

I Frari

San Polo, campo dei Frari (041 522 2637).
Vaporetto San Tomà. **Open** 9am-6pm Mon-Sat;
1-6pm Sun. **Admission** €2 (*see also p61* Chorus).
Audio-guides €1.55 individual; €2.58 for 2 people.
No credit cards. Map p304 C2.
A gloomy Gothic barn, the brick house of God known officially as Santa Maria Gloriosa dei Frari may not be the most elegant church in Venice, but it is certainly one of the city's most significant artistic storehouses after the Accademia and the Scuola di San Rocco. The Franciscans were granted the land in about 1250 and they completed a first church in 1338. At this point they changed their minds and started work on a larger building, facing the opposite way, which was finally completed just over a century later. The church is 98m (320ft) long, 48m (158ft) wide at the transept and 28m (92ft) high – just slightly smaller than Santi Giovanni e Paolo (*see p87*) – and has the second-highest campanile in the

city. And while the Frari may not have as many tombs of dead doges as its Dominican rival, it undoubtedly has the artistic edge.

This is one church where the entrance fee is not a recent imposition; tourists have been paying to get into the Frari for over a century. Entrance is via the left transept, but it's best to begin your visit from the back, where you can enjoy the long view of the building, with Titian's *Assumption* above the high altar acting as a focus.

Right aisle

In the second bay, on the spot where Titian is believed to be buried (the only victim of the 1575-6 plague who was allowed a city burial), is a loud *Monument to Titian*, commissioned nearly 300 years after his death by the Emperor of Austria. On the third altar is a finer memorial, Alessandro Vittoria's statue of *St Jerome*, generally believed to be a portrait of his painter friend.

Right transept

To the right of the sacristy door is the tomb of the Blessed Pacifico (a companion of St Francis) attributed to Nanni di Bartolo and Michele da Firenze (1437); the sarcophagus is surrounded by a splendidly carved canopy in the florid Gothic style. The door itself is framed by Lorenzo Bregno's tomb of Benedetto Pesaro, a Venetian general who died in Corfu. To the left of the door is the first equestrian statue in Venice, the monument to Paolo Savelli (died 1405). The third chapel on the right side of this transept has an altarpiece by Bartolomeo Vivarini, in its original frame, while the Florentine Chapel, next to the chancel, contains the only work by Donatello in the city: a striking wooden statue of a stark, emaciated St John the Baptist.

Sacristy

Commissioned by the Pesaro family, this contains one of Giovanni Bellini's greatest paintings: the *Madonna and Child with Saints Nicholas, Peter, Benedict and Mark* (1488), still in its original frame. 'It seems painted with molten gems, which have been clarified by time,' wrote Henry James, his eye, as ever, firmly on the prose structure, 'and it is as solemn as it is gorgeous and as simple as it is deep.' Also in the sacristy is a fine Renaissance tabernacle, possibly by Tullio Lombardo, for a reliquary holding a sample Christ's blood.

Chancel

The high altar is dominated by Titian's *Assumption*, a visionary work that seems to open the church up to the heavens. In the golden haze encircling God the Father, there may be a reminiscence of the mosaic tradition of Venice, as found in Bellini's altarpieces. The upward soaring movement of the painting may owe something to the Gothic architecture of the building, but the drama and grandeur of the work essentially herald the baroque.

On the right wall of the chancel is the monument to Francesco Foscari, the saddest doge of all. The story of his forced resignation and death from

Sightseeing

heartbreak (1547) after the exile of his son Jacopo is recounted in Byron's *The Two Foscari*, which was turned into a particularly gloomy opera by Verdi. The left wall boasts one of the finest Renaissance tombs in Venice, the monument to Doge Niccolò Tron, by Antonio Rizzo (1473). This is the first ducal tomb in which the subject is upright; he sports a magnificent bushy beard grown as a sign of perpetual mourning after the death of a favourite son.

Monks' choir
In the centre of the nave (which is an unusual position in Italy) stands the choir, with wooden stalls carved by Marco Cozzi (1468), inlaid with superb intarsia decoration. The choir screen is a mixture of Gothic work by Bartolomeo Bon and Renaissance elements by the Lombardi.

Left transept
In the third chapel, with an altarpiece by Bartolomeo Vivarini and Marco Basaiti, a slab on the floor marks the grave of composer Claudio Monteverdi. The Corner chapel, at the end, contains a mannered statue of *St John the Baptist* by Sansovino; this sensitively wistful figure could hardly be more different from Donatello's work of a century earlier.

Left aisle
Another magnificent Titian hangs to the left of the side door: the *Madonna di Ca' Pesaro*. This work was commissioned by Bishop Jacopo Pesaro in 1519 and celebrates victory in a naval expedition against the Turks led by the bellicose cleric in 1502. The bishop is kneeling and waiting for St Peter to introduce him and his family to the Madonna. Behind, an armoured warrior bearing a banner has Turkish prisoners in tow. This work revolutionised altar paintings in Venice. It wasn't just that Titian dared to move the Virgin from the centre of the composition to one side, using the splendid banner as a counterbalance; the real innovation was the rich humanity of the whole work, from the beautifully portrayed family (with the boy turning to stare straight at us) to the Christ child, so naturally active and alive, twisting away from his mother (said to be a portrait of Titian's own wife) to gaze at one of the clustered saints around him. The timeless 'sacred conversation' of Bellini's paintings here becomes animated, losing some of its sacredness but gaining in drama and realism.

The whole of the next bay, around the side door, is occupied by another piece of Pesaro propaganda – the mastodontic mausoleum of Doge Pesaro (died 1659), attributed to Longhena, with recently restored sculptures by Melchior Barthel of Dresden. Even the most ardent fans of the baroque have trouble defending this one, with its 'blackamoor' caryatides, bronze skeletons and posturing allegories; political incorrectness is the least of its faults. 'It seems impossible for false taste and base feeling to sink lower,' wrote Ruskin, and you can see his point.

The penultimate bay harbours a monument to Canova, carried out by his pupils in 1827, five years after his death, using a design of his own, intended

for the tomb of Titian. His body is buried in his native town of Possagno (*see p267*), but his heart is conserved in an urn inside the monument. The despondent winged lion has a distinct resemblance to the one in *The Wizard of Oz*.

San Nicolò da Tolentino
Santa Croce, campo dei Tolentini (041 710 806). Vaporetto Piazzale Roma. **Open** 9.30am-noon, 4-6pm Mon-Sat; 4-6pm Sun. **Map** p304 C1.
This church, usually known as I Tolentini, was planned by Scamozzi (1591-5). Its unfinished façade has a massive Corinthian portico added by Andrea Tirali (1706-14). The interior (most of which has been freshly restored) is a riot of baroque decoration, with lavish use of stucco and sprawling frescos. The most interesting paintings – as so often in the 17th century – are by out-of-towners. On the wall outside the chancel to the left is *St Jerome Succoured by an Angel*, by the Flemish artist Johann Liss, a work that anticipates the rococo exuberance of the Venetian 18th century. Outside the chapel in the left transept is *The Charity of St Lawrence* by the Genoese Bernardo Strozzi, in which the magnificently hoary old beggar in the foreground easily upstages the rather wimpish figure of the saint. In the chancel hangs an *Annunciation* by the prolific Neapolitan Luca Giordano and opposite is a splendidly theatrical monument to Francesco Morosini (a 17th-century patriarch of that name, not the doge) by Filippo Parodi (1678), with swirling angels drawing aside a marble curtain to reveal the patriarch lounging at ease on his tomb. In 1780 the priests of this church handed over all their silverware to a certain 'Romano', who claimed to have a secret new method for cleaning silver and jewellery. Guess what? He was never seen again.

San Pantalon
Santa Croce, campo San Pantalon (041 523 5893). Vaporetto San Tomà. **Open** 4-6pm Mon-Sat. **Map** p306 A2.
The dedicatee of this church is St Pantaleon, court physician to Emperor Galerius, who was arrested, tortured and finally beheaded during Diocletian's persecution of the Christians. The saint's story is depicted inside the church in one of the most extraordinary ceiling paintings in Italy – a huge illusionist work, painted on 40 canvases, by the Cecil B De Mille of the 17th century, Gian Antonio Fumiani. It took him 24 years to complete the task (1680-1704) and at the end of it all he fell with choreographic grace from the scaffolding to his death.

Veronese depicts the saint in less melodramatic fashion in the second chapel on the right, in what is possibly his last work, *St Pantaleon Healing a Child*. To the left of the chancel is the Chapel of the Holy Nail. The nail in question, supposedly from the Crucifixion, is preserved in a small but richly decorated Gothic altar. On the right wall is a fine *Coronation of the Virgin* by Antonio Vivarini and Giovanni d'Alemagna. Walking out of the church towards the canal, an alley to the left will take you

Titian's *Madonna* at the **Frari**. *See p113.*

Scuola Grande di San Rocco

San Polo 3054, campo San Rocco (041 523 4864/ www.sanrocco.it). Vaporetto San Tomà. **Open** *Apr-Oct* 9am-5.30pm daily. *Nov-Mar* 10am-4pm daily. **Admission** €5.50; €1.50 concessions. **Credit** AmEx, DC, MC, V. **Map** 304 C2.

The Archbrotherhood of St Roch was the richest of the six *scuole grandi* (*see p60*) in 15th-century Venice. Its members came from the top end of mercantile and professional classes. It was dedicated to Venice's other patron saint, the French plague-protector and dog-lover St Roch/Rock (San Rocco), whose body was brought here in 1485. The *scuola* operated out of rented accommodation for a number of years, but by the beginning of the 16th century, donations from the city's army of St Roch devotees allowed a permanent base to be commissioned.

The architecture, by Bartolomeo Bon and Scarpagnino, is far less impressive than the interior decoration, which was entrusted to Tintoretto in 1564 after a competition in which he stole a march on rivals Salviati, Zuccari and Veronese by presenting a finished painting rather than the required sketch. In three intensive sessions over the following 23 years, Tintoretto went on to make San Rocco his epic masterpiece, his *Divina commedia*. Fans and doubters alike should start here; the former will no doubt agree with John Ruskin that paintings such as the *Crucifixion* are 'beyond all analysis and above all praise', while the latter may well find their prejudices crumbling. True, the devotional intensity of his works can shade a touch too much into kitsch for the postmodern soul; but his feel for narrative structure is timeless.

To follow the development of Tintoretto's style, pick up the free explanatory leaflet and the audio guide and begin in the smaller upstairs hall – the Albergo. Here, filling the whole of the far wall, is the *Crucifixion* (1565), of which Henry James commented: 'It is one of the greatest things of art… there is everything in it.' More than anything it is the perfect integration of main plot and sub-plots that strikes the viewer; whereas most paintings are short stories, this is a novel. Tintoretto began work on the larger upstairs room in 1575, with Old Testament stories on the ceiling and a Life of Christ cycle around the walls, in which the man who possessed what Vasari referred to as 'the most extraordinary mind that the art of painting has produced' experimented relentlessly with form, lighting and colour. Below the canvases is a characterful series of late 17th-century wooden carvings, including a caricature of Tintoretto himself, just below and to the left of *The Agony in the Garden*. Finally, in the ground-floor hall – which the artist decorated between 1583 and 1587, when he was in his 60s – the paintings reach a visionary pitch that has to do with Tintoretto's audacious handling of light and the impressionistic economy of his brushstrokes. The *Annunciation*, with its domestic Mary surprised while sewing, and *Flight into Egypt*, with its verdant landscape, are among the painter's masterpieces. Admission is free on 16 August, the feast of St Roch.

into little campiello d'Angaran, where there is a carved roundel of a Byzantine emperor, which experts believe possibly dates from the tenth century. Returning to the campo, a slab in the wall by the canal indicates the minimum length allowed for the sale of various types of fish.

San Rocco

San Polo, campo San Rocco (041 523 4864). *Vaporetto San Tomà.* **Open** *Apr-Oct* 8am-12.30pm, 3-5pm daily. *Nov-Mar* 8am-12.30pm Mon-Fri; 8am-12.30pm, 2-4pm Sat, Sun. **Map** p304 C2.

If you have toured the school of San Rocco and are in the mood for more Tintorettos (perhaps after a shot of whisky or a lie-down), look no further. Built in Venetian Renaissance style by Bartolomeo Bon from 1489 to 1508 but radically altered by Giovanni Scalfarotto in 1725, the church has paintings by Tintoretto, or his school, on either side of the entrance door, between the first and second altar on the right, and on either side of the chancel. Nearly all are connected with the life of St Roch; the best is probably *St Roch Cures the Plague Victims* (chancel, lower right). The altar paintings are all difficult to see; they're high up and not very well lit. Even if you could get a good view, you might not be much the wiser: even Ruskin, Tintoretto's greatest fan, was completely baffled as to their subject matter.

Dorsoduro

Laid back to the east, hard to the west, with a nightlife mecca in between.

Dorsoduro means 'hard back'. But the eastern portion of the *sestiere* around the church of the Salute, with its air of cool, collected wealth, is more laid back than hard back, while the dockland area of Santa Marta and San Nicolò at the far western end is simply hard... or as hard as you get in Venice. Between these two social extremes is the large bustling square of campo Santa Margherita, where Venetians, tourists and students mingle and inject life – including the nocturnal variety – into the area.

Western Dorsoduro

This western corner of the city was one of the earliest to be settled. The church of San Nicolò was founded as early as the seventh century. The full name of the church is **San Nicolò dei Mendicoli** – 'of the beggars'. The locals have never been in the top income bracket and in the past were mostly fishermen or salt-pan workers. The area gave its name to one of two factions into which the Venetian proletariat was once divided: the *nicolotti*. The *nicolotti* were proud enough to maintain a certain form of

local autonomy under a figure known as the Gastaldo, who, after his election, would be received with honours by the doge.

The area is still noticeably less sleek than central Venice, although fishing was superseded as a source of employment by the port long ago and subsequently by the Santa Marta cotton mill – now converted for use by the Istituto Universitario di Architettura di Venezia. Massive redevelopment schemes are under way for much of this downbeat district, with plans to revitalise it in a vast University-meets-London-Docklands-style project, to a design by the late Catalan architect Enric Miralles Moya. The plans include an auditorium, conference hall, restaurant and huge centralised university library, thus providing Venice University with something approaching a genuine campus. *See also p31* **The shock of the new**.

Moving eastwards, the atmosphere remains unpretentious around the churches of **Angelo Raffaele** and **San Sebastiano**, with its splendid decoration by Paolo Veronese. Northwards from here, on the rio di Santa

Local *nicolotti* fought rival *castellani* on the **ponte dei Pugni**. *See p120.*

Most-photographed grocer's. *See p120.*

Margherita, are some rather grander *palazzi*, including **Palazzo Ariani**, with its magnificent Gothic tracery, almost oriental in its intricacy, and, further up, the grand **Palazzo Zenobio**, now an Armenian school and institute, containing early Tiepolo frescos (not accessible to the public) and giving on to an elaborate garden where plays are sometimes performed in the summer.

Angelo Raffaele

Campo Angelo Raffaele (041 522 8548). Vaporetto San Basilio. Closed for restoration as this guide went to press, due to reopen late 2003. **Map** p306 B1.

This is one of the eight churches in Venice traditionally founded by St Magnus in the eighth century, although the present free-standing building – one of only two churches in the city that you can walk all the way around – dates from the 17th century. The unusually high ceiling has a lively fresco by Gaspare Diziani of *St Michael Driving out Lucifer*, with Lucifer apparently tumbling out of the heavy stucco frame into the church. There are matching Last Suppers on either side of the organ (by Bonifacio de' Pitati on the left and a follower of Titian on the right). But the real jewels of the church are on the organ loft, whose five compartments, painted by Giovanni Antonio Guardi (or perhaps his brother Francesco), recount the story of *Tobias and the Angel* (1750-3). They are works of dazzling luminosity, quite unlike anything else done in Venice at the time and with something pre-Impressionist about them. The paintings and the story they recount play a significant role in Sally Vickers' novel *Miss Garnet's Angel* (2000).

Street wise

See also **Street wise** *in chapter* **Directory**.
Baccalà (fondamenta del)
'Cod'; dried cod was stored here (*see also* p260 **The joy of cod**).
Incurabili (ponte, rio degli)
A hospital of this discouraging name was founded here in 1522; Volpone is banished here at the end of Ben Jonson's homonymous play.
Malcanton (fondamenta, rio del)
'Bad corner'; history relates that the bishop of Castello, calling to demand his tithe from the parish priest of San Pantalon, was set upon by the mutinous parishioners and murdered; this is said to have been the origin of the enmity between the *castellani* and the *nicolotti*.
Maravegie (ponte delle)
Legend recounts that the 'Bridge of Wonders' was so called because it was miraculously built overnight by unknown hands; boring chronicles relate that a family of this name lived here.
Pugni (ponte dei)
One of several bridges in the city where organised punch-ups were tolerated between the *castellani* and the *nicolotti*.
Rimorchianti (campiello, calle dei)
Sailors of tug boats (*rimorchi*) lived here.
Toletta (calle, rio, ponte della)
A small *tola* ('plank'; *tavola* in Italian) served as a bridge here for years.
Turchete (ponte, calle, fondamenta delle)
A colony of Turkish women were imprisoned here, awaiting conversion to Christianity.

San Nicolò dei Mendicoli

Campo San Nicolò (041 275 0382). Vaporetto San Basilio or Santa Marta. Closed for restoration as this guide went to press; due to re-open autumn 2003. **Map** off p306 B1.

San Nicolò is one of the few Venetian churches to have maintained its 13th-century Veneto-Byzantine structure, despite numerous rearrangements and refurbishings. Between 1971 and 1977 the church underwent a thorough restoration by the Venice in Peril Fund, and traces of the original foundations were uncovered, confirming the theory that dates the church's origins to the seventh century. Film buffs will recognise this as the church from Nicolas Roeg's dwarf-in-Venice movie *Don't Look Now*. The 15th-century loggia at the front is one of only two extant examples of a once-common architectural feature (the other is on the equally ancient San Giacomo di Rialto, *see p103*); it originally served as a shelter for the homeless. The interior contains no major works of art, but a marvellous mishmash of architectural and decorative styles combines to create an effect of cluttered charm. The structure is that of a 12th-century basilica, with two colonnades of stocky columns topped by 14th-century capitals. Above are gilded 16th-century statues of the apostles. The paintings are mainly 17th century. There are also some fine wooden sculptures, including a large statue of San Nicolò by the Bon studio. As this guide went to press, the church was being restored.

In the small campo outside the church is a column with a diminutive winged lion. Across the canal is the former convent of the Terese, in the process of being converted to an extension of the Architecture University. Just around the corner from the church there was, until a few years ago, a house full of monkeys. To the dismay of his neighbours, the retired docker who lived here decided to turn his house and narrow garden into a private zoo. On his death this mini-Longleat was closed, and new homes were found for the monkeys.

San Sebastiano

Fondamenta di San Sebastiano (041 275 0642/ www.chorus-ve.org). Vaporetto San Basilio. **Open** 10am-5pm Mon-Sat; 1-5pm Sun. **Admission** €2 (*see also p61* Chorus). **No credit cards. Map** p306 B1. This contains perhaps the most brilliantly colourful church interior in Venice – all the work of one man, Paolo Veronese. One of Veronese's earliest commissions in Venice (in 1555) was *The Coronation of the Virgin* and the four panels of the Evangelists in the sacristy (open 10am-5pm Sat, 1-5pm Sun). From then on there was just no stopping him: between 1556 and 1565 he painted three large ceiling paintings for the nave of the church, frescos along the upper parts of the walls, organ shutters, huge narrative canvases for the chancel, and the painting on the high altar. The ceiling paintings depict scenes from the life of Esther (*Esther Taken to Ahasuerus, Esther Crowned Queen by Ahasuerus* and *The Triumph of Mordecai*). Esther was considered as a forerunner of the Virgin, interceding for Jews in the same way that the Virgin interceded for Christians – or (more pertinently) for Venice. These works are full of sumptuous pageantry: no painter gets more

Glossary

Amphitheatre (*ancient*) open-air oval-shaped theatre.
Apse large recess at the high-altar end of a church.
Baldachin canopy supported by columns.
Barrel vault a ceiling with arches shaped like half-barrels.
Baroque artistic period from the 17th-18th century, in which the decorative element became increasingly florid, culminating in the Rococo (*qv*).
Basilica ancient Roman rectangular public building; rectangular Christian church.
Byzantine Christian artistic and architectural style drawing on ancient models developed in the 4th century in the Eastern empire (capital Byzantium/Constantinople/Istanbul) and developed through the Middle Ages.
Campanile bell tower.
Campo Venetian for piazza or square.
Capital head of a column, generally decorated according to classical orders (*qv*).
Caryatid column carved in female shape.
Chiaroscuro painting or drawing technique using no colours, but shades of black, white and grey.
Cloister exterior courtyard surrounded on all sides by a covered walkway.
Coffered ceiling decorated with sunken square or polygonal panels.
Cupola dome-shaped roof or ceiling.

Decumanus (*ancient*) main road, usually running east-west.
Entablature section above a column or row of columns including the frieze and cornice.
Ex-voto an offering given to fulfil a vow; often a small model in silver of the limb/ organ/loved one cured as a result of prayer.
Fan vault vault formed of concave semi-cones, meeting at the apex; from beneath, gives the appearance of four backwards-leaning fans meeting.
Festoon painted or carved swag or swathe decorated with fruit and/or flowers.
Fresco painting technique in which pigment is applied to wet plaster.
Gothic architectural and artistic style of the late Middle Ages (from the 12th century), of soaring, pointed arches.
Greek cross (church) in the shape of a cross with arms of equal length.
Grisailles painting in shades of grey to mimic sculpture.
Iconostasis rood screen; screen in Eastern-rite churches separating nave from the sanctuary.
Intarsia form of mosaic made from pieces of different-coloured wood; also know as **intaglio**.
Latin cross (church) in the shape of a cross with one arm longer than the other.
Loggia gallery open on one side.

splendidly shimmering effects out of clothing, which is probably why Veronese's nude St Sebastians are the least striking figures in the compositions. These huge canvases, on the side walls of the chancel, depict, on the right, *The Martyrdom of St Sebastian* (who was in fact cudgelled to death – the arrows were just a first attempt), and, on the left, *St Sebastian Encouraging St Mark and St Marcellan* – two other Roman martyrs. Other paintings in the church include *St Nicholas*, a late painting by Titian, in the first altar on the right. Paolo Veronese and his brother Benedetto are buried here.

Campo Santa Margherita to the Accademia

Campo Santa Margherita is the pulsing heart of Dorsoduro. A long, irregular-shaped campo with churches at both ends, it is lively by day and night. During the morning there is a market, with a continual bustle of shopping housewives, hurrying students and dawdling pigeons; in the evening the various bars and cafés attract Venice's under-30s, to the continual irritation of the local residents. If Venice can be said to have a nightlife hub, this is it (*see chapter* **Nightlife**).

There are several ancient *palazzi* around the square, with Byzantine and Gothic features. In the middle is the isolated Scuola dei Varoteri, the School of the Tanners. At the north end is the former church of Santa Margherita, long used as a cinema and now beautifully restored as a conference hall for the university; the interior (sneak in the back for a quick gawp if there's a conference going on) is so unashamedly theatrical it's difficult to imagine how it was ever used for religious purposes. St Margaret's dragon features on the campanile, and the sculpted saint also stands triumphant on the beast between the windows of a house at the north end of the square; a miraculous escape from the dragon's guts for some reason makes her the patron saint of pregnant women. At the other end of the square are the **Scuola dei Carmini** and the church of the **Carmini**.

Sightseeing

Lunette semi-circular surface, usually above a window or door.
Mannerism High Renaissance style of the late 16th century; characterised in painting by elongated, contorted human figures.
Monoforate with one opening (cf polyforate), usually used of windows.
Narthex enclosed porch in front of a church.
Nave main body of a church; the longest section of a Latin cross church (*qv*).
Ogival (of arches, windows etc) curving in to a point at the top.
Opus sectile pavement made of (usually) geometrically-shaped marble slabs.
Orders classical rules governing the proportions of columns, their entablatures (*qv*) and their capitals (*qv*), the most common being the less ornate Doric, the curlicue Ionic and the Corinthian in which capitals are decorated with acanthus leaves.
Palazzo large and/or important building (not necessarily a palace).
Pendentives four concave triangular sections on top of piers supporting a dome.
Piano nobile- showiest floor of a palazzo (*qv*), containing mainly reception rooms with very high ceilings.
Pilaster column-shaped projection from a wall.
Polyforate with more than one opening (cf monoforate).

Polyptych painting composed of several panels (cf dyptych with two panels and triptych with three).
Porphyry hard igneous rock ranging from dark green to dark purple; this latter was most commonly used, and known as *rosso antico*.
Presbytery the part of a church containing the high altar.
Reredos decorated wall or screen behind an altar.
Rococo highly decorative style fashionable in the 18th century.
Romanesque architectural style of the early Middle Ages (c500 to 1200), drawing on Roman and Byzantine (*qv*) influences.
Rusticated large masonry blocks with deep joints between them used to face buildings or monuments.
Sarcophagus (*ancient*) stone or marble coffin.
Stele upright slab of stone with commemorative inscription and/or decorative relief scupture.
Transept shorter, transversal arms of a Latin cross church (*qv*).
Trilobate with three arches, used of windows, doors or ceilings .
Triumphal arch arch in front of an apse (*qv*), usually over the high altar.
Trompe l'oeil - decorative painting effect to make surface appear three-dimensional.

Gondolas in the making at the **Squero**.

Leaving the campo by the southern end you reach the picturesque rio di San Barnaba. At the eastern end of the fondamenta is the entrance to the swaggering Longhena palazzo of **Ca' Rezzonico**, home to the Museum of 18th-Century Venice.

The middle of the three bridges across the canal is **ponte dei Pugni**, with white marble footprints indicating that this was one of the bridges where punch-ups were held between the rival factions of the *nicolotti*, from the western quarters of the city, and the *castellani*, from the east. These brawls, often extremely violent, were tolerated by the authorities, who saw them as a chance for the working classes to let off steam in a way that was not disruptive to the state. However, after a particularly bloody fray, the Council of Ten banned them in 1705.

Past the most photographed greengrocer's in the world (a barge moored in the canal), is campo San Barnaba. The church of **San Barnaba** has nothing special about it except a picturesque 14th-century campanile and a *Holy Family* boldly attributed to Veronese; however, the campo is a good place in which to sit outside a bar and watch the world go by. San Barnaba has never been grand. In the final years of the Republic it was where penniless patricians used to end up, since apartments were provided here

by the state for their use. The *barnabotti*, as they were known, could make a few *zecchini* by peddling their votes in the Maggior Consiglio (*see p76* **Checks and balances**); otherwise they hung around in their tattered silk, muttering (after 1789) subversive comments about Liberty, Fraternity and Equality.

Katharine Hepburn fell into a nearby canal in the film *Midsummer Madness*, causing permanent damage to her eyesight. In *Indiana Jones and the Last Crusade*, on the other hand, Harrison Ford entered the church (which became a library in the film) and after contending with most of Venice's rat population, emerged from a manhole on to the pavement outside.

From the campo the busy route towards the Accademia crosses rio San Trovaso, a canal with twin *fondamente* lined by fine Gothic and Renaissance palaces housing secondary schools and university buildings. Off to the right is the church of **San Trovaso**, with two identical façades, one on to the canal and one on to its own campo. Backing on to the campo is a picturesque *squero*, one of the few remaining yards where gondolas are made.

The **Accademia**, Venice's art school and most important picture gallery, is just a short walk from here, situated at the foot of the reconstructed wooden bridge of the same name over the Grand Canal.

Ca' Rezzonico (Museo del Settecento Veneziano)

Dorsoduro 3136, fondamenta Rezzonico (041 241 0100). Vaporetto Ca' Rezzonico. **Open** *Apr-Oct* 10am-6pm Mon, Wed-Sun. *Nov-Mar* 10am-5pm Mon, Wed-Sun. **Admission** €6.50; €4-€4.50 concessions (*see also p61* Musei Civici Veneziani). **No credit cards. Map** p306 A2.

The Museum of 18th-Century Venice was re-opened in July 2001 after careful restoration and is now a gleaming showcase dedicated to the art of the twilight years of the Republic, complete with book-shop and café. But for most visitors the paintings on display here will appear less impressive than the fixed decoration that is the palazzo itself, an impos-ing Grand Canal affair (it's on the corner between fondamenta Rezzonico and the Canal) designed by Baldassare Longhena for the Bon family in 1667. Bon ambitions exceeded Bon means, and the unfin-ished palace was sold on to the Rezzonico family – a dynasty of rich Genoese bankers who had bought their way into Venice's register of nobility, the *Libro d'Oro*. The Rezzonicos' bid for stardom was crowned in 1758 by two events: the election of Carlo Rezzonico as Pope Clement XIII, and the marriage of Ludovico Rezzonico into one of Venice's most ancient noble families, the Savorgnan. Giambattista Tiepolo was called upon to celebrate the marriage on the ceiling of the *sala del trono* and he replied with a composition so tumbling and playful that it's easy to forget that this is all about money. Giovanni Battista Crosato's over-the-top ceiling frescos in the ballroom have aged less well but, together with the Murano chandeliers and the intricately carved furniture by Andrea Brustolon, they provide an accurate record of the lifestyles of the rich and famous at the time. There are historical canvases by Giovanni Battista Piazzetta and Antonio Diziani, plus other gems: a series of detached frescos of pulcinellas (characters from Italian folk theatre), recently restored, from the Tiepolo family villa in Zianigo by Giambattista's son Giandomenico, capture the leisured melancholy of the moneyed classes as La Serenissima went into terminal decline. There are some good genre paintings by Pietro Longhi, whom Michael Levey calls 'the Jane Austen of Venetian art', and a series of smooth pastel portraits by Rosalba Carriera, a female 'prodigy' who was kept busy by English travellers eager to bring back a souvenir of their Grand Tour. On the third floor is the Egidio Martini picture gallery, a collection of mainly Venetian works assembled by a scholar and donated to the city, and a reconstruction of an 18th-century city pharmacy, with fine majolica vases.

Santa Maria dei Carmini

Campo dei Carmini (041 522 6553). Vaporetto Ca' Rezzonico or San Basilio. Closed indefinitely for restoration as this guide went to press. **Map** p306 A1.
The church officially called Santa Maria del Carmelo has a tall campanile topped by a statue of the Virgin, a frequent target for lightning. It is richly decorated inside, with 17th-century gilt wooden statues over the arcades of the nave and, above, a series of baroque paintings illustrating the history of the Carmelite order. However, the best paintings in the church are a *Nativity* by Cima da Conegliano on the second altar on the right and *St Nicholas of Bari* by Lorenzo Lotto opposite; the latter has a dreamy landscape – one of the most beautiful in Italian art, according to art historian Bernard Berenson – containing tiny figures of St George and the dragon. In the chapel to the right of the high altar is a graceful bronze relief of *The Lamentation Over the Dead Christ* by the Sienese sculptor, painter, inventor, military architect and all-round Renaissance man Francesco di Giorgio.

San Trovaso

Campo San Trovaso (041 522 2133). Vaporetto Zattere. **Open** 8-11am, 3-6pm Mon-Sat. **Map** p306 B2.
This church, which looks on to its quiet raised campo, has two almost identical façades, one at each end, both based on the sub-Palladian church of Le Zitelle (*see p127*) on the Giudecca. The story goes that San Trovaso was built on the very border of the two areas of the city belonging to the rival factions of the *nicolotti* and *castellani*, so that in the event of a wedding between members of the two factions, each party could make its own sweeping entrance and exit. There was no saint called Trovaso: the name is a Venetian telescoping of two other names:

martyrs San Protasio and San Gervasio. There are five works by the Tintoretto family in the church; three are probably by the son, Domenico, including the two on either side of the high altar, which are rich in detail but poor in focus. In the left transept is a smaller-than-usual version of one of Tintoretto's favourite subjects, *The Last Supper*, and in the chapel to the left of the high altar is *The Temptations of St Anthony the Abbot*, featuring enough vices to tempt a saint (note the harlot with 'flames playing around her loins', as Ruskin so coyly put it).

On the side wall of this latter chapel is a charming painting in the international Gothic style by Michele Giambono, *St Chrisogonus on Horseback* (c1450); the saint is a boyish figure on a gold ground, with a shyly hesitant expression and a gorgeously fluttering cloak and banner. In the right transept, in the Clary Chapel, is a set of Renaissance marble reliefs (c1470) showing angels playing musical instruments or holding instruments of the Passion. The only attribution scholars will risk is to the conveniently named 'Master of San Trovaso'.

Scuola dei Carmini

Dorsoduro 2617, campo dei Carmini (041 528 9420). Vaporetto Ca' Rezzonico or San Basilio. **Open** *Apr-Oct* 9am-6pm Mon-Sat; 9am-4pm Sun. *Nov-Mar* 9am-4pm daily. **Admission** €5; €4 students. **No credit cards. Map** p306 A1.

Patron saint of sausage makers. *See p126.*

Sightseeing

Begun in 1670 to plans by Baldassare Longhena, the building housing this *scuola* run by the Carmelite order was spared the Napoleonic lootings that dispersed the furniture and fittings of most of the other *scuole*. As a result, we have a fairly good idea of what an early to mid 18th-century Venetian confraternity HQ must have looked like, from the elaborate Sante Piatti altarpiece downstairs to the staircase with its excrescence of gilded *putti* (cherubs).

On the upper floor is one of the most impressive of Giambattista Tiepolo's Venetian ceilingscapes. The airy ceiling panels, in the main first-floor hall, were painted from 1740 to 1743 and are best viewed with one of the mirrors provided. Don't even try to unravel the story – a celestial donation that supposedly took place in Cambridge, when Simon Stock received the scapular (the badge of the Carmelite order) from the Virgin herself. What counts, as always with Tiepolo, is the audacity of his off-centre composition. If the atmosphere were not so ultra-refined, there would be something disturbing in the Virgin's sneer of cold contempt and those swirling Turneresque clouds. The central painting fell from the woodworm-ridden ceiling in August 2000 but has been beautifully restored. In the two adjoining rooms are wooden sculptures by Giacomo Piazzetta and a dramatic *Judith and Holofernes* by Giambattista Piazzetta.

Eastern Dorsoduro

The eastern triangle of Dorsoduro, between the Accademia and the Salute, is an area of elegant, artsy prosperity, home to many real and would-be artists, writers and wealthy foreigners. Ezra Pound lived out his last years in a small house near the Zattere; Peggy Guggenheim hosted her collection of modern artists in her truncated palazzo on the Grand Canal (now the **Peggy Guggenheim Collection**; *see p123* **Peggy G**); and artists now use the vast spaces of the old warehouses on the Zattere as studios. On a Sunday morning, campo San Vio becomes some corner of a foreign land, as British expatriates home in on the Anglican church of St George. Overlooking the campo, on the other side of the canal, the **Galleria Cini** has a collection of Ferrarese and Tuscan art.

It is a district of quiet canals and cosy *campielli*, perhaps the most picturesque being campiello Barbaro, behind pretty, lopsided **Ca' Dario** (rumoured, after the sudden deaths of owners over the centuries, to be cursed). But all that money has certainly driven out the locals: nowhere in Venice are you further from a simple *alimentari* (grocer's).

The colossal magnificence of Longhena's church of **Santa Maria della Salute** brings the residential area to an end. You can stroll on past the church to the old **Dogana di mare** (Customs House) on the wedge-shaped tip of Dorsoduro. There had long been talk of this empty building being taken over by the Peggy Guggenheim Museum and detailed Tate-Modern style plans drawn up by architect Vittorio Gregotti were confidently presented in 2000. Unfortunately the plans were based on the notion that the museum would be able to spill over into the adjoining Patriarchal Seminary, but the vigorous new Patriarch of Venice (installed in 2002) has made it quite clear that not a square foot of any buildings in his keeping will be given up for such purposes. It looks as if the Dogana will remain empty for a good many more years yet.

Crowning the corner tower of the Dogana, a 17th-century weathercock figure of Fortune perches daintily on a golden ball, 'characteristic,' according to Ruskin, 'of the conceits of the time, and of the hopes and principles of the last days of Venice'. A grand view can be enjoyed from here of St Mark's, the lagoon and the islands.

Gallerie dell'Accademia

Dorsoduro 1050, campo Carità (041 522 2247/ www.artive.arti.beniculturali.it). Vaporetto Accademia. **Open** 8.15am-2pm Mon; 8.15am-7.15pm Tue-Sun. **Admission** €6.50 (*see also p61* State Museums). **No credit cards. Map** p306 B2.

The Accademia is the essential one-stop shop for Venetian painting. It's housed in three former religious buildings: the Scuola Grande di Santa Maria della Carità (the oldest of the Venetian *scuole*, founded in the 13th century), the adjacent church of the Carità, and the Monastery of the Lateran Canons, a 12th-century structure radically remodelled by Palladio. It was Napoleon who made the collection possible, first by suppressing hundreds of churches, convents and religious guilds, and second by moving the city's Accademia di Belle Arti art school here, with the mandate both to train students and to act as a gallery and storeroom for all the evicted art treasures, which were originally displayed as models for the academy's pupils to aspire to.

The collection is arranged chronologically, with the exception of the 15th- and 16th-century works in rooms 19-24 at the end. It opens with a group of 14th- and 15th-century devotional works by Paolo Veneziano and others, still firmly in the Byzantine tradition. This room was the main hall of the Scuola Grande: note the original ceiling of gilded cherubim, whose faces are all subtly different. Rooms 2 and 3 have devotional paintings and altarpieces by Carpaccio, Cima da Conegliano and Giovanni Bellini (a fine *Enthroned Madonna with Six Saints*).

Rooms 4 and 5 bring us to the Renaissance heart of the collection: here are Mantegna's *St George* and Giorgione's mysterious *Tempest*, which has had art historians reaching for symbolic interpretations for centuries. In Room 6 the three greats of 16th-century Venetian painting, Titian, Tintoretto and Veronese, are first encountered. But the battle of the

Sightseeing

Peggy G

Peggy Guggenheim, the prima donna of
modern art patronage, had the usual rich
girl's miserable childhood. Her father
Benjamin went down with the *Titanic* on his
way back from installing the lifts in the Eiffel
Tower; he left her with $460,000 and a
bulbous nose that she hated – especially
after a Cincinnati plastic surgeon had botched
an attempt to turn it into a delicate organ,
'tip-tilted like a flower'.

But if she didn't have looks, she did have
a fully functioning body and a stack of ready
cash; and Peggy set out to use both,
extravagantly. Her numerous lovers included
Samuel Beckett, Yves Tanguy, Roland
Penrose (who liked to tie her up) and Max
Ernst, to whom she was briefly married. When
asked how many husbands she had had,
Peggy replied: 'Do you mean mine, or other
people's?' She wasn't always so successful.
In his autobiography, English art forger Eric
Hebborn describes being chatted up by Peggy
next to her Marino Marini sculpture of a horse
rider with a most immodest protrusion. 'Peggy
put her hand on the bronze erection and said
in a sultry sexy kind of voice... "Eric, the
whole heat of Venice seems to concentrate
itself in this spot." With which she unscrewed
the object, and to my horror, thrust it into my
hand and invited me to kiss her. Thinking it
impolite to refuse a lady, I gave her a gallant
peck on the cheek and returned the metal
penis with: "I'm sorry, Peggy, but this is a lot
harder than mine is".'

Peggy took the same voracious approach
to art as to men. In her autobiography, *Out
of this Century*, she writes: 'My motto was
"buy a picture a day", and I lived up to it.' As
Europe steeled itself for all-out war, she was
in the middle of a spending spree. 'The day

Hitler walked into Norway, I walked into
Léger's studio and bought a wonderful 1919
painting from him for $1,000'.

She turned up in Venice in 1949 looking
for a home for herself, her poodles and her
collection. London had turned her down:
a short-sighted Tate curator described her
growing pile of surrealist and modernist works
as 'non-art'. Venice, still struggling to win
back the tourists, was less finicky, and Peggy
found a perfect, eccentric base in the shape
of the Palazzo Venier dei Leoni, a truncated
18th-century Grand Canal palazzo that looks
as though Marcel Duchamp might have
removed its upper floors (*see also p67*).

Venice has had much reason to be thankful
to Peggy since: today, the Peggy Guggenheim
Collection is the third most-visited museum
in the city, after the Palazzo Ducale and the
Gallerie dell'Accademia. There are big
European names here, including Picasso,
Duchamp, Brancusi, Giacometti and Max
Ernst, plus a few Americans such as Calder
and Jackson Pollock, whose career was jump-
started by Peggy. But it is the intensely
personal nature of the collection that makes
the Peggy Guggenheim gallery unique. The
gallery also has a charming garden attached,
best surveyed from the terrace of the café-
restaurant; temporary exhibitions of
contemporary art are held here.

Peggy Guggenheim Collection

*Dorsoduro 701, fondamenta Venier dei
Leoni (041 520 6288). Vaporetto Accademia
or Salute.* **Open** *Apr-Oct* 10am-6pm Mon,
Wed-Fri, Sun; 10am-10pm Sat. *Nov-Mar*
10am-6pm Mon, Wed-Sun. **Admission** 8;
5 concessions. **Credit** AmEx, DC, MC, V.
Map II 3B.

giants gets under way in earnest in Room 10, where
Tintoretto's ghostly chiaroscuro *Transport of the
Body of St Mark* vies for attention with Titian's
moving *Pietà* – his last painting – and Veronese's
huge *Christ in the House of Levi*. Originally commissioned as a Last Supper, this painting emerged
so full of anachronistic and irreverent detail that the
artist was accused of heresy and ordered to alter the
painting; instead, he simply changed its name. Room
11 covers two centuries, with canvases by Tintoretto
(the exquisite *Madonna dei Camerlenghi*), Bernardo
Strozzi and Tiepolo. The series of rooms beyond
brings the plot up to the 18th century, with all the
old favourites: Canaletto, Guardi, Longhi and the

soft-focus bewigged portraits by Rosalba Carriera.
Rooms 19 and 20 take us back to the 15th century;
the latter has the rich *Miracle of the Relic of the Cross*
cycle, a collaborative effort by Gentile Bellini,
Carpaccio and others, which is packed with telling
social details (check out the black gondolier in
Carpaccio's *Miracle of the Cross at the Rialto*).

An even more satisfying cycle has Room 21 to
itself. Carpaccio's *Life of St Ursula* (1490-5) tells the
story of the legendary Breton princess who
embarked on a pilgrimage to Rome with her
betrothed so that he could be baptised into the true
faith. All went swimmingly until Ursula and all the
11,000 virgins accompanying her were massacred

by the Huns in Cologne. More than the ropey legend, it's the architecture, the ships and the pageantry in these meticulous paintings that grab the attention.

Room 23 is the former church of Santa Maria della Carità: here are devotional works by Vivarini, the Bellinis and others.

Room 24 – the Albergo Room (or secretariat) of the former *scuola* – contains the only work in the whole gallery that is in its original site: Titian's magnificent *Presentation of the Virgin*.

On Saturdays (3.30-5.30pm) and Sundays (10am-noon, 3.30-5.30pm) it is possible to visit the Quadreria (no extra ticket required), which is essentially the museum's storeroom, containing paintings – including some very major works – otherwise not on show. A guided tour of the Quadreria can be taken on Tuesday afternoon at 3pm; pre-booking is essential (041 522 2247).

Galleria Cini
Dorsoduro 864, piscina del Forner (041 521 0755). Vaporetto Accademia. **Open** by appointment only. **No credit cards. Map** p307 B3.

This collection of Ferrarese and Tuscan art was put together by industrialist Vittorio Cini, who founded the Fondazione Cini on the island of San Giorgio Maggiore (*see p129*). It's small but there are one or two gems, such as the unfinished Pontormo *Double Portrait of Two Friends*, on the first floor, and Dosso Dossi's *Allegorical Scene* on the second, a vivacious character study from the D'Este Palace in Ferrara. There are also some delicate late-medieval ivories and a rare 14th-century wedding chest decorated with chivalric scenes.

Queening it: **La Salute**. *See p125.*

Literary locations Donna Leon

The American mystery writer Donna Leon published her first detective novel starring Commissario Brunetti of the Venice Questura (police headquarters) in 1992. Nine more have followed, earning her a committed following, particularly in Germany: her heady mixture of southern corruption, watery intrigue and good Italian cooking clearly appeal to something deep in the northern soul. They have yet to win over the heart of any Italian publisher.

Given Leon's extreme geographic precision, fans of her works will have no trouble tracing the Commissario's crime-solving footsteps. The writer tends to favour people and food over architecture: if she mentions a greengrocer with a wig in Barbaria de le Tole, you can be pretty certain that he and his hairpiece exist.

What follows is a selective list of top Brunetti locations.

San Marco
Bar Rosa Salva (*see p166*) in **campo San Luca** (San Marco): a popular meeting place in the centre of Venice, occasionally used by Brunetti; the best coffee in Venice, according to the Commissario.

Castello
The Questura in **campo San Lorenzo** (**map** p308 A1-2) where Brunetti works was moved to Marghera on the mainland a few years back; there is now just a small local police station, a few doors down from the imposing palazzo that once housed the central Venetian Questura (No.5053). Brunetti often nips down the fondamenta for a cappuccino at the bar by the **ponte dei Greci**.

Another Castello location is the **Arsenale**. A body is found beneath the rickety catwalk clinging to its northern wall in *Death in a Strange Country*.

Santa Maria della Salute ✶

Campo della Salute (041 522 5558). Vaporetto
Salute. **Open** *Oct-Mar* 9am-noon, 3-5.30pm daily.
Apr-Sept 9am-noon, 3-6.30pm daily. **Map** p307 B3.

This magnificent baroque church, queening it over the entrance of the Grand Canal, is probably as recognisable an image of Venice as St Mark's or the Rialto bridge. It was built from 1631 to 1681 in thanksgiving for the end of Venice's last bout of plague, which had wiped out at least a third of the population in 1630. The church is dedicated to the Madonna, as protector of the city.

The terms of the competition won by 26-year-old architect Baldassare Longhena represented a serious challenge, which beat some of the best architects of the day. The church was to be colossal but inexpensive; the whole structure was to be visually clear on entrance, with an unimpeded view of the high altar, the ambulatory and side altars coming into sight only as one approached the chancel; the light was to be evenly distributed; and the whole building should *creare una bella figura* – show itself off to good effect.

Longhena succeeded brilliantly in satisfying all these requisites – particularly the last and most Venetian one. The church takes superb advantage of its dominant position and pays homage to both the Byzantine form of San Marco across the Grand Canal and the classical form of Palladio's Redentore, across the Giudecca Canal. Longhena said he chose the circular shape with the reverent aim of offering a crown to the Madonna. She stands on the lantern above the cupola as described in the Book of Revelations: 'Clothed in the sun, and the moon under her feet, and upon her head a crown of twelve stars.' Beneath her, on the great scroll-brackets around the cupola, stand statues of the apostles – the 12 stars in her crown. This Marian symbolism continues inside the church, where in the centre of the mosaic floor, amid a circle of roses, is an inscription, *Unde origo inde salus* (from the origin comes salvation) – a reference to the legendary birth of Venice under the Virgin's protection.

Longhena's intention was for the visitor to approach the high altar ceremoniously through the main door. If visitors were able to take this route, the six side altars would only come into view upon reach the very centre of the church, where they appear framed theatrically in their separate archways. However, the main door is rarely open and often the central area of the church is roped off, so you have no choice but to walk round the ambulatory and visit the chapels separately.

The three on the right have paintings by Luca Giordano, a prolific Neapolitan painter who brought a little southern brio into the art of the city at a time (the mid 17th century) when most painting had become limply derivative. On the opposite side is a clumsily restored *Pentecost*, by Titian, transferred here from the island monastery of Santo Spirito (demolished in 1656).

The high altar has a splendidly dynamic sculptural group by Giusto Le Corte, the artist responsible (with assistants) for most of the statues inside and outside the church. This group represents *Venice Kneeling Before the Virgin and Child*, while the plague, in the shape of a hideous old hag, scurries off to the right, prodded by a tough-looking putto with a flaming torch. In the midst of all this marble hubbub is a serene Byzantine icon of the *Madonna and Child*, brought from Crete in 1669 by Francesco Morosini, otherwise known for blowing up the Parthenon.

The best paintings are in the sacristy (open same hours as church; admission €1.50). Tintoretto's *Marriage at Cana* (1551) was described by Ruskin as 'perhaps the most perfect example which human art has produced of the utmost possible force and sharpness of shadow united with richness of local colour'. He also points out how curiously difficult it is to spot the bride and groom in the painting.

On the altar is a very early Titian with *Saints Mark, Sebastian, Roch, Cosmas and Damian*, saints who were all invoked for protection against the plague; the painting was done during the outbreak of 1509-14. Three later works by Titian (c1540-49) hang on the ceiling, violent Old Testament scenes also brought here from the church of Santo Spirito: the *Sacrifice of Abraham, David Killing Goliath*, and *Cain and Abel*. These works established the conventions for all subsequent ceiling paintings in Venice; Titian decided not to go for the worm's eye view adopted by Mantegna and Correggio, which sacrificed clarity for surprise, and instead chose an oblique viewpoint, as if observing the action from

Cannaregio

Flavia Petrelli, the diva who appears in two novels, lives in an apartment in **calle Testa** near the Miracoli church. Maria, the white-haired newspaper-seller at the end of calle Testa seems to have handed the business on.

San Polo

Do Mori (*see p169*), an ancient tavern near the **Rialto Bridge**, is Brunetti's favourite bar. His top-storey apartment is near **campo San Silvestro**.

Dorsoduro

The Commissorio's father-in-law Count Falier lives in a palazzo on the Grand Canal near **campo San Barnaba**.

The Lagoon

Remote **Pellestrina** is the scandal-riddled setting of *A Sea of Troubles*.

Sightseeing

the bottom of a hill. More Old Testament rowdiness can be seen in works by Salviati (*Saul Hurling a Spear at David*) and Palma il Giovane (*Samson and Jonah* – in which the whale is represented mainly by a lolling rubbery tongue).

Le Zattere

Having rounded the Punta della Dogana, the mile-long stretch of Le Zattere, Venice's finest promenade after the riva degli Schiavoni, will take you all the way back past the churches of **I Gesuati** and **Santa Maria della Visitazione** to the city's origins in the San Nicolò zone (*see p116*).

This long promenade bordering the Giudecca Canal is named after the *zattere* (rafts) that used to moor here, bringing wood and other materials from the mainland. The paved quayside was created by decree in 1519. It now provides a favourite strolling-ground, punctuated by some spectacularly situated benches for a picnic, and several bars and *gelaterie*. The eastern end is usually quiet (although restoration work was making things noisier as this guide went to press), with the occasional flurry of activity around the vast 14th-century salt warehouses, now used by rowing clubs.

Westward from these is the church of **Spirito Santo** and the long 16th-century façade of the grimly named **Ospedale degli Incurabili**, now used as a juvenile court. Volpone's property is confiscated and sent to this hospital at the end of Ben Jonson's play of the same name; the main incurable disease of the time was syphilis.

The liveliest part of the Zattere is around the church of **I Gesuati** and the boat-stops to the Giudecca. Venetians flock here at weekends to savour good ice-cream (*see p171* **Gelateria Nico**) or sip drinks at canal-side tables

The final and widest stretch of the Zattere takes you past several notable *palazzi*, including the 16th-century Palazzo Clary – until recently the French consulate – and the Gothic Palazzo Molin, which is now used by the Società Adriatica di Navigazione.

Towards the end is the 17th-century façade of the **Scuola dei Luganegheri** (sausage-makers' school), with a statue of the sausage makers' protector, St Anthony Abbot, whose symbol was a hog.

I Gesuati

Fondamenta Zattere ai Gesuati (041 275 0642/ www.chorus-ve.org). Vaporetto Gesuati. **Open** 10am-5pm Mon-Sat; 1-5pm Sun. **Admission** €2 (*see also p61* Chorus). **No credit cards. Map** II 2B.
The official name of this church is Santa Maria del Rosario, but it is always known after the Gesuati, the minor religious order that owned the previous

church on the site; the order merged with the Dominicans – the church's present owners – in 1668. I Gesuati is a great piece of teamwork by a trio of remarkable rococo artists: architect Giorgio Massari (he of the boring but effective Palazzo Grassi on the Grand Canal, *see p82*), painter Giambattista Tiepolo and sculptor Giovanni Morlaiter.

The façade deliberately reflects the Palladian church of the Redentore opposite, but the splendidly posturing statues give it that typically 18th-century touch of histrionic flamboyance. Plenty more theatrical sculpture is to be found inside the church, all by Morlaiter. Above is a magnificent ceiling by Tiepolo, with three frescos on obscure Dominican themes (a mirror is provided for the relief of stiff necks). These works reintroduced frescos to Venetian art after two centuries of canvas ceiling paintings. The central panel shows St Dominic passing on to a crowd of supplicants the rosary he has just received from the cloud-enthroned Madonna. Tiepolo also painted the surrounding grisailles, which, at first sight, look like stucco reliefs.

There is another brightly coloured Tiepolo on the first altar on the right, *The Virgin and Child with Saints Rosa, Catherine and Agnes*; Tiepolo here plays with optical effects, allowing St Rosa's habit to tumble out of the frame. In his painting of three Dominican saints on the third altar on the right, Giovanni Battista Piazzetta makes use of a narrower and more sober range of colours, going for a more sculptural effect.

Santa Maria della Visitazione

*Fondamenta Zattere ai Gesuati (041 522 4077).
Vaporetto Zattere.* **Open** *Apr-Sept* 8am-noon, 3-7pm Mon-Sat. *Oct-Mar* 8am-noon, 3-6pm Sun. **Map** p306 B2.
Confusingly, this has the same name as the Vivaldi church on the riva degli Schiavoni (*see p91*) – though the latter is usually known as La Pietà. Santa Maria della Visitazione stands on the Zattere just a few yards from the larger church of I Gesuati (*see p126*); it is now the chapel of the Istituto Don Orione, which has taken over the vast complex of the Monastery of the Gesuati next door (entrance by appointment via the door marked 'Istituto Artigianelli').

Designed by Tullio Lombardo or Mauro Codussi and built in 1423, the church has an attractive early Renaissance façade. It was suppressed (that rascal Napoleon again) at the beginning of the 19th century and stripped of all its works of art with the exception of the original coffered ceiling, an unexpected delight that contains 58 compartments with portraits of saints and prophets by an Umbrian painter of Luca Signorelli's school (mirrors are provided). This is one of the few examples of central Italian art in Venice; the others are Andrea del Castagno's frescos in San Zaccaria (*see p88*), the Martini chapel in San Giobbe (*see p97* **Along the canal**) and the Florentine Chapel in the Frari (*see p113*). To the right of the façade is a lion's mouth for secret denunciations: the ones posted here went to the Magistrati della sanità, who dealt with matters of public health.

La Giudecca & San Giorgio

From Hanseatic Gothic to Palladian masterpiece, via the Garden of Eden.

A gondola-shaped strand of eight inter-connected islands, **La Giudecca** lies to the south of the city. It was once known as Spinalonga, from an imagined resemblance to a fish skeleton (*spina* means fish bone). The origin of the present name is disputed, some attributing it to an early community of Jews, others to the fact that troublesome nobles (who had been *giudicati*, or judged) were banished here. However, there were plenty of noblemen who came to the islands of their own free will, building villas as rural retreats. They were not alone: Michelangelo, exiled from Florence in 1529, came here to mope, and three centuries later Alfred de Musset, during his torrid affair with George Sand (who had a fling with the doctor summoned to visit the poet), praised the cool Arcadian charms of 'la Zuecca'.

During the 19th century the city authorities began to make use of the numerous abandoned convents and monasteries, converting them into factories and prisons, and building over their gardens and orchards. The factories have all closed down, while the prisons (one for drug offenders and one for women) remain in use. A great deal of low-rent housing has been created over the past century, much of it on the island of Sacca Fisola at the western end, created from mud dredged from the bottom of the lagoon.

Many of the factories remain abandoned, contributing to the run-down appearance of the south side of the Giudecca; however, work is under way on the transformation of the most conspicuous one, the colossal **Molino Stucky** at the west end. This former flour mill (the largest building on the lagoon) was built in 1895 in Hanseatic Gothic style; it was closed in 1954 and stood in rat-ridden Teutonic desolation for over 40 years. To the surprise of ever-sceptical locals, the building is now being restored to more than its former glory in an ambitious project that envisages a conference centre, a 250-room hotel, 138 apartments and a shopping centre.

The main sights of the Giudecca are all along the northern fondamenta, including **Santa Eufemia**, the Palladian churches of **Le Zitelle** (literally 'the spinsters'; the convent ran a hospice for girls from poor families, who were trained as lacemakers) and **Il Redentore**, as well as several fine *palazzi*.

Near Le Zitelle is the neo-Gothic **Casa De Maria**, with its three large inverted-shield windows; the Bolognese painter Mario De Maria built it for himself from 1910 to 1913. It is the only private palazzo to have the same patterned brickwork as the Doge's Palace.

Towards the end of fondamenta rio della Croce (No.149, close to the Redentore) stands **Palazzo Munster**, a former infirmary for English sailors. The vitriolic Anglo-Catholic writer Frederick Rolfe received the last sacraments here in 1910, after slagging the hospital off in his libelous novel *The Desire and Pursuit of the Whole*. (He then proceeded to live for two more vituperative years.) Opposite is another ex-pat landmark – the huge **'Garden of Eden'** (*see p129* **The Garden of Eden**), the pleasure ground of Frederick Eden, a disabled Englishman who, like Byron, discovered that Venice was the perfect city for those with disabilities – particularly if they could afford a private gondola and private steam-launch.

See also p279.

Street wise

See also p279.

Michelangelo (calle)
Recalls the artist's stay on the Giudecca.

Accademia dei Nobili (calle lunga)
Named after an academy founded in 1619 for the sons of penniless nobles; pupils were taught religion, grammar, humanities and nautical theory.

Convertite (fondamenta delle)
A convent for fallen women wishing to make amends for their past. The convent's first rector, Father Pietro Leon da Valcamonica, was beheaded in 1561 for drowning the fruits of his carnal relations with at least 20 of them. The convent is now the women's prison.

It is oddly difficult to get through to the southern side of the island, but worth the effort. Take calle San Giacomo, west of the Redentore; at the end turn left along calle degli Orti, and then right. At the end is a small public garden with benches looking out over the quiet southern lagoon and its lonely islands.

Il Redentore

Campo del Redentore (041 275 0642/www.chorusve.org). Vaporetto Redentore. **Open** 10am-5pm Mon-Sat; 1-5pm Sun. **Admission** €2 (*see also p61* Chorus). **No credit cards. Map** p307 C3.

Venice's first great plague church was built to celebrate the deliverance from the bout of 1575-7. An especially conspicuous site was chosen, one that could be approached in grand ceremonial fashion. The ceremony continues today, on every third Sunday of July, when a bridge of boats is built across the Giudecca Canal. Palladio (*see chapter* **Palladian Villas**), who always paid great attention to the settings of his buildings, was a natural choice as architect. He designed an eye-catching building whose prominent dome appears to rise directly behind the Greek-temple façade, giving the illusion that the church is centrally planned, as was traditional with sanctuaries and votive temples outside Venice. A broad flight of steps sweeps up to the great entrance door, an effect Palladio had often used in his mainland villas. The solemn and harmonious interior, with its single nave lit by large 'thermal' windows, testifies to Palladio's study of Roman baths. However, the Capuchin monks, the austere order to whom the building had been entrusted, were not pleased by its grandeur; Palladio attempted to mollify them by designing their choir stalls in a plain style. The best paintings are in the sacristy (closed for restoration as this guide goes to press), including a *Virgin and Child* by Alvise Vivarini and a *Baptism* by Veronese.

Santa Eufemia

Fondamenta Santa Eufemia (041 522 5848). Vaporetto Santa Eufemia. **Open** 9-11am Mon-Sat. Closed indefinitely for restoration. **Map** p306 C2.

This church has a 16th-century Doric portico along its flank. The interior owes its charm to its mix of styles. The nave and aisles are essentially 11th century, with Veneto-Byzantine columns and capitals, while the decoration consists mainly of fussy 18th-century stucco and paintings. Over the first altar on the right is *St Roch and an Angel* by Bartolomeo Vivarini (1480).

Isola di San Giorgio

The island of San Giorgio, which sits in such a temptingly strategic position opposite the piazzetta di San Marco, realised its true potential under set-designer *extraordinaire* Andrea Palladio, whose church of **San Giorgio Maggiore** is one of Venice's most recognisable

landmarks. Known in the early days of the city as the Isola dei Cipressi (Cypress Island), it soon became an important Benedictine monastery and centre of learning – a tradition that is carried on today by the **Fondazione Giorgio Cini**, which runs a research centre and craft school on the island.

Fondazione Giorgio Cini & Benedictine Monastery

041 528 9900. Vaporetto San Giorgio. **Open** *Monastery* Mon-Fri by appointment only. *Library: art history* 9am-12.45pm Mon-Fri. *Library: music, Venetian history & oriental studies* 9am-noon, 2.30-4.45pm Mon-Fri. **Admission** free. **Map** p308 C1.

There has been a Benedictine monastery on the island since 982, when Doge Tribuno Memmo donated the island to the order. The monastery continued to benefit from ducal donations, acquiring large tracts of land both in and around Venice and abroad. After the church acquired the remains of St Stephen (1109), it was visited yearly by the doge on 26 December, the feast day of the saint. The city authorities often used the island as a luxury hotel for particularly prestigious visitors, such as Cosimo de' Medici in 1433. Cosimo had a magnificent library built here; it was destroyed in 1614, to make way for a more elaborate affair by Longhena (now open only to bona fide scholars with references to prove it).

In 1800, in a final bid for glory, the island hosted the conclave of cardinals that elected Pope Pius VII, after they had been expelled from Rome by Napoleon. In 1806 the monastery was suppressed by the French, who sent its chief artistic treasure – Veronese's *Marriage Feast at Cana* – off to the Louvre, where it still hangs. For the rest of the century the monastery did ignominious service as a barracks and ammunition store. In 1951 industrialist Count Vittorio Cini acquired the island to set up a foundation in memory of his son, Giorgio, killed in a plane crash in 1949. Restoration work was carried out and the Fondazione Giorgio Cini now uses the monastery buildings for its activities, including artistic and musical research (it holds a collection of Vivaldi manuscripts and recordings, plus illuminated manuscripts), a naval college and a craft school. A portion of the complex was given back to the Benedictines; there are currently eight monks in the monastery. The foundation is not open to the public, but those with a special interest in Palladian or baroque architecture could try ringing for an appointment. There are two beautiful cloisters – one by Giovanni Buora (1516-40), the other by Palladio (1579) – an elegant library and staircase by Longhena (1641-53), and a magnificent refectory (where Veronese's painting hung) by Palladio (1561).

San Giorgio Maggiore

041 522 7827. Vaporetto San Giorgio. **Open** *Oct-Mar* 9.30am-12.30pm, 2.30-5pm daily. *Apr-Sept* 9am-12.30pm, 2.30-6.30pm Mon-Sat; 9.30-10.30am, 2.30-6.30pm Sun. **Admission** *Church* free. *Campanile* €3. **No credit cards. Map** p308 C1.

The Garden of Eden

In 1884 wealthy English invalid expat Frederick Eden bought an artichoke field on the then-rural island of the Giudecca and set to work to turn it into a garden that lived up to his surname.

He had a guiding light for his project in the shape of his sister-in-law Gertrude Jekyll, the most famous landscape designer of the age. With Jekyll's help, the six-acre plot was transformed into a paradise of long leafy pergolas and rose trellises, of white lilies and sweet-smelling pittosporum hedges along the lagoon frontage. To complete the rural idyll, a herd of 15 cattle grazed, gazing complacently on the white-clad English visitors taking tea on the immaculate lawns.

Still in private hands, the Garden of Eden remains verdant – if, reported, totally unkempt – behind its high walls, revealing its secrets only to the invited few.

This unique spot gazing across the lagoon to the Piazzetta (*see p70*) cried out for an architectural masterpiece. Palladio provided it. This was his first complete solo church; it demonstrates how confident he was of his techniques and objectives. Unlike earlier Renaissance architects in Venice, he drew no lessons from the city's Byzantine tradition. Palladio here develops the system of superimposed temple fronts with which he had experimented in the façade of San Francesco della Vigna (*see p86*). The interior maintains the same relations between the orders as the outside, with composite half-columns supporting the gallery and lower Corinthian pilasters supporting the arches. The effect is of impressive luminosity and harmony, decoration being confined to the altars. Palladio believed that white was the colour most pleasing to God, a credo that happily matched the demand from the Council of Trent for greater lucidity in church services.

There are several good works of art. Over the first altar is an *Adoration of the Shepherds* by Jacopo Bassano, with startling lighting effects. The altar to the right of the high altar has a *Madonna and Child and Nine Saints* by Sebastiano Ricci.

On the side-walls of the chancel hang two vast compositions by Tintoretto, *The Last Supper* and the *Gathering of Manna*, painted in the last years of his life. Both works emphasise the importance of the Eucharist, as laid down by the Council of Trent, and the perspective of each work makes it clear that they were intended to be viewed from the altar rails. Tintoretto combines almost surreal visionary effects (angels swirling out from a lamp's eddying smoke) with touches of superb domestic realism (a cat prying into a basket, a woman stooping over her laundry). Tintoretto's last painting, a moving *Entombment*, hangs in the Cappella dei Morti. It is possible that, as in Titian's *La Pietà*, Tintoretto included himself among the crowd of mourners: he has been identified as the bearded man gazing intensely at Christ's face. In the left transept is a painting by Jacopo and Domenico Tintoretto of the *Martyrdom of St Stephen*, placed above the altar containing the saint's remains (brought from Constantinople in 1109).

Outside the sacristy, where tickets can be bought for the lift to the top of the campanile, stands the huge statue of an angel that crowned the belltower until it was struck by lightning in 1993. The view from the top of the tower is extraordinary. Besides giving the best possible panorama across Venice itself and the lagoon, it also allows glimpses into the two inaccessible cloisters and the gardens of the monastery on the island.

Sightseeing

The Lido to Chioggia

Witness less-weird Venice: from a sleepy beach resort to a bustling fishing port.

Two long, thin sandbanks separate the southern part of the lagoon from the open sea. The northernmost strip is the Lido, an elongated seaside resort and city suburb. Sedately residential, it only really comes to life in the summer months and during the September film festival.

The more southerly strip, on the other side of the Porto di Malamocco (one of the three *bocche di porto* that are Venice's gates from the lagoon to the Adriatic), is Pellestrina – an even narrower sliver of land with straggling fishing villages, kitchen gardens and boatyards. Beyond the bottom end of Pellestrina, on the other side of the southernmost *bocca di porta*, is the lively fishing port of Chioggia, like a miniature working-class version of Venice, rationalised to include cars.

GETTING THERE AND GETTING AROUND
The main Santa Maria Elisabetta stop on the Lido is served by frequent *vaporetti* and *motonavi* from Venice and the mainland. For details of routes, *see chapter* **Directory: Getting Around**. The San Nicolò stop to the north is served by the No.14 to Punta Sabbioni, and the car ferry from Tronchetto. To the south, the Palazzo del Cinema stop (once called Casinò and still referred to as such) is active only for the two weeks of the film festival, when the No.51/52 extends its service to keep the film buffs mobile.

Bus routes are confusing: you'll need to look carefully at the destination board on stops and buses. The A (for *arancione*, orange) and the B (for *blu*) each have two routes, one going south and one north. The southward route of both (marked 'Alberoni') is the same, straight down the road along the lagoon front to Alberoni at the southern tip of the island, via Malamocco. The northward route of each (marked 'San Nicolò' or 'Ospedale') is circular; the A travels clockwise towards San Nicolò along the lagoon-front and then turns right towards the sea and the Ospedale al Mare and makes its way back to Santa Maria Elisabetta; the B does more or less the same route anticlockwise. In the summer the routes are extended to include popular beach sites. The V (for *verde*, green) does a shorter route, travelling to the Palazzo del Cinema on the seafront and ending up at via Parri, half way down the island. In the summer months there is another circular line, the C (for *celeste*, light blue), which also travels to the

Palazzo del Cinema and back again. Finally, the No.11, which departs from across the road from the main vaporetto stop, in the Gran Viale, also heads down to Alberoni but then continues on to the car ferry, across to Pellestrina island, and down as far as the village of Pellestrina.

At least one in two of the No.11 runs (check the timetable) is timed to coincide with the departure of the passenger ferry to Chioggia, from the far end of Pellestrina island (the ferry waits if the bus is late). The entire journey from the Lido to Chioggia – including the two crossings – takes just over an hour; a ticket providing unlimited travel to and fro along the Venice–Pellestrina–Chioggia line for 12 hours costs €7.75. There is also a coach to Chioggia from piazzale Roma, but the scenery is depressing and the time saved minimal, unless you are staying near piazzale Roma.

Bicycles are a great way to get around the Lido, and those with a good pair of legs might consider doing the whole 20-kilometre (12-mile) haul down to Chioggia by bike – you can put it on the passenger ferry for €3.62 as long as too many others haven't had the same idea. For bike hire outlets on the Lido, *see chapter* **Directory**.

TOURIST INFORMATION
In the summer (June-September) a tourist information office is open at Gran Viale 6A, Lido (041 526 5721/fax 041 529 8720), 9.30am-1pm, 3-6.30pm daily.

The Lido

Map p311
If – fired by the example of Dirk Bogarde in *Death in Venice* – you have come to the Lido looking for pale young aesthetes in sailor suits, forget it. These days, Venice-by-the-sea is more of a dormitory suburb than a playground for the idle rich – though there are still a few of the latter in the two big hotels, the Des Bains and the Excelsior, who keep the legend going. On the whole, though, the Lido is the place to come to escape from the strangeness of Venice to a normality of supermarkets, cars and mothers pushing prams.

Things perk up in summer when buses are full of city sunbathers with rolled-up towels and tourists staying in the Lido's overspill hotels. However, the days of all-night partying and gambling are long gone. In January 2001

Sightseeing

A leafy corner of the **Lido**, near via Lepanto.

the Lido Casinò closed (*see p142* **Chancers**).
Now the only moment when the place stirs
to anything like its former vivacity is at
the beginning of September, when the film
festival rolls into town for two weeks, with
its bandwagon of stars, directors, PR people
and sleep-deprived, caffeine-driven journalists
(*see also p200*).

The Lido has few tourist sights as such.
Only the church of **San Nicolò** on the riviera
San Nicolò – founded in 1044 – can claim
any great antiquity. It was here that the doge
would come on Ascension Day after marrying
Venice to the sea in the ceremony known as *lo
sposalizio del mare* (*see* **Festa e Regatta
della Sensa**, *p195*). Inside is the tomb of
Nicola Giustiniani, a Benedictine monk who
was forced to leave holy orders in 1172 in order
to assure the future of his illustrious family,
of which he was the sole heir. He married the
doge's daughter, had plenty of kids, and once
the job was done became a monk once more.
Soon after his death he was beatified for his
fine spirit of self-sacrifice.

Fans of art nouveau and art deco have plenty
to look at on the Lido. In the Gran Viale – the
shop-lined main street that runs between the
vaporetto stop and the beach – there are two
gems: the tiled façade of the Hungaria Hotel
(No.28), formerly the Ausonia Palace, with its
Beardsley-esque nymphs; and Villa Monplaisir

at No.14, an art deco design from 1906. Many
other smaller-scale examples can be found in
and around via Lepanto. For full-blown turn-of-
the-century exotica, though, it's hard to beat the
Hotel Excelsior on lungomare Marconi, a neo-
Moorish party piece, complete with minaret.

Malamocco & Pellestrina

The bus ride south along the lagoonside
promenade of the Lido is uneventful but passes
plenty of submerged history. Literally so in
one case: the old town of Malamocco, near the
southern end of the island, was engulfed by a
tidal wave following a seaquake in the Adriatic
in 1107; until then it had been a flourishing port
under the dominion of Padua. The new town,
built further inland, never really amounted to
much; today its sights consist of a few
picturesque streets and a pretty bridge.

Just offshore from Malamocco is the tiny
island of **Poveglia**, which once supported 200
families, descendants of the servants of Pietro
Tradonico, a ninth-century doge murdered by
aristocratic rivals. Fearing for their lives, his
servants barricaded themselves inside the
Palazzo Ducale, and only agreed to leave when
safe conduct to this new home was promised.

The Lido ends at **Alberoni**, with its golf
course, Fascist-era bathing establishments,
lighthouse and maritime control tower. Beyond

the golf course is an attractive area of woodland, mainly maritime pines; it is a well-known gay cruising area (*see p207*).

The channel between the Lido and Pellestrina is the busiest of the three *bocche di porto* between lagoon and sea, and the one used by petrol tankers on their way to and from the refineries at Porto Marghera.

The No.11 bus motors right on to the waiting car ferry for the short hop across to the island of Pellestrina – a glorified sandbar so narrow that it has more than once risked being swept away by the sea. The answer to the problem of Pallestrina's vulnerability can be seen on the left as the bus continues its journey south. The *murazzi*, solid sea walls of wooden piles and landfill clad in Istrian stone, are at their most impressive at the southern end of Pellestrina, where the width of the island dwindles to almost nothing – but the *murazzi*, 14 metres (46 feet) wide at the base, continue to march out towards Chioggia for a distance of four kilometres (two and a half miles). They were built between 1744 and 1782 to replace earlier makeshift wooden defences. Recently, sloping sandy beaches have been created to lessen the impact of waves against them. On the lagoon side, the island of Pellestrina is a straggle of smallholdings, hastily built holiday homes and boatyards, with only two settlements to speak of: **San Pietro in Volta** and **Pellestrina** itself, a fishing village with a pretty centre of pastel houses clustered around the 18th-century church of **Santa Maria**, celebrating an apparition of the Virgin to a local boy named Natalino Scarpa de' Muti. Pellestrina is divided into quarters named after the four families (Scarpa, Zennaro, Vianello and Busetto) sent there by the *podestà* (mayor) of Chioggia after the war against Genoa (*see below and p14*); it once rivalled Burano as a lace-making island, but those days are long past.

At the end of the village, next to the cemetery, is the landing-stage for the ferry to Chioggia. Beyond this the island dwindles yet further until there is little more than the wall of the *murazzi* between the open sea and the lagoon; it is possible to walk along the wall for another half-mile or so to the small wooded area of Ca' Roman at the far south of the island, popular for camping in the summer.

Chioggia

The sea approach, via the Pellestrina *motonave*, is the best introduction to Chioggia, a port whose wedding to the sea has had more of the daily grind to it than Venice's leisurely marriage of convenience. The *chioggiotti* have always been hardy fishermen and good sailors.

If Carlo Goldoni (*see p122* **Literary locations**) is to be believed, the women were hardly less formidable; the 18th-century playwright lived in Chioggia for five years in his youth, and used his memories of the town to write *Le baruffe chiozzotte*, a comedy revolving around a quarrel between a group of fishwives.

Of Roman origin, Chioggia was important enough to have its own grand chancellor and bishop in the early Middle Ages; its 15 minutes of fame came between 1378 and 1380, with the so-called War of Chioggia. This long trial of strength between Venice and its arch-rival Genoa was only ostensibly to do with the control of a small fishing port; the real prize was control over the eastern Mediterranean shipping routes. The Genoese capture of Chioggia in 1378 was a slap in the face for Venice, but the naval blockade mounted by generals Vettor Pisani and Carlo Zeno starved the Genoese into surrender by June 1380. Chioggia was almost entirely destroyed in the process and never fully recovered its former prosperity. Today, fishing is still a major employer, though the fleet has to go further and further afield to bring home the catch. You'll see plenty of *chioggiotti* in Venice, too: many put their maritime skills to use crewing *vaporetti*.

Chioggia's old town spreads over a rectangular island split down the middle by the Canal Vena; it is sheltered from the sea by the long arm of Sottomarina to the east.

Sottomarina has the big beachfront hotels, the leafy residential streets and the supermarkets; Chioggia itself has all the historical sights, the fishing port and the low, cramped houses. The topography of this older section of town is linear: from piazzetta Vigo, where the ferry docks, the long, wide corso del Popolo extends the whole length of the island, parallel to the Canal Vena. On either side, narrow lanes lead off towards the lagoon.

The only sight not on the corso is the church of **San Domenico** (open 8am-noon, 2.30-5.30pm daily), on its very own island at the end of the street that begins across a balustraded bridge (under restoration as this guide goes to press) from piazzetta Vigo. A barn-like 18th-century reconstruction, it contains Vittore Carpaccio's last painting, a graceful, poised *St Paul*, signed and dated 1520. There is also a huge wooden crucifix – possibly a German work of the 14th century – and a Rubens-like Tintoretto. More charming is the collection of naïve *ex voto* paintings placed by grateful fishermen in a side chapel; one shows a sea rescue by helicopter. Back on the corso, **Sant'Andrea** (open 8.30am-noon, 4.30-7pm daily) is a mainly baroque church with little to see inside; its sturdy 12th-century campanile once doubled as a lookout tower.

A little further on is the **Granaio**, one of the few buildings in town that predates the War of Chioggia. Built in 1322 but heavily restored in the 19th century, it was used as the municipal granary; today it hosts the fish market (open 8am-noon Tue-Sun), a photo-op riot of glistening colour that is the heart and soul of Chioggia. The small church of **Santissima Trinità**, just off the corso on piazza XX Settembre, has long been *in restauro*; if you can get inside, there are some good Mannerist panels by Palma il Giovane and other painters on the ceiling of the oratory.

Across the canal is the church of the **Filippine**, an 18th-century building (open 8am-noon, 4-7pm daily), with an extraordinary Chapel of Reliquaries (third on the right); the walls and altar-front are decorated throughout with delicate lace-like arrangements of hundreds of tiny silver reliquaries, each containing a sliver of saintly bone or nail-parings; there is even a special calendar, with a minuscule body part for each day of the year.

Midway down the corso, the church of **San Giacomo** (closed for restoration as this guide went to press), with its unfinished façade, looks like a Palladian cowshed. If you can get in, the high altar holds the *Madonna della Navicella*, a picture of a miraculous image of the Virgin as she appeared to a Sottomarina peasant in 1508, before making her getaway on a divinely steered boat. Near the end of the corso, two churches stand side by side on the right. The smaller one is **San Martino** (open only for special exhibitions), a Venetian Gothic jewel built in 1393 by the inhabitants of Sottomarina, who had taken refuge in Chioggia after the destruction of their part of town by the Genoese. The church once contained a fine polyptych attributed to Paolo Veneziano, but this is currently being restored.

Next door, the huge 17th-century **Duomo** was built to a project by Baldassare Longhena after a fire destroyed the original tenth-century church; there are few indications here that he would go on to design the Salute in Venice. Only the 14th-century 64-metre (210-foot) campanile – across the road – remains from the earlier structure. The high altar has some good marble relief work by Alessandro Tremignon; the chapel to the left of the chancel contains a series of grisly 18th-century paintings depicting the prolonged martyrdom of the two patron saints of Chioggia, Felix and Fortunatus (Happy and Lucky).

The **Torre di Santa Maria** marks the end of the old town; just beyond, in campo Marconi, is the deconsecrated church of San Francesco, which has been turned into the **Museo Civico della Laguna Sud**. This brand-new collection struggles to fill a huge space. But though patchy, the museum does provide a good introduction to aspects of life on the lagoon, with displays showing traditional land-reclamation and shoring-up techniques. On the top floor is an exhaustive collection of model fishing boats, plus a small gallery, which contains an attractive triptych by Ercole del Fiore (1436), *Justice between Saints Felix and Fortunatus*, and a number of views of Chioggia by local 19th- and early 20th-century painters.

When the museum is open, the front desk also functions as a tourist information office.

Duomo
Calle Duomo 77 (041 400 496). **Open** 8.30am-noon, 4-6pm daily.

Museo Civico della Laguna Sud
Campo Marconi 1 (041 550 0911).
Open *Sept-mid June* 9am-1pm Tue, Wed; 9am-1pm, 3-6pm Thur-Sat; 3-6pm Sun. *Mid June-Aug* 9am-1pm Tue, Wed; 9am-1pm, 7.30-11.30pm Thur-Sat; 7.30-11.30pm Sun. **Admission** €3.50; €1.75 concessions. **No credit cards**.

Where to stay & eat

There are 73 hotels in Sottomarina – most of them seasonal – and only four in Chioggia itself. Of the latter, the recently renovated **Grande Italia** (rione Sant'Andrea 597, 041 400 515, double room €91-€170) by the ferry berth in piazzetta Vigo provides all the usual four-star comforts, and offers the use of a fitness centre. The tiny **Locanda Val d'Ostreghe** (rione Sant'Andrea 763, 041 400 527, double room €60), in a narrow calle behind the church of Sant'Andrea, has 12 basic but cheap rooms above a restaurant.

Of a weekend, Venetians are apt to take a jaunt down to Chioggia for a cheap seafood lunch. The lack of tourists and the centrality of fish in the *chioggiotto* worldview mean that it is difficult to go wrong, but one reliable address is **Al Bersagliere** (via Battisti 293, 041 401 044, average €35), a family-run trattoria just off the corso, where seafood risottos and grilled fish are cooked to perfection. **Osteria Penzo** (calle larga Bersaglio 526, 041 400 992, closed 25 Dec-Jan 6, closed Tue Sept-June & dinner Mon Sept-May, average €35) brings an original approach to otherwise traditional lagoon dishes; the daily menu depends very much on what was on offer at that morning's Chioggia fish market.

Tourist information

APT *Lungomare Adriatico 101, Sottomarina (041 401 068/fax 041 554 0855/www.chioggia-apt.net).* **Open** *Oct-Mar* 8.30am-1.30pm Mon, Wed, Fri, Sat; 9am-5pm Tue, Thur. *Apr-Sept* 9am-7.30pm daily.

The Lagoon

Islands dot a fragile environment where locals escape the tourist hordes.

When you tire of the crowds around San Marco and the tourist-trappings of the Rialto, it's worth remembering that the city is surrounded by a vast stretch of quiet water, dotted with islands. Many of these are uninhabited, containing only crumbling convents or fortresses, home to seagulls and lazy lizards.

There are 34 islands on the salt-water lagoon, which covers more than 518 square kilometres (200 square miles). Painters and photographers are just as well served out here as in the city itself, especially on clear autumn and winter days, when the horizon clears to reveal the snow-capped peaks of the Dolomites beyond.

The wetlands of the lagoon are a wild, fragile environment for flora and fauna. For Venetians the lagoon is a refuge from the daily invasion of tourists. This is where they escape by boat for picnics on deserted islands, or where they go fishing for bass and bream. Others set off to dig up clams at low tide (most without the requisite licence), or organise hunting expeditions for duck, using the makeshift hides known as *botte* ('barrels', which is what they were originally, sunk into the floor of the lagoon). Many just head out after work, at sunset, to row.

From the lagoon, the precarious natural position of Venice and the uniqueness of its urban development come sharply into focus. Exploring some of the quieter corners of this waterscape is like going back to the sixth-century origins of the city. The classic tourist trip is usually limited to the three major islands of Murano, Burano and Torcello, but there are plenty of other possibilities.

EXPLORING THE LAGOON

Trips are organised by **Marina Fiorita Viaggi** (041 530 1865/fax 041 530 9567/marinafioritaviaggi@tin.it) exploring parts of the lagoon untouched by public transport. The excursions are mostly day trips with guides (English spoken), costing €22-€26 (€40-€43 with lunch); they run from March to September (groups only by appointment in winter), starting from Treporti (vaporetto 12 or 13 from Fondamente Nove). Booking is essential.

To learn more about the lagoon's ecostructure and bird life, catch the blue bus for 'Chioggia' or 'Sottomarina' from piazzale Roma, ask to get off at the WWF's **Oasi Valle Averto** (041 518 5068, open 9am-4pm Mon-Fri, Sun, admission €5, €3 6-14s, free under-6s,

guided visits at 10am, 2pm Sun, weekdays by appointment, minimum ten people).

The adventurous can rent a boat for the day. Craft with small motors don't need a permit, and can be hired from **Sport e Lavoro**, Cannaregio 2508, fondamenta della Misericordia (041 522 9535/www.noleggiobarchevenezia.it). Hire cost is €104 per day (20 percent extra on Sundays and holidays); if you want to take a guide along with you it's an extra €37 an hour; maximum six people per boat. No credit cards are accepted.

San Michele

Just opposite the fondamenta Nuove, halfway between Venice and Murano, this is the island where any tour of the lagoon begins. But for many Venetians it is their last stop, as San Michele is the city's cemetery. Early in the morning, the vaporetto (41 or 42) is packed with Venetians coming over to lay flowers. This is not a morbid spot, though: like Père Lachaise in Paris, it is an elegant city of the dead, with more than one famous resident.

An orderly red-brick wall runs round the whole of the island, with a line of tall cypress trees rising high behind it – the inspiration for Böcklin's famously lugubrious painting *Island of the Dead*. The vaporetto stops at the elegant church of **San Michele in Isola** (open 7.30am-12.15pm, 3-4pm daily). Designed by Mauro Codussi in the 1460s, this striking white building of Istrian stone was Venice's first Renaissance church, with a tripartite façade inspired by Leon Battista Alberti's Tempio Malatestiana in Rimini. The grounds of the Franciscan monastery that used to extend behind the church were seconded for burials when the city was under Napoleonic rule, in an effort to stop unhygienic Venetians digging graves in the *campi* around the parish churches. Soon it was the only place to be seen dead in. Most Venetians still want to make that last journey to San Michele, even though these days it's more a temporary parking lot than a final resting place. The island reached saturation point long ago, and even after paying through the nose for a plot, families know that after a suitable period – generally around ten years – the bones of their loved ones will be dug up and transferred to an ossuary on another island.

Visitors enter the cemetery (open Apr-Sept 7.30am-6pm daily, Oct-Mar 7.30am-4pm daily) through a dignified arch, marked by a 15th-century bas-relief of St Michael slaying a dragon with one hand and holding a pair of scales in the other. Beyond are the cool cloisters of the restored monastery where staff hand out rough maps of the cemetery, which are indispensable for celebrity hunts. In the Greek and Russian Orthodox section is the elaborate tomb of Sergei Pavlovich Diaghilev, who introduced the Ballets Russes to Europe, and a simpler monument to the composer Igor Stravinsky and his wife. The Protestant section has a selection of ships' captains and passengers who ended their days in La Serenissima, plus the simple graves of Ezra Pound and Joseph Brodsky. There's a rather sad children's section, and a corner dedicated to the city's gondoliers, their tombs decorated with carvings and statues of gondolas. Visit the cemetery on the *Festa dei morti* – All Souls' Day, 2 November – and the vaporetto is free but packed.

Murano

After San Michele, the number 42 or 41 vaporetto continues to Murano, one of the larger and more populous islands of the lagoon

(vaporettos 12 and 13 also put in there, but only at the Faro stop). In the 16th and 17th centuries, when it was a world centre of glass production and a decadent resort for pleasure-seeking wealthy Venetians, Murano had a population of more than 30,000. Now fewer than 5,000 people live here and many of the glass workers commute from the mainland.

Murano owes its fame to the decision taken in 1291 to transfer all of Venice's glass furnaces to the island because of a fear of fire in the main city. Their products were soon sold all over Europe. The secrets of glass were jealously guarded within the island: any glass-maker leaving Murano was proclaimed a traitor. Even today, there is no official glass school, and the delicate skills of blowing and flamework are only learned by apprenticeship to one of the glass masters.

At first sight Murano looks close to being ruined by glass tourism. Dozens of 'guides' swoop on visitors as they pile off the vaporetto, to whisk them off on tours of glass furnaces. Even if you head off on your own, you'll find yourself immediately in the tourist trap that is fondamenta dei Vetrai, a snipers' alley of shops selling glass knick-knacks, most of which are made far from Murano. But there are some serious glass-makers on the island, and even

San Michele in Isola: Venice's first Renaissance church. *See p134.*

Sightseeing

the tackiest of the showrooms usually have one or two gems (*see chapter* **Glass**). There's more to Murano, however, than glass.

At the far end of fondamenta dei Vetrai, the nondescript façade of the 14th-century parish church of **San Pietro Martire** holds important works of art.

Beyond the church, the fondamenta dei Vetrai terminates at Murano's Canal Grande, spanned by Ponte Vivarini, an unattractive 19th-century iron bridge. Before crossing it, it is worth looking at the Gothic **Palazzo Da Mula**, just to the left of the bridge; this splendid 15th-century building has been recently restored and transformed into council offices. In the morning it is possible to walk through it to see the remains of its courtyard, which contains a monumental carved Byzantine arch, relic of an earlier (12th- or 13th-century) building.

On the other side of the bridge, a right turn takes you along fondamenta Cavour; 200 metres further along, it veers sharply to the left, becoming fondamenta Giustinian. The 17th-century **Palazzo Giustinian**, situated reassuringly far from tacky chandeliers and fluorescent clowns, is the **Museo dell'Arte Vetrario**, the best place to learn about the history of glass. Just beyond this is Murano's greatest architectural treasure: the 12th-century basilica of **Santi Maria e Donato**, with its apse backing on the canal.

Venice's greatest love machine Giacomo Casanova was a Murano habitué. To retrace his footsteps, return to the Ponte Vivarini and keep walking along the quiet fondamenta Sebastiano Venier to its end. Here, the church of **Santa Maria degli Angeli** (open Sun for 11am mass) backs on to the convent where Casanova conducted one of his most torrid affairs, with a libertine nun named Maria Morosoni (*see p108* **Literary locations: Casanova**).

Museo dell'Arte Vetrario

Fondamenta Giustinian 8 (041 739 586). Vaporetto 41 or 42. **Open** *Apr-Oct* 10am-5pm Mon, Tue, Thur-Sun. *Nov-Mar* 10am-4pm Mon, Tue, Thur-Sun. **Admission** €4; €2.50 concessions (*see also p61* Musei Civici Veneziani). **No credit cards**.
Housed in the beautiful Palazzo Giustinian, built in the late 17th century for the bishops of Torcello, the museum has a huge collection of Murano glass. As well as the famed chandeliers, which only made their appearance in the 18th century, there are ruby-red beakers, opaque lamps and delicate Venetian *perle* – glass beads that were used in trade and commerce all over the world from the time of Marco Polo. One of the earliest pieces is the 15th-century Barovier marriage cup, decorated with portraits of the bride and groom. One room is devoted to blown-glass mirrors, a Muranese monopoly for centuries. On the ground floor there is a good collection of Roman glassware from near Zara on the Istrian peninsula.

San Pietro Martire

Fondamenta dei Vetrai (041 739 704). Vaporetto Colonna or Faro. **Open** 9am-noon, 3-6pm Mon-Sat; 3-6pm Sun. **Map** p310.
Behind its unspectacular façade, San Pietro Martire conceals two important works by Giovanni Bellini, both backed by marvellous landscapes: an

Santi Maria e Donato: a Veneto-Byzantine classic. *See p137.*

Assumption and a *Virgin and Child Enthroned with St Mark, St Augustine and Doge Agostino Barbarigo.* There are also two works by Veronese and assistants (mainly the latter), and an ornate altarpiece by Salviati that is lit up by the early morning sun.

Santi Maria e Donato
Campo San Donato (041 739 056). Vaporetto Museo. **Open** 8.30am-noon, 4-7pm Mon-Sat; 4-6pm Sun. **Map** p310.
Though altered by over-enthusiastic 19th-century restorers, the exterior of this church is a classic of the Veneto-Byzantine style, with an ornate blind portico on the rear of the apse. Inside is a richly coloured mosaic floor, laid down in 1140 at the same time as the floor of the basilica di San Marco, with floral and animal motifs. Above, a Byzantine apse mosaic of the Virgin looms out of the darkness in a field of gold.

Burano & Mazzorbo

Mazzorbo, the long island before Burano, is a haven of peace, rarely visited by tourists. The ferry generally stops here, then heads off to Torcello before tacking back to Burano, so it is often quicker to get off at Mazzorbo and walk to Burano across the long wooden bridge that connects the two islands and offers the bonus of a great view across the lagoon to Venice.

Mazzorbo was settled around the tenth century; when it became clear that Venice itself had got the upper hand, most of the large population simply dismantled their houses brick by brick, transported them by boat to Venice, and rebuilt them there. Today, Mazzorbo is a lazy place of small farms, with a pleasant walk to the 14th-century Gothic church of **Santa Caterina**, whose wobbly-looking tower still has its original bell, dating from 1318 – one of the oldest in Europe. Winston Churchill, a keen amateur painter, set up his easel here more than once after World War II. Opposite Burano is an area of attractive new low-cost housing, in shades of lilac, grey and green, designed by Giancarlo De Carlo.

Don't come to **Burano** with a black and white film in your camera. Together with the manufacture of lace, its picture-postcard houses make it a magnet for tourists.

The locals are traditionally either fishermen or lace-makers, though there are increasingly few of the latter, despite efforts by the island's **Scuola di Merletti** (Lace School) to pass on the skills to younger generations. The street leading from the main quay throbs with souvenir shops selling lace, lace and more lace – most of it machine-made in Taiwan. But Burano is big enough for the visitor to get lost in its narrow backstreets, where life goes on at a tranquill pace. It was in Burano that the Venice Carnevale was revived back in the 1970s, and

the modest celebrations here are still far more authenticly joyful than anything witnessed by the masses of masked tourists cramming piazza San Marco.

Fishermen have lived on Burano since the seventh century; they are said to have painted their houses different colours so that they could recognise them when fishing out on the lagoon (no matter that only a tiny proportion of the island's houses can actually be seen from the lagoon). Whatever the reason, the *buranelli* still go to great efforts to decorate their houses, and social life centres on the *fondamente* where the men repair nets or tend to their boats moored in the canal below, while their wives – at least in theory – make lace.

Lace began to be produced in Burano in the 15th century, originally by nuns, but was quickly picked up by fishermen's wives and daughters. So skilful were the local lace-makers that in the 17th century many were paid handsomely to work in the Alengon lace ateliers in Normandy. Today most work is done on commission, though interested parties will have to get to know one of the lace-makers in person, as the co operative that used to represent the old ladies closed down in 1995.

The busy main square of Burano is named after the island's most famous son, Baldassare Galuppi, a 17th-century composer who set many of Carlo Goldoni's plays to music and who was the subject of a poem by Robert Browning. The square is a good place for sipping a glass of prosecco. The most famous trattoria – though not the cheapest – is Da Romano, where the walls are covered with paintings accepted by the owner in payment for meals. If your artistic talents don't stretch this far, a better-value meal can be had at **Il Gatto Nero** (*see p162*) by the lively morning fish market (Tue-Sat) on the fondamenta della Pescheria. Across the main square from the lace museum is the church of **San Martino** (open 8am-noon, 3-7pm daily), containing an early Tiepolo *Crucifixion*, recently restored, and, in the chapel to the right of the chancel, three small paintings by the 15th-century painter Giovanni Mansueti; the *Flight into Egypt* presents the Holy Family amid an imaginative menagerie of beasts and birds.

Scuola di Merletti
Piazza B Galuppi 187, Burano (041 730 034). Vaporetto 12. **Open** *Apr-Oct* 10am-5pm Mon, Wed-Sun. *Oct-Mar* 10am-4pm Mon, Wed-Sun. **Admission** €4; €2.50 concessions (*see also p61* Musei Civici Veneziani). **No credit cards**.
In a series of rooms with painted wooden beams are cases full of elaborate examples of lacework from the 17th century onwards; aficionados will have fun spotting the various stitches, such as the famous

punto burano. Many of the older exhibits change every few months for conservation reasons, but if it's on display look out for the devout intricacy of the 17th-century altar cloth decorated with the Mysteries of the Rosary. There are fans, collars and parasols, and some of the paper pattern-sheets that lace-makers use. Unfortunately the school that gives the museum its name is now virtually defunct, although occasional courses are offered by some of the older generation of Burano lace-makers, who can sometimes be seen on weekday mornings at work in a corner of the museum.

San Francesco del Deserto

From behind the church of San Martino on Burano there is a view across the lagoon to the idyllic monastery island of San Franceso del Deserto. The island, with its 4,000 cypress trees, is inhabited by a small community of Franciscan monks. Getting there can be quite a challenge. Burano's one water taxi sits by the main boat quay, but the driver tends to disappear for long periods. Burano's postman will take you across on his motorboat. Either way, expect to pay at least €30 for the return ride. A better, and cheaper, option is to ask one of the local fishermen to give you a lift. They are usually willing to do so for a small fee – perhaps €15 for the return trip.

The other-worldly monk who shepherds visitors around with agonising slowness will tell the story of how the island was St Francis's first stop in Europe on his journey back from the Holy Land in 1220. He planted his stick – they say – it grew into a pine, and birds flew in to sing for him (there are certainly plenty of them in evidence in the cypress-packed gardens). The medieval monastery – all warm stone and cloistered calm – is about as far as you can get from the worldly bustle of the Rialto.

Convento di San Francesco del Deserto

041 528 6863/www.isola-sanfrancescodeldeserto.it.
Open 9-11am, 3-5pm Tue-Sat; 3-5pm Sun.
Admission by voluntary donation.

Torcello

The boat only takes a few minutes to steam over from Burano to Torcello, the sprawling, marshy island where the history of Venice began. At low tide, you could well imagine yourself in the Fens or the Camargue, and there are certainly as many mosquitoes.

Torcello today is a rural backwater with a resident population of less than 20; each time an inhabitant moves away for the bright lights of Burano or Mazzorbo, it is headline news in the Venice press. It is difficult to believe that in the

Mestre

One of the big advantages Venice has over all other major Italian cities is that its beautiful historic centre is not hemmed in by an unsightly rash of 1950s and '60s apartment blocks. The sordid sprawl exists, but at a safe distance across the lagoon. Its name is Mestre and if there is one thing it is keen on, it is to be considered as something other than a mere suburb of its glamorous neighbour.

It has no illustrious history to pride itself on. An insignificant walled town from the tenth century (the only notable remnant of these medieval fortifications is the tower in its main piazza), Mestre did not begin to grow exponentially until the last century, with the creation of the industrial port of Marghera (*see chapter* **Venice Today**). Then the lure of jobs attracted thousands of workers from all over Italy; from the 1950s, Venetians from the lagoon began to move there too, fleeing high house prices in Venice itself, or simply seeking the convenience of mainland life, with all its luxurious trappings such as cars and supermarkets.

As the population of Venice dwindled, Mestre continued to expand, sprawling outwards and upwards in grim concrete but never achieving a genuine sense of identity. This it is now striving to do. Administratively, the mainland sprawl is

14th century more than 20,000 people lived here. This was the first settlement in the lagoon, founded in the fifth century by the citizens of the Roman town of Altino on the mainland. Successive waves of emigration from Altino were sparked off by barbarian invasions, first by Attila and his Huns, and later, in the seventh century, by the Lombards.

But Torcello's dominance of the lagoon did not last: Venice itself was found to be more salubrious (malaria was rife on Torcello) and more easily defendable. Even the bishop of Torcello chose to live on Murano, in the palace that now houses the glass museum (*see p136*). But past decline is present charm, and rural Torcello is a great antidote to the pedestrian traffic jams around San Marco.

From the ferry jetty the campanile of the cathedral can already be made out; to get there, simply follow the canal down Torcello's only street (a recent attempt to repave it in concrete was fortunately blocked). To the right there's an part of Venice. But *mestrini* are petitioning for a referendum on divorce from Venice. It's not the first time: three such referendums have been held since 1979. The persistence of the promoters after three failures may seem perverse; however, support for the break from Venice has grown noticeably with each vote. With their parents' nostalgic connections with island Venice appearing increasingly irrelevant, a younger generation of *mestrini* will, sooner or later, give a definitive snip to the umbilical cord.

And the young in Mestre are a far more significant sector of the population than they are across the water. One evening visit to piazza Ferretto, the attractive (and recently refurbished) square at Mestre's heart, will suffice to get a sense of the extent to which this is a youth-oriented city. Indeed, any tourist looking for some active nightlife should consider a trip here, once the possibilities of campo Santa Margherita have been explored and exhausted. The city has more cinemas than Venice and good clubs – both straight and gay – are to be found both in the centre and the environs (*see chapters* **Nightlife** and **Gay**).

Many young *mestrini* see little point in hopping across to Venice at all, unless it be for a dutiful visit to ageing relatives. Even if they feel like a spot of Sunday afternoon tourism, they are much more likely to climb into their cars and head for Padua or Verona than mess about with the boats necessary to reach Venice.

Mestre cannot compete architecturally or artistically with Venice, although the churches of **San Rocco** (open 10.30am-noon Wed, Fri, 6-7.30pm Thur) with its 18th-century frescos, and **San Girolamo** (open 9am-noon, 4-6.30pm Mon-Sat) are worth a look, and there are some fine classical villas, particularly in the greener areas northwards on the way towards Carpenedo (which an imaginative Mestre legend says is where Icarus fell to earth).

However, Mestre has done a good deal over recent years to establish its cultural independence. Its theatres (*see chapter* **Performing Arts**) provide musical and theatrical seasons that rival anything Venice has to offer (with the exception of opera). There are lively historical societies and creative-writing workshops. In 2001 a long-promised new cultural centre was finally opened in piazzale Candiani: a five-storey building with spaces for exhibitions, workshops and multimedia events. Many major exhibitions staged in Venice now include side-events in the **Centro Culturale Candiani** (*see also p203*).

Mestre is never likely to set any hearts a-flutter with its radiant beauty, but it is doing its best to shake off its image as a drab dormitory suburb.

opulent private palazzo that still hosts extravagant parties, and just by the ponte del Diavolo (one of only two ancient bridges in the lagoon without a parapet) there is a simple *osteria*, **Al Ponte del Diavolo** (041 730 401; lunch only except Sat; Nov-Apr closed Wed) with reliable cooking and prices that are almost reasonable. Torcello's main square has some desultory souvenir stalls, a small but interesting **Museo dell'Estuario** with archaeological finds from around the lagoon, a battered stone seat known somewhat arbitrarily as Attila's throne and two extraordinary churches.

The 11th-century church of **Santa Fosca** (open Apr-Oct 10.30am-5.30pm daily, Nov-Mar 10am-5pm daily, free) looks like a miniature version of Istanbul's Santa Sophia, more Byzantine than European with its Greek-cross plan and external colonnade; its bare interior allows the perfect geometry of the space to come to the fore. Next door is the imposing cathedral of **Santa Maria Assunta**.

By the churches, the Locanda Cipriani (*see p162*) is rated as one of Venice's top restaurants, with prices to match.

The three big Cipriani concerns in Venice – the Hotel Cipriani (*see p10*), Harry's Bar (run by Arrigo Cipriani, son of the founder; *see p165*) and the Locanda Cipriani (run by Arrigo's sister Carla, who is married to Italian soft-porn director Tinto Brass) have no business links; all have been involved in a long-running legal battle for the right to use the name 'Cipriani'.

A cumulative ticket for the basilica, campanile and Museo dell'Estuario is available at the sights themselves and costs €6 (€4 groups) or €4 for the basilica and Museo. No credit cards are accepted.

Museo dell'Estuario
Palazzo del Consiglio, Torcello (041 730 761). Vaporetto 12. **Open** *Apr-Oct* 10.30am-5.30pm Tue-Sun. *Nov-Mar* 10am-5pm Tue-Sun. **Admission** €4 (with basilica).

A small but worthwhile collection of sculptures and archaeological finds from the cathedral and elsewhere in Torcello. Among the exhibits on the ground floor are late 12th-century fragments of mosaic from the apse of Santa Maria dell'Assunta, and two of the *bocche di leone* (lions' mouths) where citizens with grudges could post their denunciations. Upstairs are Greco-Byzantine icons, painted panels, bronze seals and pottery fragments, and an exquisite carved ivory statuette of an embracing couple from the beginning of the 15th century.

Santa Maria Assunta

041 270 2464/asa@patriarcato.venezia.it. **Open** *Apr-Oct* 10.30am-6pm daily. *Nov-Mar* 10am-5pm daily. **Admission** €3.

Dating from 638, the basilica is the oldest building on the lagoon. The interior has an elaborate 11th-century mosaic floor that rivals that of San Marco. But the main draws of this church are the vivid mosaics on the vault and walls, which range in date from the ninth to the end of the 12th century. The apse has a simple but stunning mosaic of a Madonna and Child on a plain gold background, while the other end of the cathedral is dominated by a huge mosaic of the *Last Judgement* (an audioguide in English provided free at the door gives a detailed explanation). The theological rigour and narrative complexity of this huge composition suggest comparisons with the *Divine Comedy*, which Dante was writing at about the same time, but the anonymous mosaicists of Torcello were more concerned with striking fear into the hearts of their audience – hence the wicked devils pushing the damned into hell.

Campanile di Torcello

041 270 2464/asa@patriarcato.venezia.it. **Open** *Apr-Oct* 10.30am-5.30pm daily. *Nov-Mar* 10am-4.45pm daily. **Admission** €2.

The view of the lagoon from the top of the campanile was memorably described by Ruskin: 'Far as the eye can reach, a waste of wild sea moor, of a lurid ashen grey.' And he concluded with the elegaic words: 'Mother and daughter, you behold them both in their widowhood, Torcello and Venice.' There is no lift, just a stiff walk up steep ramps.

Sant'Erasmo & Vignole

Sant'Erasmo (served by vaporetto 13) is the best-kept secret of the lagoon: larger than Venice itself, but with a tiny population that contents itself with growing most of the vegetables eaten in La Serenissima (on Rialto market stalls the sign *San Rasmo* is a mark of quality). Venetians refer to the islanders of Sant'Erasmo as *i matti* – the crazies – because of their legendarily shallow gene pool (everybody seems to be called Vignotto or Zanella); the islanders don't think much of Venetians either. There are cars on this island, but as they are only used to drive the few miles

from house to boat and back, few are in top-notch condition – a state of affairs favoured by the fact that the island does not have a single policeman. It also lacks a doctor, pharmacy and school, but there is a supermarket, one fishermen's bar-trattoria – **Ai Tedeschi** (lunch only Nov-Mar, closed Tue) – hidden away on a small sandy beach by the Forte Massimiliano, a crumbling Austrian fort; and a restaurant, **Ca' Vignotto** (via Forti 71, 041 528 5329, average €25-€30, closed Tue and mid-Dec to mid-Jan) where bookings are essential.

The main attraction of the island lies in the beautiful country landscapes and lovely walks past traditional Veneto farmhouses, through vineyards and fields of artichokes and asparagus – a breath of fresh air after all the urban crowding of Venice.

By the main vaporetto stop (Chiesa) is the 20th-century church (on the site of an earlier one founded before the year 1000) containing, over the entrance-door, a particularly gruesome 17th-century depiction of the martyrdom of St Erasmus, who had his intestines wound out of his body on a windlass. The resemblance of a windlass to a capstan resulted in St Erasmus becoming the patron saint of sailors.

If you're around on the first Sunday in October, don't miss the *Festa del Mosto* (*see chapter* **By Season**), held to inaugurate the first pressing of new wine. This is perhaps the only chance you'll ever get to witness – or even participate in – *gara del bisato*: a game in which an eel is dropped into a tub of water blackened by squid ink. Contestants have to plunge their heads into the tub and attempt to catch the eel with their teeth.

The number 13 vaporetto also stops at the smaller island of **Vignole**, where there is a medieval chapel dedicated to St Erosia.

Opposite the Capannone vaporetto stop on Sant'Erasmo is the tiny island of **Lazzaretto Nuovo**. Get off here at the weekend, shout across, and with luck a boat might row over to get you. In the 15th century the island was fortified as a customs deposit and military prison; during the 1576 plague outbreak it became a quarantine centre. At the peak of the epidemic more than 10,000 people were cooped up here. More recently it has become a research centre for the archaeologists of the Archeo Club di Venezia, who are excavating its ancient remains, including a church that may date back to the sixth century.

The southern lagoon

The southern part of the lagoon between Venice, the Lido and the mainland has 14 small islands, a few of which are still inhabited, though most are out of bounds for tourists.

San Lazzaro degli Armeni: from leper colony to global centre of Armenian culture.

San Servolo is home to a private university (*see chapter* **Directory: Study**). **La Grazia** was for years a quarantine hospital but the structure has now been closed. The huge **San Clemente**, once a lunatic asylum, after a period as a home for abandoned cats, was bought by Benetton and has now been sold on to the real-estate company Beni Stabili, which has turned it into one of the lagoon's plushest hotels (*see p57* **Island luxury**).

But pick up vaporetto number 20 from San Zaccaria at 3.10pm (note that only a few each day stop at San Lazzaro), and you will be one of the select few who can say that they made it to the island of **San Lazzaro degli Armeni**, just opposite the Lido.

A black-cloaked Armenian priest meets the boat and takes visitors on a detailed tour of the **Monastero Mechitarista**. This tiny island is a global point of reference for Armenia's Catholic minority, visited and supported by Armenians from Italy and abroad. Near the entrance stand the printing presses that helped to distribute Armenian literature all over the world for 200 years. Sadly, they are now silent, with the monastery's charmingly retro line in dictionaries, school and liturgical texts farmed out to a modern press.

Originally a leper colony, in 1717 the island was presented by the doge to an Armenian abbot called Mekhitar, who was on the run from the Turkish invasion of the Peloponnese. There had been an Armenian community in Venice since the 11th century, centring on the tiny Santa Croce degli Armeni church, just round

the corner from the piazza San Marco, but the construction of this church and monastery on the former leper colony made Venice a world centre of Armenian culture.

The monastery was the only one in the whole of Venice to be spared the Napoleonic axe that did away with so many convents and monasteries: the emperor had a soft spot for Armenians and argued that this was an academic rather than a religious institute.

The tour takes in the cloisters and the church, rebuilt after a fire in 1883. The museum and the modern library contain 40,000 priceless books and manuscripts, and a bizarre collection of gifts donated over the years by visiting Armenians, ranging from Burmese prayer books to an Egyptian mummy.

The island's most famous student was Lord Byron, who used to take a break from his more earthly pleasures in Venice and row over three times a week to learn Armenian (as he found that his 'mind wanted something craggy to break upon') with the monks. He helped the monks to publish an Armenian-English grammar, although by his own confession he never got beyond the basics of the language. You can buy a completed version of this, plus a number of period maps and an illustrated children's Armenian grammar, in the shop just inside the monastery gate.

San Lazzaro degli Armeni – Monastero Mechitarista

041 526 0104. **Open** 3.20-5pm daily for guided visits. **Admission** €6; €3 concessions. **No credit cards.**

Chancers

Venice and gambling go back a long way. Setting up a city in the middle of a salt lagoon was a long shot to begin with, but like so many of the Venetians' cannier bets, it was one that paid off handsomely. It wasn't until its decline as a giant of world trade, however, that Venice turned in a big way from betting on its destiny to betting as a pastime.

In 1638 the Venetian authorities granted permission to Marco Dandolo to use the back section of his palazzo near San Moisè – the so-called 'reduced quarters' or *ridotto* (now part of the Hotel Monaco and visitable through the calle Vallaresso entrance) as gaming rooms. A century later they oozed luxury, with rich furnishings and lavish frescos. Noblemen could enter bare-faced; anyone else was admitted if masked. Senators sold their furniture and women their virtue around tables where fortunes were made and lost. So out-of-hand was the situation that in 1774, the state forced the establishment to close.

No longer concentrated in one lush setting, gambling spread everywhere: to salons, cafés, theatres (which opened up special gaming rooms bored play-goers); even the little private hide-aways (*casini*) that Venetian noblemen liked to have at their disposal for extra-marital dabbling were now given over (almost) exclusively to the gaming vice.

In the 19th century, Venice's Austrian rulers barely tolerated gambling, though the lottery was kept up to give poorer citizens a comforting dream of a better life. But the only serious money in the city was that of tourists, and for the most part they had other, staider, ways of spending it.

It was not until 1937 that any major attempt was made to revive the city's spirit of play. As part of a general scheme to make the Lido a playground for the rich and famous – and to show that Fascists could have fun too – the Casinò (pronouced with the accent on the final o; *casino* with the accent on the i means 'brothel') was opened up alongside the new Palazzo del Cinema. The war, of course, put a damper on things, but after this irksome interruption the Lido enjoyed a decade or so of worldly revelling. Industrialists, film stars and royals splashed their money around freely, to the music of swing bands and the glee of the popular press. In 1959, in response to the need

for a more conveniently situated winter establishment, Ca' Vendramin was opened on the Grand Canal near the station.

This was the beginning of the end for the Lido, which gradually dropped off the revellers' A-list. Crooked croupier scandals in the 1980s and '90s tarnished the Casinò's image. But the real blow came with the opening of a bargain-basement casino across the border in Slovenia. Local chancers (who by now made up the bulk of the clients) eschewed the long slog to the Lido in favour of a quick hop by car to a less pretentious gaming establishment.

Venice counter-attacked in August 1999 with a casino at Ca' Noghera near Mestre (*see p138*). Ca' Noghera's parish priest denounced it as the 'house of the devil'.

Venice's then-Mayor Massimo Cacciari (a prickly character never averse to a little priest-baiting) defined the croupiers as *operatori sociali* (socially useful workers). From city hall's point of view, he had a point; in the year 2000 Ca' Noghera grossed 210 billion lire (roughly £70 million), a third of which went straight into municipal coffers. (In the same period the Lido Casinò earned a measly 700 million lire; in January 2001 it was ignominiously closed.)

Venice's two casinos are Europe's most profitable, but relations between the Mestre and Venice casinos remain uneasy. The Grand Canal establishment still likes to think of itself as high class but the harsh reality is that slot-machines and electronic games are infinitely greater money-spinners than roulette. Dinner jackets and the swish of silk are definitely accoutrements of the past.

Casinò Municipale di Venezia

Ca' Vendramin Calergi, Cannaregio 2040, calle larga Vendramin (041 529 7111/www. casinovenezia.it). Vaporetto San Marcuola. **Open** *Slot machines* 11am-3am daily. *Tables* 3pm-3am daily. **Admission** 5; 10 includes cloakroom, use of car-park and a fiche. **Credit** AmEx, DC, MC, V. Jacket required.

Venice Casino Ca' Noghera

Ca' Noghera, via Pagliaga 2 (041 529 7111/ www.casinovenezia.it). Bus 4/ or shuttle-service from Piazzale Roma. **Open** 10am-4am Mon-Fri, Sun; 10am-5am Sat. **Admission** 5; 10 includes cloakroom, use of car-park and a fiche. **Credit** AmEx, DC, MC, V. Casual clothes.

Eat, Drink, Shop

Eating Out

Venture into Venetian Venice, where culinary traditions are alive and kicking.

An old tourist adage has it that 'you don't eat well in Venice'. This is no longer true – if, indeed, it ever was. Venice has long and glorious culinary traditions based on fresh seafood, game and vegetables, backed up by northern Italy's three main carbohydrate fixes: pasta, risotto rice and polenta. And although some of the city's best cooks work at home, there are plenty of others who perform for paying guests.

The lagoon has a highly developed wine culture too (*see p156* **Wines of the northeast**): the vineyards of the Veneto and Friuli fuel the city's *bacari* (*see below and p144* **Bacari**) – traditional wine-and-food bars.

But in Venice more than most places, you have to know where to go. As one of Europe's most popular tourist destinations the city inevitably has its share of sharp operators who are more interested in the quick buck than the grilled duck. To eat well, one has to be prepared to forfeit the safety of the hotel restaurant or

the *menu turistico* and venture into the mysterious land that is Venetian Venice.

Even assuming one is charged the same price as the locals (not always a safe bet), eating authentically does not always mean eating cheaply. The advent of the euro did nothing to halt the onward march of prices and it has become well-nigh impossible to get a sit-down meal on the lagoon for less than €30 a head. But take a deep breath, factor it into the budget, trust the guide, and – if the force is with you – you may end up eating very well indeed in this so-called 'culinary desert'.

SQUIDS IN

At the top end, among luxury establishments such as **Locanda Cipriani** (*see p162*) or **Harry's Bar** (*see p165*), the only real movement is the reprinting of the menu every few months to take account of inflation (and then some). The cuisine in these restaurants is generally good, in a high-class-comfort-food

Eat, Drink, Shop

Alla Botte: the place to meet for a glass of wine and seafood snacks. *See p147.*

sort of way; and knowing that you'll be able to come back in three years' time and have the same meal, served, likely as not, by the same waiters, is all part of their charm. But if it's adventure you're after – the thrill of discovery, the frisson of value for money – then steer well clear.

The slow revolution in Venetian dining has come mainly from below: from the creative relaunch of the traditional hostelry – the bacaro – which has been given a new lease of life with a spate of recent openings; and from the attempt of a handful of highly motivated local chefs to strip away the *cordon bleu* subterfuge and go back to first principles.

Yesterday's revolutionaries, of course, are today's establishment. **Corte Sconta** (*see p150*) is a case in point: when Claudio Proietto opened this trattoria in the backwoods of Castello in 1980, his formula – based on the freshest seafood, cooked and marinated in the same way Venetian families do it (or rather, used to do it) at home – was a revelation. But now everyone has jumped on the bandwagon, and though Corte Sconta is still as good as ever, the prices are now in the upper range.

If the city-wide distribution of the restaurants recommended below looks a tad uneven, that's because high rents have forced the better-value operations away from the tourist hub of San Marco and into those parts of the city that still have significant numbers of resident Venetians – northern Cannaregio, eastern Castello and Sant'Elena, western Dorsoduro, the Giudecca, and the outlying islands.

There are a few rules worth bearing in mind. In more rustic eateries, menus are often recited out loud; most waiters, though, can deliver an approximate English translation of most of the dishes on the menu, and they're used to repeating things. If you are unsure of the price of something you have ordered, always ask. If there is a printed menu, note that fish is often quoted by weight, rather than by dish – generally per *etto* (100 grammes). Steer well clear of those restaurants – mainly around the San Marco district – that employ sharply dressed waiters to stand outside and persuade passing tourists to come in for a meal: an immediate recipe for rip-off prices. Always ask for a written *conto* (bill) at the end of the meal, as it is, in theory, illegal to leave the restaurant without one.

Finally, bear in mind that there are two timescales for eating in Venice. The more upmarket restaurants follow standard Italian practice, serving lunch from around 1pm to 3pm and dinner from 7.30pm until at least 10pm. But *bacari* and neighbourhood *trattorie*

tend to follow Venetian workers' rhythms, with lunch running from midday to 2pm and dinner from 6.30pm to 9pm. In other words, if you want to eat cheaply, eat early.

WHAT'S ON THE PLATE
A writhing, glistening variety of seafood swims from the morning stalls of the Rialto and Chioggia markets (*see p186* **Market day**) into restaurant kitchens; it's not always cheap, but for dedicated pescivores, there are

The best Restaurants

For cuisine
Al Covo (*p150*); Da Fiore (*p157*); Alle Testiere (*p151*).

For the wine list
Fiaschetteria Toscana (*p153*); Alle Testiere (*p151*); Vini da Gigio (*p155*).

For value
Vini da Gigio (*p155*), Alla Zucca (*p159*).

New in town
Boccadoro (*p154*); Osteria di San Marco (*p149*); Il Sole sulla Vecia Cavana (*p155*).

For non-stop daytime eating
Alla Rivetta (*p151*).

For scenic open-air eating
Acqua pazza (*p149*); Bancogiro (*p157*); Busa alla Torre (*p162*); Harry's Dolci (*p161*); Refolo (*p159*).

For that romantic tête-a-tête
Gran Caffè Ristorante Quadri (*p149*).

For fish
Boccadoro (*p154*); Corte Sconta (*p150*); Al Fontego dei Pescaori (*p155*).

For meat
Dalla Marisa (*p153*); L'Incontro (*p161*).

For vegetarians
Alla Zucca (*p159*).

For pizza
Acqua pazza (*p149*); La Perla (*p155*).

For international cooking
Mirai (*p156*).

For an unusual location
Mistrà (*p161*).

For Sunday lunch on the lagoon
Alla Maddalena (*p162*).

Eat, Drink, Shop

Bacari

The bacaro is Venice's wine-only equivalent of the British pub. With their blackened beams and rickety wooden tables, *bacari* (accent on the first syllable) are often hidden down backstreets or in quiet *campielli*. Here locals crowd the bar, swiftly downing a glass of wine (*un'ombra*) between work and home, and taking the edge off their appetite with one of the *cicheti* (snacks) that line the counter.

In some *bacari*, long wooden tables at the back of the shop or in a side room are laid on for those looking for something more substantial: a pasta dish or a risotto, a plate of *sopressa* (rustic salami) and polenta, or in those that have a full kitchen, a wide selection of *secondi*. Such places are the saving grace of the city's tourist-oriented eating-out scene and the guardians of the endangered species that is traditional Venetian cuisine.

Bacari themselves, though, are by no means endangered. In a city not known for its good-value eats, the bacaro formula appeals to locals, students and budget-conscious tourists alike. In recent years a spate of new ones has opened: some have decor so traditional they look as if they've been around for centuries; others favour a more minimalist wine bar style.

Once you've taken up your position at the bar and ordered a glass of tocai or cabernet, you can do the *cicheti* thing yourself. You'll be expected to keep tabs on how many you've consumed – though the barman should keep a fairly accurate count. Pay for drinks and snacks together at the end. It is very rare for such salt-of-the-earth *osterie* to accept credit cards, and many close early in the evening.

Bacari are listed in this chapter if they offer sit-down meals and waiter service; for those that are mainly watering holes with bar snacks and no more than one or two hot dishes, *see* chapter **Cafés, Bars & Pasticcerie**. Many of those that have moved towards full restaurant status still have bars where you can perch and swig: even Da Fiore, now Venice's most upmarket restaurant, hangs on to its entrance bar counter as if it were a family heirloom.

Best bacari for

sit-down meals Da Alberto (*p152*); Anice Stellato (*p152*); Bentigodi (*p152*); Ca' d'Oro (Alla Vedova) (*p153*); Alla Fontana (*p155*).
wine and bar snacks All'Arco (*p169*); Bancogiro (*p157*); Il Cantinone (*p171*); Cavatappi (*p165*); Alle Alpi (Da Dante) (*p166*); Da Lele (*p170*); Do Mori (*p169*); Alla Patatina (*p158*); Ai Vini Padovani (*p161*).

few better stamping grounds in the whole of Italy. To make sense of the bewildering variety of sea creatures that are to be found, *see p160* **The menu**.

There are alternatives to seafood, but you need to make an extra effort to seek them out. The once-strong local tradition of creative ways with meat – especially the more unmentionable parts – is kept alive in a couple of restaurants and one marvellous trattoria, **Dalla Marisa** (*see p153*); it can also be found in bar-counter *cicheti* (*tapas*-style snacks) like *nervetti* (veal cartilage) and *musetto* (spicy pig's intestine parcels filled with various cuts of pork).

In other parts of north-east Italy, such as Treviso or Trieste, baking and boiling are an integral and important part of the cook's repertoire. But Venice is less influenced by all those years of Austrian occupation. Pretty much the only things that are boiled in the Venetian kitchen are pasta and polenta (cornmeal); almost everything else is either grilled, fried or marinated, in true Mediterranean style.

Vegetarians may at first be horrified to realise that there is not a single veggie restaurant in the whole of the city. But Venetian cuisine relies heavily on seasonal vegetables, so it is quite easy to eat a vegetarian meal. *Secondi* are often accompanied by a wide selection of grilled vegetables: aubergine, courgette, tomato or radicchio. Many *cicheti* are vegetables: artichoke hearts, deep-fried pumpkin flowers, *polpetti* (little balls made with ricotta cheese). And several pasta dishes are vegetable-based, using *funghi porcini*, or broccoli, or oil, garlic and chilli. The sauce rarely has meat in unless it says so on the menu; if in doubt, ask: *non c'è la carne, vero?*

There is something of the Spanish *tapas* mentality about the Venetian approach to meals: not only in the tasty *cicheti* lined up on bacaro counters, but in the way the *antipasti* (hors d'oeuvres) often engulf the whole meal. If you nodded vigorously when the waiter suggested bringing 'one or two' seafood *antipasti*, you may start to regret it when the fifth plate arrives – but it is perfectly okay to just eat a plate of pasta afterwards, or to skip to the *secondo*, or go straight to dessert. Or even to stop the meal right there. There is no obligation to order the regulation three courses: flexibility is the keyword.

Except in the more upmarket restaurants and one or two born-again *bacari*, wines will mostly be local. Luckily, the wine-growing area that stretches from the Veneto north-east to Friuli is, after Tuscany and Piedmont, one of Italy's strongest, with good whites like tocai, sauvignon and soave backed up by solid reds like raboso or cabernet franc (*see p156* **Wines of the north-east**). This means that even in humbler establishments the house wine is usually drinkable, and often surprisingly refined.

PIZZERIE

Like all major Italian cities, Venice has its fair share of pizza joints, though the standard is not particularly high. Still, prices in *pizzerie* remain reasonably low – around €15 a head for a pizza and a beer, with cover and service – which makes them a good standby for a carbohydrate-and-protein injection between more expensive restaurant meals. In the rest of Italy, *pizzerie* are generally open only in the evening; tourist demand, though, means that almost all Venetian pizza emporia serve the doughy discs at lunch too. Note that beer, rather than wine, is the traditional accompaniment to pizza.

INTERNATIONAL

The locals are decidedly conservative when it comes to exploring foreign food; and few tourists come to Venice to eat Chinese. Until a few years ago, there were virtually no international restaurants in the city. The situation is a little better now, though we're barely into double figures.

READING THE LISTINGS

Average restaurant prices are based on a three-course meal for one person, with cover charge but without drinks. For *pizzerie*, average prices are for one pizza, a medium beer, service and cover charge; we give a separate average if they also do restaurant meals. For *bacari* that offer both bar snacks and full meals with waiter service, averages are for full sit-down meals; perching at the bar and ordering a plate of nibbles is a whole lot cheaper.

Times given in the listings below refer to the kitchen's opening hours – that is, when it's possible to order food; establishments may keep their doors open well after this.

To save space, we have left some names of common Venetian dishes in Italian, as they appear in the menu. For translations, *see p160* **The menu.**

San Marco

Restaurants & *bacari*

Al Bacareto

San Marco 3447, calle delle Botteghe (041 528 9336/ www.paginegialle.it/osteriaalbacareto). Vaporetto Sant'Angelo or San Samuele. **Meals served** *Sept-July* noon-3pm, 7-10.15pm Mon-Fri; noon-3pm Sat. Closed Aug. **Average** €40. **Credit** AmEx, MC, V. **Map** p307 A3.

This rustic family-run trattoria near Palazzo Grassi has tables outside in summer. Inside is a lively bar packed with locals downing wine and sampling the *cicheti*, among which the *polpetine* (spicy balls of rice, potatoes, spinach or meat) stand out; the fried sardines (*sarde fritte*) are also good. The sit-down menu revolves around Venetian classics like *bigoli in salsa*. The only drawback is the steep price leap between bar-snack and table service; get around it by turning up at 8pm on the dot, when risottos and pasta dishes are served piping hot to stand-up customers at the bar.

Alla Botte ❷

San Marco 5482, campo San Bartolomeo (041 520 9775/www.osteriaallabotte.it). Vaporetto Rialto. **Open** *Sept-July* 10am-3pm, 6-11pm Mon, Tue, Fri, Sat; 10am-3pm Wed. Closed July. **Average** €28. **Credit** DC, MC, V. **Map** p305 C4.

Osteria San Marco. *See p149.*

RISTORANTE **BIRRARIA** PIZZERIA
Antica
La Corte

V E N E Z I A

A hint of New York in the heart of Venice

A tastefully restored beer factory offering a distinctively
different and fashionable ambience, with an atmosphere that is
typically New York yet firmly rooted in the best of
Venetian traditions

The restaurant offers regional dishes in a relaxed, warm setting,
catering to Venetians and visitors alike

We also host contemporary art exhibitions throughout the year

ANTICA BIRRARIA LA CORTE – SAN POLO 2168 – 30125 VENEZIA
TEL. +39 041 2750570 – FAX +39 041 2756605

Campo San Bartolomeo is Venice's liveliest evening meeting place, and after seeing and being seen, many young Venetians head off to the nearby Botte for a quick *ombra* (glass of wine). At the tiny, barrel-like bar (hence the name: *botte* means barrel), clients jostle for wine, a seafood *cicheto* or a sandwich made with a slice from the immense mortadella on the counter. There's a back room where simple meals (*seppie in nero, fegato alla veneziana*) are served. It can get extremely packed around aperitivo time, but that's all part of the fun.

Gran Caffè Ristorante Quadri ❸

San Marco 120, piazza San Marco (041 528 9299/ www.quadrivenice.com). Vaporetto Vallaresso or San Zaccaria. **Meals served** *Apr-Oct* 12.15-2pm, 7.15-10.15pm daily. *Nov-Mar* 12.15-2pm, 7.15-10.15pm Tue-Sun. **Average** €90. **Credit** AmEx, DC, MC, V. **Map** p307 A4.

If you want to splash out on a really special meal, book for lunch or dinner at the restaurant above Caffè Quadri (*see p164*) on piazza San Marco. The setting is truly sumptuous: two neo-classical salons adorned with huge mirrors, damask wall coverings and imposing Murano chandeliers – even better if you can secure one of the four window tables that look out over the piazza. It would be easy to soft-pedal the food in such surroundings, but the chef here manages a surprisingly creative take on the Venetian tradition; there are even one or two clearly marked vegetarian options, and an unusual 'baked ice-cream' dessert (amaretto and almond mousse, served with a toasted meringue). And the final reckoning, all things considered – is not excessive. Quadri also organises wine and food tastings on Tuesdays in English and Italian (€35 a head, book in advance).

Osteria San Marco ❹

San Marco 1610, Frezzeria (041 528 5242). Vaporetto Vallaresso. **Open** 10.30am-midnight Mon-Sat. **Meals served** 12.30-2.30pm, 7.30-10pm Mon-Sat. Closed 2wks Jan. **Average** €45. **Credit** MC, V. **Map** p307 A4.

This smart new *osteria*-wine bar on a busy shopping street is a breath of fresh air in the tourist-oriented San Marco area. The four young guys behind the operation are sometimes run off their feet, but they're serious about food and wine and their attention to detail shows through both in the bar-counter selection of snacks and wines by the glass, and in the sit-down menu, which changes regularly and is based on the freshest local produce. Among the dishes that can be sampled in the long, rustic-minimalist dining area are *garganelli in salsa di zucchine e anitra* (short pieces of pasta with courgette and duck sauce) and *bocconcini di rana pescatrice in vellutata di peperoni* (angler fish with sweet pepper sauce). Prices are high, but you're paying for the area as well as the quality and the mark-up on bottles is commendably low. Note that a selection of dishes is on offer even when the kitchen is closed.

Vini da Arturo ❺

San Marco 3656, calle dei Assassini (041 528 6974). Vaporetto Rialto or Sant'Angelo. **Meals served** *Sept-July* 12.30-2.30pm, 7.30-11pm Mon-Sat. Closed 2wks after Carnevale & Aug. **Average** €70. **No credit cards. Map** p307 A3.

This tiny place just north of La Fenice, whose narrow, pannelled interior has earned it the nickname *il vagone* (the railway carriage), is a well-kept secret among Venetian gastronomes. There's not a whiff of fish on the menu, which features the best fillet steak on the lagoon, as well as a few less carnivorous (the owner describes them as 'vegetarian') options – including some creative salad tasters, served as an antipasto. For dessert, try the creamy tiramisù, or the chocolate mousse. Service is affable and the quality of food is high, but then again so it should be at these prices – and note that they don't take credit cards.

Vino Vino ❻

San Marco 2007A, ponte delle Veste (041 241 7688/ www.vinovino.co.it). Vaporetto Vallaresso or Santa Maria del Giglio. **Open** 10.30am-midnight Mon, Wed-Fri, Sun; 10.30am-1am Sat. **Average** €30. **No credit cards. Map** p307 A3.

Overlooking a canal near La Fenice, Vino Vino – an offshoot of the ultra-traditional Antico Martini restaurant – was the city's first authentic wine bar, and it still has one of the best-stocked wine cellars. You can sample vintages from as far afield as Australia, California and Spain, as well as local crus from the Veneto and Friuli regions, a fair number of which are offered *alla mescita* – by the glass. Elaborate bar snacks include the likes of quail with polenta, sautéd veal kidneys and *baccalà alla vicentina*; the same menu is on offer for sit-down customers, at a price.

Pizzerie

Acqua pazza ❼

San Marco 3808, campo Sant'Angelo (041 277 0688). Vaporetto Sant'Angelo or Santa Maria del Giglio. **Meals served** noon-3pm, 7-11pm Tue-Sun. Closed 7 Jan-7 Feb. **Average** €20 pizza; €50 full meal. **Credit** AmEx, DC, MC, V. **Map** p307 A3.

It would be hard to imagine a better location for this new Neapolitan pizzeria-restaurant: *ombrellone*-shaded tables spill on to the raised pavement of campo Sant'Angelo, an eminently Venetian square situated half-way between Rialto and Accademia. The pizzas are authentic *napoletana* high-risers, made with quality ingredients including *mozzarella di bufala* and fresh Pachino tomatoes. The rest of the menu is equally true to its roots, with dishes like *impepata di cozze* (peppery mussel sauté) and *calamari ripieni* (stuffed squid); there is also a decent range of Campanian wines. But if you stray away from pizza and beer, don't be surprised if the prices stray too.

Castello

Restaurants & *bacari*

All'Aciugheta ⑧

Castello 4357, campo Santi Filippo e Giacomo (041 522 4292/info@aciugheta-hotelrio.it). Vaporetto San Zaccaria. **Open** 11.30am-10.30pm daily. **Average** €10 wine & bar snacks; €32 full meal. **Credit** MC, V. **Map** p308 B1.

It looks like a real tourist-trap pizzeria from the outside – we're only two minutes from piazza San Marco, after all – but muscle your way through to the bar and you'll see the other face of the 'Little Anchovy': a bar packed with locals sampling some excellent wines, and fuelling up on a selection of *cicheti*. These include *polpette*, filled peppers, the trademark *pizzette* (mini-pizzas) with anchovies, and a good selection of Italian and French cheeses, to be matched with a vintage recommended by owner-barman Gianni Bonaccorsi, who also organises wine-tasting evenings. The pizzeria-restaurant side of the operation is less exalted, and less good value.

Antica Trattoria Bandierette ⑨

Castello 6671, barbaria de le Tole (041 522 0619/ www.elmoro.com/bandierette.htm). Vaporetto Ospedale. **Meals served** *Apr-Sept* noon-2pm, 7-10pm Mon-Sat. *Oct-Mar* noon-2pm, 7-10pm Mon, Tue, Thur-Sat; noon-2pm Wed. Closed 2wks Dec-Jan. **Average** €28. **Credit** DC, MC, V. **Map** p308 A2.

The bland trattoria decor leaves a little to be desired, but the locals who cram into this busy place between Santi Giovanni e Paolo and San Francesco don't come for the decor: they're here for the good, reasonably priced seafood cooking and the friendly service. Among the *primi*, the tagliatelle with scampi and spinach and the spaghetti with prawns and asparagus are especially good.

Corte Sconta ⑩

Castello 3886, calle del Pestrin (041 522 7024). Vaporetto Arsenale. **Meals served** *Feb-Dec* 12.30-2.30pm, 7-10pm Tue-Sat. Closed Jan, mid July-mid Aug. **Average** €50. **Credit** MC, V. **Map** p308 B2.

Claudio Proietto's trailblazing seafood restaurant in the eastern reaches of Castello is now such a firm favourite on the well-informed tourist circuit that it is usually a good idea to book several days in advance. The main act is an endless procession of seafood *antipasti*; the day's catch might include *canoce, garusoli* or *schie*. The pasta is home-made and the warm *zabaione* dessert is a delight. Decor is of the modern bohemian trattoria variety, the ambience loud and friendly. In summer, try to secure one of the tables in the pretty vine-covered courtyard.

Al Covo ⑪

Castello 3968, campiello della Pescaria (041 522 3812). Vaporetto Arsenale. **Meals served** 12.30-2pm, 7.30-10pm Mon, Tue, Fri-Sun. Closed mid Dec-mid Jan, 2wks Aug. **Average** €70. **No credit cards.**

Far from the tourist crowds, Al Covo is in a quiet Castello lane behind the Riva degli Schiavoni. Its deservedly high reputation is based on sapient and sapid cooking of the freshest seafood, in creative dishes that range from tepid crustacean and mollusc antipasto to *gnocchi con filetti di gò* (with goby fillets) and grilled white fish *secondi* – all caught, rather than farmed. The restaurant's charming decor, midway between rustic and elegant, should make it ideal for a romantic dinner, but the atmosphere is more serious foodie than newly-wed footsie. The welcome can even verge on the prickly if one turns up outside of the kitchen's set-in-stone hours. Chef/owner Cesare Benelli's American wife, Diane, can talk non-Italian-speakers through the daily-changing menu; she is also responsible for the sumptuous desserts, which include a knockout chocolate cake with bitter chocolate sauce.

Dal Pampo (Osteria Sant'Elena) ⑫

Sant'Elena, calle Generale Chinotto 24 (041 520 8419/os.pampo@libero.it). Vaporetto Sant'Elena. **Meals served** noon-2.30pm, 7.30-9pm Mon-Wed, Fri-Sun. Closed Christmas, 1wk May, 1wk Aug. **Average** €25. **Credit** AmEx, MC, V. **Map** p309 C4.

Right at the end of Venice – the last vaporetto stop before the Lido – in the residential neighbourhood of Sant'Elena, this rustic trat with tables outside is a good bet for a cheap plate of spaghetti or a mixed seafood grill. Officially called the 'Osteria Sant' Elena' but known to everyone as Dal Pampo – 'Pampo's Place' – after the jolly owner, it is right by the football stadium so it can be difficult to get a table on the Sundays when Venice are playing at home.

Al Portego ⑬

Castello 6015, calle Malvasia (041 522 9038). Vaporetto Rialto. **Open** 10am-3pm, 5-10pm Mon-Fri; 10am-3pm Sat. Closed 2wks June. **Average** €25. **No credit cards.** **Map** p305 C4.

With its wooden decor, this rustic *osteria* smacks of mountain chalet. Alongside a big barrel of wine, the bar is loaded down with a selection of *cicheti*, from meatballs and tunaballs to fried veg and *nervetti* stewed with onions. There are also simple but honest pasta dishes, risottos and *secondi*, such as *fegato alla veneziana*, served up for lunch (noon-2pm) and early dinner (7-9pm). Eat at the bar or queue for one of the tiny tables, as no reservations are taken.

Da Remigio ⑭

Castello 3416, salizada dei Greci (041 523 0089). Vaporetto San Zaccaria. **Meals served** 12.30-2.30pm Mon; 12.30-2.30pm, 7.30-10pm Wed-Sun. Closed Christmas to late Jan, 2wks July, Aug. **Average** €40. **Credit** AmEx, DC, MC, V. **Map** p308 B2.

Remigio is held in high esteem by local pescivores. This means that it can be extremely difficult to get a table, despite the out-of-the-way location between San Marco and the Arsenale. The walls are a dazzling shade of ochre and the acoustics are pretty awful, but any lack of ambience is easily compensated for by delicious *antipasti*, which might include

The purple artichokes of Sant'Erasmo

You won't necessarily associate farming with Venice. But not all the islands of the lagoon are densely urban. One in particular – Sant'Erasmo (*see p140*) – has for centuries been the city's market garden. Half the size of Venice proper, this green and fertile raft still provides many of the vegetables on sale at the Rialto market, where labels saying *di San Rasmo* (from Sant'Erasmo) are proudly – and sometimes fraudulently – displayed as a guarantee of quality and freshness.

Sant'Erasmo is famous above all for its artichokes, which thrive in the island's salty clay soil. Centuries of selection and isolation from the mainland have made the *carciofi* of Sant'Erasmo a variety unto themselves. Green at first, the globes turn a dark reddish-purple as they mature; never fat like Roman or Puglian artichokes, they have a delicate, elongated tulip shape. This purple artichoke, or *carciofo violetto*, has recently been adopted as one of the *presidi* (praesidiums) of Italy's Slow Food Association, one of whose aims is the salvaging of 'endangered' food products. The objective of this particular campaign is to gain quality brand-recognition for the *carciofo violetto di Sant'Erasmo* and

encourage consumers to choose it over cheaper Puglian and Tuscan imports.

On Sant'Erasmo, low ridges of earth known as *motte* protect the plants from the biting *tramontana* wind in winter and early spring. By the end of April, the first, central buds have begun to appear. Cut immediately to strengthen and fatten up the other buds, these baby *carciofi*, or *castraure*, feature as a delicacy in Venetian restaurants and *bacari* for the two weeks that they are in season. The mature globes (known as *botoi*) are harvested between May and June, and brought over on colourful *caorline* boats by the farmers.

Castraure are delicious raw, sliced very thin and marinated in oil and lemon, or fried in batter. Larger artichokes are usually lightly boiled with garlic and parsley and dressed with olive oil and black pepper; they can also be served *col garbo*, in a casserole with garlic and onion, to which vinegar and lemon are added at the end of a slow broil. A linguistic curiosity: true Venetians refer to the vegetable as *articioco* rather than the Italian *carciofo* (both come from the Spanish-Arab *al-kharshofa*).

Eat, Drink, Shop

grilled *cape longhe*, followed by filling pasta dishes (*spaghetti alla busara* – with anchovies and onions) and a range of squeaky-fresh, grilled fish *secondi*.

Alla Rivetta ⑮
Castello 4625, ponte San Provolo (041 528 7302).
Vaporetto San Zaccaria. **Meals served** 10am-10pm Tue-Sun. Closed mid July-mid Aug. **Average** €38. **Credit** AmEx, MC, V. **Map** p308 B1.
On an ancient bridge right behind the Hotel Danieli, the Rivetta has managed to preserve its neighbourhood trattoria credentials – and prices – despite the scores of tourists who troop in and out every day. At the bar, owner Stefano serves creamy *polenta con baccalà* (cod) for little old ladies to take home for lunch. Gondoliers pile in for a noisy, boozy midday meal, featuring the usual Venetian pasta classics and an unbeatable *fritto misto*. Note the kitchen's non-stop opening times.

Alle Testiere ⑯
Castello 5801, calle del Mondo Novo (041 522 7220).
Vaporetto Rialto. **Meals served** noon-2pm, 7-10.30pm Tue-Sat. Closed last wk Dec, 2wks Jan, last wk July, 3wks Aug. **Average** €50. **Credit** MC, V. **Map** p308 A1.

One of the great success stories of recent years, this tiny restaurant is today one of the hottest culinary tickets in Venice. There are so few seats that there are two sittings each evening; booking for the later one (at 9pm) will ensure a more relaxed meal. Bruno, the cook, does creative variations on Venetian seafood, many of them involving herbs and spices; the *gnocchetti* (mini-gnocchi) with cinammon-flavoured baby squid and the *filetto di San Pietro* with aromatic herbs in a citrus sauce are two mouth-watering examples. Shaven-headed sommelier Luca guides diners around a small but well-chosen wine list and a marvellously *recherché* cheese-board.

Pizzerie

Dai Tosi ⑰
Castello 738, secco Marina (041 523 7102).
Vaporetto Giardini. **Meals served** noon-2pm Mon, Tue, Thur; noon-2pm, 7-9.30pm Fri-Sun. Closed 2wks Aug. **Average** €14 pizzeria; €25 full meal. **Credit** MC, V. **Map** p309 C4.
In one of Venice's most working-class areas, in a street festooned with washing, this restaurant-pizzeria is a big hit with local families and a welcome retreat

to normality for visitors to the nearby Biennale dell'Arte. But beware of the same-name imitator in the same street: this place (at No.738) is the better of the two establishments. The cuisine is humble but filling, the pizzas are tasty (try the Gregory Speck – *speck* is Tyrolean ham), and you can round the meal off nicely with a killer *sgropin* (a post-prandial refresher made with lemon sorbet, vodka and prosecco). In summer, it's a good idea to angle for a table in the garden out back.

Cannaregio

Restaurants & *bacari*

Da Alberto
Cannaregio 5401, calle Giacinto Gallina (041 523 8153). Vaporetto Fondamente Nove. **Meals served** noon-3pm, 7-10pm Mon-Sat. Closed mid July-early Aug. **Average** €30. **Credit** MC, V. **Map** p305 C4.
This bacaro with charming trad decor, not far from campo Santi Giovanni e Paolo, has been through a couple of changes of ownership since the eponymous Alberto left to set up the Innishark pub, but it still maintains a good standard and a well-stocked bar counter. The wide sit-down menu centres on Venetian specialities such as *granseola* and *seppie in umido* (stewed cuttlefish), along with plenty of seafood pastas and risottos. A favourite with young Venetians, Alberto's is always buzzing and packed – so book ahead if you want to sit down and eat rather than just snacking at the bar.

Anice Stellato
Cannaregio 3272, fondamenta della Sensa (041 720 744). Vaporetto Guglie or Sant'Alvise. **Meals served** 12.30-2pm, 7.30-10pm Wed-Fri; 12.30-2pm, 7.30-10pm Sat, Sun. Closed 1wk Jan, 3wks Aug. **Average** €35. **Credit** MC, V. **Map** p304 A2.
Though a relative newcomer, this nouveau-bacaro has become a firm favourite with budget-conscious Venetian gourmets. The reason is simple: the ambience is friendly, and the food good and cheap. A walk-around bar at the entrance fills up with *cichetari* (locals doing some serious snacking) in the hour before lunch and evening mealtimes. Tables take up two oak-beamed rooms around and behind, and spill out on to the canalside walk in summer. The name means 'star anise', but spices have little place in the kitchen, which turns out Venetian classics such as *bigoli in salsa* along with more creative outings like tagliatelle with scampi and courgette flowers. It's hugely popular – so it's best to book.

Antiche Cantine Ardenghi
Cannaregio 6369, calle della Testa (041 523 7691/ ardenghiclub@virgilio.it). Vaporetto Fondamente Nove. **Meals served** 8pm (single sitting) Tue-Sat. **Fixed price** €50. **No credit cards**.
Map p305 C4.
You don't just come here to eat; you come for the experience. An anonymous doorway in a calle just west of Santi Giovanni e Paolo gives on to a long

Focus on fish at **Boccadoro**. *See p153.*

bar and rustic dining room, decorated with vintage photographs of Venice. Guests – who must book in advance – are plied with a succession of delicious, authentic seafood dishes, and as much house wine as they can take (red Venegazzu or white Pinto Grigio, both from decent local producers), followed by biscuits, grappa and coffee – all for a fixed price of €50. The soundtrack ranges from opera to Sinatra, and Michele, the garrulous owner, is liable to break into song at the slightest excuse.

Bentigodi
Cannaregio 1423, Calesele (041 716 269). Vaporetto San Marcuola. **Open** *Sept-July* 11am-3pm, 6pm-midnight Tue-Sat. Closed Jan. **Average** €32. **No credit cards**. **Map** p304 B2.
With its blackened beams and heavy wooden tables, Bentigodi is always full of locals engaged in passionate discussions on food, sport, politics… and sometimes all three simultaneously. The place is run by Elena, wife of Andrea of Bancogiro fame (*see p157*), who specialises in taking the basic traditions of Venetian cuisine for a creative walk. So *linguine* might come with a sauce of rocket and walnuts, while a swordish *secondo* is cooked with aubergines, and smoked goose liver is served with Calvados-flavoured apple sauce. There are still a few *cicheti* at the marble bar for snackers, but Bentigodi is more restaurant than bacaro these days. Just a shame that the absent-minded service is not always up to the same standards as the food.

Eat, Drink, Shop

Boccadoro 22

Cannaregio 5405A, campiello Widman (041 521 1021/www.osteriaboccadorove.org). Vaporetto Fondamenta Nove. **Meals served** 12.30-2.30pm, 8-11.30pm Tue-Sun. **Average** €48. **Credit** AmEx, DC, MC, V. **Map** p305 C4.

Helmed by a chef who previously worked at Al Covo (*see p150*), this creative seafood restaurant is a promising newcomer on the slow-moving Venetian scene. The focus is on fresh fish – so fresh, in fact, that most of the entrées are raw, a sort of Adriatic sashimi featuring oysters, prawns, scallops, swordfish and tuna. Pasta courses include tasty *gnocchi con cozze*, while *secondi* range from simple grilled fish to more seafood and vegetable pairings. The original wine list includes some Sardinian whites.

Ca D'Oro (Alla Vedova) 23

Cannaregio 3912, ramo Ca' d'Oro (041 528 5324). Vaporetto Ca' d'Oro. **Meals served** *Sept-July* 11.30am-2.30pm, 6.30-10.30pm Mon-Wed, Fri, Sat; 6.30-11pm Sun. Closed Aug. **Average** €34. **No credit cards. Map** p305 B3.

Deservedly famous, this is one of the best-preserved traditional *bacari* in town. Its official name is the Ca' d'Oro; but most Venetians know it as Alla Vedova – the Widow's Place. The widow has now, alas, joined her *marito*, but her family still runs the show and her spirit marches on in the traditional brasspan and wooden-table decor and the warm, intimate atmosphere. Tourists head for the tables (it's best to book), where tasty pasta dishes and *secondi* are served, while locals tend to stay at the bar snacking on a range of classic *cicheti*, from *folpetti* (octopus) to fried artichokes to the best *polpette* in Venice.

La Colombina 24

Cannaregio 1828, campiello del Pegolotto (041 275 0622/www.lacolombina.it). Vaporetto San Marcuola. **Open** *Wine bar* 6.30-8.30pm Mon, Wed-Sun. *Meals served* 8.30pm-2am daily. Closed 1wk Jan. **Average** €40. **Credit** AmEx, DC, MC, V. **Map** p305 B3.

Under new management, this wine-oriented diner in a small square just south of the strada Nuova has become more of a conventional restaurant and less of a jazzy wine bar and lost some of its funky appeal (and value for money) in the process. But it's still a good place to explore a good bottle from the excellent list, accompanied by fresh seafood dishes or Tuscan-influenced fare such as *crostini* and an excellent Chianina steak. In summer, tables fill the *campiello* outside.

Dalla Marisa 25

Cannaregio 652B, fondamenta San Giobbe (041 720 211). Vaporetto Tre Archi. **Meals served** *Sept-July* noon-2.30pm, 8-9.15pm Tue, Thur-Sat; noon-2.30pm Mon, Sun. Closed Aug. **Average** €30. **No credit cards. Map** p304 A1.

Signora Marisa, the proud descendant of a dynasty of butchers, is a culinary legend in Venice, with locals calling up days in advance to ask her to prepare ancient recipes such as *risotto con le secoe* (risotto made with a special cut of beef from

around the spine). Pasta dishes include the excellent tagliatelle in drake (ie male duck) sauce, while *secondi* range from tripe to roast stuffed pheasant. In summer, tables spill out from the tiny interior on to the fondamenta overlooking the busy Cannaregio canal. Book well ahead – this place is not just *popolare* (of the people), but popular too.

Fiaschetteria Toscana 26

Cannaregio 5719, salizzada San Giovanni Grisostomo (041 528 5281). Vaporetto Rialto. **Meals served** 7.30-10.30pm Mon; 12.30-2.30pm, 7.30-10.30pm Wed-Sun. Closed mid July-mid Aug. **Average** €55. **Credit** AmEx, DC, MC, V. **Map** p305 C4.

Don't be fooled by the name: though this was once a depot for wine and olive oil from Tuscany, today only a good selection of steaks and big Tuscan red wines betray its origins. Otherwise, the cuisine, which runs the gamut from meat to fish to game, is true to Venetian tradition, with favourites such as *schie con polenta* and *fegato alla veneziana*. Pasta is not a strong point; better to leap from the fine *antipasti* to delicious seconds like grilled John Dory, or a renowned *fritto misto*. The decor is a little tired and the service can be peremptory, but this place is a reliable, though hardly cheap, gourmet standby. Take the sting out of the bill with one of Mamma Mariuccia's fabulous desserts, and a bottle from one of the most extensive wine lists in town.

Il Sole sulla Vecia Cavana. *See p155.*

Eat, Drink, Shop

Alla Fontana ㉗

*Cannaregio 1102, fondamenta Cannaregio (041 715
077). Vaporetto Ponte delle Guglie.* **Meals served**
Apr-Oct 6-11pm Mon-Sat. *Nov-Mar* 7-10pm Tue-Sat.
Closed 10 days Nov, 10 days Jan. **Average** €33.
Credit AmEx, DC, MC, V. **Map** p304 B2.

This traditional osteria just five minutes from the
station on the Cannaregio Canal has recently completed its move from wine-and-snack bacaro to bona
fide, evening-only restaurant. 'The Fountain' now
offers a range of filling trattoria dishes with a
creative twist: tagliatelle with eel, gnocchi with turbot and courgettes, *spezzatino* (braised strips of veal)
with polenta. In summer, tables line the busy canal
pavement outside.

Al Fontego dei Pescaori ㉘

*Cannaregio 3711, sottoportego del Tagliapiera
(041 520 0538). Vaporetto Ca d'Oro.* **Meals
served** noon-2.30pm, 7-10pm Mon, Wed-Sun.
Annual closure varies. **Average** €45.
Credit AmEx, DC, MC, V. **Map** p305 B3.

This warm modern restaurant in a *sottoportego*
(arched passageway) opposite its business partner
Vini da Gigio (*see below*) is a welcome novelty. The
atmosphere is Venetian-*moderne*, while the season-
ally changing menu – based on fresh Rialto fish and
vegetables – nods in the direction of fusion without
betraying local traditions. In spring, an antipasto of
granseola and asparagus tips might be followed by
a risotto of scampi and *bruscandoli* (wild lupin
seeds). Seconds are spread fairly evenly between
fish, meat and game (pheasant or duck). It's still
early days, but Al Fontego is off to a promising start.

Il Sole sulla Vecia Cavana ㉙

*Cannaregio 4624, rio terà Santi Apostoli (041 528
7106/www.ilsolevenezia.it).* **Meals served** 7.30-
10.30pm Tue; 12.30-2.30pm, 7.30-10.30pm Wed-Sun.
Closed 1wk Jan, 2wks Aug. **Average** €50. **Credit**
AmEx, MC, V. **Map** p305 B4.

Another new arrival in a *sestiere* that is heading the
Venetian culinary renaissance. The 'Sun on the Old
Boatshed' is the brainchild of a globetrotting chef-
owner from northern Friuli. The contrast between
the exposed bricks and beams of the spacious main
dining area and the elegant table settings carries
through into the menu, which jazzes up the
Venetian, and Friulian, traditions with some more
modern touches: a tartare of raw tuna, for example,
is served with spicy basil oil and teriyaki sauce.
Soups and risottos feature strongly among the
primi, breaking the pasta stronghold; and desserts
like apple ice-cream with glazed pumpkin ravioli
and mascarpone are exceptional. Creative without
excess, this is an intriguing and likeable new kid
on the block.

Vini da Gigio ㉚

*Cannaregio 3628A, fondamenta San Felice (041 528
5140/www.vinidagigio.com). Vaporetto Ca' d'Oro.*
Meals served noon-2.30pm, 7.30-10.30pm Tue-Sun.
Closed 3wks Jan-Feb, 3wks Aug-Sept. **Average** €40.
Credit AmEx, DC, MC, V. **Map** p305 B3.

It's no longer any secret that this is one of the best-
value restaurants in Venice, so make sure you book
well in advance. Gigio is strong on Venetian
antipasti such as *crocchette di baccalà* (breaded
stockfish) and *canestrelli all griglia* (grilled razor
clams); there are also a number of good meat and
game options, like *masorini alla buranella* (roasted
Burano-style duck). As the name suggests, wine is
another forte – there are even bottles from Australia
and South Africa, and there is always a good by-the-
glass selection. The only drawback in this highly
recommended restaurant is the decidedly unhurried
service; allow at least two hours for a complete meal.

Pizzerie

La Perla ㉛

*Cannaregio 4615, rio terà dei Franceschi (041 528
5175/www.pizzerialaperla.net). Vaporetto Ca' d'Oro.*
Meals served *Sept-July* noon-2pm, 7-9.45pm Mon-
Sat. Closed Aug. **Average** €12 pizzeria; €23 full
meal. **Credit** MC, V. **Map** p305 B4.

Many locals reckon that La Perla makes the best
pizza in town; the doughy base comes garnished
with a variety of mix-and-match toppings. The
ambience is of the all-packed-in-together variety,
with tablefuls of students sawing away at the
pizzas and knocking back some good draught beer.

Mirai: classic Japanese. *See p156.*

Wines of the north-east

The Veneto produces more wine per annum than either Tuscany or Piedmont. Quantity, of course, is not always a guarantee of quality, and neither are Italy's DOC 'controlled appellation' regulations, which too often celebrate political influence rather than oenological excellence. But in recent years, the Veneto's reputation as a producer of dependable but unexciting plonk has taken a bashing from a small, energetic cluster of winemakers, spread across the region, who use local grape varieties like Corvina and Garganega to turn out some fine and complex wines. The other main wine presence in the restaurants and *bacari* of Venice is the region of Friuli-Venezia-Giulia, further to the north-east, whose Collio and Colli Orientali del Friuli appellations produce some of Italy's best white wines. The following wine zones turn out some of the best bottles in the north-east.

Soave & Recioto di Soave

Outside of Italy, this amiable white has a reputation as a cheap party lubricant. Plenty of this oblivion-juice is still around – high yields, the expansion of the DOC area, and local co-operatives (which bottle 85 per cent of the wine) see to that. But in the small Soave Classico area, a handful of dynamic winemakers is showing that this blend of garganega and trebbiano is capable of greater things: look out in particular for Pieropan's La Rocca or Calvarino selections. In the 1980s a few producers revived the tradition of Recioto di Soave, a delicious dessert wine made from raisinised garganega grapes.

Best producers: Anselmi, Ca' Rugate, Gini, Inama, Pieropan.

Valpolicella, Recioto della Valpolicella & Amarone

An often disappointing red from the hills north and west of Verona, standard Valpolicella suffers from overstretched DOC boundaries and overgenerous yields. The best, from the historic growing area around the town of Marano, is bottled as Valpolicella Classico. Valpolicella Superiore is a version of the same that has spent time in contact with the partially dried skins of the grapes that go into Amarone and Recioto, the area's two famous *passito* wines, which are made from partially-dried grapes. Recioto della Valpolicella is the

---

International

Mirai ㉜

Cannaregio 227, lista di Spagna (041 220 6517/ www.miraivenice.com). Vaporetto Ferrovia. **Meals served** 7.30-11.30pm Tue-Sun. Closed 3wks Jan. **Average** €40. **Credit** AmEx, DC, MC, V. **Map** p304 B2.

One of the few really interesting international options in Venice, this new-born Japanese restaurant has already built up a steady local following. It does all the classics – sushi, sashimi of salmon, tuna and bream, tempura – and it does them well. The classy modern decor makes for a cool refuge from the tacky lista di Spagna souvenir hell outside.

Sahara ㉝

Cannaregio 2519, fondamenta della Misericordia (041 721 077). Vaporetto San Marcuola or Orto. **Meals served** 7pm-2am Mon-Fri; noon-2.30pm, 7pm-2am Sat, Sun. **Average** €20. **Credit** MC, V. **Map** p305 B3.

At this Syrian-Egyptian restaurant on Cannaregio's trendiest fondamenta, where clients cluster around outside tables on fine summer evenings, friendly owner Mouaffak conjures up a range of unrefined but tasty couscous-and-vegetable dishes, together with grills, sharwermas and the usual sticky

desserts. Late opening and decent prices make this one of Venice's best non-Italian options, though service can be a little slow. There's usually a belly dancer on Saturday night.

San Polo & Santa Croce

Restaurants & *bacari*

Antiche Carampane ㉞

San Polo 1911, rio terà delle Carampane (041 524 0165). Vaporetto San Silvestro. **Meals served** Sept-July 12.30-2.30pm, 7.30-10pm Tue-Sat. Closed 1wk Jan, Aug. **Average** €45. **Credit** AmEx, DC, MC, V. **Map** p305 C3.

This compact trattoria between campo San Polo and San Cassiano – in what was once the red-light district – could win the prize for the hardest-to-find restaurant in Venice. The inaccessibility is reinforced by a slightly prickly attitude towards non-Venetians, enshrined in a sign by the door indicating the restaurant's current charge for tourist information. But that's Venetian humour for you; and if you manage to break the ice, the Carampane will deliver a fine (though not cheap) seafood meal in the best local tradition, crowned by an unbeatable *fritto misto*. Inside is cosy, but outside is better for balmy summer evenings.

sweet version, Amarone the dry. In the right hands, the latter can be explosive: powerful, smoky and concentrated, with bags of ripe fruit.
Best producers: Allegrini, Bussola, Castellani, Dal Forno, Masi, Quintarelli, Viviani, Zenato.

Prosecco di Conegliano & Valdobbiadene

The classic Veneto dry white fizz has conquered Italy: *un prosecco* is what most Italians will order in a bar when they want a glass of sparkle. From vineyards around the towns of Valdobbiadene and Conegliano in the rolling hills north of Treviso (*see p265*), the Prosecco grape is subjected to a double fermentation, using the Charmat method; the result is a light, dry, sparkling wine with a bitter finish. The most highly prized (and expensive) version of prosecco is known as Cartizze, from the cooler subzone where it is grown. A more rustic, unfizzy version – known as *prosecco spento* – is served by the glass in *bacari*.
Best producers: Adami, Bisol, Bortolomiol, Le Colture, Nino Franco, Ruggeri & C.

Collio & Colli Orientali del Friuli

These two adjacent wine areas nestle up against Italy's border with Slovenia. They are responsible for some delicate fragrant whites, which will appeal to those who have had it up to here with woody Austro-Californians. Tocai (only doubtfully, and acrimoniously, related to Hungarian Tokay), Pinot Grigio, Pinot Bianco, Sauvignon, Chardonnay, Malvasia and Ribolla are the main varieties; the reds produced here, around 15 per cent of the area's total production, are mainly Merlot, Cabernet Franc and Cabernet Sauvignon. More recherché wines – produced only in the Colli Orientali zone – feature the local grapes Picolit (white) and Schioppetino (red). Almost all wines bottled here are monovarietals (one grape variety per bottle). The tocai or ribolla served in Venetian *bacari* is likely to come from the less exalted Grave dei Friuli area.
Best producers: too many to list, but look out for Ascewi, Dorigo, Livio Felluga, Jermann, Kante, Lis Neris, Miani, Ronco del Gelso, Scubla, Vie di Romans and Villa Russiz.

Bancogiro ㉟
San Polo 122, campo San Giacometto di Rialto (041 523 2061). Vaporetto Rialto. **Open** 10.30am-3pm, 6.30pm-midnight Tue-Sat; 10.30am-3pm Sun. **Average** €35. **No credit cards Map** p305 C3.
The location of this updated bacaro is splendid: the main entrance gives on to the Rialto square of San Giacometto, while the back door gives access to a prime bit of Grand Canal frontage that until two years ago was open only to market traders. Downstairs, hirsute player-manager Andrea dispenses excellent wines to an appreciative crowd of locals; above, at a few well-spaced tables under the brick ceiling vaults, a light, creative menu is served. Grilled radicchio with gorgonzola, carpaccio of *branzino* with aromatic herbs, bean soups and vaguely oriental desserts: not every dish lives up to its ambitions, but it's certainly a change from *bacalà mantecato*. Allow plenty of time, though, as the service can be sluggish. In summer, the ringside view of the Grand Canal from the outside tables makes up for the wait.

Da Fiore ㊱
San Polo 2202, calle del Scaleter (041 721 308). Vaporetto San Stae. **Meals served** Sept-July 12.30-2.30pm, 7.30-10.30pm Tue-Sat. Closed Christmas to mid Jan, Aug. **Average** €90. **Credit** AmEx, DC, MC, V. **Map** p304 C2.

Restaurant critics and local gourmets are fairly unanimous in considering the Michelin-starred Da Fiore to be Venice's best restaurant. The façade and the bar at the entrance hark back to its bacaro origins; but the elegant, barge-like dining room inside is in quite a different class. Owner Maurizio Martin treats his guests – many of whom are visiting celebrities or local bigshots – with egalitarian courtesy. There's only one window, and the space can seem rather claustrophobic, but focus on what's on the plate and the panic will pass. Raw fish and seafood – a sort of Venetian sashimi – is a key feature of the excellent *antipasti*; the pasta dishes and *secondi* such as *rombo al forno in crosta di patate* (oven-baked turbot in a potato crust) work creative variations on the local tradition. There is also an exceptional selection of regional cheeses – rare in Venice – and a collection of decent desserts. You pays your money, certainly, for what is in the end a good, rather than a totally superlative, dining experience; but that's Venice for you. See it as a celebrity-sighting surcharge.

Da Ignazio ㊲
San Polo 2749, calle dei Saoneri (041 523 4852). Vaporetto San Tomà. **Meals served** noon-3pm, 7-10pm Mon-Fri, Sun. Closed 2wks Dec-Jan, 3wks July-Aug. **Average** €42. **Credit** AmEx, DC, MC, V. **Map** p304 C2.

Take a break from seafood with vegetarian dishes at **Alla Zucca**. *See p159.*

The big attraction of this tranquil neighbourhood restaurant between campo San Polo and the Frari is its pretty, pergola-shaded courtyard. The cooking is safe, traditional Venetian: mixed seafood *antipasti* might be followed by a good rendition of *risi e bisi* (risotto with peas) and grilled fish; desserts include a decent tiramisù. Don't expect any frills: just down-home Venetian cooking in pleasant surroundings.

Alla Madonna 38
San Polo 594, calle della Madonna (041 522 3824).
Vaporetto Rialto or San Silvestro. **Meals served**
Feb-Dec noon-2.30pm, 7-10pm Mon, Tue, Thur-Sun.
Closed Jan. **Average** €40. **Credit** AmEx, MC, V.
Map p305 C3.
A sort of high-class canteen, this big, bustling fish trattoria with its friendly (though brisk) service and fair (though rising) prices has been piling in loyal locals and clued-up tourists for generations. It's a minute's walk from the Rialto bridge and while the cooking will win no prizes, it offers competent versions of old Venetian favourites such as *granseola* and *anguilla fritta* (fried eel); the restaurant can also turn out pan-Italian faves like *cotolette alla milanese* (breaded veal cutlets). Bookings are not taken; you simply join the queue outside, which moves pretty fast – as does the meal itself.

Alla Patatina 39
San Polo 2741, ponte San Polo (041 523 7238/
www.lapatatina.it). Vaporetto San Tomà. **Open**
9.30am-2.30pm, 5-10pm Mon-Sat. **Meals served**
noon-2.30pm, 6.30-10pm Mon-Sat. Closed 2wks Aug.
Average €30. **Credit** AmEx, DC, MC, V.
Map p304 C2.

A favourite student and workers' haunt with both bar snacks and table service. Though officially called Al Ponte, this no-nonsense hostelry is known to all and sundry as Alla Patatina – a reference to the house speciality, chunky potato chips fried on wooden skewers. Sit-down fare is calorifically Venetian: seafood risotto, *seppie fritte* (fried cuttlefish), *polpette al sugo* (meatballs in tomato sauce). If you perch and snack, you can be in and out for under ten euros; sit-down prices are more in line with the Venetian budget norm. Alla Patatina serves dinner as well as lunch, but note the early kitchen times.

Ribò 40
Santa Croce 158, fondamenta Minotto (041 524 2486). Vaporetto Piazzale Roma. **Meals served**
12.30-2.15pm, 7.30-10.15pm Tue-Fri, Sun; 7.30-
10.15pm Sat. Closed 3wks Jan. **Average** €50.
Credit AmEx, DC, MC, V. **Map** p304 C1.
A light, bright new canalside restaurant in the eastern reaches of Santa Croce, not far from piazzale Roma and the train station. The cuisine is modern creative Venetian, without heavy sauces, and with a certain *nouvelle* flair in presentation, as in *tortino di granseola* with green beans in oil and lemon, or scampi and artichoke risotto. The ambience is in keeping: bright and airy, especially on the pretty veranda, shaded by billowing cream drapes.

Vecio Fritolin 41
Santa Croce 2262, calle della Regina (041 522 2881/
www.veciofritolin.com). Vaporetto San Stae. **Meals**
served noon-2.15pm, 7-10.30pm Tue-Sat; noon-
2.15pm Sun. Closed 1wk Jan, 1wk Aug. **Average**
€45. **Credit** AmEx, DC, MC, V. **Map** p305 C3.

This old-style bacaro hit a low patch a few years ago but has been nursed back to health as a full-on restaurant by the charming present owner. Wooden beams, sturdy *osteria* tables and the long bar at the back of the main dining room set the mood; but the menu is more creative than one might expect, with a starter of tuna marinated in three different types of pepper, or a main course of angler fish (*coda di rospo*) with croquant vegetables and saffron-flavoured potatoes. The wine list is small but select and the prices are fairly contained for Venice.

Alla Zucca  42

Santa Croce 1762, ponte del Megio (041 524 1570). *Vaporetto San Stae.* **Meals served** 12.30-2.30pm, 7-10.30pm Mon-Sat. Closed 1wk Aug, 1wk Dec. **Average** €32. **Credit** AmEx, DC, MC, V. **Map** p304 B2.

This was one of the first of Venice's 'alternative' *trattorie* and it's still one of the best. By a pretty skewed bridge in the peaceful San Giacomo dell'Orio area, the good-value, vegetarian-friendly Pumpkin offers a welcome break from all that Venetian seafood. The menu is equally divided between meat (lamb roasted with fennel and pecorino cheese, ginger pork with pilau rice) and vegetables (*penne* with aubergine and feta, pumpkin and seasoned ricotta quiche). Women dining alone will feel at home; if any men work here, they're hidden in the kitchen. In summer, book ahead for one of few outside tables, which are much in demand.

Pizzerie

Al Nono Risorto 43

Santa Croce 2338, sottoportico di Siora Bettina (041 524 1169). *Vaporetto San Stae.* **Meals served** noon-2.30pm, 7-11pm Mon, Tue, Fri-Sun; 7-11pm Thur. Closed 2 wks Jan. **Average** €10 pizzeria; €25 full meal. **No credit cards. Map** p305 C3.

There's plenty of attitude in this lively spot. If you want to hang out over a *pizza margherita* in a shady garden courtyard over Venice's bright young things, this is the place to come. It also does traditional Venetian trattoria fare, at traditional Venetian trattoria prices.

Il Refolo 44

Santa Croce 1459, campiello del Piovan (041 524 0016/www.dafiore.com). *Vaporetto Riva di Biasio or San Stae.* **Meals served** noon-2.45pm, 7-11pm Tue-Sun. Closed early Dec-end Feb. **Average** €20 pizzeria; €45 full meal. **Credit** AmEx, MC, V. **Map** p304 B2.

The 'Sea Breeze' has tables outside in one of Venice's prettiest small squares, by a canal, with a good view of the church of San Giacomo dell'Orio. Set up by a scion of the Da Fiore dynasty, it is Venice's most luxurious pizzeria – a status that is reflected in the prices. Alongside the excellent pizzas, there is also a small international-style restaurant menu featuring high-class deli fare such as marinated salmon, tunaburgers and creative salads.

International

Frary's 45

San Polo 2559, fondamenta dei Frari (041 720 050/www.arabofrarys.it). *Vaporetto San Tomà.* **Meals served** noon-3.30pm, 6.30-11.30pm Mon, Wed-Sun. **Average** €22. **Credit** AmEx, DC, MC, V. **Map** p306 A2.

A friendly, reasonably priced restaurant specialising in Arab cuisine, though there are some Greek dishes as well. Couscous comes with a variety of sauces – vegetarian, mutton, chicken or seafood. The *mansaf* (Bedouin rice with chicken, almonds and yoghurt) is good, as are the falafel, tzaziki and taramasalata. The naïve desert murals on the wall make a change from all that Tiepolo.

Dorsoduro

Restaurants & *bacari*

Antica Osteria Al Pantalon 46

Dorsoduro 3958, calle del Scaleter (041 710 849/www.osteriaalpantalon.it). *Vaporetto San Tomà.* **Open** 10am-3pm, 5-11pm Mon-Sat. Closed 3wks Aug. **Average** €30. **Credit** AmEx, DC, MC, V. **Map** p306 A2.

Frary's, for Arabic and Greek food.

Eat, Drink, Shop

The menu

Antipasti (starters)

Antipasti are so central to the local tradition, and served in such abundant quantities, that there is often no need to eat anything else. The dozens of *cicheti* – tapas-style snacks – served from the counters of the traditional bacaro (*see p144*) are essentially *antipasti*; in more upmarket restaurants, these will be joined – or replaced – by an even larger and more refined selection.

Dishes include **baccalà mantecato** stockfish beaten into a cream with oil and milk, often served on grilled polenta; **baccalà alla vicentina** stockfish poached in milk; **bovoleti** tiny snails cooked in olive oil, parsley and an awful lot of garlic; **carciofi** artichokes, even better if they are **castrauri** – baby artichokes, served raw in April/May; **canoce** (or cicale di mare) delicate, transparent mantis shrimps; **folpi/folpeti** baby octopuses – the former have a double row of suckers; *garusoli* sea snails, to be winkled out with a toothpick; **moleche** soft-shelled crabs, usually deep-fried; **museto** a boiled brawn sausage, generally served on a slice of bread with mustard; **nervetti** very strange-looking – and tasting – dish of boiled veal cartilage; **polpetta** a deep-fried spicy meatball; **polenta** this yellow or white cornmeal mush is the traditional staple of Venetian cuisine, so much so that inhabitants of the Veneto are known as *polentoni*; **sarde in saor** sardines marinated in a pungent mixture of onion, vinegar, pinenuts and raisins; **schie e polenta** tiny grey shrimps, served on a bed of soft polenta; **seppie in nero** cuttlefish in its own ink; **spienza** veal spleen – usually served on a skewer; **trippa e rissa** tripe cooked in broth.

Primi (first courses)

bigoli in salsa fat spaghetti in an anchovy and onion sauce; **gnocchi con granseola** potato gnocchi in a spider-crab sauce; **pasta e ceci** pasta and chickpea soup; **pasta e fagioli** pasta and borlotti bean soup; **spaghetti con astice** with lobster sauce; **spaghetti al nero di seppia** in thick squid-ink sauce; **spaghetti con caparosoli/ vongole veraci** with two different types of clam; **risotto di zucca** pumpkin risotto; **risotto di radicchio** risotto made with bitter red radicchio from nearby Treviso.

Secondi (main courses)

The choice of fish and seafood is almost endless – in addition to the *antipasti* mentioned above you are likely to find the following: **anguilla** (eel); **aragosta/ astice** (spiny lobster/lobster); **branzino** (sea bass); **cape longhe** (razor clams); **cappe sante** (scallops); **cernia** (grouper); **coda di rospo** (angler-fish); **cozze** (mussels); **granchio** (crab); **granseola** (spider-crab); **orata** (gilt-headed bream); **rombo** (turbot); **pesce San Pietro** (John Dory); **pesce spada** (swordfish); **sogliola** (sole); **tonno** (tuna); and **vongole/ caparosoli** (clams).

Meat eaters are less well catered for in Venice, though there are a few exceptions. **Fegato alla veneziana** (veal liver cooked in a slightly sweet sauce of onions) is a common fixture, and in autumn one may be lucky enough to find **castradina** – a lamb and cabbage broth.

Dolci

Venice's restaurants are not the best place to feed a sweet habit – there are far more tempting pastries to be found on the shelves of the city's *pasticcerie*. The classic end to a meal here is a plate of **buranei** – sweet egg biscuits – served with a dessert wine such as Fragolino. Then it's quickly on to the more important matter of which grappa to order.

This lively bacaro near the university lays on a good range of *cicheti*, including *olive ascolane* (like Scotch eggs except with olives inside) and crostini with *bacalà mantecato*. More substantial meals, firmly in the local tradition, can be ordered from a sitting position. Graduation parties – which tend to get pretty wild in Venice – are a regular feature.

La Bitta ㊼

Dorsoduro 2753A, calle lunga San Barnaba (041 523 0531). Vaporetto Ca' Rezzonico. **Open** 10.30am-3pm, 6pm-midnight Mon, Tue, Thur-Sun.

Meals served noon-2pm, 7-11pm Mon, Tue, Thur-Sun. Closed Aug. **Average** €34. **Credit** AmEx, DC, MC, V. **Map** p306 B2.

Formerly Da Sandro, this eatery's name-change has sent prices a little more upmarket. But it's still meat or nothing here – well, nothing apart from *baccalà*, which the locals don't classify as fish. At the counter, grab a *polpetta* or a *crostino di baccalà*; or sit down at a table and order from a range of pasta dishes like *penne con speck e zucca* (with ham and pumpkin), followed by braised meat or rabbit casserole.

L'Incontro ⓐ

Dorsoduro 3062, rio terà Canal (041 522 2404).
Vaporetto Ca' Rezzonico. **Meals served** *Feb-Dec*
7.30-10.30pm Tue; 12.30-2.30pm, 7.30-10.30pm Wed-
Sun. Closed Jan, 2wks Aug. **Average** €40. **Credit**
AmEx, DC, MC, V. **Map** p306 A2.

Meaty restaurants are rare enough in Venice, but
L'Incontro is unique: it's run by an able Sardinian
chef who specialises in pasta and meat dishes from
his Mediterranean island, such as *culingiones* (large
ravioli filled with saffron, ricotta, pecorino cheese
and orange peel) and *porceddu arrosto* (roast suckling pig). The steaks – especially the *tagliata di
manzo* – are out of this world, and the cellar has
some interesting Sardinian vintages. Grab a table
on the sunny terrace in summer, or enjoy the cosy
rustic interior in winter.

La Rivista ⓐ

*Dorsoduro 979A, rio terà Foscarini (041 240 1425/
www.capisanihotel.it). Vaporetto Accademia.* **Meals
served** noon-3pm, 7-10.30pm Tue-Sun. **Average**
€40. **Credit** AmEx, DC, MC, V. **Map** p306 B2.

This smart new wine and cheese bar is an
appendage of Ca' Pisani, Venice's first design hotel.
The decor is in keeping with the revisited 1930s
theme of the hotel, and the original approach carries
through into the menu, which offers something so
often missing in Venice: a selection of light salads,
main courses and cheese platters, accompanied by
a good selection of wines by the bottle and by the
glass. Service can be a little haughty, but this is
still a good standby for a light and healthy meal in
cool modern surroundings.

Ai Vini Padovani ⓐ

*Dorsoduro 1280, calle dei Cerchieri (041 523 6370).
Vaporetto Ca' Rezzonico.* **Open** 10am-10pm Mon-Fri.
Meals served noon-8pm Mon-Fri. Closed Aug.
Average €28. **No credit cards. Map** p306 B2.

A difficult place to find, in a quiet calle between the
Accademia and San Barnaba. But this friendly
neighbourhood bacaro is worth the search if good-
value, authentic, Venetian cooking in congenial
surroundings is your thing. This is a good *cicheto*
bar – a place for a quick, stand-up meal of bar snacks
– but it also doubles as a trattoria, serving up filling
plates of meat – *saltimbocca* (veal and ham strips),
cotechino sausage – and fish. It's Mondays to
Fridays only; and make sure you get here nice and
early (in true bacaro style) for dinner.

Pizzerie

Casin dei Nobili ⓐ

*Dorsoduro 2765, sottoportego del Casin dei Nobili
(041 241 1841). Vaporetto Ca' Rezzonico.* **Meals
served** noon-10.30pm Tue-Sun. **Average** €14
pizzeria; €35 full meal. **Credit** AmEx, DC, MC, V.
Map p306 B2.

Just off campo San Barnaba, this large pizzeria-
restaurant with artsy-rustic decor serves up tasty
pizzas to a mainly student clientele. There is the
usual range of Venetian *primi* and *secondi* as well, but
you'll eat better, and more cheaply, if you stick to the
pizzas. A garden out the back is a summer bonus.

La Giudecca & San Giorgio

Restaurants & *bacari*

Harry's Dolci ⓐ

*Giudecca 773, fondamenta San Biagio (041 522
4844/www.cipriani.com). Vaporetto Sant'Eufemia.*
Meals served *Apr-Oct* noon-3pm, 7-11pm Mon,
Wed-Sun. Closed Nov-Mar. **Average** €65. **Credit**
AmEx, DC, MC, V. **Map** p306 C1.

Arrigo Cipriani's second Venetian stronghold (his
first is Harry's Bar, *see p165*), towards the western
end of the Giudecca, is only open from April to
October, when the weather allows diners to enjoy
the huge terrace with stupendous views across the
Giudecca Canal. The cuisine is supposedly lighter
and more summery than chez Harry, but in practice
many dishes – such as the flagship risottos – are
identical and just as competently prepared. What
changes is the cost: prices at Harry II are around
two-thirds of those at the mother ship (though that's
still a big dent in the average wallet). Come prepared
for mosquitoes on summer evenings.

Mistrà ⓐ

*Giudecca 212A (041 522 0743). Vaporetto
Redentore.* **Meals served** noon-3.30pm Mon;
noon-3.30pm, 7.30-10.30pm Wed-Sun. Closed Jan-
mid Feb. **Average** €40. **Credit** AmEx, DC, MC, V.
Map p307 C3.

The unvisited southern side of the Giudecca is about
as far as you can get from tourist Venice and it
conceals one of the city's most unlikely gourmet
treats. Amid a sprawl of boatyards, a fire-escape
staircase leads up to this trattoria on the first floor of
a warehouse with spectacular views over the lagoon.
Once patronised exclusively by local shipwrights
and gondola-makers, Mistrà has become a word-of-
mouth success among local foodies for its excellent
fish menu and range of Ligurian specialities; game-
based *secondi* can be sampled too, if ordered in
advance. Lunch is cheap and worker-oriented,
dinner more ambitious and a little more expensive.

Lido

Restaurants & *bacari*

For restaurants in **Chioggia**, *see p133*.

Cri Cri & Tendina

Lido, via Sandro Gallo 159A (041 526 5428). **Open**
7am-9pm Mon-Sat. **Meals served** noon-2pm Mon-
Sat. Closed Jan. **Average** €25. **No credit cards.**
Map p311.

This corner *cichetteria* a good way down the Lido's
long, main lagoonside street is always full of locals
fuelling up on glasses of tocai and a good range of

Eat, Drink, Shop

Lunch on the lagoon at **Alla Maddalena**.

bar snacks. At mealtimes – especially in the summer season, when tables spill out on to the pavement – Cri Cri extends its repertoire to take in great seafood pasta dishes, like *spaghetti alle vongole*, and some serious fishy *secondi*. The only time you really need to book is during the film festival (*see p200*), when famished cineastes descend in hordes.

The Lagoon

Restaurants & *bacari*

Busa alla Torre ⑤

Murano, campo Santo Stefano 3 (041 739 662). Vaporetto Faro. **Meals served** noon-3.30pm daily. **Average** €38. **Credit** AmEx, MC, V. **Map** p310.

This is Murano's ultimate gastronomic stop-off and a perfect place for regaining your strength after resisting the hard sell at the island's many glass workshops. In summer, tables spill out into a pretty square opposite the church of San Pietro Martire. The service is deft and professional; the cuisine is reliable, no-frills seafood cooking; the excellent primi go from the classic *spaghetti alla busara* (with anchovies and onions) to homemade *ravioli di pesce*. The jovial owner, Lele, is a giant of a man, and a real character. Note the lunch-only opening.

Al Gatto Nero ⑤

Burano, fondamenta della Giudecca 88 (041 730 120/www.gattonero.com). Motonave 12 to Burano. **Meals served** noon-3pm, 7-9pm Tue-Sun. Closed 1wk Jan, Nov. **Average** €50. **Credit** AmEx, DC, MC, V. **Map** p310.

Most guidebooks point visitors coming to the lace-making island of Burano towards the more famous Da Romano or Il Pescatore-Da Paolo, both in the brightly painted main square. But a better meal is to be had by wandering past the souvenir stalls, through the backstreets, to this friendly trattoria across a canal from the fish market. It's a charming, photogenic place for an al fresco lunch. The service is attentive and the chef does a wonderfully creamy *risotto alla buranella* (with seafood) and an excellent *fritto misto*. It's not cheap, but it's within the Venetian average for this level of quality.

Locanda Cipriani

Torcello, piazza Santa Fosca 29 (041 730 150/www. locandacipriani.com). Vaporetto 12 to Torcello. **Meals served** *Feb-Dec* noon-3pm, 7-9pm Mon, Wed-Sun. Closed Jan. **Average** €65. **Credit** AmEx, DC, MC, V.

There is a lot to like about the high-class Locanda Cipriani (only distantly, and acrimoniously, related to Arrigo Cipriani of Harry's Bar fame, *see p156*), which was a favourite haunt of Ernest Hemingway. The setting, just off Torcello's pretty main square, is idyllic; tables spread over a large vine-shaded terrace during the summer. And although there is nothing remotely adventurous about the cuisine, it's good in a professional, old-fashioned way; and so are the waiters. Specialities such as *risotto alla Torcellana* (with seasonal vegetables) or *filetti di San Pietro alla Carlina* (John Dory fillets with capers and tomatoes) are done with reliable competence, and the desserts – including a calorific giant meringue – are tasty treats for rich kids. If you want to arrive in style, the Locanda provides a boat service from San Marco to Torcello for €20 per person return (ring to book). Cipriani is great place to come if someone else is paying.

Alla Maddalena

Mazzorbo 7C (041 730 151). Motonave 12 to Mazzorbo. **Meals served** 12.30-3pm Mon-Wed, Fri-Sun. Closed 20 Dec-10 Jan. **Average** €28. **Credit** AmEx, DC, MC, V.

The No.12 ferry from Fondamenta Nove takes a very pleasant 45 minutes to chug across the lagoon to the island of Mazzorbo, the stop before Torcello/Burano. Right opposite the jetty is this rustic lunch-only trattoria, which serves filling lagoon cuisine. During the autumn hunting season, there is no better place for a lunch of wild duck, sourced directly from local hunters; the rest of the year, seafood predominates on the menu. Book ahead for Sunday lunch in summer, when the waterside tables and those in the quiet garden behind fill up with Venetian families. The house wine comes from the family's own island vineyards.

> ▶ Each listed restaurant is marked on the maps at the back of the guide: look for the red numbers after each entry.

Cafés, Bars & Gelaterie

From breakfast grappa to cakes and *spritz*: Venetian bars operate non-stop.

Pitch up in any one of Venice's plethora of bars and cafés and you'll find an almost full-service establishment, generally offering everything but seated and served three-course meals: coffees, pastries, sandwiches, light snacks, mixed drinks and quality wines by the glass or bottle. The city's bars and cafés (the terms are interchangeable in Italian) are the place to take the edge off on a bone-chilling cold day with a cappuccino; to meet friends for a stuffed *panino* (*see below* **Bar talk**); or to mingle morning, noon or night while sipping a *spritz* (*see p167* **Rosy to hazy**) – for which any time is the right time.

If you're not up for the pre-breakfast grappa with which many north-eastern workers begin their day, then your first daily café-stop will be for coffee. Venice's relationship with this beverage is a long and important one. The city's first *bottega del caffè* opened in 1683. By the late 18th century as many as 24 coffee shops graced piazza San Marco alone. San Marco continues to function as the city's main and most prestigious coffee-sipping drawing room, with two landmark cafés staring each other out across the square: the **Caffè Florian** and the **Gran Caffè Quadri**, both finely preserved examples of 19th-century café culture.

Besides the usual café and bar offerings, Venice's best bars also have a staggeringly large quantity of top-quality wines by the glass; those that specialise in wine are called *enoteche* or *bacari* (with the accent on the first a; *see also p144* **Bacari**). *Bacari* are typically Venetian wine bars, usually with a range of *tapas*-like snacks on the counter, and they generally come with an in-house sommelier to guide you in your choices. In other Italian cities, wine is usually sought out at very specific addresses; in Venice, good wine by the glass is as easy to find as the next bridge.

Many bars double up as cake and/or ice-cream shops.

PASTICCERIE

As elsewhere in Italy, the Venetian day begins with a cappuccino and brioche (pronounced the French way), preferably a hot one baked on the premises. And any important lunch invitation – and that includes Sunday with family or friends – involves investing in a big tray of dainties. But in the lagoon city, cakes – be

they the dry, biscuity Venetian variety or lush cream-filled pan-Italian ones – are also a regular fixture at aperitivo time: some of the best *spritz* in town are mixed at the *pasticcerie* listed below.

Venetian specialities include: *baicoli*, a light, dry biscuit named after a small lagoon fish that it is supposed to resemble; *busolai*, a sweet S-shaped biscuit with a slight aftertaste of aniseed made on the island of Burano; and *zaleti*, a lemony-vanilla-flavoured cornmeal biscuit packed with raisins. At Carnevale time, the range is extended to include *frittelle*, fried doughnuts containing raisins and/or filled with *zabaglione* or thick cream; and *crostoli*, light thin flakes of pastry that are fried and then dusted with icing sugar. Each *pasticceria* bakes its own specialities, so no two bakeries are ever alike.

GELATERIE

Venice has always challenged the Arabs over paternity of *sorbetto* (water ice) – the forefather of *gelato* – which settlers from the icy Dolomite mountains probably brought with them when they fled to the lagoon in ages past. Nowadays ice-cream shops are almost as numerous in Venice as mask shops; and as with mask shops, quality varies greatly.

Bar talk

bar café
bicchiere glass
brioche croissant, pastry
caffè café; espresso
caffè corretto espresso with a shot of alcohol (usually *grappa*)
caffè macchiato espresso with a dash of milk
cicheto *tapas*-like snack
enoteca wine bar and/or bottle shop
a mescita (wine) by the glass
ombra small glass of wine
panino filled roll
prosecco light sparkling white wine
prosecco spento prosecco with no bubbles
scontrino receipt
spritz *see p167* **Rosy to hazy**
tramezzino sandwich

San Marco

Cafés & bars

Bar all'Angolo

San Marco 3464, campo Santo Stefano (041 522 0710). Vaporetto Sant'Angelo. **Open** 6.30am-11pm Mon-Fri, Sun. *Nov-May* 6.30am-9pm Mon-Fri, Sun. Closed Jan. **No credit cards.** **Map** p307 B3.

If you're lucky enough to be able to grab a table outside, you'll be well placed to enjoy a coffee or a *spritz* and watch the Venetians saunter through campo Santo Stefano. Inside you'll find a mixed bag of locals and tourists being served good *tramezzini* and *panini* by friendly staff.

Bar al Campanile

San Marco 310, calle larga San Marco (041 522 1491). Vaporetto Vallaresso. **Open** 8am-9pm daily. Closed 2wks Jan. **Credit** AmEx, MC, V. **Map** p307 A4.

Bar al Campanile is known for making the best *spritz* in Venice, so don't let those frozen pizzas in the display case put you off. Indulge in a strong and hearty *spritz* (€1.50) while mingling with diehard locals. It's standing room only; beware of the owner of the nearby lace shop who uses his broom to shoo away aperitivo drinkers casually leaning upon his display windows.

Bar al Teatro

San Marco 1916, campo San Fantin (041 522 1052). Vaporetto Sant'Angelo. **Open** 7.30am-midnight Tue-Sun. **Credit** MC, V. **Map** p307 A3.

Before La Fenice opera house burned down, the Teatro was filled with opera-goers every night, and it has remained a Venice institution. As well as serving drinks and fat *tramezzini* at the bar, it doubles as a newsagent's and tobacco shop – and is one of the few places where desperate smokers can find cigarettes late in the evening and on Sundays.

Caffè Florian

San Marco 56, piazza San Marco (041 520 5641/ www.caffeflorian.com). Vaporetto Vallaresso. **Open** *May-Oct* 10am-midnight daily. *Nov-Apr* 10am-midnight Mon, Tue, Thur-Sun. Closed early Dec-Christmas, 1wk Jan. **Credit** AmEx, DC, MC, V. **Map** p307 A3.

This mirrored, stuccoed and frescoed jewel of a café was founded by a certain Floriano Francesconi in 1720 as 'Venezia Trionfante'. Its present appearance, with dozens of intimate wooden *séparés*, dates from an 1859 rehaul. Rousseau, Goethe and Byron hung out here – the last in sympathy, no doubt, with those loyal Venetians who boycotted the Quadri (*see below*) across the square where Austrian officers used to meet. These days, having a drink at Florian is not so much a political statement as a bank statement – especially if you sit at one of the outside tables, where nothing – not even a humble *caffè* – comes in at less than €8.

Stop for coffee or *spritz* at **Bar all'Angolo**.

Caffè Lavena

San Marco 133, piazza San Marco (041 522 4070/ www.venetia.it/lavena). Vaporetto Vallaresso. **Open** *Apr-Oct* 9.30am-12.30am daily. *Nov, Dec* 9.30am-11.30pm Mon, Wed-Sun. Closed Jan-beginning of Carnevale (*see p194*). **Credit** AmEx, DC, MC, V. **Map** p307 A4.

Though less well known than Florian and Quadri, the Lavena has equally good historical credentials: it was founded in 1750 as the Ungheria. It is the favourite piazza bar of many Venetians, partly because there are fewer tourists and prices are slightly lower, but mainly for the coffee, which they rate as the best in the city.

Gran Caffè Quadri

San Marco 120, piazza San Marco (041 522 2105/ www.quadrivenice.com). Vaporetto Vallaresso. **Open** *Apr-Oct* 9am-midnight daily. *Nov-Mar* 9am-midnight Tue-Sun. **Credit** AmEx, DC, MC, V. **Map** p307 A4.

Though it opened more than half a century after its rival on the other side of the piazza, the Quadri was the first café in Venice to serve dark, concentrated *caffè alla turca* – the precursor of today's espresso. It has given Florian a run for its money in the famous-client race – Stendhal and Balzac were Quadri-philes, and Proust used to sit inside in winter, changing tables frequently in order to escape those horrid draughts. But Quadri became unfashionable when the Austrians chose it as their favourite hangout during their 50-year occupation of the city, and despite its similar orchestra and prices, it has never really caught up with Florian as the place to be seen. The luxury restaurant upstairs (*see p149*) is a good place in which to celebrate that lottery win/bank robbery.

Harry's Bar
*San Marco 1323, calle Vallaresso (041 528 5777/
www.cipriani.com). Vaporetto Vallaresso.* **Open**
10.30am-10.45pm daily. **Credit** AmEx, DC, MC, V.
Map p307 B4.
This historic watering hole, founded by Giuseppe
Cipriani in 1931, has changed little since the days
when Ernest Hemingway came here to work on his
next hangover... except for the prices and the numbers of tourists. But despite the pre-dinner crush and
some offhand service, a Bellini (fresh peach juice and
sparkling wine) at the bar is as much a part of the
Venetian experience as a gondola ride (and at €13
far cheaper). At mealtimes, the tables upstairs and
down are reserved for diners who enjoy the Venetian-
themed international comfort food and are prepared
to pay very steep prices (€150-plus for three courses)
to be seen chez Harry's. Stick with a Bellini, and don't
even think of coming in here in shorts.

Vitae
*San Marco 4118, calle Sant'Antonio (041 520
5205). Vaporetto Rialto.* **Open** 9am-2am Mon-Fri;
5pm-2am Sat. **No credit cards. Map** p307 A3.
This smart designer bar in a side street between
campo Manin and campo San Luca is discovered by
few tourists. A firm favourite with Venice's young
and yuppie crowd for its well-made *spritz*, Vitae gets
packed around early evening cocktail time and again
after midnight. There are a few pavement tables, at
which to munch Vitae's tasty *panini*.

Enoteche & bacari

Cavatappi
*San Marco 525, campo della Guerra (041 296
0252). Vaporetto Vallaresso.* **Open** *Apr-Oct*
9am-midnight daily. *Nov, Dec, Feb, Mar* 9am-
midnight Mon-Sat. Closed Jan. **Credit** DC, MC, V.
Map p307 A4.
The name of this *locale*, 'Corkscrew', is certainly
appropriate for this sleek bar that offers more than
30 high-quality wines by the glass at any time.
Owners Marco and Francesca's attention to detail
is clearly evident, right down to the eclectic wooden
containers that hold the munchies that generously
accompany any glass of wine or aperitivo consumed here. The *spritz* here is in the running for
one of the best in Venice.

Osteria ai Rusteghi
*San Marco 5513, campiello del Tentor (041 523
2205). Vaporetto Rialto.* **Open** *Oct-Apr* 9.30am-
3pm, 5-8.30pm Mon-Sat. *May-Sept* 9.30am-3pm,
5-8.30pm Mon-Fri. **No credit cards.**
Map pp307 A4.
This small eaterie serves some excellent wines by
the bottle or glass to accompany its delicious mini-
sandwiches, which come in 30 or more varieties,
including bacon and rosemary, egg and asparagus,
and prawns and *porcini* mushroom. There are outside tables in a hidden square a stone's throw from
bustling campo San Bartolomeo.

Uncork a local vintage at **Cavatappi**.

Eat, Drink, Shop

Pasticcerie

See also **Rosa Salva**, *p167*.

Antica Pasticceria Inguanotto
San Marco 4819, ponte del Lovo (041 520 8439).
Vaporetto Rialto. **Open** *June-Sept* 8am-8.30pm Mon-
Sat. *Oct-May* 8am-8.30pm Mon-Sat; noon-8pm Sun.
Credit MC, V. **Map** p307 A4.
Venetians like to keep the cosy upstairs room at
Pasticceria Inguanotto a secret from tourists, and
flock in the coldest months to sip rich, creamy hot
chocolate topped with foamy cream; finding a table
on Sundays can be a difficult task. There are a few
tables downstairs, too, and ample bar space to put
down a well-made *spritz* or two.

Gelaterie

Igloo
San Marco 3651, calle della Mandola (041 522 3003).
Vaporetto Sant'Angelo. **Open** *May-Sept* 10.30am-9pm
daily. *Oct, Nov, Feb-Apr* 11.30am-7.30pm. Closed Dec,
Jan. **No credit cards. Map** p307 A3.
Generous portions of homemade, creamy *gelato* in
varieties to please everyone is what Igloo is all
about. In the summer months, fruit flavours such as
fig or blackberry are made with the market's freshest ingredients. If you're thinking of becoming a
regular, it's worth taking a punch card: every ten ice-
creams earn you a free one.

Castello

Cafés & bars

See also **Inishark Pub**, *p211*.

Angiò
*Castello 2142, ponte della Veneta Marina (041 277
8555). Vaporetto Arsenale.* **Open** *June-Sept* 7am-
midnight Mon, Wed-Sun. *Oct-Dec, Feb-May* 7am-9pm
Mon, Wed-Sun. Closed Jan. **Credit** MC, V.
Map p308 B2.
Owned by siblings Andrea and Giovanna, Angiò
offers a high-quality stopping point along one of
Venice's most tourist-trafficked spots – the lagoon-
front riva degli Schiavoni. Tables line the water's
edge; ultra-friendly staff serve up Irish beer, freshly
made sandwiches and interesting selections of
cheese and wine. Take in the stunning view of San
Giorgio with a morning coffee or an early evening
aperitivo and enquire about music events held here.

Olandese Volante
Castello 5658, campo San Lio (041 528 9349).
Vaporetto Rialto. **Open** 11am-12.30am Mon-Thur,
Sun; 11am-2am Fri, Sat. **Credit** MC, V. **Map** p307 A4.
The Flying Dutchman pub is a big hit with the
local student population. Beer is the drink of choice;
there is also a big selection of salads and one or two
hot dishes available. It's lively in summer, when
the tables that spill out on to the campiello stay

crowded until late, and cosy in the winter when the
interior rooms are packed as Venetians try to stay
warm with a beer or two.

Al Vecio Penasa
Castello 4585, calle delle Rasse (041 523 7202).
Vaporetto San Zaccaria. **Open** 6.30am-11.30pm
daily. **No credit cards. Map** p308 B1.
Al Vecio Penasa offers coffee and pastries at breakfast and *panini* and delicious *tramezzini* any time of
day. Service is friendly, but taking a seat at one of
the tables inside will add a lot to your bill.

Enoteche & bacari

Alle Alpi (Da Dante)
*Castello 2877, corte Nova (041 528 5163). Vaporetto
Celestia or San Zaccaria.* **Open** 8am-9pm Mon-Sat.
Closed 1wk Aug. **No credit cards. Map** p308 A2.
Tourists? Here? If you want to slum it with the locals
in a place that is as Venetian as they come, head for
this out-of-the-way bacaro in the depths of Castello.
There's white and red wine out of demijohns, and
Dante's wife serves up specialities such as *bovoleti* –
tiny snails in garlic – and *seppiolina* (baby cuttlefish).

La Caneva
Castello 5490, calle della Malvasia (041 521 2661).
Vaporetto Rialto. **Open** 6pm-2am daily. **Credit**
AmEx, MC, V. **Map** p308 B2.
Mauro Lorenzon is irresistible in his leather apron
and signature moustache. He's the founder of
Enoteche, an association of wine bars that are committed to providing a minimum of 24 wines by the
glass at any time. He has recently set up shop here
inside the Ristorante Canaletto and currently offers
600 different labels, all of which he is pleased to
uncork, even for a single glass. Mauro's knowledge
and energy are never-ending.

Alla Mascareta
*Castello 5183, calle lunga Santa Maria Formosa
(041 523 0744). Vaporetto Rialto.* **Open** 6pm-1am
Mon-Sat. Closed Dec-mid Jan. **No credit cards.**
Map p308 A1.
A serious wine bar with lovely old-fashioned wooden
decor, marred only by seriously stroppy staff. Wines
by the glass are more expensive than at your average bacaro, but with such top-class Friulian and
Veneto vintages on offer, the extra expense is more
than justified. Platters of cheese, salami, or salad, plus
a dessert or two, are on hand to soak up the alcohol.

Pasticcerie

Da Bonifacio
Castello 4237, calle degli Albanesi (041 522 7507).
Vaporetto San Zaccaria. **Open** 7.30am-8.30pm
Mon-Wed, Fri-Sun. Closed 3wks Aug, 1wk
Christmas. **No credit cards. Map** p308 B1.
Hidden away in a narrow calle behind the Danieli
Hotel, this is a firm favourite with Venetians. As well
as a tempting array of snacks and traditional cakes

Rosy to hazy

In Venice, any time is the right time for a *spritz*. Easily spotted thanks to its lurid red or orange colouring – generally set off by a fat olive in the bottom of the glass – the *spritz* is a throw-back to Austrian rule at the end of the 19th century. The ingredients are deceptively simple: half a glass of white wine, a twist of lemon peel (never a whole slice) and a strong measure of some bitter *aperitivo*, topped up with a shot of seltzer (though this is sometimes substituted for unsatisfactory mineral water). The classic **spritz al bitter** is made with Campari: one makes the world look rosy; two make it decidedly hazy. Less lethal variations include **spritz al Aperol** (a sweeter, medicinal-tasting drink) or **spritz al Select** (a happy medium between the bitter Campari and sweet Aperol). If staying alert is a priority, go for **spritz al Gingerino**, with its similarly garish colour and bitter taste but no alcohol. All cost around 1.50.

For the best *spritz* in Venice, head for the **Bar al Campanile** (*see p164*) or **Vitae** (*see p165*).

such as *mammalucchi* (deep-fried batter cakes with candied fruit), it serves what is generally considered the finest *americano* aperitif in town.

Chiusso
Castello 3306, salizzada dei Greci (041 523 1611). Vaporetto San Zaccaria or Arsenale. **Open** 8am-1.30pm, 4-9pm Mon, Thur, Fri-Sun; 8am-1.30pm Tue. Closed 2wks Jan. **No credit cards. Map** p308 B2.
Throughout the morning, steaming trays of excellent pastries – try the one with apples and almond paste – roll out of the kitchen at the back of this diminutive bar-*pasticceria*. Take whichever one is hottest and freshest and savour it with Chiusso's excellent cappuccino.

Rosa Salva
Castello 6779, campo Santi Giovanni e Paolo (041 522 7949). Vaporetto Fondamenta Nove. **Open** 7.30am-8.30pm Mon, Tue, Thur-Sat; 8.30am-8.30pm Sun. **No credit cards. Map** p308 A1.
There are two Rosa Salva locations in which to savour the smoothest cappuccino in town. The main branch is listed below, but for all-out charm come to this lovingly restored outlet in campo Santi Giovanni e Paolo. The slow service is worth the wait. There's also delicious home-made *gelato*. **Branch**: San Marco 4589, campo San Luca (041 522 5385).

Gelaterie

Boutique del Gelato
Castello 5727, salizzada San Lio (041 522 3283). Vaporetto Rialto. **Open** *Feb-Nov* 10am-8.30pm daily. Closed Dec, Jan. **No credit cards. Map** p308 A1.
Most Venetians agree that some of the city's best *gelato* is served in this tiny outlet on the busy salizzada San Lio. Be patient, though: there is always a huge crowd waiting to be served.

Cannaregio

Cafés & bars

See also **Fiddler's Elbow Irish Pub** and **Paradiso Perduto**, *both p211*.

Algiubagiò
Cannaregio 5039, fondamenta Nuove (041 523 6084/www.algiubagio.com). Vaporetto Fondamente Nove. **Open** 6.30am-midnight daily. Closed 3wks Jan. **Credit** AmEx, DC, MC, V. **Map** p305 B4.
Situated right by the vaporetto stop, this is a great place to stop off for a cappuccino on the way to or from the northern islands. There's a terrace overlooking the lagoon, from where you can watch the boats come and go over a beer and a *panino*. The bar has branched out into neighbouring ice-cream and takeaway pizza extensions.

Bar ai Miracoli
Cannaregio 6066A, campo Santa Maria Nova (041 523 1515). Vaporetto Rialto. **Open** 6am-11pm daily. **No credit cards. Map** p305 C4.
Located just behind the beautiful church of Santa Maria dei Miracoli in a small but lively campo, this bar has outdoor tables and, when the winter cold hits, cosy booths inside. There are tasty sandwiches and sweets to snack on as you watch the world go by.

Enoteche & bacari

La Cantina
Cannaregio 3689, campo San Felice (041 522 8258). Vaporetto Ca' d'Oro. **Open** 10am-10pm Mon-Sat. Closed 2wks July-Aug; 2wks Jan. **No credit cards. Map** p305 B3.
Serving a selection of good wines, along with draught beer and some excellent *bruschette* with toppings ranging from suckling pig to dreamy gorgonzola, La Cantina is an excellent place to take the edge off your hunger as you watch the world rush by on the nearby strada Nuova.

Pasticcerie

Boscolo
Cannaregio 1818, campiello de l'Anconeta (041 720 731). Vaporetto San Marcuola. **Open** *Aug-June* 6.45am-8.40pm Tue-Sun. Closed July. **No credit cards. Map** p304 B2.

Hosteria Al Vecio Bragosso

Typical Venetian Cuisine
Home-made Pasta
Fresh fish daily

Open 12.00 - 24.00
Closed Monday

Strada Nuova, 4386 - S.S. Apostoli - 30131 Venezia - Tel. 041 5237277

Maria Boscolo runs a busy *pasticceria* that has a packed bar; locals come in to enjoy an extra-strong *spritz al bitter*. There is also an excellent assortment of Venetian sweets: *frittelle* during Carnevale, as well as *zaleti* and *pincia* (a sweet bread that is made with cornflour).

Puppa

Cannaregio 4800, calle del Spezier (041 523 7947). Vaporetto Ca' d'Oro. **Open** *Sept-July* 7am-1.30pm, 3.30-8.30pm Tue-Sat; 7am-8.30pm Sun. Closed Aug. **No credit cards. Map** p305 B4.

Roberto Puppa and his wife run this tiny *pasticceria*, which is a local favourite. It's strictly a stand-up or take-away kind of place, with the interior frozen in time circa 1970. Not only do the Puppas provide some of the city's most delicious cakes – try the *meringa* (meringue and cream) or their famous *crostella* – they also serve as good a *spritz* as you'll find anywhere.

Gelaterie

See also **Algiubagiò**, *p167.*

Il Gelatone

Cannaregio 2063, rio terà Maddalena (041 720 631). Vaporetto San Marcuola. **Open** *May-Sept* 10.30am-8pm Mon; 10.30am-11pm Tue-Sun. *Oct-mid Dec, mid Jan-Apr* 10.30am-8pm Mon; 10.30am-9pm Tue-Sun. Closed mid Dec-mid Jan. **No credit cards. Map** p305 B3.

Follow the trail of overflowing ice-cream cones between the rail station and the end of strada Nuova and you'll easily find Il Gelatone. It offers luscious ice-cream in gorgeous flavours and generous portions: the yoghurt-flavoured variety with sesame seeds and honey is especially good.

San Polo & Santa Croce

Cafés & bars

See also **Ai Postali** and **Bagolo**, *both p210.*

Da Baffo

San Polo 2346, campo Sant'Agostin (041 520 8862). Vaporetto San Stae. **Open** 7.30am-2am Mon-Fri; 5pm-2am Sat. Closed 1wk Christmas, 2wks Aug. **No credit cards. Map** pp304 C2.

Da Baffo is an excellent choice at any time of the day, whether you call in for morning coffee, lunch with grilled vegetables and generous salads or late-night drinks, which include Belgian beer. The interior is wood-beamed and a spacious bar provides extra standing room since tables tend to fill to capacity. Winter months bring evening concerts with jazz, rhythm and blues, and fusion.

Bar Ai Nomboli

San Polo 2717C, rio terà dei Nomboli (041 523 0995). Vaporetto San Tomà. **Open** 7am-9pm Mon-Fri. Closed 1wk Christmas; 3wks Aug. **No credit cards. Map** p302 C2.

A bar much adored by the student population. You'll need to summon all your decision-making skills when faced with over 85 sandwich combinations: try the Serenissima with tuna, peppers, peas and onions.

Bar Ai Tribunali

San Polo 101, campo San Giacomo di Rialto (no phone). Vaporetto Rialto. **Open** 4am-midnight Mon-Sat. **No credit cards. Map** p305 C3.

Recently restored and spruced up, everyone knows this near-legendary Rialto dive as Il Peoco (The Mussel) – a reference to the bald head of its owner, Roberto. Ai Tribunali opens at four in the morning, when clients range from market traders setting up stalls for the day, to those returning from mainland discos. Beware of his lethal cocktail, La Bomba, the ingredients of which are a closely guarded secret.

Caffè dei Frari

San Polo 2564, fondamenta dei Frari (041 524 1877). Vaporetto San Tomà. **Open** 8am-midnight Mon-Fri; 5pm-midnight Sat; 5-9pm Sun. Closed 2wks Aug. **No credit cards. Map** p304 C2.

A cosy bar with an even cosier mezzanine, which is popular with students skipping lectures at the nearby university and lawyers from surrounding offices. The walls feature art nouveau interpretations of 18th-century Venice.

Marcà

San Polo 213, campo Cesare Battisti (no phone). Vaporetto Rialto. **Open** 7am-3pm, 6-9.30pm Mon-Fri; 7am-3pm Sat. **No credit cards. Map** p305 C1.

With standing room only, Marcà has been serving Rialto market-goers since 1918. Neatly packed into this tiny space is a snack-filled case with meatballs, artichoke bottoms and mini-sandwiches in addition to more than 34 different options for *panini* toppings and an ample selection of wines by the glass.

Enoteche & bacari

All'Arco

San Polo 436, calle dell'Ochialer (041 520 5666). Vaporetto San Silvestro or Rialto. **Open** 8am-5pm Mon-Sat. Closed 2wks Aug. **No credit cards. Map** p305 C3.

If you're anywhere near the Rialto markets, don't miss this tiny bacaro in a narrow lane off ruga Vecchia. It's one of Venice's most authentic. There are a few tables outside in summer, but do the local thing: perch at the bar, and sample owner Francesco's great *cicheti*, which include difficult-to-find traditional meaty titbits like *tetina* (cow teat) and *rumegal* (oesophagus, if you really want to know), as well as gourmet rolls and *crostini* (open sandwiches) – try the *robiola* cheese, mushroom and truffle oil version.

Do Mori

San Polo 429, calle dei Do Mori (041 522 5401). Vaporetto Rialto or San Silvestro. **Open** 8.30am-8.30pm Mon-Sat. Closed 1wk Aug. **No credit cards. Map** p305 C3.

Alaska Gelateria-Sorbetteria.

The Do Mori – in a narrow lane in Rialto market territory – claims to be the oldest bacaro in Venice, and it certainly looks it. Batteries of copper pans still hang from the ceiling, and at peak times the narrow bar is a heaving mass of bodies, all lunging for the excellent *francobolli* (mini-sandwiches) and the tremendous selection of fine wines. But don't point to a label at random, as prices can sometimes be in the connoisseur bracket. You won't go far wrong if you stick to a glass of the classic *spento* – prosecco minus the bubbles.

Da Lele

Santa Croce 183, campo dei Tolentini (no phone). Vaporetto Piazzale Roma. **Open** 6am-2pm, 4-8pm Mon-Fri; 6am-2pm Sat. **No credit cards. Map** p305 C1.
There are plenty of bars around the bus station at piazzale Roma, but most of them are either sleazy or overpriced. Gabriele's (Lele's) place is the first authentic *osteria* for those arriving in Venice – or the last for those leaving. It's so small in here there isn't even room for a phone – but there are local wines from Piave, Lison and Valdobbiadene and fresh rolls are made to order with meat and/or cheese fillings.

Al Prosecco

Santa Croce 1503, campo San Giacomo dall'Orio (041 524 0222). Vaporetto San Stae. **Open** Sept-July 8am-10.30pm Mon-Sat. Closed Aug, 1wk Jan. **No credit cards. Map** p304 C2.
Sparkling white prosecco is second only to *spritz* in terms of daily Venetian consumption. The shaded outside tables at the café of the same name are at

an excellent vantage point to watch kids play, but the interior is just as welcoming for cooler days. Excellent wines are served by the glass, with a good choice of cheeses and cold meats to accompany any selection from the bar.

Pasticcerie

Rizzardini

San Polo 1415, campiello dei Meloni (041 522 3835). Vaporetto San Silvestro. **Open** Sept-July 7am-9.30pm Mon, Wed-Sun. Closed Aug. **No credit cards. Map** p307 A3.
A beautiful *pasticcerie*. When owner Paolo is behind the bar, there's never a dull moment. It's especially good for traditional Venetian pastries, and *frittelle* during Carnevale.

Gelaterie

Alaska Gelateria-Sorbetteria

Santa Croce 1159, calle larga dei Bari (041 715 211). Vaporetto Riva de Biasio. **Open** May-Sept noon-midnight daily. *Oct, Nov, Feb-Apr* noon-9pm Tue-Sun. Closed Jan, Dec. **No credit cards. Map** p304 B2.
Carlo Pistacchi is passionate about making ice-cream and experimenting with new flavours. Using only the freshest natural ingredients, his ice-cream is the creamiest around. Stick to tried and true favourites such as hazelnut or yoghurt, or branch out to sample exotic flavours such as fennel, celery, asparagus or ginger.

Dorsoduro

Cafés & bars

See also **Margaret Duchamp,** *p211;* **Café Blue, Café Noir,** *both p210.*

Al Chioschetto

Dorsoduro 1406A, Zattere (no phone). Vaporetto Zattere. **Open** June-Sept 7.30am-1am daily. *Oct-May* 7.30am-7pm daily. **No credit cards. Map** p306 B2.
A much-loved spot not only for scrumptious *panini* and snacks, but also for the tranquillity of sitting along the Giudecca Canal with views from industrial Marghera to Palladian San Giorgio Maggiore. Watch the sun rise with coffee and fresh pastries or sip a *spritz* as the evening rolls around.

Corner Pub

Dorsoduro 684, calle de la Chiesa (340 258 1448). Vaporetto Accademia. **Open** 10am-8.30pm Mon; 10am-1am Tue-Sun. Closed 2wks Aug. **No credit cards. Map** p307 B3.
In one of the quieter residential corners of Venice, this is a haven for under-30s looking for a raucous night out in what tends otherwise to be a very sedate neck of the woods.

Ai Do Draghi

Dorsoduro 3665, calle della Chiesa (041 528 9731).
Vaporetto San Tomà. **Open** *Apr-Oct* 7.30am-2am
daily. *Nov-Mar* 7.30am-10pm Mon-Wed, Fri-Sun.
No credit cards. Map p304 B1.

Throngs of happy *spritz* drinkers cram into the
small calle off campo Santa Margherita where the
entrance to Ai Do Draghi is located, and also on to
its numerous tables on the square, to enjoy draught
beers, strong *spritz al bitter* and approximately 40
wines by the glass. Not only are the staff friendly
and courteous to everyone, but the outdoor seating
provides one of the best vantage points from which
to observe the energetic and bustling pace of campo
Santa Margherita.

Da Gino

*Dorsoduro 853A, calle Nuova Sant'Agnese (041 528
5276). Vaporetto Accademia.* **Open** *Sept-July* 6am-
8pm Mon-Sat. Closed Aug, 1 wk Christmas. **No
credit cards. Map** p306 B2.

You'll always be greeted with a smile by the Scarpa
family, whether it's your first or your 100th visit.
During the warmer months tables outside along
the calle make excellent vantage points for watching the constant flow of gallery-goers making their
way towards the Accademia and the Guggenheim
Collection. Serves some of the best *tramezzini* and
made-to-order *panini* around.

Tonolo: the place for cakes and pastries.

Enoteche & bacari

Cantinone (già Schiavi)

*Dorsoduro 992, ponte San Trovaso (041 523 0034/
cantinone@mac.com). Vaporetto Accademia.* **Open**
8.30am-2.30pm; 3.30-8.30pm Mon-Sat. Closed 1wk
Aug. **No credit cards. Map** p306 B2.

Three generations of the Gastaldi family work here,
filling glasses, carting cases of wine, and preparing
huge *panini* with mortadella or more delicate *crostini* with, for example, egg, cress and sundried tomato paste. The advent of the euro has not inflated
prices and when the bar is full, the steps on the nearby bridge outside make a good background for the
Venetian ritual of *spritz* and prosecco consumption.

Pasticcerie

Gobbetti

*Dorsoduro 3108B, rio terà Canal (041 528 9014).
Vaporetto Ca' Rezzonico.* **Open** 7.45am-8pm daily.
Credit AmEx, MC, V. **Map** p306 A2.

This small *pasticceria* makes some of the most
delicious cakes in town, but it is most famous for its
chocolate mousse, which disappears soon after the
day's fresh batch is displayed. If the whole cakes are
sold out, check the display case for single servings.

Tonolo

*Dorsoduro 3764, calle San Pantalon (041 523
7209). Vaporetto San Tomà.* **Open** *Sept-July*
7.45am-8.30pm Tue-Sat; 7.45am-1pm Sun. Closed
Aug. **No credit cards. Map** p306 A2.

On a busy street that runs into campo Santa
Margherita, this is an institution popular with students and families. The coffee is excellent, and on
Sundays the place fills up with locals buying sweet
offerings to take to lunch. All the gorgeous pastries
come in miniature sizes to make sampling easier.

Gelaterie

Gelateria Nico

*Dorsoduro 922, fondamenta Zattere (041 522
5293). Vaporetto Zattere.* **Open** *June-Sept* 7.30am-
11.30pm daily. *Oct-May* 7.30am-9.30pm daily. Closed
Christmas-mid Jan. **No credit cards. Map** p306 B2.

Nico's serves a lot more than just ice-creams, including *spritz*, prosecco, pizzas and the usual range of
bar food. Dedicated bar-loungers are attracted by
the splendid view from the terrace. If you dare, try
the *gianduiotto*, a slab of hazelnut-and-chocolate ice-
cream immersed in thick whipped cream.

Gelateria Squero

*Dorsoduro 989/990, fondamenta Nani (041 241
3601). Vaporetto Accademia or Zattere.* **Open** 11am-
8pm daily. **No credit cards. Map** p306 B2.

This *gelateria* gives neighbour Nico some healthy
competition in the ice-cream market. The strawberry
mousse is so light and creamy that it's served in a
waffle cone so it doesn't land in the adjacent canal.

Eat, Drink, Shop

Shops & Services

Masks and lace abound; staples are harder to come by.

In centuries past, Venice was the gateway to the Orient and an important trading centre, with exotic spices and raw silks among the goods imported and sold by shrewd Venetian merchants. Known now for its luxurious brocades and damasks, Burano lace and the glassworks of Murano, Venice is still the ideal place for the refined shopper. Luxurious as authentic Venetian-made goods are, prices are often prohibitive. Over the last few years, however, an increasing number of young artisans – shoemakers, jewellers, carpenters, maskmakers and others – have injected a little more competition into pricing, as well as helping to keep traditional techniques alive.

Reasonably priced gifts and souvenirs produced by local craftspeople can be found all over the city – often clustered in trade enclaves, another medieval legacy. Stained glass and wrought-iron and wooden sculptures can be found in the *calle* between campo San Polo and campo San Giacomo dell'Orio. Calle della Mandola is the street for paper products and glass beads, while antique shops are thick on the ground around campo Santo Stefano. The Dorsoduro side of the ponte dell'Accademia is one of the best places to go for handcrafted masks.

The main retail areas are the Mercerie – the maze of crowded, narrow alleyways leading from piazza San Marco to the Rialto – and the streets known collectively as the Frezzeria, which wind between La Fenice and piazza San Marco. The densest concentration of big-name fashion outlets can be found around the calle larga XXII Marzo, just west of the piazza, where top names such as Prada, Valentino, Fendi, Versace and Gucci have all staked their boutiques.

Devotees of kitsch should not miss the stalls and shops near the train station, where plastic gondolas, illuminated gondolas, flashing gondolas, musical gondolas and even gondola cigarette lighters reign supreme.

For more tasteful souvenirs, Venice's glass, lace, fabrics and handmade paper are legendary – as are the made-in-Taiwan substitutes that are passed off as the genuine article by unscrupulous traders. Sticking to the outlets listed below will help you to avoid unpleasant surprises.

With the steady demographic drop has come a demise of 'useful' shops: bread, fruit and veg,

milk and meat are increasingly difficult to get hold of. And while new supermarkets have opened in Cannaregio and on the island of the Giudecca, the flipside of this is the threat now posed to the livelihood of the greengrocers, bakers and butchers that remain.

OPENING HOURS

Most food shops are closed on Wednesday afternoons, while most non-food shops stay shut on Monday mornings. During high season (which in Venice includes Carnevale in February/March, Easter, the four weeks leading up to Christmas and the summer season from June to October) many shops abandon their lunchtime closing, and stay open all day, even opening on Sundays.

It pays to be sceptical about the hours posted on the doors of smaller shops: opening times are often determined by volume of trade or personal whim. If you want to be sure of not finding the shutters drawn, call before you set out.

Incomprehensibly – given that summer is Venice's busiest season – some shops close for holidays in August, but the majority of these are smaller ones that cater more for residents than tourists, such as *tabacchi*, photocopying centres and dry-cleaners.

If you are not an EU citizen, remember to keep your official receipt (*scontrino*) as you are entitled to a rebate on IVA (sales tax) paid on purchases of personal goods costing more than €154 as long as they leave the country unused and are bought from a shop that provides this service. Look for a sign in the window and ask for the form to show at customs upon departure.

One-stop shopping

Shopping centres and department stores are few and far between in Venice proper. If you're suffering from mall withdrawal, you can always head for Mestre (*see p138*). Be warned: although prices there may be competitive, the selection is unimaginative and the trip to Mestre can be physically, emotionally and aesthetically draining.

Auchan Centro Commerciale

Via Don Tosatto 22, Mestre (041 507 4300). Free bus service to & from piazzale Roma. **Open** 1.30-10pm Mon; 9am-10pm Tue-Sat. **Credit** varies. **Map** p303.

Sabbie e Nebbie. *See p175.*

One of the largest shopping malls on the Venetian mainland with 70 shops including restaurants, a supermarket and sporting goods shops.

Centro Le Barche
Piazza XXVII Ottobre 1, Mestre (041 977 882/ www.lebarche.com). Bus 4 or 4/ from piazzale Roma. **Open** 2-8pm Mon; 9am-8pm Tue-Sat. **Credit** varies. **Map** p303.
In addition to trendy stores, you'll find the Feltrinelli bookshop with some titles in English, a theatre box office and a well-stocked record shop – and there's a food court on the top floor and a supermarket in the basement.

Coin
Cannaregio 5787, salizzada San Crisostomo (041 520 3581/www.gruppocoin.it). Vaporetto Rialto. **Open** 9.30am-7.30pm Mon-Sat; 11am-7.30pm Sun. **Credit** AmEx, DC, MC, V. **Map** p305 C4.
Stylish, above-average department store chain. Prices aren't exactly rock-bottom, but there are bargains to be had during sales. The houseware department is good for unpretentious sheets and linens.

Standa
Cannaregio 3659, strada Nuova (041 523 8046). Vaporetto Ca' d'Oro. **Open** 8.30am-7.20pm daily. **Credit** AmEx, MC, V. **Map** p305 B3.

Italy's Woolworth's. You'll find cheap clothes (not all of them awful), toiletries and a modest selection of articles for the home. There's also a well-stocked supermarket on site.

Antiques

Antique shops can be found throughout the city, though the concentration is greatest around campo San Maurizio and calle delle Botteghe (near campo Santo Stefano). There is also a Mercatino dell'Antiquariato (antiques fair) twice a year, in the week before Easter and Christmas, in campo San Maurizio (map p307 B3).

Antiquus
San Marco 2973 & 3131, calle delle Botteghe (041 520 6395/antiquus.ve@tin.it). Vaporetto Sant'Angelo. **Open** 10am-12.30pm, 3-7.30pm Mon-Sat. **Credit** AmEx, DC, MC, V. **Map** p307 A3.
This charming shop has a beautiful collection of Old Master paintings, furniture, silver and antique jewellery, including Moors' heads brooches and earrings. **Branch:** Dorsoduro 873/A (041 241 3725).

Guarinoni
San Polo 2862, calle del Mandoler (041 522 4286). Vaporetto San Tomà. **Open** 8am-noon, 3-7pm Mon-Sat. **Credit** AmEx, MC, V. **Map** p306 A2.
An assortment of antique furnishings from as early as the 16th century is sold here. The shop also has a workshop that restores gilded ceilings and the like.

Kleine Galerie
San Marco 2972, calle delle Botteghe (041 522 2177). Vaporetto Sant'Angelo. **Open** 4-7pm Mon; 10am-12.45pm, 4-7.30pm Tue-Sat. **No credit cards.** **Map** p307 A3.
The Kleine Galerie specialises in antique books and prints as well as majolica and porcelain.

Art supplies

Angeloni
Galleria Matteotti 2, Mestre (041 974 166). Bus 4 from piazzale Roma to piazza Ferretto. **Open** 9am-12.30pm, 3.30-7.30pm Mon-Sat. **Credit** AmEx, DC, MC, V. **Map** p303.
Nice service and a wide range of supplies, where real artists go. The prices are much better than anything you'll find in island Venice.

Cartoleria Accademia
Dorsoduro 1044, campiello Calbo (041 520 7086). Vaporetto Accademia. **Open** 8am-12.30pm, 4-7pm Mon-Fri; 8am-12.30pm Sat. **No credit cards.** **Map** p306 B2.
This small but well-stocked store carries a wide range of artists' supplies and is conveniently located just behind the Accademia. Cartoleria Accademia has been in the business since 1810, so it must be doing something right.
Branch: Dorsoduro 2928, campo Santa Margherita (041 528 5283).

Eat, Drink, Shop

Cartoleria Arte e Design

Santa Croce 53, campiello Mosca (041 710 269).
Vaporetto Piazzale Roma. **Open** 8am-1pm,
3-7.30pm Mon-Sat. **Credit** AmEx, DC, MC, V.
Map p304 C1.
Art supplies of all kinds, including paper of every
imaginable shape, colour and size. Mont Blanc,
Waterman and Filofax products are available, as
well as an impressive range of computer supplies.
A favourite with the architecture students.

Testolini

San Marco 1744-8, fondamenta Orseolo (041
522 9265). Vaporetto Vallaresso or Rialto.
Open 9am-7pm Mon-Sat. **Credit** AmEx, DC,
MC, V. **Map** p307 A4.
Testolini carries stationery, backpacks, briefcases,
calendars and art/office supplies. It also has an
annexe filled with computers and accessories. The
service tends towards the unfriendly but the choice
is huge… by Venetian standards.

Bookshops

Ca' Foscarina

Dorsoduro 3259, campiello degli Squellini (041 522
9602/www.cafoscarina.it). Vaporetto Ca' Rezzonico
or San Tomà. **Open** 9am-7pm Mon-Fri; 9am-
12.30pm Sat. **Credit** MC, V. **Map** p306 A2.
The official bookstore of the Università Ca' Foscari,
with the city's largest selection of books in English,
covering literature, poetry, history and travel.

Fantoni Libri Arte

San Marco 4119, salizzada San Luca (041 522
0700). Vaporetto Rialto. **Open** 10am-8pm Mon-Sat.
Credit AmEx, DC, MC, V. **Map** p307 A4.
Beautifully illustrated art, architecture, design, photography and textile books, mostly in Italian.
There's also a small selection of cookbooks and
works on Venice in English.

Filippi Editore Venezia

Castello 5284, Casselaria (041 523 6916/
filippieditore@flashnet.it). Vaporetto San Zaccaria.
Open 9am-12.30pm, 3-7.30pm Mon-Sat. **Credit** MC,
V. **Map** p308 A1.
Venice's longest-running publishing house is a
father-and-son operation with more than 400 titles
on Venetian history and folklore – all limited editions in Italian. The evocatively dark and dusty
flagship store (address below) is now often closed.
Branch: Castello 5763, calle del Paradiso (041 523
5635).

Laboratorio Blu

Cannaregio 1224, campo del Ghetto Vecchio
(041 715 819/adep2@libero.it). Vaporetto Guglie.
Open 3.45-7.30pm Mon, 9.30am-12.30pm, 3.45-
7.30pm Tue-Sat. **Credit** MC, V. **Map** p304 A2.
The only children's bookshop in Venice. Laboratorio
Blu carries a good selection of books in English and
offers courses for kids – drawing, painting, weaving and storytelling.

Libreria San Pantalon

Dorsoduro 3950, salizzada San Pantalon (041 522
4436). Vaporetto San Tomà. **Open** *Sept-May* 9am-
7.30pm Mon-Sat. *June-Aug* 9am-1pm, 3.30-7.30pm
Mon-Sat. **Credit** DC, MC, V. **Map** p306 A2.
Known to Venetians as the bookshop with the cat in
the window, Libreria San Pantalon is a place you can
spend hours. As well as a good selection of books on
music – especially opera – it carries beautiful arts
and crafts books, games, children's books and cards.

Libreria Toletta & Toletta Studio

Dorsoduro 1214, calle Toletta (041 523 2034/
info@libreriatoletta.it). Vaporetto Accademia or
Ca' Rezzonico. **Open** *Sept-June* 9am-7.30pm Mon-Sat.
July-Aug 9am-1pm, 3.30-7.30pm Mon-Sat. **Credit**
AmEx, DC, MC, V. **Map** p306 B2.
A good source of cheap books, the Toletta offers
20%-40% off its stock, depending on the publisher.
Italian classics, art, cookery, children's books, his-
tory (mostly in Italian) all feature, along with a vast
assortment of dictionaries. Next door is the Toletta
Studio, which specialises in architecture books as
well as selling T-shirts and small gifts.

Mare di Carta

Santa Croce 222, fondamenta dei Tolentini (041
716 304/www.maredicarte.com). Vaporetto Piazzale
Roma. **Open** 9am-1pm, 3.30-7.30pm Mon-Sat.
Credit AmEx, DC, MC, V. **Map** p304 C1.
A must for boat lovers, this nautical bookshop carries publications in English as well as Italian. The
bulletin board has boats for sale for anyone interested in purchasing a gondola.

Studium

San Marco 337C, calle Canonica (041 522 2382/
libstudium@tin.it). Vaporetto San Zaccaria. **Open**
9am-7.30pm Mon-Sat. **Credit** AmEx, DC, MC, V.
Map p307 A4.
Located behind St Mark's basilica, this two-room
shop has a wide selection of works on Venice,
travel books and novels in English. Its speciality is
revealed in the back room, which is filled with theology studies, icons and prayer books.

Cosmetics & perfumes

Cosmetics and toiletries can be found in the
one-stop stores listed above or in *farmacie*,
although prices tend to be higher at chemists'.
For designer names try any of the smaller, more
specialised *profumerie*. For herbal products of
any description, including aromatherapy oils,
head for an *erboristeria*.

Barbiero & Scomparin

San Polo 806, calle del Figher (041 522 3632).
Vaporetto San Silvestro. **Open** 9am-12.30pm,
4-7.30pm Mon-Sat. **Credit** AmEx, MC, DC, V.
Map p305 C3.
Make a list before you go because when you walk in
you'll be so overwhelmed with how much stuff is
crammed into such a tiny space that you'll have

forgotten what you came for. And it doesn't just sell cosmetics and toiletries: you'll find pots, pans, rugs and even some hardware goods. **Branch**: Castello 1311, via Garibaldi. (041 521 0780).

L'Erbania
San Polo 1735, calle dei Botteri (041 723 215/ nerella93@hotmail.com). Vaporetto San Silvestro. **Open** 3-7.15pm Mon; 9.45am-1.30pm, 3-7.15pm Tue-Sat. **Credit** AmEx, DC, V. **Map** p305 C3.
A quaint shop near the Rialto where a herbalist will mix up concoctions for you. Alternatively, choose from a variety of prepared creams and perfumes.

Design & household

Ceramics & china

Camilla
Dorsoduro 2609, campo dei Carmini (041 523 5277). Vaporetto Ca' Rezzonico or San Basilio. **Open** 10am-6pm Tue-Sat. **No credit cards. Map** p306 A1.
This shop stocks pottery made and decorated by Camilla herself. The imaginative motifs are inspired by the Venetian landscape.

Ceramiche La Margherita
Santa Croce 2345, sottoportico della Siora Bettina (041 723 120/www.lamargheritavenezia.com). Vaporetto San Stae. **Open** 9.30am-1pm, 3.30-7pm Mon-Sat. **Credit** AmEx, MC, V. **Map** 304 B2.
A wonderful collection of hand-painted terracotta designed by the English-speaking owner. Plates, bowls and teapots all at reasonable prices.

Domus
San Marco 4746, calle dei Fabbri (041 522 6259). Vaporetto Rialto. **Open** 9.30am-7.30pm Mon-Sat; 11am-7.30pm Sun. **Credit** AmEx, DC, MC, V. **Map** p307 A4.
Domus is good for all sorts of houseware from rustic Italian ceramic pieces to fine bone china. Murano vases and glassware by names such as Nason-Moretti can also be found. Check in the window for discounts on plate sets, bowls and cutlery. Great place if you need to get a wedding gift.

Madera
Dorsoduro 2762, campo San Barnaba (041 522 4181/www.maderavenezia.it). Vaporetto Ca' Rezzonico. **Open** 10am-1pm, 3.30-7.30pm Mon-Sat. **Credit** AmEx, DC, V. **Map** p306 B2.
Fusing minimalist design with traditional techniques, the young architect and craftswoman behind Madera creates unique objects in wood. She also sells exceptional lamps, ceramics, jewellery and textiles by other European artists.

Materia Prima
San Marco 3436, piscina San Samuele (041 523 3585/3282). Vaporetto Sant'Angelo. **Open** 11am-1pm, 4-7.30pm Tue-Sat. **Credit** AmEx, DC, MC, V. **Map** p307 A3.

Interesting and affordable objects from around the world as well as ceramic, glass and textile works produced by local artisans.

Sabbie e Nebbie
San Polo 2768A, calle dei Nomboli (041 719 073). Vaporetto San Tomà. **Open** 10am-12.30pm, 4-7.30pm Mon-Sat. **Credit** MC, V. **Map** p304 C2.
A beautiful selection of contemporary Italian ceramic pieces as well as highly refined Japanese works. Also handmade objects by Italian designers such as lamps, candleholders and notebooks.

Fabrics & accessories

Antichità Marciana
San Marco 1691, Frezzeria (041 523 5666). Vaporetto Vallaresso. **Open** 4-7.30pm Mon; 9.30am-1pm, 3.30-7.30pm Tue-Sat. **Credit** AmEx, DC, MC, V. **Map** p307 A4.
A tasteful selection of antique baubles can be found in this jewel of a shop; its speciality, however, are the richly painted velvets created by the owner in her workshop. A favourite among interior designers.

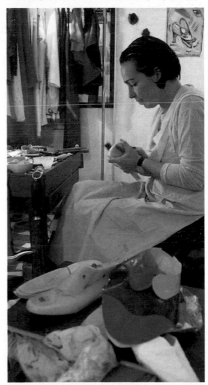

Giovanna Zanella. *See p179.*

Eat, Drink, Shop

Arras

Dorsoduro 3234, campiello Squellini (041 522 6460). Vaporetto Ca' Rezzonico. **Open** 9am-1pm, 3.30-7.30pm Mon-Sat. **Credit** AmEx, DC, MC, V. **Map** p306 A2.

Handwoven fabrics are created here in a vast range of colours and textures using silk, wool and cotton. The shop is run by a co-operative that organises weaving courses for the handicapped, whose work is on sale alongside other items.

Bevilacqua

San Marco 337B, ponte della Canonica (041 528 7581). Vaporetto San Zaccaria. **Open** 10am-7.30pm Mon-Sat; 10am-4.30pm Sun. **Credit** AmEx, DC, MC, V. **Map** p307 A4.

This small shop behind St Mark's basilica offers exquisite examples of both hand- and machine-woven silk brocades, damasks and velvets. The Venetian textile tradition is kept alive by three weavers who use original 17th-century looms. **Branch**: San Marco 2520, campo Santa Maria del Giglio (041 241 0662).

Gaggio

San Marco 3441-51 calle delle Botteghe (041 522 8574/www.gaggio.it). Vaporetto San Samuele or Sant'Angelo. **Open** 9.30am-1pm, 3.30-7.30pm Mon-Sat. **Credit** AmEx, DC, MC, V. **Map** p307 A3.

A legend among dressmakers and designers, Emma Gaggio's sumptuous handprinted silk velvets (from €150 a metre) are used to make cushions and wall hangings as well as bags, hats, scarves and jackets.

Il Milione

Castello 6025, campo Santa Marina (041 241 0722/ www.ilmilionevenezia.com). Vaporetto Rialto. **Open** 10am-12.30pm, 3-7.30pm Mon-Sat. **Credit** MC, V. **Map** p306 A1.

Handmade lamps that look like Fortuny knock-offs and are a little more affordable.

Trois

San Marco 2666, campo San Maurizio (041 522 2905). Vaporetto Santa Maria del Giglio. **Open** 4-7.30pm Mon; 10am-1pm, 4-7.30pm Tue-Sat. **No credit cards. Map** p307 B3.

The only place in Venice where you can buy original Fortuny fabrics – and at considerable savings on UK/US prices (though this still doesn't make them particularly cheap). Made-to-order beadwork masks and accessories and also available.

Venetia Studium

San Marco 2403, calle larga XXII Marzo (041 522 9281/www.venetiastudium.com). Vaporetto Santa Maria del Giglio. **Open** 9.30am-8pm Mon-Sat; 10.30am-7.30pm Sun. **Credit** AmEx, DC, MC, V. **Map** p307 B3.

Venetia Studium stocks beautiful pleated Fortuny-style silk fabrics, used for elegant pillows, lamps, scarves, handbags and other accessories in a marvellous range of colours. They are certainly not cheap, but they do make perfect gifts for those who have it all.

Hardware & kitchenware

Di Pol

Dorsoduro 3117, campo Santa Margherita (041 528 5451). Vaporetto Ca' Rezzonico. **Open** 8am-12.30pm, 3-7.30pm Mon-Fri; 8am-12.30pm Sat. **Credit** MC, V. **Map** p306 A2.

This hardware store carries a little bit of everything: paint supplies, gardening tools, detergents and staff make keys too. Most importantly, you can pick up a pair of high-water boots, even hip-high waders for those exceptionally wet days.

Ratti

Castello 5825, calle delle Bande (041 240 4600/ rattisrl@tin.it). Vaporetto San Zaccaria or Rialto. **Open** 9am-12.30pm, 3.30-7.15pm Mon-Fri; 9am-12.30pm Sat. **Credit** AmEx, MC, V. **Map** p308 A1.

If Ratti doesn't have what you're looking for, it's time to worry. There are kitchen utensils, locks and other security items, household goods, televisions, radios, adapters and all kinds of electronic gadgets. Keys cut.

Lace & linens

Lace is cheaper on the island of Burano (*see p137*) than in the centre of Venice. Bear in mind in both places, however, that if it's cheap, it's machine made, and if it's very cheap it almost certainly hails from Taiwan rather than from some dark Venetian back room where ancient crones sit hunched over their age-old craft. If you want reliable, top-quality (and exorbitant) lace without taking the trip across to Burano, stick to big names such as Jesurum and Martinuzzi.

Annelie

Dorsoduro 2748, calle lunga San Barnaba (041 520 3277). Vaporetto Ca' Rezzonico. **Open** 9.30am-12.30pm, 4-7.30pm Mon-Fri; 9.30am-12.30pm Sat. **Credit** AmEx, DC, MC, V. **Map** p306 B2.

A delightful shop run by a delightful lady who has a beautiful selection of sheets, tablecloths, curtains, shirts and baby clothes, either fully embroidered or with lace detailing. Antique lace can also be had at reasonable prices.

Jesurum

San Marco 60-61, piazza San Marco (041 522 9864/www.jesurum.it). Vaporetto Vallaresso. **Open** 9.30am-7.30pm Mon-Sat; 10.30am-6.30pm Sun. **Credit** AmEx, DC, MC, V. **Map** p307 A4.

Extremely elegant embroidered linens, towels and fabrics, from a lace company that has been going for more than 100 years. In the 19th century it was considered the only place to come for really good lace; it is still renowned for its sophisticated, traditional lacework. Be warned – quality costs. **Branch**: San Marco 4857, Merceria del Capitello (041 520 6177).

Marchini Pasticceria – very sweet, very expensive. *See p181.*

La Fenice Atelier

*San Marco 3537, campo Sant'Angelo (041 523
0578/lafeniceatelier@libero.it). Vaporetto
Sant'Angelo.* **Open** 10am-1.30pm, 3.30-7.30pm
Mon-Sat; 10.30am-7.30pm Sun. **Credit** AmEx,
DC, MC, V. **Map** p307 A3.

Slightly more affordable than Jesurum (*see p176*),
this tiny boutique has its workshop on the opposite
side of town. It produces hand-embroidered night-
gowns, towels and sheets, as well as a catalogue full
of designs for made-to-order items. Visit La Fenice
Atelier if that appeals.

Martinuzzi

*San Marco 67A, piazza San Marco (041 522 5068/
martinuzzi@inwind.it). Vaporetto Vallaresso.* **Open**
Apr-Dec 9am-7.30pm daily. *Jan-Mar* 9am-12.30pm,
3-7.30pm Mon-Sat. **Credit** AmEx, DC, MC, V.
Map p307 A4.

The oldest lace shop in Venice, Martinuzzi has exclusive designs for bobbin lace items such as place
mats, tablecloths and linens. If you have an odd-
sized bed, not to worry – Martinuzzi will create a
sheet set especially for you.

Fashion

All the big-name boutiques (Armani, Prada,
Gucci and so on) are clustered around four
streets in the vicinity of San Marco: calle
Vallaresso; salizzada San Moisè and its
continuation, calle larga XXII Marzo; calle
Goldoni; and the Mercerie. The shops listed
below offer something a little different.

Accessories

Balocoloc

*Santa Croce 2134, calle Longa (041 524 0551/
www.balocoloc.com). Vaporetto San Stae.* **Open**
1-6pm Tue-Sat. **Credit** MC, V. **Map** p304 C2.

This out-of-the-way shop offers a nice selection of
stylish and reasonably priced handmade hats. It also
stocks a line of Carnevale wear too.

Gualti

*Dorsoduro 3111, rio terà Canal (041 520 1731/
www.gualti.it) Vaporetto Ca' Rezzonico.* **Open** 10am-
1pm, 3-7.30pm Mon-Sat. **Credit** AmEx, DC, MC, V.
Map p306 A2.

One-of-a-kind jewellery creations using glass and a
resin mixture. Every piece by Gualti makes a statement – dramatic but wearable… for some.

Hibiscus

*San Polo 1060-61, ruga Rialto/calle dell'Olio (041
520 8989). Vaporetto San Silvestro.* **Open** 9.30am-
7.30pm Mon-Sat; 11am-7pm Sun. **Credit** AmEx, DC,
MC, V. **Map** p305 C2.

Viaggio nei colori – a voyage into the world of
colours – is the Hibicus motto; it is demonstrated on
jewellery, handmade scarves, bags and ceramics
with an ethnic flare. Not cheap, but a refreshing
change from glass and mask shops.

Piaroa

*San Polo 1247, campo San Aponal (041 520 2198).
Vaporetto San Silvestro.* **Open** 10am-7.30pm Mon-
Sat; 11am-7.30pm Sun. **Credit** AmEx, DC, MC, V.
Map p305 C3.

Piaroa has just about everything: clothes, sandals, slippers, bags, home decorations, incense, candles. Most articles come from either India or South America. The shop owner, originally from Uruguay, adds even more charm to this unique little shop.

Designers

Araba Fenice
San Marco 1822, calle dei Barcaroli (041 522 0664). Vaporetto Santa Maria del Giglio or Vallaresso. **Open** 9.30am-7.30pm Mon-Sat. **Credit** AmEx, DC, MC, V. **Map** p307 A4.
A classic yet original line of women's clothing made exclusively for this boutique, plus jewellery in ebony and mother of pearl.

Giovanna Zanella
Castello 5641, campo San Lio (041 523 5500). Vaporetto Rialto. **Open** 9am-1pm, 2.30-7pm Mon-Sat. **Credit** AmEx, DC, MC, V. **Map** p307 A4.
The clothes and accessories of Venetian designer Giovanna Zanella offer an alternative to the Italian standards. Beautiful colours and fabrics make each design unique.

Godi Fiorenza
San Marco 4261, rio terà San Paternian (041 241 0866/www.veneziart.com). Vaporetto Rialto or Vallaresso. **Open** 10am-12.30pm, 3.30-7.30pm Mon-Sat. **Credit** AmEx, MC, V. **Map** p307 A3.
The London-trained Godi designer sisters sell exquisite knitwear, stylish coats and chiffon evening tops. All made on the premises, and complemented with jewellery.

Trend-setters

BA BA
San Polo 2865, campo San Tomà (041 716 353/ www.katabusiness.com/ve/baba). Vaporetto San Tomà. **Open** 9.30am-8pm Mon-Sat. **Credit** AmEx, DC, MC, V. **Map** p306 A2.
All the latest from young Italian designers. Not everyone can wear it.

Diesel
San Marco 5315-16, salizada Pio X (041 241 1937/ www.diesel.com). Vaporetto Rialto. **Open** 10am-7.30pm Mon-Sat; 11am-7pm Sun. **Credit** AmEx, DC, MC, V. **Map** p307 A4.
'For successful living' is the motto of this Veneto-based company, whose kooky, club-wise styles and ad campaigns have invaded Europe. This two-storey hipper than hip store is a recent addition to the Venetian shopping scene.

Prima Visione
Cannaregio 2340, rio terà Maddalena (041 524 2356). Vaporetto Ca' d'Oro. **Open** 9am-7.30pm Mon-Sat; 10.30am-6.30pm Sun. **Credit** AmEx, DC, MC, V. **Map** p305 B3.
Stocks smaller trend-setters such as Miss Sixty, Mile, Indian Rose and Energy.

Ser Angiù
Dorsoduro 868, piscina del Forner (041 523 1149). Vaporetto Accademia. **Open** 2-8pm Wed-Sun. **No credit cards. Map** p307 B3.
Probably the only outlet store in Venice that sells discounted designer labels. Local ladies line up on Wednesdays to get first pick.

Leather goods

The big names in leather – Bruno Magli, Fratelli Rossetti and Sergio Rossi, to name but a few – are all located around piazza San Marco. For a more modest investment, try one of the following.

Francis Model
San Polo 773A, ruga Rialto/ruga del Ravano (041 521 2889). Vaporetto San Silvestro. **Open** *Apr-Dec* 9.30am-7.30pm Mon-Sat; 10.30am-7.30pm Sun. *Jan-Mar* 9.30am-1pm, 3-7.30pm Mon-Sat. **Credit** AmEx, DC, MC, V. **Map** p305 C3.
Handbags and briefcases are produced in this tiny *bottega* by a father-and-son team that has been in the business for more than 40 years.

Italo Mariani
San Marco 4775, calle del Teatro (041 523 5580). Vaporetto Rialto. **Open** 9.30am-1pm, 3-7.30pm Mon-Sat; 10.30am-6.30pm Sun. **Credit** AmEx, DC, MC, V. **Map** p307 A4.
Stylish Italian shoes for men and women at affordable prices. Bargains abound in the sale in January. **Branch:** Castello 4313, ponte della Canonica (041 522 5614).

Mori & Bozzi
Cannaregio 2367, rio terà Maddalena (041 715 261). Vaporetto San Marcuola. **Open** *June-Aug, Nov-Mar* 9.30am-12.30pm, 3.30-7.30pm Mon-Sat. *Apr, May, Sept, Oct* 9.30am-12.30pm, 3.30-7.30pm Mon-Sat; 3.30-7.30pm Sun. **Credit** AmEx, DC, MC, V. **Map** p305 B3.
Shoes for the coolest of the cool: whatever the latest fad – pointy or square – it's here. Trendy names and designer copies.

Rolando Segalin
San Marco 4365, calle dei Fuseri (041 522 2115). Vaporetto Rialto. **Open** 9am-12.30pm, 3.30-7.30pm Mon-Fri; 9am-12.30pm Sat. **Credit** AmEx, DC, MC, V. **Map** p307 A4.
'The Cobbler of Venice' has been creating shoes made to order for more than 50 years. Some of the most interesting are on display in the window, including a pair of gondola-shoes… there's no accounting for taste. Repairs are done as well.

Second-hand clothes

Laboratorio Arte & Costume
San Polo 2235, calle Scaleter (041 524 6242). Vaporetto San Stae. **Open** 10am-12.30pm, 3.30-8pm Mon-Sat. **Credit** MC, V. **Map** p304 C2.

Eat, Drink, Shop

Hidden away behind campo San Polo, this shop is jam-packed with vintage clothing, toys and God knows what in barely organised chaos. A great selection of hats from the traditional panama to stylish creations by the shop's owner. Carnevale attire can also be rented here. The shop also opens 9-11pm in July, August and over Carnevale.

Laura Crovato

San Marco 2995, calle delle Botteghe (041 520 4170). Vaporetto Sant'Angelo. **Open** 4-7.30pm Mon; 11am-1pm, 4-7.30pm Tue-Sat. **Credit** MC, V. **Map** p307 A3.
Nestling between expensive galleries and antique shops, Laura Crovato offers a selection of used clothes and a sprinkling of new items, including raw-silk shirts and scarves, costume jewellery and sunglasses. This being Venice, the shop's not giving the stuff away – even though it's second-hand.

Food & drink

For the freshest fruit, vegetables, meat and fish at the most competitive prices – plus a slice of everyday Venetian life that should not be missed – the market that's held every morning except Sunday at the foot of the Rialto bridge is difficult to beat. For (slightly) less crowded market options, *see below* **Market day**.

Grocery shops (*alimentari*) offer all the usual staples from around Italy, as well as the odd Venetian speciality such as *baccalà mantecato* (a delectable spread made with dried cod) and *mostarda veneziana* (a sweet and sour sauce made with dried fruit). Other regional favourites include olive oil from Lake Garda, flavoured vinegars, mountain honey from Belluno, fruit liqueurs and grappa, a fiery brandy distilled from the lees after the grapes are pressed (*see p269* **Moonshine**). Butchers and bakers are sadly becoming thin on the ground as the mushrooming malls across on the mainland steal their trade.

Venetians are famous for their sweet tooth. There is, therefore, an extraordinary variety of calorific delights to devour while strolling through the *calli*; *see also chapter* **Cafés, Bars & Pasticcerie**.

Alimentari

Aliani

San Polo 654-5, ruga Rialto/ruga vecchia San Giovanni (041 522 4913). Vaporetto San Silvestro. **Open** 8am-1pm Mon, Wed; 8am-1pm, 5-7.30pm Tue, Fri, Sat. **No credit cards**. **Map** p305 C3.
A traditional grocery that stocks a selection of cold meats and cheeses hailing from every part of Italy. Also on offer is an assortment of prepared dishes and roast meats.

Eat, Drink, Shop

Market day

The produce market is an integral, exhilarating part of the Italian shopping experience, and Venice and its surrounding area offer some rewarding examples. The streets immediately north-west of the Rialto bridge explode into a fruit and veg battlefield from dawn to lunchtime, Monday to Saturday. The market that sets up halfway along via Garibaldi in eastern Castello every morning but Sunday is more sedate; at the far end, make your purchases from one of Venice's few remaining boat-emporia.

Elsewhere, morning markets are once-weekly. Stalls are in operation by 7.30am and stallholders pack up by 1pm: the early bird gets the bargains.

Tuesday
Head for the Lido's Venice-facing Riviera B Marcello waterfront. Here you'll find everything: clothes, shoes, cheese, houseware, plants and freshly roasted pork. From the Santa Maria Elisabetta vaporetto stop, it's a 15-minute walk south; alternatively, take the Alberoni bus.

Wednesday & Friday
Need to go to Mestre? Plan for Wednesday or Friday when stalls selling fruit and vegetables, clothes and household goods set up behind piazza Ferretto in via Parco Ponci. *See also p138.*

Thurday
Chioggia's market begins in piazza Vigo where the boat from Venice docks. Stalls of all kinds – clothes, shoes, houseware, plants – stretch along corso del Popolo. There is also a fruit and vegetable market along the same street. The fish market is a five-minute walk towards Sottomarina and rivals the extravaganza at the Rialto. *See also p132.*

Friday
Compared to the markets above, the one held in campo della Chiesa on Sacca Fisola on Friday is small and unsophisticated. But you can be pretty sure you'll be the only non-native about.

Drogheria Mascari
San Polo 381, ruga degli Speziali (041 522 9762).
Vaporetto San Silvestro. **Open** 8am-1pm, 4-7.30pm
Mon-Sat. **No credit cards. Map** p305 C3.
Shops like this were quite common in Venice before
the onslaught of commercial shopping centres on the
mainland; now this is the only one left. It's the best
place in the city to find exotic spices, nuts, dried fruit
and mushrooms, as well as oils and wines from different regions in Italy.

Giacomo Rizzo
Cannaregio 5778, calle San Giovanni Crisostomo
(041 522 2824). Vaporetto Rialto. **Open** 8.30am-
1pm, 3.30-7.30pm Mon, Tue, Thur-Sat; 8.30am-1pm
Wed. **Credit** AmEx, DC, MC, V. **Map** p305 C4.
Offers a wide variety of traditional products, many
produced especially for the shop. The homesick
traveller should head here for imported orange mar-
malade and Betty Crocker cake mixes; it also stocks
ethnic food ingredients.

Wan Xin Store
Santa Croce 155, fondamenta Minotto/rio del
Gaffaro (041 710 920). Vaporetto Piazzale Roma.
Open 9am-1.30pm, 3-8pm Mon-Sat; 9am-1.30pm Sun.
Credit MC, V. **Map** p304 C1.
Should you tire of pasta, at Wan Xin Store you'll find
treats from the East: gunpowder tea, plum wine,
roasted seaweed, miso, ginseng chewing gum as well
as a few western favourites like Tang juice mix and
peanut butter.

Confectionery

For ice-cream, *see chapter* **Cafés, Bars &**
Pasticcerie.

Marchini Pasticceria
San Marco 676, calle Spadaria (041 522 9109/www.
golosessi.com/www.fantasychocolate.com). Vaporetto
San Marco. **Open** 9am-10pm Mon-Sat. **Credit**
AmEx, DC, MC, V. **Map** p307 A4.
Probably Venice's most famous sweet shop, and cer-
tainly the most expensive, Marchini has recently
moved to this newly remodelled location closer to
San Marco. Exquisite chocolate, including *Le Baute*
Veneziane – small chocolates in the form of
Carnevale masks. Cakes can be ordered.
Branch: San Marco 4772, calle del Lovo (041
528 7505).

Drink

See also p146 **Bacari** *and chapter* **Cafés,**
Bars & Pasticcerie.

Bottiglieria Colonna
Castello 5595, calle della Fava (041 528 5137/
botcol@libero.it). Vaporetto Rialto. **Open** 9am-1pm,
4-8pm Mon-Sat. **Credit** MC, V. **Map** p305 C4.
Extensive selection of local and regional wines.
Helpful staff will give advice on which wines to try,
and prepare travel boxes or arrange for shipping.

Eat, Drink, Shop

Thursday is market day in **Chioggia**.

QUADRI

Gran Caffè Ristorante,
since 1683,
in St. Mark's square, n° 121

Restaurant

Light - Lunch,
A' la Carte Restaurant,
Gala Dinner

Onto "the finest drawing-room in the world" with supreme quality gastronomy

Café

Welcome Coffee,
Cocktail Reception,
Caffè Concerto
After Dinner Drinks

Piazza San Marco, Venezia, Ph. 041 5222105 - 5289299 - Fax 041 5208041
http://www.quadrivenice.com   e-mail: quadri@quadrivenice.com
Closed on Monday in the winter season

Vinaria Nave de Oro

Dorsoduro 3664, campo Santa Margherita (041 522 2693). Vaporetto Ca' Rezzonico. **Open** 5-8pm Mon; 9am-1pm, 5-8pm Tue-Sat. **No credit cards.** **Map** p306 A2.
Bring your own bottles and staff will fill them with anything from Tocai and Pinot Grigio to Merlot. The latest craze is for Torbolino, a sweet and cloudy first-pressing white wine.
Branches: Castello 5786B, calle del Mondo Nuovo (041 523 3056); Cannaregio 1370, salizzada San Leonardo (041 719 695); via Lepanto 24D, Lido (041 276 0055).

Vino e... Vini

Castello 3301, fondamenta dei Furlani (041 521 0184). Vaporetto San Zaccaria. **Open** 9am-1pm, 5-8pm Mon-Sat. **Credit** AmEx, DC, MC, V. **Map** p308 A2.
A vast selection of major Italian wines from every region, plus an assortment of French, Spanish, Californian and even Lebanese wines.

Health foods

Cibele

Cannaregio 1823, campiello Anconetta (041 524 2113). Vaporetto San Marcuola. **Open** 9am-12.45pm, 3.30-7.45pm Mon-Sat. **Credit** MC, V. **Map** p304 B2.
A full range of natural health foods, cosmetics and medicines. Staff will also prepare blends of herbal teas and remedies.

Rialto Bio Center

San Polo 366, campo Beccaria (041 523 9515). Vaporetto San Silvestro. **Open** 8.30am-1pm, 4.30-8pm Mon-Sat. **Credit** AmEx, DC, MC, V. **Map** p305 C3.
A little bit of everything can be found in this shop, located behind the Rialto fish market – from whole-wheat pasta, grains, honey and freshly baked breads to natural cosmetics and incense.

Supermarkets

See also p173 **Standa**.

Billa

Dorsoduro 1491, Zattere (041 522 6187). Vaporetto San Basilio. **Open** 8.30am-8pm Mon-Sat; 9am-8pm Sun. **Credit** AmEx, MC, V. **Map** p306 B1.
One of the few supermarkets in Venice that's open seven days a week. Fruit and vegetables and other staples can be found at lower prices at Billa than in the *alimentari*.
Branches: Cannaregio 3027M, fondamenta Contarini (041 524 4786); Lido, Gran Viale (041 526 2898).

Coop

Giudecca 484, calle dell'Olio (041 241 3381). Vaporetto Palanca. **Open** 8.30am-1pm, 3.30-7.30pm Mon, Tue, Thur; 8.30am-1pm Wed; 8.30am-7.30pm Fri, Sat; 8.30am-1pm Sun. **Credit** MC, V. **Map** p306 C2.
This new supermarket on the Giudecca offers goods at good prices.

Jewellery & watches

Shops such as Nardi and Missiaglia in piazza San Marco have the most impressive and expensive jewellery, and Cartier (Mercerie San Zulian) and Bulgari (calle larga XXII Marzo) also have outlets here. The smaller shops on the Rialto bridge offer more affordable silver and gold chains and bracelets sold by weight, and you will find handmade items in workshops far from the chi-chi areas of town.

Laberintho

San Polo 2236, calle del Scaleter (041 710 017/ www.laberintho.it). Vaporetto San Stae or San Tomà. **Open** 9.30am-1pm, 2.30-7pm Tue-Sat. **Credit** AmEx, DC, MC, V. **Map** p304 C2.
A group of young goldsmiths runs this tiny *bottega* hidden away behind campo San Polo. They specialise in inlaid stones. In addition to the one-of-a-kind rings, earrings and necklaces on display, they will produce made-to-order pieces.

Sigifredo Cipolato

Castello 5336, Casselleria (041 522 8437/ sigifredocipolato@yahoo.com). Vaporetto Rialto. **Open** 11am 7.30pm Tue-Sat. **Credit** MC, V. **Map** p308 A1.
This jeweller painstakingly carves ebony to recreate the famous Moors' heads brooches and earrings.

Swatch

San Marco 4947, Mercerie del Capitello (041 522 8532). Vaporetto Rialto. **Open** 10am-8pm Mon-Sat; 11am-8pm Sun. **Credit** AmEx, DC, MC, V. **Map** p307 A4.
The Swatch store has special preview launches of new models and carries a selection of spare parts.

Beads

See also chapter **Glass**.

Antichità

Dorsoduro 1195, calle Toletta (041 522 3159). Vaporetto Accademia. **Open** 9am-1pm, 3.30-7.30pm Mon-Sat. **No credit cards.** **Map** p306 B2.
Beautiful, hand-painted antique glass beads that can be purchased individually or made into jewellery. There's also a nice selection of antiques and lace.

Anticlea Antiquariato

Castello 4719A, calle San Provolo (041 528 6946). Vaporetto San Zaccaria. **Open** 10am-1.30pm, 2-7.30pm Mon-Sat. **Credit** AmEx, DC, MC, V. **Map** p308 B1.
Packed with curious antique treasures, as well as an outstanding selection of Venetian glass beads.

Costantini

San Marco 2668A, campo San Maurizio (041 521 0789). Vaporetto Santa Maria del Giglio. **Open** 9.30am-1.30pm, 3.30-7.30pm Mon-Sat. **Credit** MC, V. **Map** p307 B3.

Eat, Drink, Shop

Constantini has a fantastic collection of Venetian glass beads sold by weight or already made up into necklaces, bracelets and brooches.

Perle e Dintorni
San Marco 3740, calle della Mandola (041 520 5068). Vaporetto Sant'Angelo. **Open** 9.30am-7.30pm Mon-Sat; noon-7pm Sun. **Credit** AmEx, DC, MC, V. **Map** p307 A3.
Buy bead jewellery or assemble your own pieces, choosing from a vast assortment of glass beads, most of which are new versions based on antique designs.

Masks

The carnival mask craze in Venice is a relatively recent phenomenon. In the early 1980s you could count the number of mask-making workshops on the fingers of one hand. With the local tourist board flogging its revamped Carnevale for all it's worth, however, these characteristic collectibles became more of a money-spinner, and Venice is now suffering from a plague of uninspired, tourist-oriented mask shops, the worst of which feature some truly nauseating designs. Don't be fooled by cheaper imported versions, or those with local decorations painted on to ready-made surfaces.

Ca' Macana
Dorsoduro 3172, calle delle Botteghe (041 520 3229). Vaporetto Ca' Rezzonico. **Open** 10am-7.30pm daily. **Credit** AmEx, DC, MC, V. **Map** p306 A2.
Easy to spot because of the eerie masked mannequin standing at the entrance, this workshop is packed with traditional papier-mâché masks from the Commedia dell'arte. A careful explanation of the mask-making process – from the clay model to moulds – is enthusiastically given by the artist in residence, who also organises courses.

MondoNovo
Dorsoduro 3063, rio terà Canal (041 528 7344). Vaporetto Ca' Rezzonico. **Open** 10am-7pm Mon-Sat. **Credit** AmEx, DC, MC, V. **Map** p306 A2.
Venice's best-known *mascheraio* offers an enormous variety of masks both traditional and modern.

Papier Mâché
Castello 5175, calle lunga Santa Maria Formosa (041 522 9995/www.papiermache.it). Vaporetto Rialto. **Open** 9am-7.30pm Mon-Sat; 10am-7pm Sun. **Credit** AmEx, DC, MC, V. **Map** p308 A1.
Established for over 20 years, this workshop uses traditional techniques to create contemporary masks. The artists draw inspiration from the works of Klimt, Kandinsky, Tiepolo and Carpaccio. The decoration determines the price, with simple designs starting at €40.

Tragicomica
San Polo 2800, calle dei Nomboli (041 721 102/ www.tragicomica.it). Vaporetto San Tomà. **Open** 10am-7pm daily. **Credit** AmEx, DC, MC, V. **Map** p304 C2.

A spellbinding collection of mythological masks, Harlequins, Columbines and Pantaloons, as well as 18th-century dandies and ladies. All are handmade and painted by an artist trained at Venice's Accademia di Belle Arti.

Paper products

Ebrû
San Marco 3471, campo Santo Stefano (041 523 8830/www.albertovallese-ebru.com). Vaporetto Accademia. **Open** 10am-7pm Mon-Sat; 11am-6pm Sun. **Credit** AmEx, DC, MC, V. **Map** p307 A3-B.
Beautiful marbled handcrafted paper, scarves, ties and other collectibles. These are Venetian originals, whose imitators can be found in a host of other shops around town.

Il Pavone
Dorsoduro 721, fondamenta Venier dei Leoni (041 523 4517/fabiopelosin@virgilio.it). Vaporetto Accademia. **Open** 9.30am-1.30pm, 2.30-6.30pm daily. **Credit** AmEx, DC, MC, V. **Map** p307 B3.
Handmade paper with floral motifs in a variety of colours. Il Pavone also stocks boxes, picture frames, key chains and other objects, all decorated in the same style. Quality products at decent prices.

Legatoria Piazzesi
San Marco 2511, campiello Feltrina (041 522 1202/ olavi@tin.it). Vaporetto Santa Maria del Giglio. **Open** *Oct-May* 10am-1pm, 4-7pm Mon-Sat. *June-Sept* 10am-7pm Mon-Sat. **Credit** AmEx, DC, MC, V. **Map** p307 B3.
The last remaining paper-maker in Venice to use the traditional wooden-block method of printing. Legatoria Piazzesi has an amazing selection of stunningly printed paper and cards.

Legatoria Polliero
San Polo 2995, campo dei Frari (041 528 5130). Vaporetto San Tomà. **Open** 10.30am-1pm, 3.30-7.30pm Mon-Sat; 10am-1pm Sun. **Credit** AmEx, MC, V. **Map** p306 A2.
This bookbinding workshop, near the Frari church, sells leather-bound diaries, frames and photograph albums. It's not cheap.

Records & music

Discoland
Dorsoduro 2760, campo San Barnaba (041 528 7229/www.discolandcd.it). Vaporetto Ca' Rezzonico. **Open** 10am-1pm, 3.30-8pm Mon-Sat. **Credit** MC, V. **Map** p306 B2.
Despite the name you won't find the Bee Gees here: jazz, rock and blues are the specialities. It's the best place in Venice for alternative sounds too.

Il Tempio della Musica
San Marco 5368, ramo dei Tedeschi (041 523 4552). Vaporetto Rialto. **Open** 9am-7.30pm Mon-Sat. **Credit** AmEx, DC, MC, V. **Map** p305 C4.
A large selection of all musical genres, though classical, jazz and opera are its forte.

Marbled and much-copied – **Ebrû**. *See p184.*

Toys & curiosities

Agile

Castello, Campo San Lio (041 923 705/347 261 3576/www.agileitalia.com). Vaporetto Rialto. **Open** 10am-7.30pm Mon-Sat (weather permitting). **No credit cards. Map** p307 A4.

An outdoor stand run by a group of professional jugglers. In addition to equipment such as high-tech yo-yos and frisbees, you'll find a fantastic selection of toys, games, puppets and hats for kids of all ages.

Bambolandia

San Polo 1462, calle Madonnetta (041 520 7502/ www.rialto.com/beatrice). Vaporetto San Silvestro or San Tomà. **Open** 10am-12.30pm, 2-6pm Tue-Sat. **Credit** AmEx, DC, MC, V. **Map** p307 A3.

Entering into this Land of Dolls can be a bit unsettling – glass eyes, wigs and limbs of all kinds are assembled here into perfect porcelain people. You'll find Tom the Gondolier, Pinocchio and many other finely dressed dolls.

Emporio Pettenello

Dorsoduro 2978, campo Santa Margherita (041 523 1167). Vaporetto Ca' Rezzonico. **Open** 9.30am-1pm, 4-8pm Mon-Sat. **Credit** AmEx, MC, V. **Map** p306 A2.

Run by the same family for more than 100 years, this toy store still has its original furnishings. Choose from marionettes, puppets, wooden toys, dolls and incredible kaleidoscopes. The shop opens on Sunday, too, in December.

Wood, sculpture & frames

Cornici Trevisanello

Dorsoduro 662, campo San Vio (041 520 7779). Vaporetto Accademia. **Open** 9am-7pm Mon-Fri; 9am-1pm Sat. **Credit** AmEx, MC, V. **Map** p307 B3.

Strategically located between the Accademia and the Guggenheim, this workshop is home to a father son-and-daughter team that makes beautiful gilded frames, many with pearl, mirror and glass inlay. Custom orders and shipping are not a problem.

Dalla Venezia

Santa Croce 2074, calle Pesaro (041 721 276). Vaporetto San Stae. **Open** 8am-noon, 2.30-7pm Mon-Sat. **Credit** AmEx, DC, MC, V. **Map** p305 B3.

Employing the traditional technique of Venetian *tira-oro* (gold leaf decoration), Dalla Venezia creates exquisite gilded frames in his enchanting studio near Ca' Pesaro.

Gilberto Penzo

San Polo 2681, calle II dei Saoneri (041 719 372/ www.veniceboats.com). Vaporetto San Tomà. **Open** 9am-12.30pm, 3-6pm Mon-Sat. **Credit** MC, V. **Map** p306 A2.

A fascinating workshop for those interested in Venetian boats of all kinds. Gilberto Penzo creates detailed models of gondolas, *sandolo*s and *toppo*s and remarkable reproductions of vaporettos. Inexpensive kits are also on sale if you would like to practise the fine art of shipbuilding.

Spazio Legno, for your customised *forcola*.

Livio de Marchi

San Marco 3157, salizzada San Samuele (041 528 5694/www.liviodemarchi.it). Vaporetto San Samuele. **Open** 9.30am-12.30pm, 1.30-4pm Mon-Fri; by appointment Sat. **Credit** AmEx, DC, MC, V. **Map** p307 A3.

Livio de Marchi has remarkably lifelike wooden sculptures of anything from paintbrushes and books to hanging underwear and crumpled jeans. Definitely something to see.

Spazio Legno

Giudecca 213B, fondamenta San Giacomo (041 277 5505). Vaporetto Redentore. **Open** 9am-6.30pm Mon-Fri. **Credit** MC, V. **Map** p307 C3.

The place to come when you need a new *forcola* for your gondola, or a pair of oars. Saverio Pastor is one of only three recognised *marangon* (oarmakers) in Venice; he specialises in making the elaborate walnut-wood rests (*forcole*) that are the symbols of the gondolier's trade; each gondolier has his own customised *forcola*, which he guards with his life. Tourists will be more interested in purchasing the bookmarks, postcards and some books on Venetian boat-works in English that are also available here.

Services

Finding conveniences in an inconvenient city such as Venice can still be frustrating, although the situation has improved over the past few years. If you're determined, it is possible to track down one-hour dry-cleaning or a swift film developing service.

Servizio Città

San Polo 1886, calle dei Botteri (041 524 2606). Vaporetto San Silvestro. **Open** 9am-12.30pm, 4-7.30pm Mon, Tue, Thur, Fri; 9am-12.30pm Wed, Sat. **No credit cards. Map** p305 C3.

Try Servizio Città for a wide range of services including domestic help, translation, plumbers, electricians and painters. With luck you might even find you can get sitters for your baby, your house or your pet.

Clothing & shoe repairs

Tolin Roberto

Dorsoduro 3769A, calle Crosera (041 524 4090). Vaporetto San Tomà. **Open** 3-7pm Mon; 8.30am-1pm, 3-7.30pm Tue-Fri; 8.30am-noon Sat. **No credit cards. Map** p306 A2.

This genuine Venetian shoemaker will make your shoes new again for a reasonable price – he usually asks all foreign clients to send him a postcard. It's a small shop and sometimes the fumes are over-whelming, but he'll get the job done.

Vidal e Fantini
Castello 5754, calle del Paradiso (no phone). Vaporetto Rialto. **Open** 10am-5.30pm Tue-Sat. **No credit cards. Map** p307 A4.
Two ladies carry out minor repairs and alterations. A hem job starts at €10 and takes about a week. If the work is urgent, the price goes up.

Carnevale costume rentals

Atelier Pietro Longhi
San Polo 2604B, rio terà Frari (041 714 478/www. pietrolonghi.com) Vaporetto San Tomà. **Open** 10am-1pm, 2.30-7.30pm Mon-Sat. **Credit** AmEx, DC, MC, V. **Map** p304 C2.
It costs between €100 and €150 to rent a garment for the first day; each additional day is half-price.

Nicolao Atelier
Cannaregio 5565, rio terà al Bagatin (041 520 7051/www.nicolao.com). Vaporetto Rialto. **Open** by appointment only 9am-1pm, 2-6pm Mon-Fri. **Credit** MC, V. **Map** p305 C4.
A very simple costume rents for €62 a day, the more elaborate ones can go up to as much as €233 a day. There is, however, a reduction for each additional day thereafter.

Dry-cleaners & launderettes

In Venice there are few self-service launderettes, and only a small number of laundries that will do your wash, charging by the kilo. Small, family-run dry-cleaners are more expensive than the chains that have opened up in recent years.

Bea Vita Lavanderia
Santa Croce 665A-B, calle delle Chioverette (348 301 7457). Vaporetto Ferrovia. **Open** 7am-11.30pm daily. **Map** p304 B1.
This coin-operated launderette is a five-minute walk from the station. Be sure to bring lots of change because the machines only operate with small bills and coins. €3.50 for 8kg, €5.50 for 16kg and €2 for the dryer. A new branch with internet café should open near the youth hostel (*see p58*) in 2003.

Centro Pulisecco
Cannaregio 6262D, calle della Testa (041 522 5011). Vaporetto Ca' d'Oro. **Open** 8.30am-12.30pm, 3-7pm Mon-Fri. **No credit cards. Map** p305 C4.
Centro Pulisecco offers dry-cleaning only. Trousers cost €2.60, jackets €3.20 and sweaters €2. A one-hour service is available.
Branch: Cannaregio 1749, rio terà del Cristo (041 718 020).

Pulilavanderia
Dorsoduro 3411, campo Santa Margherita (041 521 2609). Vaporetto Ca' Rezzonico. **Open** *Sept-Apr* 9am-1pm, 3-6.30pm Mon-Fri. *May-July* 8.45am-1.30pm, 3-6.30pm Mon-Thur; 8.45am-6.30pm Fri. **No credit cards. Map** p306 A2.
Express dry-cleaning for shirts; ironing service; clothes washed (max 8kg) for €13.

Speedy Wash
Cannaregio 1520, rio terà San Leonardo (347 359 3442/www.speedy-wash.it). Vaporetto San Marcuola. **Open** 8am-11pm daily. **No credit cards.**
This coin-op launderette charges €4.50 for 8kg, €7.50 for 16kg and €3 for the dryer.

Film & development

Cesana Photo
Dorsoduro 879, rio terà Antonio Foscarini (041 522 2020/7888). Vaporetto Accademia. **Open** 9am-1pm, 2.30-7pm Mon-Fri. **Credit** AmEx, MC, V. **Map** p306 B2.
You won't find low prices but you will find fast service at this shop near the ponte dell'Accademia: colour developing in 25 minutes and slides in an hour.

Interpress Photo
San Polo 365, campo delle Beccarie (041 528 6978). Vaporetto San Silvestro. **Open** *Nov-Mar* 3.30-7.30pm Mon; 9am-1pm, 3.30-7.30pm Tue-Sat. **Credit** DC, MC, V. **Map** p305 C3.
This is definitely one of the cheapest places in Venice for film development, and probably one of the best: 24 exposures is a mere €4. Also provides one-hour service, passport photographs, photocopies. A small selection of authentic Murano glass is also on sale.

Hairdressers

Prices are à la carte: each dab of styling foam or puff of hair spray pushes up the bill. Most salons are closed on Mondays.

Carbone
Dorsoduro 2855, calle lunga San Barnaba (041 523 7922). Vaporetto Ca' Rezzonico. **Open** 9am-5.30pm Tue-Fri; 9am-2.30pm Sat. **No credit cards. Map** p306 B2.
Where chic young Venetians (male and female) go for a trim or a full makeover.

Da Carlo
Cannaregio 2237, strada Nuova (041 719 993). Vaporetto Ca' d'Oro. **Open** 8am-noon, 4-8pm Tue-Sat. **No credit cards. Map** p305 B3.
No-frills barber for men. A haircut costs €16, a shave €8.

Stefano e Claudia
San Polo 1098B, riva del Vin (041 520 1913). Vaporetto San Silvestro. **Open** 9am-5pm Tue-Sat. **Credit** AmEx, MC, V. **Map** p305 C3.

Eat, Drink, Shop

The salon Stefano e Claudia is easily the most contemporary in the lagoon. Prices are high and an appointment is a must, but you'll have a beautiful view of the Grand Canal.

Opticians

Most opticians will do minor running repairs on the spot and (usually) free of charge.

Ottica Carraro Alessandro

San Marco 3706, calle della Mandola (041 520 4258/www.otticacarraro.it). Vaporetto Sant'Angelo. **Open** 9am-1pm, 3-7.30pm Mon-Sat. **Credit** AmEx, DC, MC, V. **Map** p307 A3.
Get yourself some unique and funky eyewear – the frames are exclusively produced and guaranteed for life. Ottica Carraro Alessandro offers extraordinary quality at reasonable prices.

Punto Vista (Elvio Carraro)

Cannaregio 1982, campiello Anconeta (041 720 453/mircorra@tin.it). Vaporetto San Marcuola. **Open** 3.30-7.30pm Mon; 9am-12.30pm, 3.30-7.30pm Tue-Sat. **Credit** AmEx, MC, DC, V. **Map** p304 B2.
Eyeglasses, sunglasses, contact lenses and saline solution. Punto Vista also undertakes walk-in eye examinations and repairs. It sells cameras too.

Photocopies & faxes

Thanks to the Università Ca' Foscari and the University Institute of Architecture (both in Dorsoduro), finding a place to make a photocopy is neither difficult nor expensive. The many *tabacchi* that send faxes usually announce the fact in their front windows, as do other service centres (for for couriers, *see p280*; internet points, *see p282*).

Ca' Foscarina Puntocopie

Dorsoduro 3224, calle Foscari (041 523 1814). Vaporetto Ca' Rezzonico. **Open** 9am-1.30pm, 2.30-6pm Mon-Fri. **No credit cards. Map** p306 A2.
Photocopies, binding and laser printing are offered. Serves stressed-out students with a thesis deadline; 5¢ per photocopy.

Micoud

San Marco 4581, campo San Luca (041 528 9275/ www.micoud.it). Vaporetto Rialto. **Open** 8.30am-2.30pm, 3-7pm Mon-Fri; 8.30am-12.30pm Sat. **Credit** DC, MC, V. **Map** p307 A4.
This tiny shop offers a variety of services: colour photocopies, fax service, binding, digital images and much more. An A4 photocopy costs 10¢. Reliable, professional service.

Ticket agencies

Tickets are also available from the tourist information office, the **APT** (*see p289*).

Bassani

San Marco 2414, via XXII Marzo (041 520 3644/ fax 041 520 4009/www.bassani.it). Vaporetto Santa Maria del Giglio. **Open** 9am-1pm, 2.30-7.30pm Mon-Fri; 9am-12.30pm Sat. **Credit** AmEx, DC, MC, V. **Map** p307 B4.
Sells tickets for concerts held in churches around town, and organises walking tours, gondola rides and visits to the islands of the lagoon. The company also functions as a regular travel agency.

VeLa

San Marco 1810, calle dei Fuseri (041 241 8029/ 240 9150/fax 041 240 9127/www.velaspa.com). Vaporetto Rialto. **Open** 8.30am-6.30pm Mon-Sat. **Credit** MC, V. **Map** p307 A4.
Through its new merchandising operation VeLa, the Venetian public transport company ACTV sells tickets to museums, concerts and exhibitions in both Venice and Mestre. Tickets can also be purchased from the following ACTV vaporetto stops: Tronchetto, Piazzale Roma, Ferrovie, Rialto, San Zaccaria and Zattere.

Travel agencies

See also above **Bassani**.

CTS (Centro Turistico Studentesco)

Dorsoduro 3252, fondamenta del Tagliapietra (041 520 5660/www.cts.it). Vaporetto Ca' Rezzonico or San Tomà. **Open** 9.30am-1.30pm, 2.30-6pm Mon-Fri. **Credit** MC V. **Map** p306 A2.
This agency caters to its own members and students in general, offering discount airfares, international train tickets and lots of information for student travellers. ISICs cost €10: bring a passport-sized photo and a document proving you are a student. It also has tickets to concerts, exhibitions and the theatre at discounted prices for members.

Stik Travel

Dorsoduro 3944, calle San Pantalon (041 520 0988/ stiktrv@interbusiness.it). Vaporetto San Tomà. **Open** 9am-1pm, 2-7pm Mon-Fri. **Credit** AmEx, MC, DC, V. **Map** p306 A2.
The Stik Travel staff are not only friendly but extraordinarily efficient. Stik offers specials to Paris and has a money-changing service too.

Video/DVD rental

Contatto Video

Castello 6153, calle lunga Santa Maria Formosa (041 522 8962/contatto.video@libero.it). Vaporetto Rialto. **Open** *June-Aug* 10am-1.30pm, 3.30-8pm Mon-Sat. *Sept-July* 10am-1.30pm, 3.30-8pm daily. **Credit** AmEx, DC, MC, V. **Map** p308 A1.
Video/DVD sales and one-day rentals; there are around 150 cassettes in English here (new releases are all DVD). Non-members pay €4 for DVDs or videos; members pay €2.50. To join, take along €15 and photo ID.

Glass

Artists use traditional materials and methods to produce contemporary work.

After an end-of-millennium boom that saw exciting new producers and galleries spring up around the city, retrenchment has become the key word on the serious Venetian glass scene, helped perhaps by an economic climate in which buyers are less and less willing to stick their necks out… and are thinner and thinner on the ground.

New galleries there are. But beware of outlets selling tired copies of works by big names. Like mask shops, glass shops are more common here than grocers'. But like mask shops, many glass shops cater for the lightning-stop visitor looking for the vitreous equivalent of the 'kiss-me-quick' hat. This chapter will help anyone looking for good glass to avoid the kitsch and the clutter.

Glass has been made in and around Venice for over 1,000 years. The industry shifted to the island of Murano in 1291, when all glass furnaces, except those engaged in faking gem stones, were ordered there to limit the fire hazard in Venice. The glass-workers enjoyed a privileged position in Venetian society that reflected the economic importance of the goods they created for an international market.

Glass manufacture — a romance of sand and fire, liquid and air — enthralled visitors to Venice in the 15th century for the same reasons that a visit to a factory fascinates today's tourist. Murano has a profusion of small- and medium-sized factories, each with its own speciality. Many of these are still in the hands of an elite group of families, who have been involved in glass production since the 13th century. A 'large' factory seldom has more than five or six *piazze* (workplaces), each occupied by a *maestro*.

Most serious production houses are not open to the public (for exceptions, *see p191* **The real Murano thing**). But opportunities to see glass being blown are not lacking. It's almost impossible to come to Venice and not be accosted by hucksters offering free trips to 'the' glass factory in Murano. These offers are usually sponsored by one of the large showrooms, which will expect to recoup its investment. If you accept the 'free' trip, you'll be met by a salesperson. There's no obligation to buy, but the pressure is difficult to resist.

Many outlets in Venice offer prices that are as low or lower than on Murano, and feature the latest Murano innovations as well. Glass gallery owners are a charming breed, who warm to serious collectors. Should your favourite glass artist not be showing when you visit, a gallerist may try to arrange a private viewing.

Showrooms & blowing

CAM Vetri D'Arte

Murano, piazzale Colonna 1B (041 739 944/ www.cam-murano.com). Vaporetto Colonna. **Open** *Apr-Oct* 9am-6pm daily (demonstrations till 4.30pm). *Nov-Mar* 9am-4.30pm daily. **Credit** AmEx, DC, MC, V. **Map** p310.
CAM specialises in mirrors, goblets, and objets d'art. Its adjoining factory offers demonstrations of traditional Venetian chandelier manufacture.

Mazzega

Murano, fondamenta da Mula 147 (041 736 888/ www.mazzega.it). Vaporetto Museo or Venier. **Open** 9am-5pm daily. **Credit** AmEx, DC, MC, V. **Map** p310.
Excellent Venetian glass of all types; demonstrations of chandelier production and glass sculpture.

Glassmaking: enthralling to watch.

Amsterdam
Andalucía
Bangkok
Barcelona
Berlin
Boston

Brussels
Budapest
Buenos Aires
Chicago
Copenhagen
Dublin

Edinburgh
Florence
Havana
Hong Kong
Istanbul
Las Vegas

Lisbon
London
Los Angeles
Madrid
Miami
Milan

Moscow
Naples
New Orleans
New York
Paris
Patagonia

Prague
Rome
San Francisco
South of France
Stockholm
Sydney

Tokyo
Toronto
Venice
Vienna
Washington, DC

The real Murano thing

Gaining access to factories, rather than
showroom outlets, is difficult. The following are
among the best, and will allow a limited numbers
of visitors, who can buy at factory prices.

Elite Murano

*Murano, calle del Cimitero 6 (041 736 168/www.
promovetro.co/aziende/elite/order.htm). Vaporetto
Venier.* **Open** 8.15am-5pm Mon-Fri. Closed 3wks
Aug. **Credit** AmEx, MC, V. **Map** p310.
Elite produces the highest-quality Venetian goblets
and reproductions of Venetian antique glassware.

Fornasier Luigi

*Murano, calle del Paradiso 70 [14] (041 736 176/
www.fornasier.it). Vaporetto Navagero.* **Open** Sept-
July 8am-1pm, 2.30-5.30pm Mon-Fri. Closed Aug.
Credit MC, V. **Map** p310.
Not easy to find, the factory of the Fornasier family
makes traditional Venetian chandeliers to order.

Fratelli Barbini

*Murano, calle Bertolini 36 (041 739 777). Vaporetto
Colonna.* **Open** 7am-6pm Mon-Fri. **No credit
cards.** **Map** p310.
Some of the best, and most original, Venetian mirrors are to be had here. The Barbini brothers have
been innovative leaders on Murano for decades.

Galleries

These galleries are dedicated to work in glass
by fine contemporary artists.

Berengo Fine Arts

*Murano, fondamenta Vetrai 109A (041 739 453/
www.berengo.com). Vaporetto Colonna.* **Open** 10am-
6pm daily. **Credit** AmEx, DC, MC, V. **Map** p310.
Adriano Berengo is establishing a fiefdom producing works in glass designed by international artists.
Branches: Murano, fondamenta Manin 68 (041 527
4198); San Marco 412/413, calle larga San Marco (041
241 0763); San Marco 3337, salizzada San Samuele
(041 522 1028).

Galleria Daniele Luchetta

*San Marco 2513A, campiello de la Feltrina (041 528
5092/www.arte-luchetta.it). Vaporetto Santa Maria
del Giglio.* **Open** 10am-1pm, 3.30-7.30pm Mon-Sat.
Credit AmEx, DC, MC, V. **Map** p307 B3.
One-offs and limited editions from designs by international artists, produced by Murano craftsmen.

Galleria Marina Barovier

*San Marco 3216, salizzada San Samuele (041
522 6102/www.barovier.it). Vaporetto San
Samuele.* **Open** 9.30am-12.30pm, 3.30-7pm Mon-Fri;
by appointment Sat. Closed Aug. **No credit cards.**
Map p307 A3.
Renowned for its collections of classic 20th-century
Venetian glass, Marina Barovier's gallery is the sole
Venetian source for contemporary glass by Lino
Tagliapietra and other contemporary artists.

Galleria Regina, Arte in Vetro

*Murano, riva Longa 25A (041 739 202/
www.galleriaregina.com). Vaporetto Museo.*
Open 10am-4pm Mon-Sat. **Credit** AmEx, MC,
V. **Map** p310.
Unique and limited-edition works by Muranese and
Italian artists principally.

Galleria Rossella Junck

*San Marco 2360, calle delle Ostreghe (041 520
7747/www.rossellajunck.it). Vaporetto Santa
Maria del Giglio.* **Open** 10.30am-7.30pm Mon-
Sat. Closed 2wks Aug. **Credit** AmEx MC, V.
Map p307 B3.
Rossella Junck shows Murano glass from the 1920s-
80s, and rare works from the 16th-19th centuries and
contemporary glass in her other branches.
Branch: San Marco 1997, campo San Fantin
(041 521 0759).

Galleria San Nicolò

*San Marco 1920, calle della Fenice (041 522 1535/
berndtl@libero.it). Vaporetto Santa Maria del Giglio.*
Open 10.30am-1pm, 3.30-7pm Tue-Sat. **Credit**
AmEx, MC, V. **Map** p306 A2.
In her new space near the opera house, Louise
Berndt specialises in established and emerging
international artists.

Contemporary design

L'Isola

*San Marco 1468, campo San Moisè (041 523 1973/
isolacm@tin.it). Vaporetto Vallaresso.* **Open** 9am-
7.30pm Mon-Sat; 10am-7pm Sun. **Credit** AmEx, DC,
MC, V. **Map** p307 B4.
Original glass pieces designed by Carlo Moretti.

Murano Collezioni

*Murano, fondamenta Manin 1D (041 736 272/
muracoll@tin.it). Vaporetto Colonna.* **Open** Apr-Oct
10am-6pm Mon-Sat. Nov, Dec 10am-5pm Mon-Sat.
Closed Jan-Mar. **Credit** AmEx, DC, MC, V.
Map p310.
This innovative retail venture provides access to the
entire collections of three glass houses: Barovier &
Toso, Carlo Moretti and Venini.

La Murrina

*Murano, piazzale Colonna 1 (041 527 4605/www.
lamurrina.com). Vaporetto Colonna.* **Open** 9.30am-
5pm daily. **Credit** AmEx, DC, MC, V. **Map** p310.
Modern glass produced to original designs.
Branch: Murano, riva Longa 17 (041 739 255).

Pauly

*San Marco 4391A, calle larga San Marco (041
520 9899/www.paulyglassfactory.com). Vaporetto
Vallaresso.* **Open** Nov-Mar 9am-6pm daily.
Apr-Oct 9am-7pm daily. **Credit** AmEx, DC,
MC, V. **Map** p307 A4.
Although it's located just off piazza San Marco,
Pauly often has a more reasonable mark-up on its
range of Murano glass than many of the outlets that
are on Murano itself.

Venini

San Marco 314, piazza San Marco (041 522 4045/ www.venini.com). Vaporetto San Zaccaria. **Open** *Nov-Mar* 10am-7.30pm Mon-Sat. *Apr-Oct* 10am-7.30pm daily. **Credit** AmEx, DC, MC, V. **Map** p307 A4.

Top-of-the-line contemporary hand-blown glass. Now owned by Royal Copenhagen of Denmark, Venini is no longer the essential point of reference it once was, but is still a must for glass fans.

Individual outlets

Some glass artists prefer to retail their own work in modest shops. Don't let the simple surroundings fool you: many of these glassmakers are noted international artists.

Antiquaria Micheluzzi

Dorsoduro 1071, calle della Toletta (041 528 2190/ maravege@tin.it). Vaporetto Accademia. **Open** 10am-1pm, 4-7pm Tue-Sat. **Credit** AmEx, MC, V. **Map** p306 B2.

Great deals on classic glass. Recently the owner, Massimo Micheluzzi, has begun to design some stunningly original pieces.

Cesare Toffolo

Murano, Bressagio 8A (041 736 460/www. toffolo.com). Vaporetto Faro. **Open** *Feb-Oct* 10am-6pm daily. *Nov-Jan* 10am-6pm Mon-Sat. **Credit** AmEx, DC, MC, V. **Map** p310.

Cesare Toffolo specialises in own-design unique and limited-series pieces, flame-worked in Pyrex. **Branch**: Murano, fondamenta Manin 75 (041 736 460).

Costantini

Cannaregio 5311, calle del Fumo (041 522 2265/ www.popweb.com/costantini). Vaporetto Fondamenta Nove. **Open** 9.15am-1pm, 2.15-6pm Mon-Fri. Closed first 2wks Aug. **Credit** AmEx, MC, V. **Map** p305 B4.

Vittorio Costantini is recognised as one of the most original Venetian lamp work specialists. His animals, insects, fish and birds are stunningly realistic.

Galleria Bellus

Dorsoduro 369, campiello Barbaro (041 523 4881/ www.bellus.it). Vaporetto Salute. **Open** *Sept-Dec* 11am-6pm Mon, Thur-Sun. Closed Jan, Aug. **Credit** AmEx, MC, V. **Map** p307 B3.

A studio-gallery, Bellus hosts works by Orlando Zennaro, his son Stefano Zennaro, and Stefano's wife Daniela Zentilin.

Genninger Studio

Dorsoduro 2793A, calle del Traghetto (041 522 5565/www.genningerstudio.com). Vaporetto Ca' Rezzonico. **Open** 10.30am-6.30pm daily. **Credit** AmEx, DC, MC, V. **Map** p306 B2.

Leslie Ann Genninger exhibits her glass jewellery and her lamps, goblets and drinking glasses in her gallery-studio on the Grand Canal. **Branch**: San Marco 1845, calle del Fruttarol (041 523 9494).

Sent Gugliemo

Murano, fondamenta Vetrai 8A (041 739 100/www. sentmurano.com). Vaporetto Colonna. **Open** *Apr-Oct* 8am-6pm daily. *Nov-Mar* 8am-6pm Mon-Fri. Closed 3wks Aug; 2wks Dec-Jan. **Credit** AmEx, MC, V. **Map** p310.

The Sent family are a reliable source of beautifully displayed craft and good design. They specialise in vases, paper weights and drinking glasses.

Susanna & Marina Sent

Dorsoduro 669, campo San Vio (041 520 8136/ sent.snc@tin.it). Vaporetto Accademia. **Open** *Feb-Dec* 11am-6pm Mon, Wed-Sat. Closed Jan. **Credit** AmEx, MC, V. **Map** p307 B3.

Among Venice's best contemporary glass jewellery.

Tiozzo Sergio di Claudio Tiozzo

Murano, fondamenta Manin 45 (041 527 4155/ www.tiozzosergio.com). Vaporetto Colonna or Faro. **Open** *Apr-Oct* 10.30am-6pm daily. *Nov-Mar* 11am-5pm Mon-Sat. **Credit** AmEx, DC, MC, V. **Map** p310.

Jewellery and objects in the Murano tradition of *murrine* (mosaic glass). The activity has recently passed from father to son; some of the latter's designs are well on the way to becoming classics.

For something different

FGB

San Marco 2514, campo Santa Maria del Giglio (041 523 6556/fgb_venezia@virgilio.it). Vaporetto Santa Maria del Giglio. **Open** 10am-7pm daily. **Credit** AmEx, DC, MC, V. **Map** p307 B3.

Handmade objects including insects, animals, plates and jewellery. Christmas tree ornaments a speciality.

Ivano Soffiato

Dorsoduro 1188, calle della Toletta (041 521 0480) Vaporetto Accademia. **Open** 9.30am-6.30pm daily Mon, Wed-Sun. Closed 1wk Feb; 1wk Aug. **Credit** AmEx, DC, MC, V. **Map** p306 B2.

One of the best places to pick up souvenirs in Venice. Ivano makes about half of the tourist goodies sold in the city: here you can watch him do it.

L'Angolo del Passato

Dorsoduro 3276A, campiello degli Squellini (041 528 7896). Vaporetto Ca' Rezzonico or San Tomà. **Open** 4-7pm Mon; 9.30am-noon, 4-7pm Tue-Sat. Closed 10 days Jan; 10 days Aug. **Credit** MC, V. **Map** p306 A2.

Giordana Naccari's small shop is where Venetian antique glass dealers go to find great buys. She specialises in Murano glass from the end of the 1800s to the present, and unique contemporary glassware.

Totem Gallery – Il Canale

Dorsoduro 878B, campo Carità (041 522 3641/ totemilcanale@katamail.com). Vaporetto Accademia. **Open** 10am-1pm, 3-7pm Mon-Sat. **Credit** AmEx, DC, MC, V. **Map** p306 B2.

Totem Gallery is full of *gioielli poveri*, jewellery made from non-precious materials. Pieces include some beautifully strung trade beads.

Arts & Entertainment

Festivals & Events

Pageantry and celebrations real and reinvented.

The city of Venice itself is a spectacular backdrop for any kind of festivity and since the earliest days of the Republic, festivals, processions and popular celebrations have been an intrinsic part of Venice's social fabric. The government of La Serenissima used pageantry both to assert the rigidly hierarchical nature of Venetian society and to give the lower orders the chance to let off steam.

The government set an example by parading whenever the occasion arose. The end of a bout of plague was always good cause for celebration. So were religious holidays, and with churches in the city dedicated to over 100 saints, each one had a feast day to celebrate. The working classes had crude entertainments such as the *corsa al toro* (bullfights) in campo Santo Stefano, or bloody pitched battles between rival sections of the populace (*see also p120*).

Some of Venice's annual festivities are modern revivals – **Carnevale** being the most successful in commercial terms. But one should not under-estimate Venetians' attachment to their own traditions – especially boat-related ones. The **Festa del Redentore** is a huge excuse for a party, while the **Regata Storica** may look like it's funded by the tourist board, but Venetians do get seriously involved in the boat races that lurk beneath the pageantry.

See also p291 **Holidays**.

Spring

Carnevale

Date 10 days ending on Shrove Tuesday.

Though it had existed since the Middle Ages, Venice's pre-Lenten Carnevale came into its own in the 18th century. Until then, religious processions had dominated the city's ceremonies; but as the Venetian Republic went into terminal decline, the city's pagan side began to emerge. Carnevale became an outlet for all that had been prohibited and controlled for centuries by the strong arm of the doge. During the carnival, elaborate, fanciful structures would be set up in piazza San Marco as stages for acrobats, tumblers, wrestlers and other performers. Masks served not only as an escape from the drabness of everyday life but to conceal the wearer's identity – a useful ploy for nuns on the lam or slumming patricians.

The Napoleonic invasion in 1797 brought an end to the fun and games, and Carnevale was only resuscitated in 1980. The city authorities and hoteliers'

association saw the earning potential of all those long-nosed masks, and today the heavily subsidised celebrations draw revellers from all over the world. The party starts ten days before *martedì grasso* (Shrove Tuesday). On the first Saturday of Carnevale there is usually a masked procession and party in piazza San Marco.

The highlight of the first Sunday is the *volo dell'angelo*. The tradition, dating back to the earliest days of Carnevale, was originally called the 'flight of the Turk' and involved a tightrope walker crossing from the campanile to the balcony of the Doge's Palace. In more recent times, a mechanical dove did the job. Since 2000, however, a real live woman has swooped down – suitably safety-harnessed – from the bell tower to the piazza below.

On *giovedì grasso* (the Thursday before Shrove Tuesday) – generally around 4pm – the competition for best costume takes place. On Friday evening there is usually a masked ball in piazza San Marco, which is open to any appropriately dressed reveller who can dance a minuet. The final Saturday sees yet

Masks make **Carnevale** go with a swing.

Arts & Entertainment

another masked procession, this time by gondola along the Grand Canal. The whole thing culminates on Shrove Tuesday with clowns, acrobats and fireworks in piazza San Marco, and a concert in the church of the Pietà (*see p91*).

Tourist offices (*see p289*) will provide you with a full Carnevale programme.

Su e Zo Per I Ponti

Information *041 590 4717/ www.suezoperiponti.org.* **Date** 4th Sun of Lent.
Literally 'Up and Down Bridges', this privately organised excursion through island Venice offers a great opportunity to get to grips with the city. Inspired by the traditional *bacarada* (bar crawl), it is an orienteering event in which you are given a map and a list of checkpoints to tick off. Old hands take their time checking out the *bacari* (*see p144* **Bacari**) along the way. Enrolment costs €3.50. Individuals can sign on at the starting line in piazza San Marco on the morning of the event; groups should phone ahead.

Benedizione del Fuoco

Basilica di San Marco. Vaporetto Vallaresso or San Zaccaria. **Date** Thur before Easter Sun. **Map** p307 B4.
Just after dusk, all the lights are turned off inside St Mark's basilica and a fire is lit in the narthex (entrance porch). Bearing the holy fire, a procession winds its way around the church, lighting all the candles one by one.

Festa di San Marco

Bacino di San Marco. Vaporetto Vallaresso or San Zaccaria. **Date** 25 Apr. **Map** p307 B4.
The traditional feast day of Venice's patron saint is a low-key affair. In the morning there is a solemn mass in the Basilica, followed by a gondola regatta between the island of Sant'Elena and the Punta della Dogana at the entrance to the Grand Canal. The day is also known as *La Festa del boccolo* ('bud'): red rosebuds are given to wives and lovers.

Festa e Regata della Sensa

San Nicolò del Lido & Bacino di San Marco. **Information** *041 529 8711/041 274 7737.* **Date** May.
Back in the days of the Venetian Republic, the doge would board the glorious state barge, the Bucintoro, and be rowed out to the island of Sant'Andrea, facing the lagoon's main outlet to the Adriatic, followed by a fleet of small boats. Here he would throw a gold ring overboard, to symbolise *lo sposalizio del mare* – Venice's marriage with the sea. Today the mayor takes the place of the doge, the Bucintoro looks like a glorified fruit boat and the ring has become a laurel wreath. The ceremony is now performed at San Nicolò, on the northernmost point of the Lido, and is followed by a regatta. Venetians pray it doesn't rain; if it does, local lore says, it'll tip down for the next 40 days ('*Se piove il giorno della Sensa per quaranta giorni non semo sensa*').

Vogalonga

Information *041 521 0544/www.vogalonga.com.* **Date** May, first Sun after Ascension.
Like San Francisco's 'critical mass'– during which bicycles clog the downtown area once a month to demonstrate against congestion and pollution – Venetians (or at least those with strength enough to complete the 33km/20.5 mile route) protest against motorboats and the damage they do by boarding any kind of rowing craft and making their way through the lagoon and the city's two main canals in this annual free-for-all. Boats set off from in front of the lagoon façade of the Doge's Palace at 8.30am.

Venezia Suona

Information *041 275 0049/www.veneziasuona.it.* **Date** Sunday closest to 21 June.
The name means 'Venice plays'… and that it does, with hundreds of bands and musicians playing anything from rock to folk to funky Venetian reggae and jazz. Music can be heard from about 4pm onwards in *campi* all over the city.

Summer

Biennale D'Arte Contemporanea & Architettura

Giardini di Castello. Vaporetto Giardini. **Information** *041 521 8711/www.labiennale divenezia.net.* **Date** *Contemporary art* (odd years) mid June-Nov. *Architecture* (even years) Sept, Oct. **Map** p309 B4.
The Biennale D'Arte, established in 1895, is the *Jeux Sans Frontières* of the contemporary art world (*see p206* **The Biennale**); its architectural counterpart, which began in 1980, draws a strong local and international crowd.

Festa di San Pietro

San Pietro in Castello. Vaporetto Giardini. **Date** week around 29 June. **Map** p309 B4.
The most lively and villagey of Venice's many local festivals. A week of events centres on the church green of San Pietro (*see p92*) in the furthest-flung eastern section of Castello: there are competitions, concerts, food stands and a puppet theatre.

Cinema all'aperto

Campo San Polo. Vaporetto San Silvestro or San Tomà. **Date** 6wks late July-early Sept. **Map** p304 C2.
In a city of small spaces, this is a unique opportunity to see movies on a big screen. *See p201.*

Festa del Redentore

Bacino di San Marco, Canale della Giudecca. **Date** 3rd weekend of July. **Map** p307 B4.
The Redentore is the oldest continuously celebrated date on the Venetian calendar. At the end of a plague epidemic in 1576, the city celebrated her deliverance by commissioning Andrea Palladio to build a church on the Giudecca, to be known as

Arts & Entertainment

'Il Redentore' – the Redeemer. Every July a pontoon bridge is built across the canal that separates the Giudecca from Venice proper, so people can make the pilgrimage to the church on foot. But what makes this weekend so special are the festivities on Saturday night. During the afternoon, boats of every shape and size gather in the lagoon between St Mark's, San Giorgio, the Punta della Dogana and the Giudecca, each holding merry-makers supplied with food and drink. This party carries on through the evening, culminating in an amazing fireworks display.

Ferragosto – Festa dell'Assunta

Date 15 Aug.

If you want Venice without Venetians, this is the time to come, as everyone who can leaves the city. Practically everything in Venice shuts down and people head to the beach. There is usually a free concert in the cathedral on the lagoon island of Torcello, Santa Maria Assunta (*see p140*), on the evening of the 15th. Tourist offices (*see p289*) have information on events.

Mostra Internazionale D'Arte Cinematografica (Film Festival)

Palazzo del Cinema, Lungomare Marconi, Lido. Vaporetto Lido. **Information** *041 272 6501/041 521 8878/www.labiennaledivenezia.net).* **Date** 12 days, starting on Tue between 29 Aug and 5 Sept. **Map** p311.

A highlight of the social calendar as well as the inter-national film year, this two-week bonanza gives locals the chance to see stars and directors shooting past in their water taxis. *See also p202*.

Regata Storica

Grand Canal. **Date** 1st Sun in Sept.

This event begins with a procession of ornate boats down the Grand Canal, rowed by locals in 16th-century costume. Once the tourist prelude is over, the races start – which is what most locals have come to see. There are four: one for young rowers, one for women, one for rowers of *caorline* – long canoe-like boats in which the prow and the stern are identical – and the last and most eagerly awaited, featuring two-man sporting *gondolini*, each painted a different colour. The finishing line is at the sharp curve of the Grand Canal between Palazzo Barbi and Ca' Foscari: here the judges sit in an ornate raft known as the *machina*, where the prize-giving ceremony takes place.

Autumn

Sagra del Pesce

Island of Burano. Vaporetto 12 to Burano. **Date** 3rd Sun in Sept. **Map** p310.

Fried fish and copious quantities of white wine are consumed in this feast in the *calli* between Burano's brightly painted houses. Rowers who have not been left legless by the festivities take part in the last regatta of the season.

Sagra del Mosto

Island of Sant'Erasmo. Vaporetto 13 to Chiesa. **Date** 1st weekend in Oct.

This annual festival is a great excuse for Venetians to spend a day 'in the country' at Sant'Erasmo (*see p140*), getting light-headed on the first pressing of new wine. The salty soil of the island does not lend itself to superior wine – which is why it's best to down a glass before the stuff has had much chance to ferment. Sideshows, grilled sausage aromas and red-faced locals abound.

Venice Marathon

Information 041 940 644/www.venicemarathon.it. **Date** last Sun in Oct.

This marathon starts out on terra firma, following the Riviera del Brenta, and finishes up on the Riva Sette Martiri in Castello. The info-packed website is in Italian and English, giving information on regis-tration, procedures and hotels. One of the best places to see the runners is on the Zattere (*see p126*).

Winter

Festa di San Martino

Date 11 Nov.

Kids armed with *mamma*'s pots and spoons raise a ruckus around the city centre, chanting the saint's praises and demanding trick-or-treat style tokens in return for taking their noise elsewhere. Horse-and-rider-shaped San Martino cakes, with coloured icing dotted with silver balls, proliferate in cakeshops.

Festa della Madonna della Salute

Church of Madonna della Salute. Vaporetto Salute. **Date** 21 Nov. **Map** p307 B3.

In 1631 Venice was 'miraculously' delivered from its last major bout of plague, which had claimed almost 100,000 lives – one in every three Venetians. The Republic commissioned a plague-deliverance church from Baldassare Longhena, and his La Madonna della Salute (*see p125*) was finally completed in 1687. On this feast day, a pontoon bridge is strung across the Grand Canal from campo Santa Maria del Giglio to La Salute so that a procession led by the patriarch (archbishop) of Venice can make its way on foot from San Marco. Along the way, stalls sell cakes and candy floss, and candles that pilgrims light once they are inside the church. Then they go home for a lunch of *castradina* – a sort of cabbage and mutton stew that tastes nicer than it sounds.

Christmas, New Year & Epiphany (La Befana)

Venice's Yuletide festivities are all pretty low-key affairs. There are two minor events: the New Year's Day swim off the Lido, when a few hardy swimmers brave the icy deep, and the Regata delle Befane on 6 January, a rowing race along the Grand Canal in which the competitors, all aged over 50, are dressed up as La Befana – the ugly old witch who gives sweets to good children and pieces of coal to bad ones.

Arts & Entertainment

Children

Let the city's magic do its work.

In her novel *The Thief Lord* – one of the many magical-mystery reads that kept children occupied in the gap between *Harry Potters* IV and V – Cornelia Funke exploits Venice's intrinsic magic to the full. The book's heroes wander the city's labyrinthine streets with hardly a moan about sore feet… a point you might like to raise from time to time if you visit Venice with kids in tow. For this city can be problematic: there's a great deal of unavoidable walking and few of the museums or major sights are geared towards children.

But any child with a jot of imagination should respond to the sheer improbability of the place. With its twisting alleys, its weird transport and its ubiquitous winged lions, it is definitely a worthy rival to Hogwarts.

GETTING AROUND

The frequent absence of any barrier between pavement and ever-present canals presents a problem for parents travelling with mobile toddlers. Those psychologically incorrect safety reins you never thought you'd stoop to might not seem such a bad idea here.

Pre-walkers present another dilemma. Remember, the only ways of getting around Venice are by boat or on foot, and there are a daunting number of bridges (*see p99* **Take it to the…**). Pushchairs mean a lot of picking up and putting down. After your umpteenth canal crossing in a day, a comfortable baby backpack may begin to look like a gift from heaven.

Vaporetto travel is far from cheap. In theory, kids more than one metre tall pay adult fares; children under that height go free. But inspectors don't carry measuring tapes; the general feeling is that you should start paying when they're about six. Still, look on the uses of transport as a Venetian experience in itself and the cost will not seem so outrageous. A complete circle on line 82 (red) from the riva degli Schiavoni will take your fascinated offspring across to the Giudecca, then up to the station and port areas, giving them a glimpse of Venice's industrial underbelly as well as a triumphal march down the Grand Canal. Small kids may enjoy a ride on the majestic *motonave* to the Lido from San Zaccaria.

Most children will clamour for the ultimate Venetian transport treat – a gondola trip – but remember that this expensive experience (*see*

p277) can be substituted by or supplemented with rides on the humbler but more useful *traghetto* gondolas that ply across the Grand Canal at points distant from bridges (*see p276*). Make the crossing more authentic by letting them stand up like a real Venetian; only tourists sit.

Sightseeing

Venice will knock all but the most cynical youngsters sideways, so keeping them amused should not take too much effort. (Of course, you may be able to bore them to death with a surfeit of churches and museums, but you'll have to work hard at it).

Under-tens, especially, are a pushover. For a start, the city's 400-plus bridges are a joy. Children will love watching boats slipping under one side and emerging from the other.

Then there are the boats themselves. Like all other cities in the modern world, Venice has to have its supplies, the only difference being that they arrive by water. So watch out for the Coca Cola boat, the builder's boat, the fire and ambulance boats, and myriad others.

For a glimpse of the more illustrious craft of the past, head for the **Museo Storico Navale** (*see p91*), where Venice's maritime history is charted in scale models of the ships built in the Arsenale through the centuries. Don't miss the model of the Bucintoro, the gold-leaf-clad vessel used by the doge in official celebrations.

When not busy building up their vast empire, the Venetians devoted much time to games and sport, a fact you and your kids can verify with a visit to the **Museo Querini Stampalia** (*see p85*), where a collection of 18th-century scenes of Venetian life includes some very unlikely amusements. Aside from the obligatory hunting parties and antics on the frozen lagoon, one painting, *La Guerra dei Pugni* by Antonio Strom, shows one of the mass boxing matches that occurred frequently. The fights took place on bridges with no railings, with the initial four competitors – before proceedings degenerated into a free-for-all – starting out with one foot on the white inlaid footprint on the corners of the top step: try it out for yourselves on ponte dei Pugni near campo San Barnaba, ponte della Guerra near campo San Zulian and ponte di Santa Fosca.

Don't forget to introduce your kids to the most famous Venetian game of all. With the

St Mark's pride of lions

In Venice, lions are everywhere: on pillars, church façades, coats-of-arms... even drain-covers. The lion is the symbol of St Mark, Venice's patron saint. But no one is sure which the city espoused first: whether Venice chose St Mark to match its emblem, or whether the lion became its emblem because St Mark was its patron.

Venice's winged lion holds a book. On it (usually) is written *pax tibi Marce Evangelista meus* (peace to you Mark my evangelist). According to popular lore, a lion holding a closed book was erected in times of war. But given that Venice was at war so often, there's a distinct lack of closed books around the city.

Most ancient lions

Piazzetta San Marco (*see p70*): the winged lion on the column is from Syria, Persia or possibly China; it was probably Venetianised with the addition of wings and book.
Arsenale (*see p90*): the four stone lions on guard outside are older than Venice; the largest is from Piraeus and bears Runic inscriptions on its side; one of the smaller ones comes from the Lion Terrace of Delos and dates from the 6th century BC, though its head is later.

Cuddliest lions

Piazzetta dei Leoncini (*see p70*): these porphyry lions have been rubbed shiny by centuries of toddlers' bottoms.

San Giorgio degli Schiavoni (*see p93*): in Carpaccio's St Jerome frescos a lion holds out his paw plaintively, while wimpish monks scatter in terror.

Feeblest lion

San Nicolò dei Mendicoli (*see p117*): on a pillar outside the church, this lion is little bigger than a kitten and hasn't sprouted wings yet.

Most melancholy lion

I Frari (*see p113*): the lion moping beside Canova's tomb bears a distinct resemblance to the one in *The Wizard of Oz*.

Most secretive lion

Calle Bernardo (Dorsoduro): near the church of San Barnaba, this is one of the few lions that escaped the sculptor employed by the French to remove all winged lions from Venice's wells.

Most watchful lion

Scuola di San Marco (*see p89*): the lion standing guard on the façade seems to be checking out visitors to what is now the hospital.

Most long-suffering lion

Giardini pubblici (*see p90*): this stone lion bears a cavorting Minerva on its back; the goddess is waving her arms drunkenly aloft, as if boasting, 'Look, no hands!'

lagoon behind you, and the lagoon-facing façade of the Doge's Palace in front of you, go to the third column from the left. Place your back firmly against it, then walk round it, all the way. Can you circumnavigate it without slipping off the shoe-worn marble pavement?

Most of Venice's museums are singularly hands-off, but some may still appeal to kids. If the vast Tintorettos and echoing halls of the **Palazzo Ducale** (*see p77*) inspire only yawns, combine your visit there with a tour of the palace's secret corridors, the **Itinerari segreti** (*see p77*), which will take you into dungeons and torture rooms. And the small collection of 18th-century costumes at **Palazzo Mocenigo** (*see p108*) brings paintings of the period to life.

In the **Scuola-Museo del Merletto** (Lace Museum, *see p137*) on the island of Burano you may, if you're lucky, find some local ladies still demonstrating this traditional craft (mornings during the week are the best time to try). On

nearby Murano, the **Museo dell'Arte Vetrario** (*see p136*) contains many examples of the island's glass-making tradition. For blowing displays, however, you'll have to visit the workshops, where the demonstration tends to be desultory and the hard sell suffocating.

As far as art goes, try breaking your children in with visits to some of Venice's less demanding exhibits, such as the **Scuola di San Giorgio degli Schiavoni** (*see p93*), where Vittorio Carpaccio's St George cycle is packed with the kind of detail that invites a game of I-spy. The grand Tintorettos in the **Madonna dell'Orto** (*see p999*), particularly *The Last Judgement,* are full of the kind of gruesome details – such as bodies with skull-heads scrabbling their way out of the earth – likely to appeal to kids.

Don't be scared off from big galleries such as the **Accademia** (*see p122*): you may link up with one of the gallery's more child-friendly

Arts & Entertainment

Most ferocious lion
Riva degli Schiavoni (*see p89*): though it snarls at the base of the Vittorio Emanuele monument, this fearsome bronze beast often acts as cosy shelter to a local cats, who sit under its outstretched wings when it rains. A bronze cousin to this animal lies underneath the Daniele Manin monument in **campo Manin** (map p307 A3).

guides, who will bend over backwards to interest your offspring in the collection. It has publications for children aged five to ten, but unfortunately only in Italian.

As for the countless churches, one way of getting a little Tintoretto-viewing time is to point out that the red marble used in so many church floors contains amazing fossils; while they go on mini-palaeontological excursions you can concentrate on the artworks.

When the culture all gets too much, take Junior up a **campanile** for a bird's-eye view of the city. The one in piazza San Marco (*see p75*) is the highest; the one attached to San Giorgio Maggiore (*see p129*) affords a more detached vantage point. Time your ascent to coincide with the striking of an hour (midday is particularly deafening). The **Scala del Bòvolo** (*see p83*) is on a smaller scale, but will give the kids the satisfaction of having made their own panting way up to the top.

Parks & entertainment

See also **Teatro del Parco** and **Teatro Toniolo**, *p217*.

Most Venetian kids spend their free time in their local *campi*. Although ball games are officially forbidden there, you will find small games going on in most of them, particularly the larger ones like campo Santa Maria Formosa and campo San Polo. Venetian kids are used to letting foreign visitors join in their games, making use of their rudimentary school English for essential communication. In one corner of campo Santa Maria Formosa by the church (*see p87*), the parish priest has kitted out a small play area for toddlers.

Although well hidden, there are public parks in the city too, and most of them have been fitted up with swings and slides. This is true of the **Giardini Pubblici** (*see p90*) and the **Parco Savorgnan** (*see p97*). At **Sant'Elena** (*see p93*) things improve with a grassy play area along the lagoon, and a roller skating/cycling rink. Sant'Elena is also where Venice's football team has its home ground (*see p223*).

In summer, break up the culture monotony with a trip across to the **Lido**, where there are some halfway-acceptable beaches. Most of the main ones are sewn up by the big hotels, which will charge you for a small stretch of sand, sometimes with deckchair and umbrella and always with huge numbers of near neighbours.

Sant'Erasmo (*see p140*) also provides a pleasant break. Green and rural, with Venice's *campanili* fading into the hazy horizon, Sant'Erasmo can be cycled around in an hour or so. There is a small beach straight across the island from the ferry landing stage.

Local feast days may also provide entertainment for your children, usually in the shape of puppet theatres. Watch walls around the city for posters announcing *feste*. Particularly picturesque is the feast of Saints Peter and Paul in the parish of San Pietro in Castello, culminating on 29 June.

Babysitting

Larger hotels should have childminders on hand; smaller ones can probably arrange them.

Books

There is an excellent children's guide to Venice (in English) – *Viva Venice* by Paolo Zoffoli and Paola Scibilia (Elzeviro, 2002) – complete with games, informative illustrations and interesting facts. *Venice for Kids* by Elisabetta Pasqualin (Fratelli Palombi, 2000) belongs to an attractive series of books on the principal cities of Italy.

Arts & Entertainment

Film

It's all quiet on the film front, except for 12 days of summer mayhem.

Directors as diverse as David Lean and Wim Wenders have rubbed their hands in glee at the prospect of making films in Venice, but the city leaves a lot to be desired as a place in which to view them. As with theatre and nightlife, the problem is simple: this is a small town, with a small and ageing population. Island Venice has only a handful of cinemas and though local film buffs are always complaining about the paltry choice, it is a pretty accurate reflection of the local demand.

There are two exceptions to this uninspiring scenario. The first is the annual **Film Festival** at the beginning of September, when the Lido shakes off its sleepy, *fin-de-siècle* deck-chair and beach-umbrella image and, for 12 days, becomes a nominee for the World Capital of Cinema award.

The second is **Circuito Cinema**, a film promotion initiative established in 1981 and run by Venice council's highly active film department. Circuito Cinema is a centre of cinema-related research and activity, but it also runs and programmes a group of local arthouse cinemas.

The newest of these is the **Giorgione Movie d'Essai**, a former porn palace in Cannaregio. Two of the other screens in the Circuito Cinema group – the **Mignon Arthouse** in Mestre and the **Aurora Movie d'Essai** in Marghera – are on the mainland; the fourth is the plushy **Sala Perla** on the Lido (Lungomare Marconi, 041 524 1320), previously open only during the Festival, but now the venue for a Friday evening series of first-run films. Local papers carry details of times and programmes.

The Lido comes alive for the **Venice Film Festival**. See p202.

Early in 2003 Venetian cinema-goers will also have their first 'multi-screen' cinema... two screens, to be precise. The **Cinema Astra** will be at via Corfu 2 on the Lido.

In Italy the dubber is king, and the dearth of original-language films is enough to make expats and cinema buffs weep. However, both the Giorgione and Circuito Cinema offer a limited selection of films in *versione originale*.

SCREENINGS AND TICKETS
Screening times in Venice are a rule unto themselves: check local press for details. Tickets cost between €4 and €7 depending on the screen and time of day.

Associations

Circuito Cinema
Santa Croce 1882, Palazzo Carminati, salizzada Carminati (041 524 1320/www.comune.venezia.it/ cinema/www.veneziacultura.it). Vaporetto San Stae. **Map** p304 C2.
The Circuito Cinema operates on various fronts: as a publisher; as a cine-club, organising a series of themed seasons and workshops; and as a promoter, via its Cinemacard, an annual (July-June) card that gives variable entry discounts to all of Venice's cinemas as well as a number of theatres, restaurants, shops, and museums. It costs €15 and can be bought from the Giorgione cinema as well as the San Polo open-air cinema in the summer.

Cinemas

Giorgione Movie D'Essai
Cannaregio 4612, rio terà dei Franceschi (041 522 6298). Vaporetto Ca' d'Oro. **No credit cards.** **Map** p305 B4.
This is a comfortable arthouse two-screener run by Circuito Cinema (*see above*); it alternates first-run fare with themed seasons, kids' films (in Italian, on Saturday and Sunday at 3pm) and original language (usually English) offerings on Tuesdays from October to May. English-language films are in the capacious Sala A, while indie material and retrospectives are shown on the miniscule screen in Sala B.

Open-air

Arena di Campo San Polo
San Polo, campo San Polo (041 524 1320). Vaporetto San Silvestro or San Tomà. **Season** 6wks late July-early Sept. **No credit cards. Map** p304 C2.
This open-air arena in one of Venice's liveliest squares has become a fixture, popular with both Venetians and tourists. With average audiences of 1,000 a night, the arena packs in more people in six weeks than any other Venetian cinema in the whole year – proof that the atmosphere of this great night out is as important as the films themselves, which

are generally repeats of first-run favourites from the previous season, and always dubbed. The exception is at Festival time, when there are sneak-preview showings of a selection of original-language films a day or two after their Lido screening.

Videotheques

Videoteca Pasinetti
Santa Croce 1882, Palazzo Carminati, salizzada Carminati (041 524 1320). Vaporetto San Stae. **Open** *Video archive* 9am-1pm Mon-Fri. *Video-projected cinema classics* Oct-May 4pm, 9pm Mon-Fri. **Admission** by membership card (€13), valid for 4mths (Oct-Jan/Feb-June). **No credit cards.** **Map** p304 C2.
Another emanation of the city council's energetic Ufficio Attività Cinematografiche, this video archive was set up in 1991 with the aim of collecting, conserving and allowing access to the huge wealth of audiovisual material that deals with Venice, in whatever format: feature film, TV documentary, newsreel, amateur video. More than 3,000 videos are kept here – around half of them feature films – and there is also a screening room where brief, ultra-cineaste film seasons are organised. Individual consultations for members can be arranged by making a reservation.

Festivals

Antenna Cinema Festival
Via San Martino e Solferino 89, 35122, Padua (049 878 9914/www.antennacinema.it), **Dates** Nov.
Antenna Cinema was founded in 1978 in Conegliano with the aim of analysing all forms of audio-visual communication and the relationship between film and TV. Participants include Channel 4, MTV, CNN and Italian public broadcaster RAI. The festival has now moved to Padua and takes place in November, although Antenna Cinema also screens retrospectives and other events throughout the year.

Asolo Art Film Festival
Info Art Film Festival, Foresto Vecchio 8, 31011 Asolo (0423 520455/www.asolofilmfestival.it). **Dates** last wk Sept. **No credit cards.**
As well as being the backdrop to Liliana Cavani's *Ripley's Game*, Asolo also hosts its own film fest, concentrating on art and artists. In 2002 it included a tribute to Venetian composer Luigi Nono. For information on accreditation and prices contact the above number or write to info@asolofilmfestival.it.

Circuito Off
Artecolica Associazione Culturale, PO Box 626, 30100 Venice (www.circuitooff.com). **Dates** first wk June. **Admission** free.
This short film festival includes competitions, retrospectives and videos. Venues include the Giorgione Cinema, the Fondazione Bevilacqua La Masa (*see p203*) and the Architecture Institute's Tolentini building. See the website for information on selection and registration.

Celluloid Venice

Undeniably atmospheric and photogenic it may be, but Venice has provided the backdrop for some cinematic dogs as well as great celluloid moments.

Luchino Visconti's sepia-tinted *Death in Venice* (1971) is a modern must-see for many film-goers... and a high-camp pastiche for others.

Paul Schrader directed the 1990 version of Ian McEwan's unsettling, needling Venetian novel *The Comfort of Strangers*. Scripted by Harold Pinter with music by Angelo Badalamenti, the film starred Christopher Walken, Natasha Richardson, Helen Mirren and Rupert Everett. Yet even this dream team couldn't rescue the production, depravity and decadence being notoriously difficult to portray on celluloid... even with Pinter behind the lines.

An author whose work translates much less problematically to the big screen is Daphne Du Maurier. Think of *Rebecca* (1940), *The Birds* (1963) – and *Don't Look Now* (1973). In Nicolas Roeg's superb 1973 adaptation of *Don't Look Now*, John (Donald Sutherland) and Laura Baxter (Julie Christie) are trying to piece together their lives after the death of their child, but they soon lose themselves, and each other, in the city's hallucinatory labyrinth.

If ever a city was made for costume drama, it's Venice. In the film adaptation of Henry James' *The Wings of the Dove*, Helena Bonham-Carter dons her umpteenth corset, to breath-taking effect. Torn between renouncing a life of wealth and privilege or her lover, Kate comes up with a diabolic scheme that just might allow her to keep both. Hossein Amini's screenplay wrenches a modern story from James's prose, but director Iain Softely serves it up with all the period trimmings.

Venice is usually cast as decadent and labyrinthine. But it also works well in more romantic guise. In David Lean's 1955 *Summertime* the preternaturally perfect Katherine Hepburn is an Ohio old maid who falls for the charms of a Venetian antiques dealer. The scene at the train station is a reminder of Lean's earlier *Brief Encounter*, but this is a much more joyful affair.

Steve McQueen got his shot at playing the American in Venice in *The Honeymoon Machine* (1961). The unlikely sight of McQueen lording it in a Venetian palazzo hotel while dressed as a marine makes the preposterous storyline a bit more palatable.

Le Giornate del Cinema Muto

Cineteca del Friuli, Palazzo Gurisatti, via Bini 50, 33013 Gemona (0432 980 458/www. cinetecadelfriuli.org/gcm). **Dates** mid Oct. **No credit cards**.
Although not actually in the Veneto, Pordenone is just an hour away from Venice and it hosts one of Europe's major silent film festivals. Accreditation costs €20 and it allows unlimited viewings except on the opening and closing nights when a silent movie with a live musical accompaniment costs €13 per screening. Non-accredited cinema-goers pay €5 per screening.

Mostra Internazionale d'Arte Cinematografica (Venice Film Festival)

Palazzo del Cinema, lungomare Marconi 90, Lido (information 041 521 8711/www.labiennale.org). Vaporetto Lido. **Date** 12 days from late Aug. **Tickets** *Season tickets* €50-€150, on sale in 2wks prior to festival from ACTV-VeLa outlets (*see p275*) or online. *Individual screenings* €5-€15, available previous day from ACTV-VeLa outlets or ticket office at the Casinò (lungomare Marconi, Lido, open 8.30am-11pm daily). Same-day tickets occasionally available. **Credit** AmEx, DC, MC, V. **Map** p311.
The 12-day Venice Film Festival takes place along the main, sea-facing Lido esplanade, between the Hotel des Bains and the Excelsior (for both, *see p58*). Between these two grand hotels is the marble-and-glass Palazzo del Cinema, where official competition screenings take place in the Sala Grande; other festival screens can be found in the gargantuan PalaGalileo and inside the Casinò. The best way to ensure the appropriate cinema overdose is to get press accreditation; the press pass, which costs €26, ensures priority access to a number of special screenings, mostly in the morning and early evening. This needs to be arranged at least two months in advance by contacting the Biennale press office (041 521 8857/fax 041 520 0569).

'Cultural' accreditation is another option; it allows access to a narrower range of screenings. Again, this should be arranged well in advance. Failing this, the next best thing is to stand in line and buy tickets for single showings. This is best done the day before the screening for competition films and anything that is being talked about. On the same day, it's advisable to get there at least an hour before the film you want to see is scheduled. *Una Settimana da leoni* is a special offer for under-26s, offering both a festival pass and accommodation; for details, consult www.venicesystem.com/ita/biennale.htm.

Galleries

Exhibitions abound as institutions take a contemporary turn.

After languishing for decades, Venice's contemporary art scene has recently been given a shot in the arm by some feisty institutions that have generated interesting new activities.

An overhaul of that mother of all contemporary art binges, the **Biennale** (*see p206* **The Biennale**), a reorganisation of the Accademia delle Belle Arti (Fine Arts Academy), an upturn in the quality of programmes at the **Fondazione Bevilacqua La Masa** and a surprising contemporary turn at the **Fondazione Scientifica Querini Stampalia** (*see p205* **La Querini**) have all contributed to injecting new life into the scene.

But though Venice is fast becoming a magnet for contemporary artists in all media, it remains resolutely averse to producing artists of its own. This situation may change after the opening of the new Art and Design department at the Architecture University (*see chapter* **Directory**) and the inauguration in Mestre on the mainland of the **Centro Culturale Candiani**, an enormous exhibition venue (*see also p138*).

But as yet there is no equivalent in Venice to those New York or London galleries where dealers invest in the growth of particular artists or movements and patrons devote themselves to the fostering of a younger artistic generation experimenting with new media. Galleries tend to be mainstream, eschewing the cutting edge for more established artists and staging exhibitions that lack true strength. All of which doesn't mean that there isn't good-quality art out there.

Beware that numerous places calling themselves galleries are really little more than outlets for the artistic output of their owner or for arty knick-knacks.

For glass – contemporary and otherwise – see chapter **Glass**.

A+A

San Marco 3073, calle Malipiero (041 277 0466). Vaporetto San Samuele. **Open** 11am-1pm, 2-6pm Tue-Sat. **No credit cards. Map** p306 A2.
An interesting, non-profit exhibition space sponsored by the Slovenian ministry of culture. It hosts various shows and events each year, most of which are dedicated to Slovenian artists or related projects.

Bugno Art Gallery

San Marco 1996A, campo San Fantin (041 523 1305/www.bugnoartgallery.it). Vaporetto Vallaresso. **Open** 4-7.30pm Mon, Sun; 10.30am-12.30pm, 4-7.30pm Tue-Sat. **Credit** AmEx, DC, MC, V. **Map** p307 A3.

A large space over two floors, which is devoted to artists working in all medias. Local artists are also included in the gallery's collection. Opening times tend to be fluid.

Il Capricorno

San Marco 1994, calle dietro la Chiesa (041 520 6920). Vaporetto Santa Maria del Giglio. **Open** 11am-1pm, 5pm-8pm daily. **Credit** AmEx, DC, MC, V. **Map** p307 A3.
This active, well-established San Marco gallery stages various shows each year. Most of them are dedicated to younger international artists working in a variety of media.

Centro Culturale Candiani

Piazzale Candiani 7, Mestre (041 238 6111/ www.comune.venezia.it/candiani). Bus 2 from piazzale Roma. **Open** 9am-7pm Tue-Sun. **Admission** varies according to event. **No credit cards.**
On the drawing board for more than 20 years, this 5,000sq m (53,800sq ft) exhibition space, which also houses concert facilities and much more was finally inaugurated in 2001. Check the website for regularly changing programmes.

Contini Galleria d'Arte

San Marco 2765, calle dello Spezier (041 520 4942/ www.continiarte.com). Vaporetto Santa Maria del Giglio or Accademia. **Open** 10am-1pm, 3.30-7.30pm daily. **Credit** AmEx, MC, V. **Map** p307 A3.
In a large though often crowded space off campo Santo Stefano, the Contini stages exhibitions of renowned artists and keeps a strong collection of 20th-century works. It has sister galleries in Mestre and Cortina d'Ampezzo.
Branch: via Ferro 11, Mestre (041 981 611).

Flora Bigai Arte moderna e contemporanea

San Marco 1652, piscina di Frezzeria (041 521 2208/041 241 3799/www.florabigai.com). Vaporetto Vallaresso. **Open** 3.30-7.30pm Mon; 10am-1pm, 3.30-7.30pm Tue-Sat. **Credit** AmEx, DC, MC, V. **Map** p307 A4.
This three-floor space, located not far from St Mark's is a recent addition to Venice's gallery scene; when this guide went to press it had staged just two exhibitions, both of works by contemporary Italian artists; the high standard of these boded well for the gallery's future.

Fondazione Bevilacqua La Masa

Exhibition space *San Marco 71C, piazza San Marco (041 523 7819/www.bevilacqualamasa.it). Vaporetto Vallaresso.* **Open** during exhibitions only 10am-1pm, 4-7pm Mon, Wed-Sun. **Map** p307 A4.

Arts & Entertainment

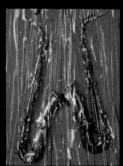

Offices & exhibition space *Dorsoduro 2826, fondamenta Gerardini (041 520 7797/8879). Vaporetto Ca' Rezzonico.* **Open** *Office* 8am-1.30pm Mon, Thur, Fri; 8am-1.30pm, 2.30-5.30pm Tue, Wed. *Exhibition space* varies. **Map** p306 B2.
Founded at the end of the 19th century when Duchess Felicita Bevilacqua La Masa left her palace of Ca' Pesaro (*see p106*) to the city, to give younger local artists a space in which to explore new trends, the institution has been given new direction and life by directors who have created a strong exhibition programme, revamped the artist-in-residence programme at Palazzo Carminati (Santa Croce 1882A, salizada San Stae, 041 523 7819, open by appointment only), and increased the exhibition and office space. The annual *esposizione collettiva* is dedicated to Veneto-based artists under 30.

Galleria Traghetto
San Marco 2543, campo Santa Maria del Giglio (041 522 1188/www.artnet.com/traghetto.htlm). Vaporetto Santa Maria del Giglio. **Open** 10.30am-12.30pm, 3.30-7.30pm Mon-Sat; by appointment Sun. **Credit** AmEx, DC, MC, V. **Map** p307 B3.
This gallery has long dealt in Venetian abstracts but has recently turned its attention to emerging artists working in various media.

Galleria d'Arte L'Occhio
Dorsoduro 181, calle San Gregorio (041 522 6550/ galleria.locchio@tin.it). Vaporetto Salute. **Open** 10am-6pm daily. **Credit** AmEx, MC, V. **Map** p307 B3.
A tiny, friendly gallery with a few solo and collective exhibitions a year devoted to younger, local and international artists in various media, mostly figurative.

Galleria Multigraphic
Dorsoduro 728, calle della Chiesa (041 528 5159/ multigraphic@infinito.it). **Open** 8.30am-6.30pm Mon-Sat. Closed 2wks Aug. **Credit** AmEx, MC, V. **Map** p306 B2.
Galleria Multigraphic has its own printing room at the back, where the graphics and etchings of the gallery's artists are produced. The gallery deals mainly in modern abstract art, and has a packed exhibition programme.

Imagina
Dorsoduro 3126, rio terà Canal (041 241 0625/ imagina.venezia@tin.it). Vaporetto Ca' Rezzonico. **Open** 3.30-7.30pm Tue-Sat. **No credit cards.** **Map** p306 A2.
The only gallery in Venice solely dedicated to photography has numerous strong shows featuring top artists to its credit. Opening times vary depending on what's going on.

La Galleria Venezia
San Marco 2566, ramo Calegheri (041 520 7415/ dvanderkoelen@xterna-net.de). Vaporetto Santa Maria del Giglio. **Open** 10am-1pm, 3.30-7.30pm Mon-Sat. **Credit** AmEx, DC, MC, V. **Map** p307 B3.
A warm space that is spread over various rooms to accommodate artworks, artist's books and scholarly volumes on established artists. The Venezia was

La Querini

Venetians have a great affection for what they call La Querini. It's here, in a quaint palazzo tucked away behind the church of Santa Maria Formosa, that Venetian students turn up late in the evening after all the city's other libraries have closed, knowing that they'll still gain access to La Querini's precious tomes (*see also p85*). And here, too, they can get a glimpse of their ancestors indulging in very Venetian pastimes in a charming set of 18th-century paintings by Gabriele Bella.

But now, in a departure from its usual role that has taken locals by surprise, the Fondazione Querini Stampalia has moved slowly but steadily into the contemporary art scene. Collaborations in the mid 1990s with Biennale-related projects and the renovation of the library and museum galleries by Mario Botta (completed in 2001) have made La Querini more aware of its possibilities and opportunities. A series of seminars on contemporary art begun in 1998 have been drawing an ever-growing audience and the 'SMF5252' project now includes occasional small-scale shows as well. The Premio Querini Stampalia-Furla per l'Arte – an award for young artists in any media, living and working in Italy – was launched at around the same time; works by the winners are shown in a special annual exhibition in the upstairs galleries.

Fondazione Scientifica Querini Stampalia
Castello 5252, campo Santa Maria Formosa (041 271 1411/www. querinistampalia.it). Vaporetto San Zaccaria. **Open** 10am-6pm Tue-Thur, Sun; 10am-10pm Fri, Sat. **Admission** 6; 4 concessions. *Library* free. **Credit** DC, MC, V. **Map** p308 A1.

recently opened by a German gallerist and scholar who has already organised numerous shows in its sister gallery in Mainz.

San Gregorio Art Gallery
Dorsoduro 165, calle San Gregorio (041 522 9296/ www.sangregorioartgallery.com). Vaporetto Salute. **Open** 10.30am-12.30pm, 3-6pm Mon, Wed-Sat. **Credit** AmEx, DC, MC, V. **Map** p307 B3.
This gallery has about three exhibitions a year, focusing on abstract and contemporary Italian art in all media.

Galleria Venice Design

San Marco 3146, salizada San Samuele (041 520 7915/www.venicedesign.com). Vaporetto San Samuele. **Open** 10am-6pm daily. **Credit** AmEx, DC, MC, V. **Map** p307 A3.

This ambitious gallery deals in all art forms, with a preference for sculpture as the form that is 'nearest to the art of living'. It represents established artists both Italian and international, and organises a few shows yearly.

Branch: San Marco 1310, calle Vallaresso (041 523 9082).

Nuova Ikona

Giudecca 454, calle dell'Olio (041 521 0101/ nuovaikona@iol.it). Vaporetto Palanca. **Open** by appointment only. **No credit cards.** **Map** p306 C2.

Established in 1993 as a non-profit association, Nuova Ikona masterminds exhibitions and events that are held in the gallery or in the tiny Oratorio San Sebastiano (Dorsoduro 2552, corte dei Vecchi, contact the gallery for opening times). The calendar of events is packed though irregular.

The Biennale

Since its inception in 1895, the visual arts bonanza officially called L'Esposizione Internazionale d'Arte della Biennale di Venezia – but better known as the Biennale – has been held in the Giardini, a series of nationally owned pavilions scattered around a leafy park at the far eastern end of the *sestiere* of Castello. The first national pavilion was built by Belgium in 1907; many other countries followed suit, commissioning architects to design fitting containers for the artists chosen to carry their flag every two years. Some of these buildings are works of art in their own right, such as Alvar Aalto's 1956 design for Finland, or Sverre Fehn's 1961 Scandinavian pavilion.

Unfortunately, these pavilions are only in use at Biennale time, leaving the pavilion end of the Giardini quite desolate during the rest of the year, when they are open to lonesome Venetians taking their dogs for a stroll. Plans to put the buildings of the Giardini to a more regular use have been in the air for some time now.

The sheer size of recent exhibitions – and the introduction of the Biennale di Architettura

in alternate years – have forced organisers to concentrate their attention on the large, abandoned and spectacular spaces of the nearby Arsenale (*see p90*), parts of which are gradually being restored to take the overflow: exhibits have spread from the Corderie (rope factory) to the Artiglierie (gun foundry), the Gaggiandre (dry docks) and still further.

Moreover, the growing importance of merely being here has forced 'have-not' countries (not to mention self-promoting artists keen to exploit the press barrage that the Biennale generates) to rent exhibition spaces elsewhere in the city, prompting a welcome influx of funds and attention.

As this guide went to press Ca' Giustinian, the Biennale's headquarters, was undergoing a slow-moving restoration programme, and the offices were divided between here and Palazzo Querini Dubois (San Polo 2004, campo San Polo, vaporetto San Silvestro, open 9am-6pm Mon-Fri). The Biennale's massive art archive, the Archivio Storico delle Arti Contemporanee (Ca' Corner della Regina, Santa Croce 2214, calle della Regina, 041 521 8700/asac@labiennale.com) has been partially closed due to restoration of the building for many years, with no reopening date yet set.

La Biennale di Venezia

Ca' Giustinian, San Marco 1364, calle del Ridotto (041 521 8711/www. labiennaledivenezia.net). Vaporetto Vallaresso. **Map** p307 B4.

Venues Giardini di Castello, vaporetto Giardini (map p309 C4); Arsenale, vaporetto Arsenale (map p308 B2). **Dates** mid June-early Nov in alternate years (odd for art; even for architecture). **Open** 10am-6pm Tue-Sun. **Admission** (allowing access to all official shows) 12; 10 concessions. **No credit cards.**

Gay & Lesbian

Infuriatingly contradictory but relentlessly romantic.

For gays, Venice can be one of the most infuriatingly contradictory cities in the world. Although its beauty and water-bound distinctiveness attract lesbians and gay men in large numbers, the city offers remarkably little in the way of dedicated gay clubs, bars, accommodation and restaurants.

If you exclude the natural attractions of **Alberoni Beach** and Il Muro (*see below*), there are no exclusively gay-identified, or even 'mixed', venues in the city. The main reason for this is the uniqueness of the city itself; it lacks the trappings of modern metropolitan life that make the gay scene what it is in Milan, Rome or even Turin. There are no cars, there's very little bustle and, excluding the thronging hordes of tourists, there are only 60,000-odd inhabitants living in island Venice. What this adds up to is a small-town feel, with all the small-town drawbacks for the gay resident or visitor.

Which is not to say that there isn't a gay scene. There most certainly is; it's just not the sort of scene that most urban gays will be used to. Cruising here is as casual and hassle- and venue-free as you can get, and generally takes place just about anywhere in the city and at any time – although it still requires a certain level of discretion, of course.

For lesbians, too, it's a comfy, homey kind of scene. You won't be hassled; you probably won't even be noticed. And if it's all too quiet for you, there's always a bit of action in summer on the beach at Alberoni.

Gays looking for something a little less oblique and a little more overt should be aware that the modern world is just a bus-, taxi-, car- or train-ride away, either in Mestre or Padua.

The national gay rights group ArciGay has a number of local chapters that sponsor activities, festivals, counselling and AIDS awareness. ArciGay membership is needed for entry to several of the venues listed below. A one-month *tessera* (membership card) for visitors costs €6.50 (you can get annual membership for €13, and if you plan to be in Italy for more than a month it's clearly worth it) and can be purchased at ArciGay Dedalo (c/o Scuola Pellico, via Costa 38A, Mestre, 041 538 4151, open 9-11pm Tue, phone enquiries 7-9pm Mon, 9-11pm Thur) or at the door of venues that require it.

Venice & Mestre

Open-air

Il Muro (The Wall)

Behind the Procuratie Nuove, by the Giardinetti Reali (at the lagoon end of the piazzetta di San Marco, turn right and keep on walking), Il Muro has seen better and more popular days as the city's after-dark cruising area. Now very rarely frequented from October to May, it can still pull a good crowd during the summer months. But even with almost no one about, the place has a romantic charm all its own, and is well worth a visit just for the view it affords of San Giorgio Maggiore across the canal.

Alberoni Beach, Lido

Bus B/(Alberoni Spiaggia) from Santa Maria Elisabetta to the last stop, then turn right and walk about 10mins towards the dunes. If you catch Bus B/(Alberoni), you'll have to walk quite a distance back to get to the beach.

Now an almost exclusively gay beach, Alberoni is *the* place to go cruising in summer. The dunes and pine forest are where the action is, and the beach area is blissfully devoid of the noisy family crowds you'd normally expect on Italian beaches from June to late August. If the weather's good, cruising starts as early as April, but if you enjoy feeling like a kid let loose in a sweet shop, go for Saturdays and Sundays in July.

Accommodation

Il Lato Azzurro

Via Forti 13, Sant'Erasmo (041 523 0642/ other.venice@flashnet.it). Vaporetto 13 to Sant'Erasmo-Capannone. **Rates** €40 single; €56 double; €75 triple; €90 quadruple; €15 for each additional bed (dinner €15). **Credit** AmEx, MC, DC, V.

This gay-owned and -operated guesthouse on Venice's vegetable-garden island of Sant'Erasmo (*see p140*) is the ideal place to stay if you're looking for a really quiet retreat. Venice and its flocks of tourists are a couple of vaporetto stops away.

Art

BAC Art Studio

Dorsoduro 862, campo San Vio (041 522 8171/ www.bacart.com). Vaporetto Accademia. **Open** 10.30am-6.30pm Mon-Sat. **Credit** MC, V. **Map** p305 B3.

An interesting gallery for important pieces or less ambitious gifts. There are sensual homoerotic works, mainly limited-edition etchings and aquatints, by Baruffaldi, and some more scenic Venetian pieces by Cadore.

Eating & drinking

For eating, drinking and evening relaxation in general, Venetian gays – like most of the city's night owls – head for campo Santa Margherita (*see p119*), with its plethora of establishments with looky-looky tables out on the campo itself.

Venice has no rainbow-flag-waving eateries but it does have establishments that are more gay-friendly than others. **La Zucca** (*see p159*) is a case in point: small and cosy, and run almost exclusively by women, it has always been a favourite with local lesbians. Other favourites include:

Antico Panificio

San Polo 945, campiello del Sole (041 277 0967). Vaporetto San Silvestro. **Open** *Aug-June* noon-3pm, 7-11pm Mon, Wed-Sun. Closed July. **Credit** AmEx, DC, MC, V. **Map** p304 C2.
Good pizza and fantastic service by Tiziano who, though married himself, is proud of his gay clientele. A two-minute walk from the Rialto.

Bagolo

Santa Croce 1584, campo San Giacomo dall'Orio (347 366 5016). Vaporetto San Stae. **Open** 6.30am-2am Tue-Sun. **No credit cards. Map** p304 C2.
A simple, typically Venetian bar that is particularly gay-friendly. Owner Gianni is striving to bring the Venetian bacaro (*see p146* **Bacari**) into the 21st century, and his efforts have made Bagolo very popular with local thirtysomethings. During the warmer months, it's a great place to sit outside, sip your *spritz* and watch campo life go by.

Sauna

Metro Venezia

Via Cappuccina 82B, Mestre (041 538 4299/ www.metroclub.it). Bus 2 or 7 from piazzale Roma/ train to Mestre, then 5min walk. **Open** 2pm-2am Mon-Fri, Sun; 2pm-3am Sat. **Admission** €14 (€11.50 after 8pm) Mon-Sat; €15 (€11.50 after 8pm) Sun; plus ArciGay membership (*see p207*). **Credit** MC, DC, V.
The first gay venue to open in the Venice area, Metro has a bar, a dry sauna, steam sauna, private room and a darkroom. Massage and hydro-massage are also available.

Tours

Venice à la Carte

Dorsoduro 3167, campo San Barnaba (041 277 0564/www.tourvenice.org). **Rates** vary according to tour. **No credit cards. Map** p306 B2.

Tailor-made, personalised holidays, catering for a wide variety of cultural interests and credit limits, are organised by American gondola-builder Thom Price and his partner Alvise Zanchi, a native Venetian and expert tour guide. The company is a member of IGLTA.

Padua

Although it was once much livelier, Padua still has a few places that gays go to, especially on Fridays and Saturdays. It's just a 20-minute drive from Venice to Padua, and the city offers the anonymity that – as any resident of Venice knows – is sorely missing on the lagoon.

We've only included those gay places that are most easily accessible by public transport or taxi from Venice or Mestre (see chapters Directory: Getting Around and Padua).

A word of caution: cruising continues to be very risky, especially around and in Padua station, and should be avoided.

Bars & entertainment

Flexo Club

Via Nicolò Tommaseo 96A (049 807 4707/ www.flexoclub.it). **Open** 9.30pm-2am Wed, Thur; 9.30pm-5am Fri; 9.30pm-7am Sat; 9.30pm-3am Sun. **Admission** €8 (incl 1 drink) Wed, Thur; €10 (incl 1 drink) Fri-Sun; plus ArciGay membership (*see p207*). **Credit** DC, MC, V.
A private club-disco arranged over four floors, with bars and labyrinthine darkrooms downstairs. It's conveniently located about ten minutes' walk from the station; the front door (ring the bell) is at the back of a courtyard on the right side of the road as you approach from the station (use the handy map on Flexo's website). If coming by taxi from Venice, be sure to specify that you want via Tommaseo in Padua and not via Tommaseo near Venice itself. Every first and third Saturday of the month Flexo organises a 'naked party': one of the four bar areas is set aside for members who must either be completely naked or at the very most clad in a pair of Y-fronts. The club's clientele is almost exclusively male, and women are not allowed beyond the downstairs bar area.

Sauna

Metro Sauna

Via Turazza 19 (049 807 5828/www.metroclub.it). **Open** 2pm-3am daily. **Admission** €14 (€16.50 Sun) until 8.30pm, then €11.50 (€14 Sun); plus ArciGay membership (*see p207*). **Credit** DC, MC, V.
Large, modern and well equipped, this place offers a proper work-those-pores Finnish sauna rather than the usual warm cabin that smells of pine. It also has private massage facilities.

Music & Nightlife

Venice has bars, but the real scene is on the mainland.

Venice was once notorious for its nightlife; nowadays it's notorious for the lack of it. But while the relentless revelry has certainly slowed down since the 18th century, when Venice was Europe's party capital, it has not ground to a complete halt.

Venetians are renowned for being partial to a tipple (or three) and a typical night out starts with a *giro de ombre* – a bar-crawl Venetian style. And if you are still standing when the traditional *bacari* (*see p146*) close, there are myriad late-opening bars for carrying on into the small hours. Native night owls gather in campo Santa Margherita, in the heart of the city's southern Dorsoduro district, or on Cannaregio's 'party' fondamenta della Misericordia, where the division between the various bars blurs to form one, long canal-front nightspot.

MUSIC

If you happen to turn up in Venice in late June, you could be forgiven for thinking you've landed in a real music mecca: the annual Venezia Suona festival hosts anything from a cappella choirs and jazz quartets to punk or Zappa revival bands, who jam in *campi* and by canals all over the city (www.veneziasuona.it). However, since a controversial Pink Floyd concert in 1989, stringent regulations and lack of adequate venues have effectively pulled the plug on large-scale live music events, Carnevale (*see p194*) and the summer festivals (*see p212*) being the exceptions.

Music industry megastars who do dates in Venice are usually confined to the extremely formal setting of one of the local theatres. Lou Reed recently played the Malibran, Paul Weller the Goldoni, Chick Corea and David Sylvian the Palafenice, and Buena Vista Social Club and Courtney Pine Mestre's Toniolo (for all, *see chapter* **Performing Arts**).

For serious jazz heads, regular series of high-quality jazz and experimental music are organised by local cultural organisations like Vortice (www.provincia.venezia.it/vortice), which has managed to pull such avant-jazzers as Dave Douglas and Elliot Sharp. Performances usually take place in the more intimate Teatro Fondamenta Nuove and Teatrino Groggia.

The local music scene itself is small but by no means dormant; internationally known home-grown talent includes: Groove Jet

producer and DJ Spiller; Pitura Freska, whose unlikely mix of Venetian dialect and reggae shot him to national fame; Radio Rebelde; and the fine jazz musicians Pietro and Marcello Tonolo, who still play in their native city.

Fortunately for Venetians and visitors alike, the tenacity of the few bar owners still willing to wrestle with red tape and put up with party-pooper petitioning neighbours has secured opportunities for playing and hearing live music in a network of *locali* across the city. Venetian vibes tend to be laid-back and these small, free gigs are almost always reggae, jazz or blues with the occasional rock, Latino or ethnic session. Clubs and venues on the nearby mainland draw much bigger acts, though resident pop pickers often travel as far as Milan or Bologna for big tour dates.

CLUBS

Venice can lay claim to only one real club, so for some serious clubbing, make for the mainland. In the winter, a short bus or train ride to Mestre or Marghera (just across the bridge and well served by night buses) is all it takes to dance until dawn. In the summer, most of the dance action moves out to the seaside resort of Jesolo Lido, the place to be for house and techno, with a smattering of Latino to swing your suntan to.

INFORMATION AND TICKETS

Day-to-day listings are carried by the two local papers, *Il Gazzettino* and *La Nuova Venezia* (*see chapter* **Directory: Media**). For a more complete overview of concerts and festivals, with English translations, the monthly listings magazine *Venezia News* is indispensable. Also keep your eyes peeled in bars or restaurants for the free *Venezia da Vivere* leaflet and around town for notices of upcoming gigs and events. Tickets should be available at the venue but can be bought in advance at the CD shop Parole e Musica, Castello 5673, salizzada San Lio (041 522 2741) or via the national ticket agency, www.boxoffice.it. For information on classical music in Venice, *see chapter* **Performing Arts**.

Late bars & bars with music

See also **L'Olandese Volante**, *p166*; **La Colombina** *p153*; and **Boccadoro**, *p153*. The following bars have no extra charge for late opening and/or live music.

Ai Postali

*Santa Croce 821, fondamenta Rio Marin (041
715 156). Vaporetto Riva di Biasio or San Tomà.*
Open 8am-3pm, 5pm-2am Mon-Sat. **No credit
cards. Map** p304 C2.
Across the bridge from the train station and down
a narrow canal, this long-established *osteria* is a firm
Venetian favourite. Locals moor their boats beneath
the outside terrace to drop in for a drink and perhaps
to linger long into the small hours.

Al Parlamento

*Cannaregio 511, fondamenta San Giobbe (041 244
0214). Vaporetto Ferrovia or Tre Archi.* **Open** 8am-
2am daily. **No credit cards. Map** p304 A1.
Don't be put off by the decor. Prices and position
ensure Parliament's popularity. Well off the tourist
trail though just behind the main drag from the station, it's packed during *spritz* hour (6-8pm; *see also
p167* **From rosy to hazy**) – when there's a choice
of 20 variations on the traditional theme – and busy
until late too. Grab a seat outside and watch the
watery world go by on the Cannaregio Canal.

Bacaro Jazz

*San Marco 5546, salizzada del Fontego dei Tedeschi
(041 528 5249/bacarojazz@iol.it). Vaporetto Rialto.*
Open noon-2am Mon, Tue, Thur-Sun. **Credit**
AmEx, DC, MC, V. **Map** p305 C4.
Venice's most central late-night watering hole,
Bacaro Jazz is a place where you'd go to meet fellow
tourists or foreign students rather than mingle with
the locals. The background jazz and wide range of
killer cocktails keep the party going into the early
hours. Try the FraBellini cocktail, a modern take on
a traditional favourite.

Da Baffo

*San Polo 2346, campiello Sant'Agostin (041 520 8862).
Vaporetto San Stae or San Tomà.* **Open** 7.30am-2am
Mon-Sat. **No credit cards. Map** p304 C2.
Named after the 18th-century erotic poet whose
saucy sonnets are on display inside, this beautifully restored bar is one of the hippest hangouts in
Venice. Locals, students and their profs all come to
sample the wide selection of Italian wines, international beers and single malts. Jazz, blues and rock
musicians from all over Italy play live on Tuesdays
from October to April.

Bagolo

*Santa Croce 1584, campo San Giacomo dell'Orio
(347 366 5016). Vaporetto San Stae.* **Open** 7am-
2am Tue-Sun. **No credit cards. Map** p304 C2.
A modern, trendy bar which has had instant success
with a diverse crowd. Sit up at the high stools inside
or sink into an armchair outside and explore the
selection of excellent Friulian grappas. Weekly live
jazz and blues in the winter.

Café Blue

*Dorsoduro 3778, calle de la Scuola (041 710 227).
Vaporetto San Tomà.* **Open** noon-2am Mon-Fri;
5pm-2am Sat, Sun. **No credit cards. Map** p306 A2.

Hip hangout: **Da Baffo**.

After serving up a delicious afternoon tea, this pub-
style bar near campo Santa Margherita turns into a
real boozer, bulging with students and an international set. Happy hour is 8.30-9.30pm and homesick
Scots can enjoy a wee dram in the Whiskeria.

Café Noir

*Dorsoduro 3805, crosera San Pantalon (041 710
925/cafenoir@hotmail.com). Vaporetto San Tomà.*
Open 7am-2am Mon-Sat; 7pm-2am Sun. **No credit
cards. Map** p306 A2.
Café Noir is a winter favourite among the university and twentysomething crowd. There's internet
access (€2 for 30mins; €3 for 1hr), tasty *panini* (filled
rolls) and the thickest of hot chocolate to warm the
cockles of the coldest heart.

Il Caffè

*Dorsoduro 2963, campo Santa Margherita (041 528
7998). Vaporetto Ca'Rezzonico.* **Open** 7am-1am
Mon-Sat. **No credit cards. Map** p306 A2.
Whether for its red exterior, or for the political lean-
ings of its core clientele, the campo's oldest bar is
known as 'Caffè Rosso'. Relaxed and bohemian, it
attracts a mixed crowd of all ages who spill out from
its single room to sip a *spritz* in the campo or to
choose from the impressive wine list. Excellent live
music, usually on Thursdays.

Cavatappi

*San Marco 525/6, campo della Guerra (041 296
0252). Vaporetto Rialto.* **Open** *May-Oct* 9am-
midnight daily. *Nov-Apr* 9am-midnight Mon-Sat.
Credit DC, MC, V. **Map** p307 A4.

This excellent new wine bar closes at midnight but has a weekly live jazz session on Thursday to accompany the fine wine and food. *See also p165.*

Easy Bar
Santa Croce 2119, campo Santa Maria Materdomini (041 524 0321). Vaporetto San Stae. **Open** 7am-2am Mon-Wed, Fri-Sun. **No credit cards. Map** p305 C3.

On one of the main routes north-west from Rialto to the station, it's easy to spot this recently restored bar, whose cool steel and stone interior stands out against the surrounding Gothic *palazzi* in the square. It livens up late when local thirtysomethings turn up for post-dinner drinks and, on Wednesdays, live rock, reggae and ethnic music.

Fiddler's Elbow Irish Pub
Cannaregio 3847, corte dei Pali già Testori (041 523 9930). Vaporetto Ca' d'Oro. **Open** 5pm-1am daily. **No credit cards. Map** p305 B3.

Expats, locals and tourists all prop up the bar in Venice's oldest Irish pub. Neighbours have put a stop to regular live music, but local bands still have play at Hallowe'en and St Patrick's Day. A screen is set up in the campo outside for sporting events.

Iguana
Cannaregio 2515, fondamenta della Misericordia (041 713 561). Vaporetto San Marcuola. **Open** 6pm-2am Tue-Sat; noon-3pm, 6pm-2am Sun. **Credit** AmEx, DC, MC, V. **Map** p305 B3.

Grappas galore at **Bagolo** *See p210.*

Perhaps not the most authentic Mexican food you'll ever eat, but the atmosphere and background beat of Brazilian blues more than make up for it. The music comes live on Tuesdays, with Latino, jazz or funk, while happy hour (6.30-7.30pm), with an extensive cocktail menu, packs in the crowds.

Inishark
Castello 5787, calle del Mondo Novo (041 523 5500). Vaporetto Rialto. **Open** 6pm-1.30am Tue-Sun. **No credit cards. Map** p308 A1.

Tucked away in a small calle on the road between the churches of San Lio and Santa Maria Formosa, this Irish-style pub has the best Guinness on tap in town and great snacks to soak up the black stuff (try the roast suckling pig and mustard sandwiches). A satellite TV is set up for important matches, packing in the football fans.

Margaret Duchamp
Dorsoduro 3019, campo Santa Margherita (041 528 6255). Vaporetto Ca' Rezzonico. **Open** Feb-Apr, Oct-Dec 9am-2am Mon, Wed-Sun. *May-Sept* 9am-2am daily. Closed Jan. **No credit cards. Map** p306 A2.

This is the campo's chicest café-bar where a seat outside is an absolute must, to see and be seen. Duchamp serves a range of international beers and bulging *panini* (filled rolls) to a hip crowd of Venetian revellers into the early hours.

Osteria agli Ormesini da Aldo
Cannaregio 2710, fondamenta degli Ormesini (041 715 834). Vaporetto San Marcuola. **Open** 10.30am-3pm, 8.30pm-2am Mon-Sat. Closed 3wks Aug. **No credit cards. Map** p304 A2.

'Aldo's Place' – or rather the unmistakable Aldo himself – is an institution among Venetians young and not-so young. They come here in droves to choose from over 100 types of bottled beer and, if conversation peters out, play board games.

Paradiso Perduto
Cannaregio 2540, fondamenta della Misericordia (041 720 581). Vaporetto San Marcuola. **Open** 7pm-2am Mon, Thur-Sun; noon-2am Sun. Closed 2wks Aug. **No credit cards. Map** p305 B3.

Probably the most famous Venetian haunt after the legendary Harry's Bar (*see p165*), this 'Paradise Lost' is well worth finding. The colourful and chaotic mix of seafood, Sambuca and succulent sounds (often somewhat impromptu renditions of mainly jazz and blues occur most nights) comes together under the watchful eye of Maurizio: owner, chef and proud possessor of the bushiest beard in town. The restaurant serves until 11pm.

Suzie Café
Dorsoduro 1527A-B, campo San Basilio (041 522 7502). Vaporetto San Basilio. **Open** 7am-8pm Mon-Thur; 7am-1am Fri & for events. **No credit cards. Map** p306 B1.

Usually all shut up by 8pm, Suzie stays open late on Fridays from April to September to host good reggae, ska and rock gigs in the square outside.

Torino@Notte

San Marco 459, campo San Luca (041 522 3914).
Vaporetto Rialto. **Open** 7pm-1am Tue-Sat. **No**
credit cards. Map p307 A4.
This dreary daytime snack bar switches management after dark and transforms into a happening
hotspot. DJ sets and live music on Wednesdays keep
the mix of students and musos grooving to acid jazz,
fusion and funky tunes.

Vitae

San Marco 4118, calle Sant'Antonio (041 520
5205). Vaporetto Rialto. **Open** 9am-2am Mon-Fri;
5pm-2am Sat. **No credit cards. Map** p307 A3.
Known as 'Il Muro' (the wall) – for reasons that are
clear *in situ* – this tiny bar behind campo San Luca
is busy long into the night with a yuppie set who
come for cocktails, mouthwatering snacks and the
background sounds of smooth soul and acid jazz.

Zenevia

Cannaregio 5548, salizzada San Cancian (041 520
6266). Vaporetto Rialto. **Open** noon-2am Mon,
Wed-Sun. **No credit cards. Map** p305 C4.
A big success with young Venetians, this new pub
offers a good choice of beers and local wines. On
Thursdays local musicians – from novices to highly talented old hands – squeeze into the back room
to play jazz, blues and acoustic rock.

Gigs & clubs

Venice

Casanova Music Café

Cannaregio 158A, lista di Spagna (041 275 0199).
Vaporetto Ferrovia. **Open** *Internet café* 9am-4am
daily. *Club* 10pm-4am daily. **Admission** free Mon-
Thur, Sun; €10 Fri, Sat (incl 1st drink). **Credit**
AmEx, MC, V. **Map** p304 B1.
Check your email, then bop till you drop in Venice's
only real nightclub, a stone's throw from the train
station. Resident ravers, passing tourists and a few
of the club's native namesakes all get down to pop
and rock from Sunday to Thursday, Latino salsa on
Friday and commercial house on Saturday.

Round Midnight

Dorsoduro 3102, fondamenta dei Pugni (041
523 2056). Vaporetto Ca' Rezzonico. **Open** 7pm-
2am Wed-Sat. **Admission** free. **No credit cards.**
Map p306 B2.
Under new management, it remains to be seen
whether this tiny DJ bar behind campo Santa
Margherita will retain its recipe for success: no
admission charge and nightly disco and Latino
sounds that keep its minuscule dancefloor busy with
bouncing students.

Summer festivals

As soon as winter loosens its grip and
temperatures start to rise, stages are set
up in squares, parks, villas and even
shopping centres to host concerts in Venice
and the surrounding mainland area. The
following are in or near Venice, although
there are a wealth of others in the region.
Look out for the posters around town. *See*
also **Venezia Suona**, *p220.*

Marghera Village Estate

Via Orsato 9, Panorama car park, Marghera
(339 671 218/www.villagestate.it). Bus 6/
from piazzale Roma. **Dates** late June-Sept
6pm-2am daily; concerts 9.30pm. Closed
Oct-late June. **Admission** free.
No credit cards.
The longest-running and best of the area's
festivals. The Village's setting – on the only
scrap of grass amid hypermarkets – might
not be awe-inspiring, but this is where
Venetians and *mestrini* of all ages spend
their summer nights. There's free nightly
live music, comedy acts and dancing as
well as a host of bars and food stands to
keep the party going.

Festa dell'Unità

Cannaregio, campo del Ghetto or campo
dei Gesuiti (041 719 907). Vaporetto San
Marcuola or Fondamente Nove. **Dates** 1wk
mid Sept. **No credit cards. Map** p304 A2.
The once-Communist Democratici di sinistra
party has renounced Marx but retained its
annual shindig, temporarily moved out of
the Ghetto for security reasons. Every night
for a week, merry supporters, neighbours
and visitors all scramble for a seat at the
long trestle tables to consume sausage and
polenta before testing their fortune in the
lucky dip tent or finding a space in front of
the stage for the live rock, jazz and blues.

Festa di Liberazione

San Polo, campo dell'Erberia
(www.rifondazionecomunistaveneto.it).
Vaporetto Rialto. **Dates** late Aug-early Sept.
No credit cards. Map p305 C3.
Rally meets rave at Rialto for the Rifondazione
Comunista party's festival. Serious debates
and film shows are followed by big nightly
concerts with salsa, rock, blues, reggae and
world music to keep the comrades up late.

Il **Caffè**: red and relaxed. *See p210.*

A new club and live music venue whose young owners have put together a truly multicultural programme of events. Argentinian tango, Indian music nights and Senegalese parties, as well as dance and percussion lessons, all take place during the week. Saturdays are reserved for rock, indie and Britpop. Regular live concerts with a firm Britpop bias pull in the fans.

Magic Bus
Via delle Industrie 118, Marcon (041 595 2151). Venice–Trieste motorway, exit Marcon; follow signs to II zona industriale. **Open** 10pm-4am Fri, Sat. **Admission** free to ARCI club members Fri (annual membership €8 at the door); €8 Sat (incl 1 drink). **No credit cards**.
In a warehouse in the industrial area of Marcon (there's no public transport; Venetians share taxis to get here), this well-known rock club has recently branched out. The indie, rock and new wave sounds remain, while a second room now features anything from reggae and soul to '80s tunes or acid jazz on Fridays. Saturdays are devoted to garage, jungle and drum 'n' bass. The club also hosts regular live concerts featuring both Italian and international talent.

Marghera Village
See p212 **Summer festivals**.

T.A.G. Club
Via Giustizia 19, Mestre (041 921 970/tagclub @tin.it). Train to Mestre. **Open** 10pm-5am Wed-Sat. **Admission** free to members (annual membership €8). **No credit cards**.
A small but lively club just behind the train station that puts on an eclectic range of concerts. Afterwards you can strut your stuff to house/techno/rock sounds; the tunes start pumping at 2am and the joint jumps until dawn.

Al Vapore
Via Fratelli Bandiera 8, Marghera (041 930 796/ www.alvapore.it). Train to Mestre, or bus 6 or 6/ from piazzale Roma. **Open** 7am-3pm, 6pm-2am Tue-Sun. **Admission** free Tue-Fri, Sun; €10 Sat (incl 1 drink). **No credit cards**.
This live music bar just behind Mestre station has been putting on quality jazz, blues and soul concerts for years and is very active on the local music scene. Gigs by local bands are on week nights; at weekends well-known Italian and international musicians perform on the tiny stage. There's no charge at the door on Fridays, but drinks cost more. During the summer months, Al Vapore moves out to Marghera Village (*see p213*).

Jesolo

The Lido di Jesolo bus (information 041 520 5530) leaves from piazzale Roma, but it's more fun to get the 12/14 *motonave* from San Zaccaria-Paglia, on the riva degli Schiavoni, to Punta Sabbioni and bus it to Cavallino or Jesolo from there. There are regular boats making the

Mestre/Marghera

041
Via Parco Ferroviario 200, Marghera (041 538 4381). Bus 6 from piazzale Roma to 1st stop in via Trieste. **Open** 11pm-4am Fri, Sat. **Admission** €5-€7. **Credit** AmEx, DC, MC, V.
DJs spin African and Latino dance sounds on Saturdays in 041, a huge former warehouse near the Holiday Inn. There are live concerts every Friday in association with the New Age, Roncade (*see p214*).

Area Club
Via Don Tosatto 9, Mestre (041 958 000/348 360 8001). Bus 3 from Mestre. **Open** 11.30pm-4am Fri, Sat. **Admission** €11-€13 Fri; €12-€14 Sat. **Credit** DC, MC, V.
The first venue in the Venice area to specialise in hardcore techno, Area Club now serves up commercial house to a well-heeled clique of clubbers.

The Blu Rooms
Via delle Industrie 29, Marghera (335 819 0377). Bus 2, 4, 4/, 6 or 6/ from piazzale Roma. **Open** 10am-4am Fri, Sat. **Admission** €12-€14. **Credit** AmEx, MC, V.
Just over the bridge from piazza Roma, this is Venice's nearest mainland dance club. There's commercial house in the main room, plus '80s and '90s music on Fridays. On Saturdays there's a salsa room.

Jam
Via della Crusca 34, Mestre (349 3555 437/www. jamclubvenice.it). Bus 12/ or 24 from piazzale Roma. **Open** 10pm-4am Tue-Sun. **Admission** free-€15 depending on event. **No credit cards**.

Fondamenta Misericordia, one long canal-front nightspot. *See p209.*

return journey, with a change at Lido between 1am and 6am. Most of the clubs on the seaside strip open at 11pm, but nobody who's anybody shows up until 1am. If you want to save money rather than face, you can usually pick up flyers for reduced entrance before 1am.

Matilda

Via Bafile 362, Jesolo (0421 370 768). **Open** *Apr-July, late Aug-Sept* 11pm-4am Wed, Fri, Sat. *1-18 Aug* 11pm-4am daily. Closed Oct-Mar. **Admission** €25-€50. **Credit** AmEx, MC, V.

Right in the centre of the Lido di Jesolo, house, jungle and drum 'n' bass are the resident sounds inside, with an ambient chill-out zone outside. Popular with a 'been there done that' older set.

Il Muretto

Via Roma Destra 120D, Jesolo (0421 371 310/ www.ilmuretto.net). **Open** *Mar-July, Sept* 11pm-4am Wed, Fri, Sat. *Aug* 11pm-4am daily. Closed Oct-Feb. **Admission** €16-€26. **Credit** MC, V.

Jesolo's legendary club has been going for more than 40 years, yet remains super-trendy. A mass of ecstactic youth floods the open-air dancefloor for serious house spun by highly respected resident DJs and guests who are living legends in clubland: Danny Rampling, David Morales and Paul Oakenfold, to name a few. Also opens for a New Year's Eve night.

Sound Garden

Via Aleardi 18A/piazza Mazzini, Jesolo (information 338 875 2823/www.soundgardencafe.com). **Open** *Jan-Mar* 10pm-4am Sat. *Apr-Aug* 10pm-4am daily. *Sept* 10pm-4am Fri, Sat. Closed Oct-Dec. **Admission** €6-€8 (incl 1 drink). **No credit cards**.

If you're tired of techno and you've had it with house, the Sound Garden is the only real alternative in Jesolo. A variety of rock, Britpop, punk, new wave and metal is on the turntable here, and on Fridays the music is

live, except in high summer. In mid July, Magic Bus *(see p213)* DJs take over, bringing the summer Sound Bus here and playing rock and indie tunes every Friday until the end of August. If you're all rocked up, you can take a break with a game of pool.

Terrazza Mare Teatro Bar

Vicolo Faro 1, Jesolo (0421 370 012/www. terrazzamare.com). **Open** *Apr-Sept* 6pm-4am daily. **Admission** free. **No credit cards**.

By the lighthouse at the south-western end of Jesolo Lido, towards Cavallino, this once-humble beach bar is more of a cultural space than a regular club, organising live music, contemporary art exhibitions and theatre productions as well as more conventional house and ambient club nights. With free entrance, no heavy-handed bouncers or labelled dress code, the informal atmosphere attracts a mixed group of groovers, who flock in their thousands for the periodic mega-events that spill over on to the beach next door.

Further afield

New Age Club

Via Tintoretto 14, Roncade (Treviso) (0422 841 052/www.newageclub.it). Venice–Trieste motorway, exit Quarto d'Altino; follow signs for Roncade. **Open** *Sept-June* 9pm-5am Fri, Sat. **Admission** *Disco* free after 12.30am for ARCI members Fri (annual membership €8 at the door); €8 Sat (incl 1 drink). *Concerts* €10-€12. **No credit cards**.

You'll need a car to get to this out-of-the-way spot but if you're a pop, rock or metal fan it can be well worth it for some of the big acts that pass through to play on its small stage. JTQ, the Fleshtones, Gomez and The Music have been among recent guests, but if the band pulls too large a crowd, the concert moves to Marghera's 041 disco *(see p213)*. A rock disco follows the gigs.

Performing Arts

Vivaldi dominates, but he's not the whole story.

'The third feast was upon St Roches day…
where I heard the best musicke that ever I did
in all my life bothe in the morning and the
afternoone, so good that I would willingly goe
an hundred miles a foote at anytime to heare
the like.' So the ever-enthusiastic traveller
Thomas Coryat described Venice's music scene
in the early 17th century.

How Coryat would rate the classical music
on offer in Venice today is a moot point. But
if quality has slipped, quantity certainly hasn't
and the contemporary visitor needn't wait for
the feast of St Rock… there are classical
concerts daily (*see p219* **Wig out**).

Venice's theatre scene was at its most
thriving a century after Coryat passed
through. Already bumbling along nicely with
the popular *Commedia dell'arte* offerings of
playwrights Pietro Chiari and Carlo Gozzi, it
went full-throttle when the Teatro Sant'Angelo
signed up Carlo Goldoni (*see p112* **Literary
locations: Goldoni**). In the 1750-51 season
alone, he calmly rolled out 16 works.

A dramatic slump followed, out of which
Venice was slow to crawl. Even today, the
productions on offer in the city at any given
time can be counted on the fingers of one hand.
The standard of performances on offer
sometimes leaves much to be desired too; but
the growth and revamping in recent years of
small theatres mean there is more drama
approaching real avant-garde.

When they tire of the mainly mainstream
programmes of the **Teatro Carlo Goldoni**
and the much younger **Teatro Toniolo** on
the mainland, Venetians head for tiny theatres
in Mestre such as the **Teatrino della Murata**
or to the **Teatro Fondamenta Nuove**,
where contemporary dance heads the bill and
the murky territory between technology and
dramatic creation is explored.

The **Teatro a L'Avogaria** and **Teatrino
Groggia** dedicate their energies to exploring
the outer reaches of Venetian and Italian
theatre, while at the **Teatro Comunale Villa
dei Leoni** along the Brenta Canal on the
mainland (*see p243*), ancient oral storytelling
traditions have been revived and revamped.

Things improve still further in summer,
when performances abound (relatively
speaking) during the **Biennale di Venezia,
Danza-Musica-Teatro** (*see p220*).

DANCE

Dance events are limited until the summer
months when the Biennale provides
contemporary performances by the resident
Accademia Isola Danza, presided over by
Carolyn Carson, as well as work from
international choreographers. The **Teatro
Toniolo** also has contemporary dance
offerings. For something yet more cutting edge,
the **Teatro Fondamenta Nuove** specialises
in interactive and multimedia productions,
mixing technology with Terpsichore. The
seasons at the **PalaFenice** and the recently
restored **Teatro Malibran** always include
the obligatory classical ballet features.

CLASSICAL MUSIC AND OPERA

With tourists far outnumbering whatever may
be left of a local music-going public, Venice has
become a victim of its own musical tradition,
with Vivaldi stealing the show. An obvious
exception is the orchestra of **La Fenice**, which
is one of the best in the country. As well as its
opera and ballet seasons, La Fenice – under
resident conductor Marcello Viotti – has at least
two concert seasons a year at its temporary
home at the **PalaFenice** (*see p216*), a tent on
the island of Tronchetto. It offers the standard
repertoire of any large orchestra, and in recent
years has shown a penchant for 20th-century
music. Unlike other musical events in town,
La Fenice's performances attract concert-goers
from deep inside the mainland.

Venice has no concert hall and, until La
Fenice is rebuilt (December 2003 according to
the latest, probably wildly over-optimistic plan),
no opera house either. The recent reopening
after 15 years of inactivity of the **Teatro
Malibran** means, however, that the PalaFenice
does not bear the weight of all opera, ballet and
classical concerts. There are also plans to
convert the Scuola Vecchia della Misericordia
(*see p98*), an elegant 15th-century Gothic
structure in Cannaregio, but for the moment the
rebuilding of La Fenice takes precedence. This
means that most musical events take place in
churches or *scuole* (*see p60*) and occasionally
Teatro Toniolo (*see p217*).

St Mark's basilica offers fewer concerts than
it used to, and they are usually of a ceremonial
nature, with the patriarch deciding who is to
attend. But lovers of church music should catch

one of two regular Sunday appointments: the sung mass at St Mark's (10.30am) and the Gregorian chant on the island of San Giorgio (11am). Venice also has a wealth of fine 18th-century organs by master organ-builder Gaetano Callido. Three of the best can be found in the churches of San Moisè (*see p83*), San Stae (*see p111*) and San Polo (*see p105*); keep an eye out for posters announcing recitals.

THE SEASON

Venice's theatre and dance season stretches from November to June – though La Fenice (in its temporary premises) keeps on going most of the year, closing only for August – but the entertainment does not stop there.

Tourist-oriented classical music concerts are held all year, as long as there's a visitor to attend (*see p218* **Wig out**). Smaller theatre groups take advantage of the summer temperatures from June and move outdoors into Venice's open spaces (*see p220* **Festivals**). But the colder months are not without their serious attractions either: look out for concerts held throughout the city during late December in a new initiative to add some Christmas sparkle with unusual venues.

INFORMATION & TICKETS

In general, tickets can by purchased at theatre box offices immediately prior to shows; the tourist information office near piazza San Marco (*see p289*) and the VeLa office (*see p275*) sell tickets for 'serious' events; most travel agents and hotel receptions will provide tickets for classical music concerts.

For high-profile or first-night productions at such major venues as the PalaFenice, Teatro Carlo Goldoni, Teatro Malibran or the Teatro Toniolo, some highly publicised shows will sell out days or even weeks in advance: in these cases, tickets should be reserved at the theatres themselves or on their websites at least ten days before performances, and picked up – in most cases – no later than one hour before the show begins. Alternatively, book through an agency (*see p188* **Ticket agencies**).

Local newspapers *Il Gazzettino* and *La Nuova Venezia* carry listings of theatrical events, as does the bilingual monthly *Venezia News* listings magazine. Ticket prices vary according to productions.

Theatres

PalaFenice

Tronchetto island (041 786 501/box office 899 909 090/www.teatrolafenice.it). Vaporetto Tronchetto. **Open** *Box office* opens 1hr before performances; also VeLa (*see p275*). *Performances* times & days vary. **Credit** AmEx, MC, V. **Map** off p304.

This huge white tent, set up on Tronchetto island near piazzale Roma soon after the La Fenice opera house was gutted by fire in 1996, hosts classical ballet, as well as the opera and classical music season. The setting is worlds apart from the central location and gilded opulence of the old opera house, but seats are always available and it's convenient for people coming from the mainland. A special vaporetto, marked 'La Fenice', leaves for the PalaFenice from the Vallaresso vaporetto stop 45 minutes before each performance, stopping to pick up at the Zattere on the way; a normal ACTV ticket is required. Alternatively, vaporetto lines 4 and 82 leave from piazzale Roma for Tronchetto every 10 minutes. Capacity in the old Fenice was 870; in the PalaFenice it's 1,200.

Teatrino Groggia

Cannaregio 3161, Parco di Villa Groggia (041 524 4665/www.comune.venezia.it/teatrinogroggia). Vaporetto Sant Alvise or San Marcuola. **Open** *Box office* 1hr before performances. *Performances* 9pm, days vary. **No credit cards**. **Map** p304 A2.

Tucked away in the trees, this little space offers evenings of poetry, multimedia performance, concerts, dance and the occasional puppet show.

Teatro a l'Avogaria

Dorsoduro 1617, corte Zappa (041 520 6130). Vaporetto San Basilio. **Open** *Performances* 8.30pm, days vary. **No credit cards**. **Map** p306 B1.

Freshly restored, this experimental theatre (entry is by voluntary donation) was founded in 1969 by internationally renowned director Giovanni Poli. Here he continued the experimental approach he had first developed in the 1950s at Venice University's drama department – another of his own creations. Through the long years when the Teatro Carlo Goldoni was closed for restoration, Poli's theatre was the city's most important. Since his death in 1979, Poli's disciples have pressed on with the master's experiments, staging works by little-known authors from the 15th to the 19th centuries. A theatre school offers two-year courses for young actors.

Teatro Carlo Goldoni

San Marco 4650B, calle Goldoni (041 240 2011/ www.teatrostabileveneto.it). Vaporetto Rialto. **Open** *Box office* 10am-1pm, 3-7pm Mon-Sat; 1hr before performances. *Performances* 8.30pm Mon-Wed, Fri, Sat; 4pm Thur, Sun. **Credit** MC, V. **Map** p307 A4.

Based in Venice's most beautiful theatre, the Goldoni's Teatro Stabile di Venezia company serves up Venetian classics by Ruzante, Chiari, Selvatico and Gallina, as well as those by Goldoni himself. But its repertoire doesn't stop there: in the 19th century, plays by Pirandello and D'Annunzio premièred here; today, some of Italy's leading directors stage works by big contemporary names. The Goldoni – which over the years has been called the San Luca, the Vendramin di San Salvador and the Apollo – was given its current name in 1875 to honour Venice's most famous literary son. The teetering structure

Arts & Entertainment

There's no shortage of Vivaldi in costume.

of this and of even older buildings were uncovered during the recent restoration. In the 17th century, this was the first of Venice's theatres to throw its doors open for anyone who could afford a ticket, rather than to the patrician class exclusively. This, however, didn't stop San Giovanni Grisostomo being a key meeting place for the elegant aristocracy and foreign visitors. When, in the 17th to 18th centuries, other theatres were bringing ticket prices down to fill seats, this one remained resolutely and expensively elitist. In 1835 the theatre was renamed as a mark of gratitude to Maria Garcia Malibran, one of the most famous singers of the time, who performed there refusing payment. When La Fenice was destroyed by fire in 1996, the Malibran became more indispensable than ever. Reopened in May 2002 after a 15-year facelift, it now shares the classical music, ballet and opera season with the PalaFenice; the atmosphere is less circus-like, but both the Malibran and the tent are a far cry from the opera house they substitute.

Further afield

Teatrino della Murata
*Via Giordano Bruno 19, Mestre (041 989 879/
www.teatromurata.it). Bus 2 from piazzale Roma,
get off at via Einaudi.* **Open** *Box office* 30mins
before performances. *Performances* 9pm Mon-Sat;
5pm, 9pm Sun. **No credit cards**.
The tiny Murata (60 seats) is situated in a former warehouse under the remains of the ancient city walls. Funded by the city and regional councils, it specialises in multicultural theatre, and provides a venue for new actors and local theatre companies.

Teatro Comunale Villa dei Leoni
*Via Don Minzoni 26, Mira (041 426 6545/www.
teatrovilladeileoni.it). Bus 53 from piazzale Roma.*
Open *Box office* 10am-1pm, 3-6pm Tue, Thur, Fri;
also VeLa (*see p275*). *Performances* 4pm, 9pm, days
vary. **No credit cards**.
Located in Mira, a small town on the Brenta Canal, this theatre focuses on upbeat productions for a younger audience, under the guiding hand of experimental writer-director-minstrel Marco Paolini, who has a huge following in Italy thanks to his (televised) one-man shows on socially committed topics.

Teatro del Parco
*Via Gori 8, Mestre (041 534 7920/www.
culturaspettacolovenezia.it/comune).* **Open** *Box office*
9am-12.30pm Mon-Fri for musical events; otherwise
1hr before performances. *Performances* times and
days vary. **No credit cards**.
As well as music, contemporary theatre and dance, Teatro del Parco often has interpretations of classic fairytales for children on Sunday evenings.

Teatro Toniolo
*Piazzetta Battisti 1, Mestre (041 274 9070/box office
041 971 666/www.comune.venezia.it/teatrotoniolo).
Bus 2, 7, 9 from piazzale Roma, get off at the*

was closed down after World War II and given a thorough overhaul before reopening in 1979. Youth theatre projects, readings, poetry afternoons and musical performances are also organised.

Teatro Fondamenta Nuove
*Cannaregio 5013, fondamenta Nuove (041 522
4498). Vaporetto Fondamente Nove.* **Open** *Box
office* 1hr before performances. *Performances* 9pm,
days vary. **No credit cards**. **Map** p304 B4.
Opened in 1993 in an old joiners' shop, the Fondamenta Nuove stages contemporary dance and avant-garde performances, and organises film festivals, symposiums, exhibitions and workshops. Experimental events exploring the relationship between artistic creativity and technology are held as part of its ongoing Art and Technology project.

Teatro Malibran
*Cannaregio 5873, calle dei Milion (041 786 603/box
office 899 909 090/www.teatrolafenice.it). Vaporetto
Rialto.* **Box office** 1hr before performances; also
VeLa (*see p275*). *Performances* 3.30pm Sat, Sun; 8pm,
days vary. **Credit** AmEx, MC, V. **Map** p304 C4.
Inaugurated in 1678 as Teatro San Giovanni Grisostomo, this 900-seater was built on the site where Marco Polo's family palazzo stood; sections

Arts & Entertainment

Finally reopened: **Teatro Malibran**. *See p217.*

hospital. **Open** *Box office* 11am-12.30pm, 5-7.30pm Tue-Sun. *Performances* 4.30pm Sun; 9pm, days vary. **Credit** MC, V.

Due to reopen by Christmas 2002 after restoration, the Teatro Toniolo in Mestre was founded in 1913. Since being taken over by the local council in 1997, it has served up a varied assortment of performances, ranging from vernacular favourites to contemporary plays, new stagings of Italian and foreign classics, cabaret, contemporary music concerts, and contemporary dance and ballet.

Churches & *scuole*

For information on musical events in Venice's churches, check the local press. *See also below* **Wig out**.

Basilica dei Frari

San Polo, campo dei Frari (041 719 308). Vaporetto San Tomà. **Map** p304 C2.

The lofty Gothic Frari (*see also p113*) is the biggest church in Venice after St Mark's and one of the best venues for catching high-standard performances of

Wig out

As long as there are pigeons in St Mark's square there will be Vivaldi pouring out of churches and *scuole*, and for many visitors a shot of Vivaldi is as quintessential a Venetian experience as being snapped while feeding the winged predators.

The recent proliferation of musicians playing in 18th-century costume is confirmation – if it were needed – that many of the musical events in Venice are little more than a quick fix for the visitor. But this doesn't mean it's all bad: if the quality of performers ranges from very average to good (including anyone from unpromising music students to professionals), the venues can be pure magic.

If your heart is set on wigs and silk-acetate, you won't have to stroll far from San Marco. Head for the Scuola di San Teodoro where **I Musici Veneziani** dish up Vivaldi every Wednesday, Friday and Sunday and a medley of opera arias on Tuesday and Saturday. On the lagoon-front riva degli Schiavoni, the **Centro di Co-ordinamento Culturale** fields three ensembles in the church of Santa Maria della Visitazione (aka La Pietà) where Vivaldi was choir master: the 12-strong string orchestra I Virtuosi di Venezia; and two costumed all-female groups, Le Venexiane and Le Putte di Vivaldi. Instrument-playing cherubs peer

down on the audience from a Tiepolo ceiling. Meanwhile, San Giacometto, one of Venice's oldest churches, hosts concerts by the **Ensemble Antonio Vivaldi** and the **Collegium Ducale** performs in the lovely church of Santa Maria Formosa.

Just because musicians are wearing costumes doesn't necessarily mean they're incompetent... however some groups spare their musicians the mortification. At performances by the **Orchestra di Venezia** – resident at Scuola Grande San Giovanni Evangelista and Palazzo Zenobio – the only baroque attire belongs to the dancers, who perform popular 18th-century numbers such as the *minuet* and the *piva*. Even more serious is the recently formed **Accademia di San Rocco**, which gives regular concerts of 18th-century music on period instruments in the Tintoretto-filled halls of the *scuola* itself. And, for highly professional renditions of Vivaldi, look no further than the church of San Vidal, where the no-frills **Interpreti Veneziani** plays several times a week.

Accademia di San Rocco

Via Ca' Venier 8, Mestre (041 962 999/www. musicinvenice.com). **Venue** Scuola Grande di San Rocco *(see p115).* **Box office** at venue 10.30am-4pm the day before concerts; from

Arts & Entertainment

sacred music. It has regular seasons in the autumn and spring, organ recitals (the church boasts three organs: two single keyboard 18th-century instruments and a 1928 Mascioni hidden behind the high altar) and a number of free or low-cost afternoon concerts, especially over Christmas and the New Year, sponsored by the local paper *Il Gazzettino*. If you go to one of the winter concerts, wrap up warm, as the church is not heated.

Santa Maria della Visitazione (La Pietà)

Castello, riva degli Schiavoni (041 522 6405/www. vivaldi.it). Vaporetto San Zaccaria. **Map** p308 B2.
Built alongside the charitable *ospedale* foundation for orphan girls where Vivaldi taught, this church (*see also p91*) is proportioned with an eye and an ear for music-making, but the excellent acoustics are not generally exploited to their full potential by the prettily costumed groups that perform arranged around the high altar. In the days of the *ospedale*, it was the sound experience that counted: Vivaldi's renowned choir could be heard but not seen as it sang from behind wrought-iron grilles in the gallery.

Scuola Grande di San Giovanni Evangelista

San Polo 2454, campiello della Scuola (041 718 234). Vaporetto San Tomà. **Map** p304 C2.
This 14th-century *scuola* with an imposing marble staircase has in recent years been the venue for an interesting series of chamber music concerts. It is also the venue for concerts by the costumed baroque outfit, Orchestra di Venezia (041 522 8125).

Scuola Grande di San Rocco

San Polo, campo San Rocco (041 523 4864/ www.sanroccofestival.com). Vaporetto San Tomà. **Map** p304 C2.
The Scuola Grande di San Rocco is best known for its magnificent interior decoration by Tintoretto (*see p89*) but it also boasts an unbroken musical tradition stretching back over half a millennium; the director of music at St Mark's was also *ex officio* director at San Rocco. The 16th-century composer Giovanni Gabrieli was organist here for 27 years, and Monteverdi also had a long association with the *scuola*. In 1958 a choral work by Stravinsky, *Threni*, had its world première here.

8.15pm on performance days. **Performances** 9pm, days vary. **Tickets** 20- 30; 25- 15 concessions. **No credit cards. Map** p304 C2.

Centro di Co-ordinamento Culturale

Via Forte Gazzera 11, Mestre (041 917 257/ www.vivaldi.it). **Venue** Santa Maria della Visitazione (*see p91*). **Box office** at venue 11am-1pm, 4.30-7pm Mon, Wed-Sun. **Performances** 9pm (winter 8.30pm) Mon, Wed, Fri, Sat. **Tickets** 25; 13 concessions. **Credit** MC, V. **Map** p308 B1.

Collegium Ducale

Santa Maria Formosa, Castello, campo Santa Maria Formosa (041 984 252/ www.collegiumducale.com). Vaporetto Rialto. **Box office** at venue from 10.30am on perforance days. **Performances** 9pm, days vary. **Tickets** 25; 20 concessions. **No credit cards. Map** p305 C4.

Ensemble Antonio Vivaldi

Chiesa di San Giacometto, San Polo, campo di San Giacometto (041 426 6559/www. prgroup.it). Vaporetto Rialto. **Box office** at venue from 11am on performance days. **Performances** 8.45pm Wed, Fri, Sun. **Tickets** 18.50; 15.50 concessions. **Credit** MC, V. **Map** p305 C3.

Interpreti Veneziani

San Vidal, San Marco 2862B, campo San Vidal (041 277 0561/www. interpretiveneziani.com). Vaporetto Accademia. **Box office** at venue 10am-8pm Mon-Sat; 10am-6pm Sun. **Performances** 9pm Mon-Sat (8.30pm in winter). **Tickets** 21; 16 concessions. **Credit** MC, V. **Map** p307 B3.

I Musici Veneziani

Scuola Grande di San Teodoro, San Marco 4810, salizzada San Teodoro (041 521 0294/www.imusicveneziani.com). Vaporetto Rialto. **Box office** at venue 10am-7pm daily. **Performances** 9pm Tue, Wed, Fri-Sun. **Tickets** 21- 31; 16- 26 concessions. **No credit cards. Map** p307 A4.

Orchestra di Venezia

Scuola Grande San Giovanni Evangelista, San Polo 2454, campiello della scuola (041 522 8125/www.orchestradivenezia.it). Vaporetto Riva di Biasio. **Map** p304 C2. *Palazzo Zenobio, Dorsoduro 2596, fondamenta del Soccorso (041 522 8770). Vaporetto Ca' Rezzonico.* **Map** p306 A1. **Box office** at Scuola 9am-7pm on performance days. **Performances** 8.30pm, days vary. **Tickets** 31; 21 concessions; free under-10s. **Credit** MC, V. **Map** p304 C2.

Arts & Entertainment

Other music venues

Fondazione Querini Stampalia

*Castello 5252, campo Santa Maria Formosa
(041 271 1411/www.querinistampalia.it).
Vaporetto Rialto.* **Performances** 5pm, 8.30pm Fri,
Sat. **Tickets** €6; €4 concessions. **Credit** MC, V.
Map p308 A1.

Offering more of a *divertissement* than a full-scale
concert, the soirées that are organised by this enter-
prising museum and cultural foundation take the
form of a half-hour recital of lesser-known (usually
Renaissance or baroque) works.

Festivals

For the cash-strapped traveller, the summer
months in Venice offer a variety of drama and
live music free of charge, as events are as much
for locals as for visitors. With the advent of
warm weather, dramatically lit performances
get under way in *campi* and courtyards. The
only possible disadvantage to outdoor
entertainment in Venice is that the urban
backdrop tends to distract one's attention from
what's going on on stage. On the other hand,
given that standards of productions vary
greatly, this is not always a bad thing.

Free festivals include **Venezia Suona**,
where live music of every variety floods the city
on the third or fourth Sunday in June. Reggae,
jazz, rock, electronic and gospel are a few of
the sounds that spill out of all bars and *campi*
possible from 4pm, until noise restrictions kill
the party at around 11pm. **Giardini d'Estate**
consoles the Venetians as summer ends with
music (generally ageing Italian rock bands)
and ethnic stalls among the trees of the Giardini
(*see p90*) in Castello.

The **Teatro in Campo** festival graces
campo Pisani near the Accademia during
August, with good-quality drama and opera.
The Teatro in Campo programme also includes
free performances on the islands of the lagoon
(Pellestrina, Giudecca and Murano).

Festival Galuppi, from late August to
October, is dedicated to the Venetian composer
Baldassarre Galuppi. It's an opportunity to hear
18th-century classical music in venues that are
otherwise inaccessible, such as the islands of
San Giorgio, San Servolo, San Francesco del
Deserto and Lazzaretto Nuovo; Vivaldi doesn't
even get a look in.

In a brave attempt to revive the
contemporary scene, the **Biennale di
Venezia** has allotted new funds to its dance,
music and theatre department. The programme
remains restricted to the summer months, but
what there is takes place in interesting newly
restored venues: the **Teatro Tese** – an open-
air space for 500 people – and the smaller
Teatro Piccolo Arsenale, both inside
the Arsenale (*see p90*) and open only for
Biennale performances.

In November, Wagner is the star of a series
of world-class concerts organised by the
Associazione R Wagner; the **Giornate
Wagneriane** also include conferences on the
great man, and visits to the house he occupied
while in Venice. In December, the **Premio
Venezia** international solo pianist competition
culminates – after closed-doors auditions and
heats – in final concerts on the 6 and 7
December by prize winners, held at the
PalaFenice with tickets available through
the Fondazione Teatro La Fenice.

For information on **Natale a Venezia**
and **Giardini d'Estate** contact local tourist
offices (*see p289*).

Biennale di Venezia, Danza-Musica-Teatro

*Ca' Giustinian, San Marco 1364A, calle del Ridotto
(041 521 8711/www.labiennale.org). Vaporetto
Vallaresso.* **Venues** around the city. **Box office**
VeLa (*see p275*). **Date** June-Oct. **Map** p307 B4.

Le Giornate Wagneriane

*Associazione R Wagner, c/o Associazione Culturale
Italo-Tedesca, Palazzo Albrizzi, Cannaregio 4118,
fondamenta Sant' Andrea (041 523 2544).*
Venues Palazzo Albrizzi; Fondazione Cini (Isola
di San Giorgio, vaporetto San Giorgio); Fondazione
Levi (San Marco 2893, calle Giustiniani, vaporetto
Accademia or San Samuele). **Box office** (at Palazzo
Albrizzi) 9.30am-12.30pm Mon-Fri. **Date** 17 Nov-30
Dec. **Map** p305 B4.

Premio Venezia

*Fondazione Teatro La Fenice, PalaFenice,
Tronchetto island (041 786 501/www.teatro
lafenice.it). Vaporetto Tronchetto.* **Box office**
tickets from Fondazione Teatro La Fenice; also
VeLa (*see p275*). **Date** 6-7 Dec. **Map** off p304.

Teatro in Campo

*Pantakin da Venezia, Giudecca 218, fondamenta
San Giacomo (041 277 0407/www.pantakin.it).*
Venue campo Pisani, vaporetto Accademia. **Box
office** (campo Pisani) from 6pm on performance
days; also VeLa (*see p275*). **Performances** 9pm,
days vary. **Date** Aug-Sept. **Map** p307 B3.

Venezia Suona

*Cannaregio 3546, fondamenta dell'Abbazia (041
275 0049/veneziasuona.it).* **Venues** around the
city. **Date** 3rd or 4th Sun in June.
Concerts are free.

Festival Galuppi

*San Marco 3972, calle Sant'Andrea (041 522
1120/www.culturaspettacolovenezia.it).* **Venues**
around the city. **Box office** at venues 2hrs before
performance; also VeLa (*see p275*). **Performances**
4pm & 8.45pm, days vary. **Date** Aug-Oct.

Sport & Fitness

Boat races on the canals and a football ground on an island.

Few cities force their inhabitants to exert themselves – covering miles on foot each day, climbing and descending innumerable flights of steps – as Venice does. Venetians' longevity and general good health into old age is testament to the success of this enforced fitness regime. However, a vaporetto trip across the lagoon will reveal what Venetians like doing best in their leisure hours: rowing around their watery backyard.

Other Venetian sports have fallen into disuse: massive tugs-of-war or competitions to build the biggest human pyramids were comparatively harmless, but boxing matches that began with two contestants often ended up involving whole *sestieri*. *Massa e pindolo* was a form of Venetian baseball, *cimbani* a local obstacle race, and *tacco* a kind of bowls played with stray heels purchased from cobblers' shops; the *tauromachia* – bullfight – in campo San Polo provided the goriest entertainment.

Unlike their landlocked counterparts, traditional water-borne competitions have stood the test of time. The **Regata Storica** (*see p196*) has been going strong since the 15th century and is just one of Venice's many water events that still succeeds in capturing the public imagination.

TAKING TO THE WATER

Among the reeds and mosquitoes of the lagoon, two activities dominate: Venetian rowing (*voga alla veneta*) and three-sail sailing (*vela al terzo*). Courses in both are available from some of the clubs listed below.

In **voga alla veneta** the rower stands up, facing the direction of travel. There are various types of *voga alla veneta* – team-rowing is one, and the impressive solo, cross-handed, two-oar method known as *voga alla valesana* is another. But the most famous type is *voga ad un solo remo* (one-oar rowing) – one of the most difficult rowing strokes of all – as practised by Venetian gondoliers. Most other forms of rowing rely on pairs of oars, whereas the gondolier only ever puts his oar in the water on the right side of the boat where it rests in a *forcola*, an elaborate walnut-wood rowlock. Pushing on the oar has the obvious effect of making the craft turn to the left. The trick consists in using the downstroke to correct the direction. It has been calculated that a gondolier uses up no more energy rowing a half-ton

gondola with three passengers than the average person expends in walking... though that doesn't quite explain why they all have such Schwarzenegger-sized biceps.

Vela al terzo was once the means of transporting goods for trade throughout the length and breadth of Venice's Adriatic dominions. But the traditional Venetian wooden flat-bottomed sailing craft is now to be found only in the lagoon, being used exclusively for pleasure and sport. Depending upon their length, these boats can hoist one or two square sails, plus the classic triangular jib. They can also be rowed in the traditional standing-up position.

ROWING RACES

There are more than 120 regattas in the lagoon each year, most of them involving Venetian rowing. The most sumptuous is the **Regata Storica** on the first Sunday in September. The regatta is much more than the extravagant pageant of tourist brochures: rowers of all ages in craft of various classes compete for glory and prizes. Perhaps even more spectacular is the **Vogalonga**, with a 32-kilometre (20-mile) route around Venice and the northern lagoon. Held in May (*see p195*), it is open to anyone who can get their hands on a boat of any kind and an oar or two. Thousands do. For a taste of history, catch the ceremonial wedding of Venice to the sea on Ascension Day (La Sensa). This is followed by a gondola regatta in which the major rowing clubs compete in multicoloured vessels.

Boating

Canottiere Giudecca

Giudecca 259, fondamenta Ponte Lungo (041 528 7409). Vaporetto Palanca. **Open** 2.30-7.30pm Mon; 9am-12.30pm, 2.30-7.30pm Tue-Sat; 9am-12.30pm Sun. **Rates** enrolment €26; insurance €5; €156 yearly membership; €6 per lesson. **No credit cards**. **Map** p306 C2.

One of the major advantages of this club is that beginners can put their seamanship to the test in the relatively tranquil waters of the lagoon behind the Giudecca. Friendly experienced rowers offer individual lessons. Options include Venetian rowing in *mascareta* (small, sporty gondola-like craft), canoes and sailboats, plus use of the gym. Hours vary in winter depending on fog and daylight.

Not just pomp and splendour at the **Regata Storica**. *See p221*.

Reale Società Canottieri Bucintoro

Dorsoduro 10, 15 & 261, Zattere (041 522 2055/520 5630/523 7933/www.bucintoro.org). Vaporetto Zattere or Salute. **Open** *Office* 2-4pm Tue, Fri. *Lessons* 9am-5pm Tue-Sat; 9am-1pm Sun. **Rates** €41 enrolment; €52 8 rowing lessons; €181 (non-members), €129 (members) sailing course. **No credit cards**. **Map** p307 C3-4.

Founded in 1882, the Reale Società Canottieri Bucintoro is one of the oldest sports clubs in Italy, and holds a slew of Olympic rowing records. The club offers canoeing, kayaking and Venetian rowing, plus a well-equipped gym.

Remiera Canottieri Cannaregio

Cannaregio 732, calle della Cereria (041 720 539). Vaporetto Tre Archi. **Open** 3-7pm Mon-Sat; 8.30am-12.30pm Sun. **Rates** €26 enrolment; €7 membership per mth; individual lessons by arrangement. **No credit cards**. **Map** off p304 A1.

Beginners' *voga alla veneta* courses by arrangement. This club around the back of the station is one of the friendliest of the lot, and in Giorgio Costantini it has one of the best instructors on the lagoon. There's a well-equipped gym too.

Società Canottiere Francesco Querini

Cannaregio 6576D, Fondamenta Nove (041 522 2039). Vaporetto Ospedale. **Open** noon-6pm Mon; 8am-7pm Tue-Sat; 8am-1pm Sun. **Rates** €25 enrolment fee; €45 10 lessons. **No credit cards**. **Map** p308 A2.

Venice's second-oldest boat club, the Querini now boasts a well-equipped gym too. The club offers rowing, canoeing and Venetian rowing.

Cycling

Cycling is not allowed in Venice and, frankly, is not much fun with a bridge to lug your bike over every 50 metres. However, it is possible – and enjoyable – to hire bikes on the (completely flat) Lido.

Bruno Lazzari

Gran Viale 21B, Lido (041 526 8019). **Open** *Mar-Sept* 8am-8pm daily. *Oct-Feb* 8.30am-1pm, 3-7.30pm daily. **Rates** €3 per hr for the first 3hrs; €9 per day (8am-8pm); €42 per wk; €52 2wks-1mth. **Credit** MC, V.

Some form of ID must be left with this Lido shop that staff keep for the entire hire period. Payment is taken on return of the bike.

Fishing

Fishing is another quintessential Venetian pastime. With all this water about, what better way to ponder on the wonders you've seen about town? Anglers can fish just about anywhere, with the Giardini embankment and the Zattere being two popular haunts. Angling needs can be satisfied at **Nautica & Pesca** (San Polo 3138, campiello San Rocco, 041 520 0617, www.ferramentadeluca.com), which offers everything from lugworms to thermal wellies, but as yet tackle is not for hire.

However, if you've been knocking back the hard stuff at Hemingway's old watering hole (*see* **Harry's Bar**, *p165*) and envisage yourself battling it out with the big boys on the high seas, get in touch with **Big Game Fishing**

(Sant'Elena, 13 campo Stringari, 041 528 5123, www.biggamesportfishing.it). Staff will rig you out and escort you on to the Adriatic. Smaller catches such as sea bass are the norm but tuna, shark and other monsters of the deep are the real quarry. Day trips cost €100 per person (maximum six people, novices welcome) and staff prefer a week's notice. No credit cards.

Football

For landlubbers, Venice offers a few sporting activities, with football at the top of the league. Despite the dearth of playing fields or anything remotely resembling a grass pitch, Venetians are just as *calcio*-crazed as the Milanese or the Neapolitans. Kids kick balls around a campo once school is out; come Sunday afternoon, supporters jump into their boats or board a vaporetto and sail off to the football stadium at Sant'Elena – the only league ground in Europe to be entirely surrounded by water.

The opposing team's supporters are met from the train, herded on to their own steamer and transported across the lagoon like a bunch of convicts heading off to Alcatraz.

For years, Venice bobbed up and down between the second and third divisions of the Italian league. Then, much to everyone's surprise, they limped back to Serie A in 1998 after an absence of 31 years, to remain there for only two measly seasons. Venezia's home matches take place on alternate Saturdays or Sundays from September to June. Tickets cost from €15 and are on sale at the ground, at main ACTV and VeLa (*see p275*) ticket offices, and at two branches of the Banca Antoniana Popolare Veneta: San Marco 5400, campo San Bartolomeo and Cannaregio 3682, strada Nuova. For further information check the club's website www.veneziacalcio.it.

Golf

Circolo Golf Venezia
Strada Vecchia 1, Alberoni-Lido (041 731 333/ http://digilander.libero.it/circologolfvenezia). Vaporetto Lido, then bus B to Alberoni. **Open** *Oct-Mar* 8.30am-6pm Tue-Sun. *Apr-Sept* 8am-8pm Tue- Sun. **Rates** €50 Tue-Fri; €60 Sat, Sun. **Credit** AmEx, DC, MC, V. **Map** p311.
Considered one of Italy's top ten courses, the Lido links have three practice courses as well as an 18-hole one. It is open to non-members, though only to those golfers with proof of membership of golf clubs elsewhere.

Gyms

The rowing clubs listed in this chapter (*see p221-2*) also have gyms.

Palestra Club Delfino
Dorsoduro 788A, Zattere (041 523 2763/www. palestradelfino.com). Vaporetto Zattere. **Open** 9am-10pm Mon-Fri; 9am-noon Sat. **Rates** €13 per day; €44 per wk; €112 per mth. **Credit** AmEx, DC, MC, V. **Map** p306 B2.
Equipped with two fully computerised Technogym fitness rooms, a solarium and massage services. Bring a fitness certificate signed by your doctor.

Eutonia Club
Dorsoduro 3656, calle Renier (041 522 8618/www. eutonia.net). Vaporetto San Tomà or Ca'Rezzonico. **Open** 10am-10pm Mon-Fri; 10am-1pm Sat. **Rates** €28 annual enrolment; €60 10 1hr sessions (valid 3mths); €35 per hr with a personal trainer; €295 for 10hrs. **No credit cards. Map** p306 A2.
This brand-new gym has three well-illuminated rooms and friendly staff to put you through your paces. Courses on offer at Eutonia range from cardio circuit to belly dancing.

Running

Deserted Venetian streets in the early morning are best for a jog. Most runners head for the wider stretches of pavement on the Zattere, on the fondamenta by the Giardini vaporetto stop, or further east under the umbrella pines of Sant'Elena. The Lido has long stretches of beach and well-paved roads offering a less knee-shattering experience than Venetian stone.

The **Venice Marathon** takes place in October, usually on the fourth Sunday of the month. The starting line for this 42-kilometre (26-mile) run is at the Villa Pisani

Arts & Entertainment

at Strà (*see p243*); the race passes along the banks of the Brenta Canal, over the road bridge to Venice, then by a specially erected pontoon over the lagoon to the finishing line on the riva degli Schiavoni. For more information, call 041 940 644 or go via the website at www.venicemarathon.it.

The less competitive **Su e Zo Per i Ponti** (*see p195*) takes place in spring in island Venice and involves desperate-looking runners getting lost all over the city.

Swimming

The sea water around Venice is not immensely appetising, although locals in their thousands brave the Adriatic and come to no harm. For public beaches, *see chapter* **The Lido to Chioggia**. There are two public swimming pools in the city, with bizarre timetables offering few possibilities for a spontaneous quick dip. All swimmers have to wear swimming caps in the water, and flip flops for the journey from changing room to pool.

Piscina Comunale Sant'Alvise
Cannaregio 3163, calle del Capitello (041 713 567). Vaporetto Sant'Alvise. **Open** 1-2.30pm, 9.30-10.15pm Mon, Wed, Fri; 3-4.15pm Tue, Thur; 3-4pm, 5.45-7pm Sat; 10am-noon Sun. **Rates** €4.50 per session; €38 10 sessions (valid 3mths). **No credit cards**.

The newest pool in town, set in the peaceful grounds of Villa Groggia, offers courses for all, from ante-natal classes to aqua-gym, with a warm mini-pool for tots and lazy adults. The pool's open daily from 9am to 10.30pm; non-course dips can be taken at the hours given above.

Piscina Comunale Sacca Fisola
Giudecca, San Biagio-Sacca Fisola (041 528 5430). Vaporetto Sacca Fisola. **Open** 10.30am-noon, 1-2.30pm Mon, Thur; 10.30am-noon, 1-2.30pm, 6.30-7.15pm Tue, Fri; 3.45-5pm Wed; 3.45-5pm, 6.30-8pm Sat; 3-6pm Sun. **Rates** €4.50 per session; €38 10 sessions (valid 3mths). **No credit cards**.

Situated in a council estate where a waste dump once stood, this pool is for serious swimmers (no mini-pool for small fry here). It's open daily from 9am to 10.30pm; hours given above are for 'free' swimming.

Tennis

Tennis Club Ca' Del Moro
Via Ferruccio Parri 6, Lido (041 770 965). Vaporetto Lido, then Bus V. **Open** 8.30am-8.30pm Mon-Sat; 8.30am-8pm Sun. **Rates** €8.25 per hr per person; €8.52 per court for 4 people for 90mins. **Pool** €10 half-day; €15 full day. **No credit cards**. This sports centre is equipped with ten tennis courts. Other facilities at the Tennis Club Ca' Del Moro include a gym, a swimming pool and pool rooms, as well as football pitches.

Chill out *alla veneta*

If you came to Venice to relax, why not do it properly and get your head (and back) straight with a bit of yoga? New yoga fads may sprout like mushrooms in an Alpine forest, but Venetians prefer the more traditional iyengar yoga. Deriving from hatha yoga, iyengar concentrates on breathing and posture. Though not as energetic-looking as the more dynamic astanga, an iyengar session at **Yoga Studio di Paola Venturini** will still put you through your paces.

Right the effects of a year spent slouching over your computer with a bit of Feldenkrais, a method that aims to alter bad postural habits and overcome limitations of movement brought about by stress, accident or general slobbiness through altering the way we move. A practitioner guides you verbally or by touch, helping you develop awareness, flexibility and co-ordination. Individual and group lessons are available with **Paolo Camia**.

And if you're thoroughly exhausted after traipsing around monuments all day, it could be that your energy channels are blocked; the best way to get them back up and running is shiatsu. This Japanese finger-pressure therapy claims to sort out problems as diverse as sports injuries and depression... not just culture-glut. Ex PE teacher **Cristina Gemin** is an experienced qualified shiatsu practitioner.

Yoga Studio di Paola Venturini
San Polo 2006, campo San Polo (041 528 9946/paolaventurini@tiscalinet.it). **Rates** 15 for 2hr session (max 12 to a group); private lessons by arrangement. **No credit cards**. **Map** p304 C2.

Paolo Camia
Santa Croce 901A, fondamenta Marin (041 524 5373/www.feldenkraisstudio.it). **Rates** 50 for 50min individual lessons; 10 per person for group lessons. **No credit cards**. **Map** p304 C2.

Cristina Gemin
Santa Croce 3707, campo San Pantalon (041 28 6154). **Rates** 25 per hr. **No credit cards**. **Map** p304 C1.

The Veneto

Getting Started

The Veneto has hills, mountains and beaches – and art and architecture too.

So overwhelming is the allure of Venice that it's easy to forget that the lagoon city is just the tip of the iceberg that is the Veneto region. And though it's a high-profile tip, the city simply doesn't cover all bases: Venice has no medieval paintings to match Giotto's frescos in the Scrovegni Chapel (*see p236* **The Scrovegni Chapel & Museo Civico**) in **Padua**, no civic Renaissance interiors quite as perfect as Palladio's Teatro Olimpico (*see p261*) in **Vicenza**, and no Romanesque churches to match San Zeno (*see p252*) in **Verona** – to say nothing of Verona's fine bevy of Roman remains.

Moreover, Venice – that most urban of cities – has little to offer in the way of landscape: for that you'll need to cross to the mainland. And if the Veneto region's natural beauties were never as striking as, say, Tuscany's, the environmental ravages of the economic miracle (*see chapter* **Venice Today**) have spared some lovely, untouched and under-visited corners, particularly in the hills and mountains. The Colli Euganei beyond Padua, and the Colli Berici south of Vicenza roll pleasantly above the industrial sprawl, dotted with their share of those Palladian villas (*see chapter* **Palladian Villas**) that pop up in the unlikeliest places in the region. Alternatively, the flat, reed-fringed waterscapes of the wildfowl-filled **Po Delta** on the southern border of the Veneto provide endless scope for messing around in boats, or on bicycles.

Further north, mountains loom and the scene changes. Still on the plain, **Treviso** has frescoed *palazzi* and an economic vitality – of which the Benetton empire is the most famous flag-bearer – that gives the town a lively, dynamic feel. In the gentle foothills of the Dolomites are the wine-producing centres of **Conegliano** and **Valdobbiadene**; **Asolo** and **Possagno,** given up respectively to the leisured laziness of *il dolce far niente* (literally, sweet doing nothing) and the cold neoclassical visions of Antonio Canova; and **Bassano del Grappa**, home of the fiery spirit that keeps the *veneti* going through those foggy winter evenings (and mornings, come to that).

Beyond **Belluno** the mountains begin in earnest, bringing hordes of *beau monde* skiers to the elegant resort of **Cortina d'Ampezzo** and queues of summer hikers to attempt one of the seven *alte vie* (high-altitude footpaths) that traverse the Dolomites.

Heading north-east from Venice, a straggle of seaside resorts with high-density beach umbrellas, campsites and discos stretches from **Lido di Jesolo** to the border of the Veneto. Beyond here, in the region of Friuli-Venezia Giulia, are the twin pulls of **Aquileia** – a tiny village with a glorious Roman past – and **Grado,** one of the pleasantest of the northern Adriatic resorts, with a quiet, island-studded lagoon of its own.

Getting around

By train

For general information on Italian trains, *see chapter* **Directory: Getting Around**.

Padua (journey time 30 minutes), Vicenza (55 minutes) and Verona (85 minutes) are all connected to Venice by frequent fast Intercity or Eurostar trains on the Venice–Milan–Turin line. Padua is where the line to Bologna

Treviso has canals too.

The Veneto

branches off, with around one fast train
an hour during the day stopping at Rovigo
(55 minutes) and Ferrara (75 minutes) along
the way; slower *interregionali* trains also
stop at smaller towns such as Monselice
(53 minutes). From the latter, the branch line
to Mantua serves the stations of Este (12
minutes from Monselice) and Montagnana
(35 minutes from Monselice), though it's a
good idea to study the timetable carefully as
these trains are infrequent.

Heading north from Venice is less
straightforward. Treviso (20-30 minutes)
and Conegliano (40-50 minutes) are on the
main line from Venice to Udine, served mainly
by *interregionale* trains. To the north-west,
Castelfranco Veneto (40 minutes) and Bassano
del Grappa (60 minutes) are served by a local
line with around 15 trains a day. Around seven
local trains a day make the agonisingly slow
but very pretty haul up the Piave valley from
Padua to Feltre (90 minutes) and Belluno (two
hours); some proceed beyond to Calalzo-Pieve
di Cadore (three hours), which is connected by
bus to Cortina d'Ampezzo (see www.dolomiti
superski.it for further travel information).

There are buses from Grado and Aquileia to
the station of Cervignano, which is on the main
Venice–Trieste line (85 minutes).

By bus

Italian long-distance buses are usually neither
as frequent, cheap or relaxing as the train. An
exception is on mountain routes, where they are
often the only mode of public transport in
existence. The ski resort of Cortina d'Ampezzo,
for example, is easiest to reach by the ATVO
(041 520 5530) bus, which leaves from piazzale
Roma at 7.50am on Saturdays and Sundays
only; the journey takes three and a half hours.

Many destinations can be reached by
combining train and bus journeys. See
individual chapters in the Veneto section for
details of bus services to more out-of-the-way
destinations. In almost all cases, Sunday
services are very limited.

By car

The larger towns in the Veneto are all connected
to Venice by fast motorway links, but note that
the tolls charged for Italian motorways
(*autostrade*, prefix A followed by the number)
are not cheap.

Surprisingly, A-roads (*strade nazionali*
or *strade statali*, prefix N or SS followed by
number) are not always as good as they further
towards the south of Italy, and often head right
through the centre of towns (with a high risk
of encountering traffic confusion) rather than
by-passing them.

For more out-of-the-way destinations and
mountain roads, a good map is essential;
those in the 1:200,000-scale series published
by the Touring Club Italiano (TCI) have
plenty of detail and are available in most
bookshops and in motorway service stations.
For information on car hire, *see chapter*
Directory: Getting Around.

The Veneto

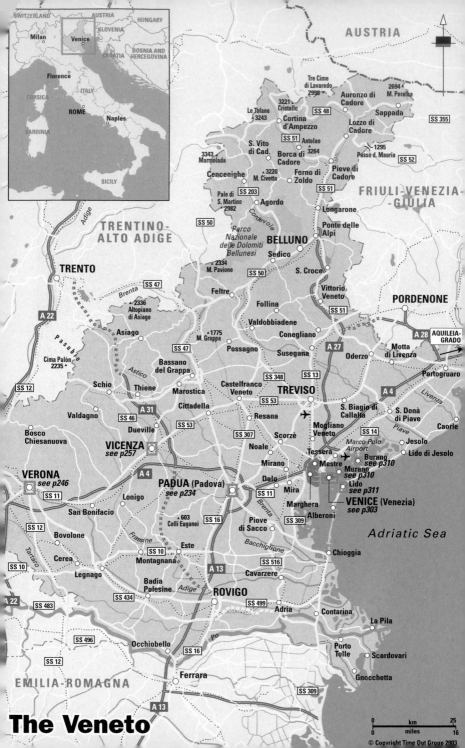

The Veneto

Palladian Villas

Palladio's architecture broke the mould.

In 1786 the German writer Johann Wolfgang von Goethe – no mean judge of talent – found himself captivated by the 16th-century architecture of Andrea Palladio in and around Vicenza. Goethe had found in Palladio both a kindred spirit and a venerable predecessor; on 19 September, he wrote: 'There is something divine about his talent, something comparable to the power of a great poet, who out of the worlds of truth and falsehood, creates a third whose borrowed existence enchants us.'

The object of such rapture, who is arguably the most influential architect in Western culture, had a lowly start in life. He was born in Padua on 30 November 1508 and baptised Andrea di Pietro della Gondola. His father, who milled grain and transported it for a living, apprenticed him at the age of 13 to a local sculptor and decorator. In 1524 Andrea moved to Vicenza and began working in the workshop of Giovanni da Porlezza, a stonecarver. The workshop, recognising his talent, put up the money for Andrea's guild entrance fee. Palladio learned to design and carve church altars, tombs and architectural elements, many of them commissioned by members of the Vicenza nobility.

Between 1530 and 1538, while working on the decorative details of a new villa on the outskirts of Vicenza, he met its owner, Count Giangiorgio Trissino, an influential and very wealthy local aristocrat who was the leader of a group of local humanist intellectuals dedicated to reviving all aspects of classical culture. This chance meeting was to change the course of Western architecture. Trissino, a poet and amateur architect, was immensely impressed with the skills and intellect of the young stonecutter and decided to take him under his wing, encouraging and funding his studies of the art and architecture of Rome.

Over the next few years, Trissino set about turning Andrea into a worthy heir to Vitruvius, the ancient architect whose treatise *De Architectura* underpinned the return to classical models in the Italian Renaissance. He began with finding a suitable name: 'Palladio' not only resonated with classical associations, but it was the name of a helpful angel in Trissino's epic poem *Italia liberata dai goti* (Italy Liberated from the Goths). In transferring the name to his protégé Trissino was expressing the hope that

Andrea would in turn liberate Italian architecture from the Gothic. Andrea was introduced to humanist circles around the Veneto, given time off to study Roman antiquities in Verona and Padua, and taken to Rome on three lengthy visits between 1540 and 1550. (Palladio made two more trips to the Eternal City on his own.) There he scrutinised, measured and sketched all the major classical remains; he also studied the buildings and plans of Renaissance greats throughout Italy, including Sanmicheli, Bramante, Raphael and Giulio Romano. In 1554 he published his Roman findings in a sort of early guidebook, *Le antichità di Roma*.

The result of this research and study was a fully developed and newly confident classical style that the architect had already begun to apply in a number of commissions for wealthy clients. Palladio's early patrons were part of the Trissino circle, who made sure the architect received both work and intellectual stimulation after Trissino died in 1550. Among these enlightened Vicentine nobles was Pietro Godi, whose villa at Lonedo di Lugo, **Villa Godi Valmarana ora Malinverni**, was Palladio's first independent commission, in 1537. Others included the Barbaro brothers, a gifted pair of scholars and statesmen who dabbled in design themselves and whose collaborative encouragement of the young architect generated one of his country-house masterpieces, the **Villa Barbaro** at Maser (1550-7). Girolamo Chiericati, another of Palladio's patrons, was on the board of commissioners who gave the architect his first big break in 1549, when plans he had submitted for the reconstruction of Vicenza's town hall (now known as the **Basilica Palladiana**, *see p259*) were accepted. This revolutionary design, in which the Gothic structure was wrapped in a huge, two-storey classical loggia, established Palladio as one of the leading architects of his day. His writings (published in user-friendly Italian, not Latin) and his prominent churches in Venice reinforced his fame. By the time of his death in August 1580, his influence was beginning to be felt from London to Moscow.

Palladio never simply copied Ancient Roman models: he reinterpreted classical motifs, creating a style that was entirely his own.

Villa Barbaro a Maser: classical symmetry outside, *trompe l'oeil* frescos inside. *See p232.*

The most instantly recognisable feature of his buildings is the use of the Greco-Roman temple front as a portico; equally innovative, though, were the dramatic high-relief effects he created on façades. He frequently employed the thermal window (a semicircular opening divided by two vertical supports) to evoke the monumentality and grandeur of the ancient Roman bath complexes. Though always unmistakably his, each of Palladio's buildings is startlingly different. He was capable both of the stark simplicity to be found at the **Villa Pisani** at Bagnolo di Lonigo, which is almost totally devoid of decorative elements, and of the immense complexity of the statue-crowned **Palazzo Chiericati** in the centre of Vicenza (now the **Museo Civico**, *see p260*). Much decoration was also functional: the gracious entrance ramp at the **Villa Emo** may also have been used as a platform for threshing grain.

But Palladio's inventiveness and sensitivity were not limited to the buildings themselves. He was also obsessed with the smallest details of the natural environment in which his buildings were to be inserted. Building near a river or canal was highly recommended by the architect; as well as allowing easy access by boat, water guaranteed cool breezes during the hot summer months and irrigated the gardens. A villa, wrote Palladio in *I quattro libri dell'architettura* (The Four Books of Architecture, 1570), should 'help conserve the health and strength of its inhabitants, and restore their spirits, worn out by the agitation of city life, to peace and tranquillity'.

What follows is a critical selection of the most important, visitable villas designed entirely or mostly by Palladio himself. For townhouses in Vicenza, *see chapter* **Vicenza**. Note that the names of villas change when they pass from one family to another, though the original owner's surname is generally retained, and occasionally some of the intermediate ones.

In the listings below we refer to the villas by their most commonly accepted names. Since the following are mostly private homes, the opening hours change frequently; telephoning in advance is always recommended. Many villas, such as the **Villa Pisani** in Montagnana (*see p242*), are not open to the public and can only be admired from the outside.

Vicenza province

All transport instructions apply from central Vicenza; unless otherwise stated, services depart from the rural FTV bus service terminal (information 0444 223 115/www.ftv.vi.it) in front of Vicenza railway station.

Villa Godi Valmarana ora Malinverni

Via Palladio 44, Lonedo di Lugo (0445 860 561/ www.villagodi.com). Bus to Thiene; change at Thiene to hourly bus for Lugo di Vicenza. **Open** *June-Sept* 3-7pm Tue, Sat, Sun. *Mar-Nov* 2-6pm Tue, Sat, Sun. Mornings and other days available for groups with reservations. **Admission** €6. **No credit cards.**
Palladio's first villa, built before he ever set foot in Rome and already completed by 1542, is in some ways one of his most radical, pared-back designs. Its matter-of-fact solidity also reminds us that most of these villas were built as working farms. Set in a vast park, the villa has some good 16th-century frescos as well as a former owner's collection of 19th-century art, artefacts and fossils (including a palm tree 5m/16ft high).

Villa Piovene

Via Palladio 51, Lonedo di Lugo (0445 860 613). Bus to Thiene; change at Thiene to hourly bus for Lugo di Vicenza. **Open** *Gardens only* Apr-Oct 2.30-7pm daily. Nov-Mar 2-5pm daily. **Admission** €4.20. **No credit cards**.

This may have been one of the architect's last commissions. The formulaic Palladian style – the portico, colonnaded wings, theatrical double staircase out front – is proof for some that self-parody was beginning to set in (or that Palladio's followers were not quite up to the level of the master). In fact, only the central block is plausibly by Palladio; the rest may be by his follower Vincenzo Scamozzi.

Villa Pisani

Via Risaie 1, Bagnolo di Lonigo (0444 831 104). Bus for Cologna Veneta. **Open** by appointment. **Admission** €6; €4 under-14s. **No credit cards**.

This early commission (begun in 1542) shows Palladio honing his style and experimenting with some features – such as rusticated arches – that would later be abandoned. Looking at the building-block simplicity of the façade, it is difficult to appreciate how revolutionary it must have seemed at the time; the revolution continues inside, where the division of rooms and design details such as the thermal windows are purely classical in inspiration.

Villa Pojana

Via Castello 41, Pojana Maggiore (0444 898 554/ pojana@iol.it). Bus for Noventa Vicentina. **Open** *Apr-Aug* 10am-12.30pm, 2-6pm Tue-Sun. *Sept-Mar* 2-5pm Tue-Sun. **Admission** €4; €2 concessions; free under-15s. **No credit cards**.

A Palladian bungalow, or one of the architect's most original creations, depending on your point of view. Dating from around 1550, the villa offers no projecting temple portico, for once, and the façade is dominated by a serliana arch (in which a central arched opening is flanked by two rectangular ones) topped by telephone-dial openings – giving an oddly contemporary feeling and suggesting that Palladio was the original postmodernist. The interior has perfectly symmetrical rooms, and is home to frescos by Bernardino India and Anselmo Canera.

Villa Rotonda

Via della Rotonda 45 (0444 321 793). Bus 8 or 13. **Open** *Gardens* Apr-Oct 10am-noon, 3-6pm Tue-Sun. Nov-Mar 10am-noon, 2.30-5pm Tue-Sun. *Interior* mid Mar-Oct 10am-noon, 3-6pm Wed. **Admission** *Gardens* €3. *Interior* €6. **No credit cards**.

Perhaps the best-known of the Veneto villas, the Rotonda – designed by Palladio between 1567 and 1570, but not completed until 1606 – was the first to be given a dome, a form previously associated with ancient temples or Renaissance churches. The successful reconciliation of the circle and the square resolved a problem that had baffled generations of architects. The Rotonda (officially called the Villa Almerico-Capra Valmarana) was planned not as a family home but as a pleasure pavilion for a retired cleric, Paolo Almerico, and thus although the structure covers a large area it actually comprises relatively few rooms. The four temple-like façades still face out on to lush green countryside on three sides, despite the villa's proximity to the city centre. Scholars (or talented bluffers) keen to examine the inside of one of the most famous buildings in Western architecture may be granted permission to visit the Rotonda's lavish interior outside the limited opening times. But those who are left outside need not complain: the building's exterior was far more influential, and circling it offers the visitor extraordinary aesthetic pleasure.

Villa Saraceno

Via Finale 8, Finale di Agugliaro (0444 891 371). Bus for Noventa Vicentina; change at Ponte Botti for local service. **Open** *Apr-Oct* 2-4pm Wed. *Nov-Mar* by appointment. **Admission** by donation. For weekly rental (sleeps 12): Landmark Trust UK (01628 825 925/www.landmarktrust.co.uk).

Until a few years ago this jewel of a villa was in a state of disrepair, in use as a barn. Then, in 1988, it was bought up by the British Landmark Trust and beautifully restored, reopening as self-catering accommodation in 1994, thus providing a unique chance to stay in a Palladian villa. The designs for the villa, published by Palladio in his *Four Books of Architecture*, show two wings that failed to materialise. Its farmyard fate was at least in keeping with the building's original function: like many of Palladio's villas, it was built for a gentleman farmer, with an attic-granary lit by large grilled windows, so that the wheat was kept well ventilated.

Villa Thiene

Piazza IV Novembre 2, Quinto Vicentino (0444 584 224/biblioteca.quinto@keycomm.it). Bus 5 (for Quinto or Lanzé) from Vicenza (piazza Matteotti). **Open** 9.30am-12.30pm, 3-7pm Mon, Thur; 9.30am-12.30pm Tue, Wed, Fri. Other times & days by appointment. **Admission** free.

Now the town hall of the otherwise unremarkable town of Quinto Vicentino, the imposing Villa Thiene is only a fraction of what was planned as an even more immense villa, designed by Palladio in 1546. The interior was frescoed in the mid 16th century by Giovanni De Mio and Bernardino India.

Treviso province

Villa Barbaro a Maser

Via Barbaro 7, Maser (0423 923 004/www. villadimaser.it). Autoservizi La Marca bus from Treviso bus station to Maser. **Open** *Mar-Oct* 3-6pm Tue, Sat, Sun. *Nov-Feb* 2.30-5pm Sat, Sun. Other days by appointment for groups only. **Admission** €5. **No credit cards.**

The Villa Barbaro is deservedly among the most famous of all Palladian villas. The charm of this out-and-out exercise in rural Utopianism derives partly from Palladio's intellectual communion with the Barbaro brothers for whom it was designed and built between 1550 and 1557, and partly from the quality of the decoration; it was only here that the architect found a painter, Paolo Veronese, capable of matching his genius. The natural setting is superb, with a rising, wooded hill behind tamed into classical symmetry by the semicircular lawn with its classical statuary in front. Two traditional parts of the Veneto farmhouse have been dressed up in a new classical disguise: those two arcaded wings flanking the main porticoed building are actually two *barchesse*, or farmhouse wings; while the mirror-image sundial-adorned chapel fronts on either end are, in fact, dovecotes. Behind is a nymphaeum – a semi-circular pool surrounded by statues. Even this served a practical function: the water flowed from here into the kitchen, from there into the garden for irrigation, and ultimately to the orchard on the far side of the road. Veronese's *trompe l'oeil* frescos inside – including the magnificent ceiling in the central Hall of Olympus – are in the same playful classical tradition as their frame. The meeting of minds is completed with work by Alessandro Vittoria, a pupil of Sansovino, who designed and carved all the statues and ornamental details. Although some of the decorative encrustation may reflect the patrons' wishes more than Palladio's, the total effect is extraordinary. By the side of the road in front of the villa is the Tempietto Barbaro, designed in the late 1570s as a memorial to Daniele Barbaro. This – Palladio's last church – is also one of his most geometrically ambitious, despite its small scale: looking back past the architect's own Redentore in Venice to the Pantheon in Rome, the design ingeniously reconciles the circle-in-a-square plan with the Greek-cross layout, a satisfying resolution of paganism and Christianity.

Villa Emo

Via Stazione 5, Fanzolo di Vedelago (0423 476 414/ villaemo@apf.it). Autoservizi La Marca bus from Castelfranco Veneto station for Montebelluna. **Open** *Apr-Oct* 3-7pm daily. *Nov-Mar* 2-6pm Sat, Sun. **Admission** €5.50; €3 concessions. **No credit cards.**

In the same mould as the Villa Barbaro but a tad more rustic, with more recognisable dovecotes at the end of the long *barchesse*, this surprisingly intimate villa was one of the first properties built as part of a Venetian scheme to encourage landowners to develop uncultivated land and exert greater government control over the terra firma. The striking beauty of the exterior resides in its austerity and proportions rather than its decoration. Still owned by the Emo family, the villa is decorated with joyous frescos by Giambattista Zelotti, one of the major fresco artists of the late Italian Renaissance.

Venice province

Villa Foscari 'La Malcontenta'

Via dei Turisti 10, Malcontenta (Apr-Oct 041 547 0012/Nov-Mar 041 520 3966/studiofoscari@ libero.it). Bus 53 from Venice's piazzale Roma. **Open** *Apr-Oct* 9am-noon Tue, Sat; other times by appointment. **Admission** €7 Tue, Sat; €6 concessions. Other times €8. **No credit cards.**

The splendid classical proportions of this villa, together with its dramatic position on a curve of the Brenta Canal close to its entrance to the Venetian lagoon, have made the Malcontenta, designed in 1555, one of Palladio's most celebrated creations. The name of the village (and nickname of the villa) refers to the land disputes of discontented peasants in the 15th century, and not – as legend claims – to an unhappy wife exiled from the fun in Venice. With its double staircase and elegant Greek temple façade, the Villa Foscari has been the model and inspiration for thousands of buildings in Europe and America. Although the graceful frescos by Battista Franco and Giambattista Zelotti are damaged and faded (and despite the present proximity to Marghera's oil refineries) the villa remains one of the most attractive and pleasant country houses in the world. It can be visited as part of the Burchiello boat excursion down the Brenta (*see p243*).

Padua province

Villa Cornaro

Via Roma 92, Piombino Dese (049 936 5017). SITA bus from Padua (piazzale Boschetto) for Trebaseleghe. **Open** *May-Sept* 3-6pm Sat; other times by appointment for groups only. **Admission** €5. **No credit cards.**

This is one of the most satisfying and elegant of Palladio's free-standing, two-storey villas (as opposed to the elongated-farmhouse style of the Villa Barbaro or Villa Emo). Probably completed between 1560 and 1570, it features a double-tiered Greek temple-style front porch with more evolved Corinthian columns (with acanthus-leaf capitals) above more primitive Ionic ones, with scrolled volutes. The interior contains some drab 18th-century frescos by Mattia Bortoloni and rather inventive stucco statues of members of the Cornaro family by Camillo Mariani.

The Veneto

Padua

Serious shopping, excellent eating and a superlative art gem.

Padua (Padova) may offer less architectural eye-candy than its more ostentatious sister on the lagoon, but it does boast one of the oldest universities in Europe (named after a tavern), a basilica piled to the rafters with religious artefacts and saintly body parts and one of Italy's greatest artistic treasures: Giotto's outstanding frescos in the Scrovegni Chapel.

Padua was established as a fishing village some time in the ninth or tenth century BC. The Romans then turned this fertile site into a thriving town, only for the barbarian hordes to knock it all down. However, plucky Padua picked itself up, dusted itself down and went on to prosper under Byzantine and Lombard rule, declaring itself an independent republic in 1164.

The city reached the height of its political power under the Carrara family (1338-1405), but the Venetians marched in and put a stop to that in 1405. Padua was governed by La Serenissima until its fall in 1797. After a period under Napoleon, Padua fell into Austrian hands (1815-66), and went on to play an active part in the struggle to free northern Italy from foreign dominion.

Apart from the incomparable Giotto frescos in the **Scrovegni Chapel** (*see p236*), Padua's prestige rests on its rags-to-riches place in the north eastern economic miracle (*see chapter* **Venice Today**). Padua now boasts some serious shopping, excellent eateries and traffic jams (and fumes) to rival those of much larger cities.

Though many in this business-like city in the Veneto's Catholic heartland bemoan the loss of traditional values, one trait remains deep-rooted: Padua's perpetual inferiority complex with regard to Venice. If La Serenissima has nurtured its aura of mystery and enigma, Padua has, since the 19th century, tried hard to compete, proudly presenting itself as a sphinx-like riddle as a city possessing 'a meadow with no grass, a café with no doors and a saint with no name'. The meadow in question is the large urban square of Prato della Valle, and the café with no doors was Pedrocchi's (which never closed).

Prato della Valle has now been turfed and, newly restored, Pedrocchi's shuts its doors at regular times (*see p237*). That leaves only the saint with no name, **Il Santo**, as the locals affectionately still call the basilica of St Anthony.

Sightseeing

Three main *piazze* stand at the heart of Padua and offer a colourful, dynamic panorama of day-to-day *padovana* life: piazza della Frutta and piazza delle Erbe flank the **Palazzo della Ragione**, known to locals as **Il Salone**; piazza dei Signori lies a little to the west.

During the morning (Mon-Sat) piazza delle Erbe and piazza della Frutta are home to bustling, picturesque fruit and vegetable markets. To the west, **Caffè Pedrocchi** and the **university** stand between the squares and the old **Ghetto**.

Piazza dei Signori is dominated by the façade of the **Palazzo del Capitanio** (1532), by Paduan architect Giovanni Maria Falconetto. This was the residence of the official who was one of the ruling authorities in the Venetian government of the city. The clock housed in the palazzo's tower is a replica of the original created in 1344, the first of its kind in Italy.

Casa di Petrarca. *See p241.*

To the left is the **Loggia del Consiglio**. This construction, again by Falconetto, housed the Maggior Consiglio, the ruling body of the city under Venetian rule. Opposite the Palazzo del Capitanio stands the church of **San Clemente**. South along via Dante, piazza del Duomo is home to Padua's cathedral.

Still further south, the once-swampy area called **Prato della Valle** had been used as a fairground for many years before 1775, when it was turned into an elegant marketplace. After years of neglect, the canal around the central island has now been dredged and cleaned, the statues lining the canal restored, the lawns replanted and the central fountain repaired. Note the statue of the notable near the southern bridge over to the island: to pre-empt inevitable future indignities, the sculptor provided this statue with its own pigeon.

South of the Prato stands one of Christendom's biggest churches, **Santa Giustina**. To the east, the **Orto Botanico** (Botanical Garden) lies between the Prato and Padua's nameless basilica: **Il Santo**. If the treasures contained in this best-loved of Paduan churches are too overwhelming, the little **Scoletta del Santo** and **Oratorio di San Giorgio**, both in piazza del Santo, offer interesting frescos on a smaller scale... and no creepy body parts to be seen.

But if you only see one thing in Padua, make it the **Scrovegni Chapel** (*see p236* **The Scrovegni Chapel & Museo Civico**) . North of piazza della Frutta, along via VIII Febbraio and corso Garibaldi, the chapel is the jewel in Padua's artistic crown.

TICKETS

The Padovacard is a multi-entrance ticket costing €13, valid for 48 hours, and allowing access for one adult and one child under the age of 12 to the Museo Civico and the Scrovegni Chapel, the Palazzo della Ragione (with limited visits when exhibitions are on), the first floor of the Caffè Pedrocchi, the Oratorio di San Rocco, the Oratorio di San Michele, and Petrarch's house in Arquà Petrarca (*see p241*). It can be purchased at the sights covered by the ticket, and at the tourist office at the train station (*see p241*). The ticket allows one visit only to each site. Further discounts on entrance fees for other main attractions are included with the ticket, plus free travel on APS buses. No credit cards are accepted.

Note that booking is obligatory for the Scrovegni Chapel. Although the chapel is included on the Padovacard, its €1 booking fee is extra. *See p236* for how and when to book. If you're prepared to wait at the entrance, you may be able to take advantage of an unclaimed place, though this is very far from certain.

Basilica di Santa Giustina

Prato della Valle (049 875 1628). **Open** *May-Oct* 8.30am-noon, 3-7pm Mon-Sat; 7am-1pm, 3-7.45pm Sun. *Nov-Apr* 8.30am-noon, 3-7pm daily.

Built in 1532-79, the Basilica di Santa Giustina is the 11th-largest Christian church in the world; its size is best appreciated as you look along its broad and bare transepts. The south transept leads to the small chapel of St Prosdocimo, the first bishop of Padua, with a fine marble iconostasis dating from the sixth century. To the east of the transept is St Luke's Chapel, which contains the tomb of Elena Lucrezia Cornaro Piscopia, the first woman in the world to get a university degree. Visits inside the chapel are on request.

Basilica di Sant'Antonio (Il Santo)

Piazza del Santo (049 878 9722/infobasilica @mess-s-antonio.it). **Open** *Nov-Mar* 6.30am-7pm Mon-Fri; 6.30am-7.45pm Sat, Sun. *Apr-Oct* 6.30am-7.45pm daily.

Popularly known as Il Santo, the Basilica di Sant'Antonio is one of the most important pilgrimage churches in Italy. St Anthony was not a local saint but a Portuguese Franciscan, a powerful preacher against the evils of usury, who died in Padua in 1231. Work on the church dedicated to him began soon after his canonisation in 1232; the main structure remained unfinished until around 1350, when the saint's body was moved to its present tomb in the Cappella dell'Arca. Visited by a steady stream of devotees, this chapel also contains one of the basilica's great artistic treasures: marble bas-reliefs of scenes from the life of the saint by artists such as Jacopo Sansovino, Tullio Lombardo and Giovanni Minello. The chapel's ceiling, by Giovanni Maria Falconetto, dates from 1533. The other great art treasures of the basilica – most of them placed so as to be almost impossible to see – are Donatello's bronze panels on the high altar (1443-50). Behind the altar, his stone bas-relief of the *Deposition* is more accessible, as are two of the bronzes – a bull and a lion, representing the evangelists St Mark and St Luke. Other works of interest held within the church include Altichiero's late 14th-century frescos in the Cappella di San Felice (on the south wall), Giusto de Menabuoi's frescos in the Cappella del Beato Luca Belludi and two fine funeral monuments – to Alessandro Contarini (died 1553) and Cardinal Pietro Bembo (died 1547) – both by the sculptor and military architect Michele Sanmicheli. At the back of the apse is the baroque Cappella del Tesoro, containing 'miraculous' relics. The reliquary containing the tongue of St Anthony was recently stolen, but then recovered, so the story goes, with the help of underworld bosses horrified that any of their confraternity could carry out such a heinous act.

In the piazza outside the church stands Donatello's famous monument to the *condottiere* (mercenary soldier) Erasmo da Narni, aka Gattamelata.

The Veneto

The Scrovegni Chapel and Museo Civi

One of the world's greatest art treasures, the **Scrovegni Chapel** is contained within Padua's **Museo Civico**. In addition to this jewel, the museum has a moderately interesting public collection and two private collections. But whatever your staying power, start with the great art treasure. Due to the 15-minute time limit for visiting the chapel, it's best to read up on the frescos before entering.

THE SCROVEGNI CHAPEL

The chapel is dedicated to the Virgin of the Annunciation, depicted on either side of the arch leading through to the altar directly opposite you as you enter. The wall frescos not only relate the story of Christ's life but also depict mainly apocryphal stories of Mary's parents Joachim and Anne.

The cycle opens (top right – alongside the *Virgin of the Annunciation*) with Joachim being driven from the temple because his marriage had so far proved infertile. Banished, Joachim wanders off into the wilderness to make an offering to God. An angel appears to both him and Anne telling them they will have a child and that when Joachim returns to Jerusalem he will encounter his wife at the Golden Gate. In the meeting scene, Giotto reveals the power of his innovative narrative realism: the embracing couple are surrounded by gossiping ladies, carelessly commenting on the coincidence of this meeting between husband and wife.

The top row on the wall opposite recounts the childhood and marriage of the Virgin. The story of Christ unfolds in the middle and lower rows, with the middle of the right-hand wall dominated by the scene of Judas' kiss. The traitor's yellow cloak enfolds Christ – but He is still the dominant figure. Note the fan of spears, clubs and torches around the central couple, leading the eye left down to St Peter as he severs the ear of the high priest's attendant.

The high dado at the base of the walls is decorated with fine grisaille paintings of the seven Virtues and Vices. Particularly striking are the figures of Envy blinded by her own serpentine tongue and Prudence equipped with pen and mirror.

THE ARCHEOLOGICAL WING

Though small, this collection of Greek, Roman and Egyptian antiquities contains some fine pieces. In Room 9 there is a noble female head of the fourth century AD, while in the ante-chamber to Room 10 is a carved Greek panel, the rear of which is decorated with a stork.

Moving into Room 10 itself there is an impressive funeral stele of a young girl slave (only the stele of women were decorated with acanthus leaves) with an inscription informing us that she was more than happy to elude the disfigurement of age by dying at the age of 19. The room also contains some stele of married couples, as well as interesting floor mosaics.

Duomo

Piazza Duomo (church 049 662 814/baptistery 049 656 914). **Open** *Church* 7.30am-noon, 3.45-7.30pm Mon-Sat; 7.45am-1pm, 3.45-8.30pm Sun. *Baptistery* 10am-6pm daily. **Admission** *Church* free. *Baptistery* €2.50; €1.50 concessions. **No credit cards**.

Paduans claim that Michelangelo designed the apse of their city's cathedral; it is obvious, however, that he didn't have much to do with its uninspiring final form. The church is worth visiting mostly for the paintings in the sacristy, by Bassano, Tiepolo and others, and even more so for the nearby baptistery, containing a series of powerfully vivid frescos by the 14th-century Florentine artist Giusto de Menabuoi.

Gli Eremitani

Piazza Eremitani 9 (049 875 6410). **Open** *Apr-Sept* 8.30am-12.30pm, 3.30-6pm Mon-Sat; 10am-12.30pm, 4-6pm Sun. *Oct-Mar* 8.30am-12.30pm, 3.30-6pm Mon-Sat; 10am-12.30pm, 4-6pm Sun.

The original building, dating from the late 13th century, was hit in an air raid on 11 March 1944: the fine

trilobate wooden ceiling is a copy of the early 14th century original. The bombs almost totally destroyed the church's artistic treasure, Andrea Mantegna's frescos of the *Life and Martyrdom of St James and St Christopher* (1454-7). Fortunately, two panels of the work, together with the main altarpiece, featuring the *Assumption*, had been removed before the raid. Two other panels – the *Martyrdom of St James* and *St Christopher Converts the Knights* – were partially reassembled from the rubble. The work is impressive even in its imperfect condition; however, the gate to the chapel is kept padlocked, making it difficult to get a good view. Also worthy of note in the church is Bartolomeo Ammanati's tomb of Marco Mantova Benavides (1544-46), on the north wall near the main entrance – a fine allegorical composition with the renowned humanist flanked by statues representing Time, Fame, Immortality, Wisdom and Labour. A further curiosity is the neo-classical bronze medallion in the west wall of the south transept commemorating Protestant hero Wilhelm George Frederick of Orange… in a Catholic church?

The Egyptian collection is mainly a tribute to the Paduan GB Belzoni, who succeeded in moving the massive bust of Ramses II from Thebes to Cairo.

THE PICTURE GALLERY

The gallery opens with two rooms of angels by 14th-century Guariento di Arpo, followed by a Giotto *Crucifixion* that originally hung in the Scrovegni Chapel; note the contrast between the very hieratic, stylised cross and the very unstylised Christ. What follows includes Squarcione's *Lazarus Polyptych*, a striking *Sailing of the Argonauts* by Lorenzo Costa and a fine *Portrait of a Young Man* by Alvise Vivarini. Don't miss some marvellous landscapes lurking behind the miserable-looking saints by the anonymous 'Pittore Veneto'. There's a very intriguing *Sacra Conversazione* by Bernardino Luini (the figures having the same blank stare as Grant Wood's American realist pitchfork-totin' farmer and wife) and two marvellous postcard-sized landscapes attributed to Giorgione.

In addition, there are fine works by the Bassano family, Pozzoserrato, Luca Giordano (note Job's comforter holding his nose in disgust at the pestilential state the poor man is reduced to in Giordano's *Job, Democritus and Archimedes*), some interesting 16th- and 17th-century Dutch and Flemish works, altarpieces by Romanino and Veronese (his surprisingly static *Martyrdom of Santa Giustina* is particularly impressive, with all the horror of death being portrayed through the rearing of the snorting horses), portraits by the early 17th-century Chiara Varotari and, to end on a bathetically light-hearted note, a portrait of a podgy Venetian captain by Sebastiano Mazzoni (1611-78).

Museo Civico & Cappella degli Scrovegni

Piazza Eremitani 8 (049 201 0020/fax 049 820 4585/www.cappelladegliscrovegni.it). **Open** *Museum* 9am-7pm Tue-Sun. *Chapel* 9am-7pm daily. **Admission** *Museum & chapel* 11. *Museum only* 9. *Chapel only* 7.50. **Credit** for bookings through website only MC, V. **Note that visits to the Scrovegni Chapel must be booked at least 72hrs in advance, or 96hrs in advance if booking on the website with a credit card. There is a booking fee of €1.** Bookings can be made at Padua's tourist offices, though make sure receipt of payment is faxed to the Scrovegni Chapel for confirmation. Booking information can be obtained by calling the number given above. At the time of writing, the chapel was also open for a temporary period in the evenings, 7-10pm, though advance booking was still required. After all this complicated procedure, you are allotted a mere 15 minutes to admire this masterpiece. But never fear: it's well worth the exasperation.

Il Ghetto

A stone's throw from piazza delle Erbe and the University of Padua medical faculty – the first in Europe to accept Jewish students (who were, however, obliged to pay double fees) – stands what was once the Jewish Ghetto, now a beautifully preserved pedestrian zone. The area only became a ghetto proper at the beginning of the 17th century, when it was shut off behind four gateways. A plaque commemorates the old synagogue, destroyed in 1943 by anti-Semitic *padovani*.

Gran Caffè Pedrocchi

Entrance from piazzetta Pedrocchi (049 820 5007/ caffe.pedrocchi@tiscali.net). **Open** *Architectural rooms* 9.30am-12.30pm, 3-7pm Tue-Sun. **Admission** €3; €2 concessions. **No credit cards.**
For café and restaurant opening times, *see p240*.
Known as 'the café without doors' because it never closed, Pedrocchi's – a mixture of neo-classical and Victorian Gothic revival – was designed by the early 19th-century architect Giuseppe Japelli. It was the scene of a student uprising in 1848, and later developed a reputation as a Fascist watering hole. After years of twilight glory, the café closed down for restoration in 1995.

It reopened in 1999, with all the renovated theme rooms on show upstairs (entrance in the right-hand wing of the side colonnade). The Greek staircase leads up to a condensed tour of Western culture: the Etruscan room leads into the Roman, then into the Herculaneum room, followed by the Renaissance – with a Gothic side-branch that goes nowhere. The whole culminates in a large white and gold neo-classical room dedicated to Rossini, on the opposite side of which is the Egyptian Room, with squatting dog-gods and starry vaults.

Oratorio di San Giorgio

Piazza del Santo 11 (049 875 5235). **Open** *Nov-Mar* 9am-12.30pm, 2.30-5pm daily. *Apr-Oct* 9am-12.30pm, 2.30-7pm daily. **Admission** €2; €1 concessions. Ticket includes the Scuola del Santo (*see p238*). **No credit cards.**

The Veneto

Il Ghetto. *See p237.*

This oratory, constructed in 1377 for the Lupi di Soragna family, contains a cycle of frescos by Altichiero (1379-84) depicting scenes from the lives of Saints Catherine and George. Altichiero is at his best here, and this place is worth a visit even after the long hike around the basilica.

Orto Botanico (Botanical Gardens)

Via Orto Botanico 15 (049 827 2119/ segreteria.ortobotanico@unipd.it). **Open** *Nov-Mar* 9am-1pm Mon-Sat. *Apr-Oct* 9am-1pm, 3-6pm daily. **Admission** €2.58; €1.55 concessions. **No credit cards.**
The Orto Botanico started life in the 1540s as a Garden of Simples (medicinal herbs), providing raw materials for the university's medical faculty. It was the first of its kind in Europe. The original layout, with stone borders enclosing the different species, has been maintained in the central section of the garden (a circle within a square).

Palazzo della Ragione (Il Salone)

Via del Municipio 1 (049 820 5006). **Open** 9am-6pm Tue-Sun. **Admission** €6; €3 concessions. **No credit cards.** Closed for restoration until spring 2003.
The Salone, as locals call it, was built between 1218 and 1219 and served as the law courts. In the early 14th century the building was raised and the external loggia of the *piano nobile* was added, giving it the structure it maintains today. Inside, the Salone proper is frescoed with signs of the zodiac and

representations of the months and seasons; it is claimed that the original frescos, destroyed in a disastrous fire in 1420, were by Giotto. However, contemporary records make no reference to what would already have been seen as a terrible loss. The impressive ship's-keel ceiling is a replacement of the 14th-century original, which was torn off by a whirlwind in 1759. The huge wooden horse was created for a tournament in 1466.

Scuola del Santo

Piazza del Santo 11 (049 875 5235). **Open** *Oct-Mar* 9am-12.30pm, 2.30-5pm daily. *Apr-Sept* 9am-12.30pm, 2.30-7pm daily. **Admission** €2 ; €1.50 concessions. **No credit cards.**
The Scuola del Santo contains 16th-century frescos, some of which Titian is said to have had a hand in.

Università di Padova, Palazzo del Bò (University)

Via VIII Febbraio 2 (049 827 3044/www.unipd.it). **Open** (Guided tours only) *Mar-Oct* 3pm, 4pm, 5pm Mon, Wed, Fri; 9am, 10am, 11am Tue, Thur, Sat. *Nov-Feb* 3pm, 4pm Mon, Wed, Fri; 10am, 11am Tue, Thur, Sat. **Admission** €3; €1.50 concessions. **No credit cards.**
The second-oldest university in Italy after Bologna occupies a building – Palazzo del Bò (bull) – that takes its name from the butchers' inn that used to stand on the site. The Old Courtyard was designed by Andrea Moroni and decorated with the coats-of-arms and family crests of illustrious rectors and students. The beautiful oval wooden-benched Anatomy Theatre on the first floor, which was built by Girolamo Fabrizi Aquapendente in 1594, was the first of its kind in the world. Galileo Galilei worked here from 1592 to 1610. Past students of the University of Padua include Copernicus, Sir Francis Walsingham and Oliver Goldsmith, all of whom are remembered in the Sala dei Quaranta, which also houses Galileo's lectern. Europe's first ever female graduate, Elena Lucrezia Cornaro Piscopia, studied here. Note that opening times are liable to change without warning.

Where to eat & drink

For the financially challenged sightseer, picnics are the best deal; the morning markets in piazza delle Erbe or piazza della Frutta and shops in the arcades around them offer a wide range of fruit, veg, cheeses and meats.

If you're too laid-back for DIY sandwiches, the finest *tramezzini* (sandwiches) and *panini* (rolls) in Padua can be found just outside the station, at the small Bar Maximilian, on the corner of corso del Popolo and via Nicolò Tommaseo (closed Saturday and Sunday).

Osteria Dei Fabbri

Via dei Fabbri 13 (049 878 1261). **Meals served** 12.30-2pm, 7.30-11pm Mon-Sat. **Average** €25. **Credit** AmEx, DC, MC, V.

The Veneto

Situated just off piazza delle Erbe and near the Ghetto, this cosy eaterie has an extensive menu that changes daily. Local staples include *pasta e fagioli* (bean soup) and home-made gnocchi. A decent wine list encourages you to tipple into the early hours and the friendly atmosphere makes Osteria Dei Fabbri a pleasant watering hole for female travellers on their own.

Le Calandre

Via Liguria 1, Sarmeola di Rubano (049 630 303/ www.calandre.com). **Meals served** noon-2pm, 8-10pm Tue-Sat. Closed 3wks Jan, 2wks Aug. **Average** €100. **Credit** AmEx, DC, MC, V.

This restaurant, 4km (2.5 miles) west of the city, has recently undergone major refurbishment but thankfully the excellent kitchen has remained intact. After the roast pigeon with duck's liver and black truffles, accompanied by wine from an excellent list, you just might need that orange and ginger sorbet to clean the palate. With two Michelin stars, Le Calandre is unmissable, bank balance permitting.

Graziati

Piazza della Frutta 40 (tel/fax 049 875 1014/ www.graziati.com). **Meals served** noon-2.30pm Tue-Sun. **Average** €20. **Credit** MC, V.

Orto Botanico. *See p238.*

Expiation for a bad dad

Among the money lenders who sit on burning earth, pelted by burning rain, in the seventh circle of hell in Dante's *Inferno* is 'one of the damned, with a blue sow on a white field painted on his bag' (Canto XVII, 64).

This family crest betrays him as Reginaldo Scrovegni, whose thriving usury business made him a fortune in Padua in the 12th century; in the frescos – paid for with Reginaldo's ill-gotten gains – that adorn his family chapel, the Scrovegni family and its crest put in an appearance.

It was Reginaldo's son Enrico who had the chapel built (between 1303 and 1305) and frescoed by Giotto, to atone for his father's mercenary practices and earn brownie points towards a more comfortable abode in the afterlife than his father. (Pious Enrico is the one presenting the model of the chapel to the Virgin in the *Last Judgement*.)

However, Enrico's act of expiation for his bad dad was not viewed as totally ingenuous by the neighbouring Eremitani monks who, in a fit of jealous pique, complained that the chapel had been built 'for pomp, vainglory and wealth rather than for praise, glory and honour of God'. Their slurs were ignored by church superiors, however, and the chapel went on to become a place of pilgrimage, not

so much for its frescos, but because those who visited in a fitting state of penitence were thought to benefit greatly in spiritual terms. Enrico managed to convince the *padovani* of his family's new-found generosity while creating a sumptuous private chapel using usurers' filthy lucre.

Usury is a recurrent theme in Giotto's frescos: usurers hang by their money bags in hell and are chased from the Temple by Jesus. For Dante, too, usurers were the scourge of the century and were named and shamed in his great work *La Divina Commedia* (*The Divine Comedy*), which he began writing at about the time Giotto was working on the frescos.

Giotto's frescos are considered as important a foundation stone of Italian art as the *Commedia* is of Italian literature. Yet by the 19th century the Scrovegni Chapel was crumbling into ruin, only to be saved – partly at least – by the indignant intervention of *The Times* of London. The Scrovegni Palace that stood alongside was not so fortunate and was demolished in 1827. In early 2002, after the latest in a series of restorations, the chapel reopened to the public looking more magnificent than ever.

Head for the **Euganean Hills** for restorative treatments. *See p241.*

Graziati is essentially a *pasticceria* (open 7.30am-8.30pm Tue-Sun), specialising in a large and calorific range of tantalising *millefeuille* pastries. For something less frivolous, however, the subterranean tearoom serves wholesome lunches. The decor is simple, the dining-room intimate and on display is a beautiful 14th-century wooden door rediscovered during recent restoration work.

Zairo
Prato della Valle 51 (tel/fax 049 663 803). **Meals served** 12-2.30pm, 7pm-1am Tue-Sun. **Average** €25. **Credit** AmEx, DC, MC, V.
Zairo's main selling point has to be its outdoor seating with the view on to the Prato (*see p235*), and its late hours. This *osteria* has its menu firmly rooted in home territory, with some international nosh to boot. Pizzas are also served.

Bars & nightlife

For gay and lesbian venues in Padua, *see p208.*

Bar dei Osei
Piazza della Frutta 1 (049 875 9606). **Open** 8am-8pm daily. **No credit cards**.
A very pleasant central bar with convenient people-watching tables outside in summer in one of Padua's busiest squares. A good lunchtime stop, with a delicious range of fresh bar snacks and sandwiches.

Gran Caffè Pedrocchi
Via VIII Febbraio 15/piazzetta Pedrocchi (049 878 1231). **Open** *Bar* 9am-9pm Mon, Tue, Sun; 9am-midnight Wed-Sat. *Restaurant*

12.30-3pm, 7-10.30pm daily. **Average** €30. **Credit** AmEx, DC, MC, V.
For centuries Padua's most elegant watering hole, and now restored to its former glory, Pedrocchi's is a landmark in its own right (*see p237*). Booking is essential for dinner.

Where to stay

Grand'Italia
Corso del Popolo 81 (049 876 1111/fax 049 875 0850/www.hotelgranditalia.it). **Rates** €135 single; €185 double; €250 suite. **Credit** AmEx, DC, MC, V.
This hotel is close to all the major sights, and the recently restored rooms are quiet and comfortable.

Majestic Toscanelli
Via dell'Arco 2 (049 663 244/fax 049 876 0025/www.toscanelli.com). **Rates** €114 single; €161 double; €197 suite. **Credit** AmEx, DC, MC, V.
All the rooms in this quiet hotel offer attractive views over the quaint streets of the Ghetto. The Majestic Toscanelli is just one minute's walk away from the town's main squares.

Sant'Antonio
Via San Fermo 118 (049 875 1393/fax 049 875 2508/www.hotelsantantonio.it). **Rates** €57 single; €74 double. Breakfast €6.70 extra. **Credit** MC, V.
Sant'Antonio is good value for money, unless you're unlucky enough to get one of the rooms looking out on to what becomes a busy street corner very early in the morning.

The Veneto

Tourist information

IAT *Padua railway station (049 875 2077/fax 049 875 5008/www.turismopadova.it).* **Open** *Sept-May* 9am-5.45pm Mon-Sat; 9am-noon Sun. *June-Aug* 9am-7pm Mon-Sat; 9am-noon Sun.

IAT *Galleria Pedrocchi, next to Gran Caffè Pedrocchi, see p237 (049 876 7927/infopedrocchi@ turismopadova.it).* **Open** 9.30am-12.30pm, 3-7pm Mon-Sat.

IAT *Piazza del Santo, opposite the basilica (049 875 3087/infosanto@turismopadova.it).* **Open** *Apr-Oct* 9am-1pm, 2-6pm daily. Closed Nov-Mar.

Getting around

By bus
City buses are operated by ACAP (049 824 1111/ www.acap.it); tickets, which must be bought before boarding, cost 85¢ and are valid for one hour. A block of ten tickets for the city costs €8 and a family day ticket (two adults, three children) costs €2.70. Destinations outside the city covered in this chapter are served by blue SITA buses (*see below*).

Getting there

By car
Padua is on the A4 La Serenissima motorway.

By train
All trains bound south-west from Venice (on the Bologna line) stop at Padua. Journey time 25-30mins.

By bus
From Venice's piazzale Roma bus terminus, orange ACTV buses trundle slowly to Padua, stopping off near several Palladian villas (*see pp229-32*) en route. Blue SITA buses (049 820 6811), on the other hand, speed along the motorway. In Padua, both stop at the bus station in piazzale Boschetti.

Around Padua

Abano Terme

To the south of Padua stand the verdant Euganean Hills. The restorative powers of the area's volcanic springs and mud were recognised in Roman times and are still exploited by the many spa hotels offering restorative treatments in such health resorts as **Abano Terme** and **Montegrotto**.

Six kilometres (four miles) west of Abano, in the village of Bresso, is the **Abbazia di Praglia**, which was founded by Benedictine monks in the 12th century, though the abbey's present buildings date from the 15th century. The monastery itself consists of an interesting series of cloisters (one of which serves as a botanical garden).

South of Abano lies **Arquà Petrarca**: it was here that the poet Francesco Petrarch (1304-74) chose to spend the last years of his life; he is buried in the church. The town has retained much of its medieval atmosphere and it is possible to visit the 14th-century house where the poet lived.

Abbazia di Praglia
Via Abbazia 16, Bresseo di Teolo (049 990 0010). **Open** *Apr-Oct* 3.30-5.30pm Tue-Sun. *Nov-Mar* 2.30-4.30pm Tue-Sun. **Admission** free (donations welcome).
A friendly monk offers guided tours every half-hour.

Casa di Petrarca
Via Valleselle 3, Arquà Petrarca (0429 718 294). **Open** *Oct-Jan* 9am-noon, 2.30-5pm Tue-Sun. *Feb-Sept* 9am-noon, 3-7pm Tue-Sun. **Admission** €3; €2 concessions. **No credit cards**.

Where to eat

Just outside Arquà's town centre is **La Cucina d'Arquà** (via Scalette 1, Arquà Petrarca, 0429 777 170, closed Mon & Tue, average €20), serving what seem to be endless courses of traditional dishes, with meat playing a major role in the second courses. It pays to work up a healthy appetite before you go.

Tourist information

IAT Terme Euganee *Via P d'Abano 18, Abano Terme (049 866 9055/fax 049 866 9053/ www.turismotermeeuganee.it).* **Open** *Nov-mid Mar* 8.30am-1pm, 2.30-7pm Mon-Sat. *Mid Mar-Oct* 8.30am-1pm, 2.30-7pm Mon-Sat, 10am-1pm, 3-6pm Sun.

Getting there

By car
Take the A13 Padua–Bologna motorway, turning off at Padova Sud for Abano, and about 20km (12.5 miles) further south at the Terme Euganee exit for Arquà; Praglia is accessible by minor roads from Abano.

By train
Frequent services (approx every 20mins) to Terme Euganee and Montegrotto for Abano on the Padua–Bologna line.

By bus
ACAP city buses and SITA buses (*see above*) run approximately every 15mins from Padua to Abano; SITA buses serve Praglia and Arquà.

Monselice

Monselice's most impressive sight is the **Ca' Marcello**, a complex that includes the 13th-century Palazzo di Ezzelino, the Palazzo Marcello, an 18th-century chapel, and a

The Veneto

crenellated structure built in the 15th century. But there's also the **Santuario delle Sette Chiese**, designed by Vincenzo Scamozzi, Palladio's most gifted pupil, who acted as guide to the English architect Inigo Jones. The church was completed between 1592 and 1593, the chapels coming later in 1605.

Tourist information

IAT *Piazza Mazzini 15 (0429 783 026/www. provincia.padova.it/comuni/monselice).* **Open** 10.15am-12.30pm, 2-3.45pm Mon, Tue, Fri; 10.15am-12.30pm Thur, Sat, Sun.

Getting there

By car
Leave the A13 Padua–Bologna motorway at the Monselice exit.

By train
Direct services on the Padua–Bologna line.

By bus
SITA buses *(see p241)* run from Padua.

Este

This town spawned the Este family, a minor branch of which moved to Germany in the 12th century and established the Brunswick-Lüneburg dynasty that would eventually become the Hanoverians, ancestors of Britain's own august royals. The more illustrious branch of the Este family was to become the dukes of Ferrara and rule over one of the most artistically fertile courts of the Italian Renaissance.

Nowadays, the town of Este reflects little of these past glories, though the **Museo Nazionale Atestino**'s picture gallery boasts a very pretty *Madonna and Child* by Cima da Conegliano.

Turning left from the museum, the via Principe Umberto takes you past the 13th-century façade and bell tower of the church of **San Martino**. Turning the other way, you come to the **Duomo** (open 10am-noon, 4-6pm daily), which contains Giambattista Tiepolo's *St Thekla Interceding with God the Father to Free the City from the Plague* (1757).

Museo Nazionale Atestino
Via Guido Negri 9 (0429 2085/www.ceramicadieste. it/museoat/museo.htm). **Open** 9am-8pm daily. **Admission** €2; €1 concessions. **No credit cards**.

Where to eat

For an unpretentious lunchtime snack, try the **Tavernetta Da Piero** (via Pescheria Vecchia 16A, 0429 2855, closed Thur, Wed

dinner Nov-Mar, average €25). This central restaurant is a bustling place full of local characters and colour.

Tourist information

Pro-Loco *Piazza Maggiore 9A (0429 3635).* **Open** *Apr-Nov* 9am-12.30pm, 4-6pm Mon-Fri; 9am-12.30pm Sat, Sun. *Dec-Mar* 9am-12.30pm daily.

Getting there

By car
Take the A13 Padua–Bologna motorway, exiting at Monselice; take the SS10 from here to Este.

By train
Direct services on the Padua–Mantua line, or change at Monselice on the Padua–Bologna line.

By bus
By SITA *(see p241)* bus from Padua.

Montagnana

Montagnana's perfectly preserved defences – composed of a total of 24 towers and intervening walls, all beautifully offset by a sweep of uncluttered grass all around – were built between 1360 and 1362.

The town boasts two other architectural gems. The first is Palladio's **Villa Pisani**. The rear view of the villa from the road alongside the garden is perhaps the most impressive.

The second, inside the town walls, is the **Duomo** (open 8am-12.30pm, 4-7.30pm daily), a striking mix of Gothic and Renaissance. Begun in 1431, it was not consecrated until 1502 and the present main portal, attributed to Jacopo Sansovino, was not added until around 1530 - a century into the church's life. The two pilasters alongside it are topped by white stone spheres that, because of the alignment of the church, are the first part of the façade to be lit up by the sun at noon.

Above the main altar is a *Transfiguration* by Paolo Veronese, while on the second altar along the south wall is an altarpiece of the *Madonna and Child Enthroned*, which is considered one of the masterpieces of the artist Giovanni Buonconsiglio. Buonconsiglio has also been credited with the two damaged panels depicting *David with the Head of Goliath* and *Judith with the Head of Holofernes* on either side of the main portal; Giorgione is another candidate.

The greatest curiosity in the church, however, is in the Rosary Chapel, on the left just before the crossing. During cleaning in 1959, the baroque altar was removed to reveal original 15th-century frescos, which form an

Arquà Petrarca – this is Petrarch country. *See p241.*

esoteric astrological allegory, with two bears
(orsa major and orsa minor) separated by the
curls of a dragon (the draco constellation)
alongside a representation of Pegasus and
the ship of the Argonauts. It has been argued
that all of these astrological figures represent
a particular conjunction of the heavenly bodies
relating to the Feast of the Annunciation. The
iconographical scheme is similar to one at the
Castle of Esztergom in Hungary; the 15th-
century physician and astrologer Galeotto
Marzio da Narni is known to have lived in
both places for some time.

Ruled by Venice from 1405, Montagnana was
renowned for its hemp, used to produce sails for
La Serenissima's fleet.

Tourist information

IAT Pro-Loco *Castel San Zeno (0429 81 320/
proloco@netbusiness.it)*. **Open** *Apr-Oct* 9.30am-
12.30pm Mon; 9.30am-12.30pm, 3-6pm Wed-Sun.
Nov-Mar 9.30am-12.30pm Mon; 9.30am-12.30pm,
3-6pm Wed-Sun.

Getting there

By car
Leave the A13 Padua–Bologna motorway at the
Monselice exit, then take the SS10 to Montagnana.

By train
Services on the Padua–Mantua line.

By bus
SITA *(see p241)* buses run from Padua.

The Brenta Canal

Goethe's memories of paddling down the Brenta
Canal in 1786 included 'the banks studded with
gardens and summer houses; small properties
stretch down to the edge of the river and now
and then the busy high road beside it'.
Nowadays, the busy high road is a more
intrusive presence and many of the gardens
and summer houses have been swept away to
make room for industrial sites. A number of
Palladian villas still grace the waterway, part
of which can be visited in a boat that chugs up
the Brenta from Venice as far as Strà, where
you are transferred on to a bus to Padua.
The journey includes visits to the **villas** of
Malcontenta (*see chapter* **Palladian
Villas**), **Widmann** and **Pisani**. The boat
trip culminates at the **Villa Pisani** in Strà,
a remarkable villa of the early-to-mid 18th
century. Note that you can cover the same route
at a fraction of the price by taking the ACTV
No.53 bus from piazzale Roma, leaving at 25
and 55 minutes past the hour.

SITA – Divisione Navigazione
'il Burchiello'
*Via Orlandini 3, Padua (049 877 4712/fax 049
876 3044/www.ilburchiello.it)*. **Services** *Apr-Oct*
Venice–Padua departure from Pietà boat stop (near

San Zaccaria) at 9am Tue, Thur, Sat; Padua–Venice departure from piazzale Boschetti at 8.15am on Wed, Fri, Sun. Closed Nov-Mar. *Rates* €62 (incl entrance to 2 villas but NOT Villa Pisani or return journey); €36 6-17s; free under-6s. Lunch €24 extra. **Credit** MC, V.
Information on the website is available in English.

The Po Delta

The Po Delta is one of Italy's three most important nature reserves. Here, river- and sea- water lagoons combine to form the largest water reserve in the country. You can travel for miles – walking or cycling along the high banks of the *valli* (fishing lagoons) – without seeing another person. The only signs of life are the *casoni* – low, peach-coloured fishing lodges with green shutters.

The *valli* fill in a lot of the dead space between the delta branches, where the meandering Po splits into a confusion of channels. In the 19th century steam-powered pumping stations allowed vast tracts of land to be reclaimed; but plenty of water has been left for the herons, eels and reed beds. Outside of the rice paddies (Italy's prized *arborio* rice is grown here), this can be poor agricultural terrain, because of the high salinity of the soil. The salt pans provide much of Italy's sea salt.

The **Bosco di Mesola** offers over 1,000 hectares of vegetation and wildlife and is the green lung of the Po Delta. Here you can meander through the undergrowth of juniper, hawthorn and butcher's broom. Watch out for red deer, hare and tortoises as you pick your way through the forest (open 8am-dusk, Saturday and Sunday). Expert guides can show you around on foot or by bike.

As the main fluvial artery of Italy's industrial heartland, the Po is heavily polluted by toxic waste. This makes the famous, fat Po eels a hazardous delicacy. Despite the pollution, the delta is a haven for wildlife, with rare birds such as the cavaliere d'Italia, red herons and marsh falcons. Some species, unfortunately, are lost for ever: beavers and pelicans were wiped out by hunters in the 17th century. But there are signs of a turnabout: spoonbills returned to the delta in 1989, and there are hopes that flamingos will one day come back to nest here.

The secrecy and inaccessibility of this waterscape has long made it a place of refuge. It was here that Garibaldi shook off his Austrian pursuers in the summer of 1849. During World War II, this was also a centre of partisan activity, later commemorated in Roberto Rossellini's film *Paisà*.

The only town of any size is **Comacchio**, which is over the border in the Emilia-Romagna region. This southern area is in many ways more interesting than the smaller Veneto slice of the delta to the north. As well as Comacchio itself, with its Venetian-style canals and famous three-way bridge (the Trepponti), there is the Abbazia di Pomposa, a magnificent Benedictine monastic complex dating back to the eighth century.

The Po is the last of Europe's four major river deltas to have been granted protected status: an inter-regional Parco Delta del Po was finally instituted at the beginning of 1998.

Where to stay & eat

Enjoy a full-immersion delta experience at the **Rifugio Parco Delta del Po** (0425 21 530/ fax 0425 26 270, www.turismocultura.it, full board €30 per person) in the tiny village of Gorino Sullam. The refuge offers cycle and canoe hire, plus guided nature treks with overnight camping stops. For a more luxurious but equally natural experience, the **Cannevié Hotel** (via Per Volano, Codigoro, 0533 719 103, www.cannevie.com, double room €72, closed Jan) is a restored 16th-century fishing lodge on the Cannevié-Porticino lagoon. The Cannevié Hotel's larger restaurant (closed Mon, average €35) occupies the old *tabarra*, where nets and fishing utensils were stored. Its more intimate restaurant, **Porticino** (closed Tue, average €40), is situated at the end of the nature trail and can be reached from the hotel on foot. Both restaurants offer typical dishes from the Po delta.

Tourist information

IAT *Piazza Folegatti 28, Comacchio (0533 310 161/ fax 0533 310 269/www.comune.comacchio.fe.it).*
Open *Nov-Feb* 9.30am-1pm, 3-6.30pm Sat, Sun. *Mar-Oct* 9.30am-1pm, 3-6.30pm daily.
This very helpful and friendly office organises boat trips around the town's canals and in the Valli di Comacchio, where a multi-sited museum of natural history and fishing techniques – accessible only by boat – has been set up.

Getting there

By car
Leave the A13 Padua–Bologna motorway at Ferrara Sud, then follow the *superstrada* to the Lidi.

By bus
SITA (*see p241*) runs early morning and late evening services from Padua.

Verona

Romeo and Juliet take a back seat amid this surfeit of architecture and art.

It would have been understandable (though not forgiveable) had Verona opted to cash in on Shakespeare's decision to set his greatest love story here. But Verona is much too staid and self-confident to turn itself into a *Romeo and Juliet* 'experience'.

It's a similar story with the city's pre-Lenten Carnevale festival, which, as any *veronese* will tell you, is Europe's oldest. Where Venice's mighty PR machine emphasises glamour and mystique, Verona is content to centre celebrations around a giant potato dumpling (*gnocco*). The 'Re del Gnoco', a chubby, red-cheeked monarch, makes his regal way though the city on a donkey, wielding a dumpling on his golden trident, and a *gnocco* binge takes place in piazza San Zeno on *venerdì gnocolar* – the Friday before Shrove Tuesday. (For the culinarily inhibited, there are also street entertainers and a boat race on the Adige river.)

No. For their self-esteem the good burghers of Verona prefer to draw on a history dating back to the Romans and a surfeit of architecture and art. The splendid – and splendidly preserved – Arena (Roman amphitheatre) testifies to the city's importance in ancient times, while a Verona native, Paolo Veronese, was to leave his vibrant mark on the art of the Renaissance.

The architecture of the Old Town betrays a strong mittel European influence, an influence that was both cultural and military. At the mouth of the Adige river valley, Verona was an important toll booth on the medieval *autostrada* bringing invaders from central Europe. As a result, the city spent much of its history dominated by other cities and powers. The home-grown Della Scala (aka Scaliger) family succeeded in controlling a swathe of northern Italy for a time, but it fell in 1387 during a fit of Montague and Capulet-style family feuding, to be replaced by the Viscontis of Milan. They were superseded in turn by the Venetian Republic, which remained in power until 1797, and finally by Austria. Only in 1866 did Verona rid itself of foreign rulers, when it joined the newly united Kingdom of Italy.

Verona was a major beneficiary of Italy's economic miracle of the 1970s. Up until then a sleepy provincial town with a mainly agricultural economy, Verona witnessed an explosion of family-run businesses producing everything from machine tools to ice-cream

making equipment. These firms have been joined in recent years by printing and pharmaceutical concerns. A booming productive sector and almost full employment acts as a magnet and Verona now has a growing immigrant community from Africa, Asia and eastern Europe, giving it a truly metropolitan and international flavour. In Veronetta – the university quarter – spices and tropical fruit abound in colourful, fragrant Afro-Caribbean shops, and oriental and Latin American restaurants – unheard of only a few years ago – continue to open.

The colossal Roman **Arena**.

Sightseeing

Verona's thumb-shaped Old Town is framed by the serpentine Adige river. Ancient Rome is an inescapable presence here, and not only because of the Arena. The streets were laid out according to a grid plan decreed by Emperor Augustus, and the Teatro Romano and ponte Pietra also help set the tone. Even the more modern buildings often have a Roman tinge. Many of them stand on Roman foundations; some have fragments of Roman marble-work inserted into their fabric (the columns in the façade of the building across from the Prada store in corso Porta Borsari is a good example).

These monuments owe their remarkable state of preservation to having been in constant use through the centuries. The fact that the nearby hills are rich in stone quarries also helped: the kind of pilfering that was so common in medieval and Renaissance Rome, for example, was simply unnecessary here.

Verona's medieval architecture dates mostly from after the great north Italian earthquake of 1117. In the building boom that followed this catastrophe, the city was adorned with some of its finest buildings: the basilica of San Zeno, the Duomo and the Gothic churches of Sant'Anastasia and San Fermo.

Piazza Brà, at the base of the 'thumb', is the gateway to the Old Town and home to the magnificent Roman **Arena**. In addition, this large square holds a number of cafés and the **Museo Lapidario** (open 1.45-7.30pm Mon, 8.30am-2pm Tue-Sun), a small private collection of Greek and Roman fragments and inscriptions.

The heart of the city lies a short walk north-east from piazza Brà in the everyday bustle of **piazza delle Erbe** and **piazza dei Signori**. Once the site of the Roman forum, piazza delle Erbe is today the site of a somewhat tacky food and souvenir market (Mon-Sat mornings). But the downmarket football jerseys and bruised fruit can't detract from the stunning buildings surrounding the square (none of which is open to the public). At the northern end is the huge 14th-century **Casa Mazzanti** with its splendid late-Renaissance frescos on the outer façade, the highly ornamented baroque **Palazzo Maffei** and the medieval **Torre Gardello**, Verona's first clock tower, built in 1370. The basin of the fountain (1368) is of Roman origin, as is the body of the statue known as the 'Madonna Verona', which stands above it; the head is medieval. The tall houses at the southern end once marked the edge of the Jewish ghetto.

A detour south-east out of piazza delle Erbe along via Cappello leads to the **Casa di Giulietta** (Juliet's house): just follow the stream of lovelorn tourists. Further down via Cappello is the **Porta Leoni**, a picturesque fragment of a Roman city gate that is now part of a medieval house; recent excavations, visible from the street, have exposed the full extent of the towered and arched structure. The Gothic church of **San Fermo Maggiore** stands where via Cappello hits the river.

The heart of medieval Verona's governance and finance, piazza dei Signori, contains the 15th-century **Loggia del Consiglio** (closed to the public) with its eight elegant arches. The building, topped by statues of illustrious Veronese residents (including the poet Catullus who was exiled from Rome to the shores of Lake Garda, thus making him an honorary citizen), marked the beginning of Renaissance architecture in Verona. While the town seems mildly embarrassed about its connection to English literature, it is quietly boastful about the fact that Dante lived in exile at the court of the Della Scala family from 1304. In fact, piazza dei Signori is also known as piazza Dante because of the statue of the poet in the centre.

Linking piazze delle Erbe and dei Signori is the 12th-century **Palazzo della Ragione** (closed to the public). Home until recently to Verona's law courts, today the palazzo houses court offices. A gateway on the piazza dei Signori side of the palazzo leads into the Mercato Vecchio courtyard, with its huge Romanesque arches and magnificent outdoor Renaissance staircase. The palazzo is dominated by the **Torre dei Lamberti** (1462). At the eastern exit from piazza dei Signori are the Della Scala family tombs (**tombe** or **arche scaligere**).

Moving towards the northern tip of the 'thumb', the narrow streets are a captivating labyrinth dotted with medieval and Renaissance *palazzi*. In via Pigna, take a look at the carved marble Roman pine cone (*pigna*) placed on a cylindrical Roman tombstone, before heading north down the narrow via San Giacomo alla Pigna towards the **Duomo**, or south towards the imposing church of **Sant'Anastasia**.

Close by, **ponte Pietra** is Verona's oldest bridge and for centuries the only link between the city centre and the suburbs beyond. The two stone arches on the left bank of the river are Roman, and date back to before 50 BC. The other three brick arches are thought to date from between 1200 and 1500. The bridge was blown up by German soldiers as they retreated at the end of World War II – as were all of Verona's bridges, including the medieval bridge of Castelvecchio – but was subsequently rebuilt with infinite care using the original stones fished from the riverbed.

Piazza delle Erbe: once a Roman forum, now a food and souvenir market. *See p247.*

The ponte Pietra leads across the river to some of Verona's most beautiful churches – including **San Giorgio in Braida**, **San Giovanni in Valle**, **Santa Maria in Organo** and **Santo Stefano** – as well as the **Museo Archeologico** and the remains of the **Teatro Romano**. From its dominating position on the hills above, **Castel San Pietro** (closed to the public) – part of the city's medieval and Renaissance fortifications, heavily redesigned by Austrian occupiers in the mid 19th century – offers a bird's-eye view of the city. Head south-east from the bridge along regaste Redentore and its continuations for the pretty **Giardino Giusti**.

Corso Porta Borsari, Roman Verona's busy main street, leads out of the north end of piazza delle Erbe towards the **Porta Borsari**, the best-preserved of the city's Roman gates. Built with blocks of local white marble, it probably dates from the reign of Emperor Claudius (AD 41-54). In a small garden along corso Cavour (a continuation of corso Porta Borsari) is the **Arco dei Gavi**, a triumphal arch attributed to Vitruvius, dating from about 50 BC. Next door, the medieval fortress of **Castelvecchio** hosts a museum and gives on to the ponte Scaligero, the other stone bridge crossing the Adige.

The basilica of **San Zeno**, the city's most stunning church, is located to the west of the 'thumb'.

TICKETS

An admission fee is charged by some churches and all museums in Verona. Cut costs by purchasing a Verona Card (€8 for one day, €12 for three days, free for under-7s), valid for all the sights that charge. It can be bought at the ticket office of any of the churches or museums participating in the scheme and includes all bus fares around the city. No credit cards accepted.

A second scheme (the *itinerario completo*) offers entrance to five of Verona's churches (San Zeno, San Lorenzo, Sant'Anastasia, San Fermo and the Duomo) for €5, as compared to the regular €2 fee per church.

Arena

Piazza Brà (045 800 3204). **Open** 1.45-7.30pm Mon; 8.30am-7.30pm Tue-Sun (hours vary during opera season). **Admission** €3.10; €1 1st Sun of mth. **No credit cards**. For opera booking details, *see p251*
A night at the opera.
The largest Roman amphitheatre in northern Italy, Verona's Arena was capacious enough to seat the city's whole population of 20,000 when it was constructed in about AD 30. Originally the site of gladiatorial games and – filled with water for the occasion – naval battles, the Arena has performed many functions over the centuries. When barbarians invaded in the fifth and sixth centuries, the city's terrified population took refuge inside. Later it was Verona's red-light district, home to the city's prostitutes and cut-throats (perhaps this is why medieval *veronesi* were firmly convinced that it had been built by the devil). Perhaps as an exercise in exorcism, the construction was used as a law court in the Middle Ages and a few unlucky heretics met their fate here. Modern-day theatre promoters were not the first to realise the Arena's attraction – it was already functioning as an open-air theatre in the 17th and 18th centuries. And in the first half of the 20th century it was also used as a football stadium.

Built with pink marble quarried from nearby hills, the Arena is in remarkably good shape. The 44 tiers of stone seats inside the 139m by 110m (456ft by 361ft) amphitheatre are virtually intact, as is the columned foyer. In large part this is because the Arena has been taken care of throughout the centuries. After the earthquake of 1117 destroyed most of the Arena's outer ring, the city repaired the damage almost immediately. Verona's Venetian

The Veneto

overlords – recognising the historic value of the building – made it illegal to pilfer the ancient stone, and carried out regular maintenance work.

Casa di Giulietta (Juliet's house)

Via Cappello 23 (045 803 4303). **Open** 1.30-7.30pm Mon; 8.30am-7.30pm Tue-Sun. **Admission** €3.10. **No credit cards**.

Verona has enough medieval buildings to be able to sacrifice one to the gods of modern tourism. The so-called Casa di Giulietta is a new – and somewhat desultory – addition to the city's attractions. The exterior walls of what is assuredly not Juliet's house have long been a blackboard for scribbled protestations of love, and tourists have long crowded underneath her balcony of renown (a 1920s addition). But now an admission fee allows you inside for a quick glimpse of... nothing at all (Romeo's house – which at least may have actually belonged to the Montague family – is tastefully not open to the public just across from the Della Scala tombs at Arche Scaligere 4.)

If everyday Juliet kitsch is not enough, then plan on being at the house around Valentine's Day, when the Club di Giulietta (via Galilei 3, 37133 Verona, 045 533 115, www.digilander.iol.it/clubgiulietta) announces the results of its annual love-letter writing competition. The most heart-wrenching entries are published in the club's bulletin and the very best are awarded a prize.

Castelvecchio

Corso Castelvecchio 2 (045 594 734/castelvecchio@ comune.verona.it). **Open** 1.45-7.30pm Mon; 8.30am-7.30pm Tue-Sun. **Admission** €3.10; €2.10 concessions. **No credit cards**.

This castle was built by Duke Cangrande II between 1355 and 1375 as an unbreachable refuge from the potential fury of Veronese citizens who were understandably upset by his famously hefty tax bills. Strong though his bolt-hole was, Cangrande was taking no chances: ponte Scaligero, the magnificent fortified medieval bridge, was intended as an emergency escape route.

The castle is now a museum and exhibition venue, with interiors beautifully redesigned in the 1960s by the Venetian architect Carlo Scarpa. The various parts of the castle are linked by overhead walkways and passages offering superb views of the city and surrounding hills. The museum itself contains important works by Mantegna, Crivelli, Pisanello, Giovanni Bellini, Veronese, Tintoretto, Gianbattista Tiepolo, Canaletto and Guardi, as well as a vast collection of lesser-known local artists. On the first floor is a magnificent collection of 13th- and 14th-century Veronese religious statuary. Note the life sized *Crucifixion with Saints* – a clear indication that Veronese artists were influenced as much by the grittier art from north of the Alps as the softer, dreamier stuff being produced in Tuscany. An

Ponte Pietra. *See p247.*

armoury contains a collection of swords, shields and some local jewellery. Admission is free on the first Sunday of every month.

Della Scala family tombs (Tombe or arche scaligere)

Via Santa Maria in Chiavica. **Open** *June-Aug* 1.30-7.30pm Mon; 9.30am-7.30pm Tue-Sun (visible from outside year-round). **Admission** €2.10; €1.50 concessions (combined ticket with Torre dei Lamberti, *see p253*). **No credit cards**.

The Gothic tombs of the Della Scala family, which ruled Verona and vast parts of northern Italy in the 13th and 14th centuries, date from 1277 to the final years of the 14th century and give a good idea of the family's sense of its own importance. Carved by the most sought-after stonemasons of the era – in particular those from the small town of Campione, now an Italian enclave in Switzerland – the more lavish tombs are topped with spires. Note the family's odd taste in first names. The monument to Cangrande (Big Dog, died 1329) above the doorway to the church of Santa Maria Antica, with its equestrian statue, shows the valiant duke smiling in the face of death. (This is a copy; the original is in the Museo Castelvecchio, *see p249*.) Poking out from above the intricate wrought-iron fence surrounding the tombs are the spire-topped final resting places of Cansignorio (Lord Dog, died 1375) and Mastino II (Mastiff the Second, died 1351). Among the less flamboyant tombs is that of Mastino I (died 1277), founder of the doggy dynasty. During the summer months, you can wander round the small courtyard for up-close examinations of the ornateness.

Castelvecchio. *See p249*.

Next door, the intimate church of Santa Maria Antica (open 7.30am-noon, 3.30-7pm daily) was the Della Scala family chapel. Intimate and lit by hundreds of candles, this exquisite building is much loved by the *veronesi*, especially stallholders from the market in nearby piazza delle Erbe.

Duomo

Piazza Duomo (045 595 627/www.veronatuttintorno.it/chiesevive). **Open** *Mar-Oct* 10am-5.30pm Mon-Sat; 1-5.30pm Sun. *Nov-Feb* 10am-4pm Tue-Sat; 1.30-5pm Sun. **Admission** €2 or by *itinerario completo* ticket (*see p248*). **No credit cards**.

Verona's cathedral, begun in 1139, is Romanesque downstairs, Gothic upstairs and Renaissance at the top half of the belltower. The elegant front portico is decorated with Romanesque carvings of the finest quality, showing Charlemagne's paladins Oliver and Roland (who feature in the *Chanson de Roland*, the medieval literary equivalent of *Saving Private Ryan*) wielding their swords while a fan club of saints looks on. Inside, the first chapel on the left has a magnificent *Assumption* by Titian. To the left of the façade is a gateway leading to a tranquil Romanesque cloister where Roman remains and mosaics are on show. In the same complex is the ancient church of Sant'Elena, with the remains of an earlier Christian basilica and Roman baths. And, at the back of the cathedral, to the right of its graceful apse, is the chapel of San Giovanni in Fonte, with a large carved octagonal Romanesque baptismal font.

Giardino Giusti

Via Giardino Giusti 2 (045 803 4029). **Open** *Apr-Sept* 9am-8pm daily. *Oct-Mar* 9am-dusk daily. **Admission** €4.50. **No credit cards**.

The dusty façades of one of Verona's most traffic-clogged streets hide one of the finest Renaissance gardens in Italy. Tucked in behind the great Renaissance townhouse of the Giusti family – the Palazzo Giusti del Giardino – the statue-packed gardens with their tall cypresses were laid out in 1580. The lower level is typically formal in the Italian style. The wild upper level climbs the steep slopes of the hill behind, which offers superb views over the city. Under every shady tree there lurks a potential picnic spot.

Museo Archeologico

Rigaste Redentore 2 (045 800 0360). **Open** 1.30-7pm Mon; 8.30am-7pm Tue-Sun. **Admission** €2.60; €1.50 concessions (includes Teatro Romano, *see p252*). **No credit cards**.

This small museum, containing a fine, though patchily labelled, collection of Roman remains, is situated in a former monastery next door to the Teatro Romano. Even visitors with the strongest aversion to yet more ancient bits and pieces are advised to take the lift from the theatre through the cliffs and up to the museum: the views over Verona and the river Adige are incomparable. Admission is free on the first Sunday of the month.

The Veneto

San Fermo Maggiore

Stradone San Fermo (045 592 813/800 7287).
Open *Mar-Oct* 10am-6pm Mon-Sat; 1-6pm Sun.
Nov-Feb 10am-4pm Tue-Sat; 1.30-5pm Sun.
Admission €2 or by *itinerario completo* ticket
(*see p248*). **No credit cards**.

At San Fermo you get two churches for the price of
one, although the bottom one tends to be a little
damp: the lower church is Romanesque and the
upper church, built in the 14th century, is Gothic.
While the lower church is intimate and solemn, the
upper part is towering and full of light. Its wooden
ceiling, resembling an upturned Venetian galleon, is
similar to that of San Zeno (*see p252*). Among the
important frescos is an *Annunciation* by Antonio
Pisanello to the left of the main entrance.

San Giorgio in Braida

Piazzetta San Giorgio 1 (045 834 0232) **Open** 8am-
11am, 5-7pm Mon-Sat; 5-7pm Sun.

This great domed Renaissance church, probably
designed by the Veronese military architect Michele
Sanmicheli between 1536 and 1543, contains some of
the city's greatest treasures. Shining in this light-
filled Renaissance masterpiece is a *Baptism of
Christ* by Tintoretto, above the entrance door, and a
moving *Martyrdom of St George* by Paolo Veronese.
But even these greats are put in the shade by a serene
Madonna and Child with Saints Zeno and Lawrence
by local dark horse Girolamo dai Libri.

San Giovanni in Valle

Via San Giovanni in Valle 36 (045 803 0119). **Open**
9am-noon daily.

Built in the Romanesque style, the current San
Giovanni is part of a much older original complex,
dating back to the eighth century. The church's
beautiful crypt (closed for renovations as this guide
went to press) contains fine examples of early
Christian sculpture.

Santa Maria in Organo

Piazzetta Santa Maria in Organo (045 591 440).
Open 8am-noon, 2.30-6pm daily.

The Renaissance church of Santa Maria in Organo
has a host of frescos by the Veronese painters
Caroto, Giolfino and Farinato, but you may want to
pass them by and make your way straight to the
apse and sacristy to see what Giorgio Vasari once
described as the most beautiful choir stalls in Italy.
A humble monk, Fra Giovanni da Verona (died
1520), worked for a quarter of a century cutting and
assembling these infinitely complex, coloured wood-
en images of animals, birds, landscapes, cityscapes,
religious scenes and musical and scientific instruments in dozens of intricate intarsia panels.

Sant'Anastasia

Piazza Sant'Anastasia (045 592 813/800 4325).
Open *Mar-Oct* 9am-6pm Mon-Sat; 1-6pm Sun. *Nov-
Feb* 10am-4pm Tue-Sat; 1.30-5pm Sun. **Admission**
€2 or by *itinerario completo* ticket (*see p248*).
No credit cards.

This imposing brick Gothic church is best visited
early in the morning, when sunlight streams in to
illuminate Antonio Pisanello's glorious fresco (1433-
8; in the sacristy to the right of the apse) of St George
girding himself to set off in pursuit of the dragon

A night at the opera

Two thousand years ago, Roman Verona's
movers and shakers didn't have to show a
ticket to get into the Arena; their names
were carved into their very own seats. Tickets
are necessary these days, but very little else
has changed. As the Arena's own website
puts it: 'People of authority and celebrities
parade in evening wear, to the delight of
the curious onlookers.'

Whether, in fact, said onlookers are
delighted by the chance to see expensively
dressed Italian industrialists getting back to
their ersatz Roman roots and perambulating
arm in arm with people who may or may not
be their spouses, or because they find
something cool about spending an evening
under the stars enjoying world-class opera in
a 2,000-year-old theatre is an open question.
Either way, a show at the Arena Opera
Festival is a unique experience.

Despite the presence of the elite, the
festival is surprisingly egalitarian. Tickets can

be had for as little as 15, and spectators
in the cheap seats can bring their own food
and drink (but no glass or cans). Since you
will be sitting on a cold stone step for three
hours, a comfy cushion is a good idea. And
whether you're in the cheap seats or not,
don't forget to bring a candle – you'll need
it for the atmosphere.

Operators on the booking line (number
given below) speak Italian, English and
German; the Arena also accepts online
bookings. Seats are sometimes available
on the day of the show, especially in quieter
midweek periods. The cheapest seats are
not numbered, so get there two hours early
to grab a decent spot.

Fondazione Arena di Verona

*Via Dietro l'Anfiteatro 6B (045 800 5151/
www.arena.it).* **Performances** *June-Aug* 9pm
Tue-Sun. **Tickets** 15- 154. **Credit** AmEx,
DC, MC, V.

that has been pestering the lovely princess of Trebizond. Carved scenes from the life of St Peter Martyr adorn the unfinished façade, while inside two delightful *gobbi* (hunchbacks) crouch down to support the holy water font; the one on the left was carved by Paolo Veronese's father in 1495.

Santo Stefano

Vicolo Scaletta Santo Stefano 1 (045 834 8529). **Open** 9am-noon, 4-7pm Mon, Wed-Sun; 9am-noon Tue.

A church has stood on this site since the sixth century, and parts of that original church can still be seen in the apse of the current building. The existing Romanesque church ranks as one of the oldest in Verona, and served as the city's cathedral until the 12th century. Santo Stefano boasts an unusual octagonal brick tower, as well as a complicated two-storey apse and a stunning 14th-century marble statue of St Peter.

San Zeno Maggiore

Piazza San Zeno 2 (045 592 813/800 6120). **Open** *Mar-Oct* 8.30am-6pm Mon-Sat; 1-6pm Sun. *Nov-Feb* 10am-4pm Tue-Sat; 1.30-5pm Sun. **Admission** €2 or by *itinerario completo* ticket (*see p248*). **No credit cards**.

One of the most spectacularly ornate Romanesque churches in northern Italy, San Zeno was built between 1123 and 1138 to house the tomb and shrine of San Zeno, an African who became Verona's first bishop in 362 and is now the city's much-loved patron saint. The façade, with its great rose window and porch, is covered with some of Italy's finest examples of Romanesque marble sculpture. Scenes from the Old Testament and the life of Christ mingle with hunting and jousting scenes, attributed to the 12th-century sculptors Nicolò and Guglielmo. The graceful porch is supported by columns resting on two carved marble lions; they serve as a frame for the great bronze doors of the basilica; the 48 panels have scenes from the Bible and from the life of San Zeno, and a few that experts have been hard-pressed to pin down, including a woman suckling two crocodiles. The panels on the left-hand door date from about 1030 and came from an earlier church. Those on the right were produced a century later. Inside the lofty church (note the magnificent ceiling built in 1386), the main altar is placed on a raised platform reached by twin staircases. A third staircase descends into the crypt, which contains the tomb of San Zeno. Dominating the altar is a stunning triptych depicting the Madonna and Child with a bevy of saints, an early work by Andrea Mantegna painted between 1457 and 1459. The lower panel, showing Christ on the cross, is a copy: the original was looted by Napoleon, and is now in the Louvre .

The enduring love affair between San Zeno and the city that adopted him may have something to do with the huge – and hugely appealing – early 12th-century marble statue of the African bishop having a grand old chuckle, which is to be found in a niche to the left of the apse. His black face, with its distinctly African

Doggy **Della Scala family tombs**. *See p150.*

features, is unique in Italian religious statuary, as is his singularly jovial and not-particularly-saintly aspect. Covering the inside walls of the basilica are frescos dating from the 12th to the 14th centuries, but perhaps more interesting than the paintings themselves is the 15th- to 17th-century graffito scratched into them by the faithful invoking Zeno's protection from earthquakes and pestilence.

To the right of the church is a massive belltower, 72m (236ft) high, begun in 1045. To the left is a lower tower, which is all that remains of the Benedictine monastery that stood on the site before the basilica was built, and which, according to local lore, stands over the grave of Pepin, Charlemagne's disinherited hunchback son. Behind is an open, light-filled Romanesque cloister.

Teatro Romano

Regaste Redentore 2 (045 800 0360). **Open** 9am-7pm Tue-Sun. **Admission** €2.60 (includes Museo Archeologico, *see p250*). **No credit cards**.

The Roman theatre, dating from around the first century BC, was buried under medieval houses until the late 19th century, when the semicircular seating was brought to light. Built into the side of the hill where Verona's earliest pre-Roman and Roman settlements were located, the theatre offers marvellous views over the city, and is an evocative venue for an annual festival of theatre (Shakespeare is a perennial favourite), ballet and jazz. For programme and booking details contact Estate Teatrale Veronese (via degli Alpini 2, 045 806 6485, www.teatroro-mano.it). Tickets cost upwards from €10 and can also be purchased at the *teatro* immediately before performances. Admission to the theatre is free on the first Sunday of the month.

Torre dei Lamberti
Cortile Mercato Vecchio (045 803 2726). **Open** 1.30-7.30pm Mon; 9.30am-7.30pm Tue-Sun. **Admission** *Lift* €2.10 (€2.60 with Della Scala family tombs, *see p250*). *Stairs* €1.50 (€2.10 with tombs). **No credit cards**.
This massive medieval tower, 83m (273ft) high, offers superb views of the city and, on clear days, a spectacular panorama of the local mountains and Italian Alps. The 368-step climb is only for the fittest.

Where to eat

Verona's cuisine is an interesting combination of Middle European heft and Italian sensibility. Boiled and roasted meats come by the trolleyful, served up with *cren*, the local take on horseradish sauce, and *peará*, made of bone marrow (BSE scares permitting), bread and pepper. Braised horsemeat (*pastissada de cuval*) is another local speciality. Vegetarians take heart, however. *Bigoli*, the local pasta, is a sort of thick spaghetti often served with meat-free sauces, and the fertile farms to the south of the city yield up excellent vegetables (pumpkin-stuffed ravioli are also a Veronese speciality).

Al Duomo
Via Duomo 7 (045 800 4505). **Meals served** *Sept-June* 11am-3pm, 6pm-midnight Mon-Sat. Closed July, Aug. **Average** €20. **Credit** MC, V.
Elderly mandolin players congregate here of a Tuesday and/or Wednesday evening to strum traditional music. Near to the Duomo, this *osteria* is much-frequented by the people of the quarter who know a well-priced meal when they see one.

Ostaria La Stueta
Via Redentore 4 (045 803 2462). **Meals served** *Sept-June* 7-10pm Tue; noon-2pm, 5-10pm Wed-Sun. *Aug* 5-10pm Tue; noon-2pm, 5-10pm Wed-Sun. Closed July. **Average** €20. **Credit** AmEx, MC, V, DC.
The menu in this tiny restaurant is limited and traditional, but unfailingly delicious. In autumn, mushrooms are a treat; try the polenta with *moscardini* (baby octopus) in summer. Helpful staff and a good wine list add to the experience. Booking advisable.

Papa & Cicia del Caciator
Via Seminario 4A (045 800 8384). **Meals served** noon-2.30pm Mon; noon-2.30pm, 7.30-10.30pm Tue-Fri, Sun; 7.30-10.30pm Sat. Closed 2wks Aug. **Average** €20. **Credit** MC, V.
This small trattoria in the Veronetta area across the river from the *centro storico* serves up a variety of tasty (and economical) lunch menus, and all the grilled meat you can stand in the evenings.

Tre Marchetti
Vicolo Tre Marchetti 19B (045 803 0463). **Meals served** 7-10.30pm Mon; 12.15-2.30pm, 7-10.30pm Tue-Sat. Closed 2wks June, 1wk Sept, 2wks Dec. **Average** €50. **Credit** MC, V.
Meals have been served on these premises just round the corner from the Roman Arena since 1291, making it one of the most ancient eating houses in Europe. It has lost none of its allure over the centuries: informal and crowded, with specialities of *bigoli* with duck, *pastissada de caval* and *baccalà alla vicentina* (*see p260* **The joy of cod**). Booking is advisable, especially during the opera season.

Bars & nightlife

Ai Preti
Interrato dell'Acqua Morta 27 (045 597 675). **Open** 6.30am-2am Mon-Sat. **No credit cards**.
Much favoured by ageing left-wing radical types, who join a heterogeneous mix of young single women, English-speaking foreigners and university teachers. Hots up – in a lukewarm kind of way – towards midnight.

Bar Leon d'Oro
Via Pallone 10A (045 595 076). **Open** 10am-4am daily. **Credit** DC, MC, V.

Much-loved **San Zeno**. *See p252*.

A bottle of red, a bottle of white

The Veneto is Italy's third-biggest wine-producing region, and the vineyards around Verona are responsible for some of the country's recognisable wines: Soave, Bardolino and Valpolicella. Unfortunately for Verona, however, these names are known more for their undiscerning Bridget Jones-type quaffing qualities than for their finesse. But that doesn't mean that good wine from the Veneto cannot be found.

In fact, the Veronese take their wine very seriously, keeping the lightweight export names for everyday use and the better-kept secrets for special occasions. Indeed, Corvina, Molinara and Rondinella – the same grapes from which Bardolino and Valpolicella are made – produce one of the great wines of Italy: Amarone, with its deep complex flavours of fruit and spice and its port-like body.

Moreover, Verona is home to the annual oenological feeding frenzy that is Vinitaly.

This fair – a five-day event usually held in early April – is not for the faint of heart. It attracts every important wine producer (and wannabe) in Italy along with hordes of trades people, journalists and the winehead public, who all jam so tight around the exhibitors' stands that quiet reflection on a sample's nuances is well nigh impossible. What it lacks in refinement, though, Vinitaly makes up for in opportunity and excitement. Wines you've never heard of, or never thought you'd get the chance to taste, are yours for the asking... even if it takes patience and a well-placed elbow or two.

Vinitaly

Fiera di Verona, viale del Lavoro 8 (information 045 829 8111/ www.veronafiera.it). **Open** to the public 9am-7pm Mon, Thur-Sun. Usually held for 5 days in early Apr. **Admission** 30; 12 concessions. **Credit** AmEx, DC, MC, V.

Late-night hangout for the city's glitterati, with a strong gay element. The bar is situated in a late 18th- century townhouse with a large front garden, where you can sip a drink under the stars on balmy summer nights.

Gelateria Pampanin

Via Garibaldi 24 (045 803 0064). **Open** 7.30am-midnight Mon, Wed-Sun. Closed 2wks Aug. **No credit cards.**
Pampanin's ice-creams are Verona's finest. Such is the popularity of Pampanin *gelato* with the well-heeled Veronese that the place is able to shut down in the hottest month of the year, just when its trade should be briskest. The reason is simple: its clientele has fled en masse to plush summer retreats.

Locanda del Fiume

Via Santa Maria Rocca Maggiore 15A (045 800 7751). **Open** 11am-2.30pm, 7pm-12.30am Tue-Fri; 7pm-12.30am Sat, Sun. **Credit** AmEx, MC, V.
Check your email (rates €4.20 per hour) while munching on the Locanda's good bruschetta.

Where to stay

Due Torri Hotel Baglioni

Piazza Sant'Anastasia 4 (045 595 0444/fax 045 800 4130/www.baglionihotels.com). **Rates** €250-€371 single; €390-€495 double. **Credit** AmEx, DC, MC, V.
This celebrated hotel (Beethoven and Goethe were among its illustrious guests) forms one side of the square and is widely considered to be the city's finest. Some of the rooms let guests go eyeball to

eyeball with Gugliemo di Castelvarco, whose tomb tops the archway across from the hotel.

Campeggio Castel San Pietro

Via Castel San Pietro 2 (045 592 037/www. campingcastelsanpietro.com). **Rates** €5-€7 per plot. €5.50 per person; €4 under-8s in addition. Closed mid Oct-mid May. **No credit cards.**
In a spectacular position above the city centre, within the old city walls, and 15 minutes' walk from the centre. Good bathroom facilities. Hires out caravans.

Hotel Antica Porta Leona

Corticella Leoni 3 (045 595 499/fax 045 595 214/ htlanticaportaleona@tiscalinet.it). **Rates** €62-€103 single; €83-€150 double. Closed 20 Dec-Jan.
Credit AmEx, DC, MC, V.
This pretty little hotel is in the pedestrian heart of Verona's old city.

Hotel Aurora

Piazzetta XIV Novembre 2 (045 594 717/597 834/ fax 045 801 0860/www.hotelaurora.biz). **Rates** €60-€65 single; €112-€123 double. **Credit** AmEx, DC, MC, V.
In a little nook off piazza delle Erbe, this simple hotel is friendly and efficiently run.

Hotel Bologna

Piazzetta Scalette Rubiani 3 (045 800 6830/fax 045 801 0602/www.hotelbologna.vr.it). **Rates** €110 single; €168 double. **Credit** AmEx, DC, MC, V.
Situated just off piazza Brà, this comfortable and unpretentious hotel is located in a perfect spot for exploring the city.

The Veneto

Resources

Hotel reservations

CAV *via Patuzzi 5 (045 800 9844/fax 045 800 9372/www.cav.vr.it)*. **Open** *Apr-Oct* 9am-7.30pm Mon-Sat; 2-7pm Sun. *Nov-Mar* 9am-6.30pm Mon-Fri. The Verona hoteliers' association, CAV, runs a free hotel-booking bureau.

Tourist information

APT *via degli Alpini 9 (045 806 8680/fax 045 800 3638/www.tourism.verona.it)*. **Open** 1-7pm Mon; 9am-7pm Tue-Sat; 9am-3pm Sun.

APT *inside the train station, piazza XXV Aprile (tel/fax 045 800 0861)*. **Open** 9am-6pm Mon-Sat. *Verona airport (tel/fax 045 861 9163)*. **Open** 11am-5pm Mon-Sat.

Getting around

By bus

The APT Verona bus company (045 805 7811) runs services (blue coaches) to towns and villages in the area around Verona, including Lake Garda and the Monti Lessini. Buses depart from the bus station, in front of Porta Nuova train station.

AMT (045 887 1111) runs the city bus service (orange buses), most of which start and terminate at the train station. Bus tickets can be purchased at the station or any tobacconist's. A 93¢ ticket is valid for one hour and should be punched on each bus boarded during that time.

By bicycle

El Pedal Scaligero (333 536 7770) is a booth located near the APT office (*see* Tourist information, *above*) in piazza Brà. Open 9am-8pm daily from April to September, it offers a variety of hourly, daily and longer-term rates.

Getting there

By air

Verona's Valerio Catullo Airport (045 809 5666) is a 20min bus ride from the train station. The shuttle bus between the airport and the train station leaves every 20mins; tickets cost €4.20 on the bus.

By train

Regular train services from Milan and Venice (75-90mins) to Verona Porta Nuova railway station (045 800 0861).

By car

Take the A4 La Serenissima motorway from either Venice or Milan.

Around Verona

Little more than an hour's drive north of Verona are the wild, rugged Dolomites, with marvellous skiing and trekking. To the west is Lake Garda, the largest of Italy's northern lakes (*see also*

Time Out Guide to Milan, the Lakes & Lombardy). The area to the south of Verona, on the other hand, is a culinary paradise with scores of rural *trattorie*.

Caldiero

Ancient Verona's inhabitants flocked to Caldiero's hot springs – the **Terme di Giunone** – to splash about in the same stone pool used by today's wallowers. Other more modern pools have been added to accommodate the crowds in this spa 18 kilometres (11 miles) east of Verona, where water bubbles up at a temperature of 28° centigrade.

Terme di Giunone

Via delle Terme 2 (045 615 1288/www. termedigiunone.it). **Open** *June-July* 9am-8pm daily. *Apr-May, Aug-Oct* 11am-6pm daily. **Admission** €8. No credit cards.

Valeggio sul Mincio

At the centre of the carriage-building industry, Valeggio went into a severe economic slump as the combustion engine edged out the horse-drawn vehicle. Salvation came at the hands of the area's canny womenfolk who, superb cooks all, opened scores of tiny restaurants serving some of the best food around. The excellent local *tortelli di zucca* (pumpkin-stuffed pasta) and the grilled fish, fresh from the nearby Lake Garda, are part of this tradition.

Where to eat

Alla Borsa

Via Goito 2, Valeggio (045 795 0093/www. valeggio.com/borsa). **Meals served** 12.15-2pm, 7.15-10pm Mon, Thur-Sun; 12.15-2pm Tue. Closed mid July-mid Aug; 2wks Feb. **Average** €30. **Credit** MC, V.
This family-run trattoria serves perhaps the most delicious pumpkin *tortelli* in existence. Informal and noisy, Alla Borsa also specialises in trout and other fish from nearby Lake Garda, plus stuffed guinea fowl, roast pork shanks and duck. Delicious home-made desserts.

Resources

Tourist information
See above.

Getting there

By bus

There are regular APT bus services (045 805 7811) for Caldiero and Valeggio sul Mincio from Verona bus station, in front of Porta Nuova train station.

The Veneto

Vicenza

One of the world's finest medieval and Renaissance cities.

Go shopping on **corso Palladio**.

Buildings matter, in Vicenza. It's to be expected. After all, Vicenza was the home of Andrea Palladio (*see chapter* **Palladian Villas**), and the great architect's works have placed Vicenza on the UNESCO roll of World Heritage Sights. But the buildings started mattering even before Palladio rolled into town (he was born in nearby Padua) in 1524.

The buildings mattered in part because Vicenza had long had the wherewithal to build them well. The city had been an important crossroads for the Romans and the resulting commerce became a way of life for the *vicentini*. Even during the cash-strapped early Middle Ages when Barbarians were looting and pillaging along the peninsula, the astute locals flourished. Today this city of 110,000 residents is one of Italy's richest, and its goldsmiths are known for producing some of Europe's finest jewellery (Vicenza hosts three bustling jewellery fairs each year).

The buildings mattered too because they were a very concrete means of self-expression. The Venetians had arrived in 1404, and the aristocratic *vicentini* chafed under their rule. One way to assuage their hurt feelings – and cock a noble snook at Venice – was to commission sumptuous townhouses and country villas. Much more than mere dwellings, the *palazzi* and *ville* became outward signs of the families' worth, tastes and perceived superiority over their upstart rulers. Palladio's success was due in part to his ability to take the *vicentino* superiority/inferiority complex and translate it into monument.

The effect of all this architecture and affluence is manifest in a walk down corso Palladio – Vicenza's main street: there's palazzo after palazzo adorned by balconies, loggias, arches and columns. On their ground floors, meanwhile, upmarket stores glisten with the city's world-class jewels, designer clothing and expensive gifts.

Sightseeing

Like much of north-eastern Italy, Vicenza benefited hugely from the economic boom of the 1970s. But in Vicenza – as in much of north-eastern Italy – there was a price to pay. Much of the surrounding countryside, which used to compare favourably with the Tuscan hills for aesthetic appeal, has been replaced with industrial sprawl. Villas, Palladian and otherwise, originally designed to blend picturesquely with the rural landscape, now sit amid factories and shopping malls.

On the bright side, however, some of the area's wealth has been channelled into restoring the city's *palazzi* and churches and creating a comfortable environment in which to view them.

While very little remains of Roman Vicetia, the town's Roman layout is still virtually intact: the main street, corso Palladio, was the *decumanus maximus*, the central axis of the Roman street grid, and runs east–west as straight as an arrow. For the most part, though, Vicenza's character is medieval and Renaissance. The walls bordering viale Mazzini, on the western side of the city, were part of the defence system built by the Della Scala family, who arrived from Verona in 1311 and stayed until the Venetians took over. The Della Scalas

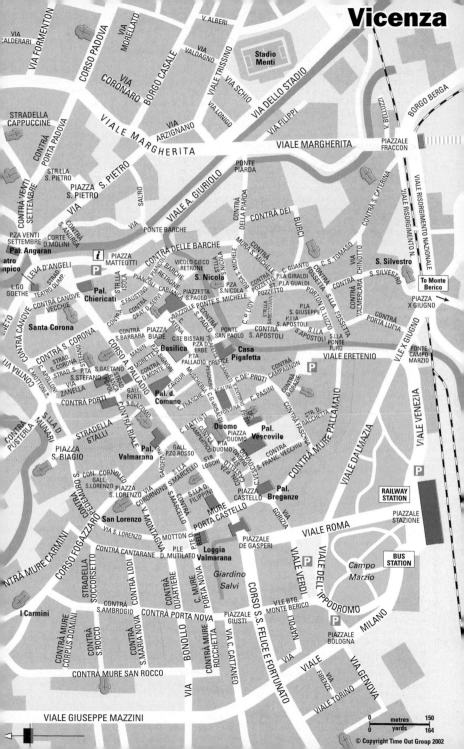

also used the city's two rivers as moats. Today, though, the Retrone and the Bacchiglione are little more than sluggish streams.

Corso Palladio begins just inside the town's western gate, **Porta Castello** (also built by the Della Scalas). But the first sight of interest is just outside the walls, in the **Giardino Salvi**. Inside this public park is Andrea Palladio's charming **Loggia Valmarana**, a Doric-style temple spanning the waters of a wide canal. Nearby, over another branch of the canal, is a baroque loggia by Baldassare Longhena. Piazza del Castello, back inside the gate, is home to **Palazzo Porto Breganze**, designed by Palladio but never finished. This tall, awkward fragment in the southern corner, with its grandiose columns and two elaborately carved windows and decorative balconies, should have extended to occupy the entire southern end of the piazza. Palladio had a hand in five of the grandiose *palazzi* lining corso Palladio (all except Palazzo Trissino are closed to the public). The first of note, on the left-hand side, is the magnificent **Palazzo Thiene Bonin Longare**, begun in 1562; note the impressive double loggia at the back of the building. At No.45 is **Palazzo Capra**, almost certainly designed by the young Palladio between 1540 and 1545. Though alterations have been made since, Palladio's original façade and doorway remain.

A quick turn right into contrà Battisti (streets in Vicenza's centre are called 'contrà' instead of the usual 'via') leads to the **Duomo**, while a detour to the left leads to the Gothic brick church of **San Lorenzo**. Back on corso Palladio, at No.92, is **Palazzo Pojana** (1564-6), which consists of two separate buildings cunningly joined together by Palladio; where the front door would normally be, the architect left room for a street to run through. **Palazzo Trissino**, at No.98, was designed in 1592 by Palladio's student Vincenzo Scamozzi.

The overwhelming presence of Palladio is to be felt once more in the vast and elegant piazza dei Signori, just south of the corso. Apart from the slender and spectacular 82-metre (269-foot) **Torre di Piazza** clock tower, which dates from the 12th century, the prevailing spirit of the square is definitely late Renaissance. Tacked gracefully on to the square side of the Gothic **Palazzo della Ragione** assembly hall (better known as the **Basilica Palladiana**, in the ancient Roman sense of the word – a public place where justice is dispensed) is Palladio's marvellous loggia. Opposite this is his **Loggia del Capitanato**, a fragment of a building that was intended to continue along most of the northern side of the square. This highly decorated brick arcade was built to celebrate Venice's victory over the Turks in the Battle of Lepanto in 1571; it was the official residence of the all-powerful Venetian governor of Vicenza. On the same side is the vast complex of the **Monte di Pietà**, the city's elegant 16th-century pawn shop, which extends on either side of the baroquified church of **San Vincenzo**.

There is a morning clothes and food market in piazza dei Signori on Tuesday and Thursday. Food stalls spill over into piazza delle Erbe, around the other side of the basilica, a square dominated by a medieval tower where Vicenza's recalcitrant wrongdoers were taken for a little tongue-loosening torture.

In the labyrinth of streets to the south of piazza delle Erbe is the **Casa Pigafetta** (contrà Pigafetta 9). Dating from 1444 and built in late Spanish Gothic style, this strange, highly decorated townhouse was the birthplace of Antonio Pigafetta, the adventurous nobleman who was one of only 21 survivors of Magellan's epoch-making circumnavigation of the globe between 1519 and 1522.

Off corso Palladio north of piazza Signori is contrà Porti, which offers a real palazzo feast. The Porto family was very rich, very influential and very clannish; all its members chose to build their townhouses in the same short street. At No.11 is the **Palazzo Barbaran Da Porto**, designed and built by Palladio between 1569 and 1571, with an interior elaborately decorated with stuccoes by Lorenzo Rubini. Currently used to house temporary exhibitions, the palazzo has long been earmarked as the site of a new museum dedicated to the life and works of Palladio – though not much has been done on this front so far.

Casa Porto (No.15) is an undistinguished 15th-century building that was badly restored in the 18th century but is of interest as the home of Luigi Da Porto (died 1529), writer of the first known account of the Romeo and Juliet story. At No.19 the exquisite, late Gothic **Palazzo Porto Colleoni** is a typical 15th-century attempt to beat the Venetians at their own game. Be sure to take a quick peek through the open gateway into the secluded back garden. **Palazzo Iseppo Da Porto**, at No.21, is one of Palladio's earliest creations.

At the far end of this street, across a bridge over the River Bacchiglione, contrà San Marco is a wide street lined with fine 16th- and 17th-century *palazzi*, including **Palazzo Da Schio**, an elegant townhouse designed by Palladio in the 1560s.

Back on corso Palladio, the huge palazzo that stands on the corner with contrà Porti is the **Palazzo Dal Toso**, a flamboyant Gothic jewel, which once boasted gilded capitals –

hence its other name, the Ca' d'Oro. The Gothic theme continues in the church of **Santa Corona** further down the corso. The **Gallerie di Palazzo Leoni Montanari** (*see below*), in contrà Santa Corona just off the corso, contains charming 18th-century genre paintings by Pietro Longhi. Almost at the end of corso Palladio, tiny **Casa Cogollo** at No.167 is thought to have been Palladio's home in later life; according to some accounts, he may even have designed it.

The main street ends in piazza Matteotti, where two of Vicenza's real artistic treats await: **Palazzo Chiericati** (1550), one of Palladio's finest townhouses, now the city's art gallery (the **Museo Civico**); and the architect's final masterpiece, the **Teatro Olimpico**.

Towering above town to the south, the **Santuario di Monte Berico** can be reached on foot in the shade of an 18th-century loggia joining it to the centre.

TICKETS
Admission to the Museo Civico (*see p260*), Museo Naturalistico Archeologico in contrà Santa Corona and the Teatro Olimpico (*see*

Urban restyling: **Basilica Palladiana**.

p261) is by *biglietto unico* only. Tickets – which are valid for three days from the date of purchase – can be bought at participating sights or at the tourist office (*see p262*). No credit cards.

The *biglietto unico* is available in three different forms:
Three museums: €7 (Museo Civico, Museo Naturalistico Archeologico in contrà Santa Corona and Teatro Olimpico).
Four museums: €8 (the above museums plus Museo del Risorgimento e della Resistenza).
Family 2 adults and 1 child or more: €12 (all four museums).

Basilica Palladiana (Palazzo della Ragione)
Piazza dei Signori (0444 323 681). **Admission** during exhibitions only; prices & times vary.
Palladio's most famous piece of urban restyling is a neat alternative to scaffolding. The original Palazzo della Regione, seat of the city government, was built in the 1450s; but the loggia that once surrounded it – and helped to support it – collapsed in 1496, making it necessary to find an elegant way of shoring up the building. The city fathers canvassed most of the leading architects of the day from 1525 onwards; luckily for Palladio – who was only 17 at this time – they dithered for 20 years before accepting the audacious solution proposed by the home contender in 1546. Palladio's double-tiered loggia, Doric below and Ionic above, encases the original Gothic palazzo in a Renaissance shell. The main *salone* is a barn-like space, with impressive ornate arches holding up the wooden ship's-keel roof. Vicenza now uses the basilica as an exhibition space, and it is only open during exhibitions.

Duomo
Piazza Duomo (0444 323 229). **Open** 10.30am-noon, 3.30-5.30pm Mon-Fri; 10.30am-noon Sat; Sun for mass only.
Founded in the ninth century, the Duomo suffered extensive damage in World War II. The Palladian dome, finished in 1574, has been painstakingly restored to its former splendour, as has the Gothic pink marble façade, attributed to Domenico da Venezia (1467). The brick interior contains an important polyptych by Lorenzo Veneziano, signed and dated 1366.

Gallerie di Palazzo Leoni Montanari
Contrà Santa Corona 25 (0444 991 291/tollfree 800 578 875/www.palazzomontanari.com). **Open** 10am-6pm Fri-Sun. **Admission** €3.30; €2.30 concessions.
No credit cards.
Situated in the recently restored baroque Palazzo Leoni Montanari, this remarkable collection of 14 masterpieces by the 18th-century Venetian genre painter Pietro Longhi, housed together with other important examples of Venetian art, should not be missed. Also on display here is a collection of Russian icons.

The Veneto

Museo Civico

Palazzo Chiericati, piazza Matteotti 37-9 (0444 321 348/fmuseocivico@comune.vicenza.it). **Open** *Sept-June* 9am-5pm Tue-Sun. *July, Aug* 9am-7pm Tue-Sun. **Admission** by *biglietto unico* (*see p259*).

The art gallery on the second floor of this Palladian palazzo contains a fascinating collection of works by local painters, Bartolomeo Montagna (1450-1523) in particular. It also houses excellent work by Van Dyck, Tintoretto, Veronese, Tiepolo and Giovanni Bellini. Outshining them all is a *Crucifixion* by the Flemish master Hans Memling, the central part of a triptych whose side panels are in New York. In the ticket office is a 16th-century portrait of the Valmarana family that allows an intimate peek at some of Palladio's keenest fans and employers.

Palazzo Trissino

Corso Garibaldi 98 (0444 221 111/www.comune.vicenza.it). **Open** 9am-1.30pm Mon-Sat; interior by appointment only. **Admission** free.

Now Vicenza's town hall, this design by Palladio's student Vincenzo Scamozzi was begun in 1592 but not completed until 1667. On the corso, a portico with Ionic columns is surmounted by a Corinthian-inspired *piano nobile*. Nobody minds if you stroll into the courtyard.

San Lorenzo

Piazza San Lorenzo (0444 321 960). **Open** 10.30am-noon, 3.30-6pm Mon-Sat; 3.30-6pm Sun.

None of the city's neo-classical or baroque places of worship can hold a candle to San Lorenzo's Gothic glory. The magnificent marble portal encases an exquisite 14th-century lunette depicting the Madonna and Child. Inside, three grandiose naves are lit by high monoforate windows. The Poiana altar in the right transept is a fine late Gothic assemblage of paintings and frescos by various artists, while the peaceful 16th-century cloister contains a pretty medieval well-head.

Santa Corona

Contrà Santa Corona (0444 321 924). **Open** 10.30am-noon, 3.30-6pm Mon-Sat; 3.30-6pm Sun.

This Gothic brick church was built between 1260 and 1270, to house a much-travelled stray thorn from Christ's crown. Its interior, consisting of three unequally sized naves, contains an *Adoration of the Magi* (1573) by Paolo Veronese in the third chapel on the right. In the crypt is the Valmarana Chapel, designed by Palladio. The church's other artistic treasure, in the fifth chapel on the left of the nave, is a *Baptism of Christ* by Giovanni Bellini (1502).

Santuario di Monte Berico

Viale X Giugno 87 (0444 320 998/www.monteberico.it). **Open** 6.15am-12.30pm, 2.30-7.30pm Mon-Sat; 6.15am-8pm Sun.

Monte Berico was where hot and bothered *vicentini* used to come for a bit of greenery and a breath of fresh air in summer. The exhaust fumes of countless pilgrim coaches grinding up to the spot where the Virgin is said to have appeared in 1426 and 1428 spoil the effect these days, though some pedestrian protection is afforded by a shady 18th-century

The joy of cod

Why is cod Vicenza's traditional dish? Vicenza, after all, is hardly a port town, with only two turgid streams to boast of. And cod isn't found in the Mediterranean in any event. Yet it's a centuries-old speciality: there are references to the *vicentini* staying alive by eating *baccalà* during a siege in 1269.

The primary reasons for the choice were the Catholic Church and food conservation. Today, many Catholics abstain from eating meat on Fridays during Lent; in the past, meat was off the menu every Friday and all of Lent. Catholics needed a lot of fish.

In pious, landlocked Vicenza, this was a tall order. Cod became the fish of choice: plentiful in the North Atlantic, the fish preserved well, allowing it to reach this far with its nutritional virtues intact.

Cod can be preserved two ways. It can be salted and partially dried (salt cod, or *baccalà* in Italian) or just dried (stockfish; *stoccafisso*). Counter-intuitively, the classic

Vicentine dish of *baccalà alla vicentina* is made not from *baccalà* but from *stoccafisso*.

The origins of this misnomer date back to 1432 when Pietro Querini, a Venetian trader, was shipwrecked off the coast of Norway. He was taken in by locals and introduced to the delights of *stokkfisk* – which would be corrupted to *stoccafisso* in Italian. When he brought his new discovery home with him, the *vicentini* decided they preferred *stoccafisso* to the *baccalà* that was already a firm fixture on their menus. *Stoccafisso*, however, is not an easy word to pronounce in the Vicentine dialect, so they kept on using the word *baccalà*.

Baccalà alla vicentina is not a dish you decide to make on the spur of the moment. The stockfish needs to be beaten, then left to soak in abundant water for several days, with the water being changed at least twice a day. After which the fish is checked carefully for pin bones, then braised for four hours in milk with onions.

The Veneto

arcade that flanks the road up to the basilica for over half a kilometre. The church itself was largely rebuilt in the 18th century. It contains Veronese's *Supper of St Gregory the Great* (1572) in the refectory (ask to see it) as well as a moving *Pietà* by local boy Bartolomeo Montagna and a fine collection of fossils in the cloister.

Teatro Olimpico

Piazza Matteotti 11 (0444 222 800). **Open** *Sept-June* 9am-5pm Tue-Sun. *July, Aug* 9am-7pm Tue-Sun. **Admission** by *biglietto unico* (*see p259*).

Palladio's last masterpiece, the Teatro Olimpico was the first permanent indoor theatre built in Europe after the fall of the Roman Empire. Palladio got to work on designing the theatre in 1579 but died just before construction began the following year. His son Silla and star pupil Vincenzo Scamozzi completed the project, taking considerable liberties with the original blueprint. The decorative flamboyance of the wood-and-stucco interior contrasts notably with its modest entrance and severe external walls. Built on the model of Greek and Roman theatres, it has 13 semicircular wooden steps rising in front of the stage, crowned by Corinthian columns holding up an elaborate balustrade topped with elegant 'antique' sculpted figures. The permanent stage set, with its five *trompe l'oeil* street scenes, represents the city of Thebes in Sophocles' *Oedipus Rex*, which was the theatre's first performance, in 1585.

The elaborately frescoed antechambers to the theatre were also designed by Scamozzi and were used for meetings and smaller concerts of the Accademia Olimpica, the learned society of humanists that commissioned the place. Don't miss the chiaroscuro fresco in the entrance hall depicting a delegation of Japanese noblemen who visited Vicenza in 1585; their presence in Vicenza gives some idea of the city's enduring economic clout.

The theatre has only recently begun to realise its potential as a venue for plays and concerts. A season of classical dramas in September and October usually includes a staging of *Oedipus Rex* (in Italian) and may take in other Greek and Shakespearean tragedies. Concerts tend to be concentrated in May and June. For information, contact the tourist office (*see p262*) or Vicenza's website (www.comune.vicenza.it).

Where to eat & drink

Vicenza's signature dish is *baccalà alla vicentina* – dried cod (stockfish) stewed in milk and oil, and almost always served with *polenta* (*see p260* **The joy of cod**). Game is a firm favourite too, particularly in the hills outside of town, as are *bigoli con sugo di anatra* (fat spaghetti with duck sauce). And bean soups keep the cold and mist out of your marrow on raw winter evenings. While the eating is fine in the town, many of the best restaurants in the area can be found in the countryside around Vicenza.

Teatro Olimpico – designed by Palladio and still in use.

The Veneto

Cinzia e Valerio

Piazzetta Porta Padova 65 (0444 505 213).
Meals served *Sept-July* 12.30-2.30pm, 8-10pm
Tue-Sat; 12.30-2.30pm Sun. Closed Aug. **Average**
€45. **Credit** AmEx, DC, MC, V.
Unquestionably Vicenza's best fish restaurant: go
for the speciality fish risottos, spaghetti with
shrimps, or *tagliolini* pasta with various shellfish.
The mixed fish grill is outstanding too, and there is
an excellent wine list.

I Monelli

Contrà ponte San Paolo 13 (0444 540 400).
Meals served 12.30-4pm, 6.30-11pm Tue-Sun.
Average €25. **Credit** DC, MC, V.
A welcoming *osteria* serving *baccalà alla vicentina*,
bigoli con sugo di anatra and *struzzo* (ostrich… really) *all'aceto balscamico* in one of the streets across
the oddly bucolic Retrone river not far from piazza
delle Erbe.

Osteria Il Cursore

Stradella Pozzetto 10 (0444 323 504).
Meals served *Sept-July* 12.30-3pm, 7.30-10.30pm
Mon, Wed-Sat; 7.30-10.30pm Sun. Closed Aug.
Average €25. **Credit** AmEx, MC, V.
Across the arched ponte San Michele is this old-fashioned *vicentino* drinking den. For a quick snack
there are bar nibbles; otherwise, the kitchen at Il
Cursore turns out excellent versions of local specialities such as *bigoli con sugo di anatra* or *baccalà
alla vicentina*.

Pasticceria Sorarù

Piazzetta Palladio 17 (0444 320 915).
Open 8.30am-1pm, 3.30-8pm Mon, Tue, Thur-Sun.
No credit cards.
One of Italy's most charming *pasticcerie*, Sorarù is
worth a look even if you don't have a sweet tooth.
The columns, marble counters and ornate wooden
shelves backed with mirrors are all 19th-century
originals; the cakes, firmly in the Austro-Hungarian
tradition, are a tad fresher. Sit at outside tables in
summer drinking coffee as you gaze across to the
basilica (*see p259*).

Al Pestello

Contrà Santo Stefano 3 (0444 323 721).
Meals served 12.30-2.30pm, 7.30-11.30pm
Mon-Sat. **Average** €30. **Credit** AmEx, DC, MC, V.
The place to go when you want to take your *baccalà*
seriously, this restaurant offers updated versions of
traditional Vicentine dishes and a good assortment
of wines from the Veneto region.

Remo

*Via Ca' Impenta 14 (0444 911 007/
ristorantedaremo@hotmail.com).* **Meals served**
Sept-July noon-2.30pm, 8-10.30pm Tue-Sat; noon-2.30pm Sun. Closed Aug, 23 Dec-6 Jan. **Average**
€35. **Credit** DC, MC, V.
Situated in an old farmhouse a little to the east of the
city, this country restaurant offers some of the best
cooking anywhere in the Vicenza area. The trolley

of boiled and roasted meats is a fixture, and Remo's
baccalà alla vicentina is spectacular. Excellent
sweets and house wine.

Where to stay

Hotels are not Vicenza's strong point, with most
focusing more on business comfort than tourist
charm. As long as you don't insist on a room
with a view, though, you can get a pleasant
night's sleep.

Camping Vicenza

*Strada Pelosa 239 (0444 582 311/fax 0444 582
434).* Closed Oct-Mar. **Rates** €4.50-€6.20 per person;
plus €5-€13.50 per camper/tent. **Credit** AmEx, DC,
MC, V.
Situated near the Vicenza Est exit of the Milan–
Venice motorway, this upmarket campsite is well
equipped; but it's a serious hike from the city centre.

Hotel Castello

*Contrà Piazza Castello 24 (0444 323 585/fax 0444
323 583/www.hotelcastello.net).* **Rates** €80-€98
single; €100-€129 double. **Credit** AmEx, MC, V.
This unpretentious hotel with 1980s-style interiors
is in the city centre close to corso Palladio and all the
main sights.

Hotel Cristina

*Corso San Felice 32 (0444 323 751/fax 0444 543
656/hotel.cristina@keycomm.it).* **Rates** €98 single;
€131 double. **Credit** AmEx, DC, MC, V.
Located just a few steps outside the Porta Castello
gate, the recently restructured Hotel Cristina offers
packages for tourists.

Hotel Giardini

*Viale Giuriolo 10 (tel/fax 0444 326 458/www.
hotelgiardini.com).* Closed Christmas & New Year.
Rates €83 single; €114 double. **Credit** AmEx, DC,
MC, V.
A small, modern hotel, located across piazza
Matteotti from Palladio's Teatro Olimpico (*see p261*).

Tourist information

Ufficio Provinciale di Turismo *Piazza Matteotti
12 (0444 320 854/fax 0444 327 072/www.
vicenzae.org).* **Open** 9am-1pm, 2-6pm daily.

Getting there

By car
Take the A4 La Serenissima motorway from Venice
or Padua towards Milan.

By train
There are regular trains to and from Venice (55mins)
and Verona (30mins).

By bus
FTV (0444 223 111) buses run from Padua to
Vicenza. The terminus is by the railway station.

Vicenza's Ponte San Michele.

Around Vicenza

Although architect Andrea Palladio and his stunning creations are undoubtedly the biggest single draw for visitors to the area surrounding Vicenza (*see chapter* **Palladian Villas**), don't let his overwhelming presence blind you to the pretty towns, villas by other architects and what remains of the beautiful countryside nearby.

Villas around Vicenza

Below is a selection of the most important country villas in Vicenza province, all of which testify to the lasting influence of Andrea Palladio. For villas in which the local architect actually had a hand, *see chapter* **Palladian Villas**.

Unless otherwise indicated, buses listed leave from the FTV terminal in front of Vicenza railway station.

Villa Cordellina Lombardi

Via Lovara 36, Montecchio Maggiore (0444 696 085). Bus to Recoaro. **Open** *Apr-mid Oct* 9am-noon Tue-Fri; 9am-1pm, 3-6pm Sat, Sun. Closed mid Oct-Mar. **Admission** €2.10. **No credit cards.**
This beautifully restored villa, built between 1735 and 1760 in the grand Palladian style, contains some flamboyant frescos by Giambattista Tiepolo. Painted in 1743, they include one of the painter's favourite Enlightenment allegories, *The Light of Reason Driving out the Fog of Ignorance*. There is also a charming French-style park and garden.

Villa Pisani Ferri 'Rocca Pisana'

Via Rocca 1, Lonigo (0444 831 625). Bus to Lonigo. **Open** *Apr-Nov* by appointment. Closed Dec-Mar. **Admission** €5. **No credit cards.**
This magnificent villa perched on a high hill was designed in 1576 on the ruins of a medieval castle by the architect Vincenzo Scamozzi, Palladio's star pupil. Like La Rotonda (*see chapter* **Palladian Villas**), La Rocca has four main windows facing the four points of the compass and a dome with a hole at the top. But whereas the Rotonda hole is covered with glass, and was conceived to allow light into the building, the hole at the Rocca is open, like the Pantheon in Rome, allowing air to circulate.

Villa Trissino Marzotto

Piazza GG Trissino 2, Trissino (0445 962 029). Bus to Recoaro. **Open** by appointment only. **Admission** *Villa* €5. *Garden* €5. **No credit cards.**
This elaborate complex, consisting of two villas (the lower one a romantic ruin), is set in one of the most charming of Italy's private parks. The upper villa and the park were designed by Francesco Muttoni between 1718 and 1722. The garden is a typically 18th-century mixture of art and nature, in which allegorical statues frame tree-lined walks; the lower villa – destroyed by lightning in 1841 – acts as a theatrical focal point.

Villa Valmarana ai Nani

Via dei Nani 2-8, Vicenza (0444 543 976/0444 544 546). Bus 8 from viale Roma. **Open** *mid Mar-Apr* 10am-noon, 2.30-5.30pm Wed, Thur, Sat, Sun; 2.30-5.30pm Tue, Fri. *May-Sept* 10am-noon, 3-6pm Wed, Thur, Sat, Sun; 3-6pm Tue, Fri. *Oct-early Nov* 10am-noon, 2-5pm Wed, Thur, Sat, Sun; 2-5pm Tue, Fri. *Early Nov-mid Mar* by appointment only for groups & scholars. **Admission** €6. **No credit cards.**
This delightful villa was designed by Antonio Muttoni in 1688; it still belongs to the Valmarana family. For once it's the interior that is the main attraction, thanks to a remarkable series of frescos painted by Giambattista Tiepolo and his son Giandomenico in 1757. The statues of dwarfs (*nani*) lining the wall to the right of the main villa are not a sign of the family's lack of taste; they bear witness instead to the sensitivity of a Valmarana father who wished to comfort his own dwarf child by giving him friendly familiars to gaze on.

Where to stay & eat

If culture and urbanity get too much for you, mountains and wilderness are never too far away. Serious hikers should ring ahead to book a bunk at the **Rifugio General Papa** (0445 630 233, open 20 June-20 Sept daily, 30 May-20 June, 20 Sept-15 Nov Sat, Sun, rates €38 per person half-board), a refuge on nearby Monte Pasubio that also provides filling meals.

To turn a visit to the Villa Trissino Marzotto (*see above*) into an indulgence, dine at **Ca' Masieri** (località Masieri, restaurant 0445 962 100, hotel 0445 490 122, www.camasieri.com, closed Sun, Mon lunch, average €50), two kilometres (1.25 miles) west of Trissino town. This charming 18th-century stone *relais* offers serious meat, game and fish cooking at fairly serious prices; it also has 12 rooms (€90 double) and suites (€130) and a swimming pool. For the ultimate gastro-treat, head for the village of Montecchio Precalcino, 15 kilometres (9.5 miles) north of Vicenza, where the Michelin-starred **Locanda di Piero** (via Roma 32-4, 0445 864 827, closed all Sun, Mon & Sat lunch, 2wks in Mar, Nov, average €50) does a *cordon bleu* take on the local tradition.

Tourist information

See p262.

Getting there

By bus

All destinations are served by FTV buses, which leave from the main terminal outside Vicenza train station; ring 0444 223 115 for timetable information. For Monte Pasubio and the Rifugio General Papa, take the bus to Pian di Fugazze.

Treviso & the Northern Veneto

Much more than the sum of its parts.

Treviso – for those who can't get enough of canals.

The area north of Venice is a simple case of the whole being more, much more, than the sum of the parts. A contemplative piazza here, a towering castle there, a rockily majestic Dolomite up yonder: the individual pieces are attractive, but they don't have the gravity to pull the visitor from the glamour of Venice. They need to be taken together: the squares in small, walled towns that have somehow managed to combine modernity and provincialism; the towns placed among the orchards and vineyards on the slopes leading up to those towering castles, or strung along deeply green valleys leading to snow-capped mountains and largely unspoilt *altopiani* – plateaux clad in the type of Alpine meadow that would make Julie Andrews weep for joy.

Treviso

Venice is not the only city in the Veneto with a watery motif. Twenty-five kilometres (16 miles) to the north, Treviso offers meandering waterways, old mill wheels, weeping willows, frescoed mansions and scope for the type of idle strolling all too rare in its bigger sister.

Piazza dei Signori is at the heart of the maze of canals and narrow, porticoed streets that make up Treviso. **Palazzo dei Trecento**, the ancient town hall, dates back to 1217, while the oversized Benetton store around the corner is a more modern reminder that the company is Treviso-based. Across from the palazzo in piazza Duomo, the **Duomo** (open 8am-noon, 3.30-6pm daily) contains an *Annunciation* by Titian (1570) and a beautiful *Adoration of the Magi* by Pordenone (1520). Two other churches in nearby piazza San Vito – **San Vito** and **Santa Lucia** (both open 8am-noon daily) – offer splendid frescos by Tommaso da Modena, considered by some to be the greatest 14th-century artist after Giotto. More works by Da Modena, including his masterpiece *The Life of St Ursula*, are tucked away in the deconsecrated church of **Santa Caterina** in piazza Giacomo Matteotti; the church has recently become an exhibition space (open during exhibitions only). For a fresco fest,

The Veneto

Bassano's showpiece, the Ponte degli Alpini. *See p267.*

head to the church of **San Francesco** (open 8am-noon, 3.30-6pm daily). Work on the ceiling of the main chapel, including the wonderful *St Francis with Stigmata* and the four evangelists in studious mode, is by an anonymous 14th-century painter, though some argue that this, too, should be attributed to Da Modena. Da Modena pops up yet again with a remarkable series of frescos in the chapter house of the Dominican monastery adjoining the Romanesque-Gothic church of **San Nicolò** (open 8am-noon, 3.30-6pm daily). Look closely at the *studiosi* pictured and you'll see the first pair of glasses depicted in art. The church itself offers interesting tombs, including one framed by pageboys frescoed by Lorenzo Lotto. Works attributed to Lotto and Titian grace the **Museo Civico**. One-off exhibitions are held in the privately run **Casa dei Carraresi** in via Palestra.

The Old Town is protected on three sides by walls put up by the Venetians in 1509. The lion of St Mark is very much in evidence in Treviso, but the city was well established before Venice took over in the 14th century, having served the Lombards as the seat of a duchy and the Romans as the city of Tarvisium. Of the walls' three gates, the **porta San Tommaso** is the most impressive, as well as a convenient place to park.

The fourth side of the Old Town is protected by the Sile river, which also provides some of the water in the canals (the rest comes from a series of streams that converge outside the walls). Once the canals were used by the city's dyers, tanners and paper mills; today, their mossy walls and small bridges offer a slightly bucolic touch to the casual *osterie* ranged alongside them offering snacks and prosecco.

Museo Civico
Borgo Cavour 24 (0422 591 337). **Open** 9am-12.30pm, 2.30-5pm Tue-Sat; 9am-noon Sun. **Admission** €3; €2 concessions. **No credit cards**.

Where to stay & eat

Toni del Spin (via Inferiore 7, 0422 543 829, closed Mon lunch, all Sun & mid June-early July average €25) is a pretty, intimate *osteria* serving local specialities at reasonable prices. **Alfredo el Toulà** (via Collalto 26, 0422 540 275, closed Sun dinner, all Mon & 3wks Aug, average €45) is Treviso's gastronomic shrine. **Osteria Al Dante** (piazza Garibaldi 6, 0422 591 897, closed Sun, average €15) dishes up splendid views and no-frills fare at the foot of the ponte Dante. **Hotel Campeol** (piazza Ancilotto 4, 0422 56 601, double room €83, breakfast €5) offers good service right in the heart of town.

Tourist information

APT *Piazza Monte di Pietà 8 (0422 547 632/ fax 0422 419 092/www.sevenonline.it/tvapt).* **Open** 9am-12.30pm Mon; 9am-12.30pm, 2-6pm Tue-Fri; 9.30am-12.30pm, 3-6pm Sat, Sun.

Getting there

By car

Take the Treviso Sud exit from the A27 motorway; alternatively, take the SS13 from Venice-Mestre.

By train

Regular Venice–Treviso services (25mins).

By bus

ACTV and ATVO buses run regularly from Venice's bus terminus in piazzale Roma.

West from Treviso

Set in a picture-postcard landscape of rolling hills covered with cypress trees, olive groves and vineyards, **Asolo** is not a place to go for serious sightseeing – the few points of interest can be covered in a dedicated half-hour. It's a place for luxuriating. And not only at the hyper-elegant Villa Cipriani hotel (*see p268*), located on a cobbled street leading into the main piazza; Asolo is also perfect for a little window shopping, a long lunch and a leisurely walk with the town's illustrious ghosts: the exiled Venetian-born Queen of Cyprus Caterina Cornaro, who set up court in Asolo in 1489; Eleonora Duse, the 19th-century actress who brought her decadent circle of intellectuals, musicians and artists here; and Robert Browning, who fell so deeply in love with Asolo that he named a collection of his poems, *Asolando* (1889), after it. And when you're through with luxuriating, Asolo is also a good base for exploring the other small gems of the area.

To the north, the tiny village of **Possagno** was the birthplace of Antonio Canova, whose marble statues were imbued with the spirit of neo-classicism, and whose works have been both slammed and hailed. The **Gipsoteca Canoviana**, a museum housed in Canova's family home, is fascinating evidence of Canova's obsession with accuracy. Carlo Scarpa's extension to the Gipsoteca, built between 1955 and 1957, is a modern architectural gem.

Scarpa, who died in 1978, was quintessentially Venetian, imbued with his city's traditional fascination with the East, as well as a desire to fuse ancient and modern in functional but striking spaces. The use of natural elements as raw material and his eye for combining inner and outer space are trademarks. For further Scarpa treats, head back to Asolo and keep going south (towards Castelfranco Veneto). The cemetery in the small town of **San Vito d'Altivole** (open 9am-7pm daily) is home to the Tomba Brion – 2,200 square metres (23,656 square feet) of pure

Scarpa, who spent over nine years (1969-78) constructing the monster. He is also buried here.

The pleasant medieval town of **Castelfranco Veneto**, surrounded by moats and a 13th-century fortified red-brick wall, is famous as the birthplace of both the painter Giorgione and a variety of *radicchio* (you have to take your accolades where you find them). Not many of Giorgione's masterpieces survive, but the **Duomo** (open 9am-noon, 3-6pm daily) has one. The **Casa Giorgione** (open 9am-noon, 3-6pm Tue-Sun, admission €2) was being restored as this guide went to press, with no reopening date set; only the most committed of fans glean much from it.

To the west of Asolo, **Bassano del Grappa** sits astride the Brenta river just as it emerges from the mountains. Monte Grappa, a few kilometres outside of town, was the scene of fierce fighting between Italian and Austrian troops at the end of World War I, and offers its name to both the town and Italy's fiery after-dinner drink (*see p269* **Moonshine**). The oldest and most famous name in grappa is Nardini, whose distillery is located in Bassano's main street, just outside the old city gates. Another famous name in grappa – Poli – can be found at the foot of Bassano's showpiece: the **Ponte degli Alpini**. Though the original bridge was probably constructed in the 1150s, what we see now is a faithful copy of Palladio's magnificent covered wooden bridge built in 1586. The copy dates back no further than 1948, Palladio's having been blown up by retreating German troops at the end of World War II.

Bassano is one of Italy's wealthiest cities, a fact easily confirmed by a stroll through the streets of the centre. The window shopping is high-end, with a rich selection of Italian fashion, jewellery, ceramics (Bassano is also known for its ceramics industry) and food. In piazza Garibaldi – one of the town's two main squares – is the **Museo Civico**, located inside the beautiful convent and cloistered gardens of the 14th-century church of San Francesco. The museum contains a fine collection of Bassano ceramics and an archaeological section devoted to the city's Roman origins. The other square – piazza Libertà – is dominated by the medieval Palazzo Municipale, which is covered with faded frescos. The **Museo degli Alpini**, with its collection of World War I memorabilia, stands at the far end of the ponte degli Alpini.

Beyond Bassano, **Marostica** offers the requisite contemplative piazza with a twist. In the middle of piazza Castello, the sharp-eyed will notice a series of marble squares. These squares are a chessboard, and come the second Friday, Saturday and Sunday of even-yeared Septembers, they are filled with live chess

The Veneto

pieces in costume. Between games, the square is a quiet place for a cup of coffee and a view of the medieval ramparts running up the hill to the **castello superiore** (hill fort).

The mountains above Bassano to the west are home to the **Altopiano Asiago**; the ride up offers spectacular views of the *pianura* (plain) below and enough hairpin turns to keep the daringest devil happy. About 1,000 metres (3,500 feet) above sea level, the Altopiano is a vast bowl of meadows, forests and cows (Asiago is one of Italy's better-known cheeses). This was the scene of fierce fighting during World War I; military cemeteries dotted around the plain bear witness to heavy British involvement. **Asiago**, the most famous of the seven towns on the Altopiano and home to the massive **Sacrario Militare** (World War I memorial; 1934), was largely destroyed during the war. Most of the buildings date from the 1920s and '30s. Today, many of the mountain trails built by opposing armies are used by hikers and Asiago is a busy resort town.

Gipsoteca Canoviana

Piazza Canova 84, Possagno (0423 544 323/www. museocanova.it). **Open** 9am-noon, 3-6pm Tue-Sun. **Admission** €4; €3 concessions. **No credit cards**.

Museo degli Alpini

Via Angarano 2, Bassano (0424 503 662). **Open** 8.30am-8pm Tue-Sun. **Admission** free.

Museo Civico

Piazza Garibaldi 12, Bassano (0424 522 235/www.x-land.it/museobassano). **Open** 9am-6.30pm Tue-Sat; 3.30-6.30pm Sun. **Admission** €4.50; €3 concessions. **No credit cards**.

Sacrario Militare

Viale degli Eroi, Asiago (0424 464 081). **Open** *Oct-mid May* 9am-noon, 2-5pm daily. *Mid May-Sept* 9am-noon, 2-6pm daily. **Admission** free.

Where to stay & eat

In Asolo, the **Hotel Duse** (via Browning 190, 0423 55 241, double room €95-€120, breakfast €6) is a comfortable three-star option in the centre of town. The **Villa Cipriani** (via Canova 298, 0423 523 411, www.starwoodhotel/italy.com, double room €328-€486) and the **Albergo al Sole** (via Collegio 33, 0423 528 111, www.albergoalsole.com, double room €160-€198) are best for full-immersion luxury. **Ca' Derton** (piazza d'Annunzio 11, 0423 529 648, closed Mon, Sun dinner & 2wks Aug, average €35) is a firm favourite with Italian foodies. In the same piazza, **Ristorante Due Mori** (piazza d'Annunzio 5, 0423 952 256, closed Wed, average €30) offers a more casual but equally delicious repast.

Up in the **Alpago**. *See p270.*

Forget restaurants and hotels in tourist-oriented Possagno, and head two kilometres (1.25 miles) east to Cavaso del Tomba, where there is an excellent hotel, **Locanda Alla Posta** (piazza XIII Martiri 13, 0423 543 112, closed 2wks July, double room €52). It has a lively bar and good restaurant (closed Wed dinner & Thur, average €25).

For such a wealthy city, Bassano can be a disappointing overnight stay, with few charming hotels and welcoming *osterie*. **Al Castello** (piazza Terraglio 20, 0424 228 665, www.hotelalcastello.it, double room €46-€82) is a reasonably priced three-star, while **Al Camin** (via Valsugana 64, Cassola, 0424 566 134, double room €80-€120) is Best Western's four-star offering, located a few kilometres outside the centre in the suburb of Cassola. In town, **Birraria Ottone** (via Matteotti 50, 0424 522 206, closed Mon dinner & Tue, average €25), serving mainly regional and Austrian dishes, is a good bet.

Asiago, as befits a resort, is chock-full of hotels. One of the most convenient, just a few steps from the main square, is the **Hotel Croce Bianca** (via IV Novembre 30, 0424 462 642, double room €68-€93). Eating is no problem, but – with many of the hotels insisting on half-and full-board – eating exceptionally well is.

The Veneto

The **Lepre Bianca**, in the nearby town of Gallio (via Camona 46, 0424 445 666, www.leprebianca.it, closed 2wks Nov, average €40), is one of the area's most highly regarded restaurants.

Tourist information

Asiago *Città d'Asiago Uffico del Turismo, Piazza Carli, Asiago (0424 464 081/www.comune.asiago. vi.it).* **Open** *July, Aug* 9.30am-12.30pm, 3.30-7pm daily. *Sept-June* 9am-12.30pm, 3-7pm Mon-Fri; 9.30am-12.30pm, 3.30-7pm Sat, Sun.

Asolo *IAT, Piazza d'Annunzio 3 (0423 529 046/ fax 0423 524 137).* **Open** 9am-12.30pm, 3-6pm Mon-Fri; 9.30am-12.30pm, 3-6pm Sat, Sun.

Bassano *APT, Largo Corona d'Italia 35, Bassano (0424 524 351/fax 0424 525 301/ infotour.bassano@tiscalinet.it).* **Open** 9am-1pm, 2-6pm daily.

Castelfranco Veneto *UIT, Via Francesco Maria Preti 66 (0423 491 416/fax 0423 771 085/ iat.castelfrancoveneto@provincia.treviso.it).* **Open** 8.30am-12.30pm Mon; 8.30am-12.30pm, 3 6pm Tue-Sun.

Getting there

By car

From Treviso, SS53 goes directly to Castelfranco Veneto. For Asolo, take SS348 to Montbelluna, then take SS248, which continues to Bassano del Grappa and Marostica. Possagno is a short distance from Asolo on marked minor roads. To get to Asiago from Bassano, take SS47.

By train

Frequent Venice–Bassano trains also stop at Castelfranco.

By bus

La Marca (0422 577 311) runs services from Treviso to Castelfranco and Bassano. Asiago and Marostica can be reached by bus from Bassano (FTV 0444 223 115).

North from Treviso

Beyond Treviso, the mountains begin to make their presence felt: the hills become a little steeper, the air a little fresher, the light a little sharper. Before the mountains proper, though, comes the **Altamarca Trevigiana**, an area of hills and valleys rich with vineyards. Sheltered from cold northerlies by the nearby Dolomites and enjoying warmer air sweeping up the Adriatic, the area between Conegliano and Valdobbiadene is home to sparkling prosecco wine production and Italy's first *strada del vino* (wine trail – an itinerary around vineyards and wine outlets), the obviously named **Strada del Prosecco**. The breathtaking combination of natural beauty and medieval architecture scattered across this zone makes it a worthwhile visit even for non-imbibers of the local bubbly.

Moonshine

Though grappa has come a long way from its humble beginnings, it shares the delightful Italian ability to be both rustic and highly fashionable. Grappa – technically a pomace brandy – began as a way to get the most from wine grapes. After the grapes are pressed for wine, 20 per cent of the fruit's total weight still remains, in the form of skins, seeds, stems and so on: this is known as the pomace. Instead of throwing it out, the frugal inhabitants of the Veneto would distil it and use it as a sort of internal central heating system during the winter… Italian moonshine, in other words.

The locals still make their own grappa: in small *trattorie* sprinkled throughout the mountains and valleys, you may be offered a *grappa nostrana* at the end of the meal, served out of a label-less bottle. While it is (almost always) safe to drink, bear in mind that it may be stronger than regular grappa, which clocks in at around 40 per cent alcohol (80 proof). Home-made grappa can easily run to 55 per cent to 60 per cent.

Elsewhere, you may be faced with a bewildering choice – some restaurants even offer a grappa trolley. Grappas come in two broad categories: *secco* (dry) and *morbido* (sweet). The classic grappas from producers such as Nardini and Poli are a combination of a number of different grapes, but there is a trend these days towards single-varietal grappas (*monovitigni*). These tend to reflect the character of the grapes, and there are as many *monovitigni* as there are varietals. In addition, grappas are often infused with herbs or fruits (*grappa aromatizzata* or *grappa al …*). *Ruta* (the bitter herb rue) and *mirtilli* (blueberry) are two popular flavourings. Of course, if the choice becomes overwhelming, you can just order yourself a *café corretto*, the espresso plus slug of grappa combination that is the classic closing note of a northern Italian meal.

The Veneto

The awe-inspiring scenery around **Lago di Santa Croce**.

The town of **Conegliano** offers a perfect base for a couple of days of wine-tasting: there is also a *strada* for red wines and Italy's first wine school. The town itself is pleasant, though not over-burdened with tourist attractions. The 14th-century **Duomo** is home to a painting of the *Virgin and Child With Saints and Angels* by the town's most famous son, Giambattista Cima, known as Cima da Conegliano. Conegliano's cultural treasures end here, but visit the **Sala dei Battuti** (open Apr-Sept 3.30-7pm Sun; Oct-Mar 3-6.30pm Sun) next to the Duomo: dedicated to a brotherhood of flagellants, it's decorated with some truly odd 15th- and 16th-century biblical frescos.

The hills change to mountains near **Vittorio Veneto**, which sprang to life in 1866 when the smaller towns of Ceneda and Serravalle were united and renamed to mark the unification of Italy under King Vittorio Emanuele II. Serravalle boasts a well-preserved medieval *borgo* (quarter), which is unfortunately situated right on the busy *strada statale*. There's not much to detain the visitor; but it's worth braving the exhaust fumes for a brief stroll through the *borgo* and an admiring glance at the frescoed Loggia Serravallese, which dates from 1462.

The reservoirs and generating stations along the Strada d'Alemagna – the main road from Vittorio Veneto to Belluno – are a reminder of the importance of hydro-electric power for Italy. It is hard not to rhapsodise about the area. **Lago di Santa Croce** is a semi-artificial mirror reflecting jagged Dolomite peaks, the

thick forests of **Bosco di Cansiglio**, and the stupendous natural bowl formed by the high valley of the Alpago. There's no shortage of awe-inspiring views, or trails to view them from. There are plenty of reasonable hotels and some wonderful restaurants, serving wild venison and boar, home-cured sausages and mushrooms fresh from the forest.

Belluno, a medieval town perched high on a rocky terrace, overlooks two rivers, the Piave and the Ardo. How high the town is perched is wonderfully illustrated by the escalator that carries visitors from the Lamboi car park to the main piazza. The escalator emerges on to a scene that is pure enchantment. Against a backdrop of mountains and tranquillity, the 15th-century **Palazzo dei Rettori** (home to the town's Venetian rulers; not open to the public) and 16th-century **Duomo** (open 7am-12.30pm, 3.30-7.30pm daily) recall the architecture along the Grand Canal. The **Baptistery** (variable hours) across from the Duomo contains an early 18th-century carving of *John the Baptist* by Andrea Brustolon. Just outside the old city walls is the new heart of the city, piazza dei Martiri. Still called Campadel by locals, this pleasant, open square with plenty of benches for relaxing and breathing in the mountain air had its name changed in 1945, in memory of the four partisans hanged from its lamp-posts.

In the mountains above here is the jet-set capital of the Dolomites, **Cortina d'Ampezzo** – beautiful, but expensive. If you're heading there, stop off at **Borca di Cadore** to check out architect Carlo Scarpa's amazing church (open 9am-noon, 4-6pm daily), built in 1959. Borca itself is a timewarp experience. Constructed by the state-owned ENI fuel company as a holiday camp for its sickly workers, this village has remained virtually unchanged since the 1950s. If you're looking for a mountain retreat that bears no resemblance to Heidi's homestead, check in to one of the village apartments or main hotel. To book, contact the Centro Vacanze at Borca di Cadore (Dolomiti Gestioni, on the SS51, 0435 487 500, open 8.30am-12.30pm, 2-6pm Mon-Sat, closed 2wks June). It can also put you in touch with the priest with the keys to the Scarpa church.

To the west of Belluno, **Feltre** was once a Roman fortress on the banks of the river Piave. Today it is a perfectly preserved 16th-century town. It owes its appearance in large part to the munificence of Venice, which financed a sumptuous rebuilding programme after its stout ally was razed to the ground in 1510 by the troops of the Holy Roman Emperor Maximilian I. Paintings and statues of the lion of St Mark are everywhere. Many of the *palazzi* along Feltre's high street, via Mezzaterra, are frescoed by local artist Lorenzo Luzzo (1467-1512); frescos on simple merchants' houses down the town's narrow alleyways are often just as striking. One of the few parts of Feltre

Belluno's escalator. *See p270.*

not perfectly preserved is its lapidaries – many of the engravings praised Venice for its aforementioned munificence. When Napoleon rolled into town, he was affronted by such lauding and ordered the words destroyed; today the town's walls are covered with stone tablets that have been chipped clean.

Where to stay & eat

For good-value local cuisine in Conegliano, try the **Trattoria Stella** (via Accademia 3, 0438 22 178, closed Sun & 3wks Aug, average €25). Alternatively, for something more upmarket, head for **Ristorante Al Salisà** (via XX Settembre 2, 0438 24 288, closed Wed, average €20) and indulge in a bottle from its excellent wine list. On the same street is the **Hotel Canon d'Oro** (via XX Settembre 131, 0438 34 246, www.hotelcanondoro.it, double room €83-€95, breakfast €9).

East of Belluno in the small town of Plois di Pieve d'Alpago (generally shortened to Pieve d'Alpago) is home to the Michelin-starred **Dolada** (via Dolada 21, 0437 479 141, www.dolada.it, closed Mon & Tue lunch in Sept-June, average €60), which doubles as a three-star hotel (double room €103, breakfast €13). The **Locanda San Lorenzo** a couple of miles south in Puos d'Alpago (via IV Novembre 79, 0437 454 048, www.locandasanlorenzo.it, closed Wed & 3wks Jan-Feb, average €55) is another fine restaurant with an excellent hotel (double room €85).

Belluno's rustic **Al Borgo** restaurant (via Anconetta 8, 0437 926 755, closed Mon dinner, Tue & 2wks Jan, average €25) offers smoked ham and sausages, and unusual, filling pasta dishes. For accommodation try the centrally located **Albergo delle Alpi** (via Tasso 13, 0437 940 545, www.dellealpi.it, double room €96).

In Feltre, the **Ristorante Aurora** (via Garibaldi 24, 0439 2046, closed Sun, average €15) offers a warming combination of casual service and down-home food.

Tourist information

For information on ski resorts in the region, consult www.dolomitisuperski.it.

Belluno *APT, Piazza dei Martiri 7 (0437 940 083/ fax 0437 940 073/www.infodolomiti.it).* **Open** 9am-12.30pm, 3.30-6.30pm daily.

Conegliano *APT, Via XX Settembre 61, (0438 21 230/fax 0438 428 777/www.comune.conegliano.tv.it).* **Open** *May-Oct* 3.30-6.30pm Tue; 9am-1pm, 3.30-6.30pm Wed-Sat. *Nov-Apr* 9am-1pm, 3-6pm Tue-Fri; 9am-1pm Sat.
Provides brochures on the *strada del vino* and will organise visits to the surrounding vineyards.

The Veneto

Feltre *APT, Piazzetta Trento e Trieste 9 (0439 2540/fax 0439 2839/www.infodolomiti.it)*. **Open** 9am-12.30pm, 3-6pm Mon-Sat; 9am-12.30pm Sun.

Getting there

By car
From Treviso take the SS13 to Conegliano, then the SS51 (Strada d'Alemagna) to Vittorio Veneto and Belluno. The three towns can also be reached by the A27 motorway. For the Alpago, turn off SS51 on to SS422d. To get to Feltre from Belluno, take SS50. For Cortina and Borca, continue on SS51.

By train
Fast Venice–Udine trains stop at Conegliano; local Venice–Belluno trains call at Conegliano and Vittorio Veneto as well. There's a local train service from Treviso to Feltre.

By bus
Services from Venice's piazzale Roma to Belluno run during the summer, stopping at Conegliano and Vittorio Veneto. La Marca (0422 577 311) runs services from Treviso's bus station to the three towns, as well as Feltre. Buses to Plois di Pieve d'Alpago and Puos d'Alpago run from Belluno (call Dolomit Bus, 0437 941 167, for information).

East from Venice

It may not seem so today, but **Aquileia** was once one of the most important cities in the Roman Empire, with a population of more than 100,000. Legend has it that an eagle (*aquila*) soared overhead as the outline of the new town was being ploughed up in 181 BC, giving it its name. In the fourth century Aquileia became one of Italy's most important patriarchates, but constant harrying by barbarian tribes forced the bishop to shift his residence to nearby Grado. The town passed to Venetian control in 1420, then to Austria in 1509.

The 11th-century **Basilica Teodoriana** (open 8am-7pm daily) contains 700 square metres (2,333 feet) of mosaic paving – remains from a fourth-century church that stood on the site – with a mishmash of imagery both Christian (Jonah and the whale, the Good Shepherd) and pagan (tortoises and cockerels). In the apse, frescos dated 1031 show the patriarch Poppo, who founded the basilica in the 11th century, with Emperor Conrad II and his wife and son, before the Virgin Mary. Twelfth-century frescos depicting the lives of Christ and Mary are to be found in the crypt beneath the presbytery (entrance is by Museo Archeologico ticket; the crypt is a more interesting sight than the museum itself).

Grado, founded by inhabitants of Aquileia fleeing barbarian invasions (and wisely staking their claim on a prime bit of future beach resort

real estate), is a far better bet for a few days of sea and sun than either Venice's cramped Lido or the tacky, downmarket Lido di Jesolo. As at any Italian beach resort, the serried ranks of umbrellas and matching deckchairs set up – and charged for – by local bathing clubs are unavoidable. But to compensate, Grado has a superb location – at the tip of a curving spit of land, between a dreamy lagoon and the Adriatic sea – and its old town centre and fishing port haven't yet been swallowed up by modern hotels. The town's sixth-century **Duomo** (open 8am-7pm daily) has a fine collection of columns with Byzantine capitals and a beautiful sixth-century mosaic floor. Mosaics of the same period are to be found in the church of **Santa Maria delle Grazie** and in the **Baptistery** between the Duomo and church.

Museo Archeologico
Via Roma 1, Aquileia (0431 91 016/www.museo archeo-aquileia.it). **Open** 8.30am-2pm Mon; 8.30am-7.30pm Tue-Sun. **Admission** €4; concessions €2. **No credit cards**.

Where to stay & eat

Of Grado's hotels, the **Antares Hotel Meublé** (via delle Scuole 4, 0431 84 961, www. antareshotel.info, double room €80-€120), pleasantly situated along the seafront, is one of very few open all year-round. A cheaper option is **Serena**, on the quiet residential island of La Schiusa (riva Sant'Andrea 31, 0431 80 697, www.hotelserena.net, double room €80-€95). The **Tavernetta all'Androna** (calle Porta Piccola 6, 0431 80 950, closed Jan-mid Feb, average €35) has the best seafood in town. More rustic – but better value – is the friendly **Trattoria de Toni** (piazza Duca d'Aosta 37, 0431 80 104, closed Wed & Dec-Jan, average €35).

Tourist information

Aquileia *APT, Piazza Capitolo 4 (0431 91 087)*. **Open** 9am-5pm Mon-Fri; 10am-1pm, 2-5pm Sat, Sun.

Grado *AIAT, Viale Dante Alighieri 72, Grado (0431 877 111/fax 0431 83 509/www.grado turismo.it)*. **Open** *May-Sept* 9am-1pm, 3-7pm daily; low season opening hours vary.

Getting there

By car
Take the Palmanova exit from the A4 Venice-Trieste motorway, then head south on the SS352.

By train
Get off the Venice–Trieste train at Cervignano, then hop on a bus (Autoservizi SAF 0431 80 055/0432 608 111) at the station.

Directory

Directory

Getting Around

By air

Venice Marco Polo Airport
Via Luigi Broglio 6/8, Tessera (central operator 041 260 6111/ flight & airport information 041 260 9260/www.veniceairport.it). **Open** *ticket counters* 5.30am-9.40pm daily.
Venice's new airport, located on the northern edge of the lagoon, opened in July 2002 and is third in Italy for air traffic volume.

Treviso Sant'Angelo Airport
Via Noalese 63E, Treviso (airport information 0422 315 131).
This tiny airport is used by Ryanair.

TO & FROM VENICE AIRPORT

By boat
Società Alilaguna (041 523 5775/www.alilaguna.com) runs its boat service hourly between 6.15am and 12.10am from the airport to San Marco and Zattere; and 4.35am (4.20am at Zattere) to 10.50pm in the other direction. Tickets (€10) can be purchased at Alilaguna's counter in the arrivals hall or on board. You should allow 70mins from or to San Marco; the service also stops at Murano, the Lido and Arsenale; after San Marco it proceeds to Zattere. A *navetta* (shuttle service) to the boat dock departs every 5mins from the airport's main entrance.

By water taxi
Consorzio Motoscafi Venezia *Marco Polo Airport, arrivals hall (041 541 5084).* **No credit cards.**
A ride from the airport right to your hotel in Venice will cost upwards of €80 depending on the number of people in your party and the stops you make. A *navetta* (shuttle service) to the boat launch departs every 5mins from the airport's main entrance.

By land taxi
Cooperativa Artigiana Radio Taxi *Marco Polo Airport, arrivals hall (041 541 6363/info 041 936 137/ switchboard 041 936 222).*

A traditional taxi ride to piazzale Roma from the airport and vice versa, takes about 20mins (depending on traffic) and will cost about €26.

By bus
ATVO
Marco Polo Airport, arrivals hall (041 541 5180/www.atvo.it). **Open** 8am-midnight daily. **Tickets** €2.70. **No credit cards.**
ATVO runs fast coach services to and from piazzale Roma to coincide with most incoming and outgoing planes. The trip takes around 25mins; buses leave hourly or more frequently between 8.30am and 11.30pm (from airport) and between 5am and 8.40pm (from piazzale Roma); from 10.20am to 6.20pm they're half-hourly.

ACTV
Marco Polo Airport, arrivals hall (041 528 7886/www.actv.it).
Bus 5 goes between the airport and piazzale Roma, leaving from the airport at 4.08am and 5.10am, and from Piazzale Rome at 4.40am, and then from both ends at 5.40am, 6.15am, 6.40am, and then every half hour until midnight; journey time 35-40mins. Tickets (77¢) can be bought at the ACTV counter in the arrivals hall or the ACTV office in piazzale Roma.

TO & FROM TREVISO AIRPORT
ATVO (timetable information 041 520 5530) buses run from Venice's piazzale Roma and back to coincide with flights. Buses leave very early to ensure your timely arrival, so make sure you check the schedule carefully. **ACTT** (0422 3271) bus 6 does the 20-minute trip from in front of Treviso train station to the airport at 10 and 40mins past the hour.

AIRLINES
Most major airlines have ticketing counters inside the departures hall at Marco Polo. If you need to purchase or change a ticket when your airline's office is closed, use SAVE in the airport departure hall (041 260 6432, fax 041 260 6429, open 5.30am-9pm daily, credit AmEx, DC, MC, V).

Alitalia
Marco Polo, departures hall (international bookings 848 865 642/ domestic bookings 848 864 641/ www.alitalia.it). **Open** 6am-8.30pm Mon-Sat. **Credit** AmEx, DC, MC, V.

British Airways
Marco Polo Airport, departures hall 2nd floor (information 041 260 6428/bookings 199 712 266/www. britishairways.com/italy). **Open** 6am-9pm Tue-Sat; 9am-9pm Mon, Sun. **Credit** AmEx, DC, MC, V.
British Airways tickets can also be bought at the general ticket office from 5.30am to 10pm daily.

Go
848 887 766/www.go-fly.com. **Credit** AmEx, MC, V.
Go services arrive and depart from Marco Polo airport.

Ryanair
Treviso Sant'Angelo Airport (information/bookings 0422 315 331/899 889 973). **Open** *Office* June-Sept 8.30-10.30am, 2-4pm, 7-10pm daily. Oct-May 8.30-10.30am, 7-9pm daily. *Booking line* 8am-6pm Mon-Fri. **Credit** MC, V.

By bus
Bus services to Venice all terminate at piazzale Roma, which is connected by vaporetto (*see p276*) to the rest of the city centre. For bus services in mainland Venice and the Lido, see *p275*. For bus services from Venice to other destinations in the Veneto, see individual chapters.

By rail
Most trains arrive at Santa Lucia station in the north-west corner of island Venice (map p304 B1), though a few will only take you as far as Mestre on the mainland, where you will need to change to a local train (every 10mins or less during the day) for the ten-minute hop across the lagoon. *See also p278.*

By road
Venice is connected to other large Italian and European cities by fast motorway links, but prohibitive parking fees make this one of the least practical modes of arrival, especially for stays of more than 24hrs. Note, though, that many Venetian hotels offer their guests discounts at car parks. The main car parks are listed below.

Autorimessa Tronchetto

Isola del Tronchetto (041 520 7555/ www.veniceparking.it). Vaporetto Tronchetto. **Open** 24hrs daily. **Rates** €18 a day. **Credit** AmEx, MC, V. **Map** off p304 C1.

Autorimessa Comunale

Santa Croce 458, piazzale Roma (041 272 7301/www.asmvenezia.it). Vaporetto Piazzale Roma. **Open** 24hrs daily. **Rates** €18.59 a day. **Credit** AmEx, DC, MC, V. **Map** p304 C1.

Parcheggio Sant'Andrea

Santa Croce 465B, piazzale Roma (041 272 7304/www.asmvenezia.it). Vaporetto Piazzale Roma. **Open** 24hrs daily. **Rates** €4.13 2hrs; €49 24hrs. **Credit** AmEx, DC, MC, V. **Map** p304 C1.

Parking Stazione

Viale Stazione 10, Mestre (041 938 021). Bus 2 from piazzale Roma or train to Mestre station. **Open** 24hrs daily. **Rates** €4.50 a day. **No credit cards.**

Park Terminal Fusina

Via Moranzani 79, Fusina (041 547 0160/www.terminalfusina.it). Vaporetto 16 to Fusina. **Open** Apr-Oct 8am-11.30pm daily. Nov-Mar 8am 5.30pm daily. **Rates** €8 for up to 12 hours; €13 for up to 24 hours. **Credit** MC, V.

Marco Polo Park

Marco Polo Airport, (041 541 5913/ www.veniceairport.it/parchegg). Bus 5 from piazzale Roma/free shuttle bus from the airport's main entrance. **Open** 24hrs daily. **Rates** €12 a day (discounts for longer periods). **Credit** AmEx, DC, MC, V.

Getting around

Public transport – including *vaporetti* (water buses) and buses – in Venice itself and in some mainland areas is run by **ACTV** (Azienda Comunale per il Trasporto di Venezia); ACTV's marketing wing is called **VeLa. ATVO** runs more extensive bus services to mainland destinations (see chapters in The Veneto section). The **Hello Venezia** (899 90 90 90) call centre provides schedule information for both ACTV and VeLa. Calls cost 40¢ a minute.

ACTV

Santa Croce 509, piazzale Roma (041 528 7886/www.actv.it). Vaporetto Piazzale Roma. **Open** 7.30am-8pm daily. **No credit cards. Map** p304 C1.
San Marco 1810, calle dei Fuseri (041 528 7886). Vaporetto Vallaresso or Rialto. **Open** 7.30am-7pm Mon-Sat. **No credit cards. Map** p307 A4.

ATVO

Santa Croce 497, piazzale Roma (041 520 5530/www.atvo.it). Vaporetto Piazzale Roma. **Open** 6.40am-7.30pm daily. **Map** p304 C1.

VeLa

518A Santa Croce, piazzale Roma (041 272 2249/www.velaspa.com). Vaporetto Piazzale Roma. **Open** 7.30am-8pm daily. **No credit cards.**
San Marco 1810, calle dei Fuseri (041 241 8029). Vaporetto Vallaresso or Rialto. **Open** 7.30am-7pm Mon-Sat. **Credit** MC, V. **Map** p307 A4.

Tickets

Individual and fixed-period tickets can be purchased at most stops, at *tabacchi*, at the main ACTV office in piazzale Roma or the VeLa office (see above). They can also be bought on board with a supplement of €1.03. Tickets must be stamped in the yellow machines at the entrance to the jetty before boarding a vaporetto. The privilege of seeing Venice from the water does not come cheap: a single ticket for one ride will set you back €3.10 – unless you're hopping from the Lido to Sant'Elena or from San Giorgio to San Zaccaria, in which case it's €1.55. If you are staying for longer than a few hours, and planning to make good use of *vaporetti*,

motonavi and ACTV buses, cut costs by investing in a 24hr ticket (€9.30), a three-day ticket (€18.08) or a seven-day ticket (€30.99).

Alternatively, three people can invest in joint one-ride (€7.75) or 24hr (€23.24) tickets; groups of four pay €10.33 for one ride and €30.99 for 24hrs; groups of five pay €12.91 for one ride and €38.73 for 24hrs.

If you are staying for longer periods, an **abbonamento** is a sound investment. Available from main ACTV and VeLa offices, this three-year pass allows you to pay the same, much lower, rates as residents of the Veneto region (who hold Cartavenezia passes). A one-off charge of €5.16 is made for the card, for which you will need one passport photo and valid photo ID. You must buy a monthly season ticket (€23.24; €15.49 students) when applying for the *abbonamento*; after the month is up, you can buy single tickets for 77¢ or a carnet (ten tickets) for €7.23.

By bus

Orange ACTV buses serve both Mestre and Marghera on the mainland, as well as the Lido, Pellestrina and Chioggia. Services for the mainland depart from piazzale Roma (map p304 C1).

Bus tickets, costing 77¢, are valid for 60 minutes, during which you may use several buses, though you can't make a return journey on the same ticket. They can be purchased from ACTV ticket booths or

Vaporetti

Strictly speaking, it is wrong to refer to all Venetian passenger ferries as *vaporetti*; only the larger, slower, more rounded boat with more room for luggage and those much sought-after outside seats at the front is a genuine vaporetto, while the sleeker, smaller and faster boat with outside seats only at the back is a *motoscafo*. As for the charming double-decker steamer that crosses the lagoon to Lido and Torcello, that's a *motonave*. Even Venetians tend to lump them all together as *vaporetti* when talking in general about the service. But disabled travellers should learn to spot the different boats, as wheelchairs can be accommodated on *vaporetti* and *motonavi* but not on *motoscafi* (see also p277).

Directory

from *tabacchi* (*see p288*) anywhere in the city. They should be bought before boarding the bus and stamped on board.

From midnight until 5am, buses N1 (every 30 minutes) and N2 (every hour) depart from Mestre for piazzale Roma and vice versa. There are also regular Lido night buses (departing at least hourly) to Malamocco, Alberoni and Pellestrina.

By boat

Vaporetti (*see also p275* **Vaporetti**) run to a tight schedule, with sailing times marked clearly at stops for each line that puts in there. Regular services run from about 5am to shortly after midnight, after which a frequent night service (N) follows the route taken by Line 82 during the day.

The main lines ply the Grand Canal, or circle the island. Without a clear idea of Venetian topography, taking the wrong boat in the wrong direction is alarmingly easy. It is worth picking up a timetable (50¢) and route map from the central ACTV/VeLa office, tourist offices (*see p289*) or any large ACTV booth. ACTV is notorious for making sudden changes to timetables as well as adding or eliminating lines.

As a rule of thumb, remember that if you're standing with your back to the station and want to make your way down the Grand Canal, take **Line 1** (slow) or **Line 82** (faster) heading left.

The stop called San Zaccaria is closest to piazza San Marco. Minimally further away, the stop now called Vallaresso used to be called San Marco; you may still find it labelled thus on old maps or timetables.

For the rarely visited southern islands (San Servolo, San Lazzaro degli Armeni) and the Lido, the starting point is San Zaccaria.

Services to islands in the northern lagoon depart from Fondamente Nove (the alternative route from San Zaccaria via the Lido is very roundabout).

Line 12 leaves about every 30 minutes from Fondamente Nove for Faro (Murano), Mazzorbo, Torcello, Burano, Treporti and Punta Sabbioni. Certain boats call at Torcello after Burano; others skip Torcello altogether. Check before boarding.

Line 13 leaves hourly from Fondamente Nove to Faro (Murano), Vignole, Lazzaretto Nuovo, Capannone (Sant'Erasmo), Chiesa (Sant'Erasmo) and Vela (Sant'Erasmo). Some boats continue for Treporti.

Lines 41 and **42** from Fondamente Nove stop at the island of San Michele (*cimitero*) before continuing to Murano.

TRAGHETTI

Traghetti are the best way of crossing from one side of the Grand Canal to the other when you're far from any of the three bridges that span it. They are also the best way to get a ride in a gondola without the kitsch trappings, and for a mere 40¢. These large, unadorned *gondole* are rowed back and forth across the canal in a service laid on by the gondoliers' cooperative, in collaboration with the city council. The jostling, chatting Venetian habitués of this unique ferry service brave the rocky wakes of passing motor boats and always ride *traghetti* standing up.

Traghetti ply between the following points:
San Marcuola-Fontego dei Turchi.
June-Sept 9am-12.30am Mon-Sat. *Oct-May* 7.45am-1pm Mon-Sat. **Map** I 2B.
Santa Sofia-Pescheria
7.30am-8.30pm Mon-Sat; 8am-7pm Sun. **Map** p305 C3.
Riva del Carbon-riva del Vin
8am-2pm Mon-Sat. **Map** p305 C3.
Ca' Garzoni-SanTomà
7.30am-8pm Mon-Sat; 8am-7.20pm Sun. **Map** p306 A2.

On foot

Much of your getting around Venice will inevitably be done on foot. Walking is the main means of locomotion for Venetians, too, which explains why they are perhaps the only Italians who stride purposefully, rather than dawdling; understandably, then, the locals take a dim view of tourists who obstruct narrow thoroughfares as they stand to gawp, or – worse still – spread out their picnics on busy bridges. A few 'road rules' will help you manoeuvre through Venice.

Traffic tends to flow in loosely divided lanes (keep right) with potential for passing. A quick acceleration on the left with a polite *scusate* or *permesso* will help part the crowds. Slow down and pull

off to the right side to consult a map or admire a building, instead of suddenly stopping, potentially disrupting the traffic flow. 'Rush hour' for Venetians is in the mornings and afternoons going to and from work; during the high season this blends into an all-day-long traffic jam clogging main arteries of the city, especially near San Marco and Rialto. Be adventurous and explore the more remote parts of the island if you want to avoid these situations. Try getting lost... with a good map to help you resurface. A leisurely stroll through the city is a definite must during your stay but should be done in the early morning or after dinner to appreciate the city's charm.

Acqua alta

If you're in Venice between September and April, there's a fair-to-middling chance that you're going to get your feet wet: a high tide, coupled with a wind driving against the tidal outflow from the lagoon, and the city's lowest points will disappear for a couple of hours under several inches of water.

The first you'll know about it is two or three hours before an exceptionally high tide, when sirens around the city sound five ten-second blasts. As the *acqua alta* (high water) makes its slow but inexorable way into city streets, you might want to head for a shop selling rubber boots, such as **Di Pol** (*see p176*).

How far you are inconvenienced will depend on how far the lagoon rises above its normal level (*see chapter* **That Sinking Feeling**). During the *acqua alta* season, trestles and wooden planks are stacked up along flood-prone thoroughfares, ready to be hurriedly transformed into raised walkways by the city rubbish department as the water level rises. If the tide rises more than 120cm (47 inches) above its average level, even the walkways begin to float, and you'd do well to find a nice, dry and preferably high place to sit it out until the tide ebbs.

Acqua alta has an etiquette all of its own. It is most evident on the raised walkways where Venetians wait their turn patiently, without the pushing and jostling that mark queues for *vaporetti* or market stalls; they then proceed along the narrow planks slowly and with consideration for other users; and they expect tourists to do the same, or risk an angry telling-off for their lack of manners.

The etiquette extends beyond the walkways, as anyone splashing, *Singin' in the Rain* style, through the high water will find out: the *calli* and *campi* may be waterlogged, but they continue to function as a municipal road network, and local road-users are understandably peeved if thoughtless tourists prevent them from reaching their destination in as dry a state as possible. Remember, too, that during *acqua alta* you can't see where the pavement stops and the canal begins.

A map posted at each vaporetto stop – copies of which are available at APT offices (*see p289*) – shows flood-prone areas, and routes covered by raised walkways. If you want to avoid *acqua alta* water altogether, study this map and stick to higher ground. The tide office (Centro Maree) provides *acqua alta* forecasts in Italian only (recorded message 199 165 165).

San Samuele-Ca' Rezzonico
7.30am-1.30pm Mon-Sat.
Map p306 A2.
Santa Maria del Giglio-Santa Maria della Salute
8am-6pm daily. **Map** p307 B3.
San Marco-Dogana
9am-noon, 2-6pm daily. **Map** p306 B2.

WATER TAXIS

Venetian water taxis are breathtakingly expensive: expect to pay €75 from the airport directly to San Marco and only slightly less from San Marco to the railway station or piazzale Roma. A quick trip along the Grand Canal will cost upwards of €80. Between the hours of 10pm and 7am there is a surcharge of €7.

Beware of unlicensed taxis, which charge even more than authorised ones. The latter have a black registration number on a yellow background.

Cooperativa San Marco

Information 041 240 6711/ switchboard 041 522 2303/ www.veneziamotoscafi.com.
Open 24hrs daily. **No credit cards.**

GONDOLE

Like the city it symbolises, the gondola has now given itself up almost exclusively to tourism. It is expensive, anachronistic and clichéd… which doesn't stop starry-eyed visitors in droves spending the most romantic hour of their Venetian holiday afloat.

There are official gondola stops on the fondamenta Bacino Orseolo (map p307 A4), in front of the Hotel Danieli on the riva degli Schiavoni (map p308 B1), by the Vallaresso vaporetto stop (map p306 B4), by the railway station (map p304 B1), by the piazzale Roma bus terminus (map p304 C1), by the Santa Maria del Giglio vaporetto stop (map p307 B3), at the jetty at the end of the piazzetta San Marco (map p307 B4), at campo Santa Sofia (map p305 C3) near the Ca' D'Oro vaporetto stop, by the San Tomà vaporetto stop (map p306 A2), by the Bauer Grundwald hotel in campo San Moisè (map p307 B4), and on the riva del Carbon at the southern end of the Rialto bridge (map p305 C3).

Fares are set by the Istituzione per la Conservazione della gondola e tutela del gondoliere (Gondola Board; 041 528 5075/www. gondolavenezia.it); in the unlikely event that a gondolier tries to overcharge you, address complaints to the Ente. Prices below are for the hire of the gondola, regardless of the number of passengers (up to six).

8am-8pm: €62 for 50mins; €31 for each additional 25mins.
8pm-8am: €78 for 50mins; €39 for each additional 25mins.

By bicycle

Be prepared to fight off hordes of wired-up, sleep-deprived journalists and film critics to get your hands on a bike on the Lido during the Film Festival in early September (*see p202*). At other times, try the following.

Giorgio Barbieri

Via Zara 5, Lido (041 526 1490). **Open** *Mar-Oct* 8.30am-7.30pm daily. **Rates** €9 a day. **No credit cards**. **Map** p311.

Bruno Lazzari

Gran viale Santa Maria Elisabetta 21B, Lido (041 526 8019). **Open** *Mar-Sept* 8am-8pm daily. *Oct-Feb* 8.30am-1pm, 3-7.30pm. **Rates** €9 a day. **Credit** MC, V. **Map** p311.

By car

For car parks, *see p275*.

Avis

Santa Croce 496G, piazzale Roma (041 523 7377/www.avisautono leggio.it). **Open** *Apr-Oct* 8am-6pm Mon-Fri; 8am-12.30pm Sat, Sun. *Nov-Mar* 8.30am-12.30pm, 2.30-6pm Mon-Fri; 8am-12.30pm Sat, Sun. **Credit** AmEx, DC, MC, V. **Map** p304 C1.
Branch: Arrivals hall, Marco Polo Airport (041 541 5030).

Europcar

Santa Croce 496H, piazzale Roma (041 523 8616/www.europcar.it). **Open** *Apr-Oct* 8.30am-1pm, 2-6.30pm Mon-Fri; 8.30am-12.30pm Sat, Sun. *Nov-Mar* 8.30am-12.30pm, 2.30-6pm Mon-Fri; 8.30am-noon Sat. **Credit** AmEx, DC, MC, V. **Map** p304 C1.
Branch: Arrivals hall, Marco Polo Airport (041 541 5654).

Hertz

Santa Croce 496F, piazzale Roma (041 528 3524-4091). **Open** *Apr-Oct* 8am-6pm Mon-Fri; 8am-1pm Sat, Sun. *Nov-Mar* 8am-12.30pm, 3-5.30pm Mon-Fri; 8am-1pm Sat. **Credit** AmEx, DC, MC, V. **Map** p304 C1.
Branch: Arrivals hall, Marco Polo Airport (041 541 6075).

Maggiore National

Mestre railway station (041 935 300/www.maggiore.it). **Open** 8am-1pm, 2.30-7pm Mon-Fri; 8am-1pm Sat. **Credit** AmEx, DC, MC, V.
Branch: Arrivals hall, Marco Polo Airport (041 541 5040).

Mattiazzo

496E Santa Croce, piazzale Roma (041 522 0884). **Open** 8am-8pm daily. **Credit** AmEx, DC, MC, V.
Map p304 C1.
Chauffeur-driven limousine hire.

By train

Many long-distance trains terminate at **Santa Lucia station** (map p304 B1) in island Venice. Others go no further than Mestre on the mainland, from where local trains run every ten minutes or less to Santa Lucia.

There is now a national rail information number: 89 20 21 (operates 7am-9pm daily). To talk to an operator – who may speak a few words of basic English – rather than coping with a recorded message in Italian, stay on the line during the initial recorded instructions. You will be given the option of *orario* (timetable) or *altro*. Say *altro* and to be connected to an operator. Recorded schedules only from 9pm to 7am.

The website www.trenitalia. com gives complete information on schedules, in English as well as Italian. In theory, tickets can be booked through the website by credit card and picked up from machines in the station; in practice, it doesn't always work.

The rail information office in the main hall of Santa Lucia station is open 7am-9pm daily. Train tickets can be purchased from windows (open 5.50am-9.30pm daily, all major credit cards), from cash and credit card vending machines in the station, or from travel agents around the city displaying the FS (Ferrovie dello Stato – state railways) logo. Alternatively, they can be ordered by phone between two months before

and the day of departure by ringing 041 275 0492, 9am-1pm, 3-6pm daily and collected from the station (Club Eurostar, platform 1-2) or sent to your home.

In Venice station check that the ticket window you are queuing for is the right one: the first three windows are for domestic travel while windows 6-11 are for reservations and international tickets.

Supplements are charged for high-speed trains – marked either ES (Eurostar), IC (Intercity) or EC (Eurocity, the same as Intercity except that it goes across a national border).

Seat bookings are obligatory (and free) on ES trains on Fridays and Sundays and all week at certain peak times of year. An R inside a square on train timetables indicates this; it is a good idea to check when purchasing your ticket. Booking a seat on IC and internal EC routes costs only €3 and is well worth it to avoid standing in a packed corridor at peak travel times, especially on Friday and Sunday evenings. If your ES or IC train arrives more than 30 minutes late and you have a seat booking, you can ask the ticket office at your destination (at the booth marked Rimborsi) to reimburse the cost of the supplement, though this is a long process.

Anyone under 26 can buy cut-rate BIGE tickets at the ticket counter or the Passaggi travel agency located in the entrance of the train station.

Remember that you must stamp your ticket – and any supplement – in the yellow machines at the head of each platform before boarding the train. Failure to do so can result in a fine, though looking foreign and contrite usually works. If you are running for your train and forget to stamp your ticket, locate the inspector as soon as possible after boarding and s/he will waive the fine.

Directory

Resources A-Z

Accommodation

For on-the-spot hotel reservations, make your way to booths run by the **Associazione Veneziana Albergatori** (Venice Hoteliers' Association, 041 523 8032/ 041 522 2264). The booths can be found at locations listed below:
the train station (041 715 288); the arrivals hall in Marco Polo airport (041 541 5133); the Comunale car park in piazzale Roma (041 522 8640/ 041 523 1397).

Addresses

Postal addresses in Venice consist of the name of the *sestiere* (*see p60*) followed by a house-number: the Doge's Palace is San Marco 1; Castello, the largest sestiere, goes up to number 6828. Armed with only this information, you will never reach your destination. In this guide we also give the calle (street)/campo (square) etc on which each place is located, though as the same street name is likely to crop up several times in different

places around the city, this is not always helpful either. When asking for directions, make sure you ascertain the nearest vaporetto stop, campo, church or other easily-identifiable landmark. Note that the Venetian attitude to spelling is very flexible.

Age restrictions

Cigarettes and alcohol cannot legally be sold to under-16s. Beer and wine can be consumed at bars from the age of 16, spirits from 18. Anyone of 14

Street wise

Venice is perhaps never more Venetian than in its place-names; this is true both of the terms describing the kind of location and the names attached to these terms. Understanding the name-system is one way of getting a grip on this slippery city.

TERMINOLOGY

The uniqueness of Venice's topography is reflected in its street nomenclature. Italian words are the exception: there is only one piazza (plus two piazzette and one piazzale); the two *vie* – Garibaldi and 22 Marzo – are 19th-century creations. The principal designations are as follows:
calle the commonest type of street.
campo literally 'field', harking back to the days of tiny communities clustered around churches on marsh-encircled islands. Smaller ones are **campielli** or **corti**.
crosera crossroads.
fondamenta street flanking a canal.
lista street where an ambassador lived.
paludo former marshland.
piscina former site of a stagnant pool.
ramo literally, 'branch'; hence a side-street (either a blind alley or a short one linking two other streets).
rio canal; the only ones within the city dignified by the name 'canal' are the Grande, Giudecca, Cannaregio, Arsenale and San Pietro.
rio terà a filled-in canal; about 40 canals have been made into streets since the 18th century.

riva some *fondamente* on the Grand Canal or lagoon have this name.
ruga street, usually with shops.
sacca originally an inlet of the lagoon.
salizada literally 'paved street, usually the most important in the neighbourhood.
sotoportego archway or covered street.

NAMES

Most Venetian toponyms fall into the following categories: churches, local families, religious icons, jobs, shops and taverns, foreign communities and local features. The same name may crop up several times around the city.

Local characteristics explain most other place names in the city: there are self-explanatory names like *calle stretta* (narrow alley) and *calle sporca* (dirty alley) and several that refer to certain curious local features, such as *pozzo roverso* (upside-down well).

The Italian tendency to name places after national worthies never caught on in Venice. Campo San Bartolomeo was officially renamed campo Goldoni when a statue was erected to the playwright, but it never caught on owing to Venetian stubbornness, and the square soon reverted to its original name. The same is true of campo Santo Stefano, officially renamed after Doge Francesco Morosini, the hero of Venice's last Turkish wars, but resolutely known by its saint.

or over can ride a moped or scooter of 50cc; no licence is required. You must be over 18 to drive and over 21 to hire a car.

Business

If you are planning to do business in Venice, a call to your embassy's commercial sector in Rome (*see p281*) is always a good idea. Note that few countries have consulates in Venice, and those that exist are often short on useful data. **Comitato Venezia Vuole Vivere** (c/o Parco Scientifico e Tecnologico, Fabbricato Lybra, Marghera, 041 549 9111), an umbrella group of local industrial and retail associations, provides useful insights into setting up and doing business in Venice.

Conferences

Venice has extensive facilities for business conferences and congresses. The same goes for the rest of the Veneto, where functions can be held in Palladian villas and other historic landmarks.

For information on trade fairs in Venice, contact **Venezia Fiere** (San Polo 2120, campo San Polo, 041 714 066/fax 041 713 151/ www.veneziafiere.it).

Most of the organisers listed below will provide hotel and boat booking services as well as the usual facilities.

Codess Settore Cultura
San Polo 2120, campo San Polo (041 710 200/fax 041 717 771/ www.codesscultura.it). **Map** p304 C2.

Endar
Castello 4966, fondamenta de l'Osmarin (041 523 8440/ fax 041 528 6846/www.endar.it). **Map** p308 B1.

Nexa
San Marco 3870, corte de l'Alboro (041 521 0255/fax 041 528 5041/ nexa@flashnet.it). **Map** p307 A3.

Studio Systema
San Polo 135, campo San Giacomo di Rialto (041 520 1959/fax 041 520 1960/www.studiosystema.iti.it). **Map** p305 C3.

Venezia Congressi
Dorsoduro 1056, calle Gambara (041 522 8400/fax 041 523 8995/ www.veneziacongressi.com). **Map** p306 B2.

Couriers

Local
Bartolini 041 531 8944/ www.bartolini.it
Executive 041 999 506/ www.executivegroup.com
Pony Express 041 957 500/ www.pony.it
SDA Express 041 595 1717/ www.sda.it
TNT Traco 041 250 0111/ www.tntitaly.it

International
DHL (toll free) 199 199 345/ www.dhl.it
Federal Express (toll free) 800 123 800/www.fedex.com/it
Mail Boxes Etc 041 985 868/ www.mbe.it
UPS (toll free) 800 877 877

Interpreters

Most of the conference organisers listed above will also provide interpreters.

Lexicon
Via Caneve 77, Mestre (041 534 8005/www.lexitrad.it).

TER Centro Traduzioni
Cannaregio 1076/C, ramo San Zuane (041 717 923/www.ter-traduzioni.com). **Map** p304 A1.

Customs

Anyone arriving from another EU country does not have to declare goods imported into or exported from Italy for their personal use.

For people arriving from non-EU countries the following limits apply: 200 cigarettes or 100 cigarillos or 50 cigars or 250 grams of tobacco; one litre of spirits or two litres of wine; one bottle of perfume (50 grams/1.76 oz). Anything above will be subject to

taxation at the port of entry. There are no restrictions on imports of cameras, watches or electrical goods.

Disabled travellers

The very things that make Venice unique make it extra-difficult for disabled travellers: no barriers between pavements and canals; hundreds of picturesque but wheelchair-unfriendly bridges; museums that are either unrepentantly inaccessible or that proudly boast that they have state-of-the-art disabled facilities – once you've made it up the stairs. The city should not, however, be automatically crossed off the holiday destination list, as there has been an effort in recent years to provide facilities and make at least some areas of the city viable for disabled travellers.

There is now a handy one-stop source of information, **Informahandicap**, which has collaborated with the local tourist board to mark in yellow on the standard free tourist map of Venice the areas of the city that are easily accessible to wheelchair-bound travellers.

The bridges that have wheelchair ramps (five in the *sestiere* of San Marco, one on the island of Burano and one on Murano) are marked, as well as the public toilets which are accessible to wheelchair-users. The map is available in APT offices (*see p290*), as are the keys for operating the automated ramps (you can keep the keys: they work for ramps all over Italy).

Public transport is one area where Venice scores higher than many other destinations, as standard *vaporetti* and *motonavi* (but not *motoscafi* – see *p275* **Vaporetti**) have a reasonably large, flat deck area, and there are no steps or steep inclines on the route between quayside and boat. The vaporetto lines that currently guarantee disabled access (though peak times should be avoided) are 1, N, 6, 12, 14 and 82. Some of the buses that run between Mestre and Venice also have wheelchair access: ring ACTV for info (041 528 7886), or go to the Informahandicap website, which is in any case worth a look before you set out.

Informahandicap

Viale Garibaldi 155, Mestre (041 534 1700/www.comune.venezia.it/ handicap). **Open** 3.30-6.30pm Tue, Thur, Fri; 9am-1pm Wed, Sat. A city council service that provides information – in English, if necessary – on disabled travel in Venice and the Veneto, and on hotels, restaurants and museums with facilities for the disabled. All the information is contained in a free guide, which can be sent on request.

COINtel

06 712 9011/www.coinsociale.it. This Rome-based organisation provides nationwide information on the wheelchair-friendliness of hotels, museums and other disabled facilities.

Transport

Contact the following numbers for further information on services for the disabled:
ACTV (buses and *vaporetti*) 041 528 7886.
FS (state railways) 041 785 570.
Marco Polo Airport 041 260 9260.

Drugs

If caught in possession of drugs of any type you will be taken before a magistrate.

If you can convince him or her that the tiny quantity you were carrying was for purely personal use then you will be let off with a fine or be ordered to leave the country. (Habitual offenders will be offered rehab. Holders of Italian driving licences may have them temporarily suspended.) Anything more than a tiny amount will push you into the criminal category: couriering

or dealing can land you in prison for up to 20 years.

It is an offence to buy drugs, or even to give them away. Sniffer dogs are a fixture at most ports of entry into Italy; customs police will take a dim view of visitors entering with even the tiniest quantities of narcotics, and are likely to allow them to stay no longer than it takes a magistrate to expel them from the country. For more information call 840 002 244.

Electricity

Italy's electricity system runs on 220/230v. To use British or US appliances, you will need two-pin adaptor plugs: these are best bought before leaving home, as they tend to be expensive in Italy and are not always easy to find. If you do need to buy one here, try any electrical retailer (*casalinghi* or *elettrodomestici*).

Embassies & consulates

There are few diplomatic missions in Venice. For most information, and emergencies, you will probably have to contact offices in Rome or Milan.

British Consulate

Dorsoduro 1051, campo della Carità (041 522 7207). Vaporetto Accademia. **Open** 10am-1pm Mon-Fri. **Map** p304 A1.
In emergencies phone 329 808 0018 (9-10am, 2-4pm Mon-Fri); outside of these hours refer to the duty officer at the Milan consulate on 335 810 6857.

South African Consulate

Santa Croce 466G, piazzale Roma (041 524 1599). Vaporetto Piazzale Roma. **Open** 9.30am-12.30pm Mon-Fri. **Map** p306 A1.
In emergencies contact the Milan consulate on 02 809 036.

Embassies in Rome

Australian 06 852 721
British 06 4220 0001
Canadian 06 445 981

Irish 06 697 9121
New Zealand 06 441 7171
South African 06 852 541
US 06 46 741

Consulates in Milan

Australian 02 777 041
British 02 723 001
Canadian 02 675 81
New Zealand 02 4801 2544
US 02 290 351

Emergencies

See also p287 **Safety & security**.

Thefts or losses should be reported immediately at the nearest police station (either of the Polizia di Stato or the nominally military Carabinieri). Report the loss of your passport to the nearest consulate or embassy (*see above*). Report the loss of a credit card or travellers' cheques to your credit-card company (*see p285*).

National emergency numbers

Polizia di Stato 113
Carabinieri 112
Fire brigade 115
Ambulance 118
Car breakdowns (Automobile Club d'Italia) 803 116
Guardia Forestale (forest rangers and mountain rescue) 1515
Coast guard 1530

Local emergency numbers

Polizia di Stato
Santa Croce 500, piazzale Roma (041 271 5511/www.polizia distato.it). Vaporetto Piazzale Roma. **Map** p304 C1.
Carabinieri
Castello 4693A, campo San Zaccaria (041 520 4777). Vaporetto San Zaccaria. **Map** p308 B1.
Fire brigade 041 257 4700
Ambulance 041 523 0000
Coast guard (Capitaneria di Porto) 041 240 5711

Domestic emergencies

To report a malfunction in any of the main public services, call the following:
Electricity (ENEL) 800 900 800
Gas (Italgas) 800 900 777
Telephone (Telecom Italia) 187
Water (Vesta) 041 521 2952

Directory

Health & hospitals

The *pronto soccorso* (casualty department) of all public hospitals provides free emergency treatment for travellers, but it is also worth taking out private health insurance (*see below*).

If you are an EU citizen and need minor treatment, take your E111 form (*see below*) with you to any doctor for a free consultation. Drugs he or she prescribes can be bought at chemists at prices set by the Health Ministry.

Tests or specialist examinations carried out in the public system (*Sistema sanità nazionale*, SSN), will be charged at fixed rates (*il ticket*) and a receipt issued.

For urgent medical advice from local health authority doctors during the night call 041 529 4060 in Venice, 041 526 7743 on the Lido and 041 534 4411 in Mestre (8pm-8am Mon-Fri; 10am Sat-8am Mon).

Contraception

Condoms are on sale near the checkout in supermarkets, or over the counter at chemists. The contraceptive pill is freely available on prescription at any pharmacy.

Dentists

Dental treatment in Italy is on the expensive side and may not be covered by your health insurance. For urgent dental treatment at weekends, go to the *Ambulatorio Odontostomatologico* at the Ospedale Civile (*see below*).

Hospitals

The public relations department of Venice's Ospedale Civile (041 529 4588) provides general information on being hospitalised in Venice.

The hospitals listed below all have 24-hour *pronto*

soccorso (casualty) facilities. For an ambulance-boat, call 041 523 0000.

Ospedale Civile
Castello 6777, campo Santi Giovanni e Paolo (041 529 4111/casualty 041 529 4516/668). Vaporetto Ospedale. **Map** p306 A1.
Housed in the 15th-century Scuola di San Marco, Venice's main hospital has helpful staff and doctors who are quite likely to speak English.

Ospedale al Mare
Lungomare D'Annunzio 1, Lido (041 529 4111/casualty 041 529 5234). Vaporetto Lido. **Map** p311.
Smaller than the Ospedale Civile, and offering a smaller range of services, but with fine sea views.

Ospedale Umberto I
Via Circonvallazione 50, Mestre (041 260 7111).
A modern hospital on the mainland.

Ospedale di Padova
Via Giustiniani 2, Padova (049 821 1111).

Ospedale di Verona
Piazzale Stefani 1, Verona (045 807 1111).

Pharmacies

Pharmacies (*farmacie*), identified by a red or green cross above the door, are run by qualified chemists who will dispense informal advice on and assistance for minor ailments, as well as filling doctors' prescriptions. Over-the-counter drugs such as aspirin are more expensive in Italy than in the UK or US.

Most chemists are open 9am-12.30pm, 3.45-7.30pm Mon-Fri; 9am-12.45pm Sat. A small number remain open on Saturday afternoon, Sunday and at night on a duty rota system, details of which are posted outside every pharmacy and published in the local press.

Most pharmacies carry homeopathic medicines. All will check your blood pressure. If you require regular medication, bring adequate supplies of your drugs with you. Ask your GP for the chemical rather than the brand

name of your medicine: it may only be available in Italy under a different name.

Insurance

EU citizens are entitled to reciprocal medical care in Italy provided they leave their own country with an E111 form, available from local health authorities. If used for anything but emergencies (which are treated free anyway in casualty departments, *see above*), it will entail dealing with the intricacies of the Italian state health system. For short-term visits, it may be advisable to take out private health insurance.

Non-EU citizens should review their private health insurance plans to see if they cover expenses incurred while travelling. If not, travel insurance should be obtained before setting out from home. If you are a student, you may want to check with your student travel organisation: some offer basic health cover with the purchase of their IDs.

If you rent a car, motorcycle or moped while in Italy, make sure you pay the extra charge for full insurance cover.

Internet

A number of Italian providers offer free internet access, including Caltanet (www.caltanet.it), Libero (www.libero.it), Tiscali (www.tiscalinet.it), Kataweb (www.kataweb.com) and Fastweb (www.fastweb.it).

Cyber-cafés have mushroomed in the area; if you plan to surf or check your email from a hotel or private house, check that the phone jack on the end of the cable works in an Italian phone socket; US jacks (RJ11) are fine, British ones not. If you need an adaptor for a British jack, buy it before you leave home. Some places still have old three-pin

Directory

phone sockets; adaptors for these can be found in large supermarkets, and phone and electrical shops.

Rialto Net

San Polo 279, calle Prima de la Donzela (041 241 3862/www. rialtonet.it). Vaporetto Rialto or San Stae. **Open** 9.30am-11.30pm daily. **Rates** *Non-members* €2.40 for 20mins. *Members* €1.40 for 20mins. *Students* €2 for 20mins (monthly fee €4). **No credit cards. Map** p305C3. There are 24 computers in this peaceful Internet point tucked behind the Rialto market stalls, plus fax, photocopying facilities, webcam, word-processing, scanner, colour printing, CD-burning and other services.

Left luggage

Most hotels will look after your luggage even after you have checked out.

Santa Lucia railway station

041 785 531. **Open** 6am-midnight daily. **Rates** €3 per item per 12hrs; €2 extra after 12hrs. **No credit cards. Map** p304 B1.

Marco Polo airport

Arrivals hall (near Post Office) (041 260 6111/329 926 7336). **Open** 6am-9pm daily. **Rates** €2.32 per item per day. **No credit cards.**

Piazzale Roma bus terminus

041 523 1107. **Open** 6am-9pm daily. **Rates** €2.58 per item per day. **No credit cards. Map** p304 C1.

Legal help

If you are in need of legal advice, your first stop should always be your consulate or embassy (*see p281*).

Libraries

You will need some form of photo ID to get into all the libraries listed below.

Archivio Storico delle Arti Contemporanee (ASAC)

Santa Croce 2214, calle della Regina (041 521 8700/www.labiennale divenezia.net/it/asac). Vaporetto San Stae. **Map** p305 C3.

The archive of the Venice Biennale contemporary art festival was closed for long-term restoration at the time of writing and accessible only by written request to the curator.

Archivio di Stato

San Polo 3002, campo dei Frari (041 522 2281/www.archivi. beniculturali.it). Vaporetto San Tomà. **Open** 8.20am-6pm Mon-Thur; 8.20am-2pm Fri, Sat. **Map** p304 C2. Houses all official documents relating to the administration of the Venetian Republic, and a host of other historic manuscripts. Material must be requested between 8.30am and 1pm.

Biblioteca Nazionale Marciana

San Marco 7, piazzetta San Marco (041 520 8788/www.marciana. venezia.sbn.it). Vaporetto Vallaresso. **Open** 8.10am-7pm Mon-Fri; 8.10am-1.30pm Sat. **Map** p307 B4. The city's main public library, the Marciana has medieval manuscripts and editions of the classics dating back to the 15th century.

Biblioteca Fondazione Scientifica Querini Stampalia

Castello 5252, campo Santa Maria Formosa (041 271 1411/www. provincia.venezia.it/querini). Vaporetto Rialto or San Zaccaria. **Open** *Reading room & catalogues* 4pm-midnight Mon-Fri; 2.30pm-midnight Sat; 3-7pm Sun. *Catalogues only* 9am-2pm Mon-Fri (or online 24hrs daily). **Map** p306 A1. The Querini Stampalia library is attached to the museum of the same name (*see p85*) and has a fine collection of works on Venice and all things Venetian. Post-graduate students and professors may ask to use the library's quiet study rooms.

Biblioteca Generale dell'Università di Ca' Foscari

Dorsoduro 3199, calle Bernardo (041 234 6169/www.biblio.unive.it). Vaporetto Ca' Rezzonico. **Open** 8.30am-10.45pm Mon-Fri; 8.30am-1.30pm Sat. **Map** p306 A2. The university library is strong on the humanities and economics.

Biblioteca Centrale Istituto Universitario di Architettura di Venezia

Santa Croce 191, fondamenta Tolentini (041 257 1106/http:// iuavbc.iuav.it). Vaporetto Piazzale Roma. **Open** 9am-midnight Mon-Fri; 2pm-midnight first Mon of the mth. **Map** p304 C1.

The library of one of Italy's top architecture faculties has a vast collection of works on the history of architecture, town planning, art, engineering and social sciences.

Biblioteca Fondazione Giorgio Cini

Isola di San Giorgio Maggiore (041 528 9900/www.cini.it). Vaporetto San Giorgio. **Open** *Art history & music* 9am-4.45pm Mon-Fri. *History* 9am-12.45pm Mon, Wed, Thur; 9am-noon, 3-6pm Tue, Fri. *Literature & theatre* 9am-12.45pm, 2.30-4.45pm Mon-Fri. *Venice & the East* 9am-noon, 2.30-4.45pm Mon-Fri. **Map** p308 C1. Specialises in art history, with sections dedicated to the history of Venice and the Venetian state and society, literature, theatre and music. There's a large archive of microfilms and photographs. Apply for permission to use the library prior to your visit.

Biblioteca Museo Correr

San Marco 52, piazza San Marco (041 522 5625/www.comune.venezia. it/museicivici). Vaporetto Vallaresso. **Open** 8.30am-1.30pm Mon, Wed, Fri; 8.30am-5pm Tue, Thur. **Map** p307 A4. Part of the Museo Correr (*see p75*), this small library contains books on Venetian history and art history.

Lost property

Your mislaid belongings may end up at one of the *uffici oggetti smarriti* listed below. You could also try the police (*see p281* **Emergencies**), or ring VESTA, the city's rubbish collection department, on 041 729 1111.

ACTV

Santa Croce, piazzale Roma (041 272 2179). Vaporetto Piazzale Roma. **Open** 7.30am-6pm daily. **Map** p304 C1. For items found on *vaporetti* or buses.

Comune (City Council)

San Marco 4136, riva del Carbon (041 274 8225). Vaporetto Rialto. **Open** 8.30am-12.30pm Mon-Fri.

FS/Stazione Santa Lucia

Santa Lucia railway station, centro accoglienza clienti (041 785 670). Vaporetto Ferrovia. **Open** 7am-9pm daily. **Map** p304 B1. All items found on trains in the Venice area and in the station itself are brought to this deposit.

Marco Polo Airport

Arrivals Hall (041 260 9222). Bus 5 to Aeroporto. **Open** 9am-8pm daily.

National dailies

Italian newspapers can be a frustrating read. Long, indigestible political stories with very little background explanation predominate. On the plus side, Italian papers are delightfully unsnobbish and happily blend serious news, leaders by internationally known commentators, and well-written, often surreal, crime and human-interest stories.

Sports coverage in the dailies is extensive and thorough, but if you're not sated there are the mass-circulation sports papers **Corriere dello Sport**, **La Gazzetta dello Sport** and **Tuttosport**.

Corriere della Sera

www.rcs.it.
To the centre of centre-left, the solid, serious but often dull Milan-based *Corriere della Sera* is good on crime and foreign news.

Il Manifesto

www.ilmanifesto.it.
A reminder that, though the Berlin Wall is a distant memory, there is still some corner of central Rome where hearts beat Red.

La Repubblica

www.repubblica.it.
The centre-ish, left-ish *La Repubblica* is good on the Mafia and the Vatican, and comes up with the occasional major scoop on its business pages.

La Stampa

www.lastampa.it.
Part of the massive empire of Turin's Agnelli family – for which read Fiat – *La Stampa* has good (though inevitably pro-Agnelli) business reporting.

Venice dailies

Il Gazzettino

www.gazzettino.it.
One of Italy's most successful local papers. A conservative broadsheet, it provides national and international news on the front and local news inside, with different editions for towns around the region.

La Nuova Venezia

www.nuovavenezia.it.
Local coverage dominates in this small-circulation daily, which emerged in 1984. Young, lively and strong on crime stories, *La Nuova* (as locals call it) carries Venetian news and listings.

Foreign press

The *Financial Times, Wall Street Journal, USA Today, International Herald Tribune* (with its Italy Daily supplement) and most British and European dailies can be found on the day of issue at newsstands all around town – especially those at the station, within striking distance of St Mark's and the Rialto, and at the large *edicola* at the Accademia vaporetto stop. US dailies take a day or two to appear.

Magazines

News weeklies **Panorama** (pro-Berlusconi) and **L'Espresso** (anti-Berlusconi) provide a general round-up of the week's events , while **Sette** and **Venerdì** – respectively the colour supplements of *Corriere della Sera* (Thursday) and *La Repubblica* (Friday) – have nice photos, though the text often leaves much to be desired.

For tabloid-style scandal, try **Gente** and **Oggi** with their weird mix of sex, glamour and religion, or the execrable **Eva 3000**, **Novella 2000** and **Cronaca Vera**.

Internazionale (www. internazionale.it) provides an excellent digest of interesting bits and pieces gleaned from the world's press the previous week. **Diario della Settimana** (www.diario.it), is informed and urbane with a flair for investigative journalism.

But the biggest-selling magazine of them all is **Famiglia Cristiana** – available from newsstands or in most churches – which alternates Vatican line-toeing with Vatican-baiting, depending on the state of relations between the Holy See and the idiosyncratic Paoline monks who produce it.

Listings & classified ads

Venezia News

€2.20
A bilingual listings magazine out on the first of each month, *Venezia News* includes music, film, theatre, art and sports listings, plus interviews and features.

Gente Veneta

€1
This weekly broadsheet, produced by the local branch of the Catholic Church, blends cultural and religious listings with reports on Venetian social problems.

Boom

A small-ads paper thrust free through every letterbox each week. The place to look for flats, jobs and lonelyhearts.

Aladino

Issued every Thursday, it has classified ads for everything from flats for rent to *gondole* for sale.

Television

Italy has six major networks (three are owned by state broadcaster RAI, three belong to Silvio Berlusconi's Mediaset group). When these have bored you, there are local stations to provide hours of channel-zapping, compulsively awful fun.

The standard of TV news and current affairs programmes varies; most, however, offer a breadth of international coverage that makes British TV news look like a parish magazine.

Local radio

Radio Venezia

FM 100.95 & 92.4
News and pop music with the Venetian housewife in mind.

Radio Capital
FM 98.5
Heavy on advertising, but generous with information on events and news in the city. In between you'll hear '80s and '90s classics and a sprinkling of current hits.

Radio Padova
FM 103.9 & 88.4
Only the best popular chart music, with concert information for the Veneto area.

Money

In February 2002 the euro replaced the lira as Italy's currency. It was hardly a seamless transition but the tourist trade has whole-heartily accepted the new currency. One euro is worth L1,936.27. There are euro banknotes of €5, €10, €20, €100, €200 and €500, and coins worth €1 and €2 as well as 1¢ (*centesimo*), 2¢, 5¢, 10¢, 20¢ and 50¢. Notes and coins from any Euro-zone country are valid in Italy.

ATMs

Most banks have 24-hour cash-point (Bancomat) machines, and the vast majority of these accept cards with the Maestro and Cirrus symbols. Most cashpoint machines will dispense cash to a daily limit of €250.

Banking hours

Most banks are open 8.20am-1.20pm and 2.45-3.45pm Mon-Fri. All banks are closed on public holidays and work reduced hours the day before a holiday, usually closing at 11am. Banks are listed under *Banche ed Istituti di Credito* in the Yellow Pages.

Foreign exchange

Banks usually offer better exchange rates than bureaux de change (*cambio*). Commission rates in banks vary considerably. Don't be fooled by 'no commission' signs in exchange offices: these usually mean that the exchange rate is dire.

It's a good idea to take your passport with you, especially if you want to change travellers' cheques or draw money on your credit card.

American Express
San Marco 1471, salizzada San Moisè (041 520 0844/amexvenezia @tin.it). Vaporetto Vallaresso. **Open** *May-Oct* 9am-7.45pm Mon-Sat; 9am-5.20pm Sun. *Nov-Mar* 9am-5.30pm Mon-Fri; 9am-12.30pm Sat. **Map** p307 B4.
Exchange with no commission, travellers' cheque refund, card replacements, 24-hour money transfers, plus a variety of extra services such as hotel reservations, car rentals, train and plane tickets, and tour organisation. There is also an ATM.

Travelex
San Marco 5126, riva del Ferro (041 528 7358/roberto.formentin @travelex.it). Vaporetto Rialto. **Open** 9am-7pm Mon-Sat; 9.30am-4.30pm Sun. **Credit** MC, V. **Map** p305 C3.
Cash and travellers' cheques exchanged with no commission. Mastercard cardholders can also withdraw cash.
Branches: San Marco 142, piazza San Marco (041 277 5057); Marco Polo Airport, arrivals (041 541 6833).

Credit cards

Plastic has made great inroads into what was until very recently a cash-only country, but you still can't rely on every shop, hotel and restaurant to accept it happily. However, most hotels of two stars and over will take most major credit cards.

Report lost credit or charge cards to the appropriate emergency number listed below. All the lines are toll-free, operate 24 hours a day, and have English-speaking operators.
American Express 800 864 046
American Express (cheques) 800 872 000
Diners' Club 800 864 064
Eurocard/CartaSì 800 868 086
Mastercard 800 874 299
Visa 800 877 232

Postal services

Besides its main post office (*see below*), Venice has smaller branches in each district that are open 8.10am-1.30pm Mon-Fri, 8.10am-12.30pm Sat and 8.10am-noon on the last working day of the month. There is also a branch at Marco Polo Airport open 8.30am-2pm Mon-Fri, 8.30am-1pm Sat (041 541 5900).

Posta Centrale (Central Post Office)
San Marco 5554, salizzada del Fontego dei Tedeschi (041 271 7111). Vaporetto Rialto. **Open** 8.30am-6.30pm Mon-Sat. **Map** p305 C4.
The main post office is housed in the 16th-century Fontego dei Tedeschi, once a base for German merchants in the city and formerly frescoed by Giorgione. You can purchase stamps, send packages, faxes or telegrams. The office also provides information for philatelists and a *fermo posta* (poste restante) service.

Stamps & charges

Italy's postal service (www.poste.it) is generally reliable and you can be more or less sure that your letters will arrive in reasonable time.

Italy's equivalent to first-class post, *posta prioritaria*, works very well: it promises delivery within 24 hours in Italy, three days for EU countries and four or five for the rest of the world; more often than not, it delivers. A letter of 20g or less to Italy or any EU country costs 62¢ by *posta prioritaria*; outside the EU the cost is 77¢; special stamps can be bought at post offices and *tabacchi* (*see p288*) and posted in any box.

Stamps for slower regular mail are also sold at post offices and *tabacchi* only. A 20g letter costs 41¢ to European countries and 52¢ to a further-afield destination.

The CAI Post-Posta Celere service (available only in main post offices) guarantees 24-hour delivery to major cities

Directory

in Italy and two- to three-day delivery to major cities abroad; you can track the progress of your letter or parcel on the service's website (www.postacelere.com) or by calling (803 160, operates 8am-8pm Mon-Sat).

Registered mail (*raccomandata*, only at post offices) costs €2.58 extra (€2.69 extra outside the EU).

Letter boxes are red and distributed throughout the city. They have two slots: *Per la città* (for Venezia, Mestre and Marghera), and *Tutte le altre destinazioni* (for all other destinations).

Telegrams & telexes

The main post office provides these services during normal business hours. Telegrams to any destination can be sent and dictated over the phone by dialling 186 from a private phone, which will be billed automatically for the service.

Faxes

The main post office will send faxes during regular business hours. The service is costly, however. Most photocopy and *tabacchi* shops offer fax services, too; ask for prices before you send your fax, as they vary significantly.

Religion

Mass times vary from church to church, and are posted by front doors. The church of San Zulian (041 523 5383; map p307 A4) has mass in English between May and September at 9.30am on Sunday. Listed below are the non-Catholic denominations in the city:

Anglican
St George's, Dorsoduro 870, campo San Vio (041 520 0571). Vaporetto Accademia. **Services** *Sung Mass* 10.30am Sun. *Vespers* 6pm daily. **Map** p307 B3.

Greek Orthodox
San Giorgio dei Greci, Castello 3412, fondamenta dei Greci (041 522 5446). Vaporetto San Zaccaria. **Services** 9.30am, 10.30am Sun. *Vespers* 6pm Sat. **Map** p308 B1.

Jewish
Cannaregio 2899, campo del Ghetto Nuovo (041 715 359/museoebraico @codesscultura.it). Vaporetto San Marcuola. **Services** after sunset Fri; 9.30am Sat. **Map** p304 A2. You may be asked for your passport.

Lutheran
Cannaregio 4448, campo Santi Apostoli (041 522 7149). Vaporetto Ca' D'Oro. **Services** 10.30am 2nd & 4th Sun of mth. **Map** p305 C4.

Methodist (Valdese)
Castello 5170, fondamenta Cavagnis (041 522 7549). Vaporetto Rialto. **Services** 11am Sun. **Map** p308 A1.

Relocation

Bureaucracy

You may need any or all of the following documents if you plan to work or study in Venice.

Permesso di soggiorno (permit to stay)
The key document for anyone staying in Italy for more than a short period, the *permesso di soggiorno* can be obtained from the Questura (police HQ). Get there early (7am) and take your passport and a photocopy of it; three passport photos; proof that you are enrolled in a course or that you are in Italy on a scholarship (for students); or a statement from your employer; freelancers should take a bank or tax statement showing you have means of support; and a €10.33 *marca da bollo* (official stamp) available from some *tabacchi* and the post office.

Questura *via Nicolodi 22, Marghera (041 271 5701/041 271 5744). Bus 6/ from piazzale Roma.* **Open** 8.30am-noon Mon-Fri.

Carta d'Identità (identity card)
This official Italian ID card is not strictly necessary for foreigners, who can use their own national IDs and passports as a means of identification. Obtainable from the *Ufficio anagrafe* of the town hall. Take your ID, your *permesso di soggiorno*, and three photographs.

Ufficio anagrafe *San Marco 4142, calle Loredan (041 274 8221). Vaporetto Rialto.* **Open** 8.45am-1pm Mon-Sat. **Map** p307 A3.

Codice Fiscale (tax code)
A *codice fiscale* is required to work legally in Italy, or to open your own business. You will need one to open a bank account or get a phone line, and for some kinds of treatment under the Italian national health service. Take your passport and *permesso di soggiorno*.

Agenzia delle Entrate, Ufficio locale Venezia 1 *San Marco 3538, campo Sant'Angelo (041 271 8111). Vaporetto Sant'Angelo.* **Open** 8.45am-12.45pm Mon, Wed, Fri, Sat; 8.45am-12.45pm, 2.45-4.45pm Tue, Thur. **Map** p307 A3.

Partita IVA (VAT number)
Freelancers or company owners may need a VAT number for invoicing. There is a form to be filled in, but no charge.

Ufficio IVA *San Marco 3538, campo Sant'Angelo (041 271 8111). Vaporetto Sant'Angelo.* **Open** 8.45am-12.45pm Mon-Fri; 8.45am-12.45pm, 2.45-4.45pm Tue, Thur. **Map** p307 A3.

Permesso di lavoro (work permit)
Non-EU citizens must have a work permit to be legally employed in Italy. Employers will usually arrange this; if not, pick up an application form at the address given below, get it signed by your employer and return it with a photocopy of your *permesso di soggiorno*.

Ufficio provinciale del lavoro *via Ca' Marcello 9, Mestre (041 531 8880/dpl-venezia@minlavoro.it). Train to Mestre.* **Open** 9am-noon Mon, Wed, Fri; 9am-noon, 3-5pm Tue, Thur.

Certificato di residenza (residence permit)

Necessary if you want to buy a car or import your belongings without paying customs duties, the *certificato di residenza* can cause diplomatic rows with your landlord: to obtain it, the tax on rubbish collection (*nettezza urbana*) must have been paid for the property you reside in – which means that either you have to volunteer to pay it (and landlords renting out property but not paying taxes on the income run the risk of being discovered), or you have to persuade the owner to. In either case, you'll need to present your passport and *permesso di soggiorno*.

Ufficio anagrafe *San Marco 4142, calle Loredan (041 274 8221). Vaporetto Rialto.* **Open** 8.45am-1pm Mon-Sat. **Map** p307 A3.

Work

Openings for picking up casual employment in Venice are few, though language schools (*Scuole di lingua* in the Yellow Pages) are sometimes on the lookout for native English speakers, especially with TEFL experience. Women *di bella apparenza* (as the advertisements put it) might try conference organisers, or the smart boutiques in the Frezzerie area around San Marco, which sometimes advertise for *commesse* (sales assistants). The more exclusive hotels may have openings for experienced babysitters. The main Ca' Foscari university building at Dorsoduro 3246, calle Foscari (vaporetto San Tomà) often has employment opportunities posted on the noticeboards. Alternatively, try the following agencies:

Manpower

Via Piave 120, Mestre (041 935 900/ www.manpower.it). Bus 2 from piazzale Roma. **Open** 9am-6pm Mon-Fri.

Temporary

Via Manin 38A, Mestre (041 979 048/www.temporary.it). Bus 7 from piazzale Roma. **Open** 9am-12.30pm, 2-6pm Mon-Fri.

Accommodation

Expect to pay upwards of a €500 a week for a very basic apartment in Venice. Cheaper student-type shares can be found through the noticeboards at Ca' Foscari university (*see above*), local listings magazines (*see p284*) or *Il Corriere Immobiliare*, a free weekly newspaper that has information on rentals in the Veneto area.

Otherwise, an agency is your best bet; it will take the equivalent of one month's rent as a commission. Landlords will demand at least one month's (and sometimes as much as three months') rent as a deposit.

Immobil Veneta

San Polo 3132, campiello San Rocco (041 524 0088/immobilvenetasnc @libero.it). Vaporetto San Tomà. **Open** 9.30am-12.30pm, 4-6pm Mon-Fri. **Map** p304 C2.
A reliable agency with apartments at reasonable prices.

Giaretta

San Marco 511, campo della Guerra (041 528 6191/www.giaretta.com). Vaporetto Rialto. **Open** 9am-1pm, 2-7pm Mon-Fri. **Map** p307 A4.
Pleasant if pricey apartments to let.

Safety & security

Venice is, on the whole, an exceptionally safe place at any time of day or night, and violent crime is almost unknown. Lone women would be advised to steer clear of dark alleyways late at night, though even there they are more likely to be harassed than attacked (*see p291* **Women**). Bag-snatchers are a rarity, mostly because of the logistical difficulties Venice presents for making quick getaways. However, pickpockets operate in crowded thoroughfares, especially around San Marco and the Rialto, and on public transport, so make sure you leave passports, plane/train tickets and at least one means of getting hold of money in your hotel room or safe.

If you are the victim of theft or serious crime, call one of the emergency numbers listed under **Emergencies**, *see p281*. The following rules will help avoid unfortunate incidents:

● Don't carry wallets in back pocket, particularly on buses or boats. If you have a bag or camera with a long strap, wear it across your chest and not dangling from one shoulder.

● Keep bags closed, with your hand on them. If you stop at a pavement café or restaurant, do not leave bags or coats on the ground or on the back of a chair where you cannot keep an eye on them.

● Avoid attracting unwanted attention by pulling out large wads of cash to pay for things at street stalls or in busy bars. It's a good idea to keep some small bills and change easily accessible.

● Crowds in general offer easy camouflage for pickpockets. Be especially careful when boarding buses or boats, and entering museums.

● If you have your bag or wallet snatched, or are otherwise a victim of crime, go immediately to the nearest police station to report a *scippo* (*see p281* **Emergencies**). A *denuncia* (written statement) of the incident will be made for you. Give police as much information as possible, including passport number, holiday address and flight numbers. The *denuncia* will be signed, dated, and stamped with an official police seal. It is unlikely that your things will be found, but you will need the *denuncia* for making an insurance claim.

Smoking

Smoking is not permitted in public offices or on public transport. For where to buy cigarettes, *see p288* **Tabacchi**.

Study

All lectures and exams – the majority of which are oral in the Italian system – at Venice's two main universities are in Italian, making a thorough knowledge of the language essential if you wish to get the full benefit of studying here.

Directory

To find out about entrance requirements and contact numbers, consult the faculty websites at www.iuav.unive.it (**Istituto Universitario di Architettura di Venezia**) or www.unive.it (**Università degli Studi di Venezia Ca' Foscari**).

EU citizens have the same right to study at Italian universities as Italian nationals. You will need to have your school diplomas translated and authenticated at the Italian consulate in your own country before presenting them to the *ufficio studenti stranieri* (foreign students' department) of any university.

Both universities run exchange programmes with foreign institutions and partipated in the EU's Erasmus scheme.

A third university – the **Venice International University** (041 271 9511/ www.viu.unive.it) – was created recently on the island of San Servolo. Students currently registered at one of the Venice International member universities (Duke University, Ca' Foscari, Istituto Universitario di Architettura di Venezia, Universitat Autònoma de Barcelona, Ludwig Maximilians Universität and Tel Aviv University) are eligible to apply for VIU undergraduate activities.

Language courses

ASCI-Onlus – Associazione Socio-Culturale Internazionale

Dorsoduro 3861, calle larga Foscari (041 504 0433/www.ascionlus.com). Vaporetto San Tomà. **Open** *mid Jan-mid June* 6.30-8.30pm Mon, Wed, Fri. **No credit cards. Map** p306 A2.
Courses in Italian, French, German, Spanish, Greek, Arabic, Hindi and Chinese. If languages aren't your thing, try computing, tango or belly-dancing.
Branch: Corso del Popolo 81, Mestre (041 504 0433).

The Venice Institute

Dorsoduro 3116A, campo Santa Margherita (041 522 4331/www. istitutovenezia.com). Vaporetto Ca' Rezzonico. **Open** 9am-1pm, 3-5pm Mon-Thur; 9am-3pm Fri. **Credit** MC, V. **Map** p306 A2.
Courses in Italian for foreigners; group and individual sessions.

Tabacchi

Tabacchi or *tabaccherie* (identified by signs with a white T on a black or blue background) are the only places where you can legally buy tobacco products. They also sell stamps, telephone cards, individual or season tickets for public transport, lottery tickets and the stationery required when dealing with bureaucracy. Most of Venice's *tabacchi* pull their shutters down by 7.30pm. If you're gasping for nicotine late in the evening or on Sunday, you'll have to go to the one in the main hall of the railway station, or try the Bar Al Teatro (*see p164*) which stays open until 11pm Tue-Sun.

Telephones

Phone numbers

All Italian land-line numbers must be dialled with their prefixes, even if you are phoning within the local area. Numbers in Venice and its province begin 041; numbers in Padua province begin 049; in Vicenza 0444; in Verona 045. Phone numbers generally have seven or eight digits after the prefix; some older ones still have six, and some switchboards five. If you try a number and cannot get through, it may have been changed to an eight-digit number. Check the directory (*elenco telefonico*) or ring directory enquiries (12).

Numbers beginning with 800 are freephone lines. Numbers beginning 840 and 848 are charged at a nominal rate. These numbers can be

called from within Italy only, and some are available only within certain regions.

Cell phone numbers begin with a 3. Until recently they began 03.

Rates

The pressure of competition has led to continual price cuts, and Italy's once-exorbitant telephone company (Telecom Italia) is edging its rates down.

The minimum charge for a local call from a private phone is about 2¢ (20¢ from a public phone). Phoning abroad remains expensive. You can keep costs down by:

● phoning off-peak (10pm-8am Mon-Sat, all day Sun).

● not using phones in hotels, which usually carry extortionate surcharges.

● using international phone cards, purchasable at *tabacchi* (*see above*) Operators such as Happiness, Planet, Welcome and Europa offer €5 & €10 cards, which can be used from public, cell or land-line phones and will cut costs significantly.

● not calling cellphones from land lines and vice versa.

Public phones

There are public phones in Venice along the tourist routes. Some bars also have payphones. Most public telephones operate only with phonecards (*schede telefoniche*). Some newer models take major credit cards, while the few remaining old-style ones take 10¢, 20¢ and 50¢ coins. Phonecards costing €2.50, €5 and €7.50 can be purchased at post offices, *tabacchi* and some newsstands, or from the occasional vending machine near banks of public phones; to use your card, tear off one corner as marked, insert it into the appropriate slot and dial. Your credit balance will be displayed on the phone. Check the expiry date on your phonecard: no matter how much credit remains, you can't use it after that date.

Telecom Italia also supplies international phone credit cards (*schede telefoniche internazionali*) at various prices. Similar cards for the rival phone company Infostrada (155) can be found at some *tabacchi* shops. While you can't use the Infostrada cards from Telecom public phones, it is worth looking into because the rates are often cheaper.

International calls

To make an international call from Venice dial 00, then the country code (Australia 61, Canada and USA 1, Ireland 353, New Zealand 64, UK 44, South Africa 27), then the area code (usually without the initial 0) and the number. International directory enquiries is on 4176. When calling an Italian land line from abroad, the whole prefix, including the 0, must be dialled, so dial 00 39 041… for Venice from the UK.

For operator-assisted calls abroad, dial 170. To make a reverse-charge (collect) call abroad through an operator in the country you are calling, dial 172 plus the appropriate four-digit country code listed in the 'Country Direct' service instructions in the phone directory (00 44 for BT in the UK; 1011 for AT&T in the US; 1161 for Optus in Australia).

Operator services

Other services provided by Telecom Italia include:
170 problems with national calls
4176 problems with international calls
4114 alarm call
186 telegrams
4161 speaking clock
4197 interrupts a conversation on an engaged line

Mobile phones

Owners of GSM phones can use them in Italy on both 900 and 1800 bands, though

reception in Venice can be patchy. American phones operate on a 1900 band and are therefore useless in Europe. Some phones now have a tri-band system, which operates on all three frequencies.

Time

Italy is one hour ahead of London, six ahead of New York, eight behind Sydney, and 12 behind Wellington.

Tipping

There are no hard and fast rules on tipping in Italy, though Venetians know that foreigners tip generously back home and therefore expect them to be liberal. Some upmarket restaurants (and a growing number of cheaper ones) will add a service charge to your bill: feel free to ask *il servizio è incluso?* If it isn't, leave whatever you think the service merited (and remember that Italians rarely leave more than five to ten per cent).

Bear in mind that all restaurants charge a cover fee (*coperto*), which is a quasi-tip in itself.

Toilets

Public toilets can be found in Venice by following the blue and green signs marked WC. Maintained by the council, they are relatively clean and charge 50¢.
Academia Bridge *Academia side.* **Open** 8am-8pm.
Rialto Market *campo Rialto Novo.* **Open** 7am-5pm.
Campo San Bartolomeo *calle della Bissa.* **Open** 8.30am-8pm.
San Marco *Giardinetti.* **Open** 9am-8pm.

Tourist information

Getting hold of comprehensive tourist information in Venice has become easier of late.

Most hotels will provide you with a copy of *Un Ospite di Venezia/A Guest in Venice*, a bilingual booklet compiled by hoteliers, which contains useful addresses and timetables. It is published every fortnight in high season and monthly in winter.

The official tourist board, along with the Promove association, produces a free quarterly magazine in English and Italian called *Pocket Venice* (www.meetingvenice.it), available at APT offices (*see p290*). The local press is another source of useful information on events (*see p284*), as are the posters plastered on walls all over the city. *Venezia da Vivere* and *Leo* are good resources for information on nightlife and concerts.

DISCOUNT CARDS
The **Venice Card** (www.venicecard.it), produced by the city council, is a one-, three- or seven day card that gives discounts and access to services around the city. You must book your ticket at least 24 hours in advance: you can do this online or by calling 899 909 090 (041 271 4747 from abroad). There are two types of cards, blue and orange: the blue card allows you to use public transport, toilets and baby changing facilities while the orange card also includes admission to the Musei Civici museums (*see p61*). Tickets can be bought at any VeLa office (*see p275*), the Alilaguna (*see p274*) office in the airport or the ASM desk in the San Giuliano car park (*see p290*).
Blue One-day €11; €7 under-30s. Three-day €23; €17 under-30s. Seven-day €41; €39 under-30s
Orange One-day €26; €16 under-30s. Three-day €42; €30 under-30s. Seven-day €58; €51 under-30s

Visitors between the ages of 14 and 29 can sign up for the **Rolling Venice** programme, organised by the town council

Directory

and youth organisations. Holders of a Rolling Venice card are eligible for discounts at selected hotels, museums (up to 50 per cent) and restaurants and shops (10-15 per cent) around the city, as well as cut-price (€12.91) three-day vaporetto passes and 50 per cent off tickets for concerts (not operas) at La Fenice. The card costs €2.58; to get it, take two passport-sized photos and a valid document to any VeLa (see p275) or APT office (see below).

Tourist information offices

See chapters in **The Veneto** section for information offices outside Venice.

Azienda di Promozione Turistica (APT)

San Marco 71F, piazza San Marco (041 529 8711/fax 041 529 8740/ www.turismovenezia.it). Vaporetto Vallaresso. **Open** 9.30am-3.30pm daily. **Map** p307 A4.
APT provides maps of the city and surrounding areas, plus information on sights and events, and a list of hotels. It will also put you in touch with registered guides, and give details of official fees for guided tours. The Palazzetto Selva branch (map p307 B4) has a selection of books, sells concert tickets, and provides Internet access too. Main offices tend to become very crowded in high season, when supplementary kiosks are set up around the city. Offices are open daily throughout the year; most branches remain open into the late afternoon or early evening.
Branches: San Marco 2, Palazzetto Selva, Giardinetti Reali (041 522 5150); Venice-Santa Lucia railway station (041 529 8727); Marco Polo

Airport arrivals hall (tel/fax 041 541 5887); ASM Garage, piazzale Roma (041 241 1499); Viale Santa Maria Elisabetta 6A, Lido (June-Sept only 041 526 5721/fax 041 529 8720).

Tours

Cooperativa guide turistiche

San Marco 750, calle Morosini de la Regina (041 520 9038/fax 041 521 0762/guideve@tin.it). Vaporetto San Zaccaria. **Open** 9am-1pm, 2-6pm Mon-Fri; 9am-1pm Sat. **Rates** €113 for 2hr tour for groups of up to 30 people; €3.50 for every extra person. **No credit cards. Map** p307 A4.
Has around 40 guides on its books, offering made-to-measure tours in Italian, English, French, Spanish, German and various other languages. The only drawback is the €113 minimum charge, which is pricey for small groups. In high season, book at least a week in advance.

Museum card

In spring 2003 Venice plans to launch what is tentatively being called the **Carta dei Musei di Venezia/Venice Museum Card**. Costing 30 (20 concessions), it will be valid for a year and will allow access to 40 sights. The card will be available at all the participating museums, galleries etc, and at tourist offices (see p289), VeLa outlets (see p275) and probably at tabacchi (see p288) around the city. Payment by credit card will depend on facilities available where the ticket is purchased. The ticket will cover:
Biblioteca Marciana/Libreria Sansoviniana (p74)
Ca'D'Oro – Galleria Franchetti (p95)
Ca' Pesaro – Galleria Internazionale d'Arte Moderna (p106)
Ca' Pesaro – Museo d'Arte Orientale (p108)
Ca' Rezzonico – Museo del Settecento Veneziano (p120)
Casa di Carlo Goldoni e Biblioteca di Studi Teatrali (p113)
Gallerie dell'Accademia (p122)
Museo & cattedrale, Torcello (p140)
Museo Archeologico Nazionale (p75)
Museo dell'Arte Vetrario (Glass Museum) (p136)
Museo Correr (p75)
Museo Ebraico (p101)
Museo della Fondazione Querini Stampalia (p85)

Museo Fortuny (p82)
Museo dell'Istituto Ellenico (p90)
Museo del Merletto (Lace Museum) (p137)
Museo Storico Navale (p91)
Museo di Storio Naturale (Natural History Museum) (p64)
Palazzo Ducale (Doge's Palace; p77)
Palazzo Mocenigo (p109)
Scala Contarini del Bovolo (p83)
Scuola Grande di San Rocco (p115)
Scuola Grande di Santa Maria dei Carmini (p121)
Sinagoghe (p101)
Torre dell'Orologio (p79)

CHURCHES
See also p61 **Chorus**.
(I Frari) Santa Maria dei Frari (p113)
I Gesuati (Santa Maria del Rosario) (p126)
Madonna dell'Orto (p99)
Il Redentore (p128)
San Giacomo dell'Orio (p110)
San Giovanni Elemosinario (p105)
San Pietro in Castello (p92)
San Sebastiano (p118)
San Stae (p111)
Sant'Alvise (p101)
Santa Maria Formosa (p87)
Santa Maria del Giglio (p83)
Santa Maria dei Miracoli (p102)
Santo Stefano (p82)

American Express

San Marco 1471, salizzada San Moisè (041 520 0844/amex venezia@tin.it). Vaporetto Vallaresso. **Open** *May-Oct* 9am-7.45pm Mon-Sat; 9am-5.20pm Sun. *Nov-Mar* 9am-5.30pm Mon-Fri; 9am-12.30pm Sat. **Map** p307 B4.
American Express offers daily guided tours in several languages at reasonable prices.

Visas

For EU citizens, a passport or a national identity card valid for travel abroad is sufficient. Non-EU citizens must have full passports. Citizens of the US, Canada, Australia and New Zealand do not need visas for stays of up to three months. In theory, visitors are required to declare their presence to the local police within a few days of arrival, unless they are staying in a hotel, where this will be done for them. In practice, you will not need to report to the police station unless you decide to extend your stay, and you apply for a *permesso di soggiorno* (permit to stay, *see p286*).

Water & drinking

Forget *Death in Venice*-style cholera scares: the water is safe to drink and checked regularly. For information visit www.vestaspa.net.

When to go

Holidays

See also chapter **Festivals & Events**.

On public holidays (*giorni festivi*) public offices, banks and post offices are closed. So, in theory, are shops – but in tourism-oriented Venice, this rule is often waived, especially in high season. Some bars and restaurants mayobserve holidays: if in doubt, call ahead. You'll be hard pushed to find much open on Christmas Day and New Year's Day.

Public transport is reduced to a skeleton service on 1 May, Christmas Day and New Year's Day, and may be re-routed or curtailed for local festivities (*see chapter* **Festivals & Events**); details are posted at vaporetto stops and at the bus terminus in piazzale Roma.

Holidays falling on a Saturday or Sunday are not celebrated on the following Monday. By popular tradition, if a public holiday falls on a Thursday or Tuesday, many people will also take the Friday or Monday off as well, a practice known as *fare il ponte* (doing a bridge). The public holidays are:

1 January New Year's Day (Capodanno)
6 January Epiphany (Befana)
Easter Monday (Pasquetta)
25 April Liberation Day (Festa della Liberazione) and patron saint's day (San Marco)
1 May Labour Day (Festa del Lavoro)
15 August Assumption (Ferragosto)
1 November All Saints' Day (Ognissanti)
21 November Festa della Salute (Venice only)
8 December Immaculate Conception (L'Immacolata)
25 December Christmas Day (Natale)
26 December Boxing Day (Santo Stefano)

Weather

Venice's unique position does nothing at all for its weather: high levels of humidity often make winter days seem colder than their average of a few degrees above zero, and summer days become humid as soon as the thermometer rises above 25°C. Strong north-easterlies in winter, coming off snow in the mountains (snow in the city is rare), may drive temperatures finger-freezingly low, but they turn the sky a glorious shade of turquoise and make Venice's colours zing. Autumn and spring are generally mild, though November and March are also the rainiest months.

Women

Venice is an exceptionally safe place for women travellers, both by day and by night. A solitary female may attract the usual gaggle of local male pursuers, but however dogged they seem, remember, the vast majority of them are all bark and no bite.

If you want to play extra safe at night, keep away from quieter, more outlying islands, and from the Tronchetto car park. Stick to main through-routes to avoid getting lost in dark alleyways; if in doubt, cut walking to a minimum by taking the vaporetto to as near to your destination as possible.

Tampons (*assorbenti interni*) and sanitary towels (*assorbenti esterni*) are cheaper in supermarkets, but can also be found in pharmacies and in some *tabacchi* shops.

Women suffering gynaecological emergencies should make for the *Pronto soccorso* (emergency ward) at the Ospedale Civile (*see p282*).

Family planning

Consultori familiari are run by the local health authority, and EU citizens with an E111 form are entitled to use them, paying the same low charges for services and prescriptions as locals. Non-EU citizens may use the service and, depending on their insurance plan, claim refunds. The *consultori* are staffed by good gynaecologists (book ahead for a visit).

The pill is available on prescription. Abortions are legal when performed in public hospitals.
Dorsoduro 1454, campo della Lana (041 529 4004). Vaporetto Piazzale Roma or Ferrovia. **Map** p304 C1.
Giudecca 936, campo Marte (041 528 9258). Vaporetto Zitelle. **Map** p307 C4.
Ospedale al Mare, Lungomare D'Annunzio 1, Lido (041 529 5327). Vaporetto Santa Maria Elisabetta. **Map** p311.

Directory

Vocabulary

In hotels and restaurants you'll generally find someone who speaks English; further off the tourist track, however, some Italian is useful. Italian is pronounced as it is spelled. Stresses usually fall on the penultimate syllable; a stress on the final syllable is indicated by an accent. There are two 'you' forms: the formal third-person *lei* and the informal second-person *tu*. Masculine nouns and their accompanying adjectives generally end in 'o' (plural 'i'), female nouns and their adjectives in 'a' (plural 'e').

VENETIAN

The distinctive nasal Venetian drawl is more than just an accent: locals have their own vocabulary, too, some of it from Byzantine roots. Venetians tend to ignore consonants, running vowels together in long diphthongs (explaining how *vostro schiavo* – 'your servant' – became *ciao*.) *Xè* is pronounced 'zay'; *gò* sounds like 'go' in 'got.' For further information consult www.veneto.org/language.

Pronunciation

Vowels
a – as in ask
e – like a in age (closed e) or e in sell (open e)
i – like ea in east
o – as in hotel (closed o) or in hot (open o)
u – as in boot

Consonants
c before a, o or u is like is c in cat
c before an e or an i is like the ch in check (sh as in ship in Venetian)
ch is like the c in cat
g before a, o or u is like the g in get
g before an e or an i is like the j in jig
gh is like the g in get
gl followed by an i is like lli in million

gn is like ny in canyon
qu is as in quick
r is always rolled
s has two sounds, as in soap or rose
sc before an e or an i is like the sh in shame
sch is like the sc in scout
z has two different sounds, like ts and dz

USEFUL PHRASES
(Italian/*Venetian*)
Hello and goodbye – ciao; used informally in other parts of Italy; in any and all social situations in Venice
Good morning, good day – buon giorno
Good afternoon, good evening – buona sera
I'm sorry – mi dispiace/ *me dispiaxe*
I don't understand – non capisco, non ho capito/ *no gò capio*
Do you speak English? – parla inglese?
Please – per favore, per piacere
Thank you – grazie
Open aperto – *verto.*
Closed – chiuso
When does it open? – quando apre?
It's closed – è chiuso/*xè serà*
Where is… ? – dov'è…?/ *dove xè?*
Excuse me – mi scusi (polite), scusami (informal) *scusime/ me scusa*
Exit – uscita
Left – sinistra; **right** – destra
Ticket/s – biglietto/i
**I would like a ticket to… –
Vorrei un biglietto per…**
Postcard – cartolina; **stamp** – francobollo
Bedroom – camera
Booking – prenotazione
Boy/girl – ragazzo/a/*fio/fia*
Good-looking – bello/a/*bèo/a*
Old – vecchio/a/*vecio/a*

The come-on
Do you have a light? – hai d'accendere?/*ti gà da accender, ti gà fógo?*

Do you have a boy/ girlfriend? – hai un ragazzo/ una ragazza?
Come over to my place – Vieni al mio magazzino/*vien ala mia carbóna*
Would you like an ice-cream? Vuoi un gelato?/ *ti vol un geáto?*

The brush-off
I'm married – sono sposato/a
I'm tired – sono stanco/a/ *so fato/a*
I'm going home – vado a casa
I have to meet a friend – ho un appuntamento con un amico/una amica

Days & times
Monday – lunedì; **Tuesday** – martedì; **Wednesday** – mercoledì; **Thursday** – giovedì; **Friday** – venerdì; **Saturday** – sabato; **Sunday** – domenica; **yesterday** – ieri; **today** – oggi/*ancùo*; **tomorrow** – domani; **morning** – mattina; **afternoon** – pomeriggio; **evening** – sera; **this evening** – stasera; **night** – notte; **tonight** – stanotte

Numbers, money & shopping
0 zero; **1** uno; **2** due; **3** tre; **4** quattro; **5** cinque; **6** sei; **7** sette; **8** otto; **9** nove; **10** dieci; **11** undici; **12** dodici; **13** tredici; **14** quattordici; **15** quindici; **16** sedici; **17** diciassette; **18** diciotto; **19** diciannove; **20** venti; **21** ventuno; **22** ventidue; **30** trenta; **40** quaranta; **50** cinquanta; **60** sessanta; **70** settanta; **80** ottanta; **90** novanta; **100** cento; **1,000** mille; **2,000** duemila.

Money – soldi/*schei*
Shop – negozio/*botéga*
How much does it cost/is it? – quanto costa?, quant'è?/ *quanto xè?*
Do you accept credit cards? – si accettano le carte di credito?
Can I pay in pounds/dollars? posso pagare in sterline/dollari?

Directory

Further Reference

Books

Non-fiction

Svetlana Alpers, Michael Baxandall *Tiepolo and the Pictorial Intelligence*
Stoutly defends Tiepolo against the charge of frivolity.
Anton Gill, *Art Lover: A Biography of Peggy Guggenheim.*
Recent bio tells all about the seedier side of Peggy G's life.
Deborah Howard *The Architecture of Venice*
The definitive account just rereleased by Yale University Press.
WD Howells *Venetian Life*
US consul's (1861-5) account of Venetian life before mass tourism.
Frederick C Lane *Venice: A Maritime Republic*
The best single-volume scholarly history of Venice.
Ian Littlewood *A Literary Companion to Venice*
Interesting compendium of accounts by literary visitors from Coryat on.
Mary McCarthy *Venice Observed*
Witty account of Venetian art.
Michael Marqusee *Venice, an Illustrated Anthology*
An excellent selection of words and images.
Wortley Montagu *The Letters of Lady Wortley Montagu*
The 18th-century traveller lived in Venice for the last years of her life.
Jan Morris *Venice*
Impressionistic history.
John Julius Norwich *A History of Venice*
More readable/rambling than Lane.
John Pemble *Venice Rediscovered*
Essays on the 19th-century English obsession with things Venetian.
John Ruskin *The Stones of Venice*
Ruskin's prose hymn to Venetian Gothic architecture.
Tony Tanner *Venice Desired*
Romantic Venice through studies of Byron, Ruskin, Pound et al.
Gary Wills *Venice: Lion City*
Fascinating blend of history and art criticism.

Fiction & literature

Lord Byron *Childe Harold's Pilgrimage* and *Beppo*
Venice as a dream (*Childe Harold*) and at Carnevale (*Beppo*).
Giacomo Casanova *Story of My Life*
The great seducer's escapades paint a vivid picture of life in mid-18th century Venice.
Michael Dibdin *Dead Lagoon*
Aurelio Zen returns to his native city.

Anthony Hecht *Venetian Vespers*
A moving modern *Childe Harold* by this American poet.
Ernest Hemingway *Across the River and into the Trees*
Aka *Across the Canal and into the Bar.*
Henry James *The Wings of the Dove*
Venetian melodrama concealed behind a wall of elegant prose.
Donna Leon *Acqua Alta*
One of a series featuring detective commissario Guido Brunetti.
Ian McEwan *The Comfort of Strangers*
A rich, menacing stranger disturbs a couple's rocky marriage.
Thomas Mann *Death in Venice*
Disease, decadence, indecision, voyeurism – they don't write 'em like this any more.
Ezra Pound *The Cantos*
Full of abstruse Venetian details.
William Rivière *A Venetian Theory of Heaven*
Atmospheric novel set among the 1980s English community in Venice.
Frederick Rolfe (Baron Corvo) *The Desire and Pursuit of the Whole*
Camp, vitriolic account of the late-19th-century expat community.
William Shakespeare *The Merchant of Venice* and *Othello*
The bard's Venetian offerings are far from politically correct.
Barry Unsworth *The Stone Virgin*
A statue links three stories across as many centuries.
Sally Vickers *Miss Garnett's Angel*
Elderly English lady's staid life is overturned by angelic encounters.

Film

See also p202 **Celluloid Venice**
The Comfort of Strangers
(Paul Schrader, 1990)
Dysfunctional couple have salt rubbed in their emotional wounds in Harold Pinter's halting adaptation of Ian McEwan's novel.
Death in Venice
(Luchino Visconti, 1971)
Dirk Bogarde chases sailor-suited boy around cholera-plagued Venice.
Don't Look Now
(Nicolas Roeg, 1973)
Chilling tale of a couple (Donald Sutherland and Julie Christie) in Venice after the death of their daughter, drawn into greater horror.
Eve
(Joseph Losey, 1962)
Budding novelist Stanley Baker is ensnared by temptress Jeanne Moreau.
Senso
(Luchino Visconti, 1954)
Venetian countess Alida Valli falls violently in love with sadistic

Austrian soldier Farley Granger, betraying her husband and her country in her blinding passion.
Vampires in Venice
(Augusto Caminito, 1988)
Nosferatu (Klaus Kinski) is summoned to Venice by a Transylvanian princess, and wreaks the usual kind of vampire-havoc.

Music

Lorenzo Da Ponte (1749-1838)
Expelled from Venice for his fast and loose behaviour, Father Lorenzo Da Ponte fled to Vienna, where he penned *libretti* for Mozart's *Marriage of Figaro, Don Giovanni* and *Così fan tutte.*
Andrea Gabrieli (c1510-1586)
Organist of St Mark's basilica, Gabrieli senior's madrigals were Venetian favourites.
Giovanni Gabrieli (c1556-1612)
Nephew and student of Andrea, Gabrieli junior composed sacred and choral music, particularly motets for a number of choirs stationed at different points around churches to create a stereophonic effect; *In ecclesiis* is perhaps his masterpiece.
Antonio Vivaldi (1678-1741)
There's no escaping his *Four Seasons* in Venice. But there are nearly 500 more concertos and 16 surviving operas to choose from too.

Websites

The first port of call for information on museums and exhibitions in Venice is the cultural heritage ministry's informative (but Italian-only) site at www.beniculturali.it. Other useful sites include:
www.virtualvenice.net
Historical, cultural, and events information (Italian).
www.venezia.net
Everything from apartment rents to online booking for concerts (English).
www.venetia.it
History, useful phone numbers and good links (English).
www.doge.it
Cultural information, courses, and online hotel booking (English).
www.comune.venezia.it
City council's site with useful practical information (Italian).
www.regione.veneto.it/cultura
Cultural offerings and happenings around the Veneto region. Parts (including museum info) in English.
www.turismo.regione.veneto.it
Information on Venetian hotels and events.
www.veniceword.com
News magazine with current events and entertainment in English.

Index

Advertisers' Index

Please refer to the relevant pages for
addresses and telephone numbers

Maps

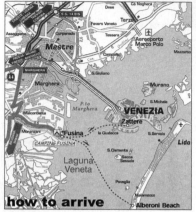

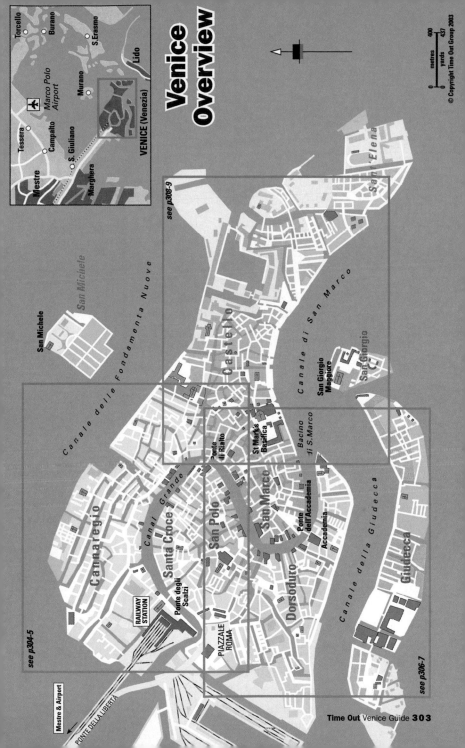

Venice Overview

VENICE (Venezia)

Torcello
Burano
S. Erasmo
Marco Polo Airport
Murano
Lido
Tessera
Campalto
Mestre
S. Giuliano
Marghera

© Copyright Time Out Group 2003

0   metres   400
0   yards   437

San Michele

San Michele

Canale delle Fondamenta Nuove

see p308-9

San Giorgio

San Giorgio Maggiore

Canale di San Marco

Castello

St Mark's Basilica

Bacino di S.Marco

Cannaregio

Canal Grande

Santa Croce

Ponte di Rialto

San Polo

San Marco

Accademia

Ponte dell'Accademia

Dorsoduro

Canale della Giudecca

San Elena

Giudecca

see p304-5

Ponte degli Scalzi

RAILWAY STATION

PIAZZALE ROMA

see p306-7

Mestre & Airport

PONTE DELLA LIBERTÀ

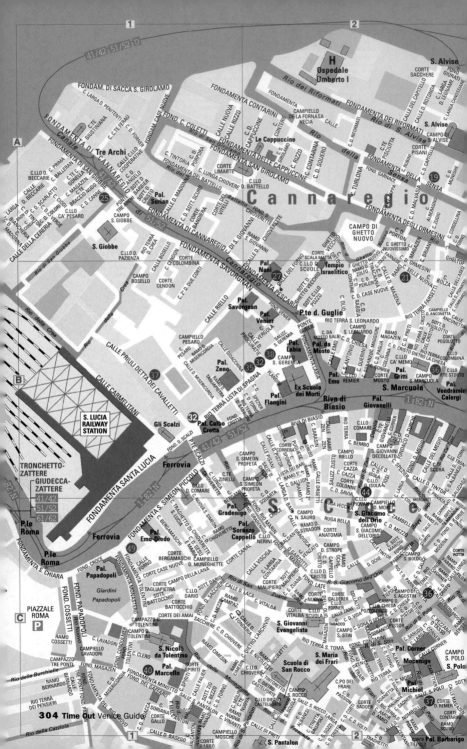

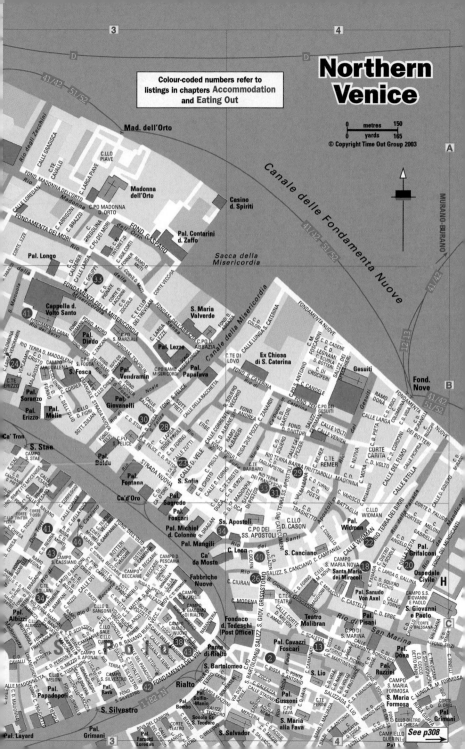

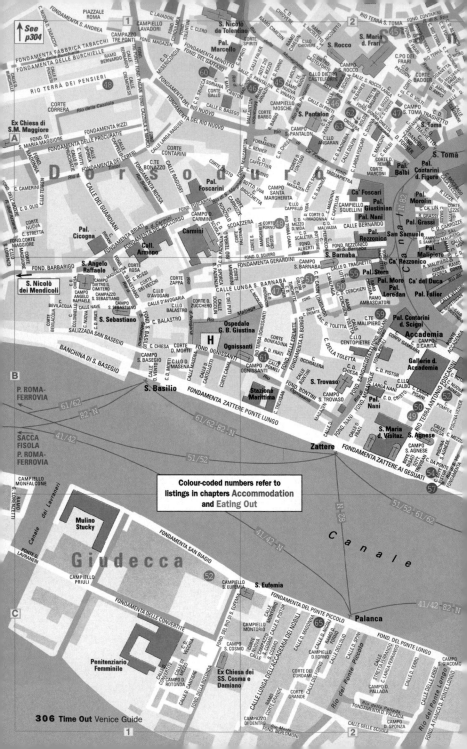

Colour-coded numbers refer to
listings in chapters **Accommodation**
and **Eating Out**

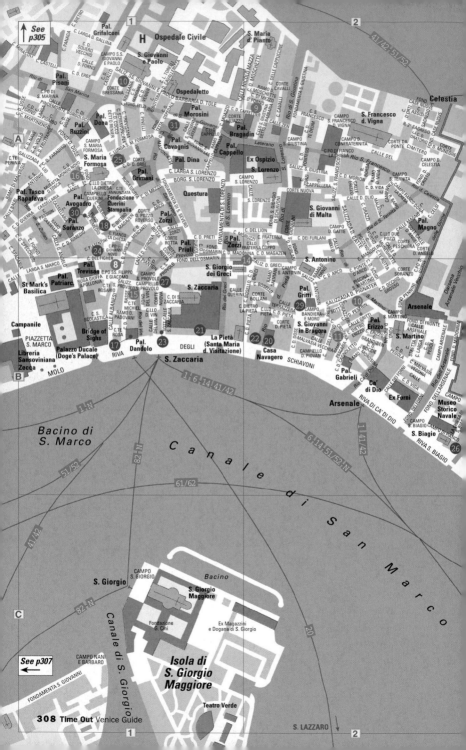

See p305

1

2

Pal. Grifalconi

Ospedale Civile

S. Maria
d. Pianto

H

S. Giovanni
e Paolo

Celestia

Pal.
Pisani

San Marina

Ospedaletto

Pal.
Ruzzini

10

CORTE
BRESSANA

Pal.
Morosini

Pal.
Bragadin

S. Francesco
d. Vigna

CORTE DA
PONTE CIMITERO

Pal.
Donà

31

9

Pal.
Cappello

A

Pal.
Cavagnis

S. Maria
Formosa

25

Pal. Dina

Ex Ospizio

S. Lorenzo

16

Pal.
Grimani

CAMPO
S. LORENZO

Pal. Tasca
Rapafava

Fondazione
Querini
Stampalia

30

Pal.
Avogadro

Pal.
Soranzo

18

Questura

Pal.
Zorzi

S. Giovanni
di Malta

Pal.
Magno

24

Pal.
Priuli

Pal.
Zorzi

S. Antonino

8

14

Pal.
Trevisan

27

S. Giorgio
dei Greci

St Mark's
Basilica

Pal. Patriarc

S. Zaccaria

Pal.
Gritti

29

Arsenale

10

Campanile

17

Bridge of
Sighs

15

Pal.
Dandolo

23

21

S. Zaccaria

DEGLI

La Pietà
(Santa Maria
d. Visitazione)

22

20

Pal.
Erizzo

S. Giovanni
in Bragora

11

S. Martino

Piazzetta
S. Marco

Palazzo Ducale
(Doge's Palace)

RIVA

S. Zaccaria

SCHIAVONI

Casa
Navagero

Pal.
Gabrieli

Ca'
di Dio

Ex Forni

Libreria
Sansoviniana
Zecca

B

MOLO

1 · 6 · 14 · 41/42

Arsenale

RIVA DI CA' DI DIO

RIVA S. BIAGIO

S. Biagio

Museo
Storico
Navale

26

1 · N

51/52

*Bacino di
S. Marco*

82 · N

C a n a l e   d i   S a n   M a r c o

6 · 14 · 51/52 · N

1 · 41/42

61/62

41/42

82 · N

S. Giorgio

CAMPO
S. GIORGIO

Bacino

S. Giorgio
Maggiore

20

CAMPO NANI
E BARBARO

Fondazione
G. Cini

Ex Magazzini
e Dogana di S. Giorgio

Canale di S. Giorgio

See p307

FONDAMENTA GIOVANNI

*Isola di
S. Giorgio
Maggiore*

C

Teatro Verde

S. LAZZARO

1

2

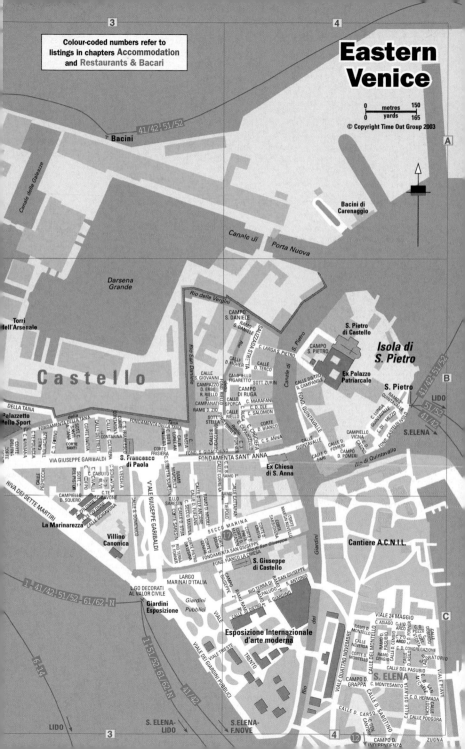

Eastern Venice

0   metres   150
0   yards   165
© Copyright Time Out Group 2003

3   **4**

A

Bacini

41/42. 51/52

Bacini di Carenaggio

Canale di Porta Nuova

Darsena Grande

Rio delle Vergini

CAMPO S. DANIELE

S. Pietro di Castello

Torri dell'Arsenale

C a s t e l l o

Isola di S. Pietro

B

Ex Palazzo Patriarcale

S. Pietro

41/42. 51/52

LIDO

51/52

41/42

S.ELENA

Rio San Daniele

CAMPO DI RUGA

CAMPO S. PIETRO

DELLA TANA

Palazzetto dello Sport

FONDAMENTA DELLA TANA

FONDAMENTA SANT'ANNA

Ex Chiesa di S. Anna

FOND. S. GIOACCHINO

VIA GIUSEPPE GARIBALDI

S. Francesco di Paola

RIVA DEI SETTE MARTIRI

La Marinarezza

Villino Canonica

V.LE GIUSEPPE GARIBALDI

SECCO MARINA

FONDAMENTA SAN GIUSEPPE

S. Giuseppe di Castello

Cantiere A.C.N.I.L.

Giardini

17

1. 41/42. 51/52. 61/62. N

LARGO MARINAI D'ITALIA

L.GO DECORATI AL VALOR CIVILE

Giardini Esposizione

Giardini Pubblici

S. ANTONIO

IL GIARDINO

C

VIALE 24 MAGGIO

Esposizione Internazionale d'arte moderna

S. ELENA

1.51/52. 61/62. N

41/42

VIALE DEI GIARDINI PUBBLICI

VIALE TRIESTE

TRENTO

VIALE QUATTRO NOVEMBRE

VIALE DEL MONTELLO

CALLE DEL PASUBIO

ORATORIO

VIALE PIAVE

LIDO   S. ELENA-LIDO   S.ELENA-F.NOVE   CAMPO D. INDIPENDENZA   ZUGNA

3   **4**   **12**

Murano

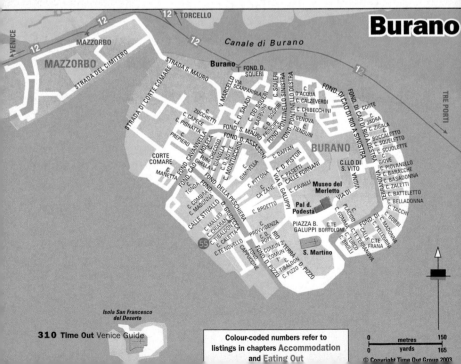

Burano

Colour-coded numbers refer to
listings in chapters **Accommodation**
and **Eating Out**

© Copyright Time Out Group 2003

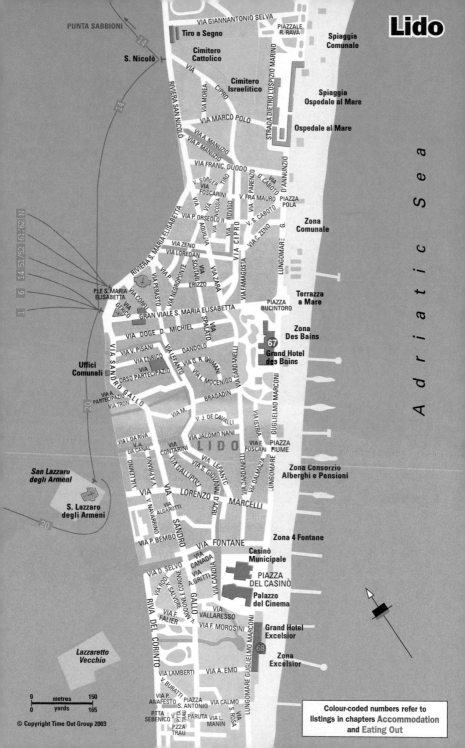

Street Index

Cason c.llo del p305 C4
Castelli c. p305 C4
Catecumeni c. p305 C4
Cavallo c.te p305 A3
Cendon c. p304 A1
Cendon c.te p304 B1
Cereria c. della p304 A1
Chiesa c. della p304 B2
Chiesa c.llo della p305 B3
Chiesa fond. della p305 B3
Chiesa r.t. della p304 B2
Chiovere c. lunga p304 A1
Chioverette c. della p304 A2
Chioverette fond. della p304 A2
Ciodi c. p304 A1
Civran c. p305 C4
Coletti fond. p304 A1
Colombina c. p305 B3
Colombina c.llo p304 B2
Colombina c.te p304 A1
Colonna c. p304 B2
Colori c. dei p304 A1
Colori c. dei p305 B4
Comello c. p305 C4
Contarina c. p304 A2
Contarini fond. p304 A2
Contarini fond. p305 A3
Conterie c. p304 A2
Conterie c. p304 B2
Cooperative c. delle p304 A1
Cooperative c.llo delle p304 A1
Corda c. p304 A1
Cordellina c. p304 A2
Cordoni c. dei p305 B4
Corrente c. p305 B3
Correr c. p304 B2
Cortese c. p305 C4
Crea r.t. d. p304 A1
Cristo c. del p304 B2
Cristo c. del p305 B3
Cristo c.te del p305 B4
Cristo r.t. del p304 B2
Cristo sott. del p304 A1
Croci c. dei p305 B4
Crociferi c. dei p305 B4
Crotta fond. p304 A1
Diamante sott. p305 B3
Diedo fond. p305 B3
Doge Priuli c. larga p305 B3
Dolfin c. p305 C4
Donà ramo p305 B4
Duca c. del p305 B4
Due Corti c. p305 A3
Due Corti c. 2 delle p304 B1
Due Pozzi ruga p305 B4
Emo c. p304 B2
Erbe c. delle p305 B3
Erizzo c.te p305 B3
Facchini c.te dei p305 B3
Farnese c. p304 A2
Farsetti r.t. p304 B2
Feraù c. p304 A1
Feraù c.te p304 A1
Fiori c.llo dei p305 B3
Flangini c. p304 B2
Fornasa Vecia c. della p304 A2
Fornasa Vecia c.llo della p304 A2
Fornasa Vecia fond. p304 A2
Forner c. del p305 A3
Forner fond. del p305 B3
Forno c. del p305 A3
Forno c. del p304 B2
Forno c. del p304 B2
Forno c. del p305 B4
Foscarini c. p305 B4
Franceschi r.t. del p305 B4
Fumo c. del p305 B4
Gabriella c. p305 C4
Gallina c. larga p305 C4
Garnace fond. p304 A2
Gesuiti c.po dei p305 B4
Gheltof (Loredan) c. p304 A2
Ghetto Nuovissimo c. p304 A2

Ghetto Nuovo c.po di p304 A2
Ghetto Nuovo fond. p304 B2
Ghetto Vecchio p304 A2
Ghetto Vecchio sott. p304 B2
Gioacchina c. p304 B1
Giurati fond. p304 A2
Giustiniana c.te p304 A1
Gonella c.te p304 A1
Gradisca c. p305 A3
Gregolina c. p305 A3
Grimani fond. p305 B3
Gruppi c. p305 B3
Guglie ponte p304 B2
Labia fond. p304 B2
Larga c. p305 A3
Legname c. larga del p304 A2
Legnami c. del p305 B4
Leon c. p305 C4
Lezze c. larga p305 B3
Lezze c.te p305 A3
Lista di Spagna r.t. p304 B1
Lombardo c. p304 B2
Loredan c. p305 A3
Maddalena c.po p305 B3
Maddalena r.t. p305 B3
Madonna c. della p304 A1
Madonna c. della p305 B4
Madonna dell'Orto c.po p305 A3
Madonna dell'Orto fond. p305 A3
Magazen c. del p304 A1
Magazen c. del p304 A2
Magazen ramo p304 B2
Maggioni c. dei p305 C4
Maggiore c. p304 B2
Malvasia c. p305 B3
Malvasia c. della p304 A2
Masena c. della p304 B2
Masena ramo della p304 B2
Meloni c. dei p305 C4
Milion c. dei p305 C4
Milion c.te dei p305 C4
Miracoli c. dei p305 C4
Misericordia c. della p304 B1
Misericordia c.po p305 B3
Misericordia fond. della p305 B3
Misericordia ramo della p304 B1
Misericordia ramo della p305 B3
Mora c. p305 B4
Mori c.po c. p305 A3
Mori fond. del p305 A3
Moro fond. p305 B3
Mosto Ca' da p304 B2
Mosto c.te p304 B2
Muneghe c. delle p304 A2
Muti c.te del p305 B3
Muti ramo del p305 A3
Nuova strada p305 B3
Nuova c. p304 A1
Nuova c. p304 B2
Nuove fond. p305 B4
Oca c. dell' p305 B4
Olio c. dell' p304 B2
Ormesini c. degli p304 B2
Orto c. dell' p304 A2
Paglia c. della p304 B2
Paludo c.te d. p305 C4
Pazienza c.llo della p304 A1
Pegolotto c.te del p304 B2
Pegolotto sott. del p304 B2
Penitenti c. larga dei p304 A1
Perleri c. dei p304 B2
Pesaro c. p304 B1
Pesaro c.llo p304 B1
Pescaria fond. p304 B2
Piave c. larga p305 A3
Piave c.llo p305 A3
Pietà c. della p305 B4
Pignater/del Tabacco c. p304 B2

Pignate c. delle p305 B3
Pisani c.te p304 A2
Pisciutta c.te p304 A2
Pistor c. del p305 B3
Pistor sal. del p305 B4
Ponte Storto c.llo p304 B2
Porpora c. della p304 A1
Porton c. del p304 A2
Posta c. della p305 B4
Pozzo c.llo p304 B2
Pozzo sott. del p304 B2
Preti c. del p304 B2
Preti sott. dei p305 B3
Prima c. p304 A1
Priuli c. p305 B4
Priuli fond. p305 B4
Procuratie c. delle p304 B2
Propria c. p305 B4
Querini c. p304 B2
Rabbia c. della p305 B4
Racchetta c. della p305 B3
Remer c. del p305 B4
Remer c.te del p305 B4
Remier c.llo p304 B2
Riello c. p304 B1
Riformati c. dei p304 A2
Riformati fond. dei p304 A2
Rizzo c. p304 A2
Rotonda c. della p304 A2
Ruzzini c. p305 B4
Rubini c. p304 A2
Sacca S. Girolamo fond. p304 A1
Sacchere c.te p304 A2
Salamon c. p305 B3
S. Andrea fond. p305 B4
S. Antonio c. p304 B2
S. Antonio c.po p305 B4
S. Canciano sal. p305 C4
S. Caterina c. lunga p305 B4
S. Caterina fond. p305 B4
S. Felice c. p305 B3
S. Felice c.po p305 B3
S. Felice fond. di p305 B3
S Fosca c.po p305 B3
S. Geremia c.po p304 B2
S. Geremia sal. p304 B2
S. Giobbe c.po p304 A1
S. Giobbe fond. p304 A1
S. Giovanni c. p304 A2
S. Giovanni Cristostomo
(Grisostomo) sal. p305 C4
S. Girolamo c. p304 A1
S. Girolamo fond. p304 A2
S. Leonardo c.po p304 B2
S. Leonardo r.t. p304 B2
S. Lucia fond. p304 B1
S. Marcuola c.po p304 B2
S. Maria Nova c.llo p305 C4
S Maria Nova c.po p305 C4
SS. Apostoli c.po de p305 C4
SS. Apostoli r.t. p305 B4
Sartori c. d. p305 B4
Sartori fond. p305 B4
Savorgnan fond. p304 B1
Scala Matta c.te p304 A2
Scalzi fond. degli p304 B1
Scalzi ponte p304 B1
Scarlatto c. p304 A1
Scuola dei Botteri c. p305 B4
Scuole c. dietro le p305 C4
Scuole c.llo delle p304 B2
Scuro c. di sotto p304 A1
Selle c. p304 B2
Sensa fond. della p304 A2
Seriman sal. p305 B4
Soranzo c. p304 B2
Spagna see Lista di Spagna
Specchieri sal. p305 B4
Spezier c. del p305 B4
Squero c. del p305 B4
Squero Vecchio c. del p305 C4
Squero Vecchio ramo d. p305 B4
Stazione Santa Lucia p304 B1

Stella c. p305 B4
Stua c. della p305 B3
Tagliapietra c. p305 B4
Tagliapietra ramo p304 B1
Teatro Malibran c.te del p305 C4
Testa c. della p305 C4
Tintor c. del p304 A1
Tintoretto c. del p305 A3
Tintoretto c.te p305 A3
Tintoria c. p304 A1
Tiracanna c. del p304 B2
Traghetto c. del p305 C4
Trapolin fond. p305 B3
Trevisan c. p305 B3
Trevisan c.llo p305 B3
Turlona c. p304 A2
Valmarana c. p305 B4
Varisco c. p305 B4
Vecchia c.te p305 B3
Vele c. delle p305 B3
Vendramin c. p305 B3
Vendramin fond. p305 B3
Vendramin c. larga p305 B3
Venier c. p305 B4
Venier fond. p304 B2
Verde c. del p304 A1
Vergola c. p304 B2
Vida c. d. p305 B4
Vitelli c.te dei p304 A1
Vittorio Emanuele via p305 B3
Volti c. dei p305 B4
Volto c. del p305 B4
Widman c. p305 C4
Widman c.llo p305 C4
Zanardi c. p305 B4
Zappa c.te p304 A2
Zen fond. p305 B4
Zoccolo c. del p305 B3
Zolfo c. del p304 B2
Zolfo ramo del p304 B2
Zotti c. p305 B3
Zudio c. p304 A2
Zulian sott. p305 B3

San Polo

Albanesi c. degli p304 C2
Albrizzi c. p305 C3
Albrizzi c.llo p305 C3
Amor degli Amici c. p304 C2
Angelo c. dell' p305 C4
Archivio c. dietro l' p304 C2
Arco c. dell' p305 C3
Badoer c.te p304 C2
Banco Salviati c. p305 C3
Barzizza c. p305 C3
Battisti c.po p305 C3
Beccarie c. delle p305 C3
Beccarie c.po p305 C3
Bernardo c. p304 C2
Bernardo ramo p304 C2
Bianca Cappello c. p305 C3
Bo c. del p305 C3
Bollani c.te p305 C3
Botta c. della p305 C3
Botteri c. dei p305 C3
Businello c. p305 C3
Businello fond. p305 C3
Caffettier c. p304 C2
Calderer c.te p304 C2
Calice c. del p304 C2
Campanile c. del p305 C3
Campazzo c. del p304 C1
Campazzo ramo del p304 C1
Cappeller c. del p305 C3
Cappeller sott. del p305 C3
Cassetti ramo p304 C2
Castelforte c. dietro p304 C2
Castelforte c.llo d. p304 C2
Cavalli c. del p305 C3
Centanni c. p306 A2
Chiesa c. della p304 C2
Chiesa c.po della p304 C2
Chiovere c. delle p304 C1
Chiovere c.llo delle p304 C2
Cimesin ramo p304 C1
Cinque c. dei p305 C3